W9-BLK-712

Living Literature

Using Children's Literature to Support Reading and Language Arts

Wendy C. Kasten
Kent State University

Janice V. Kristo
University of Maine

Amy A. McClure
Ohio Wesleyan University

Abigail Garthwait
University of Maine

PEARSON

Merrill
Prentice Hall

Upper Saddle River, New Jersey
Columbus, Ohio

Library of Congress Cataloging in Publication Data

Kasten, Wendy C., –
   Living literature: using children's literature to support reading and language arts / Wendy
Kasten, Janice V. Kristo, Amy A. McClure.
     p. cm.
   Includes bibliographical references and index.
   ISBN 0–13–398199–1
     1. Reading. 2. Language arts 3. Children—Books and reading. 4. Children's
literature—Study and teaching. I. Kristo, Janice V. II. McClure, Amy A. III. Title.

LB1573.K333 2005
372.64—dc22

2004050550

Vice President and Executive Publisher: Jeffery W. Johnston
Senior Editor: Linda Ashe Montgomery
Editorial Assistant: Laura Weaver
Senior Development Editor: Hope Madden
Production Editor: Mary M. Irvin
Copy Editor: Melissa M. Gruz
Design Coordinator: Diane C. Lorenzo
Text Design: Kristina D. Holmes
Cover Designer: Kristina D. Holmes
Cover Image: Santiago Cohen
Photo Coordinator: Lori Whitley
Production Manager: Pamela D. Bennett
Director of Marketing: Ann Castel Davis
Marketing Manager: Darcy Betts Prybella
Marketing Coordinator: Tyra Poole

This book was set in Goudy Sans by Carlisle Communications, Ltd. It was printed and bound by Courier Kendallville, Inc.
The cover was printed by Coral Graphic Services, Inc.

Photo Credits: provided by Judy Blume, p. 298; Jacques Chenet/Woodfin Camp & Associates, p. 258; Kenny Comerford, p. 284 (top); Scott Cunningham/Merrill, pp. 1, 58, 122, 146, 274, 316; Laima Druskis/PH College, p. 292; Cynthia Farah, p. 39; Michael Greenlar, p. 15; provided by Virginia Hamilton, p. 133; Linda Hickson, p. 228; Jean Hobbs, p. 319; Katherine Lambert, p. 60; provided by J. Patrick Lewis, p. 92; Kenneth S. Lewis, p. 200; provided by Daniel Lunghi and the authors, pp. 2, 6, 7, 8, 18 (top and middle), 19 (top and bottom), 20, 21, 27, 48, 51, 54, 72, 98, 108, 114, 118, 125, 134, 138, 139, 140, 154, 177, 180, 186, 233, 238, 249, 265, 267, 270 (top, middle, and bottom), 271 (bottom), 272, 273 (top), 281, 284 (bottom), 286, 296 (left and right), 310, 317, 321, 322, 329; Anthony Magnacca/Merrill, pp. 18 (bottom), 22, 36, 176, 216, 218 (bottom), 271 (top), 302; Mario D. Mercado, p. 161; Michael Newman/PhotoEdit, pp. 215, 217 (top); provided by Katherine Paterson, p. 305; Pearson Learning, pp. 88, 217 (bottom); provided by Jack Prelutsky, p. 4; provided by Jon Scieszka, p. 266; Silver Burdett Ginn, p. 220; Tom Watson/Merrill, pp. 218 (top), 273 (bottom); Shirley Zeiberg/PH College, p. 256.

Copyright © 2005, by Pearson Education, Inc., Upper Saddle River, New Jersey 07458.
Pearson Prentice Hall. All rights reserved. Printed in the United States of America. This publication is protected by
Copyright and permission should be obtained from the publisher prior to any prohibited reproduction, storage in a
retrieval system, or transmission in any form or by any means, electronic, mechanical, photocopying, recording, or
likewise. For information regarding permission(s), write to: Rights and Permissions Department.

Pearson Prentice Hall™ is a trademark of Pearson Education, Inc.
Pearson® is a registered trademark of Pearson plc
Prentice Hall® is a registered trademark of Pearson Education, Inc.
Merrill® is a registered trademark of Pearson Education, Inc.

Pearson Education Ltd.
Pearson Education Singapore Pte. Ltd.
Pearson Education Canada, Ltd.
Pearson Education—Japan

Pearson Education Australia Pty. Limited
Pearson Education North Asia Ltd.
Pearson Educatión de Mexico, S.A. de C.V.
Pearson Education Malaysia Pte. Ltd.

10 9 8 7 6 5 4 3 2 1
ISBN: 0–13–398199–1

To my most supportive friend through some trying times, Garrett.

W.C.K.

To Maine teachers, my students, and colleagues at the University of Maine who inspire and teach me new ways to bring literature into the lives of children. And to Dr. Roger Frey, whose good humor and support I cherish and appreciate.

J.V.K.

To my students, friends, and colleagues at Ohio Wesleyan who have taught me much about life and literature. And to my patient family who provide love, laughter, and a daily dose of reality.

A.A.M.

To my patient friend, husband, and pal: Wayne.

A. G.

Preface

A teacher's job is to teach children not only to read, but to want to read.

This may sound like a tall order in today's classroom climate. What time will there be for quality children's literature with so much else to cover? The great news is that there *is* time! In classrooms in which particularly good things are happening with children's reading and writing, even in the content areas, students are immersed in literature. In our own teaching, and in those classrooms in which we've been privileged to observe and participate, books play a prominent role.

Teachers are sharing and using children's literature throughout the class day—*living literature*—to develop effective readers and writers as well as to foster a lifelong enjoyment of books and reading.

Living Literature: Using Children's Literature to Support Reading and Language Arts marries children's literature and K–8 classroom practice in order to prepare the best teachers possible. In this text you will find the tools you need to instill a true love of reading in students while you improve their reading and language arts skills. Your teaching will thrive and grow, and your students will blossom into readers who love books, when you explore the joy of children's literature in your classroom.

Who Will Find This Book Helpful?

This text is designed as a resource that both novice and veteran teachers can turn to for classroom-tested strategies solidly grounded in research and practice. We share our love of literature and a wealth of ideas for making children's literature come alive in K–8 classrooms in a style ideal for block courses in children's literature and reading or children's literature and language arts.

- ☺ The rich presentation of the literary genres will ground discussions and instill enthusiasm for reading and sharing these beloved books.
- ☺ The thorough and insightful coverage of methods for integrating the literature into typical reading activities, such as the teaching of comprehension and vocabulary, and strategies for using literature with drama, independent reading, read-alouds, shared and guided reading, and literature circles, come together in this invaluable resource for teachers.

The text will help you understand the children you teach, build your knowledge of quality children's literature, and assist you in developing practical teaching methods. It is an outstanding resource for modeling the integration of children's literature and language arts in your classroom.

Know Yourself and Your Students

Part I of the text will help you get to know yourself as a reader, know the students you teach, better understand the importance of the diverse classroom, and prepare you for the journey you will take with your students toward living literature.

You'll find chapters devoted to the philosophical and foundational aspects of teaching in classrooms where literature plays a prominent role. As is consistent with our constructivist perspective, we proceed from the standpoint that what teachers believe about learners, books, and the process of schooling will affect how they choose to teach. We'll consider such topics as establishing a reading/writing classroom, honoring learners in all possible ways, and teaching from a standpoint of success for all students. Students will learn from your careful modeling and demonstrations of what it is to be a member of a book-rich classroom community.

Know the Literature

Part II will help you live the literature yourself. We are former classroom teachers with a combined 60+ years of teaching experience and a passion for children's literature. We continue to find joy in the literature written for children, which has long crowded our home and office bookshelves. We've shared laughs, shed some tears, traded knowledge, and lingered over the language of these books.

Good children's books, like good friends, create lasting and positive memories. The genre chapters in this section will help you learn more about the different genres, help you determine quality books from "cute" titles, and give you the tools and the titles to develop your own knowledge and love of children's literature.

We stand committed to multicultural and diversity education. Recognizing that, even for us, this goal is a continuous learning process, we continually present a diversity of authors and examples that attempts to weave the tapestry of our global community into our work.

Chapter Format

Succinct genre chapters provide detailed information on each type of literature. Working as complements to the genre coverage are companion sections that take you right into the classroom. Filled with teacher-tested ideas, this material will help students appreciate and learn about each type of literature.

Know the Best Teaching Methods

Part III is what we believe teachers need to know to teach literature well. After decades of research and well-tested practice, this section represents the best strategies for the teaching of literature in K–8 classrooms. These chapters will help you learn the teaching methods that will have the best effect with your learners. Chapters dedicated to read-alouds, guided and shared reading, independent reading, literature circles, and writing give you the tools you'll need to use literature effectively with children.

Special Chapter Features

We're very proud of the special features included in *Living Literature: Using Children's Literature to Support Reading and Language Arts*. These will deepen your appreciation for the literature by sharing the remarkable stories behind the stories. They will broaden your vision of teaching by inviting you into living literature classrooms. And they will solidify your grasp on the strategies, lessons, and activities best suited for integrating literature and reading or language arts.

Focused on Literature

- ☺ *Guidelines for Choosing Good Literature* – Teachers must know how to choose the best titles children's literature has to offer. How can you tell a literary classic? How can you guide your students to the book that will move, touch, and engage them? These guidelines are meant to become a basis for the criteria to evaluate children's books.
- ☺ *Meet the Author* – We invited our favorite authors, illustrators, and poets share their insights on reading and writing as well as about their own literacy development. You'll find this feature in every chapter and on the CD-ROM as well. (*See Multimedia Notes for a detailed CD description.*)

Focused on Teaching

- ☺ *Living Literature Classroom* – In each part in the book, we visit a classroom that is living literature. These inspiring teachers will model classroom practice that not only engages children, but develop their reading and language arts skills as they become lifelong lovers of reading.
- ☺ *Text Sets* – Sprinkled throughout chapters are groupings of interrelated titles ideal for read-aloud, literature circles, and teaching units. The text set will become a staple of your living literature classroom, and the samples throughout the text and on the CD will serve as a model for you to create your own text sets for your classrooms. The database on the CD is the ideal tool for composing text sets!
- ☺ *Action Research for Teachers* – At the end of every chapter, we include an in-depth look at classroom practice. The action research done by teacher scholars with whom we have worked has helped us learn more about teaching literature and reading, and these excerpts of their studies will inform you, too.
- ☺ *Terms for Teachers* – Every area of study contains technical jargon and vocabulary that aids the learner in fully understanding content. The *Terms for Teachers* features throughout chapters clearly define the specialized vocabulary of children's literature, literary study, and literature teaching to help you deepen your own understanding of these topics.

Focused on Multimedia

- *Tech Notes* – Peppered throughout chapters are notes leading you to extend and expand your study with the resources available on our Companion Website and the CD-ROM included in the text.
- *CD-ROM* – Housing a large database of the best children's literature titles, as well as author bios, teaching resources, student artifacts, and sample text sets, this multimedia tool will help you throughout this course, and throughout your teaching career.
- *Companion Website* – A robust set of materials awaits you at our Companion Website. Chapter objectives and self-assessments help you make sure you completely understand chapter concepts; extension activities provide you with meaningful experiences to use yourself or take into your classroom; Web links connect you immediately to important sites on the Internet related to children's literature and teaching.

Supplements
CD-ROM

Free, and enclosed with each text, this CD-ROM contains a wealth of teacher resources, including a database of thousands of children's literature titles to support teachers as they choose appropriate books for kids or generate text sets for teaching, dozens of author profiles, annotated bibliographies, and tech notes.

Video

Conversations with Children's Literature Authors and Illustrators Video, free to adopters, includes interviews with many excellent children's book authors and illustrators, such as Eve Bunting, Floyd Cooper, Paula Danziger, Brian Pinkney, Jack Gantos, and many more.

Instructor's Manual

Free to adopters, this electronic manual provides chapter-by-chapter supplements to enrich each class meeting. You'll find an extensive test bank, as well as suggested activities, objectives and overviews, suggested readings, and other tools for teaching.

Companion Website
The Companion Website: A Virtual Learning Environment

Built on and enhancing text content, the Companion Website offers many valuable tools for broadening and deepening the reader's feel for living literature.

For the Student

- *Chapter Objectives* – serve as an overview to each chapter's main points
- *Interactive Self-quizzes* – both multiple choice and essay, these quizzes help students gauge their understanding of chapter concepts
- *Extension Activities* – provide you with meaningful experiences to use yourself or take into your classroom
- *Web Links* – links to www sites, including awards, lesson plans, and author/illustrator sites, as well as other sites providing meaningful tools to novice and experienced teachers
- *Message Board* – serves as a virtual bulletin board to post—or respond to—questions or comments to/from a national audience

For the Professor

- An extensive PowerPoint presentation – chapter-by-chapter PowerPoints will enrich every class meeting.
- *Syllabus Manager™* – provides you, the instructor, with an easy, step-by-step process to create and revise syllabi, with direct links into Companion Website and other online content without having to learn HTML.
- Students may logon to your syllabus during any study session. All they need to know is the web address for the Companion Website and the password you've assigned to your syllabus.
- After you have created a syllabus using **Syllabus Manager™**, students may enter the syllabus for their course section from any point in the Companion Website.
- Clicking on a date, the student is shown the list of activities for the assignment. The activities for each assignment are linked directly to actual content, saving time for students.
- Adding assignments consists of clicking on the desired due date, then filling in the details of the assignment—name of the assignment, instructions, and whether or not it is a one-time or repeating assignment.
- In addition, links to other activities can be created easily. If the activity is online, a URL can be entered in the space provided, and it will be linked automatically in the final syllabus.
- Your completed syllabus is hosted on our servers, allowing convenient updates from any computer on the Internet. Changes you make to your syllabus are immediately available to your students at their next logon.

To take advantage of the many available resources, please visit the *Living Literature: Using Children's Literature to Support Reading and Language Arts* Companion Website at www.prenhall.com/kasten

Acknowledgments

We deeply appreciate the varied contributions from so many who made *Living Literature* a reality. This was a huge project that could not have been accomplished without the knowledge and goodwill of so many. We sincerely hope we have not omitted anyone, and if we did, please forgive us.

We wish to acknowledge the expertise, wisdom, and insights from university colleagues: Ellen Almquist, Tanya Baker, Rosemary Bamford, Lucie Boucher, Barbara Elleman, Danielle Gruhler, Sara Holbrook, Suzy Kaback, Rich Kent, Paula Moore, Jill Ostrow, Brenda Power, Melanie Quinn, Yvonne Siu Runyan, Jane Wellman-Little, Jeff Wilhelm, Sandip Wilson, Shelby Wolf, and Belinda Zimmerman.

A special thanks goes to Richard T. Vacca, our colleague, catalyst, and inspiration.

Many educators shared the remarkable work they do to bring literature into the lives of their students: Adele Ames, Darlene Armstrong, Mary Bagley, Carli Banks, Jaclyn Baumann, Rachel Beckwith, Kelly Berube, Judy Bouchard, Joan Bownas, Jody Breindel, Kim Breton, Maria Brountas, Teresa Cianchetti, Tracy Cobb, Shelia Cochrane and the teachers at Newport Elementary School, Karen Desrosier, Joan Diamond, Jan Elie, Jennifer Estabrook, Mary Evans, Julie Foley and the teachers at Davey Elementary School, Kim Gerdes, Kim Gilbert, Penny Grant, Katie Greenman, Tracy Hallee and the teachers at Manson Park School, Andrea Harris, Peggy Harrison, Judy Hendershot, Karen Hildebrand, Lisa Hume, Kathy Jesenovec, Ed Kelly, Anjie Knarr, Kim Lane, Peter Lemos, Tom Leonard, Kate Mailman, Judy Markham, Kylee Mathieu, Kathleen Miller, Chris Mockler, Shelly Moody, Jody Workman and the teachers at Atwood Tapley School, Eileen Nokes, Peggy Oxley, Raelene Parks, Candis Penley, Jane Phillips, Sue Pidhurney, Darcie Plessis, Cassi Raslavsky, Peg Reed, Betty Robinson, Patricia Robinson, Melinda Roy, Julie Royal, Priscilla Sawyer, Mylese See, Sarah Seekins Lea Sereyko, Mary Seward, Cindy Shepley, Judy Smith, Candy Staley, Allison Staples, Jewel Stevens, Alexis Stigge, Cathy Tower, Colleen Walsh, Lillian Webb, Peg Welch, Sharen Wilson, Linda Woolard, and Lori Krug Wilfong.

To all the teachers who conducted action research and offered their work here, more than would fit within the space constraints, thanks so much for your scholarship and generosity.

To friends and family for your unending support and encouragement: Roger Frey, Bonnie Blake-Kline, Tiara Denise Kasten, Amy Chen, Billy McGrath, Garrett Cumpson, Lynda Cornett, Jodi Dodds-Kinner, Rusty McClure, Kaci McClure, Haileigh McClure, Gail Robinson, Sara Jane Kasten, and Onna Kristo.

We also extend appreciation to staff and graduate assistants: Karen Brothers, Valentyna Hamrick, and Betsey Shanahan at Kent State University; Bonny Harris, Theresa McMannus, Dottie McKenney, and Ralph White at the University of Maine; Laurie George, Nancy Groome, and Kimberly Strain at Ohio Wesleyan University; and special thanks to the staff of the Virginia Hamilton Conference at Kent State University.

We also thank our talented photographers: Daniel Lunghi, Roger Frey, Jeff Bates, and Russ Van Arsdale.

We are deeply grateful to the authors, illustrators, poets, and editors from publishing houses who generously contributed their time, talents, and insights. Thanks to you all.

We would like to thank the reviewers of our manuscript for their insights and comments: Bonnie Armbruster, University of Illinois at Urbana–Champaign; Diane Bottomley, Ball State University; Linda DeGroff, University of Georgia; Shirley B. Ernst, Eastern Connecticut State University; Cyndi Giorgis, University of Nevada Las Vegas; Nancy L. Hadaway, University of Texas at Arlington; Judith Hendershot, University of Akron; Rebecca Kaminski, Clemson University; Kathryn Mitchell Pierce, School District of Clayton, MO; Barbara Smith Reddish, University of Maine at Presque Isle; Olivia Saracho, University of Maryland; Marilou Sorensen, Professor Emerita, University of Utah and Adjunct Professor, Brigham Young University; April Whatley, University of New Orleans; and Nillofur Zobairi, Southern Illinois University at Carbondale.

And our editors at Merrill/Prentice Hall—Linda Montgomery, Hope Madden, Mary Irvin, and Melissa Gruzs.

Foreword

Richard T. Vacca

Growing up in a large Italian-American community, as I did, in East Harlem, New York in the early 1950s was not without its challenges or its joys. One of my joyful memories is that most people in my neighborhood used a narrative discourse to communicate with one another. Everybody I encountered seemed to have a story to tell, whether it involved a walk to the grocery story, an incident in the neighborhood, or an admonition from my mother "to stay out of trouble" as I ventured outside our apartment to play "on the block." As a child I was immersed in story—living the literature of everyday life—without really being consciously aware of the powerful role narrative was playing in my life.

Story made my world come alive, sparking my imagination and creating a sense of wonder and enjoyment. Even the most mundane, everyday story that a relative or neighbor told was often sprinkled with adventure and intrigue. Reading a draft of Kasten, Kristo, and McClure's book, *Living Literature,* reminded me of my early days on the block and the importance of stories in our lives. Their book's title, with its emphasis on "living literature," resonated with me immediately and brought a flood of memories from my childhood as well as my adult years as a public school teacher.

As a young, novice teacher, I often taught what I now recognize as the "mechanics" of literature, e.g., plot structure, setting, foreshadowing, etc., but often neglected to make literature come alive for my students. In the early years of my teaching career, my students didn't live literature, but rather, they endured it. While the elements of literature are important to study and understand, equally important from an instructional perspective is to help young, maturing readers to live literature in ways that this book, which is a significant addition to the literature on teaching reading through literature in elementary and middle schools, suggests. Kasten, Kristo, and McClure are masterful in combining the teaching of reading, supported by a transactional model of literacy learning, with a thorough treatment of literary genres in children's literature.

One of the major strengths of this book is the emphasis on culturally responsive classrooms. Language and culture are inextricably connected. Native speakers learn language in social settings, and in the process, they also learn their culture's norms for using language. How can today's teachers be responsive to linguistic and cultural diversity in their classrooms while maintaining high standards for teaching the reading of children's literature? Understanding the cultural and linguistic differences between mainstream and nonmainstream learners is an important first step in helping students live literature as they develop reading strategies for narrative texts. Most of us probably don't think much about what it means to be immersed in a culture, just as fish probably don't think much about what it means to be immersed in water. Culture embodies the shared beliefs, values, and rule-governed patterns of behavior that define a group and are required for group membership. On one level are the surface features of a culture—its foods, dress, holidays, and celebrations. On another level are the deeper elements which include strongly held values and beliefs systems. In this book, you will develop in-depth understandings of the role culture plays in teaching and learning.

Another strength of this book is the emphasis on teaching reading strategies within a transactional model of learning. The authors place major emphasis on children's response to literature. Not only do readers engage in thinking as they read, but they also respond to text on an affective level. *Reader response* helps to explain why learners react to what they read with both thought *and* feeling as they engage in comprehending and learning with literary texts. As you study the various chapters of this book, you will develop an understanding and appreciation for the dynamic interplay that exists between the *reader*, the *text*, and the *instructional activities* that teachers design to engage students in the comprehension of literature. Kasten, Kristo, and McClure carefully show you how to design instruction to engage your students in a response to various text genres associated with children's literature. Moreover, they show you how to build on the knowledge of the world that students bring to text as they engage in literary transactions with the author of the text. These reader-author transactions serve as the basis for developing reading strategies that will make literature come alive for students.

I am pleased to have had the opportunity to share my enthusiasm for this book with its readers. Kasten, Kristo, and McClure have provided the teaching profession with a theoretically sound, practitioner-centered instructional guide that will make a difference in your lives as teachers, and in turn, will help students "live literature" as they develop skills and strategies that will make a profound difference in their literate lives.

Contents

NOTE: Every effort has been made to provide accurate and current Internet information in this book. However, the Internet and information posted on it are constantly changing, so it is inevitable that some of the Internet addresses listed in the textbook will change.

Part I
Foundations for the Literature Classroom

I Met a Dragon Face to Face

I met a dragon face to face
The year when I was ten
I took a trip to outer space,
I braved a pirate's den,
I wrestled with a wicked troll,
And fought a great white shark,
I trailed a rabbit down a hole,
I hunted for a snark.

I stowed aboard a submarine,
I opened magic doors,
I traveled in a time machine,
And searched for dinosaurs,
I climbed atop a giant's head,
I found a pot of gold,
I did all this in books I read
When I was ten years old.

"I Met a Dragon Face to Face" by Jack Prelutsky, from
ONCE UPON A TIME by G. P. Putnam's Sons, copyright
© 1986 by G. P. Putnam's Sons. Used by permission of G. P.
Putnam's Sons, A division of Penguin Young Readers Group,
A Member of Penguin Group (USA) Inc., 345 Hudson St.,
New York, NY 10014, All rights reserved.

BELIEVING IN LIVING LITERATURE

"A teacher's most important role (in my humble opinion) is first to teach the art of reading and then to foster in every possible way a child's enjoyment of books. The nicest thing to happen to me is when a teacher or parent comes or writes to me saying 'Thank you for being responsible for opening my child/children's eyes to the pleasure of being able to enjoy reading.'" (Dick King-Smith, author of *The Sheep-Pig*, which became the movie "Babe"; personal communication, September, 1999)

Tech

A profile and a photo of Dick King-Smith are available on the CD-ROM that accompanies this book.

ooks, books, and more books—and falling in love with books—are what *Living Literature* is all about. Jack Prelutsky's poem perfectly painted with words this feeling about stories, rhymes, and exciting information that feeds the mind and the soul. Mr. King-Smith describes our role as teachers in this process: The reading adventure and love affair with books should be nourished in classrooms by teachers who know and love books, and who know how to make them come alive for students. This book will help you become that sort of teacher.

In this chapter, we discuss the following questions:

※ What is a living literature classroom?

※ What role do teacher beliefs play in effective teaching that reaches all students?

※ What are the goals of a living literature classroom?

※ What does research tell us about developing good reading attitudes?

※ What is an appropriate framework for organizing a literacy curriculum?

※ What principles guide teaching literature and reading?

What It Means to Live Literature

Many teachers in kindergarten through grade eight set the stage for wonderful reading and writing experiences by sharing a variety of genres or types of children's literature with their students—picture books, fantasy, contemporary realistic fiction, historical fiction, traditional literature such as folktales and myths, international and multicultural literature, poetry, and nonfiction. High-quality literature for children is well written and memorable. It has powerful plots, richly developed characters, varied writing styles, beautiful poetic language, and interesting and accurate information.

Students are engaged readers in living literature classrooms.

Teachers share and use children's literature throughout the class day—"living literature"—to develop effective readers and writers as well as to foster a lifelong enjoyment of books and reading. In the process, teachers work toward several important goals: to help students appreciate all the different reasons why we read; to foster the importance of books in a technologically driven world; and to build awareness that reading is personally useful, satisfying, pleasurable, and powerful.

You see literature everywhere in classrooms like Judy Smith's, where it is an integral part of daily activities. Books are everywhere: on shelves, displayed next to learning centers or interest areas, and spilling out of desks. A special set of shelves is reserved for poetry books, some of which are student-created anthologies. Colorful bulletin boards feature student writings, famous sayings related to books and reading, a display dedicated to the author of the month, and other displays on the social studies topic. A graffiti board is covered with comments about ongoing projects, responses to favorite books, sample poems, and notes to friends.

Judy and teachers like her know that books are significant tools for learning. Literature is not only the backbone of the reading program, but also a major source for students to learn content knowledge in science and social studies, and a resource

Tech Note

On the CD-ROM that accompanies this book, you will find many resources for making literature come alive in your classroom. This text features living literature classrooms: Tracy Hallee's first grade, Judy Smith's third grade, and Alexis Stigge's multiage intermediate, with examples for applying some of these resources.

Teachers and librarians are powerful people. I believe that. Through the books they share with young readers, they teach values and attitudes.

Part Mora, author; personal communication, September, 1999

Meet . . . Jack Prelutsky

Author/poet of *The New Kid on the Block; A Pizza the Size of the Sun; Ride a Purple Pelican; My Parents Think I'm Sleeping; Nightmares: Poems to Trouble Your Sleep; Zoo Doings; Beneath a Blue Umbrella; Rainy Rainy Saturday;* and others.

"I'm a very lucky person, because I'm doing exactly what I was meant to do. Ever since I was a teenager, I knew that I would spend my life in the arts but I didn't know exactly how. I tried many things: opera and choral singing, folk music, photography, pottery, sculpture, acting, and drawing.

"In my early 20s, I drew a series of imaginary creatures, silly stuff that just sprang out of my head. They were things with eleven heads, round lumps that looked like they were made out of rubber tires, strange beings with holes in their middles or sporting hundred foot-long tongues.

"One evening I took a good look at these drawings and for some reason I still can't explain, I decided they needed poems to accompany them. I sat down for a couple of hours and wrote about two dozen little verses, one for each drawing. A few months later I showed these drawings and poems to an editor, Susan Hirschman, who told me that while I was an amateurish artist, I had a natural gift for verse. Susan Hirschman has been my editor for all those 35 years and we're still producing books together."

Mr. Prelutsky (who grew up in the Bronx, a few subway stops from Yankee Stadium) claims that over the years, his writing has been influenced by other writers, but also by hours he spent at the Bronx Zoo, and the American Museum of Natural History. "I owe an immeasurable debt to books—they opened the doors to my imagination."

Mr. Prelutsky now lives on Mercer Island, in Washington.

---

for learning more about the fine arts and mathematics. The value of literature also lies in its power to increase our understanding of ourselves and our place in the world. Reading and talking about good literature can also be a transformative experience for readers—it can literally change how we think and act.

In many schools, however, books aren't so visible; textbooks mainly dominate the curriculum. In other schools, there is a happy marriage of textbooks and children's literature, not only for reading instruction but also across the curriculum. Sharing good books, though, has been a priority for many teachers around the country for decades. These teachers have always known the power of a good read-aloud. They see the necessity and value of organizing a high-quality classroom library and understand that students need time to read from actual books (not just textbooks), as well as time to think and talk and to respond

> *Literature is like music. If it has a purpose at all, it is meant to draw young people into the world of careful thought and imagination. The best children's literature is built of the bricks and mortar of emotional content. Its only message is "you are not alone."*
>
> *Rosemary Wells, author; personal communication, September, 1999*

in powerful and memorable ways to these books. In the 1970s and 1980s, many teachers learned the importance of organizing much of their teaching around children's literature. More classrooms began to look like Judy Smith's, and also Tracy Hallee's.

If you visit Tracy Hallee's first-grade classroom, what will you see? Today it might be a small group of children involved with the teacher in a *symbolic story representation* (Wilhelm, 2002), in which students talk about where they see themselves fitting into the story world. You might see children intently working on their animal projects while referring to the checklist of expectations for the project. You might observe Tracy assisting a small group of students in editing their poems and short stories for their class anthology.

Perhaps you will peek in when she shares aloud *The Other Side,* by Jacqueline Woodson (2001), a book about

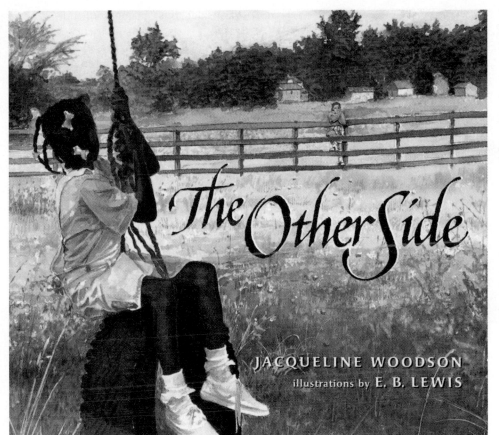

The Other Side

JACQUELINE WOODSON
illustrations by E. B. LEWIS

Illustrations by E. B. Lewis, copyright © 1998 by E. B. Lewis, illustrations from THE OTHER SIDE by Jacqueline Woodson. Used by permission of G. P. Putnam's Sons, A Division of Penguin Young Readers Group, A Member of Penguin Group (USA) Inc., 345 Hudson Street, New York, NY 10014. All rights reserved.

Whereas teaching reading once was a separate entity in most classrooms, educators began to understand and then advocate that reading and writing support each other toward lifelong literacy (Hansen, 2001; Heller, 1991; Morretta & Ambrosini, 2000; Optiz, 1998; Short, Harste, & Burke, 1996).

As soon as we think about teaching reading from good books and teaching students about writing from good literature, then as a field we move toward making children's literature the content of the reading program. Children's literature began to enjoy a greater presence in American schools in the 1980s (Veatch, 1986; Watson, Burke, & Harste, 1989).

As this trend progressed, children's books became a source for instruction across the entire curriculum, as well as for enjoyment. Educators have learned a great deal in the last two decades about the influence and impact of using literature as the foundation of teaching for K–8 classrooms (Borders & Naylor, 1993; Langer, 1995; Laughlin & Swisher, 1990; Laughlin & Watt, 1986; McMahon & Raphael, 1997; Moss, 1996; Purves, Rogers, & Soter, 1990; Stover, 1996).

Our aim in *Living Literature* is to build on this foundation, and to teach educators effective ways to bring students and books together. After all, our job

two neighbor children, one black and one white, separated by a fence between the two houses. The teacher uses questions from the "Tell Me Framework" (Chambers, 1996a) to both stimulate and challenge thinking. The conversation gets heated as students scramble to share their viewpoints about fairness and the courage to do what's right. Or, you might step into this classroom when students are engaged in dramatic enactments based on stories they've heard read aloud (Wilhelm, 2002). These are all descriptions of what takes place on a regular basis in Tracy Hallee's first-grade classroom.

> *My early life was paved with good books and poetry which I shared with my mother. A classroom teacher has a golden opportunity to teach the joys of sharing.*
>
> *Jean Fritz, author; personal communication, September, 1999*

as teachers of reading has two parts, as Dick King-Smith suggests at the beginning of this chapter. The *first* is to teach students to read. But the *second* part, teaching students to *want to read*, is the bigger challenge.

For decades, educators have studied the best way to teach reading and the other language arts. Over the years, thinking about how best to teach reading has shifted.

Examining Your Beliefs

Here is where your belief system is put to the test. Do you truly believe you can or should teach your students to want to read? to love to read? Or is it sufficient if they can

Living literature classrooms have high-quality literature and places for students to enjoy it. Teacher Tracy Hallee, Grade 1, Maine.

Consider this example of how a teacher's beliefs might influence students. One of our colleagues recalls elementary school vividly when the teacher had arranged the movable classroom desks into two groups. The larger group sat on one side of the room; the smaller group of six—mostly boys—was segregated off to one side. Even in the distant memory of this colleague, she recalls that when the teacher addressed the small group, she used her "mean voice." Those students did different, less interesting, and less attractive work. The teacher's voice changed to be pleasant, even nurturing, when addressing and teaching to the larger group.

As years passed, the members of the small group gradually disappeared. They weren't at high school graduation. At a class reunion years later, the colleague asked her old classmates what had become of these people, whose names she somewhat remembered. Oddly, not only did no one know what had become of them, they didn't even recall their presence in that third-grade classroom years before. The invisible children had vanished even from most people's memories.

The actions and beliefs of one teacher, and perhaps others, were at least partly responsible for these children's feeling unwelcome and unwanted in her classroom. Her actions succeeded in "weeding the learning garden." This teacher believed that not all children can learn. She made no effort to change the label, the expectations, or the destiny of the invisible children (Kasten & Lolli, 1998).

What you believe will influence your teaching, so knowing yourself is an important exercise that deserves some time and attention. Think about those invisible children from the anecdote mentioned earlier: Where are they today? Are they successful? Do they read for pleasure and use libraries? Do they read to their own children? Are books part of their lives in any way? How would things be different if a teacher had believed in them, and had advocated for their right to books and to literacy? If they, as adults now, have to vote on a tax that will help schools deliver the kind of education we want for our children, will they vote "yes"? These are some things to ponder and discuss with your colleagues.

read functionally? If only *some* of your students profess a love of books and welcome the learning opportunities they afford, then have you, as a teacher of reading and literature, done your job?

A multiage primary teacher meets regularly for 45 minutes before school with her readers who are struggling most. She uses her Reading Recovery background to support these students. One morning, she had a disconcerting encounter with a teacher colleague. This colleague, also in the building early, queried her curiously. "Why are you doing this?" the colleague scolded. "You don't get paid any more than anyone else for all this extra work," and she added, "some children just can't learn." The hardworking reading teacher, who both liked and respected her colleague, was more than a little surprised that not all teachers believed as she did: All children can learn.

What do *you* believe? Take some time to examine your beliefs in this regard. If you believe that all children can learn, you will teach accordingly, and will make certain curricular and instructional decisions. These decisions will obviously affect outcomes. What we believe and how we teach have long-term effects on our students, their future children, the degree to which the next generation supports education and teachers in their efforts.

> *The teacher is a critical player in shaping the minds of young children. The teacher's theory will determine how she designs her curriculum, how she assesses her students, and how she responds to their intellectual needs.*
>
> *Dorn & Soffos, 2001, p. 1*

Believing in Children

We believe that all children can learn, and can learn to read, no matter what their cultural or economic background. If some children are not learning, or are not thriving, the onus is on teachers and the wider educational community to figure out how best to teach them. We accept that this presents huge challenges. We know that some children are far more difficult to teach than others, and that it takes a variety of approaches to meet the needs of all learners. This view also requires accepting responsibility for children's failures. If children fail, we need to figure out how best to teach them.

Believing in Literacy

We believe in the power of books and reading to be empowering and transformative in the lives of people. We believe in this for all people in today's world, but the power of literacy also was felt throughout history when it was denied to some people. For example, author Katherine Paterson (1981) quotes from the autobiography of former slave Frederick Douglass who, as a small boy, was taught some rudiments of reading by a kind mistress on the plantation where he was enslaved. When the master of the plantation learned of this, he was enraged. He reminded the mistress that it was illegal and immoral to teach a slave to read, and that it would, in fact, ruin the slave, render him useless to the plantation.

Douglass overheard this conversation. Even as a youngster, he wondered what it was about reading that the wealthy plantation owners feared. Considering this point, he became determined to read, no matter what, concluding that the power of reading must be the key to freedom of the mind and the spirit.

Katherine Paterson (1981) makes the point that to some people, reading and literature are dangerous. Reading and books are tools for thinking and could open the "floodgate" of information. The frightening truth is that certain books still are considered dangerous to particular people or groups, because attempts at censorship persist.

Students in Tracy Hallee's first grade are sharing stories—a common sight in living literature classrooms.

The idea that reading and books may be dangerous and, in the eyes of some, need to be controlled became clear for one of us who has hosted graduate students from former Soviet countries. Meeting these students who have just gained access to the information we take for granted is sobering. One student, on his first visit to a large bookstore, simply gasped at the sight of so many books accessible and for sale. He asked if a time could be arranged for him to spend the entire day at the bookstore. The sight of so many books brought tears to his eyes.

Teachers and librarians are the conduits of knowledge in any culture. But as a teacher of reading and literature, you need to be aware that the culture in which we live and the political climate influence what and how we teach. You may discover that someone thinks a book you've made available to students should not be in the

Text Set — *Frederick Douglass*

Burchard, P. (2003). *Frederick Douglass: For the Great Family of Man*. New York: Atheneum.

Douglass, F. (2003). *Narrative of the Life of Frederick Douglass, an American Slave/Written by Himself with Related Documents* (D. W. Blight, Ed.). Boston: St. Martin's Press.

Welch, C. A. (2003). *Frederick Douglass*. Minneapolis: Lerner.

An attractive reading corner filled with books and related materials brings a living literature classroom alive. Teacher Candy Staley, Grade 2, Ohio.

development, of pedagogy or learning and teaching processes, and of the content they teach. *There are no exceptions to this.* We all need to keep professionally active by being readers ourselves—reading professional journals and books, keeping current with children's literature, and exploring genres of literature we are less informed about. We also need to be professionally active by attending conferences, workshops, and courses. Our children and the future deserve good teaching and the greatest expertise available.

Part of this expertise comes from understanding the discourse—not the terms you'll use with your students, but the terms of the trade. In many chapters in this text, you will find an aid to developing your expertise in Terms for Teachers. See the feature to learn or review the discourse of teaching and of children's literature.

classroom. A local school board or even the state or federal government may prohibit teaching a particular topic or may mandate that a topic be taught. Each of these bodies or constituencies has values and beliefs about the job you do as a teacher of reading. Learn to recognize the stance from which other groups speak. Know what your values and beliefs are. Sooner or later, you may need to defend them.

Believing in Professional Development

We believe that the processes of learning never stop—for students or teachers. Teaching people of any age is an extremely complex process. Teaching children is not easier because the participants are younger; quite the opposite, in fact, is true. Teaching is an intellectually challenging act at all grade levels; teachers must constantly make judgments—about students, curricular choices, how to present a lesson, how long to continue a unit, how much to review, how to assess student learning, etc.

Because of the responsibility of making so many judgments, teachers need to continue to be lifelong learners, to grow in their knowledge of students and their

> *You, the teacher, are the mirror your students look into to catch their own reflections.*
>
> *Karen Hesse, author; personal communication, September, 1999*

What We Believe Influences Decisions About How We Teach

Our beliefs influence what and how we teach, even when we don't realize it. Sometimes the messages we convey, overtly or subtly, can encourage or discourage, invite or deny, include or exclude. This is true for literature and teaching as well as for other areas of study. If we choose to be the teacher who "weeds the classroom garden and waters only the roses," then we will not introduce the same quality of books, discussions about books, and excitement about books to all of our students. The tendency to give students who struggle a less rigorous, less interesting, less equitable education in literacy is well documented (Allington & McGill-Franzen, 1989; Cousin, Weekley, & Gerard, 1993; Koppenhaver, Coleman, Kalman, & Yoder, 1992; Lipsky & Gartner, 1989; Poplin, 1988; Thomas, 1976; Truax & Kretschmer, 1993; Wang, 1989). However, students who struggle need us to teach our very best; they need many opportunities for exciting and engaging reading and writing experiences. And, they need as much time reading and writing for authentic purposes as do our more able students.

If we believe all students have the right to read high-quality literature and to fall in

Terms for Teachers

Anthology – A collection of stories, poems, or any combination of literature or music presented in a single binding, edited, and often with a purpose (e.g., instruction) or a theme (e.g., ghost stories, works of Edgar Allan Poe, short stories, and poems about dogs).

Basal Reader – An instructional anthology of shorter texts used in the teaching of reading. Many publishers create basal readers as the foundation of a reading program. These anthologies vary in focus and in story quality. Typically, there are teacher's manuals and other accompanying instructional materials available for purchase.

Best Practices – Strategies or practices in education that have a sound basis in research with evidence of effectiveness in K–12 schooling. Also called *Effective Practices.*

Constructivism – Based on the work of Piaget and others, a view of learning that learners must construct their own knowledge based on their experiences, and must make sense of new learning in their own ways, attaching new ideas to known ones.

Effective Practices – See *Best Practices.*

Intermediate Grades – Generally grades 3 (ages 8–9) through 6 (ages 11–12), although third grade is sometimes considered primary and sixth grade is sometimes considered middle school. Typically corresponds to late childhood years (ages 8–12).

Middle School – Corresponding to early adolescent years, middle school sometimes includes grade 4 (ages 9–10), grade 5 (ages 10–11), and grade 6 (ages 11–12), and almost always grades 7 and 8 (ages 12–14). Middle schools are meant to meet the unique needs of students during this time of life, with a strong emphasis on exploratory curricula to help blossoming teens better understand themselves and their strengths.

Multiage Classroom – A classroom of students deliberately grouped across ages to enhance what cross-aged learning has to offer. Students in multiage classes (such as K–1, K–2, 3–4, and 5–6) typically stay with the same teacher for more than one year.

Primary Grades – These grades roughly correspond to early childhood years once children enter K–12 schooling. These may include kindergarten (called "Prep" in Australian schools, ages 5–6), grades 1 (ages 6–7), 2 (ages 7–8), and 3 (ages 8–9).

Trade Book – A book that has been published for the regular bookseller's market, whether it is a picture book, a novel, nonfiction, an anthology, etc. Trade books can be obtained from booksellers in stores, from catalogs, and on-line (as opposed to books and materials created for instructional purposes that typically are obtained from a specialized publisher or division, and through catalogs and websites marketed to teachers and school districts).

Whole Language – A philosophical stance within education, based on theory, research, and practices pertaining to reading, writing, literature, and language arts. Whole language emphasizes meaning-centered learning, teacher empowerment and professionalism, multicultural considerations, and constructivist teaching. Whole language is not, never has been, and cannot be one practice or one set of materials.

---

love with books, then we all need to know about good books and how to use them, how to select them for our libraries, for our classrooms, and for individual students who need to find books they love. So many books are published annually that no one can keep up with all the new titles available, so we all need to know how to find books through media specialists, resource books, library databases, book reviews in reputable journals, and the advice of colleagues.

If we value higher-level thinking and responses to books and if they are the desired outcomes of our teaching of literature, then how we assess reading and literature must also be different. Our assessment practices need to be consistent with what we value, with our goals for our children.

Books change people's lives, in the short run and the long term. Although bringing students and books to-gether may be the challenge for the teacher of reading and literature, it is also the joy that brought many of us to this love of children's literature and that keeps us here.

Goals for Living Literature

Many teachers who view literature as the backbone of the curriculum (Fredericks, Blake-Kline, & Kristo, 1997) are also literature lovers themselves. They're excited about newly discovered titles and love to share and talk about them with their students. Their enthusiasm for books and reading is evident everywhere you look in their classrooms—both in the environment and through their teaching.

From OUT OF THE DUST by Karen Hesse. Published by Scholastic Press & Scholastic Inc. Jacket illustration copyright © 1997 by Scholastic Inc. Used by permission. Jacket photograph copyright courtesy of Library of Congress Prints and Photographs Division Farm Security Administration Collection.

Classroom teaching practices are rooted in the beliefs teachers hold about learning and literacy (International Reading Association, 1996; 2002). Our teaching practices are also influenced by our own experiences with reading, the role books played in our lives as children, the ways in which we learn best, as well as myriad other factors.

Teaching Children to Read and to Want to Read

As teachers of reading and literature, we have two goals. The first and most obvious one is to teach our students to read. National data suggest that, all in all, we have done a fairly good job at this (NAEP Report, 2003).

The second goal is to teach our students to *want* to read—to create lifelong consumers of print materials from which they will derive pleasure and information. This is the goal where, as a nation, we have fallen down (NAEP Report, 2003). In a talk in Sarasota, Florida, on November 4, 1989, Donald Graves said that 95% of all the books published in the United States—which is many thousands—are purchased by only 5% of the people. This statement is staggering. If 95% of our population doesn't buy books, then what is the likelihood that they are all taking books out of their public libraries? In our experience, people who use libraries are the same ones who buy books. What does this tell us about the results of our literacy teaching over the past few decades?

As a teacher, you will be asked to make many judgments about teaching reading and literature in your classroom. Sometimes there will be materials you will be required to use. At other times, you will have more discretion in what to offer your students. No matter what the requirement, the various materials, such as basal readers and workbooks, offered or expected as part of your reading program are not sufficient for building good attitudes toward reading. As professionals, we know a great deal about developing good reading attitudes. One important idea to note: We don't know of a single study or case where students have fallen in love with reading from using a basal reader and/or a workbook. One of your most important jobs, then, is to provide access to books and to literacy and to foster lifelong reading attitudes in your students.

Developing Good Reading Attitudes

Here is what we know about creating good and lasting attitudes toward reading:

- ☺ Students enjoy reading in school more when their classrooms use literature-based instruction, as opposed to using only work sheets, workbooks, or other decontextualized activities (Thames & Reeves, 1994).
- ☺ Students improve in reading attitudes when they have opportunities to teach and to help younger students (Leland & Fitzpatrick, 1994), such as in cross-aged tutoring.
- ☺ Students are motivated to read when they have choice in their reading (Allington, 2002; Fountas & Pinnell, 2001; Sweet, Guthrie, & Ng, 1998).

- Students are motivated when they can socialize and discuss books with peers (Allington, 2002; Au, Carroll, & Scheu, 1997; Conniff, 1993; Gambrell & Almasi, 1996; Gambrell, Codling, & Palmer, 1996).

On the other hand:

- When students become teenagers, interest in reading declines (Tunnell, Calder, & Phaup, 1991). Middle school teachers have the awesome responsibility of trying to prevent this decline.
- Poor reading attitudes are likely when reading instruction is limited to prescribed texts and does not include engaging literature (Sweet, Guthrie, & Ng, 1998).
- When students are grouped for reading by ability, lower-ability groups never earn high scores on reading attitude surveys, and they are not motivated to read (Schooley, 1994).

These are important points to keep in mind and to address when teaching. We teachers need to be able to build on what we know about developing positive attitudes toward reading, and to counteract or avoid the elements that build poor attitudes. The living literature classroom is built with these points in mind.

You will create an environment for rich learning and lasting engagement with literature by knowing your students; by reflecting on your own beliefs; by becoming familiar with the classroom practices that engage readers and writers and that build on their natural curiosity to develop content-area knowledge, reading and writing skills, and a love of literature; and by modeling a love of literature.

Modeling Living Literature

One former elementary teacher (Vacca, Vacca, & Gove, 2000) started each school year by reading from her "big red notebook." This notebook was her collection of personal writings saved from the time she was an elementary-aged student. With no commentary, she would just sit down after her third graders arrived and begin reading poems and little stories she had written decades ago. Through her sharing, this teacher modeled for her students her developing love of reading and writing.

We have often seen posters or greeting cards or bookmarks that are inscribed "Children learn what they live." This saying applies to classrooms; it describes what we call *modeling*. Too many of us overlook the power of modeling. When students see teachers excited about reading and writing, they are more likely to become excited. When students are read to from wonderful books, they are more likely to have a high opinion of books. Our students watch everything we do, and they learn from what we do—even when we don't think we are teaching.

Planning for Living Literature

As you read through this book, hear about exciting classrooms and incidents, and either plan or rethink your own classroom, you may wonder—as teachers always do— How do I do it all? How do I ensure that I provide all that students need? How much of this and that should I do? Where is the framework I should use as I plan and think about my curriculum? To plan for living literature, teachers need an understanding of curriculum and of the six language arts, a framework for that curriculum, and living literature principles to implement.

The Literacy Curriculum Framework

Harste (2003) states that good curriculum in the 21st century needs three things: meaning making, language study, and inquiry-based learning. He and his coauthors see curriculum as a metaphor for the lives we want to live and the people we want to become (Short, Harste, & Burke, 1996). These three things apply to a living literature classroom in that we make meaning with language, we study language, and we inquire through books and other resources, through student research that is meaningful, relevant, and highly engaging. Accomplishing all these learning processes can be difficult at first, but having a framework will help. The processes through which we accomplish them are the six language arts.

Understanding the Six Language Arts

An important part of the living literature model is the six language arts.

1. *Reading.* Reading is defined as gaining meaning from print. Reading is *receptive written language.* That is, when we read, we interact with written language, and we decode it, understand it, and take it in cognitively. Once a reader is fluent, this process occurs rapidly and effectively.
2. *Writing.* Writing is the reciprocal of reading. When we write, we encode (as opposed to decode) written language. Writing, then, is *productive written language.*
3. *Listening.* Listening is half of the oral language pair. When we listen, we receive and make sense of the oral language of others. Listening is *receptive oral language.*

4. *Speaking.* Speaking is the reciprocal of listening. When we talk, we produce language. Speaking, then, is *productive oral language*. Speaking and listening together are sometimes called *oracy*.

5. *Viewing.* There is only a fine line between gaining meaning from regular language-type print and other material that is printed and/or viewed. For example, most literacy scholars now recognize that interpreting symbols such as picture road signs, popular commercial logos, and all the icons on a computer desktop is another sort of reading. But viewing in the 21st century goes beyond that to include interacting with television, computer-generated images (websites, DVDs, etc.), movies, video, graphs and charts, and anything else we look at and wish to gain meaning from. Because these visual modes have increasing importance in daily life, they are considered part of the language arts (Tompkins, 2005). Viewing, then, is a *receptive language arts skill*.

6. *Visually representing* parallels writing in that an individual produces something other than typical language, such as in art, creating web pages, movies, drawings and paintings, and nonprint media of other kinds. Visually representing, then, is another *productive* language arts skill (Tompkins, 2005). Some refer to this newer area of the language arts as a visual literacy expressed as learning to "make meaning not only from text but from vast amounts of visual information conveyed through images" (Smolin & Lawless, 2003, p. 571).

These processes are all interrelated elements in teaching language arts, reading, and literature (Tompkins, 2002). Figure 1.1 shows how these six language arts fit together, how they are interrelated and are therefore difficult to treat or teach separately.

Literacy curriculum can be looked at in different ways, or in models proposed by different people. We describe two popular models here, along with our own.

The Four Blocks Model

Patricia Cunningham and Dorothy Hall offer an appealingly simple Four Blocks Literacy Model (2001). In this model, four blocks consist of *guided reading, self-selected reading, writing,* and *working with words, in equal proportions*. The Four Blocks Literacy Model has a research base and offers somewhat different guidelines for primary, intermediate, and middle school. Emphasizing reading most heavily, this otherwise useful model does not highlight literature and its importance in the overall literacy curriculum.

The Ohio State University Model

Another popular framework that many schools use is the Ohio State University Model Literacy Collaborative Framework (Fountas & Pinnell, 1996; 2001). The components of this comprehensive framework are: *reading aloud, shared reading, guided reading, independent reading, shared writing, guided writing, independent writing, writing workshop,* and *letter/word study*. This model incorporates all the important areas of literacy study, and is well grounded in theory and research.

The Living Literature Curriculum Framework

In Figure 1.2, we offer our curriculum model for creating and sustaining a living literature classroom. Our model is consistent with current theory, research, and effective practice, and places literature and teachers who know and love books at its center.

To create a classroom abundant with literature to structure appropriate and exciting learning experiences, teachers start with their own excitement and knowledge about books, and with their commitment to bringing students and good books together. Flowing into that heart of the model is the teacher's knowledge of literature's value as (a) the content of the reading program, (b) the tools for learning in other content areas (math, science, social studies), (c) a source for understanding ourselves and others, and (d) fuel for the learner's imagination.

The living literature teacher incorporates these values into her beliefs and principles, shown in the box immedi-

Figure 1.1 The Six Language Arts

	Receptive Language		Productive Language
Written Language	Reading	⟷	Writing
Oral Language	Listening	⟷	Speaking
Visual Literacy	Viewing	⟷	Visually Representing

ately below the heart of the model. These have all been presented in this chapter. Our beliefs include that all children, no matter who they are or how different they are, *can* learn, and that in recognizing this fact, we consider that diversity is an asset, albeit sometimes a challenge as well; that learning (ours and our students') is meant to be lifelong; and that what we believe will influence how and what we teach.

Following these beliefs are the living literature principles, presented in the pages that follow: providing access to high-quality books; understanding that the six language arts are all interrelated and need to be integrated with each other and with content; building a climate and a culture of inquiry for ourselves and our students; using strategic and explicit teaching based on judgments about learners and our curriculum; and providing students with

focused and specific feedback that helps them grow and improve.

The right side of our model is about book knowledge. Knowing the genres and forms of literature and how to teach them is the content of Part II of this book: poetry (chapter 5), traditional literature (chapter 6), picture books (chapter 7), fiction—contemporary, historical, and fantasy (chapter 8), and nonfiction (chapter 9).

The left wing of our model is the use of *effective practices* for the teaching of reading with literature. These researched and tested practices are the content of Part III of *Living Literature:* reading aloud (chapter 10), shared and guided reading (chapter 11), independent reading (chapter 12), literature circles (chapter 13), and students as authors (chapter 14), which focuses on writing within the living literature classroom.

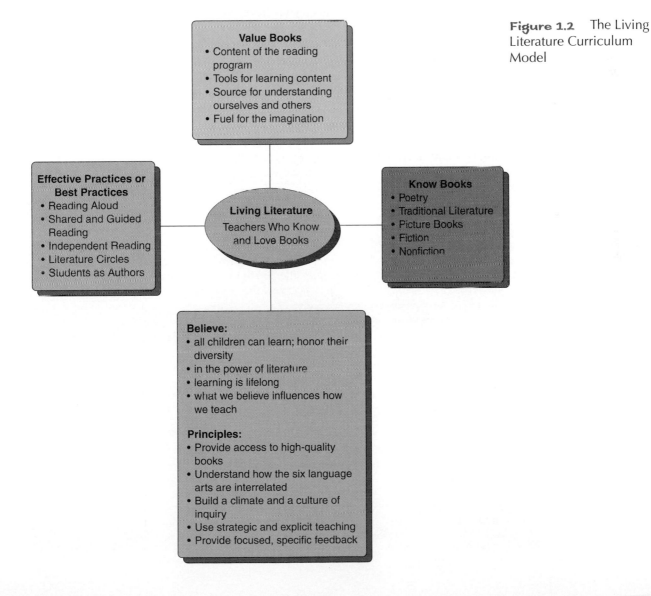

Figure 1.2 The Living Literature Curriculum Model

We believe this model fosters the sort of learning community that we would like to teach and learn in, and where we would want our own children to live for their K–8 learning lives and beyond.

Developing Your Library Collection

To have a strong literacy program and to create a classroom where children are living literature, you need to know how to build your classroom and school library collection. Students need ready access to good books that suit their interests, their cultures, and school content curriculum. Collections in classrooms and in schools should reflect the students in the school and the nation as a whole, and they should offer children windows to the world beyond.

Building a collection starts with knowing what to buy. A source of good titles is children's book awards. Books that have received awards or honorable mentions have been scrutinized by experts and sometimes by young readers as well.

Many classrooms with a good selection of books also offer attractive places in the room to read. Providing places to read makes a strong statement that reading is important. Figure 1.3 explains more about developing a reading corner.

Award-Winning Books

Two kinds of book awards tell teachers and media specialists about good books. The first is given by experts—teachers, librarians, and those in higher education who teach children's literature. The second kind of award is given by children—the readers themselves. Various "children's and young adult choice" awards mean that young readers have voted for their favorites.

Tech Note

Descriptions of popular awards for readers and lists of award-winning books are available on the CD-ROM accompanying this book and on the companion Website.

Understanding Text Sets and Using Books Effectively

Once you have lots of high-quality books in your classroom and access to even more, the next step is using them effectively in curriculum. One way is by creating text sets. You will find text sets presented throughout this book. By clustering books in various ways, we make

Tech Note

You can create text sets using the database on the CD-ROM. Use the search function to search by themes, authors, or any other field.

Figure 1.3   The Reading Corner

How a classroom is organized communicates a teacher's values. If books are important, then having a book corner or reading corner with a cozy and inviting place to read demonstrates that books are valued. Strong literature teachers generally design such a place into their room. Here are some ideas:

- ☼ Find movable shelves or racks to hold books. Consider garage sales, used furniture stores. If you tell vendors you are buying items for a classroom, they might then consider donating.

- ☼ Ask civic organizations for funds or help in creating your book corner.

- ☼ Find comfortable seats for students: an old couch, rocker, pillows, carpet remnants, beanbag chairs. Some teachers have a loft built, or they may solicit furnishings from parents or the community. Even an old bathtub or row boat can become a reading place.

- ☼ Learn safety rules and local rules for fire prevention, escape, etc. Fabrics may need to be sprayed with fire retardants; shelving may need to be secured. Consult your custodian or fire department for assistance.

- ☼ Find ways to give students access to the area as a learning station, as a free-choice option, during independent reading, etc. Decide how many students can use the reading corner at one time.

them appropriate for so many creative uses. Figure 1.4 presents ideas for organizing text sets.

Principles of Living Literature

The following principles will guide you in creating an environment where literature comes alive for your students.

Providing Students With the Best in Children's Literature

Living literature classrooms have high-quality collections across genres of books and other print sources appropriate for children: fiction, nonfiction, poetry, traditional literature, periodicals, and reference books. Even when money is tight, teachers find ways to provide books through book clubs, donations, grants, student-authored works, libraries, and their personal collections.

Using the Six Language Arts

Teachers design literacy experiences that encompass the six language arts—reading, writing, listening, speaking, viewing, and visual representation (Tompkins, 2005).

Trade books, or children's literature, are the key sources for reading. Children's books are models for writing. Students listen to the beauty of words through read-alouds. They engage in literary talk about what they read and what they hear read aloud. They dramatize, design visual responses to books, and craft other rich and memorable responses to literature.

In Tracy Hallee's classroom, literature, including student-written poetry anthologies, is everywhere, spilling from baskets, bookshelves, desks, and centers. Tracy, a first-grade teacher, uses literature to address all the language arts in the ways just listed. Through these activities and experiences, she helps students make thoughtful and insightful connections to their own lives as well as to the world and to other books (Keene & Zimmermann, 1997).

Integrating the Language Arts

Curriculum is more meaningful and lasting when it is integrated and inquiry based, and when content areas connect and support each other. In real life, reading, writing, science, social studies, and math are not separate subjects or entities. The more content areas teachers can coordinate with literacy and literature, the more relevant and meaningful learning becomes.

At the same time, it is important for students to learn specific content in areas such as science and social studies, so content must not be sacrificed in an attempt to integrate all areas. Students need to clearly understand how science works as a discipline, for example—how

---

Text sets are teacher-created (or media specialist–created, or student-created) clusterings of books that suit instructional purposes. These sets of approximately 5 to 20 titles can be of mixed genres or focus on one genre, such as nonfiction.

Teachers use text sets to enhance units of study, and they create text sets to suit any classroom purpose. Depending on purpose and goals, text sets can be organized by:

- Topic—A blend of genres, including fiction, nonfiction, poetry, and traditional literature, on the Rainforest, Ancient Egypt, Japan, spiders, communities, aging, whales, Benjamin Franklin, etc.

- Genre—A focus on one genre, such as nonfiction to study content in science and social studies.

- Theme—Titles in mixed genres that have a theme such as change, war, loss, friendship, and strong female role models.

- Author—Books by the same author or illustrator (or both).

- Variants, variations—Text sets could be created of all *Cinderella*-type stories (variants) or multiple variations on *The Three Bears*.

- Mentor text sets—These text sets are composed of books selected to teach specific aspects of writing, or a particular feature of a genre (Anderson, 2000). For example, a text set of books containing unusually good metaphors can be used to teach about metaphor.

Figure 1.4   Understanding Text Sets

scientists think, how they gather data, and how they write about science. This also holds true for history and for other content areas.

In Alexis Stigge's multiage intermediate class, content-area learning is always infused with literature. In her class's study of ancient Greece, for example, students choose a topic within the culture, such as citizenship, weapons, games, government, structures, clothing, architecture, music and drama, or economics. To implement individual investigations, each student works on specific components, such as a piece of nonfiction writing, fictional writing, something interactive (such as a quiz, game, or puzzle to share with a classmate), and a model made to scale for mathematical application.

Creating a Climate of Inquiry

Teachers cultivate a climate of inquiry, where curiosity is expected, modeled, and lived; where raising difficult questions is considered exciting; where literacy skills and content are very engaging and personally rewarding.

In the same multiage intermediate learning community, Alexis and her two coteachers work with students to select topics that meet district goals but that are also highly interesting to early adolescents. This year, their overarching theme is "human cultures." Alexis and her colleagues, who use no textbooks for the content areas, have narrowed their focus to "ancient cultures" for the next 6 weeks, and more specifically to ancient Greece, ancient China, and ancient Egypt. Alexis's room will become ancient Greece, and the other two will focus on China and Egypt. Students in all three classes choose which of the three cultures they would like to specialize in during their daily 9:00–11:00 integrated-learning block. Each student will enter into a contract about what he or she wishes to learn, how he or she will conduct inquiry, and how he or she will share results and be evaluated. All the language arts will be used, books will be everywhere, and everyone will be very busy learning, including the teachers.

Using Strategic and Explicit Teaching

Teachers appreciate that students need to be supported as learners. Simply providing lots of books in the classroom will not, on its own, teach students how to read or how to become better readers. Students need teachers who carefully observe learning and plan instruction. They grow and mature as learners from the teacher's instructional support or scaffolding when they are learning something new. As students develop as readers and writers, teachers provide opportunities for students to become more independent in their learning (Graves & Graves, 2003).

Tracy Hallee believes that it's important to have not only the products of student learning on the classroom walls but also artifacts of her teaching displayed for children to use as resources for their learning. For example, she posts a word wall listing high-frequency words the children are learning, and a chart of her expectations for the children's animal projects. Nearby is another chart with information about what to look for in good nonfiction: a glossary, sidebars, a table of contents, etc.

Encouraging Experimentation

Teachers encourage experimentation as children respond to literature through reading and writing. Because students construct knowledge, all learners need to try out ideas, make mistakes, and take risks in order to grow in their literacy development. Mistakes are powerful learning tools and have value in themselves; students and teachers both learn from mistakes. Teachers find assessment opportunities and learning insights from their thoughtful observations of students.

Because Judy Smith loves poetry and does so much with it in her classroom, many of her students experiment with reading and writing poetry. At one point, she stopped the class so Brandon could read the second draft of his poem to the group. She praised him for changing the words around to create a more pleasing poetic arrangement, encouraging others to try the same strategy with their own work.

Providing Focused, Specific Feedback

Students of all ages learn from feedback that is honest and specific. Students aren't motivated if they don't know what they are doing right, and they can't improve if they don't know what they are doing wrong. Feedback isn't a letter grade (that's a label, not feedback); it isn't red marks on papers; it isn't vague comments orally or on paper; and it isn't a test score (that's an evaluation). Specific feedback is teachers interacting with students and responding to their work; it's more capable peers responding to each other as they too begin to gain critical skills.

Judy gives her students explicit feedback throughout the day. For instance, when she found Elise, Melissa, and Susanne at the butterfly cage, pencils in hand, struggling to think of just the right word to describe the insect's movement and color for acrostic poems they were writing, she asked, "What can you explain to me about how you came up with different words for your poems?"

"You know how you take the name of an animal or person, write their name down a line, then write words to describe it?" replied Elise. "We wanted to write something about our butterflies so we started with 'beautiful.' Then we thought 'unusual insects' would be good for the next line. But then we put 'extraordinary' on the next line and we didn't like it." Judy helps them brainstorm several words until they decide on "energetic." "That fits better because it means they show a lot of energy and it makes a better rhythm in the poem," says Elise.

Judy's parting comments to the girls are focused: "When you work on a poem, you say it over and over to yourself, and you find places where a word might make it better. Sometimes you leave it just the way it is. But sometimes you keep saying it to yourself, even when you're in bed at night and you discover something new to add or change. Good revising, girls."

By implementing the living literature principles within a well-grounded curriculum model, we can accomplish what we believe about teaching literature. We not only help our students learn to read, but also help them to love books and reading.

Summary

Teachers who believe that all their students can learn, and that those students have a right to be literate, provide access to high-quality literature of various types, tastes, and genres. Such teachers strive to meet the needs of all their students, not only for teaching reading but also for introducing them to the joys of books and reading. To do this, teachers need good collections of books, knowledgeable others to help with book currency and selection, and continuous professional development.

A comprehensive literacy curriculum has beliefs and books at the center, with the six language arts as the learning modes, and the strategies that are learned throughout this book. Good teachers are scholarly and inquiring and try to instill in their students a love of learning as well as of literature.

Action Research for Teachers

Implementing a Child-Centered Literacy Program

Tamara Bialota
Grade 3

Tamara was preparing to change to teaching a third-grade class in an inner-city urban school, and she wondered how she could implement a child-centered, language-rich environment into her new grade level. She knew her new class would be diverse in terms of ethnicities and capabilities.

In a yearlong study, she worked to design a balanced literacy program, implementing large blocks of time (1 hour 40 minutes) to focus on literacy learning. She began each day with a classroom meeting to build community and ownership. She tracked discipline referrals to see if meetings improved classroom climate. For her language arts block, she implemented shared reading, guided reading, independent reading, and word study. She had students keep journals about their feelings toward school in general. She tracked the number of books students chose to read on their own. She gave a reading attitude survey twice; she collected oral reading samples on audiotapes, and she conducted periodic reading inventories to document increased reading abilities. She set up learning centers in the room, and on occasion observed the centers to track how students acted at them and how they used their time.

Tamara realized a few weeks into her study that she had too many goals. To adjust, she tracked 11 students representing different abilities instead of all 29 children. She also realized that parents would be a good source of feedback and sent home two brief questionnaires on their perceptions about their children's progress.

All students showed progress throughout the year. All students scored higher in their attitudes toward reading. Parent surveys showed a 24% increase in students wanting to read at home. Tamara concluded that she had started to become a more skillful teacher and that she would continue to improve her literacy instruction.

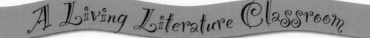
Judy Smith's Third Grade

Step into Judy Smith's busy classroom, where literature, particularly poetry, holds an important role in the curriculum. The classroom is organized somewhat informally. Although children have their own desks where they store materials, they are encouraged to move about and to interact with peers. Thus, numerous informal writing and reading communities form, disband, and then reform, depending on interests and needs.

No matter where you look, you see books. They're on display, on shelves, and in students' hands. They color every aspect of the children's school day. The students themselves write classroom poetry anthologies, which Judy stores alongside the works of masters for all to share. You might find a display highlighting the work of one author, bulletin boards covered with student writing, and dozens of other clear signs of Judy's love of literature.

Writing Workshop

Judy uses the early part of the day for writing workshop. As you walk around today, you see children engrossed in reading and writing. Some students have stories in progress. Some groups are doing research reports, and one group is doing a play. Because Judy loves poetry and does so much with it in her classroom, many students are writing poems.

Minilesson in Writing Workshop

Soon it's time for the minilesson segment of writing workshop, so the children gather around in the rug area. Today, Judy is discussing the use of repetition in poetry. She reads aloud Robert Frost's poem "The Pasture Spring," which includes a repeating line at the beginning of each stanza: "I'm going out to ___ " and one at the end of each stanza: "I shan't be gone long—you come too." The group discusses the effect of these lines; how they give the listener a feel for the gentle, repetitive nature of farm life. They then decide to write a class poem emulating Frost's style. The students break into small groups, each of which creates a stanza. These are then combined into a group poem.

Third Grade Group Poem
I'm going out to climb the birch
That stands behind the barn
It's swaying in the wind and bending down
I shan't be gone long—you come too.

I'm going out to see the little chicks
I'll feed them only barely, corn and grain
They'll squawk and run around.
I shan't be gone long—you come too.

I'm going out to ride the shiny horses, black and brown
They stomp their feet and gallop through the woods
We'll chase the winds that blow south to the bay
I shan't be gone long—you come too.

Independent Reading

Afternoons are used for independent reading, read-alouds, and literature study groups. During independent reading time, students read self-selected materials for 30 minutes. They can read virtually anything: high-quality picture books, chapter books, nonfiction, magazines, and so on. They can browse through the poetry collection Judy has in the classroom. Or they can read purposefully to find a specific poem that connects to some aspect of a novel they're reading or that extends their understanding of a social studies or scientific concept.

Some children read alone, and others prefer to read poems to a partner, talking and sometimes giggling over each one.

Once independent reading time is over, the group meets briefly to share some of their favorites that they've marked with self-stick notes. Today, for example, Susanne has selected "Whispers," by Myra Cohn Livingston, from McGovern's *The Arrow Book of Poetry* to share. "I love the way she [Livingston] repeats the word 'whisper.' It makes the poem really sound like whispering," she says.

Brandon and Jason ask to share "Honeybee," from Paul Fleischman's *Joyful Noise: Poems for Two Voices*. " We like to read the two parts, and this poem's got interesting words," they say. The class applauds their spirited reading of the poem.

Literature Circles

Judy also uses literature circles in her classroom. Today, the children are reading and discussing novels that they selected from four choices she provided. As one group gathers with her to discuss *Charlotte's Web*, by E. B. White, other children are at their seats, reading their own books, writing in their response journals, or working on extension projects related to their books.

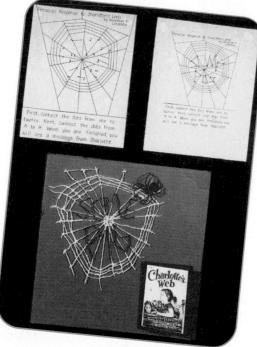

The discussion group arrives, books and response journals in hand, to discuss how the characters of Wilbur and Charlotte have changed through the course of the story. They have completed Venn diagrams documenting the changes. James has found a spider poem from the text set Judy prepared that reflects his perception of Charlotte. Lively conversation ensues as the children share the ideas from their own papers to create group diagrams. They also discuss what they think will happen next in the book.

Text Set  Spiders

Crewe, Sabrina. (1997). *The Spider.* (Illustrated by Colin Newman). Austin, TX: Raintree.

Fowler, Allan. (1996). *Spiders Are Not Insects.* New York: Scholastic.

Glaser, Linda. (1999). *Spectacular Spiders.* (Illustrated by Gay Holland). Camp Hill, PA: Millbrook Press.

Joosse, Barbara M. (1983). *Spiders in the Fruit Cellar.* (Illustrated by Kay Chorao). New York: Knopf.

Jukes, Mavis. (1987). *Like Jake and Me.* (Illustrated by Lloyd Bloom). New York: Holiday House.

Kimmel, Eric. (1997). *Anansi and the Talking Melon.* (Illustrated by Janet Stevens). New York: Holiday House.

Llamas, Andreu. (1997). *Spider Spins a Story: Fourteen Legends from Native America.* (Illustrated by Benjamin Harjo). Phoenix: Northland Publishing.

Temple, Frances. (1998). *Tiger Soup.* New York: Orchard Books.

White, E. B. (1998). *Charlotte's Web.* New York: Harper & Row.

Tech Note

Lists of popular titles for literature circles organized by grade levels are located on the CD ROM that accompanies this book.

Reading Aloud

The final literary activity of the day is reading aloud. Judy reads all kinds of materials during this time. Often she reads more than one thing, perhaps pairing a poem with a picture book or a nonfiction trade book with a newspaper article. Today, she is reading aloud *Century Farm: One Hundred Years on a Family Farm*, by Peterson and Upitis, to increase the students' understanding of their social studies unit on how America has changed over time. She also reads a poem that addresses the concept of change.

How Is Literature Alive in This Classroom?

Judy's students are living literature. Literature permeates everything they do, helping them make sense of and understand their lives. Her classroom is an active, living example of the guiding principles for teaching and learning literature.

- Judy surrounds her students with excellent literature, particularly poetry.

- She lets them make their own choices about what to read, but also provides guidance through choice and example.

- Judy constantly models the kinds of strategies she wants her students to use in their own reading and writing.

- She also provides focused, explicit instruction when appropriate.

- Judy allows and encourages informal sharing because she has found that children's written and oral responses become more complex and more numerous as a result.

- She encourages her children to revise their writing.

- She tells children specifically and directly what they are doing well and provides suggestions for possible changes or new directions.

CULTURALLY RESPONSIVE CLASSROOMS

"One of the major goals of my work and my life (aside from communicating the things I believe in) is to help foster understanding and respect for each other—whatever our nation, race, or gender—and for all life upon this Earth. It's the message I've been hearing for many decades now from traditional elders all around the world, a message that we all need to heed. As a person of mixed European and Native American ancestry, I've found myself in a unique position to see more than one world and to try to work as a translator between." (Joseph Bruchac, author; personal communication, September, 1999)

The world is always changing. People from all walks of life and from many cultures and backgrounds now commonly attend the same schools. Teachers 50 years ago didn't always need an extensive knowledge of cultures beyond the communities in which they taught. But communities have changed to become more diverse, and children of all ethnicities have come to the same schools, as peoples from around the world have immigrated to places where more opportunities are available.

These changes require more from teachers. Our goal in this chapter and throughout this text is to show you the scope of the issues involved in teaching children from diverse backgrounds.

In this chapter, we concentrate on the following questions:

- ☼ What is culture?

- ☼ What is the need for culturally responsive classrooms?

- ☼ How can teachers meet the needs of all learners, including culturally diverse students?

What Is Culture?

Once we all thought of culture as knowing about and appreciating the finer things in life, such as music, theater, and architecture. But culture actually is *ways of knowing, believing, valuing, and thinking* among a group of people (Au, 1993; Heath, 1983). A genuine study of culture goes beyond what different people wear and eat, what holidays they celebrate, and the types of homes they dwell in. These features make up *surface culture*, because they are most readily apparent to someone from outside the particular culture.

I am very committed to having our literature reflect the verbal richness that is the country, our full heritage. I am convinced that teacher leaders and librarian leaders of good conscience will settle for nothing less. I want teachers and librarians to realize their power to affect what cultures are and are not published.

Pat Mora, author; personal communication, September, 1999

Tech Note
Check the CD-ROM that accompanies this book for a profile of Pat Mora and other authors, including Ashley Bryan, Laurence Yep, Alice Faye Duncan, Nikki Grimes, Gloria Jean Pinkney, Jerry Pinkney, and Julius Lester.

Deep Culture

A true exploration of culture refers to *deep culture*—characteristics, values, and beliefs that are not so apparent, but that teachers need to understand about their students. Deep culture refers to ways people think about the world, including relationships in their community and with people outside their community, spiritual aspects of daily life, what is or isn't considered important, how life and death are viewed, and what it means to live a happy, successful life. Deep culture includes what is considered polite in any situation, how children relate to elders, and what kinds of talk are allowed, encouraged, or discouraged among a cultural group.

Aspects of deep culture are so ingrained in people that each value, practice, or belief is generally taken as universal by members of that culture. To better understand this notion of cultural differences, think about this: Do you recall the first time you ate a meal or stayed over at a friend's house? Perhaps the rules at the dining room table were different from those at your house. Maybe the people in your friend's home were more affectionate or more formal than what you were used to. Perhaps certain rituals were new to you and appeared odd considering your family's way of doing things.

School Culture

In schools, cultural differences are a far more serious consideration. Noted Alaskan historian and teacher Father Michael Oleksa (1994) likens the system of deep culture to the rules in a game, such as American football. If everyone plays the same game, then everyone knows the rules of the game: rules for passing the ball, scoring points, how to win and lose, and what is considered a foul. Consequently, the game proceeds smoothly, and skillful players experience a successful and familiar game.

However, a cultural mismatch occurs when one group in the game has been playing soccer all their lives. They know the rules for soccer as well as all the terminology. The soccer players enter school. However, as they proceed, they are rebuked for dribbling, even asked to leave the game for playing incorrectly. The new players are confused, perhaps angered by their treatment. No one has told them they are playing American football. No one has explained that the game is quite different from soccer.

Back at home, the soccer players are successful. Their communities applaud and reward their playing. The gulf between home and school is annoying, confusing, even devastating. The soccer players feel they do not belong. Oleksa's apt analogy suggests why the "soccer players" begin to operate on the edge of the football world. They

Meet . . . Joseph Bruchac

Author of *Pushing up the Sky*; *Crazy Horse's Vision*; *Squanto's Journey*; *Sacajawea*; *Bowman's Store*; and many others.

Joseph Bruchac believes he's in a unique position, being of mixed native and European descent, to bridge more cultures. "I've also found that even though I've traveled the world, I keep coming back to my roots in this place where I was raised by my grandparents and still live. I've learned so much from family, from Native earth and from listening. My autobiography, *Bowman's Store*, is one place you might look for more information about me. But, aside from autobiography, the best thing that I think a writer can do is be invisible. Hear the voices of the stories I tell, don't let my life or my voice get in the way. Literature is one of the best ways to understand yourself and the world around you. Look for yourself in books and learn the lives of others as you see the world through their eyes."

Bruchac goes on to explain that if you want to be a writer, you should do four things: "1. Read (a lot). 2. Write (a lot). 3. Rewrite (even more than you write). 4. Then rewrite again."

Joseph Bruchac makes his home in the Adirondack Mountain foothills of Greenfield Center, New York, in the same house where his maternal grandparents raised him. Much of his writing draws on this land and his part-Abenaki heritage.

Crazy Horse's Vision

BY JOSEPH BRUCHAC • ILLUSTRATED BY S. D. NELSON

CRAZY HORSE'S VISION text copyright © 2000 by Joseph Bruchac. Illustrations copyright © 2000 by S. D. Nelson. Permission arranged with Lee & Low Books Inc., New York, NY 10016.

become "marginalized" within our educational system.

Schools, like communities, have a culture. Schools have timeworn ways of doing things that are generally accepted and often unquestioned, such as the schedule for the beginning and ending of the school day, grade-level classes, the organization of the school day, homework, certain instructional practices (such as spelling bees and memorizing times tables), discipline and management systems (such as staying inside at recess if you don't get your work done, parent-teacher conferences, after-school sports, honor rolls, etc.). Each of these practices or systems, however common they may be, come from a cultural value or belief. The honor roll, for example, is seen as a motivator or reward for distinguishing hard work and achievement in some belief systems. The schedule comes from valuing a day that begins and ends predictably and conveniently and that works in concert with transportation needs. After-school sports stem from a value that extra activities build character, team spirit, cooperation, and a healthy sense of competition.

Tech Note

A videotape series by Father Michael on culturally responsive schooling is available through National Public Television and is appropriate for teacher workshops.

Text Set

Prejudice

Coerr, E., & Himmel, R. (1999). *Sadako and the Thousand Paper Cranes*. New York: Penguin Putnam.

Dr. Seuss. (1961). *The Sneetches and Other Stories*. New York: Random House.

Dr. Seuss. (1984). *The Butter Battle Book*. New York: Random House.

Hesse, K. (2001). *Witness*. New York: Scholastic.

Ikeda, D. (1992). *Over the Deep Blue Sea*. New York: Knopf.

Kellogg, S. (1971). *The Island of the Skog*. New York: Dial Books.

Speare, E. G. (1958). *The Witch of Blackbird Pond*. New York: Bantam Doubleday Dell.

Spinelli, J. (1990). *Maniac Magee*. Boston: Little, Brown.

Taylor, M. D. (1976). *Roll of Thunder, Hear My Cry*. New York: Viking Penguin.

Voight, C. (1986). *Come a Stranger*. New York: Simon & Schuster.

Mismatched Cultures

None of the values or cultural aspects we have presented are inherently good or bad; they are what they are. The point here is not to criticize them, but rather to acknowledge that they all have a value base. The problem, however, is that the values underlying these practices tend to match those of white, middle-class, Western European, heterosexual, male-dominated culture. Many children who come to school are from this demographic group, but many others are not.

If your culture matches the culture of school, then you, as a student, are more likely to feel comfortable and accepted in school. You are more likely to succeed and to get positive feedback about your ideas, responses, who you are as a developing person, and your worthiness. You are also more likely, statistically, to graduate. On the other hand, if your culture does not match that of school, you are more likley to feel uncomfortable, to be disciplined, and to be referred for special education for having a "learning disability"; you are also less likely to graduate (Au, 1993; Moll, 1994; Ogbu, 1994).

Because of this cultural mismatch, we have serious issues in schools. Evidence is clear that certain demographic groups are better served than others in today's school systems. Those least served are minorities, includ-ing Latinos, Native Americans, native Alaskans, native Hawaiians, and African Americans (Au, 1993; Delpit, 1995; Ladson-Billings, 1994; Moll, 1994; Ogbu, 1994). In addition to these groups who have historically been un-derserved, new immigrant populations present new challenges as teachers learn to accept and adapt to teaching children who are Hmong, Polynesian, Guatemalan, Mexican, Korean, Vietnamese, Middle Eastern, Japanese, and Haitian—to name a few of the many. Figure 2.1 provides suggestions for helping English language learners.

The Need for Culturally Responsive Schooling

Many may believe that it's up to students to make cultural shifts and to adjust to school, but as Au (1993) and others have shown through their research, many students cannot and do not make the shift. They simply fail in the system, or they leave it. Teachers and schools must face the challenges of culturally responsive schooling (Brown, 2002; Gilliland, 1988).

The challenges are two-fold. First, educators need to become aware that school culture is a mismatch for many youngsters. Second, they need the opportunity to know, in depth, their students' backgrounds, families,

> *I would encourage young readers to seek out stories and images of themselves and the diversity of the peoples of the world. Children loving their ancestry will strengthen their roots and grow strong within.*
>
> *Ashley Bryan, author/poet/illustrator; personal communication, September, 1999*

> *I'll never know if perhaps I didn't dream of being a writer because as a child, I never saw or read a writer who was like me, Mexican-American, bilingual. One of the messages when I visit a school is that writers come in many shapes and sizes.*
>
> *Pat Mora, author; personal communication, September, 1999*

Figure 2.1 Tips for Helping English Language Learners

Develop a culture in your classroom that values and respects all students' backgrounds, cultures, and languages. Language-minority students need caring and patience from those who teach them.

Label objects in your classroom, such as doors, windows, desks, walls, and chairs, in English and in the language(s) of students in your room.

Involve the students' families where possible: ask for help to understand the culture(s), secure available reading materials in other languages, and perhaps have caregivers and the children teach the class something from their home cultures.

Involve the newer student in social activities such as jump rope that use talk, other games with songs and chants, and play at learning centers.

Make use of cross-age or peer tutoring, having classmates or older students help the newer students with their work.

Include content in your curriculum that is especially relevant to your newer students so that they can feel smart and successful and so that other students learn as well.

Note that English language learners may need assignments that support their language growth when other assignments would be too difficult.

Involve English language learners in functional uses of language such as writing notes, corresponding with pen pals, and using newspapers.

Whenever possible, make instruction *whole to part*, using a story before teaching features of print (such as letter names, sounds, and key words).

When talking to language-minority students, speak more slowly and clearly, and use simple language without slang until they become more proficient.

Encourage English learners to read and write in their home language at times, to make books about their home communities or countries, and to share those books with your school.

When students speak to you, model simple but correct English in your replies without directly correcting their mistakes.

Find out if there are bilingual adults in your community who can visit periodically to help you better understand the culture and to help the learners with their work.

Explore computer software that supports language learning to assist your English learners.

Remember how difficult the transition to a new language can be, and be patient.

Source: Based on Freeman & Freeman, 1992; 1994

home experiences, and values. Moll (1994) believes that we must know our students better to value the knowledge and abilities they bring to school. We must learn about and make use of their *funds of knowledge.*

Funds of knowledge are the stores of information that all students bring to school. They have knowledge from and about their communities, ethnicities, family hobbies, vocations, and other varied experiences. Too often, teachers know little of these experiences, and tend to think only about the experiences that prepare students well for school curricula.

For example, teachers may value the knowledge of the child whose family has read to him or her extensively, because it supports the teaching of literacy. However, they may not think to acknowledge and value the child who knows everything about the world of cotton and

A group of students create a collaborative artistic response to Eloise Greenfield's poem "Africa Dream" using collage.

agriculture because the child and his or her family are migrant workers who harvest cotton yearly, or the child who has been tending sheep beside his elders as the community has done for a thousand years or more.

All of our students will benefit if we take the time to find out what they know, and to build on those strengths in the classroom. This can be a difficult task, but teachers who get to know their students better, as well as the culture and norms of the communities they serve, will be able to adapt instruction to best meet the needs of their students.

Culturally Responsive Model

Au (1993) proposes a model by which schools can become culturally responsive. Here are the four elements she suggests.

1. *Incorporate Cultural and Linguistic Identity.* Students need to believe that their home language and culture are good, are valued, and are accepted, and that some aspects of that language and culture are part of classroom life, including appropriate multicultural literature. In the classroom, incorporating different cultures can be accomplished in many ways. For example, objects around the room can be labeled in the languages of all class members. One school in Melbourne, Australia, has everything, including doors and bookcases, labeled four times in each principal language spoken in the school; the message is clear that those languages have a place and are valued. These labels extend beyond classrooms to common areas

such as the clinic, office area, and cafeteria. Children who have knowledge and languages to share are encouraged to teach them to their classmates.

2. *Community Participation.* One way to get to know the students and their unique culture and needs is to invite their families or caregivers and extended communities (elders, religious leaders, community leaders) to visit the school so that they can participate in events, and share their knowledge with teachers and other school personnel. This not only creates good will, but also makes the home culture publicly valued and welcomed in school in front of the children from these communities.

For example, a native tribal run school in Florida had members of the Miccosukee community employed at the school to teach the Miccosukee language. Once per month, school children were transported to a replica of a native village nearby where elders would instruct children in beadwork, sewing the elaborate Miccosukee/Seminole quilted clothing, making pumpkin bread and fry bread, canoe making, and other important skills for the Everglades habitat. These skills were foreign to the mostly white teaching staff, who learned new skills side by side with their students.

Another example is an "Afro-Centric" school located in a dense urban area. Older people from the community have made a continuing commitment to be part of this neighborhood school. These "elders" attend school regularly in African garb, and they teach students about African sayings, drums, stories, and values. They participate in many aspects of school life and are a constant presence and source of pride. The school values these community members, and they are encouraged to help raise their inner-city children with knowledge and pride in their common heritage.

Inviting participation must go beyond sending home a form letter asking families to visit the school. Groups who have not had good experiences with schools may view a written invitation as insincere or even offensive. Family members who disliked school may not be excited to visit, especially if the invitation shows little effort or seems impersonal. Many cultures respond best to personal contacts, face-to-face invitations, or invitations through trusted community leaders, ministers, or elders.

Schools with diverse populations have special challenges to get to know the community they serve. Teachers and principals will likely need to interact within that community to gain family trust and to understand community dynamics. These efforts may include shopping in the local neighborhood, eating at local food establishments, inviting family members for informal chats over refreshments, making home visits and personal phone calls, and even occasionally attending community churches or other religious institutions (Ladson-Billings, 1994). Such efforts can go a long way toward building the foundations on which participation can begin.

3. *Pedagogy.* The manner in which teaching takes place (pedagogy) and has been orchestrated within a classroom or other setting has cultural implications. Traditional transmission-style teaching (in which the teacher stands in front of the room and lectures) can be problematic for students who are unaccustomed to learning in this fashion. Many Native American communities, for instance, utilize demonstration and modeling as a primary learning tool (Kasten, 1992). Rarely would it be appropriate to directly dictate information separate from the context in which the information is to be used. It may also be inappropriate while lecturing to another to make direct eye contact during communication.

Many cultural groups learn best in cooperative peer groups where students must work together, rather than calling attention to themselves as individuals or competing with classmates (Au, 1993; Gilliland, 1988, Kasten, 1992). Among certain cultural communities, having mixed-sex groups can cause a lesson idea to fail. Girls and boys are separated in some cultures during school years and rarely work together in a learning setting (Au, 1993). For all these reasons and many more, it is important for teachers to get to know each student's cultural background.

Communication style can also be a cultural obstacle for some teachers. A common practice is for a teacher to begin a lesson with a question such as "Who knows who the Pilgrims were?" The purpose is for children to respond with their ideas and to build on those ideas in a subsequent presentation, or to check for understanding from a previous lesson. Obviously the teacher/questioner already knows who the Pilgrims were, and so the question is not an authentic one. It's more like a school game that has some unwritten rules.

In a diverse classroom, children will respond to this situation very differently. Some children may wonder why the teacher is asking a question for which he or she already knows the answer (Heath, 1983). This situation may feel odd and unfamiliar to them. It is possible their parents never used this "I-know-the answer-to-the-question-I-am-asking-you" game. Depending on the audience and the purpose, teachers will want to consider the kinds of questioning they use.

Other students will have an association with Pilgrims quite different from the teacher's. They may associate this knowledge with stories that mark the destruction of their societies and ways of life (Heidenreich, Reyhner, & Gilliland, quoted in Gilliland, 1988). Aside from the nega-

tive connotation of Pilgrims, native American students may be unlikely to respond to the question. In some cultures, raising hands to answer as an individual is impolite; it's inappropriate to distinguish oneself from the class as a whole and to make peers look bad for not responding. Believing that something is inappropriate creates a highly uncomfortable situation at school (Gilliland, 1988).

This communication style has still other ramifications. The teacher is undoubtedly making informal assessments and judgments about the students. This teacher may be noting, for example, who the active learners appear to be, who seems knowledgeable, and who participates well; he or she might also be assuming that other students who don't respond are less motivated, less capable, or less smart. This teacher is totally unaware that he or she is playing a game in which not all learners know the rules. Although it is well intentioned, a kind of pedagogy has been practiced that empowers mainstream learners and marginalizes minority students.

Getting to know students is challenging. Here are some basic principles:

- Get to know as much as possible about the child's culture.
- Remember that not all members of a cultural group or ethnicity are the same, so get to know students as individuals.
- Acknowledge your own biases—we all have some. You may believe that some groups are better students, poorer students, more this, less that—the list goes on. Challenge yourself to become aware of your attitudes, and work to improve them.

4. *Assessment.* Assessment practices, like aspects of schooling, are built on underlying values. It is not surprising, then, that many minority children don't perform well on assessments, causing some educators to believe the students are poorly educated, learning disabled, or less capable.

When students perform poorly on tests, do you question the capabilities of the students, or do you question the validity and reliability of the tests? Throughout our educational history, educators and the public have viewed testing failure as a problem with the students or with the teachers, instead of raising serious and critical questions about the nature of the tests and whether they are appropriate, biased, or even racist in their construction (Gipps & Murphy, 1994; Murphy, 1997; Perrone, 1991; Valdes & Figueroa, 1994).

Rhodes (1989), for example, studied why native American university students in Arizona continually failed to make the cutoff scores on the California Achievement Tests (CAT), which were used to retain university students between lower and upper divisions of study. Rhodes studied native learners by asking them to think aloud as they proceeded through the test.

Rhodes's findings are stunning. He divided them into two categories he called *product bias* and *process bias*. The first, product bias, concerned the choice of content. The CAT included questions such has "Who discovered America?" The test makers' response of "Columbus" was in no way appropriate to a native American student. Not only would a Native American not consider Columbus a "discoverer" ("conqueror" and "terrorist" would be more appropriate terms), the individual culture from which the subjects came made telling an untruth a serious taboo. So even if a native student knew what the test maker had in mind, conscience would not permit a response that was considered a lie. See *Rethinking Columbus: The Next 500 Years.* (Bigelow & Peterson, 1998).

Another item asked for the first settlement in North America; the question did not say "White" settlement. The communities to which some Arizona native peoples belong have been stable and continuous since the 14th century; no American Indian would in good conscience respond with "Jamestown" or "St. Augustine."

Darling-Hammond, Ancess, and Falk (1995) call for assessment that not only informs instruction and helps know student progress, but that also is equitable among cultural groups. Clearly much assessment is not. This is well exemplified in Rhodes's (1989) second finding, which he termed process bias. For example, standardized achievement tests are timed, even though it is not clear where theory or research about testing has established that a person who completes a task faster is necessarily better. These tests are timed strictly under the guise of being uniform, fair, and standard.

However, some native peoples are taught a careful and deliberate process for making decisions that calls for the most careful and thoughtful consideration of all alternatives; there is no discarding of any that may seem frivolous or silly on the surface until they are carefully considered and deliberated upon for any possible worthiness (Rhodes, 1989). This carefull process takes time. The subjects in Rhodes's study used this painstaking process to complete a multiple-choice subtest. However, when the time for the subtest was over, few items had been answered.

Au (1993) points out that high-quality assessment can empower students when they participate in it, learn

> *By identifying, for the span of a book, with another culture, another economic stratum, students see others' ways of being. With thoughtful discussion, readers increase their broader understanding of the world and begin to put their own life experience into perspective.*
>
> *Karen Hesse, author; personal communication, September, 1999*

about their own learning, and find assessment as a meaningful aspect of personal learning. We observed this in a Colorado suburban school, where a teacher of a multiage intermediate class has family members of each student come to school one evening per month as part of an ongoing assessment and self-assessment process. These evenings are often coordinated with other activities, such as the parent-teacher association meeting.

Students always accompany parents and guardians on these evenings and have prepared a presentation for their caregiver about their recent learning and their upcoming goals. All students present at the same time, so the room is noisy, but the result is highly productive. Everyone knows what is going on. Family members feel informed and also involved and consulted. Students are compelled to reflect upon their own learning and take responsibility for their strengths and needs. This is a highly successful assessment practice that fulfills the need for authenticity and equity.

Meeting the Needs of All Learners

The issues we have raised here may seem complex and overwhelming. "How can I know about all the children I will teach?" you may be wondering. Obviously, no teacher is completely prepared with intricate and intimate knowledge of every child and his or her culture. The best most of us can hope for, as we continue to educate ourselves on multicultural features and aspects, is to know what questions to ask about the students we teach. Following are some suggestions. Note that it may not be appropriate to ask these questions directly: You may have to obtain this information via colleagues, research, observation, and other means. Figure 2.2 summarizes and extends the array of questions teachers may need to ask.

What Does This Have to Do With Teaching Literature?

Knowing your students influences how you teach them, including the books you make available for reading, browsing, and sharing aloud. Issues include the need for

Figure 2.2
Questions to Ask
About Students and
Their Cultures

☼ **Who is the head of the family?** Is the structure of the family matriarchal (children have the mother's surname and/or clan membership) or patriarchal (the students have the father's surname or clan name)? Or, is the family power balanced between male and female leaders? *You need to know this before you communicate with a family member.*

☼ **Has the child learned to view males and females as possessing similar or differing degrees of authority?** In some societies, the child's principal disciplinarian is the father. Sometimes it is the mother or the mother's uncles; or various members may contribute differently to the raising of children. *You need to know this if, for example, you are a female teacher, and in the child's family and/or home country, only males have authority for discipline.*

☼ **What are the home rules for touching?** Is touching okay, or is it demeaning or inappropriate? *You need to know this because you may like to hug students or give them a friendly pat, but you risk offending someone or may give an unwanted message. On the other hand, you may come from a culture where little physical contact is normal or expected but have students who relate to others through casual touching.*

☼ **What are the rules for eye contact?** Some cultures consider eye contact an excellent way of establishing rapport, maintaining discipline, and sustaining attentiveness. In other cultures, eye contact is far too personal for a teacher–student relationship, a sign of disrespect between an older person and a younger one, or even a highly intimate conduit to the spiritual self that can result in some diminishing of the individual's well-being—or even perhaps illness (Kasten, 1992). *You need to know this because it is common practice in schools to control mildly off-task behavior by making eye contact with a student. You may feel it is productive to confront undesirable behaviors directly with a face-to-face talk. However, this maneuver may backfire if eye contact is viewed differently in the child's culture.*

☼ **How do children learn in their home?** What kinds of parent–child interactions take place? The way children learn in their home is the foundation for schooling. If they are accustomed to learning through modeling, through the use of stories, for example, they will be confused and surprised to find learning different in school. They will not know the rules for the game. *You need to know this because children cannot adapt easily to a totally different learning milieu. As they adjust to a new system, they may appear less ready, less capable, less communicative, and less active. Unfortunately, these perceptions are often solidly in place in well-intentioned professionals before students learn how to operate in the foreign system.*

☼ **What is the view or value of competition in the home culture(s)?** The value of competition in different cultural groups ranges from it's the way to do everything, to a little competition is a good thing, to it's an undesirable feature, to it's totally inappropriate and taboo. *You need to know this because many common features of schooling are competitive, either overtly (such as team sports) or subtly (such as honor-roll lists, lists of books that students have read, and games to reinforce skills). Mores about competition are highly ingrained in cultures and will not be changed by the rules of schooling.*

multicultural literature for both minorities and mainstream students; the role of story in cultures; the way children respond to literature; multiple ways of knowing; and literature and oral narrative as models for the writing that children do.

I want students of all ages to believe that they can add their voice to our national literature. It's hard to believe if you don't see yourself in the literature presented, promoted, and honored.

Pat Mora, author; personal communication, September, 1999

"We Read to Know We Are Not Alone"

In the movie *Shadowlands*—the story of the life of writer C. S. Lewis—one of Lewis's Oxford students says, "We read to know we are not alone." It's true. We

Figure 2.2
(continued)

☼ **What are the narrative styles of oral and written forms?** All homes have language in them. In some, books and printed texts are highly valued; in others, oral stories are frequent and highly valued. As a teacher of literacy, you may place more value on the home that values the written texts. All cultures have stories or texts associated with history, family, or spirituality. The forms of these stories vary greatly. *You need to know this because when students begin writing, they will write in forms they are most familiar with.*

☼ **What do you know about family background, interests, and vocations?** Children generally know a great deal about what their family does for a living, as well as family hobbies. However, children don't always realize they have unique knowledge, because most have not lived in more than one family. For example, the child of a carpenter likely has a tool vocabulary that extends far beyond the typical classroom vocabulary lessons; the child whose family raises animals will know a lot about biology, animal care, life spans, and associated technical vocabulary. The list goes on. This information is worth knowing about your children not only to teach them and to make use of in the classroom, but also for assisting them in selecting reading material and in making connections with new knowledge. *You need to learn these things because otherwise you cannot help your students build on their strengths or recognize and make use of their resident expertise.*

☼ **What is the makeup of the family and/or past families of your students?** The child who lives with a single parent may be hurt or embarrassed when teachers address communication to "Dear Mom and Dad," or just to mothers, for example, when men are sole heads of household. Many children are being raised by other family members such as grandparents, aunts, and uncles, or by one parent and the parent's same-sex partner. Still other children are adopted or live in foster homes. Do you know the family situation of each of your children? *You need to know these things so you can address communications properly, and also because foster homes have little knowledge of birth families. The children rarely have baby pictures, and the time lines of their lives can be sources of embarrassment. Teachers who plan to ask students to bring in pictures, research family origins, or make time lines of their lives must carefully consider the student body.*

☼ **What home responsibilities do children have?** Sometimes children care for siblings after school, help in the family business, or have animals to tend. Older children may be expected to help hunt or fish, prepare meals, or help run the household. These responsibilities may compete with homework assignments. *You need to know those these things about your students, especially if you teach outside the community in which you were raised. It is easy to assume that children live at home as you did. These school intrusions may be unfair to the family, may cause economic hardship to the household, and will not strengthen home–school rapport. Teachers need to know and understand the communities in which their students live.*

read because in books, we not only learn things, we discover we are not alone. We see that others share our loves, doubts, fears, growing up, values, and dilemmas. From books, we affirm that our lives are normal, that life has ups and downs, that people triumph over tragedy, that one person can make a difference in the world, and much more.

What, then, if no one in the books we read looks like us? What if no one feels like us? What if no one has anything happen to them with which we can empathize because of past experience? Of course, *we feel alone*. More

seriously, we feel alone in school, where many of our concepts, labels, ideas about ourselves and our worthiness further separate us from our school experiences. After all, school—good or bad—is an institution of authority. It has the power to pass, to fail, to expel, and to nurture (Brown, 2002; Delpit, 1995; Locust, 1988; Paul, 1981).

Students who feel alone also feel they do not belong. Students who feel they do not belong are less likely to stay. Students who don't stay, don't graduate. When drop-out rates are high, the system needs to be scrutinized (Au, 1993; Delpit, 1995).

We Read to Learn About Those With Whom We Share This Planet

Classrooms need ample supplies of multicultural literature that appeals to a variety of students, and in which students can find themselves and their values and dilemmas. "Multicultural literature" does not mean a few authors of color, but rather authors who write about different kinds of families, different economic circumstances, different ethnicities, experiences, home settings, sexes, ages, interests, information, regions, and lifestyles.

Building collections of multicultural literature in a variety of genres isn't only about appealing to minority students in a school. Books educate us about our world. Informational books that focus on a different place or culture teach us about people, places, and things we need to know. Fiction helps us get to know people who are like us, but who live in very different times and places and show us that we have a great deal in common. Fiction teaches us to empathize, to become compassionate, because the lessons we learn from our books carry over into our lives and our future careers. Poetry also can teach us all of these lessons. Unless we have the opportunity to travel around the world and meet all its different peoples, how else can we know them, understand them, appreciate their uniqueness, and build a tolerant global society?

> Dedicated teachers seek out literature for their students that reflects the diversity of the peoples of the United States.
>
> *Ashley Bryan, poet; personal communication, September, 1999*

Learners With Another Kind of Difference: Special Education

One of our teacher friends once remarked that getting to know and work with students with exceptionalities was not unlike the challenges we associate with getting to know a new culture—there was new terminology, new ways of thinking about learners, and new teaching practices to learn. In our inclusive classrooms of today, we have students who need educational accommodations. These students require our best intentions and efforts in meeting their specific teaching and learning needs.

Some students identified as needing special education services have only mild disabilities that cause them to learn more slowly, learn less easily, or simply need more practice. Others have extraordinary needs that go beyond the scope of this book. No matter the need, we still must do our best to teach reading, writing, and literature to all students. All require both access to good literature and opportunities to find characters in books they can identify with, and to understand that they, too, are not alone.

Stories Mean Different Things to Different People

Different people value different things when it comes to books and stories, both written and oral. Some people

Text Set

Disability Awareness

Bergman, T. (1990). *Going places: Children Living with Cerebral Palsy*. Milwaukee: Gareth Steven Books.

Brown, T. (1984). *Someone Special Just Like You*. New York: Holt, Rinehart and Winston.

Carter, A. R. (1999). *Dustin's Big School Day*. Morton Grove, IL: Albert Whitman.

Gordon, M. A. (1999). *Let's Talk About Deafness*. New York: Rusen Publishing Group.

Krementz, J. (1992). *How It Feels to Live with a Physical Disability*. New York: Simon & Schuster.

Kuklin, S. (1986). *Thinking Big*. New York: Lothrop, Lee & Shepard.

McMahon, P. (1995). *Listen for the Bus*. New York: Boyds Mill Press.

Meyer, D. (1997). *Views from our Shoes: Growing Up with a Brother or Sister with Special Needs*. Bethesda, MD: Woodbine House.

Powell, J. (1999). *Talking About Disability*. Austin: Raintree.

Rogers, F. (2000). *Extraordinary Friends*. New York: Putnam.

Sanders, P. (1992). *Let's Talk About Disabled People*. New York: Gloucester Press.

prefer to read to learn; others read to escape. Certain stories, creation stories, for instance, are sacred in some cultures. Some sacred stories are shared; some are not.

Storyteller Paula Underwood shared a Native American learning story entitled *Who Speaks for Wolf?* (Underwood, 1991). Although some native stories are not meant to be shared with the outside world, this one has been, and from it we have learned a function of a story that many of us did not know. *Who Speaks for Wolf?* is both a simple and a complex story of a native elder relating an often-told tale of a time when the people have to move to a new place.

In the tale, scouts are sent out to find a good place where the people will be safe, have ample food sources, and enjoy a good life. The problem arises because one scout has not returned when all the others have, and the chief becomes pressured to make a decision. One scout's input will be missing in the decision-making process, which in this case may be a life or death decision for an entire community.

Plans and ideas are shared and deliberated. Someone asks "Who speaks for Wolf?" in the absence of the yet-returned scout, who is known as Wolf's Brother. The question is dismissed for lack of time. A decision is made, and the community relocates.

In time, it becomes clear that the new site is uncomfortable, perhaps unsafe, because it has been located in an area that is a primary wolf habitat and hunting ground. Suddenly humans and wolves no longer enjoy the harmony that they have shared for eons. A decision must be made about how to resolve the situation that will meet the needs of the human and the wolf communities.

Although this story has no stated lesson or moral, much is implied. In the community from which the story originated, it would be inappropriate, perhaps insulting, to state any moral. It is accepted that people will interpret the story differently; each person derives an appropriate lesson suited to his or her time and learning needs. Interpretations of this story are vast; there is no "right" answer, nor is there supposed to be.

In many diverse communities, stories are told in this manner: Listeners know there is a lesson embedded in the story, and they listen with a learning stance. The storytellers and the listeners all know the story is important and has a purpose. The purpose of the story varies with the listener, but the selection is not an accident.

Imagine for a moment the child in your classroom who has been a member of such a culture. For this child, stories form the very fabric of learning about communities, values, mores, and specific historical lessons. These students have high expectations and a certain reverence for stories. Now picture that child in a classroom where the reading lesson is a story selected because it is next in the basal reader. The story connects to nothing else; it has a contrived format with short sentences and a limited vocabulary. How does the child from the rich oral culture react?

This is another example of cultural mismatch. The student examines the story for its purpose and meaning, but it has little semantic or literary value. Perhaps the only meaning was to teach the consonant cluster "tch," so the story is called "The Dutch Witch." The student who does not know that there is no major point to the story is confused as, once again, the teaching in school uses a different set of rules than those of home.

When Stories in School Are So Different From Stories at Home

One of us was teaching a short course in multicultural literature to practicing teachers. Not surprisingly, the group was multicultural: There were participants from Latino cultures, two women who were of African American descent and described themselves as "Primitive Baptists," and a woman who identified herself as Jewish.

One goal of this course was to have participants experience literature circles (the subject of chapter 13; literature circles are heterogeneous student-led groups in which students read, discuss, and respond to trade books), but to make things more interesting, the instructor deliberately placed these teachers in groups with books outside their culture. For example, the two women who described themselves as "Primitive Baptists" were placed in the group reading Jane Yolen's Holocaust story, *The Devil's Arithmetic* (1991). These teachers acknowledged that they knew little of Jewish traditions.

The first chapter of *The Devil's Arithmetic* is set in an early World War II–era Jewish home at the family's Seder (a dinner-type ceremony at the start of Passover that involves sacred readings and the eating of symbolic foods) immediately prior to Nazi occupation of the town. Although the two women of African American descent were highly competent readers, they had difficulty relating to what was taking place, because they were unfamiliar with the word *Seder* or the scene the book described. They could understand, however, that the scene was an honored family tradition and had spiritual meaning to the characters in the book. In their literature response journals (journals in which they record their literature responses; see chapter 4), they could not summarize the chapter but wrote about the ceremony in their own church that involved the washing of feet before entering church. Their schema was so different than the demands of the reading situation that reading became difficult.

Had these readers been children, and had the teacher been unschooled in culturally responsive teaching, their inability to summarize the first chapter of a novel might have been interpreted as poor reading comprehension. They might have been judged as less capable readers than others in their class, and been placed in a lower reading group. It is important to note how difficult it is to read outside one's culture and to comprehend meaning if one has not had experience with the concepts in the texts.

How many students in school are put daily in this position? Reading texts outside one's culture is a valuable tool, once you are a fluent reader and ready to broaden your experiences and take on challenges. But newer experiences are better taught with additional teacher support.

Discussions can be valuable by providing readers with support as they experience new kinds of books and styles of writing (additional prereading strategies are addressed in chapter 3).

During writing time, children who come from other cultures also write stories in the tradition of their own culture. Stories from different cultures have varied forms and styles. Although teachers might expect all stories to have a clear beginning, middle, and end and incorporate a specific number of details, stories from non-European traditions are often structured differently: Some forms may be more recursive than sequential; others (such as *Who Speaks for Wolf?*) have no end at all, because readers are expected to draw their own conclusions; still others may utilize repetition for the sake of cadence or emphasis.

Sometimes when children write stories in the tradition of their culture, the writing is assessed and evaluated on a rubric related to knowledge of Western European narrative styles. Consequently, writing is judged less capable when, for example, it may use the conventions and forms from the home community.

From THE BUTTERFLY by Patricia Polacco, copyright © 2000 by Patricia Polacco. Used by permission of Philomel Books, A division of Penguin Young Readers Group, A Member of Penguin Group (USA) Inc., 345 Hudson St, New York, NY 10014. All rights reserved.

From AUNT HARRIET'S UNDERGROUND RAIL-ROAD IN THE SKY by Faith Ringgold, copyright © 1992 by Faith Ringgold. Used by permission of Crown Publishers, an imprint of Random House Children's Books, a division of Random House, Inc.

Tech Note

On the CD-ROM that accompanies this book, there are exercises on culturally relevant issues that are suitable for class discussion or teacher in-services.

As in the football analogy, no one explicitly tells students that the writing rules are different in school. Likewise, teachers do not set out to cause their students to fail. But teachers may not have sufficient knowledge of other story forms, and the committee that created the rubric and the evaluation methods may have been similarly uninformed (Delpit, 1991; Ferdman, 1991; McLaren, 1991).

Global Books for Everyone

Most of us still have a great deal to learn about the complex human world we live in. We may be familiar with some unique cultures and totally unaware of others. One of the best ways for us all to learn about each other is through books that challenge us to become different and more experienced in our knowledge and our views.

These issues are woven throughout *Living Literature*. We do not confine our discussion of sociocultural issues with literature to this chapter. Becoming literate today means seeking literature from a variety of authors and traditions.

Summary

Students come in all sizes, shapes, ability levels, colors, and ethnicities. No matter who they are or where they come from, and whether they are longtime Americans, immigrants into this country, or temporary residents, we must teach them to the best of our ability. To do a good job, we must know them and their background—to understand what they believe, care about, and aspire to do. Getting to know their cultures and what they bring to school is a challenging task, but it can assist us in better meeting their learning needs.

Obviously, literacy is a primary area of need. All children deserve equal access to literacy and to good literature. Schooling must not ignore the factors of culture, race, class, and origin or pretend that they have nothing to do with school. Living literature classrooms work to accommodate and enrich all students with rich experiences with many high-quality books.

Action Research for Teachers

Teaching Tolerance With Multicultural Literature

Evelyn Francis
Grade 6

Following the tragedies of September 11, 2001, Evelyn decided her inner-city sixth graders needed to know more about the various cultures of the world. Could she make them more tolerant and aware by using quality multicultural books? She chose multicultural titles, implemented literature circles, and had students keep specific journals about their learning of other cultures. Evelyn administered a pretest to determine what sterotypes students had of various ethnic groups, and she posttested them at the end of her yearlong study. She additionally planned explicit lessons about tolerance through the literature experiences.

Evelyn kept a researcher log of her own journey through this venture.

Throughout the year, as Evelyn included more multicultural literature in her classroom, student interest in the books and issues increased, and they chose to read about diverse cultures more often. Student journals showed more evidence that students were thinking critically about books and the issues in them. Student posttest scores showed a decrease in stereotypic thinking. Evelyn also found that she enormously enjoyed teaching multicultural books, and planned after her research to make it an ongoing part of her classroom.

Chapter

UNDERSTANDING WHAT WE READ:
Comprehension, Vocabulary, and Discussion

"We learn to read, and we learn through reading, by adding to what we know already. Thus, comprehension and learning are fundamentally the same process." (Frank Smith, 1982, p. 53)

very summer, our Masters-level clinical practicum graduate teachers work with struggling readers who have been identified by their public school teachers as needing tutoring support. Often, when teachers first listen to these struggling readers, they sound fluent and competent—until the teachers check for comprehension. They ask their students to talk about what they have read; surprisingly, some readers who sounded so good have comprehended little of the story.

In this chapter, we address the following questions:

* ☀ What is reading comprehension? What is the relationship of vocabulary to comprehension?

* ☀ What is the role of the teacher in comprehension and vocabulary instruction?

* ☀ What is a transactional view of comprehension?

* ☀ What is the notion of "readability"?

* ☀ How can teachers activate prior knowledge with prereading activities?

* ☀ How can teachers encourage critical thinking?

* ☀ What are ways to assess comprehension?

* ☀ What are strategies for building student vocabulary?

* ☀ How can we facilitate good discussions in school settings?

* ☀ How do discussions contribute to comprehension and to the reading/literature program?

What Is Comprehension?

Comprehending is the process of understanding, or making meaning from what we read; simply put, comprehension is *thinking*. It can also be explained as bridging the new to the known (Pearson & Gallagher, 1983), or as relating what we read to the world around us and to what we already have in our heads (Smith, 1982).

One's view of comprehension is related to how one defines reading. A popular definition of reading is *gaining meaning from print* (Goodman, 1986; Weaver, 1994). In this

definition, comprehension and reading are essentially the same thing. In other words, if there is no understanding, then there also is no reading—only decoding of print.

Frank Smith (1978; 1982; 1990) aptly describes the process of comprehending as the interaction between the visual information a reader perceives (letters, words, and other symbols), and the nonvisual information (ideas, concepts) that the reader connects to the symbols. Comprehension has multiple components. First the eyes (or the hands in the case of a person with limited sight reading Braille) take in the symbolic information. Then the brain attempts to attach meaning to the symbols. That meaning takes the form of pictures in the mind of the reader, or associations with the symbols based on the reader's prior knowledge, or *schema* (the plural is *schemata*). This knowledge includes understanding the encountered words and the concepts they represent.

The example presented in chapter 2 of the diverse group of teachers reading Jane Yolen's *The Devil's Arithmetic* is useful here. The two teachers who struggled to understand the opening chapter had no prior experience, or schema, to which they could attach the word "Seder". They had never before encountered the word, had never attended a Seder, and had little to make a direct connection to the word and the concept. The Jewish woman in the group, by contrast, would have had a great deal of schemata to draw upon if she were reading that chapter, because her family participated in this ritual every year. The text would be a good match to one learner's schema, and quite alien to some others.

Schemata can be compared to a jukebox: Once you press the button for a song (see visual information such as a word or sentence or paragraph), a mechanism becomes activated that searches the available recordings to match the button pressed to a particular recording. Readers search in similar ways to attach meaning, perhaps pausing when a connection is made, and are satisfied when the result has been successful.

During this searching process, if readers are unable to make a connection because they have no relevant schemata, then comprehension may be poor or even nonexistent.

Tech Note
A profile of Diane Stanley is available on the CD-ROM that accompanies this book.

A child who reads good books will prosper. She will develop her vocabulary, increase her knowledge, and come to understand others better. She will pass dull moments in pleasure, receive comfort in hard times, and experience moments of sheer joy. What else could possibly be better?

Diane Stanley, author; personal communication, September, 1999

Reading instruction, then, involves helping readers make, expand, and deepen those connections. The more background, or schemata, one has when beginning a reading experience, the more one also takes away from it.

This comprehending process is a "most human, cognitive activity, needed for functioning in most societies" (Taylor, Graves, & van den Broek, 2000, p. 1). Its goal is to produce a useful and coherent mental representation of what is being read. Comprehension involves a network of meaning that includes meaningful relations and referential relations that enable readers to track characters and events as they proceed in their reading.

The Role of the Teacher

In the literature program, the role of the teacher is to enable and support comprehension. This role takes several forms. First of all, teachers match students' interests and their reading ability to ensure a successful reading experience. As students read in areas related to their interests and experiences, the schemata they possess about reading and about the topic are utilized, enhanced, and expanded. Generally, teachers and media specialists help match students to books for their independent reading experiences.

Of course, not everything students read can comfortably suit their interests and their schemata. An important part of instruction is expanding readers' repertoires, so that they continue to develop their reading skills. Consequently, teachers maneuver students into selections that challenge them somewhat, but through good instruction, they provide them with the needed and supportive scaffolding.

Scaffolding is supportive teaching that includes questioning, modeling, feedback, and instruction with the idea that adult support is gradually withdrawn as learners become more autonomous (Harris & Hodges, 1995, p. 226). The goal of instruction with scaffolding is to enable readers to grow, and to make them as independent as possible so that they have the skills to continue to develop when teachers are not available. Many of the prereading strategies presented later in this chapter foster scaffolding. Scaffolding is based on the work of Vygotsky; the term itself is believed to have been coined by Wood and Middleton (1975). Using the metaphor of a construction scaffold, readers can picture in instruction building a framework (like the one outside a wall being painted) upon which students can climb as they gain understanding of the matters at hand.

The goals in reading comprehension instruction, then, are to enhance reader comprehension, to enlarge a reader's vocabulary and word knowledge, which assists in their growing comprehension, and to foster meaningful student responses to literature (detailed in chapter 4). The teacher continually makes judgments about what students know and what they need to know, and helps them get there. Teachers can select the types of strategies presented in this chapter and throughout *Living Literature* to assist students in better understanding what they read.

A Transactional Theory of Comprehension

In the 1930s, a remarkable educator, Louise Rosenblatt, changed the way reading researchers and theorists thought about comprehension. Until then, the prevailing belief was that comprehension was a process of remembering and of getting an accurate account of what the author wrote, as well as a correct interpretation. Meaning was invested into a text by the author, and the reader's job was to get the meaning right.

Rosenblatt's (1938; 1978) view of reading defined how readers read differently for different purposes, and she proposed a continuum to describe them. For example, when people read strictly for fun and pleasure, they are reading aesthetically. Few demands are placed on the reader for aesthetic reading, and the process can be a quick one, even a less precise one. Aesthetic reading is the sort of reading one does on the beach, on an airplane, or while relaxing on a rainy afternoon.

However, not all reading is aesthetic, Rosenblatt argued. Tackling a difficult textbook in a course or the directions for doing one's taxes is a very different reading experience. She labeled this sort of reading as *efferent*. Efferent reading is a much more demanding process and requires more work. During efferent reading, readers are more likely to slow down, reread passages, attempt to read every word, and sometimes struggle with particular parts to gain meaning.

Most reading, Rosenblatt would contend, falls somewhere between totally efferent and totally aesthetic. How efferent or aesthetic it is depends on the background of the reader to cope with the text, the degree to which the reading was a choice, the purpose for the reading, and the nature of the writing. Clearly, readers don't get to choose everything they read. And sometimes readers make deliberate choices to challenge themselves, explore different genres of writing, or tackle a text because of their desire, knowing it will be difficult.

Meet . . . Pat Mora

Author of *This Big Sky; Tomás and the Library Lady; The Rainbow Tulip; My Own True Name: New and Selected Poems for Young Adults; Napantla: Essays from the Land in the Middle; House of Houses;* and more.

"I spent most of my life in my hometown of El Paso, Texas, a city on the U.S./Mexican border, a city in the Chihuahua desert. All four of my grandparents came to Texas at the time of the Mexican Revolution in 1910. These facts of geography and family influence my writing.

"I love writing both for children and for adults. Keenly aware of the need for more Latino authors, I feel fortunate to spend at least some of my time writing and also speaking to groups across the country." Ms. Mora was influenced to become a reader and writer by a mother who read to her, by a nun at school who loved literature, and by an aunt who was a wonderful storyteller. "I write because playing with words is a unique pleasure. I hope that my readers of all ages will find delight in the words I've knitted together and in the power of words to make us laugh, cry, sigh, remember."

Ms. Mora takes her role as a Latino writer seriously. "I am very committed to having our literature reflect the verbal richness that is the country, our full literary heritage. I am more and more convinced that when Latinos fully participate in all aspects of children's book publishing, as publishers, editors, reviewers, conference chairs, award committee chairs, publicity and art directors, scholars, and journals editors, then we will see more work by Latino illustrators and writers, not only published but reviewed and promoted and included as part of the history of this (nonfiction) genre. I am convinced that teacher leaders and librarian leaders of good conscience will settle for nothing less. I want teachers and librarians to realize their power to affect what cultures are and are not published. We are all committed to excellence for children. It won't be easy to make our home, this Earth, a place where a book is judged not by the heritage of the author but by the words and how they move us. I'm counting on teachers and librarians to be the change."

Ms. Mora now lives in Kentucky. Her website is www.patmora.com.

Louise Rosenblatt (1978) also suggested another stance toward reading and reacting to texts: Because readers are unique and have varied experiences, each reader gleans quite different meanings from texts. Rosenblatt called this process a reading transaction. She explained that a transaction has three parts: the reader, the text, and the poem or message.

1. The *reader* brings a unique set of experiences to reading, including personal background, reading background, culture, and ways of knowing. Consequently, teachers don't control what readers get from a text, nor should they try to. The reader is one part of the transaction.

2. The second part of the transaction is the *text*. Once written, a text is static, and the author has no more control over it.

3. The *poem*, or *message*, is the meaning the author intended. However, just because the author had a particular meaning does not guarantee that readers will re-

act as expected. For example, most of us have written something that was misinterpreted or misconstrued. We look back at our text to see how it ended up sounding different to a reader than what we meant: It was too cold or too short, or it had an unfortunate choice of words. Consequently, the reader can gain a meaning that the writer didn't intend. Thus, there is a difference between the printed text and the sentiment that the author meant to convey. This phenomenon is part of the reading transaction.

The last important aspect of a reading transaction is that whenever these three parts—the reader, the text, and the message—come together, there is a change in the reader. This change may be big or little, subtle or explicit, but whenever we read (or write), we learn and grow, gaining new meanings and expanding our personal literacy repertoire.

Readability

There have been attempts in reading education to assign a readability (Fry, 1978, and others), or difficulty, level to particular passages. Although the notion of matching students to books and stories that are suited to their ability is appealing, in reality, it is impossible to ensure readability. All these formulas take into account only the text and its writing style, usually examining sentence length and word length as measures of difficulty. However, these aspects of texts have never been proven to make reading more difficult. Maurice Sendak's popular book *Where the Wild Things Are*, for example, is fairly easy to read, but the book is one long sentence that runs 16 pages.

Even educational materials that have been designated with a readability level should be questioned.

No readability formula can take reader experience into account. All veteran teachers who deal with reading have met readers who sometimes choose to read texts that seem to be too difficult. But readers who are determined and motivated often succeed. What would we as teachers accomplish by preventing their risk taking? Sometimes risk taking is fruitful.

Because readers need to be taken into account, teachers can consult the suggestions of booksellers for broad recommendations, while remembering these are *only* guidelines. In the final analysis, finding the right book for a student is a combination of teacher judgment, purpose for reading, student interest and motivation, and trying out books. Sometimes it's okay to try. Sometimes it's okay to abandon something tried and start again.

Because experience is a crucial factor, readability formulas should be used cautiously. A better way to find out if a text is suitable is to let a student try it out for a few pages. If it is too difficult, he or she will generally become frustrated. Ultimately, readers need to begin to learn to select texts that are suitable for themselves.

Building Comprehension

There are several steps in building reader comprehension as teachers implement their literature and reading program: activating or supplying prior knowledge; guiding reading; reinforcing concepts; and encouraging critical thinking and inquiry.

Activating or Supplying Prior Knowledge

Sometimes students know a great deal about a topic: They may have read books on the same topics or by authors with a similar style, or the topics presented may be familiar in their experience and culture. At other times, students may not be prepared to handle a particular literature selection.

Lack of familiarity may happen for any of the reasons already mentioned. The readers may not know critical concepts that are needed to make sense of a selection. For example, a story could be about a holiday such as Christmas. Students who are familiar with Christmas will immediately relate to a story about Santa Claus, Christmas trees, or caroling. Not all students will make the needed connection, however. Often, these students

Copyright © 1963, 1991 Maurice Sendak.

are culturally different from their teacher, who needs to consider that some students will have no reference from which to understand what they will read. A young child raised in a traditional Korean family, a Jewish family, a Chinese family, or a Vietnamese family, for example, may have had little or no experience with the concept of Christmas.

> There are many complaints from inside and outside schools about the quality of student thinking. These complaints are venerable and probably unanswerable. Parents for generations have been convinced that their children are not taught as well as they were.
>
> Frank Smith, 1990, p. 6

Teachers eventually learn not to make assumptions about their students, and instead carefully consider the relevance of different selections for students in a classroom. They generate a good discussion about the needed concept where students who do know about a topic can share their experiences with students who are unfamiliar with it. They often select key words associated with a topic or selection to present or review, either formally or incidentally.

Through discussion or even in lessons before reading a selection, students gain some useful schemata that will assist them in making meaning when they read. Keeping these issues in mind will enable more students to benefit from the story.

Consider again the example of Jane Yolen's *The Devil's Arithmetic* (1990). How might a teacher of intermediate-aged students prepare, or scaffold, them before reading this book? As you may recall, the opening scene is a family Seder, set in a modern Jewish household.

Activating or supplying prior knowledge is an important part of teaching reading comprehension. For this book, a teacher can help readers by asking a Jew to share items used during a Seder or explain the custom of the Seder, or by locating a picture or explanation of a Seder. Some students, such as those who have been raised in Jewish homes, may be able to share their family experiences. With help from parents or local community members, a teacher might be able to simulate the ritual of the Seder in the classroom prior to reading the story.

Guiding Student Reading

In chapter 11, we discuss guided reading in depth. Here, we use the term more generally to mean anything a teacher does that guides any reading of students.

Sometimes, teachers lead a discussion prior to the reading, provide experiences, or show items that relate to a story, as just described; these experiences lead off a discussion that sets a purpose for the reading. "Read to find out what happens at the end of the Seder" might be a good suggestion to help readers forge ahead in *The Devil's*

Arithmetic with some anticipation of what is to come. Thus, setting a purpose for reading is one way teachers guide their students' reading.

At other times, when reading selections are longer, teachers segment the selections to guide the reading. They may choose a natural break a few pages into a text; they ask readers to stop when they reach that point and then hold a short discussion about what has happened so far and to predict what will happen next.

Breaking the selection into more manageable parts can support struggling readers. One caveat, though: Sometimes this approach can be counterproductive. Too much stopping to talk can interfere with readers' becoming engaged and absorbed in the material, and students who must wait for classmates to get to the same point can become bored in the process. This strategy should be used carefully, thoughtfully, and judiciously.

One way teachers guide reading with younger readers is to take them on a "picture walk"; this simply means browsing a picture book's illustrations before beginning to read it. Having students identify and label objects in each illustration and asking them what they think is going on in each illustration can help activate students' knowledge, help them predict what they will read, and build anticipation for the reading event.

A comparable way that middle school teachers sometimes guide reading is by throwing a "teaser." Seventh-grade teacher Kim Gerdes designs teasers for her classes that can take several forms: Sometimes she will read aloud an especially exciting text excerpt; at other times, she will post a copy of some exciting text in the classroom for students to discover. This could be accompanied by some thought-provoking questions about the piece. Whatever form the teaser takes, it succeeds in getting kids interested and ready to read.

Reinforcing Concepts

In the course of reading, words and concepts may arise that students know little about. Skilled teachers assess these needs as they interact with readers and discuss texts with them. In this way, they know what to teach further, what to highlight, and what misconceptions to correct. For example, one student talking about her reading of Arthur Clarke's short story *Space Pet* never understood that the setting was a space station; she believed the story talked about a gas station. If a reader doesn't know about space stations, then the rest of the story doesn't make a lot of sense.

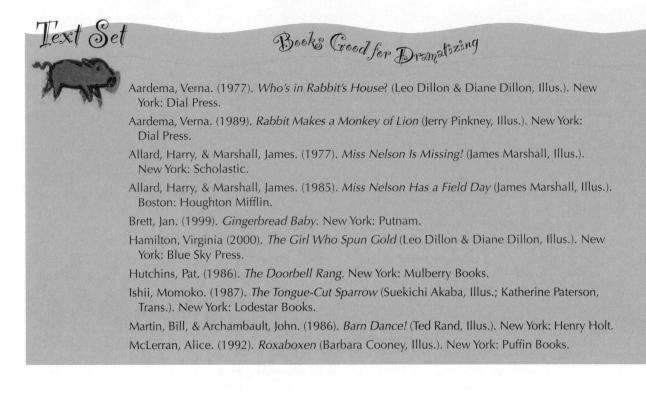

Text Set   Books Good for Dramatizing

Aardema, Verna. (1977). *Who's in Rabbit's House?* (Leo Dillon & Diane Dillon, Illus.). New York: Dial Press.

Aardema, Verna. (1989). *Rabbit Makes a Monkey of Lion* (Jerry Pinkney, Illus.). New York: Dial Press.

Allard, Harry, & Marshall, James. (1977). *Miss Nelson Is Missing!* (James Marshall, Illus.). New York: Scholastic.

Allard, Harry, & Marshall, James. (1985). *Miss Nelson Has a Field Day* (James Marshall, Illus.). Boston: Houghton Mifflin.

Brett, Jan. (1999). *Gingerbread Baby*. New York: Putnam.

Hamilton, Virginia (2000). *The Girl Who Spun Gold* (Leo Dillon & Diane Dillon, Illus.). New York: Blue Sky Press.

Hutchins, Pat. (1986). *The Doorbell Rang*. New York: Mulberry Books.

Ishii, Momoko. (1987). *The Tongue-Cut Sparrow* (Suekichi Akaba, Illus.; Katherine Paterson, Trans.). New York: Lodestar Books.

Martin, Bill, & Archambault, John. (1986). *Barn Dance!* (Ted Rand, Illus.). New York: Henry Holt.

McLerran, Alice. (1992). *Roxaboxen* (Barbara Cooney, Illus.). New York: Puffin Books.

An excellent way to reinforce concepts in some stories is to dramatize them. Acting out stories such as *The Keeping Quilt* (Polacco), *Barn Dance!* (Martin & Archambault), and *Abiyoyo* (Seeger) with some simple props can help readers reinforce meanings and enhance comprehension. When students act out the events in a story, many word and sentence meanings, and consequently the concepts that underlie them, become clear.

Dramatization is an important support for comprehension that is underutilized in classrooms. Many students enjoy dramatizing, and are unaware of the excellent learning value of the drama. While dramatizing, readers and actors hear the story again for review (and repeated readings are an important aspect of developing fluency) (Wilhelm, 2002).

Learners of all abilities can readily participate in dramatization. Considering multiple intelligences (Gardner, 1993), drama better suits learners whose strengths are in bodily-kinesthetic learning. Teachers report that drama works in many contexts. Some feel strongly that drama is good for special education students. Providing struggling students with opportunities to act out stories is good for building both skills and attitudes. Other teachers feel just as strongly that drama is a wonderful strategy for honors or advanced students.

Encouraging Critical Thinking and Inquiry

Teachers often talk about their goal of encouraging critical thinking and inquiry with their students. But knowing how to encourage critical thinking can be challenging.

One thing is certain: Simply asking comprehension questions is usually ineffective and inadequate. For example, a few decades ago, Ken Goodman wrote a passage entitled "The Mardsen Giberter," from which many of us have learned some things about reading. Goodman substituted nonsense words such as "Mardsen" and "Giberter" for real words, spelling these new words using logical English spelling. High-frequency words such as "the" and "for" remained the same (Whitmore & Goodman, 1996). Many teacher education students have read the almost nonsense passage, and then answered some "comprehension" questions at the end, much like common reading and content-area assignments. It is interesting to note that most students can answer the five comprehension questions even without having any idea what the story is about.

What happens is that readers who have been playing at doing school for years have learned how to find the responses to literal questions in an assignment by looking for key words in a selection. By matching those key words,

Cover from BARN DANCE! written by Bill Martin Jr. and John Archambault. Illustrated by Ted Rand. Illustrations copyright © 1986 by Ted Rand. Reprinted by permission of Henry Holt and Company, LLC.

and reading what comes next, they can often write the expected answer, although they may not know the meaning of the words being written!

What does this tell us? Literal questions—those that are answered explicitly in a text—are a poor measure of reading comprehension. In fact, one could say they are inappropriate, because readers can game-play in this strategy without comprehending anything at all. This is not the goal of good reading instruction.

Learning to ask *good* questions is an important part of teaching for comprehension. Although there is nothing wrong with asking a few literal questions at the beginning, questioning should move into other areas, asking students to infer, compare, conclude, synthesize, raise questions, and take other perspectives. Skilled teachers learn to put all sorts of questions into a discussion that will suit the needs and abilities of varied learners.

One middle school teacher we work with ensures that everyone in her class will be successful: She often begins lessons with some literal questions or some very obvious questions. She builds up to more inferential, higher-level questions, making sure that all readers are also challenged. By doing this, special education students as well as her most successful learners are all engaged and participating.

This same teacher asks students to bring in a favorite old book from their earlier reading days. Using this favorite book, seventh graders create their own questions about the story, using literal, inferential, and application-type questions. Then they teach a reading lesson to a class of younger students in the school. By doing this, they learn how to ask questions about stories, and how to be better prepared for questions they will be asked.

Figure 3.1 lists types of questions one might ask to elicit deeper understanding in readers. Not every reading lesson needs to include all question types. Teachers develop judgment about good questioning that lend themselves to particular selections.

Assessing Comprehension

The task and the challenge of assessing a reader's understanding of a selection are complex, because teachers want to know not only whether students are comprehending, but also how well they are comprehending. This process is further complicated by the fact that students have different communication skills. Teachers thus rely on a variety of strategies to assess comprehension.

As Figure 3.1 shows, thoughtful questions are useful tools for teachers. Because many of those questions have no one right answer, teachers must develop judgment about student responses to get the most accurate picture of their understanding. Figure 3.1 shows how

Figure 3.1
Questions for
Levels of Compre-
hending: *The Three
Little Pigs*—The
Traditional Tale

Literal Questions—These questions can be answered simply by locating information in the text. They show whether students can retrieve information, but are not helpful for assessing more sophisticated understanding of a selection.

Examples: How many little pigs were there? What kind of house did the first little pig build?

Inferential Questions—Answers to these questions are suggested in the text but not explicitly stated. For example, a character comes into a room from outside, his clothes and hair are dripping wet, and he is folding a wet umbrella. The reader infers that it was raining outside, but the text does not state this.

Examples: How are the three little pigs related to each other? (You infer they are siblings, but it is not stated.) What do you infer about the intelligence of the three pigs?

Comparison and Contrast Questions—Comparing means finding similarities; contrasting means finding differences.

Examples: What do the three little pigs have in common? How are the first and third little pigs different? How is this folktale different from Jon Scieska's *The True Story of the 3 Little Pigs!* (1989)?

Synthesis Questions—These questions combine understandings, draw conclusions, or in some way require readers to think differently about the material in the story. Synthesis questions ask readers to detect patterns and to learn from those patterns.

Example: What might wolves learn from the Big Bad Wolf about the building habits of little pigs?

Application Questions—These questions involve identifying information or perceptions from a text and asking questions that demand readers to apply this knowledge to a new situation.

Example: If you were to plan your own home or advise someone else in their planning, what lessons from the little pigs might be helpful?

Critical Questions—These types of questions raise awareness of different points of view, ask readers to make judgments, or have readers extend knowledge with cause-and-effect thinking. Critical questions can lead to further inquiry.

Examples: What would this story be like if it were told from the wolf's point of view? How might this story be partly responsible for people having negative views of wolves? Why has the wolf, and not the pigs, been portrayed as a bad character?

Connection Questions—These questions address the extent to which readers can relate an idea in the story to their own lives, including personal experience and experiences with other texts, including movies and television programs. (See Keene & Zimmerman, 1997).

Examples: What other story can you think of where wolves are bashed for being big and bad? Was there a time in your life when doing something quickly and poorly was not a wise course of action?

Cause-and-Effect Questions—Students gradually learn to predict plot and character actions based on life experiences. These questions probe their growing sense of cause-and-effect thinking, which is an essential human skill.

Examples: What choices did the first little pig make about building his house? Why was his choice an unwise decision? How might the story have been different if the wolf had started at the home of the third little pig instead?

Theme Questions—A theme is an underlying idea or premise about a story. It may communicate a universal lesson or truth.

Example: What can someone learn about life from the story of the Three Little Pigs? (Taking the time to do something well will pay off in the end.)

questions can become more challenging and use more critical thinking.

Other strategies for assessing comprehension include retellings, shortcut miscue analysis, story mapping, comic strip writing, sketch-to-stretch, symbolic story representation, think alouds, and writing to learn.

Retellings

One way to find out what learners got from a story is to ask them. Using an audio recorder, teachers first suggest that students tell everything they remember about the story from the beginning to the end; this invites a full recounting of the story. This *unaided* retelling—where the examiner does no helping or prompting—is uninterrupted as the reader retells. The teacher does not pose any questions or prompts, but instead listens carefully (Goodman, Watson, & Burke, 1987). Unaided retellings can also be done in writing.

During an oral retelling, the teacher can proceed to an *aided* retelling, in which the teacher poses questions based on what the reader has already volunteered. The teacher does *not* ask about ideas the reader has not already brought up; thus the reader is not incidentally coached to retell

based on questions. For example, if a teacher asks how many houses are in the story of the Three Little Pigs and the student never mentioned houses, then the reader is already coached that there was more than one house; the reader may or may not have already understood that point. Such questions interfere with getting accurate notions of the student's understanding.

On the other hand, if the student mentioned that a pig was in the story, the teacher could ask a more open-ended question such as "What else can you tell me about the pig you mentioned?" Even simply asking "What else can you tell me about the story?" is a good way to elicit more responses. Figure 3.2 lists good open-ended questions for retelling or for conferencing about books. It is important to remember that teachers may not need to use this process with all their students. Collecting this kind of information from struggling students is a sensible approach. It's important to continue this process until you believe you've gotten everything possible from the student. If an audio recorder is not available for this process, teachers need to take notes and listen very carefully as students retell.

Figure 3.2 Open-Ended Questions for Conferencing About Books

- Tell me something you noticed about today's reading.
- What does today's reading remind you of?
- How does today's reading make you feel?
- Why do you think the author wrote this?
- Are there any more people or animals in the story you recall?
- What was the problem in the story?
- How did this story begin?
- How did this story end?
- What do you think about the way this story ended?
- Is there something in this story you could learn from?
- Is there something in this story you plan to remember for the rest of your life?
- Was there one part of this reading that was most exciting?
- Is there one part of this book you'd like to tell your friends about?
- Was there something or some part of this reading that you did not like?

After hearing both the aided and unaided retellings, the teacher can assess the degree to which the story was retold. Thinking of an entire story as 100%, the teacher can then list story events to determine the proportion of the events the students has appropriately shared. If half of the story has been related, then a 50% retelling score could be assigned.

Often teachers will prepare a retelling outline listing events in a given story or selection, where they can check off events the reader mentions and easily determine if any events are missing. Next they calculate the percentage of the story that has been related. Also, it is considered appropriate to allow some "wiggle room" for raising a student's score if, for example, he or she shared insights about the story that went beyond the text (about 5–10% "wiggle room").

Figure 3.3 presents the guidelines for conducting and scoring a retelling.

There are other ways to use retellings as a reading strategy in classrooms; one way is after a class read-aloud. In *Read and Retell* (1987), Brown and Cambourne discuss numerous ways to engage students in retelling or summarizing text in writing after hearing the teacher read aloud, which

they call "oral-to-written retelling." They describe it this way: "This form of retelling can be used with both immature and mature readers/writers. It can also be used to gain insight into learners' listening skills and/or degrees of control over the written forms of language" (p. 29).

Brown and Cambourne also mention variations of this strategy, such as having students draw after the read-aloud. They explain that if students discuss their illustrations, teachers will learn more about the students' listening comprehension and ability to express meaning orally.

A variation on oral-to-written retelling is seventh-grade teacher Kim Gerdes' retelling journal. As Kim reads aloud *The Midwife's Apprentice* (Cushman), she stops at critical points to pose questions that will scaffold students' written retelling at the end of the read-aloud session. Kim says, "Each day when I finish reading I usually have my students respond in their journals to a prompt concerning what was read. For example, in *The Midwife's Apprentice* I might ask them to respond to: Do you think Alice should put up with the mean midwife or go back to fending for herself?" (personal communication, June, 2003).

Figure 3.3
Executing and Assessing a Retelling

1. Choose a text appropriate to the student's reading level. Prepare a list of events in the story.

2. Have the student read the selection. Be sure to tell the student prior to reading that you will be asking for a retelling. The student can read orally or silently.

3. Afterward, ask the student to tell you everything he or she can remember about the reading or selection. We recommend you tape-record this retelling.

4. Once the student has supplied all he or she can, probe further by building on what the student said, but without introducing any new material or ideas: "Tell me more about _____ (insert names of characters or events the student mentioned)." Continue until you feel you have gotten all the student has to offer.

5. As the student retells (or as you listen to the tape), note on your list which events are covered fully or partially. Keep track of the events the student recalled.

6. Retelling the plot and events of a reading can be worth a total of 60% of the score. For example, if the student supplies four out of five story events, that student's score for this part is 48% $(4 \div 5 \times .60)$.

7. Identifying characters and the setting in the reading can be worth 40% of the score. Distribute this percentage according to the importance you give to characters and the setting; for example, you might make characters worth 30% and the setting 10%, or both might be worth 20%. Do not assign much value to minor characters or setting if the setting is "Once upon a time."

8. Add up the assigned scores, the proportion of the 40% and the 60% that you have judged based on the retelling. Add up to 10% if you believe a reader has provided some inferences or insights. All these together become *your student's retelling score.*

Structured retelling is a strategy that some teachers use after reading a story aloud to a class. It helps them know whether students listened effectively, and it serves as a review for everyone, especially struggling readers. Here's how a structured retelling works.

As soon as you have finished reading aloud a picture book or a chapter to your students, initiate questioning: "Who can tell me how this story started?" (or "today's reading" if it was an excerpt). Once someone has offered a good explanation of the beginning, ask, "Who can tell me what happened next?" Continue asking "Who can tell me what happened after that?" or something similar until you feel you have enough responses to ask, "Who can tell me how today's reading ended?"

Structured retelling is especially good with younger students or with struggling readers. Like all strategies, however, you shouldn't use it every time you read. Sometimes, it's acceptable just to read, and to let children listen without having any agenda.

Shortcut Miscue Analysis

Miscue analysis (Goodman, Watson, & Burke, 1987; Wilde, 2000) is an individual and authentic assessment tool that helps a teacher understand a reader's strengths and needs. By listening to a student read and by examining the errors or miscues the student makes, the teacher can determine the extent to which a reader's patterns may interfere with the gaining of meaning. Even most skilled adult readers make miscues when they read. Making miscues in itself is not a problem; it is the nature of the miscues that is examined that determines whether the construction of meaning is supported or not.

Although conducting a full miscue analysis is an important skill for reading and literature teachers, the whole of it is too extensive to cover here. However, a shortcut that will help a teacher get insights into a student's reading is described in Figure 3.4. More about miscue analysis is available in other sources (Goodman, Watson, & Burke, 1987; in press).

Figure 3.4
Miscue Analysis Shortcut

- ☼ Have a student read aloud an unfamiliar passage at least two pages in length, or a short story appropriate to the student's interest and ability. The story should contain few, if any, pictures. Tape-record the student's reading.

- ☼ Listen to the student's tape as you look at a copy of the text. Indicate where the student substitutes words by writing in the miscue above the intended word. Add words the student inserts with an editing caret, and circle or cross out words the student omits. If the piece is short, follow this procedure for the entire piece. For a longer selection, analyze 10 consecutive sentences near the end of the selection when the reader has had a chance to get engaged with the piece. If the student has corrected miscues along the way, deal only with what was not corrected.

- ☼ Number a paper from 1 to 10. Say each sentence as the student last read it, including any corrections the student made. Ask yourself, "As the student read this sentence, will it change meaning in the story?" In other words, if the miscues were not important, you may well answer "no change." You can answer "change" for sentences you feel were changed enough that meaning was altered. Answer "partial change" where the change in meaning was slight.

- ☼ Add up the number of sentences for which you judged partial change or no change. If this student had no change or partial change for 80% of the sentences, the reader is likely reading fairly effectively, even if the reading sounds less than smooth, and if the student is making corrections along the way.

- ☼ If you combine this technique with a retelling score, you will have some excellent data about the student's reading. If the miscue score was high but the retelling score was low, then the student has sufficient decoding skills but needs the sorts of comprehending strategies mentioned in this chapter, such as story maps, comic strips, written conversations, and sketch-to-stretch, in addition to opportunities for writing to learn.

- ☼ If the miscue score is low, such as under 70%, then the passage may have been too difficult, the student may need more prior knowledge activated or supplied, or he or she would benefit from reading the passage with another student (buddy reading).

(Based on Goodman, Watson, & Burke, 1987)

Story Maps

Story mapping is an artistic postreading strategy that helps develop and assess reader comprehension. These are typically done cooperatively in small groups, enabling students to benefit from classmates' perceptions, compare notes about texts, and challenge each other's thinking. Using large poster-sized paper, the group segments a story into several parts (they have to decide how many), and represents each part artistically.

Each member of the group must participate. At the conclusion of the mapping, the group shares their map and explains their reasoning and representations to the class, which essentially results in retelling the story. These also can be preserved and posted on classroom walls and hallways to share informally what groups are reading. Often teachers will have students add the story title and the author/illustrator.

Comic Strips

A useful and motivating postreading strategy for checking story comprehension is to have students create a comic strip. Students fold a piece of paper into four frames, and they draw any four consecutive scenes from the book or story. As in a real comic strip, readers can add speech balloons to indicate characters talking to each other. Teachers examine student work to gain insights into their thinking about the selection.

Sketch-to-Stretch

This artistic postreading strategy is done by individual students of any age after reading a provocative, interesting text. Teachers give students a piece of drawing paper and instruct them to "draw whatever the story means" to them. Developed at Indiana University (Leland & Harste, 1994; Siegel, 1984), this strategy enables readers to artistically express some aspect of a story, after which they are invited to orally share about their drawing.

Symbolic Story Representation

While reading or after reading a story, students create cutouts of the characters, similar to paper dolls, using art supplies or magazine cutouts as props to represent characters (Wilhelm, 1997).

Using these props, students dramatize story events, with the teacher as audience. The act of dramatizing with the props is a powerful way to develop and enhance comprehension. This helps students see themselves in the story and is a way to assess understanding. Some teachers videotape these dramatizations for other students to view, or for assessment purposes. Students enjoy this strategy because it is similar to play and involves use of other artistic intelligences. The photo on this page shows symbolic story representation.

Writing to Learn

In the 1980s, theorists and researchers came to understand that writing is a cognitive strategy (Emig, 1981; Flower & Hayes, 1981; Holly, 1989; Perl, 1980). They realized that when people write, they are also learning, and are demonstrating learning. The processes used during writing are multifaceted and complex, and they require a great deal of brainpower. Recall a time when you finished writing a paper for a course and were mentally exhausted as a result of the writing experience; the term "brain drain" comes to mind.

Having students write what they know can be a most effective assessment tool. Many teachers have implemented writing as a part of literature, math, science, or foreign language learning. The writing fosters the development of thinking about the subject area.

First graders have done a symbolic story representation of a Robert Munsch book, *Purple, Green and Yellow*.

In the teaching of literature, students can write as part of literature circles (see chapter 13), or they can write in response to literature in a variety of ways (see chapter 14). The important point here is that through writing, teachers have a window into students' comprehension. Many teachers find this an assessment not only of student learning or of misconceptions, but also of the effectiveness of their teaching.

> *Vocabulary is a must—even more critical than knowing the meaning of a word is knowing how the word is correctly and effectively used in a sentence. That is learned through reading.*
>
> *Ken Mochizuki, author; personal communication, September, 1999*

Think-Alouds

Thinking aloud is a powerful strategy for both teaching and assessing understanding that allows learners to hear what is going on inside the mind of the teacher (Wilhelm, 2002a). In this strategy, teachers essentially share what they are thinking about as they read. This experience is critical for students because it provides them a window into the mind of a more sophisticated reader. Effective readers are active readers. They have an inner narrative running through their minds as they process and think about what they read. Think-alouds show children what capable readers do.

Think-alouds are a versatile strategy that can be applied across the curriculum for different purposes. Here we share how the think-aloud strategy can be incorporated into a read-aloud to teach comprehension strategies. Jill Ostrow, a former elementary teacher, designed a plan for incorporating the teaching of important comprehension strategies: making connections, asking questions, inferring, using visual and sensory imagery, and synthesizing into a read-aloud. See Figure 3.5 for a plan using the book *The Big Box* (Morrison & Morrison).

This plan shows how Jill incorporates what she is thinking as she applies a variety of strategies for comprehending the story. Typically the think-aloud time is a teaching time, one

Tech Note
An author profile of Ken Mochizuki is available on the CD-ROM that accompanies this book.

THE BIG BOX

Written by Toni Morrison with Slade Morrison

Illustrated by Giselle Potter

FORMAT:

Picture Book written in poetic style

POSSIBLE TOPICS OF STUDY:

Personal Freedom, Poetry, Social Activism

OVERVIEW:

This is my new favorite book! I was astounded when I read it. Written in Toni Morrison's characteristic poetic style, this book talks about the personal freedom of children. Beautifully written, the words are strong and purposeful.

Not abiding by rules set up by the adults around them, three children are sent to live in the "big box." There they are given food and presents. However, the strong message here is that you can't substitute creativity and freedom with things.

The illustrations complement the book, but the words stand on their own.

MODELING MAKING CONNECTIONS:

The teacher thinks aloud how the box in the story reminds her of a classmate she once knew who was constantly breaking the law. Eventually, the student went to jail, and this was just like being in a box.

The teacher invites students to share any connections they have made, such as a time they felt they were in a box, or someone they knew who had a similar experience.

Figure 3.5
Example of a Think-Aloud to Teach Comprehension Strategies (created by Jill Ostrow)

(continues)

Figure 3.5
(continued)

MODELING ASKING QUESTIONS:

- (Page 1) Why do the kids have to live in a box?
- (Page 2) Why don't they live with their parents?
- Why do they get all of the food and all of those gifts?
- (Page 3) I wonder what the authors meant when they wrote, "Those kids can't handle their freedom?"
- (Page 5) A Cure?! Was she sick?
- Why do adults always say, "You can't handle your freedom"?
- (Page 9) But is Mickey hurting anyone?
- (Page 10) With so many rules, where *was* his freedom?
- (Page 14) But aren't they acting free? They can be free with themselves!
- What is the difference between personal freedom and acting in a way that is not accepted in a community or a society? What are those boundaries?

MODELING INFERRING:

- (Page 4) I'm inferring that Patty might be what some teachers call a "behavior problem." (I HATE that term! Poor Patty!)
- (Page 6) I think by saying, "But if freedom is handled just *your* way then it's not my freedom or free," she is saying that everyone has a different definition of freedom.
- (Page 8) I'm inferring that the authors write about the animals because the active nature of kids is natural! You wouldn't say that animals can't handle their freedom . . . they do what comes naturally.
- (Page 12) I think the parents think that they will make the kids happy by giving them gifts, but personal freedom is more important than toys!
- (Page 20) I think this page means that you can impose "locks" but you can't take away someone's personal boundaries.

MODELING USING VISUAL AND SENSORY IMAGERY:

- I can hear the rhythm throughout the book. It sounds like a song.

MODELING SYNTHESIZING:

- Three children are accused by the adults in their life of not being able to handle their freedom because they are not acting the way the adults want them to.
- The children are sent to live in the Big Box where their parents visit them and bring them gifts and food. The parents think the presents will "calm" them down. The children still "break out" of the box.

SPECIAL NOTES:

This book is awesome! I'd use this book to model questioning and inferring. But, more, this book would spark a very deep conversation on personal freedoms and boundaries. So many questions arise from rereading this book. A good example of why it is important to reread.

in which teachers demonstrate their thinking depending upon their purpose. Jill may focus on only one agenda, such as students making connections. Or she might return to an interactive read-aloud in which she asks students to make their own connections as she reads to them (see chapter 10). This is an important teaching strategy for helping students become more powerful readers themselves—all done through the vehicle of sharing books

aloud. It becomes an informal assessment tool when teachers listen to and analyze think-alouds.

What's in My Lexicon?

An advanced sixth-grade reader needs to look up the word *farce*, which is on her vocabulary list. She locates it, but the definition includes the word *sham*, and she does not know the meaning of that word. Accordingly, she looks up *sham* in her dictionary; the definition of *sham* includes the word *feign*, and she does not know what that means either. So, she looks up *feign*, and the definition says it's a *sham*. For all her effort, this student knows little more than she did when she started her vocabulary exercise, and in fact feels very frustrated by this experience. Furthermore, she still will have a difficult time comprehending the piece she is reading.

Learning vocabulary is much more than looking up in a dictionary words you don't know . And unfortunately, if you don't know much about the words you are looking up, using the dictionary is not all that helpful, as the preceding example shows.

When readers read something new, the degree to which they comprehend is related to the words they understand. Expanding students' vocabulary, or personal lexicon, is both a goal and an outcome of reading.

Getting to know new words is not an easy process. How we come to understand meanings depends on whether the new words represent objects, actions, feelings, or ideas. Readers most easily assimilate objects and actions. Words for feelings and ideas can be extremely complex in that readers may first need to learn underlying concepts before fully understanding a particular word (Kibby, 1995).

Teachers struggle with how to expand students' reading and speaking vocabulary. One traditional approach has been to present students with new or less familiar words, and have them look up these words in a dictionary and then use them in sentences. *This is a common but highly ineffective practice.*

Researchers generally agree about ways to develop meaningful vocabulary in our readers, but that does not mean that teaching vocabulary is easy (Dole, Sloan, & Trathen, 1995; Kibby, 1995). Here are some key points to remember.

Vocabulary is best learned in context rather than in isolation (Dole, Sloan, & Trathen, 1995; Kibby, 1995; Nagy & Herman, 1985). Although teachers who present students with lists of words to learn have good intentions of helping to expand student vocabulary, there is no evidence to suggest that students will retain much from these lists. The nature of the human mind is that people remember what they need to know or what is personally interesting and relevant to them; a list of words selected by someone else is neither of those things.

A better practice would be to have students become responsible for identifying words they would like to know more about and working at making these words their own.

Students need multiple encounters with words to have a lasting understanding of their meanings (Blachowicz & Lee, 1991; Kibby, 1995; Nagy & Herman, 1985; and others). Rarely can anyone learn a new word permanently after only one encounter; generally the process by which we come to know a word is a gradual one. On a first encounter, we perceive it and try to find a place in our schema to hang it. In doing this, we try to make associations, or find knowledge we can relate it to. Generally, this process occurs the next several times we encounter a word, especially if the word represents an abstract notion, such as *heuristic, epistemology, hermeneutics*, or *hegemony*.

Students who read independently 25 minutes per day in school have a stronger vocabulary than students who do not have this opportunity (Nagy & Herman, 1985). One effective way to learn new words is incidentally and in context, and the best place to learn them is in good literature. Students who read more have a better personal lexicon. The breadth and scope of what is learned through real reading cannot be duplicated in any contrived way in a classroom lesson.

Learning vocabulary does not necessarily improve reading comprehension (Dole, Sloan, & Trathen, 1995). Although reading authentically and regularly does increase vocabulary, the explicit and deliberate teaching of

Listening centers are easy and natural ways to build vocabulary and fluency by having students listen to audio books and follow along. Students enjoy listening centers. Teacher Sheila Cochrane, Grade 4, Maine.

vocabulary has not been shown to have any effect on reading comprehension. Including more reading time for students will influence both reading and vocabulary more than will adding separate vocabulary lessons.

> *Reading, like anything else, improves with practice. Not only vocabulary, but also inferential reading between the lines will become stronger and easier to assimilate the more you read.*
>
> *Christopher Collier, historian, author, teacher; personal communication, September, 1999*

Reading narrative writing lends itself better to vocabulary training than nonfiction texts (Klesius & Searls, 1991). In narrative, this vocabulary is used by good writers in a context where a student has a fair chance of discerning meaning and a likelihood of meeting that word more than once to reinforce it, as well.

Students benefit the most when instruction provides tools for figuring out unfamiliar words through study of roots, affixes, derivations, morphology, etc. (Blachowicz & Lee, 1991; Kibby, 1995; Nagy, 1988; Scott & Nagy, 1997). Al-

though most of us have complained about how irregular the English language is, in actuality there is more logic to the way words are written and spelled than is readily apparent. Learning the history of words and word parts, the languages that help create the mosaic of English, and how those parts work will be the most effective type of vocabulary instruction that can take place in schools. If you know word parts, you often can guess the meaning of a new word.

Consider the example of our first experience with the word *comorbidity.* Most people know that "co" is a piece of a word (morpheme) that means there is more than one thing happening together, such as in *cooperation, coordination,* and *cohabitation.* Thinking further about "morbid," one immediately thinks of words having to do with death or dis-

Figure 3.6
Presenting Vocabulary in Multiple Contexts

Word: **Farce**

Read the word in each of these contexts. Then answer the question below.

a. This play, which Jan had wanted to see for many years, was being produced locally. This example of a delightful <u>farce</u> was written in the 19th century.

b. The student was shocked when he heard that the school administration had proposed to make the school grounds safer on weekdays and thought the plan was an absolute <u>farce</u>!

Write what you glean from context about the underlined word in each sentence.

Now look up a definition in an on-line or print dictionary. Write what it says here:

Now write about what you can relate this word to in your own experience.

Check the one that applies:

_____ I now know this word forever.

_____ I have some knowledge of this word but would not like to use it yet.

_____ I am still uncertain about this word and need more exposure to it.

ease or interests in such things. Because the word appeared in a passage about students who are ADHD and who are being evaluated for learning disabilities, it becomes readily apparent that *comorbidity* is the occurrence of more than one affliction or disorder together in an individual. If you know word parts, you don't always need a dictionary.

The goal of vocabulary instruction is to teach students to infer meanings in context (Nagy, 1988). The best use of vocabulary instruction is to help students become independent in tackling new words. In adult life, their continued development will occur in real and authentic contexts, and the tools teachers give them in school will be helpful. Vocabulary lessons that fo-

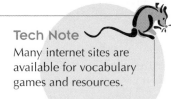

Tech Note
Many internet sites are available for vocabulary games and resources.

cus on placing or discerning a word that appears in multiple contexts will be more helpful than creating arbitrary lists of words to try to learn. Figure 3.6 shows one way to generate an instructional context for students to infer meaning.

A teacher can create excitement and enthusiasm for word study that will enhance student attitudes toward vocabulary instruction (Kibby, 1995). If a teacher expresses enthusiasm for words and their meanings, many students will realize that learning words can be fun and personally useful. A number of teachers have done action research studies to find more useful ways to teach vocabulary (Holly, Arhar, & Kasten, 2005). Using some ideas mentioned in this chapter as well as other vocabulary strategies, these teachers have succeeded in diminishing the moans they used to hear from students when they started vocabulary lessons. Figure 3.7 shares some popular vocabulary-teaching strategies.

Figure 3.7
Vocabulary Strategies for Classrooms

Comic Search—Students love comic strips. Comics are not typically written for naïve audiences and often contain interesting vocabulary. Let students search newspapers for comics with words they would like to learn. These can be added to a personal learning list or recommended to the teacher for inclusion in a vocabulary strategy.

Sniglets—This popular strategy is one students love. Because word parts have meanings, students use word parts to invent words of their own. Study affixes such as *dis-, un-, re-, mis-, co-, mal-, dys-, -ology, -otomy, graph-, phono-, mega-* and *-pathy.* Create a new word by adding an affix to a known word. Write your own logical definition for each new word. Examples:

mal-lexicon-ology—the study of bad or boring vocabulary lessons.

teacher-pathy—the state of teachers who are tired and need a vacation.

word-isis—the state of thinking vocabulary lessons are way too important.

literature-maniac—someone hopelessly in love with literature!

Puns—Puns are plays on words that appeal to students' sense of humor. Encourage students to create puns and then display them in a pun-o-gram or a project the students create. Here are a few examples:

John jogged in the local **cemetery** and became winded after 3 miles. "My, I think I am in a very **grave** situation," he concluded.

Tiara was asked to get out the potato peeler for her Mom and cut up some potatoes for home fries. "I think this is very **ap-peeling**," she replied.

Oxymorons—These are uses of language that when considered literally are contradictions. For example, the military uses the term "friendly fire" when soldiers are killed by their own side's bullets. (How can fire of that sort be friendly?) Locate oxymorons used in the press, in books, and in other public places. Create some of your own. Display them in the classroom along with the name of the person who found or created the oxymoron (and who would like to draw a moronic ox for the poster?).

Portmanteaus—A blending of two or more words to make a single word, a portmanteau sometimes becomes a new word in our language. *Motel* began as a portmanteau from "motor hotel"; *brunch* began as a combination of "breakfast" and "lunch." Create some portmanteaus of your own. Here are some examples: *raincess*—a rainy recess period when you can't go out; *snoliday*—a holiday that occurs when school is called off because of snow; *flead*—read by flashlight.

We Have So Much to Talk About! Generating Good Discussions

Although the term "discussion" is widely used in classrooms and appears frequently in lesson plans, what happens typically in the name of discussion isn't really a discussion at all. When a teacher and students talk about a text the class has read and the teacher looks for students to supply correct answers, this is not a discussion. A transcript of the typical "classroom discussion" would reveal that the teacher is talking most of the time, and is mostly in control of what happens during the "discussion" time. On the other hand, a true discussion enables multiple people to talk, to share opinions and insights, to raise questions, and to seek the

> Exploratory talk is an acceptable, even necessary way for speakers to bring their tacit knowledge, or 'personal knowledge' to a talking place where, through socialization, they can construct new meanings.
>
> Dorothy Watson, in Wilde, 1996, p. 243 ("personal knowledge" is a term coined by Polanyi, 1958)

perceptions of others. In a discussion, a teacher can initiate talk, but then needs to step back and let students have the floor, which can be very difficult at first.

Some of the best discussions take place when the teacher lets a student be the leader, or when teachers deliberately situate themselves behind the student circle, at a student desk, or even in another part of the classroom. Physical presence can signal who is and is not in charge.

Discussion plays a very important role in comprehension and in building vocabulary. We learned earlier that vocabulary is best learned incidentally, rather than presented as a teacher-generated list. Prereading and postreading discussions are a good time to work in the newer vocabulary that has come up in the reading and literature context.

We also saw that teachers often need to supply appropriate scaffolding or schemata for students to better understand a selection. Some of this seaffolding is developed through discussion. The section that follows presents some more specific examples.

Prereading Discussions

Sometimes teachers delve into the reading portion of a lesson without enough prereading preparation; however, what we do before reading can make the difference for many students in effective comprehending. Consider Gary Soto's 1993 picture book, *Too Many Tamales*. This story of a Latino family at Christmastime involves a little girl who loses a ring inside the newly made tamales and who eats a bunch of them to find the ring.

Most students in the southwestern United States will have no difficulty connecting with all parts of this story, because they will be familiar with both Christmas and tamales. But suppose our students are in northern Maine or a predominantly Asian area of Los Angeles, or are Alaskan native children or recent immigrants from the Ukraine. Students who come from predominantly Christian cultures will understand the Christmas part but are less likely to know about tamales. Some of the Asian students, for example, may not be familiar with either.

Another example would be for a group about to read a classic story such as *Time of Wonder* (McCloskey). Students who live in fishing villages or other marine environments will feel right at home with this story set in coastal Maine, but many students will be unfamiliar with terms mentioned throughout the book. Discussion can bring up many of these words, perhaps with pictures or maps to place these ideas in context.

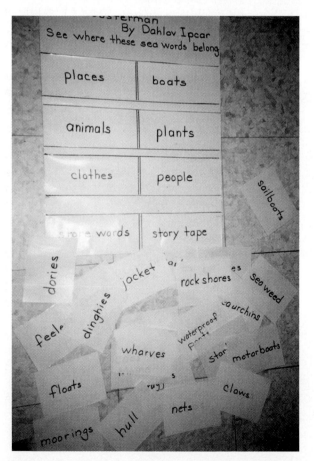

Maine students sort vocabulary words after reading *The Lobsterman*, by D. Ipcar, in Maria Brountas's first-grade classroom.

Text Set   *Southwest Themes*

Baylor, B. (1974). *Everybody Needs a Rock* (Peter Parnall, Illus.). New York: Scribner.

Baylor, B. (1975). *The Desert Is Theirs.* New York: Macmillan.

Baylor, B. (1994). *The Table Where Rich People Sit* (Peter Parnall, Illus.). New York: Scribner.

dePaola, Tomie. (1996). *Legend of the Bluebonnet: An Old Tale of Texas.* New York: Putnam.

Krumgold, Joseph. (1984). *And Now, Miguel* (Jean Charlot, Illus.). New York: Harper.

Mora, Pat. (2001). *The Bakery Lady* (Pablo Torrecilla, Illus.). Houston, TX: Pinata Books.

O'Dell, Scott. (1970). *Sing Down the Moon.* New York: Dell.

Soto, Gary, & Martinez, Ed. (1993). *Too Many Tamales.* New York: Putnam.

Tapahonso, Luci. (1999). *Songs of Shiprock Fair* (Anthony Chee Emerson, Illus.). Walnut, CA: Kiva.

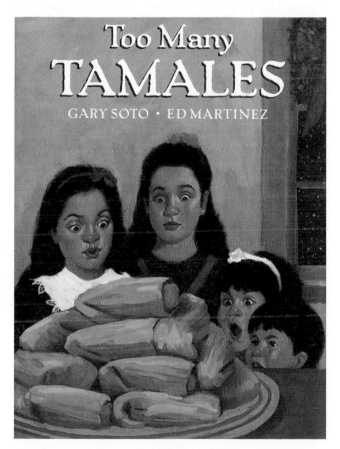

Cover from TOO MANY TAMALES by Gary Soto, illustrated by Ed Martinez, copyright © 1993 by Ed Martinez, illustrations. Used by permission of G.P. Putnam's Sons, A Division of Penguin Young Readers Group, A Member of Penguin Group (USA) Inc., 345 Hudson Street, New York, NY 10014. All rights reserved.

The teacher's role, then, is to anticipate students' needs. Perhaps discussing Christmas or other winter holidays will be one start for scaffolding. Having a picture of tamales, or maybe even the real thing, would scaffold students about the tamales in *Too Many Tamales* (consult with a local Mexican restaurant for help).

Another role for the teacher is to encourage contributions from students who are more reticent to speak in groups. Dominant voices will have little trouble contributing in the classroom, but to hear most or all voices, the teacher may need to make overt invitations to particular students. This is especially true when some students are second language English speakers. Newer speakers are often more comfortable in a small group of peers than in a whole-class discussion. Once their language confidence grows, they will be more likely to participate with the entire class.

Sometimes a discussion will begin with the entire class and then break into smaller units; then the smaller groups allow more students the opportunity to share. Of course, it is important to consider the makeup of the groups when splitting the class into ad hoc discussion groups. Once the groups are formed, the teacher can move about the room and eavesdrop, enough to know how well conversation is flowing and what points may be useful to reiterate with the entire class at the close of the small-group discussion. Ensuring you have one strong talker in each group generally helps things proceed smoothly.

Creating a rich discussion before reading a challenging story or book can make a big difference in the anticipation of students reading the selection and gaining meaning. In spite of time constraints, sometimes it is necessary to give a discussion time to simmer.

Postreading Discussions

Just as with prereading discussions, teachers may wish to pose provocative questions after reading. Again using *Too Many Tamales* as an example, a teacher might ask, "Suppose you found yourself in the same predicament as Maria in the story. Do you agree with what Maria did?"

In these sorts of discussions, students may not have had any prior experiences personally. However, they may have read books or seen movies that can help them respond, and they may be able to draw on vicarious experiences to relate to the question posed.

Discussion is an important part of literature teaching. It not only promotes vocabulary learning and comprehension, but also provides time for students to deepen their understandings of the issues in literature, and perhaps the incentive to read more and learn more about issues that arise. Of course, these discussions are not confined to teaching literature, because social studies and science topics come up as well through the study of literature.

Summary

In this chapter, we have defined reading comprehension and how it works from a transactional perspective. The most critical factors in reading comprehension are under-standing readers and what they bring to the experience. Although the difficulty of passages does matter, there is no one way to assess readability based on text language—only in regard to knowing readers, listening to them, and learning to match readers to reading material and helping them learn to select their own.

The components of reading comprehension are activating prior knowledge, guiding student reading, reinforcing concepts, and encouraging readers to think critically about what they read.

Assessing comprehension is never simple, but using retellings, miscue analysis, and artistic renderings such as story mapping are all ways to get at what readers understand about their reading.

Building student vocabulary goes hand in hand with comprehension. Students do not learn words by looking them up in dictionaries but through authentic, multiple encounters, such as exposure to good literary works that are age appropriate. Eliciting good student discussions is another important way to scaffold reading, provide time for students to share perspectives, and extend students' understanding of what they read.

Action Research for Teachers

Will Peer Interaction Promote More Authentic Vocabulary Learning?

Carol Stefanko
Urban Middle School

Carol felt that vocabulary instruction in her classroom was boring and ineffective. She hoped to find something more interesting and more effective to accomplish vocabulary instruction. Knowing that discussion is an important part of learning, she wondered if including more peer interaction with learning words would improve vocabulary instruction.

First she surveyed her students about their attitudes toward vocabulary learning (they mostly thought it was boring). She had students write in learning logs about new words they were learning, and she audiotaped sessions when students were studying words together.

She then presented students with target words to learn. Each week, she introduced a variety of strategies and experiences for vocabulary learning, such as concept maps, and "sniglets" (described in this chapter). Carol analyzed the audiotaped discussion, student learning logs, and the pre- and poststudy surveys as her data sources for this inquiry.

All in all, Carol learned that interaction about vocabulary was an important ingredient. Students reported liking the new instruction better and feeling they were really learning the new words. She also saw that learning vocabulary takes more time and repetition than teachers typically allow. She sought ways to give students more time and practice with newer words, and adjusted her expectations to focus on quality learning instead of a certain predetermined quantity of new words each week.

RESPONDING TO LITERATURE

"Don't forget that a book is a private contract between a writer and a reader. Don't try to force another reader to share your contract. And, above all, don't kill the joy." (Katherine Paterson, author; personal communication, September, 1999)

hree fourth graders chose *Julie of the Wolves* (George, 1972) for their literature circle book. The story is set in Alaska and describes the adventures and challenges faced by Julie, a young girl who runs away and lives out on the tundra with a wolf pack. The teacher had some questions ready to get the discussion going when the group gathered to talk about the book. However, she soon found she couldn't get a word in. The children were so interested in the story that they spent over an hour debating Julie's choices, how the actions of each wolf illuminated its personality, and what they thought might happen after the book concluded.

Seven-year-old Haileigh was an advanced reader for her age. Usually she selected beautiful picture books, poetry, and humorous transition books such as Louis Sachar's *Wayside School* series to read. One day, she came home with *Maniac Magee* by Jerry Spinelli, a complex novel that blends fantasy and realism to tell the story of a boy who unites a racially divided town. She told her mother that the running feet on the cover had attracted her. However, after reading about one third of the book, she abandoned it because she said it was boring. One year later, she stayed up all night to devour *Bud, Not Buddy*, a book by Christopher Paul Curtis with many similarities to *Maniac Magee*. "This is the best book I've ever read," she told her mother, "He [the main character] feels just like me."

A sixth-grade teacher read aloud Robert Coffin's "Crystal Moment," a complex poem in which the poet describes a perfect suspended moment of time when he observed life and death "running beautifully together" as he witnessed a deer being pursued by hunting dogs. After the teacher read the poem, there was total silence for several minutes. Several children broke the silence, asking her to read it again. After the second reading, the group started talking about hunting (a common pastime in their community) and how they hated killing animals. Soon they began sharing their feelings about death. After the group dispersed, Stacie and Carrie remained. They asked their teacher for the book she'd just read from. Turning to "Crystal Moment," Stacie exclaimed, "Oh, I just love this poem. Read it to me again." She closed her eyes and rocked quietly in the chair as her friend Carrie read the poem to her.

These examples of children responding to literature show us a few of the many ways children connect to books. When children make a unique personal connection with a story or poem they're reading, the world around them almost disappears as they become totally engrossed in the world created by the story. Through books, they can solve mysteries, go on adventures to distant and magical lands, and laugh over a character's humorous antics.

As teachers, we want to nurture this positive response to books, engaging children's minds and hearts; this is how we can create lifelong, enthusiastic readers. We also want to help children deepen their connections, going back into books to discover what the author did to touch them, make them think more deeply or help them discover some new insight about their world. To do all this, we must know children's books. But that is not enough. We must also know our children — how they learn, their life experiences, and what their expectations are for future encounters with books.

Reader response is the interaction that occurs in the minds of readers when they experience literature. We generally think about this interaction the same way we think about comprehension as composed of three facets: (1) the reader, (2) the text, and (3) the context (Cullinan & Galda, 1998). We first discuss each facet of response. Then we describe how readers integrate these elements as they interact with texts. Finally, we present ways teachers can support children's responses to what they read.

Specifically, we address the following questions:

- What are the characteristics of reader, text, and context that influence response?

- How do these factors—reader, text, and context—interact to create a reader's unique response to text?

- What opportunities can teachers provide to support and deepen children's responses to books?

Response: The Reader

In chapter 3, we learned that everything readers bring to a reading event influences how well they will comprehend. Similarly who we are, our past experiences with literature and the world, our interests, the books we've read, the places we've been, the people we've known, our ages—everything about us—influence how we respond to a book. Response, then, is highly idiosyncratic. Knowing this, we need to carefully observe our students, documenting their understandings about books, their preferences for certain kinds of books and the connections they make to books. We also need to know where they are developmentally: how they think, what they know about language, how they view justice and morality. We can then make informed decisions about which books will connect and resonate with them. Let's examine these factors more fully.

Meet... Phyllis Reynolds Naylor

Author of *Shiloh; Shiloh Season; Saving Shiloh; Achingly Alice; All but Alice; An Amish Family; Beetles, Lightly Toasted; Boys Against Girls; Shadows on the Wall; The Keeper; Sweet Strawberries; A Spy Among the Girls;* and many more.

"I was no overnight success as a writer. My first story was published when I was 16, but I wrote short stories for 15 years before I ever attempted a book. I have now published over 2000 short stories and articles and over a hundred books, but I've accumulated 10,337 rejection slips along the way.

"Perhaps the biggest influence on me as a writer was the fact that our parents read aloud to us every night until we were well into our teens. I was caught up in the plot, characters, the lyrical sounds of their voices as they interpreted different roles. At some point, I must have decided that if it was this much fun listening to stories, it must be even better writing them."

About teachers, Ms. Naylor shares that "whenever a teacher cries when reading one of my books aloud in the classroom, or laughs so hard she has to hand the book to someone else, children write and tell me about it. They are fascinated that the story affects their teacher as much as it touches them, and this is the most important lesson of all."

She recommends a good writing exercise for developing writers. "Think about the times in your life you were the angriest, the most scared, or sad, or embarrassed. Write a few sentences down about it, and then turn it over in your imagination. Play with it, change it, put on a new ending or beginning, make it happen to someone else. This way you are starting with something emotional that truly affected you, and then give it wings, and see what happens."

Ms. Naylor lives in Bethesda, Maryland.

Experiential Background

In chapter 3, we learned about schemata; these life experiences have a great influence on how we respond to a book. Knowledge obtained from school, family, travel, and other experiences creates a foundation that influences how we respond to everything in our world, including literature. For example, a child who has lived on a farm will have different expectations, perceptions, and understandings when she reads E. B. White's *Charlotte's Web* than will an urban child who has never been on a farm. Readers approach the world, including literature, from a certain perspective. Yet the text extends our perspectives. So the readers' knowledge of the world and experience keep changing and growing.

Children also have different life experiences with books and reading. Some come to school having had many pleasurable experiences; they may have been read to frequently, learned to read easily, and were supported as they voiced their opinions in response to their interactions with books. In contrast, you may have students who see reading as a race—something to do as quickly as possible so they can move to the next activity or level of the reading series. Worse might be the child who has had frustrating experiences with reading and views any interactions with books negatively or fearfully. Past experiences explain to a great degree whether a student responds enthusiastically to a wide range of books and related activities or avoids the task. And in some instances, children arrive at school with little or no experience with books, and have no preconceived notions about reading at all. In such cases, teachers provide children with positive book experiences right from the start.

> When we read something and we feel a jolt of recognition, we understand that we are part of the continuum of humanity. Realizing that others share their fears and emotions can make children feel less alone in the world. Then when we read about a person's experiences vastly different from our own and can imagine what it is like to be that person, we can grow.
>
> Cynthia De Felice, author; personal communication, September, 1999

Interests

It makes sense that students will respond more positively to literature that interests them than to stories or poems they find boring. Teachers can use student interests to help them

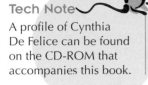

Tech Note

A profile of Cynthia De Felice can be found on the CD-ROM that accompanies this book.

find books that will engage them and to which they will positively respond. They can also extend students' interests by observing what they currently enjoy, and then help them learn to appreciate a broader range of ideas and topics.

Teachers can discern student interests in several ways. One of the easiest is just to *ask* them. You can do this in whole-class sharing sessions, through written surveys, or in individual conferences. A series of questions such as those in Figure 4.1 should give you useful information for guiding book selection and response. You can also have older students create a "reading biography" that details their personal history as a reader.

Tomlinson and Lynch-Brown (2002) suggest yet another strategy to help you create a classroom library based on students' interests.

1. Collect 30 to 40 books that are new to your students and that you think might be interesting to them. Be sure you have selected books from a wide range of genres and topics.
2. Number the books with paper bookmarks.
3. Create one response sheet per book on which children indicate whether they would like to read each book.
4. Hold up each book and give a short summary of its content. Then place the books around the room.
5. Have students rank order the top three to five classroom favorites.

Preferences

Whereas interests are personal and individual, preferences reflect broad patterns across gender, age, ability, or other developmental factors. Students' preferences are usually identified through survey research that presents options from which they must choose. So, for example, if students are asked if they preferred to read a mystery, a romance novel, or an adventure story and they responded "mystery," you might infer that students of this age prefer mysteries. However, the way these studies are conducted (forced choices, varying methodologies, differences in populations of children studied) makes it difficult to make

---

☼ What are your favorite things to do?

☼ Are you really good at something? Tell me about it.

☼ What would you like to learn more about?

☼ Do you like fiction, nonfiction, or poetry?

☼ What kind of books do you like to read? Tell me about some of your favorites.

☼ Is there a type of book you don't like to read?

☼ Do you have a favorite author?

☼ What kinds of stories do you like to hear?

☼ How do you choose books to read?

☼ Do you read with anyone at home?

☼ Why do you read?

☼ When do you like to read?

☼ Where is your favorite place to read?

☼ What is hard for you when you're reading?

☼ What would you like to do better as a reader?

Figure 4.1
Questions to Aid in Book Selection

(Adapted from Szymusiak & Sibberson, 2001, p. 60.)

SHILOH Phyllis Reynolds Naylor

(Artwork by Lynn Dennis 1991.)

generalizations. Nevertheless, a few patterns can be determined (Huck, et al., 2004; Lynch-Brown & Tomlinson, 2002; Norton, 2003):

- There are no significant differences in the reading preferences of boys and girls before age 9.
- Both boys and girls in middle grades (ages 10 to 13) prefer mystery, adventure, and horror stories. To a lesser degree, they enjoy humor, adventure, and animal stories.
- Poetry is at or near the bottom of preference studies at all ages and for both boys and girls.
- Boys seldom prefer books they consider "girl" books, but girls are likely to read "boy" stories.
- Boys tend to gravitate to nonfiction as they get older, and girls show increasing preferences for romantic fiction.
- Preferences of boys in the middle grades include action, adventure, and sports stories.
- Girls in the middle grades tend to prefer fantasy and animal stories as well as stories about people.
- Young children enjoy fairy tales, but middle-grade students are more interested in realistic stories where characters go on adventures or must survive on their own.
- Favorite topics with young people of many ages are animals, humor, action, and suspense. This changes somewhat with age: Students at age 12 prefer more subtle humor than 6-year-olds do; older students prefer realistic animal stories in which something tragic or dramatic occurs, whereas younger children enjoy books about fantasy animals.
- Early adolescents begin choosing magazines for the short, current articles in areas of interest.

However, remember that these are generalized preferences; there are girls who never love romance stories

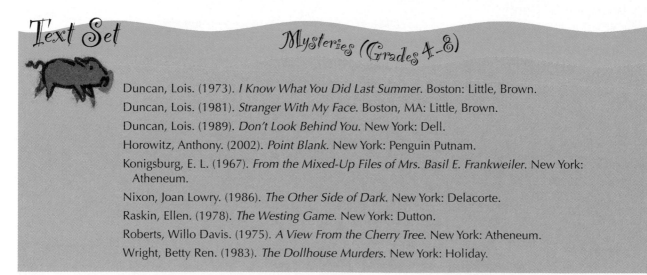

Text Set   Mysteries (Grades 4–8)

Duncan, Lois. (1973). *I Know What You Did Last Summer*. Boston: Little, Brown.

Duncan, Lois. (1981). *Stranger With My Face*. Boston, MA: Little, Brown.

Duncan, Lois. (1989). *Don't Look Behind You*. New York: Dell.

Horowitz, Anthony. (2002). *Point Blank*. New York: Penguin Putnam.

Konigsburg, E. L. (1967). *From the Mixed-Up Files of Mrs. Basil E. Frankweiler*. New York: Atheneum.

Nixon, Joan Lowry. (1986). *The Other Side of Dark*. New York: Delacorte.

Raskin, Ellen. (1978). *The Westing Game*. New York: Dutton.

Roberts, Willo Davis. (1975). *A View From the Cherry Tree*. New York: Atheneum.

Wright, Betty Ren. (1983). *The Dollhouse Murders*. New York: Holiday.

and boys who prefer fantasy over nonfiction. As both boys and girls gain more experience with books, they may share interests (Sturm, 2003) as well as have greater appreciation and enthusiasm for increasingly diverse, more complex books.

Also, we wonder if these choices reflect real preferences or conformity to social expectations. We suspect that both factors are influencing these responses. Additionally, remember that these preferences are based on forced choices: A child may have been asked if she preferred mystery or nonfiction, when actually her first love was fantasy. For these reasons, information on children's preferences should be used only to gain a general sense of

the kinds of books students might prefer. Helping students find books they will like can be challenging. Figure 4.2 has some helpful suggestions.

Developmental Issues

Children's cognitive, linguistic, moral, and, to a lesser extent, physical development also influence their response to books. Just as Haileigh's taste in books (described at the beginning of the chapter) changed as she matured, so do all students' responses change as they develop. Because this book focuses on working with learners in grades K–8, we discuss only developmental changes for children at these ages. Figure 4.3 details

Figure 4.2
Helping Students Have Access to a Wide Range of Books

Teachers and librarians sometimes struggle with helping students choose books that they can read successfully. Here are some tips:

- Informally interview students about their reading habits. Find out how often they choose to read as a free-choice activity; what types of books they prefer; what recent titles they have read; how they feel about reading longer texts; whether they consider themselves good readers.

- If a reader appears less than confident, be more careful to suggest or help him or her select a book that will be an easy read. Success with an easy read will help build confidence.

- Consider having the student read aloud the first page to you or another adult. Listen to the reading. All readers will make miscues, so listen to the *kind* of miscues the reader is making: Miscues that seem far off base or that the reader does not self-correct will likely signal a too-difficult text. A reader who is shaky but who corrects most miscues, or who makes miscues that do not alter the meaning of the passage, may be suited to reading the book. (Note also that there is no magic or maximum number of miscues that suggests a text is too difficult.) Ask readers after reading the page whether they believe the text is suited to them or is too hard. Usually they know.

- Remember that students who are unusually motivated to read a book, regardless of its difficulty, should be allowed to try. Praise them for wanting or attempting to read a difficult book, even if they realize after a few pages that they have taken on too difficult a text.

- A student can read a more difficult text when paired with a somewhat more proficient reader. Consider having the students read the book aloud together in a quiet corner.

- Having a more capable reader or adult read aloud the first chapter of a book to a student can help jump-start reading. This experience gives the reader a chance to hear the nature of the language, learn place names and characters names that may be frustrating even though they may have little to do with comprehending.

- Talk with readers about strategies they will use when they come to something they don't know. Help them identify the words that are not essential to struggle with while reading. These can be skipped and looked at later. Unfamiliar words that may hinder understanding can be solved by quietly asking someone for help.

- Telling students to look up words they don't know in a dictionary is not a particularly effective strategy. The interruption can be annoying to the process of engagement and to comprehending the story, and may be counterproductive in the long run. Using the dictionary is time-consuming and could take up too much time set aside for reading.

Developmental Characteristics	Implications for Instruction	Books Interesting to Children at This Age Level
Kindergarten/Primary, Ages 5–7		
Children are concrete operational thinkers. Learning is based on hands-on, direct, concrete experience.	Children can conceptualize and solve problems but must have a concrete referent. They try to make sense of new experiences and relate new ideas or experiences to what they already know. They can't mentally manipulate abstract ideas.	*Corduroy*—Don Freeman *Where the Wild Things Are*—Maurice Sendak *The Very Hungry Caterpillar*—Eric Carle *Harry the Dirty Dog*—Gene Zion
Children's learning is integrated.	Children benefit from an integrated curriculum, where they study topics that cross discipline areas and use knowledge and skills from one area to learn another.	*Alexander and the Terrible, Horrible, No Good, Very Bad Day*—Judith Viorst *There's a Nightmare in My Closet*—Mercer Mayer
Children are acquiring a background of experience to which they can link new ideas and concepts.	Children need and respond to books that introduce them gradually to new ideas and concepts that are still close to their own experiences.	*Ira Sleeps Over*—Bernard Waber Frog and Toad books—Arnold Lobel
Language gradually becomes more complex—children understanding multiple meanings and simple word play.	Children need books with simple language that also extend their basic language skills by presenting more advanced vocabulary and sentence structures.	*Tell Me a Story, Mama*—Angela Johnson *The Snowy Day*—Ezra Jack Keats *Koala Lou*—Mem Fox
Children enjoy humor, particularly humor that evolves from language.	Children enjoy books featuring verbal jokes, tongue twisters, and riddles.	*Jamaica and Brianna*—Juanita Havill *Monster Mama*—Liz Rosenberg
Gender identification becomes connected to culturally acceptable roles and expectations, and influences children's choices of friends and behavior.	Children enjoy stories about their own gender, although girls sometimes read books with male characters. They use books to discover acceptable ways of behaving.	*Dog Breath*—Dav Pilkey *Talking Like the Rain*—X. J. Kennedy & Dorothy Kennedy Arthur series—Marc Brown
Children show a marked preference for same-sex playmates and reject the opposite gender.	Children tend to read what everyone else does. They typically will not select books with characters of the opposite sex. They need opportunities to discuss books and hear recommendations from others.	Bailey School series—Patricia Reilly Giff Clifford books—Norman Bridwell
They form their first genuine friendships with give-and-take, shared experiences, and mutual trust.		*Miss Nelson Is Missing!*—Henry Allard
Response is very physical—children talk back to the story, and move in response to it. They retell stories rather than answer questions or summarize.	Children need opportunities to respond to books through action—drama, movement, chanting, etc. Spontaneous dramatic play or story language is often observed as a response to stories.	

Figure 4.3   Selecting Books by Development and Age

Developmental Characteristics	Implications for Instruction	Books Interesting to Children at This Age Level
Kindergarten/Primary, Ages 5–7 (continued)		
Children are better able to consider and understand right and wrong. They are aware that others can have different perspectives, thoughts, and feelings from their own.	Children need stories that present simple moral dilemmas that are close to their own experiences.	*The Art Lesson*—Tomie dePaola *Nathaniel Talking*—Eloise Greenfield *A Chair for My Mother*—Vera Williams *Traveling to Tondo*—Verna Aardema
Children show true empathy only to people they know. They show some concern for others' physical and emotional needs, but they lack a true understanding of other people's perspectives. They develop a "conscience" (although it's often excessively strict). They obey rules because more powerful people created them. Children are very concerned about fairness, and are beginning to consider the concept of merit in decisions about fairness. "Wrong" behaviors are those that will be punished.	Children benefit from books that question their perceptions of morality to create disequilibrium that will move them to a higher level of judgment.	*Mailing May*—Michael Tunnell *Dim Sim for Everyone*—Grace Lin *Too Many Tamales*—Gary Soto *Island of the Scog*—Steven Kellog *Strega Nona*—Tomie dePaola
Children seek independence and want to work things out for themselves, but they need to do this in a limited fashion.	Children need opportunities to select their own books. They like to see characters who are responsible and who are going on age appropriate adventures.	
Children respond to parts of a story rather than to wholes.	Children should be encouraged to comment on aspects of a story that they can associate with their own experience. They should respond during read-alouds and storytelling, rather than waiting until the end of a story.	
Children don't understand the concepts of past and future time; they are very rooted in the present.	Children generally prefer realistic stories or folklore with vague time references. They can be introduced to some historical fiction, as long as it focuses on children like themselves.	
Children have a powerful urge to master skills held by older children and adults in reading, writing, math.	Children enjoy stories where the main character gains competence or skill in a familiar, everyday task.	
Children take an interest in the wider world and in how things work.	Children enjoy stories that broaden their experience, but that are still rooted in familiar experiences.	
Children learn through imaginative play.	Children enjoy stories that can be dramatized.	

Figure 4.3

(continues)

Developmental Characteristics	Implications for Instruction	Books Interesting to Children at This Age Level
Middle Elementary Grades, Ages 8–9		
Children are in the concrete-operational stage of cognitive development; thinking becomes flexible and reversible.	Children can handle more complex plot structures such as flashbacks and multiple plots to a limited extent. Also, they enjoy longer books—particularly transitional chapter books.	*A Bear Called Paddington*—Michael Bond *James and the Giant Peach*—Roald Dahl *Charlie and the Chocolate Factory*—Roald Dahl
Children use and understand more complex sentence structures than they can produce. Vocabulary is rapidly expanding.	Children benefit from and enjoy being read aloud to. Books should provide the opportunity to hear more complex language so children's ability to use language expands.	*Charlotte's Web*—E. B. White *Jumanji*—Chris Van Allsburg *Sarah, Plain and Tall*—Patricia MacLachlan
Peer-group acceptance becomes increasingly important.	Children need opportunities to share opinions about books with peers. They need group approval that reading is a worthwhile activity. They need opportunities to recommend books to each other.	Little House series—Laura Ingalls Wilder The Boxcar Children series—Gertrude Chandler Warner
Children are beginning to realize that rules aren't all the same and that breaking a rule is not always wrong. They are better able to consider a person's intention in deciding if actions are right or wrong but still define right and wrong in terms of consequences to themselves.	Children should experience disequilibrium in books that question their perception of morality and show them that moral decisions aren't easy. Books should present dilemmas that aren't easily solved.	*Ramona the Pest*—Beverly Cleary *Superfudge*—Judy Blume Magic School Bus series—Joanna Cole & Bruce Degen *The Random House Book of Poetry for Children*—Jack Prelutsky
Children realize that others have thoughts and feelings different from their own but still perceive these in a simplistic, one-dimensional fashion. They lack true empathy for others' perspectives, needs, or feelings.	Children enjoy stories with simple morals.	*Cousins*—Virginia Hamilton *The Best Christmas Pageant Ever*—Barbara Robinson *Sideways Stories From Wayside School*—Louis Sachar
Children are beginning to develop a sense of autonomy.	Children enjoy stories where child characters exhibit independence and autonomy in safe, structured situations.	Junie B. Jones series—Barbara Park *Amelia Bedelia*—Peggy Parish *Bunnicula: A Rabbit-Tale of Mystery*—James Howe
Children can begin to summarize rather than just retell a story. They can classify books into genres or topics, and can recognize themes in stories. They tend to judge a book based on their personal response to it (e.g., "It's boring") rather than on its literary qualities.	Children can discuss books in greater depth so teachers can implement sustained literature circles.	*The Chocolate Touch*—Patrick Catling *The New Kid on the Block*—Jack Prelutsky *Where the Sidewalk Ends*—Shel Silverstein Ramona series—Beverly Cleary

Figure 4.3   (continued)

Developmental Characteristics	Implications for Instruction	Books Interesting to Children at This Age Level
Middle Elementary Grades, Ages 8–9 (continued)		
Children acquire more developed concepts of time.	Children enjoy simple biographies and historical fictional, as long as the plots are active and they can identify with the characters.	*26 Fairmount Avenue*—Tomie dePaolo
Children are beginning to read independently and with enjoyment. However, there is a wide variation in ability.	Children need time for uninterrupted silent reading and help selecting books that are engaging and appropriate for their level. They are ready for longer chapter books.	Matt Christopher Sports Series—Matt Christopher *Chocolate Fever*—Robert Kimmel Smith
There is variation in children's reading interest. Other interests and pursuits become more important for some children.	It is critically important that children select books that relate to their interests; they must get "hooked" into reading.	
Children's sense of humor is becoming more sophisticated. Their cognitive level allows them to notice subtle word plays, absurdities in everyday life, etc.	Children enjoy jokes, puns, tall tales, and humor in everyday situations.	
Upper Elementary, Ages 10, 11		
Children are still concrete operational thinkers, but they are beginning to move to more symbolic, abstract thinking. Their cognitive development is characterized by more systematic, flexible thinking. They can take on different points of view.	Children start enjoying mysteries and more complex plots with flashbacks or stories within stories.	*The Lion, the Witch and the Wardrobe*—C. S. Lewis *Hatchet*—Gary Paulsen *Holes*—Louis Sachar *Bud, Not Buddy*—Christopher Paul Curtis
This age is characterized by "cognitive conceit"—the idea that children are as smart and as competent as adults.	Children like books where protagonists survive on their own.	*Tuck Everlasting*—Natalie Babbitt *My Brother Sam Is Dead*—James Collier & Christopher Collier
Language continues to expand. Children are comfortable with complex sentence structures and are beginning to understand abstract language concepts.	Children can comprehend longer books with advanced vocabulary, concepts, and sentence structures.	*Joyful Noise: Poems for Two Voices*—Paul Fleischman *Number the Stars*—Lois Lowry *Shiloh*—Phyllis Reynolds Naylor
Boys and girls are developing a sense of gender identity.	Children like books that provide examples to help define gender roles. They also can respond to books that provide opportunities for open discussions about gender differences.	*Missing May*—Cynthia Rylant

Figure 4.3

(continues)

Developmental Characteristics	Implications for Instruction	Books Interesting to Children at This Age Level

Upper Elementary, Ages 10, 11 (continued)

Developmental Characteristics	Implications for Instruction	Books Interesting to Children at This Age Level
Peers are even more important, offering social and emotional support.	Children enjoy stories about children like themselves, particularly when stories show evolving friendships, struggles with peers, etc.	*Maniac Magee*—Jerry Spinelli
		Roll of Thunder, Hear My Cry—Mildred D. Taylor
Children advocate moral behavior on the basis that it's the "right" thing to do and that they will be liked or appreciated if they help, but they hold stereotypical views of "good" and "bad" behavior. At the same time, they realize that others may have mixed and possibly contradictory perceptions of a situation. They realize that people's actions may not reflect their feelings and that people sometimes do things they don't intend to do. Girls may see moral issues differently from boys.	Children enjoy stories where characters face moral dilemmas that involve more complex issues than at an earlier age. Resolution of these issues should be fairly straightforward.	*Harry Potter series*—J. K. Rowling
		Because of Winn-Dixie—Kate DiCamillo
		Bridge to Terabithia—Katherine Paterson
		Stepping on the Cracks—Mary Downing Hahn
		Morning Girl—Michael Dorris
		On My Honor—Marion Dane Bauer
		Joey Pigza Swallowed the Key—Jack Gantos
Children are beginning to develop autonomy, a sense of self, along with an awareness that it takes effort and perseverance to succeed.	Children enjoy stories about struggle and survival, particularly when characters are their own age.	*Where the Red Fern Grows*—Wilson Rawls
		Passage to Freedom: The Sugihara Story—Ken Mochizuki
Children can restate ideas from a story in general terms. They begin to see that their feelings about a book are related to identifiable aspects of the writing, (e.g., "I like the book because the author made the characters seem real.") They still judge books according to the fit with their own perception for reality. They can discuss books using general statements that are less tied to a specific text. They are beginning to understand the idea of literary analysis.	Children can discern the moral of a fable or a story theme (as long as it is straightforward).	*Ella Enchanted*—Gail Carson Levine
		All the Small Poems—Valerie Worth
	Children can formulate specific responses to books that focus on literary aspects such as characters or theme (but typically are not interested in abstract literary analysis).	*Where the Sidewalk Ends*—Shel Silverstein
		The True Story of the 3 Little Pigs—Jon Scieszka
		Walk Two Moons—Sharon Creech
		Are You There God? It's Me, Margaret—Judy Blume
		The Tale of Despereaux—Kate DiCamillo
Physical development varies widely; puberty has begun in some children.	Children have a growing interest in books about boy/girl relationships.	*A Taste of Blackberries*—Doris Buchanan Smith
Children have a more developed sense of chronology of past events and are developing an understanding of how the present relates to the past.	Children can read more advanced historical fiction that presents issues and problems not easily resolved and not necessarily tied to a present-day context.	*Tales of a Fourth Grade Nothing*—Judy Blume
		Nothing's Fair in Fifth Grade—Barthe DeClements

Figure 4.3   Selecting Books by Development and Age (continued)

Developmental Characteristics	Implications for Instruction	Books Interesting to Children at This Age Level
Middle School, Ages 12, 13, 14		
Children can reason logically, deal with abstractions, view a situation from alternate perspectives, and tolerate ambiguity. Thinking is sometimes more abstract and flexible, and they can manipulate symbolic language.	Children read more complex stories, particularly high fantasy and historical fiction that call for complex logic and that have multiple plots. Figurative language is more easily understood. Children can be introduced to literary analysis and abstract reasoning related to books.	*Holes*—Louis Sachar
		The Golden Compass—Philip Pullman
		A Wrinkle in Time—Madeleine L'Engle
Children understand the meanings of many words. They know connotative and denotative meanings and how one's intent or purpose can influence meaning. They comprehend complex sentence structures, and can understand and talk about subtle language use such as metaphors, point of view, and persuasion.	Children can participate in literature discussions featuring vocabulary for abstract and subtle concepts. They can appreciate books that use language in subtle, well-crafted ways.	*The Well*—Mildred D. Taylor
		Freak the Mighty—Rodman Philbrick
		Scorpions—Walter Dean Myers
		Pink and Say—Patricia Polacco
		An Island Like You: Stories of the Barrio—Judith Ortiz Cofer
		Harry Potter series—J. K. Rowling
		The Giver—Lois Lowry
Peers are critically important: They provide social and emotional support, often to the exclusion of adults. They are agents of socialization (reinforce actions appropriate for age, sex, ethnic group, etc.), and often are very comforting.	Children enjoy social interactions involving books. They enjoy small-group discussions around books, and need to share favorite titles with one another. Reading must be seen as a desirable, "cool" activity or they may be reluctant to read. They need books with characters like themselves.	*Red Scarf Girl: A Memoir of the Cultural Revolution*—Ji-li Jiang
		A Wizard of Earthsea—Ursula Le Guin
		Lyddie—Katherine Paterson
		Catherine, Called Birdy—Karen Cushman
Children have strong needs for companionship, affection, and security, particularly from peers.	Children need opportunities to discuss books in a trusting, nonjudgmental environment.	*The True Confessions of Charlotte Doyle*—Avi
		Our Only May Amelia—Jennifer Holm
Children generally make moral decisions based on what actions will please others. They take others' perspectives and intentions into account in decision making.	Children benefit from ideas in books that challenge their perceptions of right and wrong, causing disequilibrium in their thinking. Particularly appropriate are situations where the right decision is ambiguous and is dependent on contextual factors.	*Nightjohn*—Gary Paulsen
		The Witch of Blackbird Pond—Elizabeth George Speare
		The Outsiders—S. E. Hinton
Children are capable of expressing true empathy for another person's situation and willingness to help others is based on those empathic feelings. They can be genuinely concerned with the well-being of others and are able to perceive a situation from another's perspective. Girls and boys may view moral issues differently.		*Shabanu, Daughter of the Wind*—Suzanne Fisher Staples
		Nothing But the Truth—Avi
		Journey to Jo'Burg—Beverly Naidoo
		Dragonwings—Laurence Yep
		The Dark Is Rising series—Susan Cooper

Figure 4.3

(continues)

Developmental Characteristics	Implications for Instruction	Books Interesting to Children at This Age Level
Middle School, Ages 12, 13, 14 (continued)		
They can see things from their own and from another's perspective but can also take an "outside" perspective of the two-person relationship. They appreciate the need to satisfy both themselves and another simultaneously and understand the benefits of cooperation, compromise, and trust.	Children enjoy fantasy, adventure, and realistic stories where characters face conflicts and moral dilemmas, and resolve dilemmas both external to and within the character. The issues presented in these stories are often complex, with no easy answers.	*Before We Were Free*—Julia Alvarez *Homeless Bird*—Gloria Wheland *A Single Shard*—Linda Sue Park *Walk Two Moons*—Sharon Creech
Children experience a new kind of egocentrism—they imagine themselves as the center of attention and feel their problems are unique.	Children begin to enjoy introspection and self-analysis. They often identify with characters who are focused on exploring their own problems.	
Response to literature becomes more evaluative and analytic. Children are able to consider how texts work and how a text reflects an author's worldview. They can use literary terminology to analyze character motivation, plot structure, and theme, but their understanding of literacy terms is incomplete. They can go beyond personal reactions to see how parts function in the story as a whole.	Children begin to do some literary analysis of books, although personal response should always be emphasized.	
Physical changes result in puberty.	Children have a strong interest in sexuality and in knowing more about physical changes in both sexes.	
Children have well-developed concepts of past and future time.	Children can contend with flashbacks, flash forwards, and other complex manipulations of time in stories.	

Figure 4.3   Selecting Books by Development and Age (continued)

some of the important developmental patterns for children in the elementary grades along with the kinds of books, themes, topics, etc., they tend to prefer at particular stages of development.

As with the studies on reading preferences, we caution you to remember that these are just patterns. Growth has wide variations; children change at different rates, and their development is affected by many social, cultural, and biological factors. Additionally, research suggests that children who have had many experiences reading and responding to books often exhibit more sophisticated responses than might be expected if one is considering just their developmental stage. For example, Lehr (1991) found that children in classrooms where they encountered many books and had many experiences with literature could understand and discuss more abstract concepts such as theme and character motivation and could also make generalizations about stories. McClure (1990) found that children in classrooms where discussion and writing of poetry were emphasized had more sophisticated responses to that genre. Kasten and Clarke (in Kasten & Lolli, 1998) found that students in a class that emphasized literature were better able to talk articulately about their preferences, stating favorite authors, titles, and genres, than students in classrooms that used mostly basal readers with little other supplemental literature. So although general patterns can tell us a great deal about choosing appropriate books, classroom practices also play a key role.

Literacy Skills

Students who are proficient readers, enjoy reading, and have advanced literacy skills are likely to enjoy literature and respond positively to it. They can pay attention to subtle nuances in characterization or debate complex issues presented in books. Conversely, children who struggle to comprehend, lack fluency, and have difficulty decoding will be more concerned with the mechanics of reading than with engaging with ideas they encounter in books. However, if less able readers have a strong interest in reading a particular book, this desire can often transcend their reading level (Conniff, 1993; Shapiro & White, 1991; Thames & Reeves, 1994).

Ronnie, a fifth-grade student, is a good example of this. Ronnie was classified as a low-achieving reader; he could spell only phonetically, and his response journal entries were typically only a few sentences long. However, Ronnie wanted to read Esther Forbes's *Johnny Tremain*, a challenging book set during the American Revolution, with the advanced literature circle group. His teacher encouraged him to try.

Ronnie labored for days, taking the book home at night, reading during every free moment, even getting his reading tutor to help. When he met with his literature group, Ronnie took the lead. He debated ethical issues raised in the book. He shared his knowledge of the American Revolution and the Sons of Liberty. In short, he responded in very sophisticated ways to a lengthy, complex novel, far beyond what would normally be expected of him—because he was motivated. Students who are highly motivated to read a book will often be successful. Teachers need to make judgments in some instances and give even struggling readers a chance to try something difficult.

Another example is a second-grade boy who was reading the 734-page *Harry Potter and the Goblet of Fire* (Rowling). No one would have thought that the fourth book in the Harry Potter series would be appropriate second-grade reading because it is vastly longer than most selections chosen by 7- and 8-year-olds. However, this very small boy was motivated to read it, and so he did. He was conversant with the details of the first three books—clearly he had read and comprehended them. He wore a tee-shirt that said "Hogwarts" on it (the fictional school in the series) and used a literature response journal with a Harry Potter motif on it that someone had purchased for him. Who would prevent this child from reading a book he wanted to read that badly? Remember, then, that preferences and developmental issues discussed in this chapter do not take the place of good teacher judgment.

Response: The Text

Characteristics of the text also affect how a reader responds to a particular book. Different types of text generate different responses. For example, when we read nonfiction, we tend to approach the experience as a task to gather information. In contrast, when reading a novel, we usually become absorbed in such things as determining relationships among characters, following a sequence of events, and forming opinions about the theme. Our response is often more emotional.

Different genres also require different skills to read them. Young children typically have more experience with narrative text structures. This means that they naturally know what to expect when reading fiction, for example, and how to respond to it. Teachers generally read aloud to younger students from narrative text, forgetting that nonfiction can also make a good read-aloud experience.

Expository text structure is markedly different from narrative structure. Students must learn how visual features (diagrams, photos, tables, etc.), organizational structures (subheadings, presentation of material, etc.), and other special qualities of nonfiction facilitate a reader's understanding. These details are described in depth in chapter 9.

One's experience or lack of experience with text, then, determines one's response to it. The more experience you have with nonfiction text and the more interest you have in reading it, the more comfortable you will be reading and responding to it on a more complex level. Teachers help their students gain this experience.

The extent to which the content of a book engages a reader also influences response. If we are personally involved, barely aware of the world around us as we turn page after page, our response will be markedly different than if we are bored or unable to personally connect with the book. Whether we've chosen to read the book also makes a big difference. If we are reading it to fulfill an assignment, we will likely have a quite different response than if we are reading for our own pleasure or purposes. Sometimes, of course, readers will connect with a book they were required to read, but choice still plays a big factor. The description at the beginning of this chapter of the students reading *Julie of the Wolves* is an apt example of how engagement with content can influence response.

Response: The Context

We have come to understand that although reading is a solitary activity, response to reading is often shaped by a social context. Through interaction with others (adults

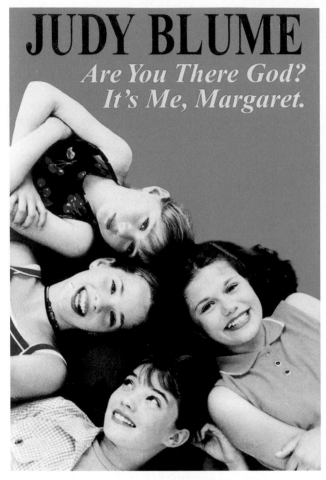

Jacket Cover of ARE YOU THERE GOD? IT'S ME, MARGARET by Judy Blume. Used by permission of Dell Publishing, a division of Random House, Inc.

Other teachers can no doubt recall many of their boys getting hooked on R. L. Stine's horror books, the Chronicles of Narnia books by C. S. Lewis, or the Encyclopedia Brown (Sobol) books. These preferences can sail through a classroom like a wave, introduced by one or two students and catching on like the common cold.

Peers also help evoke and shape each other's responses to books. Hepler (1982) demonstrated this in a research study showing that in a classroom environment designed to encourage response, a "community of readers" developed that nurtured and supported various response activities. Interactions with peers validated initial responses and provided opportunities for children to try out their half-formed responses. Then, readers refined those responses through interactions with other readers. Barnes (1976) also reported that talking and writing in groups gave children the opportunity to work through meanings they may not have articulated or had only partially considered.

However, peers are not the only important aspect of social context; teachers also play a major role, particularly in encouraging, nurturing, and deepening response. Researchers (Hepler, 1982; Hickman, 1979) remind us that as teachers, we serve as important models for reading, both as readers ourselves and as the leaders of the reading community in our classrooms. We help children make significant connections between what was read in the past and what they are currently reading. Teachers also extend students' initial responses through scaffolding: They help students make their own associations and connections with litera-

Tech Note
You will find a photo and a profile of popular author Judy Blume on the CD-ROM that accompanies this book.

and peers) negotiating ideas, understandings, and varying perspectives, students develop increasingly more thoughtful, sophisticated responses. They learn how to respond to books by listening to others as well as by getting feedback to their own responses.

Peers have a particularly powerful influence on response. You may remember all the girls in your fourth-grade class reading the *Babysitter's Club* series or Judy Blume's *Are You There God? It's Me, Margaret.* In one sixth-grade classroom, a particular Judy Blume book was so popular that students developed their own written waiting list of who would get it next, and the paperback cover was completely worn off from all the readers' hands that held it.

> A memory
>
> A memory is a story remembered for generations.
> It smells like sweet honeydew.
> It looks like a fluttering humming bird.
> It taste like sugar, so sweet.
> It sound like a babbleing brook.
> A memory feels like something in which nobody can explain.
>
> —by Jeffrey

This student's original poem is a personal response to reading *Wilfred Gordon McDonald Partridge,* by Mem Fox.

ture as well as show them how to connect literature with their own experience.

Teacher expectations also influence the kinds of responses children make to books. If you always expect students to answer teacher- or publisher-created questions following their reading, and if students must all read the same books in lockstep fashion, you will likely find that your students respond superficially and unenthusiastically to books. However, if you surround your students with books and give them time and opportunity to explore many genres, topics, ideas, and cultural perspectives, you will likely discover that your students become enthusiastic readers who are capable of responding to books in increasingly complex, sophisticated ways.

A teacher's perspective on what constitutes a "good" response also makes a critical difference. If you accept only one response to a book or poem as "correct," you will stifle original thought, honest feelings, and personal engagement with books. Sometimes students have a new way of looking at a book or poem that diverges from what we expect or consider "correct." We can reject these divergent ideas or we can value them, considering the perspective and thinking that influenced children to construct their opinions. Teachers who value divergent ideas help their students articulate their thoughts and encourage them to respond in personally satisfying ways. These actions will create an environment that nurtures honest, personal, and thoughtful responses to literature.

Readers, and especially young readers, respond most readily to literature as an embodiment of human personalities, human situations, human conflicts and achievements. The life situations and interests of students [are] more often seen as the bridge between them and books.

Louise Rosenblatt, 1938/1976, p. vii

Journeying among children responding to literature is a pleasant voyage filled with bright moments and sudden insights.

Bernice L. Cullinan, 1993, p. 322

Cultural Influences and Response

Students will always respond to literature based on their unique backgrounds, and a large part of this background is cultural. In chapter 2, we discussed the complexities and intricacies of cultures and how different students' and teachers' experiences can be. You will recall the example of the teachers who had difficulty relating to the Seder scene at the beginning of Yolen's *The Devil's Arithmetic*. Issues such as this will be equally pronounced in students, but they may not be able to articulate that their culture is what is causing them difficulty.

Salisbury (1967) offers an illustrative, funny example of how some Alaskan native children reacted to those old readers from Scott Foresman featuring Dick, Jane, Sally, Spot, and Puff. The Alaskan children, whose rural subsistence culture differed so extraordinarily from the stories in the reading books, could not figure out why Father kept leaving for a place called "office" and never returned with any food for the family dinner. The Alaskan students of the 1960s also could not comprehend incidents in these stories where a police officer helped children to cross a street. The Alaskan children wondered if the children were disabled in some way that they needed help with such an ordinary task. They were further confused as to why Dick and Jane and Sally kept going to visit grandparents on something called a "farm." The Alaskan children, responding from their own cultural context, wondered what taboo the grandparents must have broken to be ostracized from the rest of their family and made to live with animals!

Students respond from their own cultural perspective, and they generally don't know that their perspective may differ from the characters in the story. In the case of the Alaskan native children, no teacher realized the cultural divide between those students and the setting and cultural context of the stories. However, some skilled scaffolding could have introduced the students to life in another area of the country and to a context called "the suburbs." If such scaffolding had taken place, then the children might have been better prepared to understand the basal reader story, even though it was highly foreign to them.

Today's teachers are better prepared than the teachers of the 1960s to understand cultural differences. As we discussed in chapter 2, it's not possible to be knowledgeable about all cultures one may meet in one's career. But knowing enough to ask questions and to work at becoming familiar with students' cultures will help teachers decide how and when scaffolding is needed, and to prepare themselves for unusual or unexpected responses to books.

Reader and Text: A Literary Transaction

Traditionally, the study of literature emphasized the author, or the historical and social factors that influenced the text. A new Critical Formalism Movement arose in the 1930s, questioning this notion. New critics asserted that literature study should focus on examining the text to discern a "true" meaning that was supposedly inherent in that text. The perspective of the reader or any other factors extraneous to the text were virtually ignored.

Teachers believed students needed knowledge of literary conventions, structures, and vocabulary to discover the meaning of a literary work. To this end, students were first taught to recognize specific elements such as plot structure in stories and rhyme schemes in poetry. They were then expected to use this knowledge in a logical, orderly way to uncover the correct meaning of a story or poem. The teacher acted as judge of what constituted the correct interpretation, controlling both procedure and student response. Readers were not encouraged or expected to bring self or context into this process.

Transactional Response Theory

In chapter 3, we introduced transactional theory from the works of Louise Rosenblatt. In her groundbreaking book *Literature as Exploration* (1938/1976), she transformed our perception of how literature could be taught, providing a theoretical basis for moving beyond the text to consider the perspective of the reader in the response process. To describe the evolution of our thinking concerning response, she used the metaphor of a darkened stage on which the figures of author and reader appear with the literary work between them. The spotlight initially focused on the author, with reader and text essentially invisible. At this point, meaning was thought to reside in the author's mind. Then the spotlight shifted to the text. The reader remained in the shadow, and meaning relied solely on the printed word. Next the spotlight moved to the reader, who gained new importance as an active participant, one who shaped and influenced reading. As Rosenblatt's "play" ends, all three characters — author, text, and reader—are spotlighted and seen as essential elements of response.

As stated, this theory of response regards author, text, and reader as important in constructing meaning. Eve Merriam, in her poem "I, Says the Poem" (from *It Doesn't Always Have to Rhyme*), eloquently describes the relationship between reader and text. The poem begins by declaring itself "a golden mystery," then adds, "But . . . I cannot speak until you come. Reader, come, come with me." Readers are active participants who construct personal

> *Literature . . . helps readers develop the imaginative capacity to put themselves in the place of others—a capacity essential in a democracy, where we need to rise above narrow self-interest and envision the broader human consequences of political decisions.*
>
> Louise Rosenblatt, 2000, p. 158

> *A good work of fiction is a jewel with many facets. Which ones shine depends on where you're standing.*
>
> Ann Cameron in McClure & Kristo, 1996, p. 229

responses to literature based on their view of the world. This worldview is created through readers' experiences, conceptions, and perceptions that cause them to distill multiple meanings from what they read.

The text, by virtue of its content, style, and purpose, evokes responses from readers while also guiding and constraining their construction of meaning. Iser (1974) explains that there are many possibilities in any one text, and one reading event would never exhaust the many possibilities that exist. In reading and responding to text, then, the reader moves back and forth between text and self, forming expectations that are confirmed or rejected as reading progresses. This means that readers often step back and rethink their previous understandings, checking them with what they know about the world, before moving on. It is a process of "reciprocal interaction"—of looking forward to the next part of text, then looking back, then forward again (Iser, 1974). Finally, the reader moves out of the world created by the text and considers what has been learned or experienced in the reading experience (Langer, 1995).

Efferent and Aesthetic Response

In chapter 3, we introduced what Rosenblatt (1978) calls "stance" when approaching the reading of a text, and her terms *efferent* and *aesthetic reading*. Readers who respond from an efferent stance focus on information or analysis rather than on the experience of reading. They might retell or summarize the story and evaluate its believability, or they might describe information and facts they learned. Older children might analyze the author's use of various literary elements or text structures (Cox, 1991; Many, 1990, 1991). Figure 4.4 shows two literature response journal entries (by 11-year-old boys) written from an efferent stance.

You will recall that, in contrast, aesthetic reading is concerned with what Rosenblatt terms the "lived through experience" that occurs when readers focus on the sounds and feelings the text evokes. When readers identify with a story's characters, marvel at the imagery created in a poem, or are moved by the events described in a piece of nonfiction, they are reading aesthetically. In aesthetic reading, readers draw heavily on their past experiences with texts and the world. They respond emotionally to the sounds of the words, and they identify with the characters

Figure 4.4
Examples of
Efferent Responses

November 7

It is amazing how some people can see a book one way (author) and someone else can see it from a totally different point of view (me). Not that I didn't enjoy today's reading. The author must have written pages 95–102 in about a day or so because he's not putting the same feeling into it as in the other chapters. It's turning into more of a history book instead of an enjoyable story book.

Treasure Island—Robert Louis Stevenson

When we just read, I noticed that Robert Louis Stevenson could write about anything. I say this because the poems he wrote were about happy things and we got used to that, and then when we started reading this, it just got real serious and life-like, unlike some other books where all the author can write about is positive things, where nothing goes wrong. Those books are boring because they are not realistic.

and events as they compare them to their own perspective. They become involved in sensing, clarifying, structuring, and savoring the reading as it unfolds. With aesthetic reading, both the mind and the heart are engaged.

When children respond aesthetically, they focus on parts of the story or poem that intrigue them. They cite their favorite parts. They wonder or hypothesize about events, characters, and themes. They may also make connections to other stories as well as to their own feelings and experiences. Young children sometimes talk to characters or add sound effects or actions, particularly if they're responding to a story that has been read aloud to them (Cox, 1991; Many, 1990, 1991). Figure 4.5 presents a literature response journal entry (by an 11-year-old boy) written from an aesthetic stance.

Although you might think readers respond to texts either efferently or aesthetically, this is not always the case: Most reading is a mixture of the two, although readers typically adopt a predominant stance. Readers constantly move between efferent and aesthetic, blending emotion and the search for information as they read a text. Differ-

ent genres tend to dictate a predominant stance (i.e., we typically read nonfiction efferently). However, the same text can be read both efferently and aesthetically. It is the reader's stance that makes the difference.

The notion that readers can read a text both efferently and aesthetically does not mean children must understand or "comprehend" a text efferently before they can respond aesthetically. Aesthetic reading is not an "add-on," efferent reading with an extra affective dimension. Rather, the aesthetic stance

> produces a meaning in which cognitive and affective, referential and emotive, denotational and connotational, are intermingled. The child may listen to the sound, hear the tone of the narrative "voice," evoke characters and actions, feel the quality of the event, without being able to analyze it or name it.
>
> Rosenblatt (1982, p. 269)

Thus, the literacy experience has two facets: first, the transaction between reader and text, and second, the concurrent

Figure 4.5
Example of an
Aesthetic Response

Across Five Aprils—Irene Hunt

Dear Teacher,

The part we read today put me on the edge of my seat. We read about how Ellen is addicted to coffee and how she needs it to soothe her headaches. I think that's bad because if you usually get addicted to something, your body decides to use that thing instead of doing it by itself.

We also read about how Jethro went in town to Newton. I think when he got there it was sad how they talked about Bill and how he took a trip to the South. I don't think that is good that we went to the South, but that was his decision and he has a freedom of movement. And I think they should respect that.

Tech Note
You will find a profile and a photo of Sharon Creech on the CD-ROM that accompanies this book.

A lot goes on under the surface when a reader reads, and sometimes that cannot be — should not be — tested. I like to think that literature can encourage us to expand our thinking and see things in different ways, but sometimes it is enough to let readers read.

Sharon Creech, author; personal communication, September, 1999

stream of reactions to the evoked work in that experience. It is both processes — transaction and reaction — that constitute response.

Teaching From a Literary Transaction Perspective

Rosenblatt's ideas suggest, first, that teachers must recognize and support the active role of readers. Readers construct images, savor the effect of the language, form opinions, make connections, pause to reflect, revise original expectations — all in an active search for meaning and a personal connection. They are not passive recipients of the information a teacher sees in the text, following a prescription for discerning some assumed inherent textual meaning. This is consistent with how children learn according to a constructivist perspective.

This perspective on response, in turn, suggests we abandon the notion that there is one correct interpretation of a story or poem. Because readers have different expectations, life experiences, cultural backgrounds, and experiences with literature, they will construct different meanings from reading a text, meanings that are personal to them. Thus our emphasis should shift from examining a meaning that supposedly resides in the text to examining the *many* meanings readers construct as they transact with text. It is this view of reading as a transaction that forms the philosophical basis for the instructional practices we espouse in this book.

Additionally, Rosenblatt's ideas suggest that we should view response from a broader perspective by encouraging

children to use both efferent and aesthetic stances. In particular, the aesthetic stance is the most neglected in schools (Rosenblatt, 1982). We must actively encourage our students to take an aesthetic stance when reading, "savoring the images, words, actions, associations and feelings" (Rosenblatt, 1982, p. 271) evoked by the reading experience. Too often, teachers hurry children through a personal response so they can get to what they see as the "important stuff": comprehension questions, analysis of facts, or evaluation of literary elements. Certainly there is a place for efferent response. However, we believe the teacher's priority should be to encourage an aesthetic stance, particularly while reading fiction and poetry. When readers respond aesthetically to a book, they are more likely to interpret story events, generalize and abstract concepts, and apply their experiences with literature to life (Cox & Many, 1992a, 1992b; Many, 1990, 1991). Figure 4.6 lists questions to elicit both aesthetic and efferent responses.

They are also more likely to become engaged readers. Engaged readers are essentially unaware of how many pages they've read or how long they've been reading. They don't focus on phonics skills, vocabulary, or gathering information to answer comprehension questions. Rather, they read for personal reward: to find more information on a topic that interests them, to vicariously experience someone else's experiences, emotions, and dilemmas, to enjoy language—and they are likely to seek out these continued pleasurable experiences with reading throughout their lives. We want children to be engaged with what they read.

The teacher of literature, above all, needs to keep a firm grasp on the central fact that he is seeking always to help specific human beings—not some generalized fiction called the student—to discover the pleasures and satisfactions of literature.

Louise Rosenblatt, in Kridel, 2000, p. 2

To me the highest accolade comes when a young reader tells me, I really liked your book. The young seem to be able to say really with a clarity, a faith, and an honesty that we adults have long forgotten. That is why I write.

Christopher Paul Curtis, Newbery Award winner, in Scales, 2000, unpaged

Rosenblatt's ideas also tell us that children should have opportunities to reflect more deeply on their reading. There are many ways to encourage and support children's thinking about stories. Some of these can be done immediately after reading to capture initial thoughts and feelings. Children's initial responses are often half-formed; they may not even be sure about the meaning of what they just read. Readers need time to explore some of these hazy responses.

Efferent Stance	Aesthetic Stance
☼ Can you retell the story in your own words?	☼ What did you think about the story?
☼ How does the author reveal the characters? What do they do? say? How do they interact with others? What do others say about them?	☼ What feelings did you experience as you read?
	☼ What are some things you want to say about this reading?
☼ What does the main character learn through the story?	☼ Is there a particular part of the story that moved you that you would like to tell about?
☼ How is the setting significant to the story (or, do you think the setting is significant)?	☼ Did you wonder about anything in the story? Did anything puzzle you? frighten you? make you sad?
☼ How does the author create suspense (humor, sadness, etc.)?	
☼ What does the author do to give you emotional feelings about the book?	☼ Did you agree with the decisions the characters made?
☼ How does this author's style in this story compare to other books he/she has written?	☼ What does the reading remind you of in your own experiences?
☼ How do the illustrations (if there are any) contribute to the story's meaning? What style of art was used? Is that style appropriate to the story?	☼ What other stories, movies, or television shows does the reading remind you of?
☼ Do you want to know more about this topic after reading this book?	
☼ Do you think the person who wrote this book is passionate about the topic he or she was writing about? Why or why not?	

Figure 4.6
Questions to Elicit Stances

Often, this takes the form of writing (typically in literature journals), drawing, and discussions. Children can then be encouraged to explore books more deeply, through sustained activities they see as memorable and engaging. In this way, their responses become more authentic, richer, and more informed. The next section of this chapter gives you a range of options you can provide for this purpose.

> The teacher's job, in its fundamental terms, then, consists in furthering a fruitful interrelationship between the individual book or poem or play and the individual student.
>
> Louise Rosenblatt, in Kridel, 2000, p. 2

their ideas and feelings with teachers and peers through movement, talk, writing, drama, and art helps them grow in their ability to respond in richer, more complex ways. Let's look at the various types of activities you can use to stimulate both spontaneous and sustained responses to books. In this section, we suggest some general types of response activities. Specific variations within each general type are addressed throughout the rest of the book, particularly in the genre chapters in Part II.

Activities for Deepening Children's Responses to Literature

Children become more thoughtful readers when they have opportunities to think about books and then express those thoughts in a way they find personally satisfying. Sharing

Writing

Through writing, children can record both initial and more thoughtful responses to books. Writing provides a permanent way to record the thinking they engage

Tech Note
Find out more about Patricia Lauber on the CD-ROM that accompanies this book.

in as they clarify their understandings, form opinions, and raise questions about their reading. Typically, writing in response to books is shared with peers in discussions (such as during literature circles), in writing groups, or with the teacher in a private conference. The responses of these listeners to what is shared then shapes and extends the writing. Following are some typical ways elementary children respond to books through writing.

When you read, notice what makes some books better reading than others.

Patricia Lauber, author; personal communication, September, 1999

Exploring books through a variety of response activities often helps students develop a greater understanding of and appreciation for what they read. Further, the opportunities for response that we provide ought to help them become more aware of their own responses, of how the story that they have created is a function both of their own experiences and of the text that they read.

Lee Galda, 1993, p. 313

student saw the book as a chore; the teacher's well-intentioned assignments had killed any aesthetic response. Somewhere in 19 packets of three-page handouts, the joy of a piece of very beautiful literature had been lost.

Overteaching a book in this manner will kill any true personal response and likely will cause children to dislike the book. Instead, children can write in their journals every day, respond at regular intervals as they progress through the text, or wait until they finish a book before responding

Literature Response Journals

Response journals are a repository of wonderings, wanderings, speculations, questions, and elaborated thoughts recorded during and/or after reading (Hancock, 1993). Some teachers give children the freedom to write whatever they want to say about a particular book, whereas others provide general questions. One thing we suggest you avoid doing is requiring your students to answer a lengthy list of questions day after day.

One of our own children read *Where the Red Fern Grows* (Rawls) in middle school. Every night, this student had to complete a three-page handout of vocabulary and detailed questions about this coming-of-age novel. Picking up her daughter's copy of the book, the mother shared about the days when she read this book to her sixth graders and everyone sat crying and didn't want to go out to recess. This middle schooler looked at her mother incredulously that others kids had actually *liked* the book. Clearly this

to it. Teachers usually have students respond to journals on some regular basis to get a sense of what children are thinking and how their responses change over time.

Variations on the typical literature journals include *dialogue journals*, where children and teachers or peers write back and forth to each other (often in letter format), and *character journals*, where readers pretend to be one of the book's characters and create a series of journal entries from that person's perspective. *Double-entry journals* are divided into two columns; the reader records quotes, descriptions, events, and other aspects of the book on one side of the page, and then writes responses to these on the other side. In *sketchbook journals*, another variation, children incorporate drawings, charts, and other visuals into the written response. This works particularly well with young children who often need to create a visual image as a prelude to writing, and with students who have difficulty expressing themselves in writing.

Text Set   Novels With a Coming-of-Age Theme

Anderson, Laurie Halse. (2000). *Fever 1793*. New York: Aladdin.

Avi. (1990). *The True Confessions of Charlotte Doyle*. New York: Orchard Books.

Curtis, Christopher Paul. (1999). *Bud, Not Buddy*. New York: Delacorte.

McKinley, Robin. (1982). *Blue Sword*. New York: Greenwillow.

Naylor, Phyllis Reynolds. (1991). *Shiloh*. New York: Atheneum.

Paterson, Katherine. (1980). *Jacob Have I Loved*. New York: Avon.

Peck, Robert Newton. (1972). *A Day No Pigs Would Die*. New York: Dell.

Rawls, Wilson. (1961). *Where the Red Fern Grows*. New York: Bantam.

Writing From Literature Models

Writing activities can also imitate the structure and format of a children's book. For example, children can create a research report on a topic following the format of a nonfiction book they've read; they can create a poem following the pattern of a favorite poem written by a professional poet; or they can imitate the stylistic techniques of a fiction writer in their own creative stories. This helps them understand how authors craft their stories and deepens their understanding and awareness of the conventions of various genres. More ideas of this sort are offered in chapter 14, "Writing: Students as Authors."

Dictated Responses

Younger children who have difficulty writing can have teachers record their thoughts. Often this is done in a group where the teacher writes children's ideas on chart paper. Teachers can also write dictated captions, sentences, or stories to accompany children's drawings.

What About Book Reports and Commercially Published Activity Forms?

We suspect you remember doing book reports. Maybe you knew children who read the book flap or jacket, wrote a quick summary, added a one-sentence opinion and turned it in—all without ever reading the book! We think this still happens far too often, and it is counterproductive to our goal of nurturing thoughtful, enthusiastic responses to literature. Book reports are boring to write and time-consuming to grade. Students have been cheating on them for generations. Consequently, we recommend you do away with traditional book reports, or at least revise this activity to make it more meaningful. Figure 4.7 features some alternative assignments.

Be wary also of commercially produced literature response forms or activity sheets. They often are little more than book reports in disguise, or the same kind of literature basalization mentioned earlier for *Where the Red Fern Grows*. And these both can be overwhelming. Providing 50 questions, 10 vocabulary words, and 14 extension activities for a picture book such as Eric Carle's *The Very Hungry Caterpillar* will destroy children's engagement with this delightful book. Scrutinize these commercially published materials carefully and use them only as guidelines for starting discussions or as general prompts for journal writing. Don't substitute published materials for your own teacher judgment and the good ideas you learn about using literature.

Oral Responses

Responses evoked through oral language activities are some of the most common and earliest kinds of responses children exhibit. Spontaneous comments, joining in on repetitive chants, clapping and singing to a beat are very natural ways that young children, in particular, respond to a book. Older students can respond in rap, writing their own material. In one classroom of seventh graders, for example, five students showed up to literature class wearing baggy clothing and sunglasses and performed a rap they had made about Mildred Taylor's novel *Let the Circle Be Unbroken*.

Cover art by Max Ginsburg, from LET THE CIRCLE BE UNBROKEN by Mildred Taylor, copyright © 1991 by Max Ginsburg, cover art. Used by permission of Puffin Books, A Division of Penguin Young Readers Group, A Member of Penguin Group (USA) Inc., 345 Hudson Street, New York, NY 10014. All rights reserved.

Figure 4.7 Better Than Book Reports: Ways to Respond (Adapted from Goodman, Bird, & Goodman, 1991)

Assignments Incorporating Writing

- Write a play based on a book. Plan to act it out for your class.
- Write a book review for a magazine or newspaper. Consider publishing the reviews in a school publication (or start a school publication!).
- Write a letter recommending a book to a friend or relative. Explain how it would particularly interest that person.
- Write to tell a story to go with a wordless picture book.
- Write and send a letter to a living author through his or her publisher or website. Compliment the author and ask questions related to insights about the book. Include a return self-addressed, stamped envelope if you use regular mail.
- Write about why one of the characters in a book would make a very good or very poor friend.
- Write a poem or rap based on a story.
- Pretend you are a newspaper reporter reporting on one of the major plot events in the book. Write a headline article of 200–300 words based on this event.
- Rewrite a story in rebus form (using pictures for some of the words).
- Use appropriate software to write a play on the computer based on your book.

Assignments Incorporating Art

- Make a poster advertising a book. Display it in your classroom or school.
- Illustrate a character from your book. Make a full-size portrait showing clothing appropriate to the setting's time and place.
- Design a board game based on the book that can be played by two to four players. Develop questions to accompany the game that players have to answer after they have read the book.
- Make a comic strip based on the plot of a book.
- Create a dust jacket that you think would sell a book. Laminate the jacket and put in on the book.
- Create a "tableau" by posing classmates dressed in costumes as characters in your book. Decide on one or more scenes to re-create this way. Take digital photos of your tableaus.
- Make a bulletin board based on your story or book. Try to make it interactive—things on your board that classmates can try out, read, do.
- Dress old dolls as characters in your book, or make paper dolls to accompany the book.

Assignments Incorporating Research

- Research the life of the author. Find any similarities between the author's life and events in the book.
- List five interesting facts you learned from a book. Verify or amplify with additional sources.
- Develop a time line of events in the story.
- Develop a cast for your book among real actors as if your book were to be made into a movie. Consider finding photos of these people on the Internet as part of your work.
- In cases where food is mentioned in a book, find out about that food and make it for your classmates.

Figure 4.7
(continued)

Assignments Incorporating Talk

☀ Prepare a short speech on something you liked or disliked about the book. Back yourself up with quotations or examples from the book.

☀ Discuss with a classmate how your personal experiences have been similar to or different from those of a character in a book.

☀ Explain orally or in writing how a book could be made into a continuing TV series.

☀ Find a classmate who read another book by the same author. Write or discuss the similarities and differences between the two (or more) books.

☀ Broadcast a book review or advertisement over your school public address system.

☀ If your book taught you how to do something, prepare a demonstration of that procedure to the class.

Assignments Incorporating Dramatics/Performance

☀ Create a musical accompaniment for your book using musical instruments or a computer music writing program.

☀ Share poetry from a book you read through choral reading, with illustrations, with musical accompaniment, perhaps with rhythm instruments, clapping, or drums.

☀ Write a monologue that a book character might say, and pretend you are the character when you perform it.

Children also spontaneously and enthusiastically make comments about their reading to partners or small groups of peers, sharing discoveries, insights, intriguing facts, or illustrations that catch their eye. Teachers should encourage the sharing of spontaneous oral responses because they offer informative glimpses into children's thinking as their interaction with a book unfolds.

Teachers can also provide opportunities for children to respond orally in more structured and focused ways. Some typical activities include the following.

Retelling/Storytelling

Students have a natural affinity for telling stories to others. You've probably seen them at play, making up stories or retelling familiar tales to a classmate or caregiver; this is a valuable activity. Through tellings and retellings, students learn and practice story structure and expand their oral language. You can encourage this by creating dramatic play centers with puppets, felt board story sets, costumes, toys from popular stories, tape recorders, props related to specific books and other story-related materials, along with literature books that have been read aloud to the children. You can also provide time following read-alouds, shared reading, guided reading, and literature circles for these oral response activities. Some teachers have a large box or tub in their room full of old hats, scarves, costume jewelry, sheets, tablecloths, shawls, headbands, masks, and other items from people's closets; in there, students find appropriate props to help them get into the mood of their story.

Book Talks

Students can be encouraged to share information about the books they're reading. Often this activity is done before or after reading time or following sustained silent reading. Book talks can involve reading aloud favorite passages, telling part of the story and encouraging listeners to read the book for themselves, pointing out interesting illustrations, or providing an enthusiastic personal recommendation. Sometimes students dress as a book character, or use a prop or two to help with their talks.

Book Discussions

Large- and small-group discussions allow students to share their thoughts about books in a more structured context. During these discussions, children build on each other's ideas, extend their own thinking, and develop richer, more informed responses through talk. The teacher sometimes leads these discussions, showing children how to express opinions, work through disagreements, manage time, and extend each other's ideas. Chapter 13, "Literature Circles," provides a wealth of information for implementing this approach.

Choral Speaking

Choral speaking can be done at any age level and with groups of different sizes. It can range from joining in on a repeated refrain from a book read aloud to a four-part reading of a poem, and is an excellent way to develop appreciation for language in literature. Chapter 5 provides extensive guidelines for using poetry for choral speaking with children.

Responding Through Drama

Creative drama, the form of drama most often used for response to literature, usually evolves out of spontaneous retelling and storytelling. Creative drama is more structured than retelling, although the informal, spontaneous process of "playing" is emphasized. A finished, polished performance can evolve from the reading of stories or poems. Typically, however, a quick scene can be created to explore a character's dilemma, re-create a favorite folktale, or reread a favorite section. Then the scene is concluded, and the group moves on to another activity. Children who learn best through physical activity particularly enjoy responding to books in this way.

Which drama strategy you select for use in your classroom depends on the book and your purposes. Typically, the performance aspect is less important than is helping children explore stories from multiple perspectives and articulate more thoughtful understandings about a book.

Edmiston (1993), recommends using drama to expand student understanding. He suggests that

> rather than putting our energies as teachers into getting the story right, we can work with our students to create dramatic situations in which they may all take up perspectives on certain aspects of the story. . . . They may see the story world through the eyes of characters or others, and, in doing so, the students will have experiences from inside the story world. If they reflect on those experiences, they may well discover new insights into the characters, the themes, and themselves

(p. 252). Using drama is not only memorable, but also supports comprehension and acknowledges the multiple intelligences (Gardner, 1993) of students. Following are some recommended ways you can use drama to support student's responses to literature.

> *Students take to these strategies like ducks to water, enactments enliven and engage students, and get them interacting with texts in profoundly different ways. . . . Enactment strategies are the most powerful strategies I use.*
>
> *Jeff Wilhelm, 2002, pp. 13–14*

Story Dramatization and Improvisation

When students dramatize a story, they reenact events essentially as these unfold in the book. Students can also select parts of stories to reenact, sometimes freezing the action to discuss cause and effect, character motivation, or other aspects of the story. Improvisation goes beyond the basic story line to creating new chapters, alternative choices characters might make, what happens after a story ends, or other "what ifs" the children might wish to consider. Then discussing why children created a particular response to an improvisation prompt can be a powerful way to extend their responses to a story.

Pantomime

You can also have children act like a character or re-create a scene without using words. In this technique, the story is conveyed solely through gestures, facial expressions, or other body language. This strategy is most effective with short stories that students know well, or with picture books. Students can pantomime while another student narrates.

Reader's Theatre

Reader's Theatre is an informal performance activity where students read from scripts that have been adapted from literature. Usually, the language of the story or poem is closely followed, although sometimes changes are made for smoother scripting and transitions. Lines aren't memorized and costumes are kept to a minimum. Little staging occurs. Rather, it is up to the readers to breathe life into the story through their interpretive reading. Reader's Theatre is sometimes handled like a radio play behind a screen or hanging barrier.

Puppetry

Children enjoy using puppets to play out a story. Shy children, in particular, can gain much from the opportunity to retell or create stories while hidden behind a puppet stage. Puppets work well with many genres, although they are particularly effective with folklore and picture books. As in other creative drama activities, emphasis should be on creatively acting out a story rather than preparing a formal script.

Responding Through Art and Music

Many students enjoy expressing themselves through art or music. Both can be effective media for supporting children's responses to books. Students can create a painting of a book's setting, construct a mobile of significant characters, find music that fits a story's mood, or explore techniques used by a favorite picture-book artist, to name a few examples. Far from being "busy work," these activities require students to go back into the text, verifying that their artistic or musical representation reflects the characters, events, settings, and other elements they are responding to.

Artistic responses also can serve as rehearsals for written and oral responses. Young children, in particular, often must create drawings or constructions before they can respond in other ways. If you allow young children to respond first through art, you may find that their subsequent responses are more thoughtful and more fully developed.

First-grade teacher Lisa Siemens uses art in her classroom for supporting responses. She muses, "I think a lot of their wonderful pieces come from their art. Art is another form of expression. I have found myself when I sit down and paint or draw, even if you don't end up writing about it, that it seems to take you to a place in your head that allows you to accent words, parts, language, whatever you may not have been able to do before. I think maybe it is that focus, by sitting and drawing, that you are really focusing on something and letting go of the words. Then the words come back to you, fuller and more developed" (personal communication, January, 2002). Knowing how she works as an artist, Lisa allows drawing to play an important role in response.

A well-stocked art center can be a wonderful catalyst for encouraging responses through art: fabric, yarn, buttons, socks, toilet-paper and paper-towel tubes, wire, Styrofoam, egg cartons, various kinds of paints, pipe cleaners, empty plastic bottles, doilies, ribbons, glue, tape, stamps (for printing purposes), and miscellaneous objects found around the school or home (pine cones, grasses, packing foam, etc.) can stimulate creative artistic responses to books. Interesting papers such as grocery bags, construction paper, tissue and textured papers, wallpaper samples, cardboard, oak tag, and cut-up packing boxes can also stimulate children's imaginations. Figure 4.8 lists some common ways for children to respond to literature through art and music.

Explorations of Illustrators' Media and Style

Students can learn much about the relationship between art and story when they replicate the work of a favorite illustrator. For example, children can use watercolors or water-soluble acrylic paints to create decorated papers that are then cut up and used to create collages like those in Eric Carle's *The Very Hungry Caterpillar*. Or they can use doilies, rubber stamps with designs carved on them, tissue paper, and watercolors to replicate Leo Lionni's *Swimmy*. Other artistic media children can explore include scratchboard, marbleized paper, stencils, and chalk.

Response Through Music

Some students will enjoy finding appropriate background music for dramatizing or reading a story aloud. Some books come with a CD that can be played to convey a mood while the book is shared aloud. Children can also create their own songs and music for presentations of stories or poetry. For example, second-grade teacher Candy Staley has her students compose an opera, complete with lyrics and music.

Young children also enjoy singing some of their favorite stories that were often written for this purpose. Books such as John Langstaff's *Oh, A-Hunting We Will Go;* Raffi and Wescott's *Down by the Bay; The Hokey-Pokey,* by Larry La Prise, Charles Macak, and Tafft Baker and illustrated by Sheila Hamanaka; and Merle Peek's *Mary Wore Her Red Dress* are typical books that can be used for this activity.

Graphic Organizers

Graphic organizers help students organize and synthesize their responses to books. Teachers usually create them as part of a group brainstorming session during which children's ideas are recorded on a chart. Sometimes art is added to extend understanding and increase the visual impact of the display. You will see numerous ways to use these techniques with students throughout this book. The following are some of the most common ones:

Semantic maps: An idea, theme, or concept is placed at the center of the chart with spokes radiating to related words, ideas, or concepts from a text.

Word webs: A variation of semantic map in which the concept of a particular word is explored and mapped. A key word is placed on a chart; related words and concepts are used to create a weblike graphic.

Figure 4.8 Art and Music Response Activities

Drawings and Paintings—Using paints, inks, chalks, crayon, etc.

Collages—Mixing paper, fabric, and other media on a picture.

Dioramas—3-D scenes from a book, built in a box.

Murals—Art in any medium using large rolls of paper that may cover an entire wall. Some schools permit students to use real interior house paint to paint murals on the school wall that will be painted over at the end of the year to make way for new art and artists.

Wall Hangings—Large pieces of fabric decorated with scenes from the book, main characters, etc. that are suspended from a rod.

Mobiles—Objects pertaining to a story suspended from X-shaped rods or clothing hangers.

Roller Movies—Rolls of paper are used as scrolls and placed into a box cut to resemble a television set.

Sculptures—Using papier-mâché or clay, students can make a bust or model of a character.

Computer Graphics—Students create simple pictures or multiple pictures in a PowerPoint presentation. Some pictures can be original and others captured from websites, or scanned into the presentation from student photography.

Filmstrips, Slides, and Movies—Media specialists can assist students and teachers in creating films and filmstrips, using computer software.

Story Boxes or Jackdaw Kits—Collections of artifacts related to a story.

Puppets or Figures—Students create a puppet or a life-size scarecrow figure of a story character.

Raps or Rhymes—Students create a rap or poem based on a story that they can perform using their available resources to add rhythm to the performance.

Ballads—Students create a poem that tells the story—a ballad—and set it to music. Those in the group with instrumental talents might accompany the performance on available instruments.

Dance—Students perform a simple dance that they think shows something about their book, having characters dance their role or feelings that are important to the story. Sometimes they invite their classmates to participate.

Text Set

Books for Talking About Collage Art

Carle, Eric. (1969). *The Very Hungry Caterpillar.* New York: Philomel.

Carle, Eric. (1984). *The Very Busy Spider.* New York: Philomel.

Carle, Eric. (1990). *The Very Quiet Cricket.* New York: Philomel.

Carle, Eric. (1995). *The Very Lonely Firefly.* New York: Philomel.

Lionni, Leo. (1960). *Inch by Inch.* New York: Astor-Honor.

Lionni, Leo. (1988). *Six Crows.* New York: Knopf.

Venn diagrams: Used to compare two books, characters, ideas, etc. Two overlapping circles are drawn on the chart. Children brainstorm how the two ideas being compared are alike and different. Qualities in common are written in the area where the circles intersect; differences are written in the nonintersecting areas of each circle.

Comparison charts: A way to organize thought and talk about several books or about several concepts related to one book. For example, children might compare and contrast books by one author. Or they might compare variations of one folktale, tracing similarities and differences among characters, action, and resolution of the story.

Plot diagrams: Used to help children see how a plot is structured by charting out the initial problem, events, rising action, climax, and resolution of the story. This could look like a flow chart or diagram.

Summary

Our goal throughout this chapter has been to acquaint readers with the importance, depth, and scope of reader response. We have discussed reader response theoretically as framed by Rosenblatt's work, and practically through the many examples. Responses are the rooting of lifelong loves of literature. When we feel, sense, and respond to books, we are making memorable book connections that are the foundation for future reading.

Varying these opportunities for response can suit learners as we provide ways for students to respond in writing, orally, through drama, through art, through technology, and through music. These kinds of activities are exciting for both teachers and students.

Action Research for Teachers

Increasing Student Response and Comprehension Through Book Discussions

Lisa Starr

Lisa's action research project concerns the implementation of literature circles in a second-grade classroom as a means of increasing student response and comprehension.

Each week during the study, students chose books to read in literature circles. After reading their selected book, students responded through writing and drawing, and contributed to group discussions spawned by their drawings and writings. Lisa chose five focus students, and tracked their progress. Each week, she tape-recorded the target students' discussions, and then analyzed tapes. Additionally, Lisa kept a researcher log, noting changes in student behavior, insights, and reflections about what was taking place.

In the beginning, discussions were not very interesting or engaging. However, as the study pro-

gressed, Lisa noticed that students began to trust each other, genuinely interacted with each other, and began to build on each other's attempts to construct meaning. Through analysis of the tapes and observations, Lisa found that student discussions began to improve. Students were more on-task with their talk, they were delving more deeply into the book's characters, and she heard in their comments more instances of higher-level thinking. The entries in their literature response journals also showed that they were more deeply engaged with the selections they read. Both their written responses and their discussions become more sophisticated and included more literate talk about books. Lisa made a decision to continue teaching with literature circles and response.

Part II

Learning About Literature

Books in Winter

SUMMER fading, winter comes —
Frosty mornings, tingling thumbs.
Window robins, winter rooks,
And the picture story-books.

Water now is turned to stone
Nurse and I can walk upon;
Still we find the flowing brooks
In the picture story-books.

All the pretty things put by,
Wait upon the children's eye,
Sheep and shepherds, trees, and crooks,
In the picture story-books.

We may see how all things are,
Seas and cities, near and far,
And the flying fairies' looks,
In the picture story-books.

How am I to sing your praise,
Happy chimney-corner days,
Sitting safe in nursery nooks,
Reading picture story-books?

From *A Child's Garden of Verses*,
Robert Louis Stevenson,
1905—Charles Scribner's Sons.

Chapter 5

POETRY

"I think, when you write a poem, one of the things you always hope to do is to surprise a reader. Surprising yourself comes as a bonus. And, just to keep everything from being tied up in a neat little package, there is a strange power of poetry to present something new and fresh while at the same time making it so right, so true, that it feels familiar; we seem to be discovering something we've always understood. I love that paradox of poetry." (Alice Schertle, poet; personal communication, September, 1999)

hird-grade teacher Linda Woolard loves sharing poetry with her students. She reads poems aloud every day, encouraging her children to listen for powerful descriptive words, feelings, and interesting rhythms. She has memorized poems to share at opportune moments. The children immerse themselves in hundreds of poetry books, sharing their favorites with each other and compiling personal anthologies. They also write their own poetry in poetry journals; Chelsea's "Moon" was created during one of these daily writing sessions. She describes how the poem evolved: "We were writing poems in the classroom and I looked up at a painting Miss Woolard has hanging on the wall. It has shooting stars and swirls and reminded me of the moon. I just kept looking at it and a poem just started coming to my mind."

First-grade teacher Adele Ames also loves conveying her enjoyment of poetry to children. "Each year, poetry runs rampant in our first-grade class," she says. "We read poetry off and on throughout the day. We read it at morning meeting, after lunch, before story time, and I often read poetry as part of a reading and writing workshop minilesson. I carefully choose poets who are diverse. Hopefully, the children will find at least one they connect with."

Third-grade teacher Kathy Perfect also loves poetry and uses it regularly with her children. She says, "I could not imagine teaching a day without poetry in my classroom. It starts our day, shapes our day and sometimes helps us get through our day. It doesn't take long for students to be captivated by the allure of poetry once it begins to weave its magic in the classroom" (1999, p. 728).

Living the joys of poetry: That's what Linda Woolard, Adele Ames, Kathy Perfect, and many other teachers invite their children to do every day, through many positive, enjoyable, and memorable experiences with this genre. Commitment and enthusiasm are the key. Think about poetry as one of the major entrees on the literary buffet table. Invite your students to sample from a feast of savory morsels served up by the skilled wordsmiths of poetry.

This chapter addresses some of the important ideas related to poetry as well as helps you discover ways to bring children and poetry together. Here are the questions we examine:

☀ What is poetry? What are the ingredients that make good poetry work?

☀ What do we look for in high-quality poetry?

☀ What should be included in your classroom poetry library?

☀ What is your personal history with poetry, and how might this experience influence what you do with poetry in the classroom?

☀ What should you consider when selecting poetry for sharing with children so it will resonate with them and cause them to be poetry lovers?

☀ What are some recommended strategies for helping children appreciate the crafting (literary qualities) of fine poetry without forcing them to dissect or interpret it?

☀ How can we support children as they write their own poetry?

What Is Poetry?

Poetry is musical language. It skips, it sings, it tugs at you with an insistent voice that rings through your head. Poets love the harmony of sound and rhythm that words create. They get inside and around words, going beyond surface definitions to discover their sounds, textures, rhythms, and connotative qualities. They hope this exploration will help them use words to capture the precise emotions and images they want to convey.

This elusive, emotional, eclectic quality of poetry makes it difficult to define precisely. Poet Myra Cohn Livingston (1996) agrees and asks:

What definition is there to encompass all the poems that have meaning and appeal to children? Do not definitions belong, rather, to science, to the laboratory? Our varying emotions, our needs as human beings, are not so easily stuffed into formulas and test tubes. The language of experience, of feeling, is not, as Ciardi [a fellow poet] so well points out, the language of classification, and the point of poetry is not to arrive at a definition but to arrive at an experience — to feel, to bring our emotions and sensitivities into play (p. 223).

It's also interesting to consider children's definitions of poetry. Fisher (1994) reports that children in second through

Moon

Big light rock,
your brightness
shines
into my heart.

Sunbeams dance
away from the sun
then glisten
off of you,
Moon.

Protect me
in the dark.
Help me
see my way to daylight.

Chelsea Rae Gough
Grade 3
Newark, Ohio
Teacher:
Linda Woolard

fifth grades typically don't understand what poetry is or how it differs from narrative. When asked to define poetry, the children in this study made statements such as, "It just is . . . " or "It needs more adjectives to be a poem." Some focused on the superficial aspects of how poetry is written: "It has capitals on every line, and it's printed in the center and it's short." They had no understanding of the differences among poetic forms or how a poem's lines and phrasing can make a critical difference (Fisher, 1994, p. 55).

In contrast, children who have been exposed to many examples of good poetry and have written poetry on their

> *Poetry is many things. It's the music of language. It's the stuff that doesn't have to extend to the margin. It's the stuff that can have meter and rhythm. It's the stuff that at its finest says things that prose cannot say. Very often it's something that's comforting to the poet. It's a distillation of experience. But most of all it's communication, right up there with sculpture, photography and painting and music.*
>
> *Jack Prelutsky, poet; author interview, in Zinsser, 1990, pp. 102–103*

own possess a remarkable understanding of the genre. When one group of first- and second-grade children with much experience with poetry were asked to define the genre, they said things such as: "Poetry is like a picture taken without a camera," "poems grab me because they are so nice and comfortable . . . they give me a good feeling," and "poetry has a satisfaction to it that books don't have. A book doesn't have time to focus on one part but a poem does" (McClure, 1990, p. 45). These children have a keen sense of what poetry is all about; they know it should nourish the heart and mind as well as the ear. They know this because they have been exposed to many

Douglas Florian creates whimsical, humorous poetry about animals ranging from birds to sea creatures. *Lizards, Frogs, and Polliwogs* celebrates reptiles and amphibians. Book cover from LIZARDS, FROGS, AND POLLIWOGS, copyright © 2001 by Douglas Florian, reprinted by permission of Harcourt, Inc.

examples of the best this genre has to offer.

It seems poetry has many possible definitions. For our purposes, however, we define poetry as the written form that results from the exquisite polishing of words. Poetic language is crafted in such a way that words are chosen carefully and concisely to say, in an economical way, just what the poet had in mind. However, crafting is not enough. Skillful poets also often express a unique truth or make an observation that invites us to look at our world in a new way. It's the combination of the two that makes good poetry. For example, Nikki Grimes causes us to reconsider the meaning of a common, everyday word in her poem "Shower."

I think in a way, a poem is like a museum. It's a place where you can keep safe the things you love or that you find interesting. You can keep a beautiful snakeskin in a poem, and you can keep the look of the sun shining through it. You can keep the papery feel, and the rustle the skin makes when you pick it up. You can keep the excitement.

In a poem, you can keep things you could never put in a real museum—things like a ride on a merry-go-round. You can keep feelings of sadness and joy. You can keep love, safe forever.

Patricia Hubbell, in Janeczko, 1990, p. 115

Shower

This word wets my pocket.
I have to stay indoors
Until my blue jeans dry.
SHOWER is a clean word—
Soap and water for the sky.

Nikki Grimes, in A Pocketful of Poems

The Elements of Poetry

Just as narrative and nonfiction writers use various elements to craft their pieces, poets use rhyme, rhythm, figurative language, and shape to create poetry that is imaginative, evocative, and unique. Writers of other genres use these elements as well. However, in well-crafted poetry, these tools are the essence of the writing. Even though contemporary poets are constantly breaking rules and pushing the boundaries, these elements still comprise the palette from which poets draw for their work, particularly when writing for children.

We want to offer one caveat: Using these terms to then analyze poetry with children is not a good idea. Drilling children on various rhyme schemes, measuring rhythmic patterns, or translating a poem into prose to get the "real" meaning are practices that can lead to poetry disaster! Rather, it's helpful to know the vocabulary associated with sophisticated poetry so you can use the right words with children. Then you can develop their taste for better poetry by helping them discover how poets use language to create a total composition.

Sound

The sounds of poetic language are what make it seem musical to the ear. Experienced writers of poetry are wordsmiths. They delight in playing with how language sounds, in the rhythm and rhyme of well-turned phrases and artfully orchestrated words. They are crafters of language, carving and polishing their words until they create just the right image and sound. That's why poetry is so often at its best read aloud. The sounds are what contribute to that pleasing sensation that tickles your ear and tongue. Poets use all the elements of sound—rhyme, alliteration, assonance, onomatopoeia, and rhythm—to create the appealing music that draws people to poetry.

Rhyme

One of the most salient aspects of sound in poetry for children is rhyme. The appeal of rhyme helps explain the attraction of Mother Goose, jump-rope chants, and other kinds of simple verse that children love. It also explains the enduring popularity of traditional poets such as Robert Louis Stevenson as well as those who are more contemporary, such as Mary Ann Hoberman, Eloise Greenfield, Karla Kuskin, and X. J. Kennedy, who often use rhyme. Consider the following poem by J. Patrick Lewis:

Sand House

I built a house
    One afternoon
With bucket, cup
    And tablespoon,

Then scooped a shovel-
    ful of shore
On top to add
    The second floor.

But when the fingers
    Of the sea
Reached up and waved
    A wave to me,

It tumbled down
    Like dominoes
And disappeared
    Between my toes.

J. Patrick Lewis, in Earth Verses and Water Rhymes

Meet... J. Patrick Lewis

Author of *The Tsar and the Amazing Cow; A Hippopotamusn't and Other Animal Poems; Two-Legged, Four-Legged, No-Legged Rhymes; Earth Verses and Water Rhymes; The Moonbow of Mr. B. Bones; One Dog Day; July Is a Mad Mosquito; The Fat-Cats at Sea; Ridiculous Nicholas;* and many others.

"Sister Poetry introduced herself to me late in life, just on the sunlight side of forty. I had labored in other fields for many years (teaching college economics), and thought I would continue to do that until the sun eloped with the moon. So, better late than never is a cliché I swear by. My first efforts at writing poetry were, how should I put this? Dreadful. Why? Because the only thing I knew about poetry was that I loved it. So I stopped writing for three years, and did nothing but read the classics, for adults and children, until I thought I knew something about the craft of poetry. That's when I began writing again.

"Luckily, I'm a twin. My twin is my best male friend and first reader. Always has been. I show him alone everything I write before sending manuscripts off to my editors. Our parents were blue ribbon all the way. They read nursery rhymes, fables, and tall tales to us as children, and I believe that made a world of difference for each of us. Somehow we came to believe that words were golden keys that had the power to open doors to other lands. And it turns out we were right."

To teachers, Mr. Lewis would suggest to discourage children from rhyming. He considers *sound* every bit as important as *sense* and he believes when young children connect with poetry, it is similar to the way they connect with music. "As I have said elsewhere, poetry is ear candy." But, he adds, rhyming is not one of your holiday games. "Like painting or learning to play the piano, writing poetry takes a slow hand. For writers in rhyme, the bar of excellence for rhymes rises a notch or two because contrived, hackneyed rhymes are so easy to write and so painful to read. A child coming to writing invariably chooses the easy rhyme that's completely forced. The results are woeful. Instead, encourage children to do what they do best, which is to revel in surprising, sometimes wholly original metaphors and similes that are the envy of all poets. They have a knack for 'saying the darndest things' until they lose that natural ability about the age of 11 or so."

Mr. Lewis lives in Chagrin Falls, Ohio.

Tech Note

Interviews with several other children's poets can be accessed on the CD-ROM that accompanies this book.

The rhymes provide unity by linking the words with each other, creating a pleasant, musical effect. Further, the rhymes fit the meaning of the poem. Unrhymed poems are pleasing to the ear in a different way; the music is more subtle and sometimes discordant but nevertheless has a memorable effect on the listener. Arnold Adoff often writes unrhymed poetry. Read aloud "Dear Mom" and consider how the poem sounds.

I figure I might as well just fool around with words and let an idea happen. The tremendous fun of writing in rhyme is reeling in whatever it is you've caught and being surprised by it. If you're lucky, you just keep landing one line after another, like a fisherman stacking up his limit. When things go swimmingly, a sleek idea will come thrashing up to the surface right there and then, while you write.

X. J. Kennedy, in Janeczko, 1990, p. 37

Dear Mom,

First: Keep momming

Second:
      I'm really thanking you.

Third: I'm serious.

Fourth:
      Don't laugh.

Fifth: Please kiss
      Only
        On
       The
      C h e e k.

Your Big Son: The Kid Himself.

Arnold Adoff, in Love Letters

Alliteration, Assonance, and Onomatopoeia

Alliteration is the repetition of similar consonant sounds, and assonance is a repeating internal vowel sound that provides a partial rhyme. Say the following poem by Rebecca Kai Dotlich to yourself and notice the effect of the repeating "s" sound.

Lemonade Sun

We pour
its liquid sweetness
from a tall
glass pitcher,
splashing
sunshine
on frosty squares of ice,
lemon light
and slightly tart,
we gulp its gold—
licking our lips
with summer.

Rebecca Kai Dotlich, in Lemonade Sun

In this example, the alliteration is so smooth the words are tied together, almost without our being aware of it. Sometimes, however, alliteration produces a sharp, staccato effect, waking us up to the sound of the words clanking together. Eve Merriam does this effectively in her poem "A Jamboree for J" (from *Jamboree: Rhymes for All Times*), where she describes "J" and says "It jiggles, it joggles, it's juicy, it's jamful"(p. 88). The words almost bounce off the page.

Assonance is typically more subtle. Read the following poem aloud and notice the repetition of the two sounds for "o."

Brother

I had a little brother
And I brought him to my mother
And I said I want another
Little brother for a change.

But she said don't be a bother
So I took him to my father
And I said this little bother
Of a brother's very strange.

But he said one little brother
Is exactly like another
And every little brother
Misbehaves a bit, he said.

So I took the little bother
From my mother and my father
And I put the little bother
Of a brother back to bed.

Mary Ann Hoberman, in The Llama Who Had No Pajama

When words in a poem imitate actual sounds, then the poet is using onomatopoeia; words such as "smash," "oink," or "clink" are all examples of this use of sound. In David McCord's "Pickety Fence" (from *One at a Time*), onomatopoeia—the clicking sound a stick makes as it's dragged along a wooden fence—comprises the entire poem.

Rhythm

Rhythm is the heartbeat of a poem. Young children naturally respond to rhythm: even before they can understand language, they respond to songs and poems with rhythmic movement. Poets use rhythm in different ways. Sometimes the words and lines are organized so that the rhythm propels the poem forward, as in Karla Kuskin's "Spring."

Spring

I'm shouting
I'm singing
I'm swinging through trees
I'm winging sky-high
With the buzzing black bees.
I'm the sun
I'm the moon
I'm the dew on the rose.
I'm a rabbit
Whose habit
Is twitching his nose.
I'm lively
I'm lovely
I'm kicking my heels.
I'm crying "Come dance"
To the freshwater eels.
I'm racing through meadows
Without any coat
I'm a gamboling lamb
I'm a light leaping goat
I'm a bud
I'm a bloom
I'm a dove on the wing.
I'm running on rooftops
And welcoming spring!

Karla Kuskin, in In the Middle of the Trees

Poets also use repetition to develop the rhythm of a poem. This repetition can be as simple as repeating one word at the beginning of the line, or it can involve a more complex pattern, where the poet repeats stanzas or weaves repetitive words and lines throughout the poem. The effect can be hypnotic and comforting, such as when Robert Frost repeats "and miles to go before I sleep" in his familiar *Stopping by Woods on a Snowy Evening*. Or the repetition can create unity in the poem that results in a satisfying pattern, such as Karla Kuskin's repetition of "I" in "Spring."

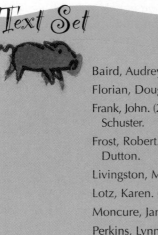

Text Set

Winter Poetry

Baird, Audrey. (2002). *A Cold Snap: Frosty Poems*. Honesdale, PA: Boyds Mills Press.

Florian, Douglas. (1999). *Winter Eyes: Poems and Paintings*. New York: Greenwillow.

Frank, John. (2003). *A Chill in the Air: Nature Poems for Fall and Winter*. New York: Simon & Schuster.

Frost, Robert. (1978). *Stopping by Woods on a Snowy Evening* (Susan Jeffers, Illus.). New York: Dutton.

Livingston, Myra Cohn. (1987). *New Year's Poems*. New York: Holiday House.

Lotz, Karen. (1993). *Snowsong Whistling* (Elisa Kleven, Illus.). New York: Dutton.

Moncure, Jane. (1985). *In Winter*. Chicago: Children's Press.

Perkins, Lynne Rae. (2003). *Snow Music*. New York: Greenwillow.

Rogasky, Barbara. (2003). *Winter Poems*. New York: Simon & Schuster.

Schnur, Stephen. (2002). *Winter: An Alphabet Acrostic* (Leslie Evans, Illus.). New York: Clarion.

Whipple, Laura. (2003). *A Snowflake Fell: Poems About Winter* (Hatsuki Hori, Illus.). Cambridge, MA: Barefoot Books.

Yolen, Jane. (1997). *Once Upon Ice*. Honesdale, PA: Wordsong/Boyds Mills Press.

Yolen, Jane. (2003). *Snow, Snow*. Seattle, WA: Mountaineers Books.

Figurative Language

The impulse to make metaphor is a fundamental quality of human intelligence. We seem driven to use metaphor to explain our new experience in terms of how it relates to our past experience. Through these connections, we create relationships that challenge our accepted vision of reality and provide us with fresh perspectives and new insights (McClure, Harrison, & Reed, 1990, p. 205).

How do poets create meaning through imagery? When writers compare one thing to another, using "like" or "as" to connect them, they have created simile. Metaphor, on the other hand, is a direct comparison (without "like" or "as"). It is important that the image resulting from the comparison be unique, providing us with a new perspective on the objects being compared. For example, in "Polliwogs," by Kristine O'Connell George, polliwogs are described as "chubby commas." The comparison is fresh and causes us to say, "I never thought of frogs quite that way before."

Polliwogs

Come see
What I found!
Chubby commas,
Mouths round,
Plump babies,
Stubby as toes.
Polliwogs!
Tadpoles!

Come see
What I found!
Frogs-in-waiting—
Huddled in puddles,
Snuggled in mud.

Kristine O'Connell George, in
The Great Frog Race and Other Poems

Some metaphors are subtle; you have to read carefully to notice them. Others are sustained throughout the entire poem and are more obvious, as when William Jay Smith compares a toaster to a dragon in his poem "The Toaster" (from Dunning, *Reflections on a Gift of Watermelon Pickle and Other Modern Verse*).

Personification is a comparison in which an inanimate object is described as having human qualities. For example, in "The Toaster," Smith uses personification when he tells how the toaster "hands" the toast to you when it's done. Constance Levy uses personification when she describes the sea as the "Earth's old wild heart beating" in "Ocean Rhythms."

Ocean Rhythms

Wave after wave,
each wave
a beat
each beat
repeating
can stretch

receding.
This is Earth's
old wild heart
beating.

Constance Levy, in Splash! Poems of Our Watery World

Figurative language shows children how language can awaken our awareness to the world around us. It helps them appreciate how poetry can give us a fresh view of the world through an imaginative juxtaposition of images.

Shape

Shape is a poem's visual display on the page: how the words are written, how many are placed per line, and the meaning of the whole poem in relation to its indentations and punctuation. Some poems begin each line with a capital letter and have an orderly succession of lines; others have words scattered all over the page, or use punctuation in creative ways for emphasis and to extend the poem's meaning. Shape is important: It affects how you read a poem, defining the rhythm as well as the speed at which the poem unfolds.

Poets use print creatively to emphasize particular letters or words, as when "SPLASH" is written in capitals to denote the loud sound a wave makes as it crashes against the beach during a storm. Some poets create a visual image that mirrors their meaning. Two examples are Brad Burg's "Swing" and "Sand Castle" (from *Outside the Lines: Poetry at Play*): "Swing" is written in a shape that suggests the arc made by a swing as it moves back and forth, and "Sand Castle" fits the poem's words on various parts of the illustration of a giant sand castle. Joan Bransfield Graham is a poet who has created several collections of "concrete poetry," in which the poems are written in the shape of the object being described: "Flashlight" is one of her most distinctive pieces.

F
L
A
S
H
LIGHT

click
one flick
I am the SUN,
I chase the shadows
one by one, growing scary,
jagged, tall — with brilliant beams
I'LL MELT them ALL!

Joan Bransfield Graham, in Flicker Flash

Although how a poem looks usually is not its driving force, shape can nevertheless have a significant influence on its meaning and effect.

Emotional Force

The elements of poetic crafting are of little significance, however, unless they work together to create an emotional response in the reader. Poems must start with a feeling, then the other elements work together to convey that feeling. One poet described this coordination of craft and feeling in the following way: "A poem should fill you up with something and make you swoon; stop you in your tracks, change your mind or make it up; a poem should happen to you like cold water or a kiss" (Heard, 1989, p. 74). This is particularly evident in Joyce Carol Thomas's "Brown Honey in Broomwheat Tea." The speaker conveys strong emotion softly but intently.

Brown Honey in Broomwheat Tea

My mother says I am
Brown honey in broomwheat tea
My father calls me the sweetwater of his days
Yet they warn
There are those who
Have brewed a
Bitter potion for
Children kissed long by the sun
Therefore I approach
The cup slowly
But first I ask
Who has set this table

Joyce Carol Thomas, in Brown Honey in Broomwheat Tea

Insight

Although all the elements discussed so far contribute to a good poem, a poem doesn't linger in our minds long after we initially experience it unless it startles us with its insight. These insights don't have to be sophisticated and complex; sometimes they amaze us with their simplicity, such as when Deborah Chandra describes her skin as like "a canvas tent/that's stretched/from bone to bone" (in "Tent," from *Balloons and Other Poems*) or when Nikki Grimes describes a spring shower as "soap and water for the sky" (from *A Pocketful of Poems*). But it is the sense that the poem has given you a new perspective or made you feel differently about something that is the hallmark of truly fine poetry. It is the "concentrated clarity of understanding" (Temple, Martinez, Yokota, & Naylor, 2002, p. 259) that makes us return to poetry again and again.

Forms of Poetry for Children

Children are not particularly concerned about the forms of poetry. Thus, we don't recommend that you drill them on defining forms or have them write poems in a particular form. For example, many teachers introduce students to poetry by having them write haiku because it seems like such an easy form to emulate. However, haiku is very complex.

The strict numbers of lines and syllables are difficult to get right and still make sense. Because of haiku's brevity, ideas are implied, and connections are often symbolic. No wonder most surveys of poetry preferences list haiku as the most disliked poetic form. You should expose students to many poetic forms so they have opportunities to discover what they enjoy. This will help expand their preferences. The Terms for Teachers feature that follows presents some of the most common poetic forms used with students.

Terms for Teachers

Common Poetic Forms Used With Students

Narrative—Tells stories. Can rhyme or be in free verse. Can be humorous, sad, adventurous. Many of the popular traditional ones are now available in picture-book format. Most popular form with children.

Examples: Traditional—*Ernest Lawrence Thayer's Casey at the Bat*, by Christopher Bing; "The Cremation of Sam McGee," by Robert Service (from *Collected Poems*); *Now We Are Six*, by A. A. Milne; Contemporary—much of the poetry by Jack Prelutsky and Shel Silverstein; *Brown Honey in Broomwheat Tea*, by Joyce Carol Thomas; *Meet Damitra Brown*, by Nikki Grimes

Lyrical—Melodious; focuses on descriptions or observations, conveying an image, feeling, or insight. Most children's poetry is written in this form.

Examples: *Out in the Dark and Daylight*, by Aileen Fisher; *Heartland* and *Cave*, by Diane Siebert; *Splash* and *When Whales Exhale and Other Poems*, by Constance Levy; *Sun Through the Window*, by Marci Ridlon; *Advice for a Frog*, by Alice Schertle; *Lemonade Sun: And Other Summer Poems*, by Rebecca Kai Dotlich

Free Verse—Nonrhyming; usually has rhythm, although it is not always patterned or consistent. Typically not as popular with students until they gain some background with poetry.

Examples: *Love Letters*, by Arnold Adoff; *All the Small Poems*, by Valerie Worth; *The Dream Keeper*, by Langston Hughes; *Confetti: Poems for Children*, by Pat Mora; *19 Varieties of Gazelle: Poems of the Middle East*, by Naomi Shihab Nye

Limericks—Five lines; thought to be Irish in origin. Humorous nonsense poems with an aabba rhyme scheme. Fifth line is usually a humorous concluding statement. Rhythm also follows prescribed rules. Popular with students.

Examples: *The Hopeful Trout and Other Limericks*, by John Ciardi; *Uncle Switch: Looney Limericks*, by X. J. Kennedy; *A Lollygag of Limericks*, by Myra Cohn Livingston; work by Edward Lear

Haiku—Ancient Japanese three-line form. First and third lines have five syllables; second line has seven syllables. Most haiku poems make an observation about nature and a statement of mood. Students tend not to like haiku until they have extensive experience with poetry.

Examples: *Cool Melons—Turn to Frogs!*, by Matthew Golub; *Black Swan, White Crow*, by J. Patrick Lewis; *Cricket Never Does: A Collection of Haiku and Tanka*, by Myra Cohn Livingston; *Stone Bench in an Empty Park*, by Paul Janeczko; *Don't Step on the Sky: A Handful of Haiku*, by Miriam Chaikin

Concrete Poetry—Written in the shape of the poem's subject. Can be rhymed or free verse. Purpose is to be seen rather than heard.

Examples: *Outside the Lines*, by Brad Burg; *Summersaults*, by Douglas Florian; *Splish Splash* and *Flicker Flash*, by Joan Bransfield Graham

Acrostic—Form in which a word is written vertically on a page; each letter of the word begins a line of the poem. Not typically a recognized poetic form, although a few poets have begun experimenting with it.

Examples: *Winter; Spring; Summer; Fall*, by Stephen Schnur

Poetry Novels—Series of poems (usually free verse) that tell a continuous story. Typically, characterization, theme, setting, and other elements of fiction are important elements in the poetry.

Examples: *Out of the Dust*, by Karen Hesse; *Girl Coming in for a Landing*, by April Wayland; *Becoming Joe DiMaggio*, by Maria Testa

Guidelines for Choosing Literature

Criteria for Evaluating Poetry

☼ Is it pleasing to your ear? Is it enjoyable to say aloud?

☼ When the poem has rhythm and rhyme, are they likely to appeal to students? When it is free verse, does it have some quality — usually imagery or interesting word choice — that will appeal to children?

☼ When the poetry rhymes, are the rhymes interesting and fresh, or are they predictable and contrived? Do the rhymes enhance the meaning or get in the way?

☼ Is it poetry your students will be able to understand? Be cautious of poetry written many years ago: It might be pleasurably nostalgic to you but seem irrelevant to your children, because of archaic vocabulary and references.

☼ Are the images created by the poet fresh and interesting to children, yet still true to life?

☼ Is the figurative language relevant to students' lives, and does it include comparisons that children can understand?

☼ Does the content relate to students' lives?

☼ Does the poem appeal to students yet extend their taste of what they consider "good" poetry?

Choosing Quality Poetry

What are the best examples of this genre that you should share with your students? How do you select the best? The Guidelines for Choosing Literature feature above lists criteria to help you evaluate what this genre has to offer.

Awards for Excellence in Poetry

Another way to determine excellence in poetry is to examine what has won awards. For example, the National Council of Teachers of English (NCTE) gives its Award for Excellence in Poetry for Children to a living American poet in honor of that person's aggregate body of work (members of our author team are proud to have served on the selection committee for this award). The award was given annually from 1977 until 1982, when it was decided that the award would be given every 3 years. Figure 5.1 lists the winners of this award. NCTE's website, www.ncte.org, provides information on the current winner.

An excellent resource for showcasing the work of the NCTE award winners is Bernice Cullinan's *A Jar of Tiny Stars: Poems by NCTE Award-Winning Poets* (1996). This useful book presents several poems by each of the NCTE award–winning poets. All have been field-tested with children. This book also provides a brief biographical sketch and a memorable quote by each poet.

The Lee Bennett Hopkins Poetry Award, administered by the Pennsylvania Center for the Book at The Pennsylvania State University, is granted annually to an American poet or anthologist for the most outstanding new book of

Tech Note

The CD-ROM that accompanies this book lists past winners of both of these awards and websites to access for more information on the awards.

☼ 2003—Mary Ann Hoberman

☼ 2000—X. J. Kennedy

☼ 1997—Eloise Greenfield

☼ 1994—Barbara Juster Esbensen

☼ 1991—Valerie Worth

☼ 1988—Arnold Adoff

☼ 1985—Lilian Moore

☼ 1982—John Ciardi

☼ 1981—Eve Merriam

☼ 1980—Myra Cohn Livingston

☼ 1979—Karla Kuskin

☼ 1978—Aileen Fisher

☼ 1977—David McCord

Figure 5.1   NCTE Excellence in Poetry for Children Award Winners

One student's personal response to *A Jar of Tiny Stars,* by Bernice Cullinan.

children's poetry published in the previous calendar year. The Lee Bennett Hopkins Promising Poet Award is given every 3 years by the International Reading Association to a children's poet who has published no more than two books of children's poetry. Winners of this award include Deborah Chandra, for *Rich Lizard and Other Poems,* Kristine O'Connell George, for *The Great Frog Race and Other Poems,* and Craig Crist-Evans, for *Moon Over Tennessee: A Boy's Civil War Journal.*

Categorizing Poetry

Works of poetry can be categorized in several ways: by author, type of collection, literary device used, theme, etc. To give you a sense of the diverse range of topics for which you can find poetry, we have categorized some of the best books by themes that have been popular with children. Figure 5.2 presents some of these themes, along with representative books that explore that theme by both traditional and contemporary poets. Brief descriptions of each book can be found on the CD-ROM that accompanies this book. Certainly some books could be placed in more than one group. And, of course, there are many other themes and good books that could be included. Nevertheless, this list can be a catalyst for stimulating your own explorations.

Building a Classroom Library of Poetry

A classroom poetry collection is an excellent catalyst for generating interest in poetry. But you might wonder about the essential titles and kinds of books you should definitely include. You might start with poetry by Silverstein and Prelutsky because their work will surely entice your children into this genre. But our job as teachers is to help move children beyond their comfort level to explore new poetry territory because there is so much to sample from the vast "poetry buffet table." Just as no one could survive on a constant diet of fast food and chocolate candy, so you should vary your students' poetry diet.

As you build your poetry collection, consider students' interests as well as their previous experiences with this genre. You will want to find poetry that is focused on their interests and experiences while also extending their tastes. To accomplish this, you will want to include poetry on topics such as humor, animals, nature, everyday life, and sports. Figure 5.2 has suggestions for excellent books on a range of themes that appeal to students.

Figure 5.2
Common Themes
in Poetry for
Children

Poetry of Nature

Arnold Adoff: *In for Winter, Out for Spring*

Francisco X. Alarcón: *From the Bellybutton of the Moon and Other Summer Poems; Iguanas in the Snow*

Frank Asch: *Cactus Poems*

Audrey Baird: *Storm Coming!; A Cold Snap: Frosty Poems*

Byrd Baylor: *Your Own Best Secret Place; Everybody Needs a Rock; I'm in Charge of Celebrations; Desert Voices*

John Bierhorst: *In the Trail of the Wind: American Indian Poems and Ritual Orations; On the Road of Stars: Native American Night Poems and Sleep Charms*

Joseph Bruchac: *Thirteen Moons on Turtle's Back: A Native American Year of Moons*

Rebecca Kai Dotlich: *Lemonade Sun*

Barbara Esbenson: *Echoes For the Eye: Poems to Celebrate Patterns in Nature*

Aileen Fisher: *Out in the Dark and Daylight*

Ralph Fletcher: *Ordinary Things: Poems From a Walk in Early Spring*

Douglas Florian: *Summersaults; Winter Eyes*

Robert Frost: *You Come Too: Favorite Poems for Young Readers*

Kristine O'Connell George: *The Great Frog Race and Other Poems; Old Elm Speaks: Tree Poems; Toasting Marshmallows: Camping Poems*

Lee Bennett Hopkins: *Rainbows Are Made: Poems by Carl Sandburg*

Tony Johnston: *An Old Shell: Poems of the Galapagos; Once in the Country: Poems of a Farm*

Jane Kurtz: *River Friendly, River Wild*

Constance Levy: *When Whales Exhale; A Crack in the Clouds; Splash! Poems of Our Watery World*

J. Patrick Lewis: *Earth Verses and Water Rhymes*

Myra Cohn Livingston: *A Circle of Seasons; Sky Songs; Earth Songs; Sea Songs*

Lilian Moore: *Poems Have Roots: New Poems*

Lillian Morrison: *Whistling the Morning In*

Judith Nichols: *The Sun in Me: Poems About the Planet*

Paul Paolilli & Dan Brewer: *Silver Seeds: A Book of Nature Poems*

Barbara Rogasky: *Leaf by Leaf: Autumn Poems; Winter Poems*

Alice Schertle: *A Lucky Thing*

Steven Schnur: *Winter; Spring; Summer; Fall*

Diane Siebert: *Cave; Mojave; Heartland*

Ann Turner: *Moon for Seasons*

Nancy Van Laan: *When Winter Comes*

Jane Yolen: *Weather Report; Once Upon Ice; Snow, Snow: Winter Poems for Children; Color Me a Rhyme; Least Things: Poems About Small Natures*

Charlotte Zolotow: *Seasons*

Everyday Experiences

Arnold Adoff: *Street Music: City Poems*

Francisco X. Alarcón: *Laughing Tomatoes and Other Spring Poems*

Jorge Argueta: *A Movie in My Pillow/Una película in mi almohada*

Gwendolyn Brooks: *Bronzeville Boys and Girls*

Lori Carlson: *Cool Salsa*

Ann Nolan Clark: *In My Mother's House*

Emanuel di Pasquale: *Cartwheel to the Moon: My Sicilian Childhood*

Paul Laurence Dunbar: *Jump Back, Honey*

Tom Feelings: *Soul Looks Back in Wonder*

Kristine O'Connell George: *Swimming Upstream: Middle School Poems*

Nikki Giovanni: *Spin a Soft Black Song*

Isabel Joshlin Glaser: *Dreams of Glory: Poems Starring Girls*

Ruth Gordon: *Pierced by a Ray of the Sun: Poems About the Times We Feel Alone*

Eloise Greenfield: *Honey, I Love; Under the Sunday Tree; Nathaniel Talking*

Nikki Grimes: *Meet Damitra Brown* (and other Damitra Brown Collections), *A Dime a Dozen*

Monica Gunning: *Not A Copper Penny in Me House*

Mary Ann Hoberman: *The Llama Who Had No Pajama; Yellow Butter, Purple Jelly, Red Jam, Black Bread*

Sara Holbrook: *The Dog Ate My Homework; I Never Said I Wasn't Difficult; Walking on the Boundaries of Change; Am I Naturally This Crazy?*

Charlotte Huck: *Secret Places*

Simon James: *Days Like This: A Collection of Small Poems*

Karla Kuskin: *Dogs and Dragons, Trees and Dreams*

Claudia Lee: *Messengers of Rain and Other Poems From Latin America*

Sandra Liatsos: *Bicycle Riding and Other Poems*

Myra Cohn Livingston: *A Song I Sang to You; I Like You, If You Like Me; Remembering and Other Poems; Celebrations*

Kam Mak: *My Chinatown: One Year in Poems*

Salley Mavor: *You and Me: Poems of Friendship*

David McCord: *One at a Time*

(continues)

Figure 5.2
(continued)

Everyday Experiences (continued)

Jane Medina: *My Name Is Jorge: On Both Sides of the River*

Eve Merriam: *You Be Good and I'll Be Night; Blackberry Ink*

A. A. Milne: *The World of Christopher Robin*

Pat Mora: *Confetti*

Cynthia Rylant: *Waiting to Waltz*

Carol Diggory Shields: *Lunch Money and Other Poems About School*

Gary Soto: *Fearless Fernie: Hanging Out With Fernie and Me; Canto Familiar; Neighborhood Odes*

Robert Louis Stevenson: *A Child's Garden of Verses*

Luci Tapahonso: *Songs of Shiprock Fair*

Joyce Carol Thomas: *Gingerbread Days*

April Halprin Wayland: *Girl Coming in for a Landing*

Janet Wong: *A Suitcase of Seaweed and Other Poems; Good Luck and Other Poems*

Jane Yolen: *Street Rhymes From Around the World*

Poetry About Sports and Movement

Arnold Adoff: *The Basket Counts*

Barbara Esbenson: *Dance With Me*

Lee Bennett Hopkins: *Sports! Sports! Sports! A Poetry Collection; Extra Innings; Opening Days; Song and Dance: Poems*

Paul Janeczko: *That Sweet Diamond*

X. J. Kennedy: *Elympics*

Sharon Bell Mathis: *Red Dog Blue Fly: Football Poems*

Lillian Morrison: *The Sidewalk Racer and Other Poems About Sports and Motion; Rhythm Road: Poems to Move To; At the Crack of the Bat*

Charles R. Smith Jr.: *Rimshots: Basketball Pix, Rolls and Rhythms; Short Takes: Fast-Break Basketball Poetry*

Michael Strickland: *My Own Song and Other Poems to Groove To*

Ernest Lawrence Thayer's Christopher Bing: *Casey at the Bat: A Ballad of the Republic Sung in the Year 1888*

Humorous Poetry

N. M. Bodecker: *Hurry, Hurry, Mary Dear*

William Cole: *Poem Stew; Oh, What Nonsense!*

Robin Hirsch: *FEG: Ridiculous Poems for Intelligent Children*

Belinda Hollyer: *The Kingfisher Book of Family Poems*

X. J. Kennedy: *Exploding Gravy: Poems to Make You Laugh; Brats; Fresh Brats*

Bruce Lansky: *Kids Pick the Funniest Poems*

Edward Lear: *The Complete Nonsense of Edward Lear; The Jumblies; Of Pelicans and Pussycats: Poems and Limericks*

Dennis Lee: *Dinosaur Dinner (With a Slice of Alligator Pie); Alligator Pie; Jelly Belly; The Ice Cream Store*

J. Patrick Lewis: *A Hippopotamusn't; Good Mousekeeping and Other Animal Home Poems; Riddle-icious; Riddle-Lightful: Oodles of Little Riddle-Poems*

Colin McNaughton: *Who's Been Sleeping in My Porridge?*

Eve Merriam: *Poem for a Pickle; Higgle Wiggle: Happy Rhymes*

Richard Michelson: *Animals That Ought to Be*

Jeffrey Moss: *Butterfly Jar*

Jack Prelutsky: *The New Kid on the Block; For Laughing Out Loud: Poems to Tickle Your Funny Bone; Something Big Has Been Here; A Pizza the Size of the Sun; It's Raining Pigs and Noodles*

Laura Richards: *Turra Lura, Rhymes Old and New*

Shel Silverstein: *A Light in the Attic; Where the Sidewalk Ends*

William Jay Smith: *Laughing Time*

Nancy Van Laan: *With a Whoop and a Holler*

Fresh Perspectives on Ordinary Things

Arnold Adoff: *Touch the Poem*

Sylvia Cassedy: *Zoomrimes: Poems About Things That Go*

Deborah Chandra: *Balloons and Other Poems; Rich Lizard*

Barbara Esbenson: *Who Shrank My Grandmother's House?*

Ralph Fletcher: *Twilight Comes Twice*

Charles Ghigna: *A Fury of Motion: Poems for Boys*

Joan Bransfield Graham: *Flicker Flash; Splish Splash*

Nikki Grimes: *A Pocketful of Poems*

Mary Ann Hoberman: *A House Is a House for Me*

Lee Bennett Hopkins: *School Supplies: A Book of Poems*

J. Patrick Lewis: *Doodle Dandies: Poems That Take Shape*

Figure 5.2
(continued)

Fresh Perspectives on Ordinary Things (continued)

Eve Merriam: *Fresh Paint*

Naomi Shihab Nye: *Come With Me: Poems for a Journey*

Marci Ridlon: *Sun Through the Window*

Alice Schertle: *Keepers*

James Stevenson: *Popcorn; Candy Corn; Sweet Corn; Cornflakes*

Brian Swann: *The House With No Door; Touching the Distance*

Nancy Willard: *The Moon and Riddles Diner and the Sunnyside Café*

Janet Wong: *Night Garden*

Valerie Worth: *All the Small Poems; Peacock*

Charlotte Zolotow: *Snippets: A Gathering of Poems, Pictures and Possibilities*

Family Life

Arnold Adoff: Black Is Brown Is Tan

Lori M. Carlson: *Sol a Sol*

Dori Chaconas: *On a Wintry Morning*

Ralph Fletcher: *Relatively Speaking*

Eloise Greenfield: *Night on Neighborhood Street*

Margo C. Griego: *Tortillitas Para Mama*

Nikki Grimes: *My Man Blue; Poems Stepping Out With Grandma Mac*

Carol and Daniel Hittleman: *A Grand Celebration: Grandparents in Poetry*

Mary Ann Hoberman: *Fathers, Mothers, Sisters, Brothers*

Angela Johnson: *Running Back to Luddie*

Myra Cohn Livingston: *Poems for Mothers; Poems for Fathers*

Richard J. Margolis: *Secrets of a Small Brother*

Pat Mora: *Love to Mama: A Tribute to Mothers*

Javaka Steptoe: *In Daddy's Arms I Am Tall*

Dorothy and Michael Strickland: *Families: Poems Celebrating the African American Experience*

Joyce Carol Thomas: *Brown Honey in Broomwheat Tea*

Janet Wong: *The Rainbow Hand: Poems About Mothers and Children*

Jane Yolen and Heidi Stemple: *Dear Mother, Dear Daughter*

Animals

Anne Carter: *Birds, Beats and Fishes: A Collection of Animal Poems*

Rebecca Kai Dotlich: *Sweet Dreams of the Wild: Poems for Bedtime*

Barbara Esbenson: *Words With Wrinkled Knees*

Aileen Fisher: *Feathered Ones and Furry*

Paul Fleischman: *Joyful Noise: Poems for Two Voices; I Am Phoenix*

Douglas Florian: *Lizards, Frogs and Polliwogs: Poems and Paintings; Insectlopedia; Mammalabilia; On the Wing; Bow Wow, Meow, Meow; Beast Feast; In the Swim*

Kristine O'Connell George: *Little Dog Poems: Little Dog and Duncan*

David Harrison: *Farmer's Garden: Rhymes for Two Voices*

Georgia Heard: *Creatures of Earth, Sea, and Sky*

Mary Ann Hoberman: *Bugs!*

Lee Bennett Hopkins: *Hoofbeats, Claws & Rippled Fins; Dinosaurs*

Tony Johnston: *It's About Dogs; Cat, What Is That?*

Kate Kiesler: *Wings On the Wind*

Nancy Larrick: *Cats Are Cats; Mice Are Nice*

Constance Levy: *When Whales Exhale and Other Poems*

Myra Cohn Livingston: *Dog Poems; Cat Poems; If the Owl Calls Again; If You Ever Meet a Whale*

Jack Prelutsky: *Tyrannasaurus Was a Beast: Dinosaur Poems*

Alice Schertle: *I Am the Cat; How Now, Brown Cow?; Advice for a Frog*

Jury Sierra: *Antarctic Antics*

Marilyn Singer: *Turtle in July*

You will also want to include poetry from many cultures in your collection. Diverse voices have traditionally been underrepresented in children's poetry, but you will want to find poetry written by poets whose voices reflect the multicultural experience. For example, in *Danitra Brown Leaves Town*, poet Nikki Grimes details the life of a young African American girl through poetry. You may be familiar with the work of African American poet Langston Hughes, but know few other voices from diverse cultures. You will likely want your students to have a broader background.

The best multicultural poetry portrays a particular culture honestly and accurately while giving us all insights into what it's like to be of that culture. It also addresses universal themes, emotions, and experiences familiar to all children. Contemporary poets write from many cultural perspectives, including African American, Middle Eastern, Latino, Caribbean, and Asian American. Some of the best collections are listed in Figure 5.3. In addition, the text set highlights poetry books that celebrate the Latino experience.

Poetry that supports the study of content areas is another category of books that should be part of your

Figure 5.3 Some Recommended Multicultural Poetry Collections

Author	Title
☼ Arnold Adoff:	*In for Winter, Out for Spring; Touch the Poem; Black Is Brown Is Tan; Street Music: City Poems; The Basket Counts; I Am the Darker Brother*
☼ John Agard & Grace Nichols:	*A Caribbean Dozen: Poems from Caribbean Poets; No Hickory, No Dickory, No Dock: Caribbean Nursery Rhymes; Under the Moon & Over the Sea*
☼ Francisco X. Alarcón:	*From the Belly Button of the Moon and Other Summer Poems; Iguanas in the Snow; Laughing Tomatoes and Other Spring Poems*
☼ Jorge Argueta:	*A Movie in My Pillow/Una pelicula in mi almohada*
☼ Barbara Brenner:	*Voices: Poetry and Art From Around the World*
☼ Gwendolyn Brooks:	*Bronzeville Boys and Girls*
☼ Joseph Bruchac:	*Thirteen Moons on Turtle's Back: A Native American Year in Poems*
☼ Lori Carlson:	*Cool Salsa; Sol a Sol*
☼ Nancy W. Carlstrom:	*Midnight Dance of the Snowshoe Hare: Poems of Alaska*
☼ Emanuel di Pasquale:	*Cartwheel to the Moon: My Sicilian Childhood*
☼ Paul Laurence Dunbar:	*Jump Back, Honey*
☼ Tom Feelings:	*Soul Looks Back In Wonder*
☼ Nikki Giovanni:	*Spin a Soft Black Song*
☼ Ruth Gordon:	*Peeling the Onion*
☼ Eloise Greenfield:	*Honey, I Love; Under the Sunday Tree; Night on Neighborhood Street; Nathaniel Talking*
☼ Margot C. Griego:	*Tortillitas Para Mama*
☼ Nikki Grimes:	*My Man Blue: Poems; Stepping Out With Grandma Mac; Meet Damitra Brown (and other Damitra Brown collections); A Dime a Dozen; A Pocketful of Poems*
☼ Monica Gunning:	*Under the Breadfruit Tree: Island Poems; Not a Copper Penny in Me House*

Figure 5.3
(continued)

Author	Title
☼ Mingfong Ho:	*Maples in the Mist*
☼ Mary Ann Hoberman:	*My Song Is Beautiful: Poems and Pictures in Many Voices*
☼ Angela Johnson:	*Running Back to Ludie*
☼ Claudia Lee:	*Messengers of Rain and Other Poems From Latin America*
☼ Hugh Lupton:	*The Songs of Birds: Stories and Poems from Many Cultures*
☼ Kam Mak:	*My Chinatown: One Year in Poems*
☼ Jane Medina:	*My Name Is Jorge on Both Sides of the River: Poems; The Dream on Blanca's Wall*
☼ Adrian Mitchell:	*Strawberry Drums: A book of poems with a beat for you and all your friends to keep*
☼ Pat Mora:	*Confetti; Love to Mama: A Tribute to Mothers*
☼ Naomi S. Nye:	*The Space Between Our Footsteps: Poems and Paintings From the Middle East*
☼ Annette Ochoa, Betsy Franco, & Tracy L. Gourdine:	*Night Is Gone, Day Is Still Coming: Stories and Poems by American Indian Teens and Young Adults*
☼ Michael Rosen:	*Itsy-Bitsy Beasties: Poems From Around the World*
☼ Charles R. Smith Jr.:	*Rimshots: Basketball Pix, Rolls, and Rhythms; Short Takes: Fast-Break Basketball Poetry*
☼ Gary Soto:	*Fearless Fernie: Hanging Out With Fernie and Me; Canto Familiar; Neighborhood Odes*
☼ Javaka Steptoe:	*In Daddy's Arms I Am Tall*
☼ Dorothy & Michael Strickland:	*Families: Poems Celebrating the African American Experience*
☼ Michael Strickland:	*My Own Song and Other Poems to Groove To*
☼ Brian Swann:	*The House With No Door; Touching the Distance*
☼ Véronique Tadjo:	*Talking Drums: A Selection of Poems from Africa South of the Sahara*
☼ Luci Tapahonso:	*Songs of Shiprock Fair*
☼ Joyce Carol Thomas:	*Brown Honey in Broomwheat Tea: Gingerbread Days*
☼ Uzo Unobagha:	*Off to the Sweet Shores of Africa and Other Talking Drum Rhymes*
☼ Carole Weatherford:	*Remember the Bridge: Poems of a People*
☼ Janet Wong:	*The Rainbow Hand: Poems About Mothers and Children; Night Garden; A Suitcase of Seaweed and Other Poems; Good Luck and Other Poems*
☼ Jane Yolen:	*Sleep Rhymes Around the World*

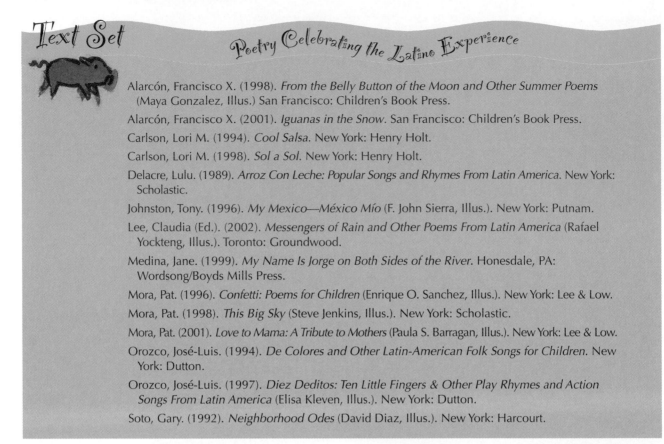

Text Set   Poetry Celebrating the Latino Experience

Alarcón, Francisco X. (1998). *From the Belly Button of the Moon and Other Summer Poems* (Maya Gonzalez, Illus.) San Francisco: Children's Book Press.

Alarcón, Francisco X. (2001). *Iguanas in the Snow*. San Francisco: Children's Book Press.

Carlson, Lori M. (1994). *Cool Salsa*. New York: Henry Holt.

Carlson, Lori M. (1998). *Sol a Sol*. New York: Henry Holt.

Delacre, Lulu. (1989). *Arroz Con Leche: Popular Songs and Rhymes From Latin America*. New York: Scholastic.

Johnston, Tony. (1996). *My Mexico—México Mío* (F. John Sierra, Illus.). New York: Putnam.

Lee, Claudia (Ed.). (2002). *Messengers of Rain and Other Poems From Latin America* (Rafael Yockteng, Illus.). Toronto: Groundwood.

Medina, Jane. (1999). *My Name Is Jorge on Both Sides of the River*. Honesdale, PA: Wordsong/Boyds Mills Press.

Mora, Pat. (1996). *Confetti: Poems for Children* (Enrique O. Sanchez, Illus.). New York: Lee & Low.

Mora, Pat. (1998). *This Big Sky* (Steve Jenkins, Illus.). New York: Scholastic.

Mora, Pat. (2001). *Love to Mama: A Tribute to Mothers* (Paula S. Barragan, Illus.). New York: Lee & Low.

Orozco, José-Luis. (1994). *De Colores and Other Latin-American Folk Songs for Children*. New York: Dutton.

Orozco, José-Luis. (1997). *Diez Deditos: Ten Little Fingers & Other Play Rhymes and Action Songs From Latin America* (Elisa Kleven, Illus.). New York: Dutton.

Soto, Gary. (1992). *Neighborhood Odes* (David Diaz, Illus.). New York: Harcourt.

collection; many wonderful poetry books are available for use with science, social studies, mathematics, music, and art. Using poetry across the curriculum provides a unique aesthetic dimension that helps children look beyond the "facts" they might learn in their textbooks to discover the rich nuances and textures that underlie a topic. So, when studying American history, for example, they could experience *Hand in Hand: An American History in Poetry*, selected by Lee Bennett Hopkins; *We the People*, selected by Bobbi Katz; Ann Turner's *Mississippi Mud: Three Prairie Journals*; and Ted Rand's picture-book version of *Paul Revere's Ride*. A scientific study of sea life could be enhanced by reading Myra Cohn Livingston's *Sea Songs*, Tony Johnston's *An Old Shell: Poems of the Galapagos*, and Jane Yolen's *Sea Watch: A Book of Poetry*. Additionally, Lee Bennett Hopkins's *Spectacular Science* features poems on a variety of scientific topics. Many books on counting and early mathematical concepts are written in verse. For example, Richard Michelson and Dave Saunders's *Ten Times Better* focuses on multiples of 10, and Barbara Esbenson's *Echoes For the Eye: Poems to Celebrate Patterns in Nature* uses free verse and exquisite language to describe spirals, polygons, circles, and other interesting mathematical patterns. *A World of Wonders*, by J. Patrick Lewis, presents poetry about various geographic

Cover art copyright © Floyd Cooper. Used by permission of HarperCollins Publishers.

Text Set

Poetry About Geography and Geology

Asch, Frank. (1996). *Sawgrass Poems: A View of the Everglades* (Ted Lewin, Photog.). San Diego: Harcourt Brace.

Asch, Frank. (1998). *Cactus Poems*. (Ted Lewin, Photog.). San Diego: Harcourt Brace.

Fisher, Aileen. (2001). *Sing of the Earth and Sky: Poems About Our Planet and the Wonders Beyond*. Honesdale, PA: Boyds Mills Press.

Hopkins, Lee Bennett. (2000). *My America: A Poetry Atlas of the United States*. New York: Simon & Schuster.

Lesser, Carolyn. (1997). *Storm on the Desert*. San Diego: Harcourt Brace.

Lewis, J. Patrick. (2001a). *Earth & Us Continuous: Nature's Past and Future*. Nevada City, CA: Dawn.

Lewis, J. Patrick. (2001b). *Earth & You: A Closer View: Nature's Features*. Nevada City, CA: Dawn.

Lewis, J. Patrick. (2002). *A World of Wonders: Geographic Travels in Verse and Rhyme*. New York: Dial Books.

Livingston, Myra Cohn. (1986). *Earth Songs*. New York: Holiday House.

Locker, Thomas. (2001). *Mountain Dance*. San Diego: Harcourt Brace.

Mora, Pat. (1994). *Listen to the Desert* (Francisco X. Mora, Illus.). New York: Clarion.

Mora, Pat. (1998). *This Big Sky* (Steve Jenkins, Illus.). New York: Scholastic.

Peters, Lisa. (2003). *Earthshake: Poems From the Ground Up*. New York: Greenwillow.

Siebert, Diane. (1989). *Heartland*. New York: Crowell.

Siebert, Diane. (1991). *Sierra*. New York: HarperCollins.

Siebert, Diane. (1998). *Mojave*. New York: HarperCollins.

Siebert, Diane. (2000). *Cave*. New York: HarperCollins.

Siebert, Diane. (2001). *Mississippi* (Greg Harlin, Illus.). New York: HarperCollins.

---

features around the world. The text set on this page provides additional titles you can use when teaching geography and geology.

You can also find wonderful poetry to enhance your study of the arts. This is a natural partnership, because the work of poets is similar to that of artists: Just as artists use paint and canvas or composers use rhythm and melody, poets use the elements of poetry to create something fresh and unique. Poetry about music, dance, art, and drama enhances students' understanding of the arts and the role they play in our lives. Excellent collections for this purpose include *Song and Dance*, selected by Lee Bennett Hopkins, *Dance With Me*, by Barbara Esbenson, *Celebrate America: In Poetry and Art*, created by the staff at the National Museum of American Art, *My Own Song: And Other Poems to Groove To*, by Michael Strickland, and *Heart to Heart: New Poems Inspired by 20th Century Art*, by Jan Greenberg.

You will also want to include poetry books of varying formats in your collection, including anthologies, books by individual poets, and picture-book editions of single poems.

Anthologies

Comprehensive poetry anthologies serve as the backbone of your collection. These usually are divided into themed sections with many poems on each topic and often feature a balance of contemporary and traditional poets.

Tech Note

The CD-ROM that accompanies this book features a list of some of our favorite poetry books that focus on topics across the curriculum.

From A WORLD OF WONDERS: GEOGRAPHIC TRAVELS IN VERSE AND RHYME by J. Patrick Lewis, illustrated by Alison Jay, copyright © 2002 by J. Patrick Lewis, text. Used by permission of Dial Books for Young Readers, A Division of Penguin Young Readers Group, A Member of Penguin Group (USA) Inc., 345 Hudson Street, New York, NY 10014. All rights reserved.

Some we've found that work well with a wide range of children are *The Random House Book of Poetry*, selected by Jack Prelutsky; *Sing a Song of Popcorn*, selected by Beatrice Schenk de Regniers, Eva Moore, Mary Michaels White, and Jan Carr; and *Reflections On a Gift of Watermelon Pickle*, edited by Stephen Dunning. Several that are suitable for young children are *Talking Like the Rain*, selected by X. J. and Dorothy Kennedy, and *Side by Side: Poems to Read Together* and *Climb Into My Lap: Poems to Read Together*, both compiled by Lee Bennett Hopkins. Figure 5.4 lists some excellent anthologies that will provide you with many poems on a variety of topics for classroom use.

Because permissions to use poems in anthologies have become more expensive, some anthologists have created short, more specialized anthologies that focus on a topic as interpreted by different poets. For example,

Myra Cohn Livingston, Lee Bennett Hopkins, and Jack Prelutsky have all created many short anthologies of poems by diverse poets on a variety of subjects from animals, holidays, and families to sports, science, humor, and music. You will want to look for books by these anthologists and others as you search for books on specialized topics.

Single-Poet Collections

In contrast to anthologies, which typically feature the work of diverse poets, many collections focus on the work of a single poet. Getting to know some poets and their trademark styles, themes, and forms will enable you to select poetry from their books to match the needs of your children and your curriculum. The winners of the NCTE Poetry Award are a good place to start. These poets have many wonderful collections that have engaged students for decades. Other contemporary poets we suggest you become familiar with, in addition to Shel Silverstein and Jack Prelutsky, include Alice Schertle, Janet Wong, Kristine O'Connell George, Rebecca Kai Dotlich, Lee Bennett Hopkins, Nikki Grimes, Ralph Fletcher, Tony Johnston, J. Patrick Lewis, Sara Holbrook, Jane Yolen, Judy Sierra, Nikki

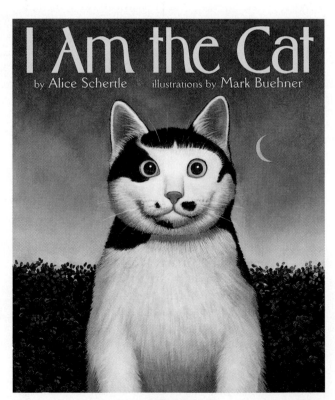

Cover art copyright © Mark Buehner. Used by permission of HarperCollins Publishers.

☼	Arnold Adoff, *I Am the Darker Brother: An Anthology of Modern Poems by Black Americans*
☼	John Agard & Grace Nichols, *Under the Moon & Over the Sea*
☼	Liz Attenborough, *Poetry by Heart*
☼	David Booth, *Till All the Stars Have Fallen*
☼	Catherine Clinton, *I, Too, Sing, America: Three Centuries of African-American Poetry*
☼	Joanna Cole, *A New Treasury of Children's Poetry; Old Favorites and New Discoveries*
☼	Bernice Cullinan, *A Jar of Tiny Stars: Poems by NCTE Award-Winning Poets*
☼	Tomie dePaola, *Tomie dePaola's Book of Poems*
☼	Beatrice Schenk de Regniers, *Sing a Song of Popcorn*
☼	Bobbye Goldstein, *Inner Chimes*
☼	Donald Hall, *The Oxford Book of Children's Verse in America*
☼	Lee Bennett Hopkins, *Side by Side: Poems to Read Together*
☼	Paul Janeczko, *Wherever Home Begins: 100 Contemporary Poems; The Music of What Happens: Poems That Tell Stories; Preposterous Poems of Youth; The Place My Words Are Looking For; Seeing the Blue Between*
☼	X. J. Kennedy, *Knock at a Star: A Child's Introduction to Poetry*
☼	X. J. & Dorothy Kennedy, *Talking Like the Rain: A First Book of Poems*
☼	Lilian Moore, *Sunflakes: Poems for Children*
☼	Naomi Shihab Nye, *The Tree Is Older Than You Are: A Bilingual Gathering of Poems & Stories From Mexico; The Space Between Our Footsteps: Poems and Paintings From the Middle East; This Same Sky: A Collection of Poems From Around the World*
☼	Neil Phillip, *Singing America: Poems That Define a Nation*
☼	Jack Prelutsky, *The Random House Book of Poetry*

Figure 5.4 Recommended Comprehensive Poetry Anthologies for Children

Giovanni, Monica Gunning, Pat Mora, Naomi Shihab Nye, Douglas Florian, and Ashley Bryan.

Well-known poets who have written excellent poetry appropriate for children include Carl Sandburg, Robert Frost, Emily Dickinson, Robert Louis Stevenson, and Langston Hughes. The work of these traditional poets is especially enjoyed by children who have encountered much good poetry by contemporary writers.

Single Poems in Picture Book Format

Some poems have been put into picture books accompanied by beautiful illustrations that make these poems accessible and engaging to today's children. For example, Susan Jeffers created hauntingly evocative illustrations for Robert Frost's "Stopping by Woods on a Snowy Evening."

Copyright © 2003 Jan Spivey Gilchrist. Used by permission of HarperCollins Publishers.

books that are appropriate just for them. Young children have a natural affinity for poetry; they love play rhymes, raps, and playground chants. If you watch them play, you will see them make up their own rhymes or create variations on familiar verses. You can capitalize on this by sharing much excellent poetry with them and providing them with poetry books they can read themselves. Although some people consider these more verse than poetry, we believe they deserve a place in your poetry collection because they provide a wonderful entrée for young children into the world of poetry.

A number of good poetry books are written specifically for beginning readers. These feature simple vocabulary and sentence structures on topics appealing to young children. Lee Bennett Hopkins has created several excellent ones, including *Surprises*, *More Surprises*, *Questions*, and *Sports! Sports! Sports!* Jack Prelutsky has created several to share at holiday time: *It's Thanksgiving*, *It's Halloween*, and *It's Valentine's Day*. Charlotte Zolotow's *Seasons* is another excellent collection. We suggest you purchase multiple copies of these books for guided reading, literature circles, and other small-group reading activities.

Christopher Bing overlaid mementos, artifacts, and baseball memorabilia, even yellowing the edges of the 1888 *Mudville Monitor*, to provide readers with a sense of the cultural context of Ernest Lawrence Thayer's *Casey at the Bat*. The poetry of some contemporary poets is also now being featured in picture books; Eve Merriam's *Bam Bam Bam*, illustrated by Dan Yaccarino, Rebecca Kai Dotlich's "A Family Like Yours," illustrated by Tamie Lyon, and Eloise Greenfield's *Honey, I Love*, illustrated by Jan Spivey Gilchrist, are some good examples. These "poetry picture books" provide children with an excellent opportunity to study a poem and discover the effect illustrations have on our response to it.

Special Considerations for Young Children

If you are building a poetry collection for young children, you need some additional

A representative classroom poetry collection for young children.

Poetry in the Living Literature Classroom

During a late-afternoon spring rain shower, one of us was driving her then 3-year-old daughter, Kaci, home from the sitter's. As they chatted about the day, Kaci called out from the backseat, "Mommy, the rain is tickling the roof!" Many people might think a preschooler would be incapable of making such an abstract comparison. But her mom wasn't surprised: She'd been sharing poetry with Kaci since she was a baby, so Kaci was familiar with using metaphor to describe the world around her. Poetry was a natural part of her life.

This section provides you with ways to make poetry a memorable, positive experience for children so that poetry becomes part of their lives. How often you share and talk about poetry, combined with your own comfort level with the genre, will leave lasting impressions on students. You will learn how you can make poetry memorable and enriching as children read and respond to it.

Looking Back Into Your History With Poetry

Before you can generate enthusiasm for poetry in your students, you need to love it yourself. Unfortunately, for most of us, our experiences with poetry were not very positive. How would you describe your journey into poetry? Was it clear sailing or rocky going? When it comes to poetry, do you like reading it, hearing it read aloud, or writing it?

If your history with poetry was a positive one, then you'll naturally want to bring that enjoyment with this genre into your work with children. Perhaps you recall teachers who enjoyed poetry: They shared it often, and there was a spirit of fun, with the sounds of poetry filling the air. The poems they read aloud captured your ear and were on topics close to your heart or experience. Maybe you remember memorizing your favorite poems, keeping an anthology of the best-loved ones, and even writing your own. You will likely have many good ideas for sharing poetry with children along with enthusiasm for the genre.

One of our favorite examples of a good poetry teacher is Miss Stretchberry in *Love That Dog*, by Sharon Creech. In this story, Miss Stretchberry nurtures, supports, and encourages children to love poetry and to find their own

voice for writing it. One of her students, Jack, initially says in his journal that only girls write poetry, and he tells her:

> I tried
> Can't do it.
> Brain's empty. (p. 2)

However, as the year progresses and he has experience with reading poetry by diverse skilled poets and writing his own pieces, Jack comes to appreciate how poetry can help him come to terms with a personal tragedy.

Conversely, you may have bad memories of poetry. Maybe your experiences mirrored those of Jack Prelutsky (1990):

> When I was a kid I heard poems about hills and daffodils and things like that. The teacher would recite a boring poem:
>
> > Blah, blah, blah, blah, the flower
> > Blah, blah, blah, blah, the tree,
> > Blah, blah, blah, blah, the shower,
> > Blah, blah, blah, blah, the bee.
>
> And of course I didn't care much for that. If I had wanted to hear poems back then—and I wasn't convinced that I did—I wanted to hear poems about kids like myself. Or poems about MONSTERS, OUTER SPACE, DRAGONS, DINOSAURS, WEIRD PEOPLE, SPORTS—things kids can relate to. (pp. 104–105)

We know what Jack Prelutsky means. We remember from our own "not so good" experiences with poetry that teachers sometimes chose poetry that was too sophisticated for us, far beyond our experiential level, or oversentimental. We may not even have been aware that there was poetry written expressly for children! We remember being assigned to memorize poems to recite in front of the class, dissecting poems to find their "real" meaning (like dissecting a frog in biology class), analyzing the structure and rhyme schemes, and doing poetry work sheets. Poetry was viewed as a cryptic word puzzle in which poets hid their meaning or put it into a code that could be deciphered only through an orderly process of deductive analysis.

Sometimes, to our dismay, we were asked to write a poem. Writing poetry is not

> *Too often a fence of formality is built around the idea of poetry in our lives . . . make poetry accessible to children and they will have a form of self-expression as satisfying as singing and shouting.*
>
> *Karla Kuskin,* Near the Window Tree, *p. 6.*

a bad thing; in fact, it's important that children write some poetry. Our poetry-writing experiences were disastrous because we read and talked about few poems before we were asked to write them: The teacher didn't lay the groundwork for writing poetry or provide the support for successful experiences.

The result of such experiences is that kids grow to hate poetry. Survey after survey reveals that these approaches create intense dislike of the genre (Benton, 1992; Craven, 1980; DeLawter, 1992; Dias, 1992; Hecht, 1978; Lockward, 1996; Painter, 1970; Shapiro & Shapiro, 1971). And no wonder: Just as that frog dissected in biology class is dead, so is the dissected poem devoid of all energy and life.

We need to change our approach. Teachers can create an environment where children have positive experiences with poetry. Children can experience delight in playing with language and the satisfaction of discovering how poets use words in fun and interesting ways.

You also need to enjoy poetry yourself. Before you can enthusiastically share poetry with students, you should become familiar with it, savoring how the words roll off your tongue and resonate in your heart and mind. Wrap yourself around a good poem. Linger with it, saying it aloud again and again to appreciate the sounds, the words, and the images created in your mind. We've selected two of our favorite poems to get you started. First, think back to childhood summers. Do you remember dusk falling; how the time between dark and light seemed magical? You might have had the experience of catching fireflies in a jar and watching their lights blink through the glass. Rebecca Kai Dotlich has captured this activity perfectly in the following poem:

Firefly

Sliver of moon
Slice of star
Rhinestone in
a jelly jar.
Twinkling treasure
snatched
From sky;
neon
sparkle-
Firefly!

Rebecca Kai Dotlich, in Lemonade Sun

Here is another well-crafted poem. It's fun to say, and it's also filled with interesting tidbits of information.

Deer Mouse

get   get   get   get   get
  get
    out of the nest

get
    into the cold
get   get   get   get
get
    food
    lots of food
get
    seeds
    berries
    nuts
    bugs
    bark
get enough to last
get enough to store
get more
get   get   get   get   get
  get going
    move
      hustle
don't rustle
don't squeak
    beware
    danger in the air
get busy
get done
get   get   get   get   get
  get out of here
    run

Marilyn Singer, in Turtle in July

These poems are very different, but both are enjoyable. The more you practice them aloud, the more you will appreciate how carefully each poet chose just the right words to convey the message and placed those words on the page to make the poem sound pleasing—and the more you will come to appreciate the power of poetry to make us marvel and to reconceptualize our notions about the world.

Poet Constance Levy says that "any teacher who is not yet comfortable with poetry has only to dig in and become familiar with the many wonderful poems for children. I suggest sitting in the library for an hour or two at a time . . . reading book after book. You will not only be entertained, but also develop a comfortable feeling and find favorites to share with the children. They will love you for it. They will love words too" (personal communication, September, 1999). We invite you to do as Levy suggests. Take time to read lots of good poetry written especially for children. Move beyond the poetry you know from your childhood and familiarize yourself with the fine work of diverse writers. Find poems that personally tickle your ear or that provide you with a different perspective on some everyday phenomena you previously took for granted. Sharing these discoveries with your students will ignite your love of poetry and will nurture their positive responses to this genre.

Children's Poetry Preferences

Children have some strong opinions about what they like in poetry; survey after survey consistently confirms this (Fisher & Natarella, 1982; Ingham, 1980; Kutiper & Wilson, 1993; Simmons, 1980; Terry, 1974). The results of these surveys tell us:

☺ Children prefer narrative and limerick poetic forms. Haiku and free verse are the most disliked forms.

☺ Poetry that is humorous and focused on familiar experiences and animals is most popular. Poems about nature are not preferred.

☺ The elements of rhyme, rhythm, and sound are enjoyed, whereas complex visual imagery and figurative language are least enjoyed.

☺ Younger children enjoy poetry about imaginative events and people.

☺ Younger children prefer contemporary poems.

These results are rather discouraging: It seems children can enjoy only a very limited kind of poetry. Is this inevitable? Are children capable only of appreciating light, humorous poetry? What would happen to student poetry preferences if they were introduced to a steady diet of increasingly complex poetry by teachers who were knowledgeable about the genre and enjoyed it themselves?

If children are continually exposed to high-quality poetry through read-alouds, discussions, and choral readings; allowed to read poetry extensively on their own; and encouraged to write poetry, their preferences change. Although they do not abandon the light, humorous material, their preference for poetry that features unusual imagery, carefully selected words, and complex meanings is significant. They become familiar with a wider variety of poetry and also seem more appreciative of elements such as figurative language and abstract forms such as haiku (Krogness, 1995; Lenz, 1992; McClure, 1985; Perfect, 1999; Siemens, 1996).

Selecting Poetry to Share With Students

Choosing the poetry you will read to your students is an important decision. You may want to begin with poetry styles that children are comfortable with so that they develop positive attitudes toward poetry. Yet you also want to share poetry that will stretch their literary tastes so that they develop an appreciation for more sophisticated writing.

Humorous poems are usually a great starting place, especially for poetry-resistant students. Humorous poems tend to break the icecaps around the word "poetry" and lure children in to explore. Two poets who have mastered the art of humorous writing are Shel Silverstein and Jack Prelutsky; their poetry is an excellent place to start. Then move to other poets such as X. J. Kennedy, Dennis Lee, and J. Patrick Lewis, who delight and amuse us with their silliness, especially with word plays. Using poetry like this will help children develop positive attitudes toward the genre as well as a desire to hear more.

Next, you can begin drawing students into experiences with other kinds of poetry. Many poems can serve as a bridge between children's initial preferences for light, humorous pieces and those that require more thoughtful contemplation to enjoy. Reading several poems on the same topic or theme also often works well for this purpose. Using the topic of dogs, for example, you could first read aloud Irene McLeod's "Lone Dog" (from *Favorite Poems, Old and New*, edited by Helen Ferris). This poem is popular with children because of its compelling rhythm and internal rhyme that convey the feel of a tough, stray dog on the run. It can then be contrasted with these poems portraying dogs: "Dog," from *All the Small Poems*, by Valerie Worth, and *Little Dog Poems*, by

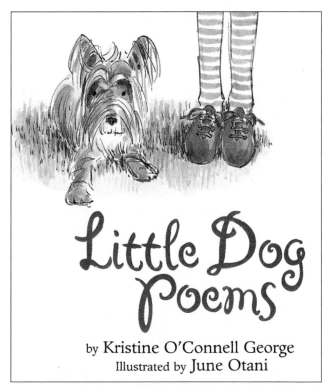

by Kristine O'Connell George
Illustrated by June Otani

Cover from LITTLE DOG POEMS by Kristine O'Connell George, illustrated by June Otani. Jacket illustrations copyright © 1999 by June Otani. Reprinted by permission of Clarion Books/Houghton Mifflin Company. All rights reserved.

Kristine O'Connell George. The poems describe different dogs and skillfully use poetic language to create those images. Once children have heard several poems describing an object or a feeling from multiple perspectives, they are often ready for pieces that are more challenging or abstract. For the topic of dogs, you could use Judith Thurman's "Flashlight" (from *Flashlight and Other Poems*), featuring a unique metaphor in which a dog on a leash is compared to a flashlight.

Puzzle or riddle poems can also help children think more carefully about poetry and thus develop an appreciation for how poets skillfully use language. Omitting the title while reading Worth's "Safety Pin" (from *All the Small Poems*) or Chandra's "Balloons," for example, causes children to look closely at words and how the poet has conveyed meaning. Have children guess what the poet is describing and say what words or phrases caused them to make that guess. Showing the object after guessing, then reading the poem again, will heighten the effect of the words and should stimulate thoughtful discussion of how poets carefully select their words to accurately yet cre-

atively describe the subject. Some helpful collections for this purpose are Lewis's *Riddle-icious*, Worth's *All the Small Poems*, and Nims's *Just Beyond Reach*.

Poems that clearly and accessibly use specific poetic elements are another way to extend your students' tastes in poetry. For example, Kuskin's "Spring" has a compelling rhythm that perfectly illustrates this poetic element. Starbird's "December Leaves" (1963) compares leaves on snow to breakfast cornflakes in a bowl of milk, a metaphor most children can identify with. Figure 5.5 has additional suggestions of poems you can use to help children become familiar with various poetic elements.

The most important thing to remember, however, is not to worry about choosing the "right" poem. Find poems that match the ages, stages, and interests of your students, yet that stretch their literary tastes. Be the adult who leads children to the good poets. As your own taste and enthusiasm expand, you will naturally begin sharing more sophisticated pieces while not abandoning those that are fun. Students seem to need both kinds; and isn't

Rhyme	Figurative Language	Rhythm
"Sneeze," by Maxine Kumin (from Moore, *Sunflakes: Poems for Children*)	"Comma in the Sky," by Aileen Fisher (from *In the Woods, in the Meadow, in the Sky*)	"Street Song," by Myra Cohn Livingston (from *A Tune Beyond Us: A Collection of Poetry*)
"Mice," by Rose Fyleman (from Prelutsky, *The Random House Book of Poetry for Children*)	"Rags," by Judith Thurman (from *Flashlight, and Other Poems*)	"The Swing," by Robert Louis Stevenson (from *A Child's Garden of Verses*)
"The Furry Ones," by Aileen Fisher (from Cullinan, *I Heard a Bluebird Sing*)	"The Toaster," by William Jay Smith (from Dunning, *Reflections on a Gift of Watermelon Pickle and Other Modern Verse*)	"Hello and Goodbye," by Mary Ann Hoberman (from *The Llama Who Had No Pajama: 100 Favorite Poems*)
"Keep a Poem in Your Pocket," by Beatrice Schenk de Regniers (from *Inner Chimes: Poems on Poetry*)	"Steam Shovel," by Charles Malam (from Dunning)	"Spring," by Karla Kuskin (from *Dogs and Dragons, Trees and Dreams*)
"Whisper," by Myra Cohn Livingston (from *Whispers and Other Poems*)	"December Leaves," by Kaye Starbird (from *Don't Ever Cross a Crocodile*)	"Pickety Fence," by David McCord (from *One at a Time*)
"Poem to Mud," by Zilpha Keatley Snyder (from *Today Is Saturday*)	"Polliwogs," by Kristine O'Connell George (from *The Great Frog Race and Other Poems*)	"Honey, I Love," by Eloise Greenfield (from *Honey, I Love and Other Poems*)
"This Is My Rock," by David McCord (from Kennedy & Kennedy, *Talking Like the Rain: A First Book of Poems*)	"Fueled," by Marci Hans (from Dunning)	"Dog," by Valerie Worth (from *All the Small Poems*)
"Catalog," by Rosalie Moore (from Dunning)	"Autumn Leaves," by Deborah Chandra (from *Balloons and Other Poems*)	"Cloud Dragons," by Pat Mora (from *Confetti: Poems for Children*)
	"Paper Clips," by Rebecca Kai Dotlich (from Hopkins, *School Supplies: A Book of Poems*)	
	"Becoming the Tea," by Joyce Carol Thomas (from *Brown Honey in Broomwheat Tea*)	

Figure 5.5   Some Suggested Poems for Poetry Conversations: Examples of Poetry Elements

that true for adults as well? It is a love for poetry that leads us to crave more.

Sharing Poetry With Children: Discussions

Your students' knowledge and enjoyment of poetry are directly related to repeated positive encounters with it. Thus, they need constant exposure to this genre, ideally every day. Poetry should be a natural part of children's daily classroom experiences, shared both purposefully and spontaneously throughout the day. Don't stop at the primary levels. Older students can gain much from repeated experiences with fine poetry.

One of the easiest ways to extend children's appreciation of poetry is through discussion following a read-aloud. We don't mean reading and then asking the question, "So . . . what is the meaning of this poem?" Silence will inevitably follow. This doesn't mean you should never help children appreciate the crafting of poetry, or that you should never explore how a poet has selected just the right words or carefully connected sounds or discovered the most apt metaphor. These explorations are also part of experiencing poetry. However, they should follow experiences in which you and your students delight in the sound and sense of poetry. So what can you do to make the experience of sharing and discussing poetry delightful and informative? We suggest the following general questions for guiding poetry discussions:

☺ What sounded appealing to you in the poem?
☺ What were your reactions to this poem?
☺ How did the poem make you feel? Why?
☺ What did the poem make you think about? (McClure, Harrison, & Reed, 1990)

These questions focus on aesthetic responses from students and are nonthreatening, open-ended, and a good place to begin a conversation about a poem. The emphasis should be on conversation. Invite many responses to your questions to learn how different students feel and react to the poetry.

You can also add your thoughts, not as the expert, but as one more respondent. This should occur later in the conversation so as not to give the impression that your interpretation is the correct one. The purpose of contributing your opinion is to offer a new perspective, support an opinion already stated, or describe how a student made

> If we can get teachers to read poetry, lots of it, out loud to children, we'll develop a generation of poetry readers; we may even have some poetry writers, but the main thing is, we'll have poetry appreciators.
>
> Eve Merriam, poet; 1981, p. 964

you think about a poem in a totally new way. This latter response is very powerful modeling: It shows that you, the teacher, don't have the final word or the right way to respond.

Once students become comfortable with poetry and responding to how it makes them feel or see things differently, they can begin to consider one more question:

☺ What does the poet do to make this poem memorable?

Elements such as rhythm, figurative language, word choice, imagery, and form can be discussed at this point. Again, we caution you not to overdo this. Enjoyment should be the focus; help children deepen their enjoyment so the enjoyment is more informed. Our experience suggests that once teachers initiate this kind of talk, they find that students start noticing various poetic techniques themselves and also begin using them in poetry they write.

Some teachers have students keep notebooks to deepen their thinking in response to poetry. Third-grade teacher Danielle Gruber has her students keep a poetry notebook of the poems they discuss every week. On Monday, she shares a poem several times and invites personal reactions. On subsequent days, the poem is again shared and the children explore the poet's use of interesting words, imagery, shape, and so on. Students record their discoveries in their notebooks. On Friday, the poem is performed several times using only limited props, so the children must use their voices to convey the flavor of the poem. They then take a copy of the poem home for sharing with their families. Poet Georgia Heard (1989) suggests that children create a two-column journal entry after hearing a poem read aloud. In one column, they write their perceptions of what the poem said; in the other, they write how they think the poem connects to their lives.

Sharing Poetry With Children: Informal Activities

Children also need opportunities to read and share poetry in more spontaneous, informal ways. It's a good idea to give students the opportunity just to browse through poetry books. Some teachers designate one day a week during independent reading time as "poetry day"; on that day, everyone reads poetry.

Students can mark favorites with self-stick notes for sharing with the whole class, and can write comments on the notes about what was particularly pleasing about the poems. Subsequent readers of the poems can add their own comments. This process often evolves into small-group poetry-sharing sessions as children begin to share their favorites spontaneously with friends. Some schools designate a "Poetry Break" reading and sharing time for the entire school. When the principal announces "Poetry Break," everyone drops what they're doing to share a favorite poem or two. Students can also collect their favorite poems into personal anthologies (or class anthologies can be created). Once the poems have been selected, they can be organized by theme, form, or author, or the children can devise a classification system.

Following are some additional ways teachers can incorporate poetry into their classroom routines. All help children become more familiar with many kinds of poetry as well as with diverse poets. In turn, this familiarity should generate enthusiasm and heighten interest in the genre.

Older students create a poster in response to studying the work of Eloise Greenfield.

⊚ *A Time Line of Poetry: Celebrating Poetry Throughout the Year.* Celebrate each month of the school year with poetry. Designate some wall space around your room to keep a monthly record of all your classroom activities. The centerpiece for each month will be poems that help tell the story of classroom life that particular month. Poems by published poets that reflect events of the month—holidays, theme studies, class accomplishments, etc.—can also be included. This poetry time line shows students that the events of our lives can be connected to poetry. It's also illuminating on the last day of school to review the poetry from the whole year. Teachers who have used this idea often remark how children's tastes in poetry have changed as the year progressed.

⊚ *Festival of Poetry.* For one day a month, showcase poetry by having a school or grade-level festival of reading and sharing poetry. On that day, everyone reads poetry and shares their favorites with a larger group. Students can also do in-depth studies of poets independently or with partners. They find bibliographic information and photos of the poet, and they can share favorite poems by the selected poet. Students can also write poems in the style of the selected poet. Other possible activities are preparing anthologies of favorite poems by the poet, making comparison charts or graphs comparing and contrasting the poems in a variety of ways, illustrating favorite poems, and writing to the poet via the publisher.

⊚ *Playground Chants, Raps, and Jump-Rope Rhymes: Moving With the Rhythms of Poetry.* You can help students build an early love for language and playing with sounds. Locate books such as *Miss Mary Mack and Other Children's Street Rhymes* and *Juba This and Juba That: 100 African-American Games for Children* for examples of fun chants, rhyming games, finger plays, raps, and jump-rope games. Teach these to students by writing them on large pieces of chart paper for a shared reading activity. Older students can research examples of these for themselves. One group of third graders adapted this activity for their first-grade buddies. After locating some viable choices, the third graders copied them into small booklets for their buddies. These were shared on the playground during buddy reading time, and soon everyone was performing the poetry by chanting, singing, clapping, and jumping rope to the rhymes and rhythms of the poems.

⊚ *Poetry Slams.* Once your children have a good repertoire of poems they love, you can organize a "poetry slam": This is a group poetry-sharing activity in which students take turns reading poetry aloud. They take turns spontaneously as they find connections among their favorite poems based on common themes, poetic devices, characters, or other qualities. For example, one child might read aloud Constance Levy's poem "Fog" (from *Splash! Poems of Our Watery World*), which compares walking through fog to walking through clouds. A second child might link into the concept of clouds or of fog by next spontaneously sharing Sandburg's "Fog" (from *Complete Poems*), which describes fog as coming "on little cat feet." A third child might then pick up on the concept of a cat walking stealthily and read "Cat," by Karla Kuskin (from *Near the Window Tree*), which includes the line "The cat comes and goes on invisible toes." This activity is particularly useful for helping students make connections between poems with similar themes and images. It works best with groups who are familiar with many well-written poems so they can readily make thematic connections.

⊚ *Poetry Hunts.* Encourage students to collect examples of poetic language they encounter in everyday life: advertisements, popular songs, playground chants, etc. They can even find short phrases or brief descriptions that "sound poetic"; these can be shared and posted in the classroom. This activity helps children realize how poetry permeates their lives.

⊚ *Poetry Café.* On Friday afternoons, fifth-grade teacher Patricia Robinson lowers the lights, puts snacks and lemonade on tables, and opens her poetry café. While soft background jazz plays, students take turns reading poetry—some from published poets and some of their own work. Many have memorized their poems, although this is not required. After each reading, the group snaps their fingers to show appreciation.

Performing Poetry

Another excellent way to stimulate interest in poetry is through choral speaking and poetry performance. Choral speaking involves dividing a poem so that individuals or groups of readers read certain parts. In poetry performance, movement is added. The benefits of these activities are many. Students learn much about interpreting poetry as they consider various alternatives for planning their performances. They must read and reread, trying out various ways to put words into lines, movements, and interpretations until they find the performance combination that is most appropriate for conveying the meaning of the poem. They also learn how to negotiate and cooperate as they work together to create their reading. Additionally, they get the opportunity to savor the rhythms and sounds of poems that become familiar through repeated readings.

Don't worry too much about polishing the performance. Keep it spontaneous and light so students have an enjoyable, anxiety-free experience with poetry.

Several ways of organizing choral readings are appropriate for students.

Call/Refrain

One person (teacher or student) reads a verse or section of the poem. The others join in on a refrain or repeating line, or they repeat each line after the leader. Some good

poems for this activity are "Went to the Corner," by Eloise Greenfield (from the edition of *Honey, I Love* illustrated by Leo and Diane Dillon), and Myra Cohn Livingston's "Whispers" (from *A Song I Sang to You*) and "My Little Sister" (from *Jump for Joy*).

Line by Line

Different children take turns reading consecutive lines of a poem. This technique works best for poems that are "lists" of items, comments, observations, or descriptions. Sometimes the group joins in on beginnings, endings, or repeated sections. Poems that work well for this technique are: "I Brought a Worm," by Kallie Dakos, in *If You're Not Here, Please Raise Your Hand: Poems About School*; "Junk Food," in Sonja Dunn's *Butterscotch Dreams*; "When I Misbehave," by Eloise Greenfield, in *Nathaniel Talking*; and Sara Holbrook's "Full Blast" (from *Wham! It's a Poetry Jam*).

Poems for Two Voices

Paul Fleischman's poems in *Joyful Noise: Poems for Two Voices* and *I Am Phoenix*, David Harrison's *Farmer's Garden: Rhymes for Two Voices*, and Kristine O'Connell George's "Two Voices in a Tent at Night," from *Toasting Marshmallows*, are excellent models for two-voice reading. In these poems, two columns of words are placed side by side. Two readers (or groups of readers) take turns reading the columns; sometimes the voices alternate and sometimes they are joined. The sounds and images blend together to create a musical montage. Children can practice this technique with these poems, and then write their own two voice poems that they can then perform. Or children can put two similar poems together and create a new two-voice poem. Children who become proficient at performing two-voice poems might want to take on a new challenge with Fleischman's *Big Talk*, which features poems designed for four voices.

Cumulative

A cumulative style of choral reading can be used to interpret a poem that builds to a climax. A few students read the first line or verse, and then more and more children join in on the subsequent lines until everyone speaks at the end of the poem. Or everyone can start, and then drop out until only a few voices remain at the end of the reading. Some good poems for this type of arrangement are: "Snow," by Mary Ann Hoberman (from *The Llama Who Had No Pajama*), "Snowfall," by Deborah Chandra (from *Balloons and Other Poems*), and "Eraser," by Louis Phillips (from Lee Bennett Hopkins's *School Supplies*).

Poetry Performance

Children can get creative during choral reading performances by adding props, sounds, or movements to their interpretations. They can consider what will enhance a characterization, a series of sounds, or an image in the poem. For example, students performing Myra Cohn Livingston's "Street Song" (in Moore, *Sunflakes*), a bouncy, rhythmical poem that celebrates eating potato chips, planned movement and sounds to accompany their reading: Part of the group chanted "ch, ch, ch" as the others read the words, everyone snapped their fingers to the beat, and one student walked rhythmically in front of the group while munching potato chips. An excellent resource for planning poetry performances is *Wham! It's a Poetry Jam*, by poet Sara Holbrook (2002).

Writing Poetry

Once students have been exposed to many examples of good poetry through read-alouds and exploration on their own, they can experiment with their growing awareness of poetic language and form by trying it out for themselves. It is a rewarding challenge to help students develop enthusiasm for writing poetry as a way to make sense of and appreciate the world.

However, children must first have many experiences with good poetry. Teachers sometimes expect students to write poems, even specific forms such as haiku or limerick, without having any real understanding of what they're being asked to create. This typically results in poems that may be technically correct but that are devoid of voice or feeling. So give your students many and varied poetry encounters, and then introduce the idea that they can write their own.

Getting Started

Most teachers find that when students write about what they know, they write their best poetry. Georgia Heard's book *For the Good of the Earth and Sun: Teaching Poetry* (1989) is a good reference for helping your students learn about becoming poets. She describes her own process for starting to write a poem in the following way:

> Most of my poems begin with a feeling, some deep

urge. Sometimes it's so strong I actually feel something inside of me move. It can happen anytime; it happens about ideas, memories, things I see every day. Often I start with an image, a picture in my mind. I use this as a resource to guide me in the making of a poem. (p. 10)

This is excellent advice for students. They too should be encouraged to find the feelings and images in their own lives that they want to write about. Let them know that poets can write about anything and they will usually discover something to help them get started. Tell them to delve into their writing journals and observation notebooks to discover nuggets of thought or interesting words and phrases that can be turned into poems. Heard (1989) also offers several other suggestions for children who need help finding an idea:

- ☺ Sit for a while with your eyes closed and see if anything comes to mind.
- ☺ Walk around to see what other people are writing about.
- ☺ Look through some of your stories to see if there's any poem material there.
- ☺ Walk to the window and look outside; take your paper and see if there's anything interesting to see.
- ☺ Try free-writing. (p. 28)

Occasionally, students need even more specific help: They can't find an intriguing idea, they create rhymes with no sense, and they just don't seem to know how to go about writing a poem. When this happens, you should encourage them to return to browsing the classroom poetry collection, helping them discover that virtually anything can be the "stuff" of poetry. Show them that poetry can be found in the simplest everday phenomena such as a glistening spider web spotted on the way to school, the slap of the jump rope on the playground, or the metamorphosis of the classroom caterpillar.

Some teachers, particularly those who work with younger children, encourage their students to emulate the work of a published poet to jump-start their creative juices. For example, teachers might share a poem, and then suggest that students create their own pieces following the same model. Or they

---

Stupefied

A poem, a poem
I can't write a poem
Cause my brain won't work,
My pencil won't write
And I think I've lost my appetite
With all this untouched white
Staring up at me.

Katy, Grade 3

Ideas for poems come to me when I pay attention to the world. When I truly see how a hawk cups the sky under its wings. When I notice how my little dog fits perfectly inside the sunny spot on the carpet. When I see a maple seed flutter by my kitchen window and I wonder: Where is it going? These moments of discovery are when a poem will tap me on the shoulder.

Kristine O'Connell George, poet, in Janeczko, 2002, p. 35

might encourage children to write in the style of their favorite poet, even sometimes borrowing words or phrases they've grown to love through repeated readings of that person's work. The poem in Figure 5.6, by Leah, is based on Paul Fleischman's *I Am Phoenix: Poems for Two Voices*.

> *I know a poem is finished when I can't find another word to cut. My favorite poems are like vitamins. They are capsules of feelings, pictures, sounds. Rhythmic combinations of words that give new energy to language. Warning: Rhyme is fun, but it can get bossy! Use it to say what you want to say. Don't let it take over your ideas!*
>
> *Bobbi Katz, in Janeczko, 1994, p. 52*

This borrowing is not considered to be plagiarism. Rather, it is an opportunity to try out the language of poetry. As students gain experience, they will find their own voices and move away from models. One child demonstrated this transition from models as she wrote a caterpillar poem. She used the phrase "creeping through a forest of green"—a paraphrase of a line in an Emily Dickinson poem—to describe a caterpillar's movement through grass because the phrase "sounds more poetic . . . poets don't just say stuff, they turn the words around," she explained. That child was beginning to understand the craft of poetry but initially needed the support of another poet until she developed her own voice.

You can also help students understand how poetry writing "goes" by having them create group poems. Often teachers first read aloud poems similar to the ones they will ask the group to create. Children can then offer ideas, and the group negotiates which words and phrases to include in the poem. At other times, the class might be divided into smaller groups or partners to create lines or stanzas that are then combined into one piece. The third-grade Living Literature Classroom vignette beginning on page 18 in chapter 1, in which children wrote a collaborative poem based on Robert Frost's "The Pasture Spring," is an example of how the writing of a group poem might evolve.

Encouraging Revision

Once students become immersed in writing poetry, you can help them shape their pieces to be pleasing to the ear. Revision is an important part of writing poetry. Because poetry is so compact, poets must be sure they have selected the best words and phrases to convey their meaning. Thus they must carefully sift among alternatives, experimenting with various possibilities until they get just the right combination of words and images.

Students usually resist revision, however; they write a poem in a few minutes and are eager to move on. It takes gentle, insistent prodding to encourage them to return to a piece, rethinking it, playing with different words and ideas. But most children appreciate the results once they've made the effort. One child we know compared the process of writing poetry to looking through all the keys on your key ring to find the one that unlocks a magic door. Another likened the revision process to lightening your load on a trip by throwing out the excess baggage—in this case, unnecessary words or superfluous ideas.

Following are some ideas you can suggest to students as you help them revise their poems:

☺ Is the image or comparison you've created true to life?
☺ Have you looked closely at what you're describing? Have you become a part of it so you really see it?
☺ Are there any words you can eliminate to keep the rhythm steady?
☺ Do your lines and spacing help the rhythm?
☺ Can you play with different possibilities of words to get the best one for saying what you want to say?
☺ How could you use what you know about poetry to make your piece more interesting?
☺ Have you said something new, or something old in a new way?
☺ Do you like the way the poem sounds read aloud? (McClure, Harrison, & Reed, 1990)

Night

Night is peaceful	Night is peaceful
night is dark	
	night is quiet
you can hear the bugs	
	screaching
peeping	
	rusling
chirping	
moving	in the night
in the night	stars
stars	so bright
so bright	you can hear
you can hear	sounds
sounds	at
night	night

by Leah Conn

Figure 5.6 A Child's Poem Based on Fleischman's *I Am Phoenix*

A child writes a poem and creates an illustration to extend the meaning to the poem. Teacher Peg Reed, grade 5, Ohio.

Summary

In this chapter, we have introduced some of the common terms people use to discuss poetry as well as the most typical forms of poetry for children. We have shared some ways you can identify the best examples of this genre. We have also provided many examples of excellent poetry along with strategies for bringing poetry and children together so that poetry becomes a powerful presence in your classroom.

As teachers help their students become attuned to the rhythms and images of poetic language, they find that students begin hearing the poetry all around them: in the crunching of leaves on a warm fall day, the quiet stillness of snowflakes on a cold winter's night, and the crack of a bat on a baseball. They begin to memorize and recite poems they love on the playground, during the walk home from school, or before falling asleep in bed. They can't wait to get to school to spill the images they've created onto paper. They are truly living and loving poetry.

Kellie, a sixth grader, says it best in the following poem:

> Please pass the poetry
> on the platter over there.
> Not the stories all loaded
> up with fat.
> Not the songs with a
> lifetime of sugar.
> Not the rhymes overcooked
> and hard,
> But poetry, a warm feast
> to delight in.
>
> *Kellie*

Action Research for Teachers

The Influence of Poetry on Intermediate Literacy

Molly Hinkle
Language Arts Teacher,
Upper Arlington City Schools

"Do you know how many poems I wrote in my journal last year?" Nat asked one March afternoon. "Six. I found it and counted. This year, my poetry journal is full!"

Joshua joined us in the after-school conversation. "I didn't use to care for poetry, but you introduced us to different kinds and I learned it doesn't have to be serious or rhyme. I found the kind I like, and now I'm good at it."

Nat and Joshua were typical fifth graders, but this year, they had learned to love poetry. That had been my goal as I initiated an action research project, the intent of which was to immerse students in poetry, where they heard, read, wrote, and shared it frequently. Nat and Joshua's conversation provided evidence that enthusiasm for poetry begets enthusiasm for poetry.

Major Questions Studied

My research questions were the following:

- ☼ How does original poetry written by students change over time?
- ☼ How do the poems students select for poetry collections and poetry shares change over time?

Procedures

Students were immersed in poetry through a variety of experiences. I read a daily poem to or with the class. Poetry workshop occurred weekly and consisted of a minilesson, journal writing, poetry browsing, and sharing. Minilessons ranged from the introduction of a specific poetic form (list, haiku, concrete, riddle, limerick) or device (simile, personification, alliteration) to the sharing of poems that served as inspirations for students' own poems.

While browsing poetry, students collected at least one poem each week for a personal collection. They illustrated the poems, then shared and displayed them. Students collected both poetry by published authors and classmates and their own poems, recording them in a log. In May, they created special displays to house these personal collections.

To emphasize the joy of sharing poetry, monthly poetry shares were held with a neighboring fifth-grade class. Students shared poems they found or wrote according to a chosen theme. A special evening event was held for parents in May.

Poetry was given a special place during a 6-week study of poet J. Patrick Lewis. Students read or heard each of Pat's books, conducted research, wrote poetry, and created diverse projects, including a life-size portrait of Mr. Lewis. Students performed *The Fat-Cats at Sea* for an audience at the Ohio State University Children's Literature Conference that included Pat himself.

Finally, field trips to a nearby park occurred in November and May for observing the natural environment and writing poetry. In November, students and adults worked together to write and perform small group poems. In May, students worked in pairs or groups of three to create and share poems for multiple voices, using the work of Paul Fleischman as a model.

Throughout the project, I conducted conferences to assist with and assess student work. For the purpose of data collection and analysis, I selected four students (two boys, two girls) who represented a range of abilities and interests to serve as my sample group. I also conducted two class surveys to gather further information.

Outcomes

An exciting trend emerged from analysis of poetry collections: Fully 78% of the poetry collected was original work, suggesting that my students were confident as writers of poetry and trusted that their own work was worth publishing. Three of the students also included at least one poem written by a classmate. This suggests that sharing and displaying original poetry created a community where students valued and supported one another as writers.

Survey results confirmed the positive influence of a classroom environment that valued poetry. When asked to respond to the statement "I am a better poetry writer now than before this school year," every student agreed, with 16 of 19 strongly agreeing. Similarly, 89% of the class agreed with the statements "I enjoy poetry more now than before this school year" and "I enjoy more *types* of poetry now than before this school year." An anonymous student added, "I love poetry!!!" to the survey, and Matthew referred to the teacher in *Love That Dog* in his comment, "You're like Ms. Stretchberry! I like it!" Ben commented that "writing poetry a lot builds your confidence."

Personal Reflections

As the project emerged and as I began to analyze student work, the word *change* caused difficulties. Perhaps I asked the wrong questions, because I found myself increasingly studying the nature of the teaching/learning cycle. A more appropriate question might have been "What types of learning experiences lead students to a greater command of and appreciation for various poetic forms, language, and devices?" The greatest trend to emerge from the project is the basic premise for teaching in general—students will try what is taught and modeled. Students attempted new poetic forms and devices introduced and explored in class, and chose to publish many of these. Students' enthusiasm for poetry grew as I shared my own enthusiasm.

I was reminded throughout the study of the importance of emergent curriculum. An unexpected February thunderstorm provided a "drop everything and write" opportunity in which many students independently applied what they had learned about personification. An article in *Time for Kids* prompted us to respond to Walt Whitman's "I Hear America Singing," and Langston Hughes's "I, Too, Sing America" elicited some of the most thoughtful poetry written by my students during the year.

The results of the study may not have supported *changes* in students' reading and writing, but the implication is clear: Teachers who want students to value poetry must set aside time for students to read, write, and share poetry as a community of learners. Where the teacher leads, students *will* follow.

The following poems by Nathan and Ben are examples of pieces written by my students.

River Side View
by Nathan

I hear a stream,
a gentle calm feeling
from where I stand.
Here lies before me
a mother's touch of water,
of breeze,
and a soft touch of warmth.

The sound of raindrops,
of a stream,
Mother clutching her baby
as it cries.

I'm here alone,
standing in a world of color,
of sound,
of you, Mother.
As I'm alone and
company sails away,
I hear in a baby
the long cries of the stream.

As I pack up and say farewell,
I keep the memories in my heart
for you . . . Mother Nature.

I Will
by Ben
Inspired by Langston Hughes's I, Too

I will sing America.
I may be the lighter brother
but I will stand alongside
the darker brothers.
I will fight for what is right.
There will be riots,
but I will douse the flames.
They will think I am wrong,
but I know that I am right.
I will sing America.

Chapter

TRADITIONAL LITERATURE

"The only universal language which breaks across barriers of race, culture, time is the language of fairy tale, fantasy, myth, parable, and that is why the same stories have been around in one form or another for hundreds of years." (Erich Fromm, 1951, p. xii)

raditional stories, whether oral or written, are a part of every culture: Wherever there are people, there are also stories. In this chapter, we present an anthropological or cultural perspective on traditional literature. Because much of traditional literature is rooted in the oral tradition of a particular culture, we study this genre from the perspective of culture: the values, beliefs, ways of knowing and living that characterize a social group.

Specifically, we explore the following questions:

- ☼ What is traditional literature? What are the distinctive literary qualities of this genre?

- ☼ What forms of traditional literature are appropriate for children?

- ☼ How do we determine what constitutes high-quality traditional literature?

- ☼ What are some of the best examples from this genre that should be part of your classroom library?

We also focus on how you can use traditional literature effectively in your classroom while respecting the cultures from which the stories arise.

- ☼ What strategies help children examine the literary qualities of these stories?

- ☼ How can discussion, storytelling, and drama activities help children explore traditional literature?

- ☼ What are some appropriate writing activities you can use to encourage thoughtful response to traditional literature?

What Is Traditional Literature?

Traditional literature is the written form of stories that are part of the oral tradition of a culture; *culture* can refer to an ethnic group, a nationality, or a subgroup within a national border. Oral stories became written ones with the advent of the printing press. However, not all stories have been written

Underneath their fanciful trappings, the old tales had a lot to say about human nature; about cruelty, vanity, greed, despair . . . and about the "magic" that overcomes them: kindness, compassion, generosity, faith, persistence and courage.

Terri Windling & Ellen Datlow, 2003, p. viii

In some ways folklore is a lot like the popular party game, telephone. Each time someone hears a story or song and repeats it, he or she changes it slightly. A gray dress becomes a blue blouse, a woman who lives in a shack in the woods suddenly moves to a cabin on a hill, a boy who owns a spotted dog gives him up for a black one. And other changes occur as a story is passed from person to person. Each teller infuses in the tale a part of himself or herself, filling it with his or her ideas about the world, its people, and its creatures.

Amy Cohn, 1993, p. xiii

down — nor should they be. The rich oral tradition that is the hallmark of many cultures could be damaged by written documentation of stories. Additionally, writing down some stories could destroy their esteemed place as oral narratives.

Traditional stories mirror the values and mores from which they arise, and they serve many functions. Some stories explain the unknown, such as the origin of geographical features; others preserve significant events that define a group and shape its culture, teach values and the foundations of cultural beliefs to the young, explore human consciousness, and entertain (Campbell, 1988). Stories are affected by the geography and the linguistic and social contacts of the culture from which they originated as well as by the course of history (Thompson, 1946). Because the stories have been handed down through time, they have no known author. Rather, stories of this sort have always been part of everyday life, mainly for the purpose of educating a culture's youth (Jaffe, 1996). Thus, hearing and reading traditional stories can provide children with a fascinating glimpse of a particular culture as well as teach them about values and codes of behavior.

Another reason children should know these stories is that the characters, language patterns, and themes are often referred to in everyday life. For example, people in Western cultures who have been exposed to traditional stories know what it means when someone is described as acting like a "wolf" or is "going up against Goliath." Such expressions often become sufficiently common that most members of the cultural group understand them even without knowing the specific stories they come from.

This intertextuality—referring to a story in another context—can create bonds, but also problems in a multicultural society. In American culture, for example, references often come from Western European and Biblical stories. Non-Christians and those who grew up in other cultures are less likely to know the stories or the related references, which can lead to alienation or, at the very least, marginalization. Thus, teachers need to be sensitive when sharing stories from many cultural traditions so students develop understanding, awareness, and appreciation of diverse cultures.

Literary Elements of Traditional Literature

Traditional stories are characterized by many of the same elements found in fiction, including plot, setting, characters, style, and theme. However, because of the origins of traditional stories, these elements typically possess unique qualities that help distinguish this genre from others. Although the use of these elements can vary across cultures and the different forms traditional tales take, we can draw some generalizations.

Plot

Plots in traditional tales are usually simple and often sequential. Characters, setting, and conflict are quickly described, then the teller goes straight to the action. Once the story is told, it is concluded swiftly with a brief phrase such as "and they lived happily ever after" or "snip, snap, snout, my tale's told out." Plots in stories with Western European traditions are generally quite predictable, with easily identifiable beginnings, middles, and ends.

Some plots are cumulative, that is, the events repeat, building on one another as the story progresses. The story of "The Gingerbread Boy" (Galdone) who runs away only to be chased by a growing progression of characters is one example of a cumulative tale from the Western tradition. Another is Simms Taback's "I Know an Old Lady Who Swallowed a Fly," in which the lady eats increasingly bigger animals; each page reviews all the previously eaten animals before adding the new one. In some plots, repetition of phrases, chants, or other responses is often used to encourage audience participation and as an aid to listeners for remembering the plot.

Stories from other cultures, particularly Asian, sometimes feature other plot structures, such as a cyclical organization. For example, in Gerald McDermott's *The Stonecutter*, a Japanese folktale, a man who cuts stone for a living wishes to be more powerful. As he wishes, he becomes powerful, only to find something else more powerful than he. The main character, who transforms many times, ends up exactly as he was in the beginning of the story, making this a good example of a cyclical plot.

Setting

Settings in traditional literature are often deliberately vague, using descriptions such as "Once upon a time," "In the dreamtime," "Back in the beforetime," "Long ago and far away," or "In a beautiful castle." Stories with more specifically delineated time and place have them because

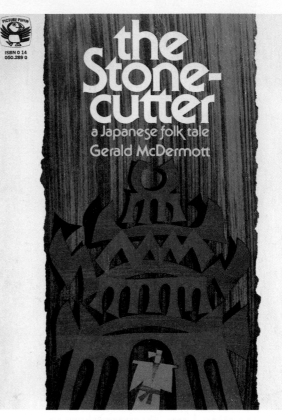

From THE STONECUTTER by Gerald McDermott, copyright © 1975 by Gerald McDermott. Used by permission of Viking Penguin, a Division of Penguin Young Readers Group, A Member of Penguin Group (USA) Inc., 345 Hudson Street, New York, NY 10014. All rights reserved.

they are important to the story's events, as in the King Arthur hero tales or many of the American tall tales. Settings of stories from a specific cultural group are set in the geographical region and habitat associated with the group's homelands. In these cases, settings often make reference to the indigenous plants, animals, weather, and terrain of the area when these are relevant to the tale.

Characterization

Characters in traditional stories are frequently symbolic and are rarely developed as actual people with strengths, weaknesses, personalities, and idiosyncrasies. Rather, they tend to be sterotypes: all good, all evil, all wise, or all foolish, depicting fundamental human qualities. This tends to be true even if the main character is based on a historical figure, such as John Henry or Daniel Boone. Physical qualities might be mentioned, but typically readers are ex-

Older students create a rebus in response to reading traditional literature.

Reprinted with the permission of Atheneum Books for Young Readers, an imprint of Simon & Schuster Children's Publishing Division from BEAUTIFUL BLACKBIRD written and illustrated by Ashley Bryan. Copyright © 2003 Ashley Bryan.

pected to form their own mental images of the characters as the tale unfolds.

Style

Because traditional stories arose from the oral storytelling tradition, they provide readers with the opportunity to hear the cadences and common expressions of the culture where the story originated. Margaret Hurst uses Caribbean dialect in *Grannie and the Jumbie: a Caribbean Tale* to enhance the storytelling quality of this tale:

> *Emmanuel is a very small chile. He hear about ghost, spirit, and Jumbie once in a while. Grammie, she tell him the spirit story so that he minds: like keepin' your cap on in the right ju all the time. (unpaged)*

Ashley Bryan uses a similar technique in his adaptation of *Beautiful Blackbird* (2003), a tale from the Ila-speaking people of Zambia. When all the birds are asked who is the most beautiful, they circle Blackbird in a Beak and Wing Dance, singing,

> *Beak to beak, peck, peck, peck,*
> *Spread your wings, stretch your neck.*
> *Black is beautiful, uh-huh!*
> *Black is beautiful, uh-huh! (unpaged)*

Some tales imitate animal sounds or use musical, repetitive language to enhance the telling and delight the ears of listeners. Thus, in *Why Mosquitos Buzz in People's Ears*, a retelling of an African tale, Verna Aardema describes the slithering of a python into a rabbit's hole as "wasawasu." The gingerbread figure who escapes pursuer after pursuer chants, "Run, run, run, as fast as you can. You can't catch me, I'm the Gingerbread Man." Dialect can make a story sound authentic but may need to be explained to children so understanding is not lost.

Theme

Because the purpose of traditional stories is not only to entertain but also to instruct, they usually feature themes important to the culture from which they originated. For example, kindness, humility, concern for the downtrodden, courage, and hard work are usually rewarded. Evil is vanquished, sometimes in graphically violent ways. Often, the powerless triumph through perseverance, hard work, and intelligence.

Some adults have voiced concerns about violent themes in traditional stories, fearful that they may lead children to commit violent acts. Consequently, they advocate rewriting a tale such as "The Three Little Pigs" so that the wolf isn't eaten at the end. In one sanitized version, the wolf sits down to a feast (supposedly vegetarian) with the pigs!

IN THE RAINFIELD
Who Is the Greatest?

ISAAC O. OLALEYE · ANN GRIFALCONI

Nigerian folktale in which Wind, Fire, and Rain gather to see who is the greatest. Rain demonstrates the power of gentleness. Illustration by Ann Grifalconi from IN THE RAINFIELD, WHO IS THE GREATEST? by Isaac O. Olaleye. Published by the Blue Sky Press, an imprint of Scholastic Inc. Illustration copyright © 2000 by Ann Grifalconi Reprinted by permission.

However, most adults contend that the violence in these stories is quickly described and is rather bloodless. And much of the cruel punishment is meted out to truly evil characters. Thus, we believe that children will clearly understand that evil must be destroyed so good can prevail. Children need this message of hope—that despite seemingly insurmountable obstacles and bleak prospects, it is possible to vanquish evil and live happily. Traditional stories provide this hope.

Motifs

Literary elements that recur across many stories are called *motifs*. They can be characters, objects, plot elements, or other aspects important to the culture from which the story originated. Thus, for example, the motif of transformation (an animal taking on human form or the reverse) can be seen in stories ranging from Marianna Mayer's *Beauty and the Beast* (France) to Sumiko Yagawa's *The Crane Wife* (Japan) to Paul Goble's *The Girl Who Loved Wild Horses* (Native American). The motif of a magical pot that won't stop producing can be found in stories from European to Russian to Native American cultures. The "trickster" character is another popular motif found in diverse cultures. For example, Anansi the Spider is a popular African trickster. Coyote is often featured as a trickster in stories from the Southwest and Latin America, and Brer Rabbit is a favorite wily character in stories arising from the African American tradition. Figure 6.1 lists some common motifs that can be identified in traditional stories from around the world.

Variants

As stories have come down to us through countless retellings over time, their details have changed and evolved. Many of the world's traditional stories surprisingly resemble each other: Similar characters, episodes, and plots appear across many cultures. These stories have endured and are remembered because they explore universal human concerns in entertaining ways. However, each culture leaves its unique mark on a story, sometimes changing major characters or plot elements to more closely suit the perspective of that culture. A story is considered a variant of a tale if it has many fundamental similarities but differs in terms of details, such as character names, setting, or motifs.

For example, "The Three Little Piggies and Old Mister Fox," a Scottish American variant of "The Three Little Pigs," features a fox who is continually outwitted by the third pig until he eventually jumps into her butter churn and is turned into butter. "Big Pig, Little Pig, Speckled Pig, and Runt" is an African American variant featuring four pigs in which the wolf is "burnt to a crackling" in the end. In "The Three Geese," a traditional tale from Italy, each successive goose kicks its sibling out of the house, and the youngest goose cooks pasta for the wolf, then pours the scalding water on him. (The variants described here all come from Sierra's *Can You Guess My Name? Traditional Tales Around the World.*) Studying variants can help children identify similar elements in folktales across cultures while also seeing the influence of a culture on the telling of a tale.

Motifs are the recurring elements that run through texts, much as music has melodies that are used over and over again in a longer composition. Here are common motifs:

Figure 6.1
Motifs in
Traditional
Literature

☼ **Magic**—Creatures may use magic, and objects may be magical, such as magic rings, gems, goblets, lamps, doors, and fairies. Example: *Aladdin and the Magic Lamp* (Trussell-Cullen)—the lamp has powers.

☼ **Transformations**—A character changes from animal to human, or human to animal, or animal to another animal, or human to object. Example: Galdone's *The Frog Prince*—the frog becomes a man.

☼ **Journeys and Quests**—Characters in tales are often journeying somewhere to seek or save something. Typically there are trials and obstacles along the way. Example: In Aardema's *Traveling to Tondo* (1991), the cat and his three friends are journeying to a town for the cat's wedding, but they get distracted along the way by obstacles.

☼ **Trickery**—Some character in tales often outsmarts others, playing tricks on them. Example: In Galdone's *The Gingerbread Boy,* the cookie outsmarts the fox.

☼ **Flying**—Especially in the tales of people who have a history of oppression, flying occurs often. There are examples of this in *The People Could Fly* (Hamilton, 1985).

☼ **Numbers**—Many cultures attach special significance to certain numbers, and these numbers appear in their traditional literature. The use of 3 is common in Western European tales (three wishes, three bears, three goats, three little pigs, three obstacles, etc.). The use of 4 is common in tales of *indigenous peoples* (the home of the winds, North, South, East, and West).

☼ **Repetitive Phrasing**—A common convention that traditional literature inherited from storytelling is the use of repetitive phrases, which add emphasis and cadence to the tale. Example: "Run, run, run as fast as you can. You can't catch me, I'm the Gingerbread Man."

Categorizing Traditional Literature by Form

Before we present categories of traditional literature, you should know that these categories have been devised by scholars of traditional literature. Storytellers did not preserve these tales for the purpose of categorizing them. Not all stories will fall neatly into a particular category; some have elements that could meet the criteria of several. And children's literature sources don't all agree on the definitions of these categories. So although these terms are useful for thinking about stories and their features, categorizing stories should be subordinate to sheer enjoyment of them.

Typically, traditional literature can be classified into two major categories: nonprose and prose forms. Nonprose narratives include jokes, riddles, play rhymes, short proverbs or "old sayings," ballads, and nursery rhymes. Riddles such as "Why did the chicken cross the road? To get to the other side" (American) or "What is it that never gets tired of motioning people over? The earflaps of the teepee" (Native American) (*Lightning Inside You and Other Native American Riddles*, edited by John Bierhorst) and sayings such as "The mouth is the guard for the heart" (Middle Eastern) are examples of this type of traditional literature. Every generation transmits sayings like these to other generations via school playgrounds, ceremonial gatherings, campfires, back porches, and so on—wherever people congregate.

The major prose forms of traditional literature include folktales, fairy tales explanatory stories (myths, creation stories, and pourquoi tales), fables, and legends. These are longer stories with well-defined plots. Often they are designed to be told over extensive periods of time. The Terms for Teachers feature on p. 128 defines the different forms of traditional literature and provides examples of each.

Terms for Teachers
Forms of Traditional Literature

Nonprose Narratives

Jokes and Riddles—Using language in humorous ways; jokes and riddles are favorites with children.

Example: What's black and white and "red" all over? The newspaper!

Proverbs and Sayings—Cultures have short common sayings that communicate some collective wisdom about life.

Examples: "People in glass houses shouldn't throw stones." Origin unknown; before you criticize, be careful that the same criticism doesn't apply to you.

"Two man-rat can't live in the same hole." Caribbean; two people with strong, assertive personalities are not compatible.

"The patience of a lion is mistaken for timidity only by a fool." Nigeria; used to teach about the power of patience and good judgment.

"Without an appetite for hard work, inspiration is useless." Ukraine; be willing to work for a dream.

Ballads—Longer texts, often set to music, that tell a story some believe is true or has origins in a true story.

Examples: "Barbara Allen." Story of a woman whose lover dies, she then dies of sorrow and is buried next to her lover.

"Robin Hood and the Tanner." Robin Hood meets a man in the woods who he thinks may be a thief, but discovers he is a good and honest man.

Folk Songs—Songs with no known author often exist in multiple variations, just as other traditional literature does. Different cultures have their own folk songs, as do different groups such as slaves, sailors, and miners.

Examples: "Abiyoyo." Seeger; story of an annoying boy with his ukulele and an equally annoying father who could make things disappear; the two later save their town from a giant and are no longer considered annoying. Believed to be of African origin.

"Michael Row Your Boat Ashore." Story of someone named Michael crossing the River Jordan. Origin unknown.

"Two Winds." Tells of slaves wanting wings to fly away, and wanting their sins to be washed away. American slave origin.

Nursery Rhymes—Rhymes shared with very young children. Often rhythmical, rhymed, and alliterative. The ones in Western European culture are often called Mother Goose rhymes.

Examples: "Jack Be Nimble, Jack Be Quick, Jack Jump Over the Candlestick." Refers supposedly to King John, son of Henry II, who reputedly was low in intelligence.

Arroz Con Leche: Popular Songs and Rhymes From Latin America. Latin America (collected by Lulu Delacre); a collection of traditional children's songs, rhymes, singing games. Both Spanish and English versions included.

Street Rhymes Around the World. Edited by Jane Yolen. Counting games, songs, and chants representing children from 17 countries as diverse as Armenia, Denmark, and Brazil.

Jump-Rope Rhymes and Other Game-Related Sayings—Chants and little poems or sayings often accompany children's play and are passed on from child to child.

Examples: "Teddy Bear, Teddy Bear, Turn Around; Teddy Bear, Teddy Bear, Touch the Ground" (jump-rope rhyme) (Brown).

"One potato, two potato, three potato, four. Five potato, six potato, seven potato more" (from Colgin's *One Potato, Two Potato, Three Potato, Four: 165 Chants for Children*). Helps to choose who will go first in a game.

"Scissors, paper, stone." On a given signal, children are supposed to thrust forward a stone (first), scissors (two fingers extended), or paper (palm flat). Scissors cut paper, paper covers stone, stone dulls scissors—this determines who goes first or gets the first pick of something (Colgin).

Prose Narratives

Folk Tales—Longer stories that feature human and/or animal characters. Some are meant to entertain, and others teach community values and social mores. "Little Red Riding Hood" and "Hansel and Gretel" are two you might be familiar with. Folktales are generally categorized into subgroups such as the following:

Trickster Tales. The main character plays tricks in some way. Generally this character initially seems weak or is in a position of little power but eventually outsmarts those in power.

Examples: *Iktomi and the Buffalo Skull.* Blackfoot, Native American (Goble); recurring trickster Iktomi is always getting into trouble—this time, he gets his head stuck in a skull. Iktomi appears in native stories in the form of a person, spider, or coyote.

Uncle Remus (Lester). African American stories; Brer Rabbit uses language mischievously to outwit his pursuers.

Brother Rabbit. Cambodia (retold by Minfong Ho); Brother Rabbit outwits toothy crocodiles and angry elephants.

Noodlehead Stories. Folktales that feature a fool, noodlehead, or other silly character. Probably showed the dangers of poor judgment. The characters' poor judgment and their subsequent actions lead to dire consequences such as a porridge pot boiling over uncontrollably or being captured by an evil being.

Examples: *Epossumondas.* Southern United States (retold by Colleen Salley); Possum takes everything he hears far too literally and misunderstands his mama's directions.

"Lightening the Load." Turkish, European; a rider puts a sack on his own shoulders to lighten the load of the beast he's riding on.

Beast Stories. Folktales that feature animals as the main characters. Often the animals are anthropomorphized because the tales are meant to teach human foibles.

Examples: *Panchatantra Tales.* India; lions, monkeys, and crocodiles are used to present moral lessons.

"*Three Billy Goats Gruff.*" Germany (retold by Janet Stevens); three goats try to cross a bridge under which a troll lives. The troll is outsmarted.

"Puss 'n' Boots." Western Europe; a cat helps his master win the king's daughter's hand and becomes a prince.

Myths—Stories whose function is to explain. Early peoples needed to explain events, places, and occurrences, so they created stories to answer their questions. Classifying these tales as myth, creation, or pourquoi (*pourquoi* means "why" in French) depends on the perspective of the individual. Pourquoi stories typically are secular; they explain everyday phenomena such as how the tiger got his stripes and why rabbits have long ears. Creation stories are more serious and explain the origin or creation of a group of people or a place. Myths are usually considered sacred; often they are associated with spirituality and ritual, particularly when they tell how a group of people came to live in a place or how they were created.

Pourquoi Stories—"Why Deer Have Short Tails." Shawnee (retold by Jane Curry); this pourquoi tale explains that deer have short tails because they were kicked hard by a

hunter when the chief deer had attempted to make the lovely sister of a hunter man his wife.

"How Turtle Got a Cracked Back." West Indian (retold by Grace Hallworth); Turtle's shell, once mirrored, is used by vain animals who fail to invite Turtle to a party because he's not a flying animal. He disguises himself as a bird, pasting feathers onto his shell to attend the event. His deceit is discovered, birds pull off his feathers while in flight, and he crashes to the ground, breaking his shell.

Greek and Roman Myths. Most Greek myths were retold and collected by the eighth-century poet Hesiod. Roman culture adopted Greek myths in variations. Some of these myths resemble fables in that what they explain can teach a lesson about human vices.

Examples (from Bolton; Osborne): "The Golden Fleece." Explains one of the signs of the zodiac, Aries, the ram.

"Arachne." Explains vanity and greed through a spider/maiden character.

Creation Myths. In the Beginning: Creation Stories From Around the World (Hamilton). Stories explaining the beginning of humans, earth, and sky from cultures as diverse as China, Guinea, and Alaska.

Moon Was Tired of Walking on Air. South America, Charote Indians (retold by Natalie Belting); tells of how moon wanted solid ground to walk on so he created earth, then grass, then seeds, then crops.

The Boy Who Found the Light. Inuit (retold by Dale deArmond); explanation of how daylight came to the Inuit peoples through the effort of an orphan boy.

Fairy or Wonder Tales—A type of folktale generally containing fairies, witches, heroes, dragons, serpents, or some element of magic. They have "happily ever after" endings. A person or an object may possess supernatural powers such as the ability to cast spells or transform people or things.

Examples: "Cinderella." European; a stepdaughter who is mistreated finds happiness when a fairy godmother enables her to attend a ball where she meets a handsome prince and they fall in love and live happily ever after. This tale has many variants across diverse cultures.

"The Serpent Slayer." Chinese (retold by Katrin Tchana); A huge serpent lives in a cave and must feed on flesh, killing many animals and people. One brave girl becomes a sacrifice for the serpent, but uses cunning and bravery to successfully defeat it.

"Sleeping Beauty." European (retold by Mercer Mayer); a fair maiden, really a princess, is raised apart from the

(continues)

Prose Narratives (continued)

kingdom, put to sleep in a spell by a jealous witch, and awakened by a handsome prince.

"Aladdin and His Magic Lamp." Middle Eastern (from Dawood); with the aid of a genie from a magic lamp, Aladdin fights an evil magician and wins the hand of a beautiful princess.

Note: Stories written by authors such as Hans Christian Andersen are commonly categorized as fairy tales. However, because these stories are written by a known author rather than springing from the oral tradition, they are considered fantasy.

Fables and Learning Stories—Fables teach cultural values and have an explicit or implicit moral.

Example: Aesop's "The Boy Who Cried Wolf."

Learning stories also teach values but are longer, more complex texts with morals not always explicitly stated. In many cultures, discussion and argument are expected following the telling of a learning story.

Examples: "Lotus Sutra." Buddhist; children of an alchemist accidentally drink poison, then refuse to take the antidote. He pretends to be dead. In shock, the children drink the antidote. Listeners are asked to consider if the alchemist is guilty of lying.

Legends and Tall Tales—These prose narratives are thought to be true by their tellers. Through countless retellings, the characters and events take on super-human qualities. Ghost stories are legends in which paranormal events occur: hauntings, alien abductions, visits from those "beyond the grave." Tall tales are

highly exaggerated legends, such as Kellogg's *Paul Bunyan,* whose ax created the Grand Canyon. Tall tales are most common in American lore, but such stories have been documented in other cultures as well. These tales usually feature a male hero, although some with female protagonists have been documented.

Examples: *Three Strong Women.* Japanese (retold by Claus Stamm); when a famous wrestler tickles a plump little girl, the consequence is that he must be trained by her, her mother, and her grandmother.

Legends of King Arthur. British Isles; stories (such as those retold by John Matthews) of a king said to have lived in the British Isles. Known for his goodness and bravery.

Ramayana (Krishna). Epic legend of India that tells how the noble Rama, his devoted brother, and his beautiful wife, Sita, defeat the evil demon Ravana.

Ghost Stories (retold by Alvin Schwartz). "The Big Toe." Southern United States; a boy digs up a toe, which his family eats for supper. That night, a voice is heard demanding "Where is my to-o-o-o-e?" The voice comes closer and closer, then shouts, "You've got it!" Example of a "jump" story.

"The Hitchhiker." United States; a girl found on the side of the road is given a ride home. She asks for the driver's sweater/coat because she's cold. The driver returns to the place where the girl was dropped off, only to find that she died many years ago. The coat/sweater is later found draped over her grave. (Example of story where unhappy spirit haunts site of its demise.)

In addition to the books cited, you can find information on traditional tales at the following websites:

http://www.manythings.org/proverbs/proverbs1.html—index and quiz of common American proverbs for ESL speakers to learn
http://www.pbm.com/~lindahl/ballads—about ballads
http://darkwing.uoregon.edu/~rbear/ballads.html—about lyrical ballads
http://www.gwu.edu/~e73afram/ag-am-mp.html—oral tradition of African Americans
http://www.spiritandsky.com/folklore/literature/riddles/collections/—website devoted to riddles from the oral tradition

Guidelines for Selecting High-Quality Traditional Literature

Because traditional literature has evolved from so many cultures, it is difficult to evaluate, and it is challenging to apply the same criteria to all stories. Each tale is situated in the culture from which it is derived, thus expectations for plot structure, characterization, and style are culturally bound.

Another important consideration in selecting traditional literature for use in the classroom is whether the story is considered sacred by the storyteller. The next logical question, then, is, For whom is it sacred? When a story or myth comes from one's own religion or culture, it is often considered sacred. An outsider might find the story interesting, yet not hold it in as esteemed a position. There are many stories for which this judgment differs, depending on the listener's point of view. Thus, we think it's important to consider this issue when evaluating traditional stories. We ask if the person presenting the

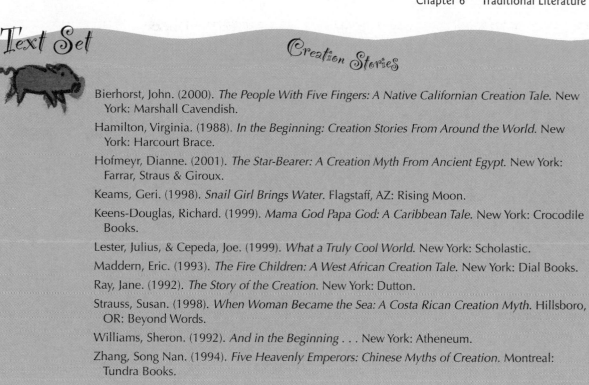

Text Set

Creation Stories

Bierhorst, John. (2000). *The People With Five Fingers: A Native Californian Creation Tale.* New York: Marshall Cavendish.

Hamilton, Virginia. (1988). *In the Beginning: Creation Stories From Around the World.* New York: Harcourt Brace.

Hofmeyr, Dianne. (2001). *The Star-Bearer: A Creation Myth From Ancient Egypt.* New York: Farrar, Straus & Giroux.

Keams, Geri. (1998). *Snail Girl Brings Water.* Flagstaff, AZ: Rising Moon.

Keens-Douglas, Richard. (1999). *Mama God Papa God: A Caribbean Tale.* New York: Crocodile Books.

Lester, Julius, & Cepeda, Joe. (1999). *What a Truly Cool World.* New York: Scholastic.

Maddern, Eric. (1993). *The Fire Children: A West African Creation Tale.* New York: Dial Books.

Ray, Jane. (1992). *The Story of the Creation.* New York: Dutton.

Strauss, Susan. (1998). *When Woman Became the Sea: A Costa Rican Creation Myth.* Hillsboro, OR: Beyond Words.

Williams, Sheron. (1992). *And in the Beginning . . .* New York: Atheneum.

Zhang, Song Nan. (1994). *Five Heavenly Emperors: Chinese Myths of Creation.* Montreal: Tundra Books.

story (orally or in writing) is also a member of that culture. Or we might ask if he or she has intimate and first-hand knowledge of that culture and its stories. Consequently, we propose here that we evaluate traditional literature differently when we are cultural insiders than when we are outsiders.

The Guidelines for Choosing Literature feature on p. 132 outlines considerations for evaluating a selection of traditional literature. Because evaluating literature from another culture is difficult, we also recommend that educators search for recommendations from book reviews, websites, professional societies, and knowledgeable members of the target culture. This feature also suggests some literary qualities you should look for in traditional literature.

We should also be wary of judging stories by contemporary standards. Because traditional literature reflects attitudes, gender roles, and class systems from the distant past, the content of some stories might surprise or offend today's readers. Some adults are concerned about violence, such as when Hansel and Gretel shove the witch into an oven or when Cinderella's sisters cut off their heels and toes. Others worry about the universal optimism these stories appear to advocate, where good always triumphs over evil, because this doesn't always happen in real life. Still others worry about the gender roles and racial portrayals. Although there are some strong female characters in traditional literature (Hamilton, 1995; Riordan, 1985), the more

common scenario is that the heroes are males and women are passive objects rewarded to men for their heroic deeds. Chinese people are typically shown as deferential or menacing. Dwarves are simple-minded (as in "Snow White") or evil (as in "Rumpelstiltskin").

These are valid concerns. However, they can be addressed by presenting tales to children that include strong, active women characters or people from a culture in non-stereotypical roles. We also believe you can discuss these issues with children; the final section of this chapter offers some suggestions for doing this.

Awards for Traditional Literature

The Aesop Prize is conferred annually by the Children's Folklore Section of the American Folklore Society (AFS) to English-language books for children and young adults. Both fiction and nonfiction works are considered. The AFS website, www.afsnet.org, lists the following criteria for consideration:

☺ Folklore should be central to the book's content and, if appropriate, to the illustrations.

☺ The folklore presented in the book should accurately reflect the culture and worldview of the people whose folklore is the focus of the book.

☺ The reader's understanding of folklore should be enhanced by the book, as should the book be enhanced by the presence of folklore.

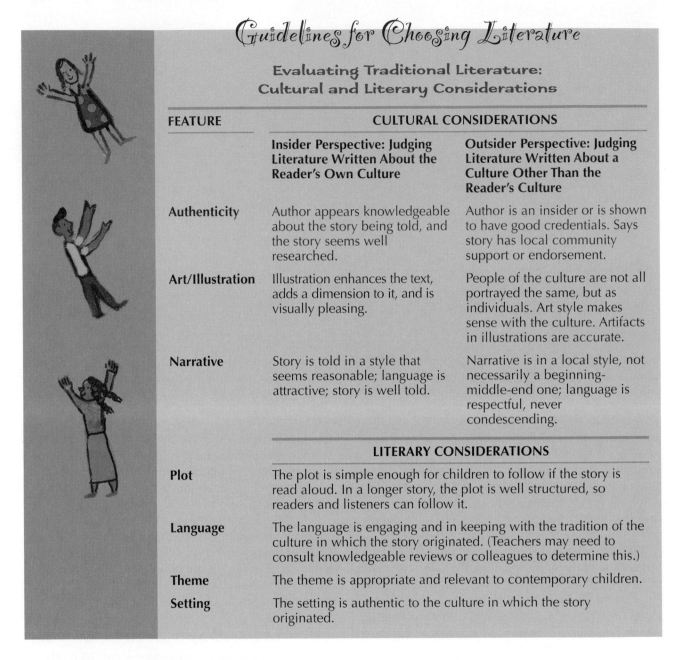

Guidelines for Choosing Literature

Evaluating Traditional Literature: Cultural and Literary Considerations

FEATURE	CULTURAL CONSIDERATIONS	
	Insider Perspective: Judging Literature Written About the Reader's Own Culture	**Outsider Perspective: Judging Literature Written About a Culture Other Than the Reader's Culture**
Authenticity	Author appears knowledgeable about the story being told, and the story seems well researched.	Author is an insider or is shown to have good credentials. Says story has local community support or endorsement.
Art/Illustration	Illustration enhances the text, adds a dimension to it, and is visually pleasing.	People of the culture are not all portrayed the same, but as individuals. Art style makes sense with the culture. Artifacts in illustrations are accurate.
Narrative	Story is told in a style that seems reasonable; language is attractive; story is well told.	Narrative is in a local style, not necessarily a beginning-middle-end one; language is respectful, never condescending.
LITERARY CONSIDERATIONS		
Plot	The plot is simple enough for children to follow if the story is read aloud. In a longer story, the plot is well structured, so readers and listeners can follow it.	
Language	The language is engaging and in keeping with the tradition of the culture in which the story originated. (Teachers may need to consult knowledgeable reviews or colleagues to determine this.)	
Theme	The theme is appropriate and relevant to contemporary children.	
Setting	The setting is authentic to the culture in which the story originated.	

Tech Note

Winners of the Aesop Prize can be accessed on the American Folklore Society website at www.afsnet.org. You can also link to this site through the Companion Website.

☺ The book should reflect the high artistic standards of the best of children's literature and should have strong appeal to the child reader.

☺ Folklore sources must be fully acknowledged and annotations referenced within the bound contents of the publication.

Other awards often honor exemplary works of traditional literature. The Caldecott Award in particular has often named a beautifully illustrated book of traditional literature as an award winner. The Notable Books for a Global Society Award Committee of the Children's Literature and Reading Special Inter-

Tech Note

A list of current and past winners of the Notable Books for a Global Society Award is published in *The Dragon Lode* and can also be accessed at www.csulb .edu/org/childrens-lit.

Meet... Virginia Hamilton

Author of The Mystery of Drear House; M. C. Higgins, the Great; Sweet Whispers; Brother Rush; Bluish; Her Stories; The People Could Fly; In the Beginning; Many Thousand Gone; The Dark Way; Cousins; Second Cousins; and many more.

"I am a full-time writer and I write exclusively for young people, and I want them to enjoy my works most of all rather than study them. I want kids to really enjoy the stories. My family supported me and thought it was a very good idea that I wanted to be a writer. I liked writing stories.

I hope everybody will read, not only in the classroom but in their spare time and that it would be part of their lives, just as sports are and music perhaps. Reading is something we all have to do in all parts of life; it doesn't matter what you do when you grow up, you are going to have to read. I think reading is very important in the classroom and outside of it. Reading out loud is wonderful for getting people involved with stories. I would suggest that everybody take part in reading aloud in classrooms and at home with their family."

Ms. Hamilton lived most of her life in Ohio with her husband, poet Arnold Adoff.

From an oral interview conducted by Miss Tiara Kasten, April, 2000.

Tech Note

Interviews with traditional literature authors and retellers Demi, Ashley Bryan, and Verna Aardema can be accessed on the CD-ROM that accompanies this book.

---

est Group of the International Reading Association also frequently honors traditional literature from cultures around the world.

Building a Classroom Library

For your students to live and love traditional literature, you will need to provide a wide variety of examples from this genre in your classroom collection. One of the most efficient ways to start a collection of traditional tales is to locate good anthologies of stories that suit the age and interests of your students. Some collections are broad in scope, and others focus on a specific cultural group or a particular form such as tall tales or fables.

Look carefully at anthologies that claim to include stories from around the world. Check the table of contents to ensure that "the world" has a representative sampling from all major regions, not just North America or Western Europe. Good collections also provide accurate information about the origins of the tales and how they were selected for inclusion. Students will prefer illustrated collections, but collections that are not illustrated can be used as teacher references or as sources for oral storytelling activities.

Some anthologies of traditional literature target a specific cultural group or type of story. Patricia McKissack assembled *The Dark-Thirty: Southern Tales of the Supernatural*, which presents stories rooted in African American culture. Many of Virginia Hamilton's anthologies feature stories with African American themes (*The People Could Fly*), dark spiritual themes (*The Dark Way: Stories From the Spirit World*), or creation stories (*In the Beginning: Creation Stories From Around the World*). Other examples are *Cric Crac: A Collection of West Indian Stories* (Hallworth), *My Grandmother's Stories: A Collection of Jewish Folk Tales* (Geras), *American Indian Myths and Legends* (Erdoes & Ortiz), *Ashley Bryan's African Tales, Uh-Huh* (Bryan), and *The Ox of the Wonderful Horns and Other African Folktales* (Bryan). It's important for diverse students to see themselves in stories, but children from mainstream cultures also should be exposed to stories outside their cultural experiences to expand their minds as well as their understanding of the world.

Beautifully illustrated picture books of single tales are another important component of the traditional literature collection. Many well-known picture-book artists have illustrated stories from a variety of cultures. Be sure you examine the text and illustrations for authenticity, as much as possible. Sometimes an illustrator who is an outsider from

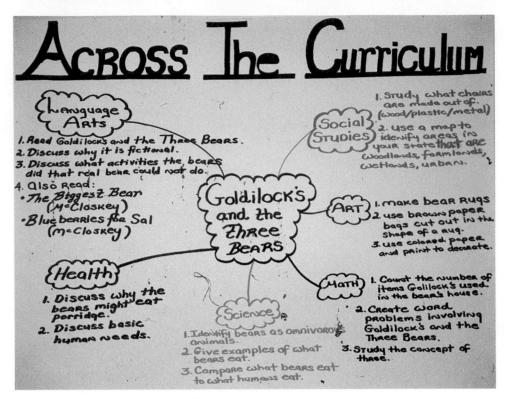

Even a simple folktale such as "Goldilocks and the Three Bears" can be webbed and integrated across the curriculum.

the culture will include details in an illustration that are not culturally authentic.

Social studies lessons often lead students into learning about other cultures. Because sharing traditional literature from a culture is a wonderful way to learn about its values and mores, you may want to include stories from diverse cultures to complement your social studies curriculum. You can also share stories from several cultures for later cross-cultural study of traditional literature.

You may also want to provide examples of particular story forms, literary elements, and stories that meet special interests. Thus, you can locate folktales, legends, or tall tales that are appropriate for the age of your students and are interesting to them. You could establish a special section of variants, such as all the Cinderella or Rumpelstiltskin stories. Locate some stories that use particular motifs or present common themes. Because traditional literature typically is male dominated, stories with strong female characters might comprise another special section of your collection. The "Strong Women in Traditional Literature" text

Often the only way to look clearly at this extraordinary universe is through fantasy, fairy tale, and myth.

(Madeleine L'Engle, author; personal communication, September, 1999)

set on p. 135 provides some examples of excellent books that meet this need.

Special Considerations for Young Children

If you are a primary-grade teacher, you will want to provide books that appeal particularly to younger children. In addition to well-illustrated versions of familiar stories, these could include books of nursery rhymes and playground chants and predictable books with distinct rhyme and rhythm.

There are many beautifully illustrated Mother Goose and nursery rhyme collections for children; many are done by such well-known artists as Tomie dePaola, Arnold Lobel, James Marshall, Robert Sabuda, and Rosemary Wells. Additionally, some individual Mother Goose rhymes are now available in picture-book format. These books feature only one rhyme or a few rhymes on a common theme. They allow you to focus on one rhyme in depth, encouraging children to particularly

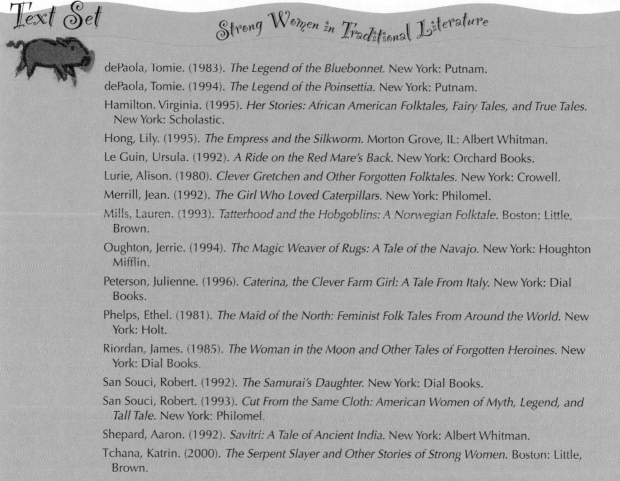

Text Set — *Strong Women in Traditional Literature*

dePaola, Tomie. (1983). *The Legend of the Bluebonnet*. New York: Putnam.

dePaola, Tomie. (1994). *The Legend of the Poinsettia*. New York: Putnam.

Hamilton. Virginia. (1995). *Her Stories: African American Folktales, Fairy Tales, and True Tales*. New York: Scholastic.

Hong, Lily. (1995). *The Empress and the Silkworm*. Morton Grove, IL: Albert Whitman.

Le Guin, Ursula. (1992). *A Ride on the Red Mare's Back*. New York: Orchard Books.

Lurie, Alison. (1980). *Clever Gretchen and Other Forgotten Folktales*. New York: Crowell.

Merrill, Jean. (1992). *The Girl Who Loved Caterpillars*. New York: Philomel.

Mills, Lauren. (1993). *Tatterhood and the Hobgoblins: A Norwegian Folktale*. Boston: Little, Brown.

Oughton, Jerrie. (1994). *The Magic Weaver of Rugs: A Tale of the Navajo*. New York: Houghton Mifflin.

Peterson, Julienne. (1996). *Caterina, the Clever Farm Girl: A Tale From Italy*. New York: Dial Books.

Phelps, Ethel. (1981). *The Maid of the North: Feminist Folk Tales From Around the World*. New York: Holt.

Riordan, James. (1985). *The Woman in the Moon and Other Tales of Forgotten Heroines*. New York: Dial Books.

San Souci, Robert. (1992). *The Samurai's Daughter*. New York: Dial Books.

San Souci, Robert. (1993). *Cut From the Same Cloth: American Women of Myth, Legend, and Tall Tale*. New York: Philomel.

Shepard, Aaron. (1992). *Savitri: A Tale of Ancient India*. New York: Albert Whitman.

Tchana, Katrin. (2000). *The Serpent Slayer and Other Stories of Strong Women*. Boston: Little, Brown.

Uchida, Yoshiko. (1994). *The Wise Old Woman*. New York: McElderry.

pay attention to rhythm, rhyme, and word play, while also helping them consider how the illustrations affect their perception of the story.

Once children become familiar with many nursery rhymes, they often enjoy the books that feature games or activities based on their knowledge. For example, *Each Peach Pear Plum* (Ahlberg & Ahlberg) presents an "I Spy" game in which children find various nursery rhyme characters hidden in the pictures. Eric Hill's *Nursery-Rhyme Peek-A-Book* and Lee Bennett Hopkins's *People From Mother Goose* feature rhyming questions about various Mother Goose characters: The child must lift the flap to find the answer to the question as well as the entire rhyme (the entire nursery rhyme is under the flap).

Many popular songs and playground chants are now available in picture-book format. Children can sing or chant along during a read-aloud session while they enjoy the beautiful illustrations that complement and extend these songs. These activities develop understanding of phonemic awareness: the ability to hear and segment sounds in words. These books in enlarged format also make excellent texts for shared, guided, and independent reading.

Special Considerations for Middle School Students

Middle school students are ready for more complex traditional stories including legends and epics such as *The Iliad* (Lattimore), *The Odyssey* (McCaughrean), *The Ramayana* (Krishna), and the King Arthur tales. Long ballads such as *The Cremation of Sam Magee* (Service) and *Casey at the Bat* (Bing) appeal to this age group. Traditional mythology from ancient cultures such as Greece, Rome, and Egypt are also often popular. Additionally, this age group enjoys ghost stories and other literature designed to scare the listener.

Traditional Literature in the Living Literature Classroom

Teaching about traditional literature provides opportunities for increasing appreciation of diverse cultures and how literature reflects the values, language, and customs of those cultures. Traditional literature can be used with all ages of children. In primary grades, traditional stories can be the impetus for shared and guided reading experiences, especially if the selections have predictable, repetitive story structures. Traditional stories, with their musical language and engaging plots, are also a wonderful resource for read-alouds.

As children mature, they can begin discerning the various forms and appreciate more complex plot structures, such as those in myths, legends, or epics. Middle-level students can assume an anthropological stance toward stories, studying the cultures that produced them, considering what can be learned about people and their humanity from a culture's stories. They can also consider what these stories tell us about how to live our own lives.

However, there are challenges to using this genre. Investigating the stories of a culture bears a certain responsibility because readers and listeners are eavesdropping on that culture. We must ensure our students are properly respectful.

Teachers must also be sure they provide opportunities for children to thoroughly study a particular form of traditional literature before they are asked to respond to it, particularly through writing. Students need multiple encounters with a particular form or body of literature from a culture, including exposure to many models, demonstrations of expected responses, and opportunities for guided practice, before they are asked to emulate a form in a writing assignment.

Another challenge arises when we use traditional literature with children who come from cultures having a rich oral instructional tradition. Native American and Native Alaskan children, for example, are often accustomed to hearing traditional stories and perceive them as having an honorable place in daily life. Their expectations may differ from children of other cultures where the function of stories is to entertain. Thus, teachers must be certain not to trivialize stories or ask children to respond to stories in ways that might be disrespectful to their culture.

Selecting Traditional Tales for Classroom Activities

Selecting traditional tales for classroom use and enjoyment involves a number of decisions. The reading level of most tales makes them accessible to a wide audience, but the content may be unsuitable or too mature for some ages; after all, traditional literature was not necessarily created for children. Today, many editions are geared for the youthful audience, but some tales have gory elements, such as dragons, witches, ghosts, and monsters, that could frighten some children. When you are uncertain about content, we suggest you consult a knowledgeable media specialist, librarian, or colleague for advice.

You also need to consider the community in which you work when you select traditional literature. Some communities, for example, find stories about supernatural phenomena, particularly haunted houses, ghosts, or witches, offensive. Knowing community norms and attitudes can guide your planning as to what you should include and whether you need to inform parents in advance of class activities, giving them an opportunity to respond. Although these attitudes do not necessarily mean controversial aspects of traditional literature should never be addressed in school, teachers should be aware of potential problems before beginning a unit.

For example, one teacher we know who was using Navajo folktales in her social studies lessons received a challenge from a parent that the tales addressed spiritual issues. The parent complained that the material in the story differed from her children's religious beliefs and that alternative beliefs were being taught in a public school classroom. The school principal adeptly defused the situation, explaining that the fifth-grade teacher's job was to teach about culture. Therefore, the stories were a legitimate part of a study about the culture and did not constitute teaching religion.

Sharing and Discussing Traditional Literature With Students

Hearing traditional stories read aloud complete with dialect, expression, gestures, and visuals can be an enjoyable experience for both teachers and students. Following the reading, discussions could center on how the story reflects the value of the culture and what its purpose might be in that culture (e.g., to entertain? to instruct? to explain?).

Another activity that leads to critical analysis and thoughtful discussion is to read several versions of a story that have strikingly different illustrations. For example, you might share Trina Schart Hyman's *Little Red Riding Hood*, illustrated in a cozy, folklore style, along with Lisbeth Zwerger's *Little Red-Cap*, which features pastel watercolors and an older heroine. Then share Marjorie Priceman's pop-up version or Ed Young's *Lon Po Po: A Red Riding Hood Story From China*, which uses ancient Chinese panel art combined with a contemporary palette of watercolors and pastels. The contrasts in these illustrations, as well as differences in story details, typically evoke quite diverse responses from children.

> *The more you tell a simple tale like "Cinderella" or "Jack and the Beanstalk," the more you know about it; and the more you learn not only about the wisdom these old tales are full of, but also about technical things like structure, shape, timing, suspense . . .*
>
> Philip Pullman, 1997/1998, p. 16

Storytelling

Because traditional tales arose from the oral tradition, storytelling is a perfect medium for sharing this genre. Not only does storytelling allow for face-to-face, more intimate contact, but the story can be paced and modified to fit the particular audience hearing it. Difficult vocabulary and plot lines can be explained and audience participation encouraged.

Stories for telling should be carefully selected to maximize the advantages of this medium. The story should have a clear, simple, active plot. Cumulative stories, based on repeated action by a series of characters, are particularly good because the repeated action makes it easier for both teller and audience to remember the plot.

Introductions that quickly draw readers into the story through a compelling incident or an interesting character, for example, work well for focusing listeners' attention. Folktales and tall tales are particularly suited to this purpose. It also helps to select stories with only three or four main characters so as to use various voices effectively, enabling listeners to more easily keep characters straight. A minimum of props, visuals, or special effects should be used because these can be confusing to listeners and difficult for the teller to manipulate.

Once you have selected your story, you need to prepare the telling. It's not necessary to memorize it, but you do need to plan. It helps first to mentally sequence the events, then add the details in subsequent rehearsals. You should practice the story several times by yourself, adding different vocalizations for characters and eventually including props. Felt boards (small boards covered with felt that can act as backgrounds for felt-backed figures), objects from the story, puppets, paper folding, music, posters, and other visuals can all be used to enhance the telling.

Once students have heard many stories told orally, they can begin telling stories themselves. They can use familiar stories for this purpose, or they can find appropriate ones previously unknown to them. Students can also be encouraged to seek out stories to share from their own family histories or the history of someone in their community. They can practice by telling their stories to a mirror, then to a partner, then to a large audience. They should be encouraged to visualize the story sequence and to speak in an informal manner rather than memorizing every word. Props are particularly helpful in supporting children's ability to remember the plot sequence as long as they are minimal and relate to the main elements of the story.

Using Graphic Organizers to Help Children Examine the Literary Qualities of Traditional Literature

Graphic organizers can facilitate discussion and critical thinking in response to the sharing of traditional literature. Several useful organizers for this genre are story maps, literary element charts, matrices, and Venn diagrams.

Story Maps

You can examine plot structure by creating story maps, which are artistic visual representations of a story's plot. Because folktale plots tend to be simple and direct, this form of traditional literature is particularly well suited to story mapping. Students can visually "map out" the journey of a character, such as the fox in Hogrogian's *One Fine Day*, an Armenian folktale, or they can depict the progression of action. We suggest that you have students segment the plot, then represent it in art, using no words when creating a story map; this helps them think visually about the story. The groups can then use their maps to retell stories to each other. Retellings strengthen understanding and offer opportunities for oral expression.

Story maps can also be used as the basis for board games. Students can map out the story line on poster board, add illustrations, direction cards, and squares on which to land playing pieces, then play each other's games.

Literary Element Charts

As part of the discussion for a traditional tale, the group can create charts of various literary elements. This activity helps students identify and think more critically about various aspects of stories. For example, they could chart all the motifs found in a particular story (magical objects, symbolic numbers, "stereotypical" characters such as sly foxes, etc.). They could then look for these elements in other forms of writing or in everyday language (e.g., "He has that Midas touch!"). Fantasy novels based on traditional stories are an excellent resource for literary element charts.

This activity can be adapted to the study of other literary aspects of traditional tales. For example, children could examine many tales with a cumulative plot structure, then create a chart comparing what accumulates in various stories. Or students can find elements in traditional literature that are still used in our language today, such as "crying over spilt milk" or "that's a Herculean task."

Folktale Matrix: Comparing Variants

The purpose of this teaching strategy is to identify and compare variants of traditional stories across cultures. This is an excellent strategy for showing children how a culture can leave its unique mark on a story, changing characters, settings, and plot structure of the tale. It can also be used to highlight literary elements and enable students to think more critically about story parts. It is most often used with folktales, but could be adapted for studying other forms of traditional literature. An excellent story for this purpose is "Cinderella" because there are so many variants of this story. In fact, virtually every culture has a form of "Cinderella" story.

Begin by selecting a traditional tale with a good number of variants. Collect variants of the story from diverse cultures. Or you can collect variants from cultures you are currently studying in your classroom. After reading them with your students, begin a matrix on a large sheet of paper with headings such as "Reteller," "Origin of Tale," "Main Character," "Main Character's Foil," "Problem," "Obstacle to the Solution," "Evil Character," "Helpful Character/ Guide," and "Ending." The specific categories you use will depend on the story and its particular characteristics. Create a column or row every time your students read a new variant, filling in the chart for that story. When the chart is completed, have students examine it for similarities and differences. Lead a discussion on how the values and mores of a culture influenced each variant.

This idea can be adapted to studying other aspects of traditional tales. For example, various themes commonly found in traditional stories such as "good triumphs over evil," "kindness is rewarded," and "pride goeth before a fall" can be identified. As students read stories, they can chart which stories exemplify the identified themes.

Venn Diagrams

Venn diagrams also give students the opportunity to discuss similarities and differences between stories. Venn diagrams differ from matrices in that only two stories are compared at a time. The tales compared can be variants of a story, two different stories from the same culture, two stories that have the same form, etc. Typically, the stories selected for the activity will have something in common along with some significant differences, such as two creation myths or two pourquoi tales from different cultures that explain the same natural phenomenon.

Tech Note

The CD-ROM that accompanies this book features a sample matrix for "Cinderella" variants from one class of students. This class focused on the type of enchantment, role of the father, ending, and relationship with the family after Cinderella and the Prince were married. A bibliography of "Cinderella" variants can be found with this activity.

Changing the Point of View

Often in a traditional tale, the reader will identify one character as the good one and another as evil; no evidence is given as to why the evil character is bad—he or she just is, and readers accept that. A good classroom writing lesson would be to have students—individually or in groups—take the point of view of another character in the tale. In the same way that Jon Scieszka has us consider the wolf's views in the modern fairy tale, *The True Story of the*

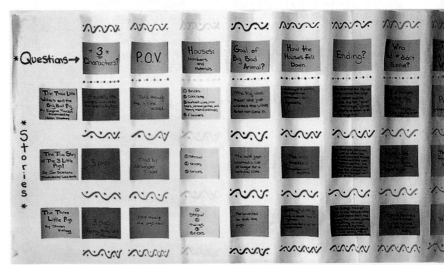

Students compare three variants of "The Three Little Pigs" in a large matrix on the classroom wall.

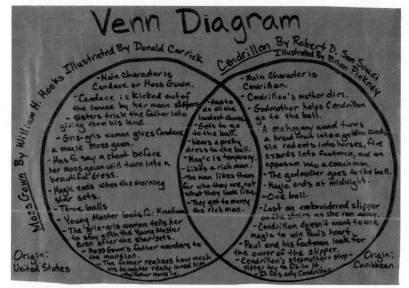

Two "Cinderella" variants are compared and contrasted with a Venn diagram, a useful strategy for comparing texts.

3 Little Pigs!, students can consider the point of view of someone else.

In Zelinsky's *Rumpelstiltskin*, for example, readers identify the miller's daughter as good and Rumpelstiltskin as bad. But suppose Rumpelstiltskin has been given a bad name and wants only to be a good father but can't have any children of his own? Has anyone considered that Cinderella's stepmother might have tried hard to raise her and that the girl may well have been spoiled and self-centered and done things to make her stepsisters resent her? Helping students consider a different point of view in traditional literature can help them raise questions about characters in other literature as well. It will also help them understand that in real life, people are complicated, seldom all good or all bad.

Discussing Issues of Racism and Sexism

Rather than ignoring or glossing over issues of racism and sexism in traditional literature, teachers can use these stories as sources for helping children recognize bias in literature. They can have students tally the number of tales they encounter that feature male and female main characters. Similarly, they can tally stories that prominently feature stories with peasants or minorities as the main characters. These activities will be useful resources for a discussion about the representation of various peoples in these stories. The conversation could focus on questions such as "Who are the heroes?"; "Who solves problems?" Students may begin to notice ideas, such as how many

traditional tales have more evil women characters (wicked stepmothers, witches, etc.) than evil male characters. You can then share traditional stories that shatter these stereotypes.

Dramatizing Traditional Tales

Dramatizing traditional literature provides engaging opportunities for students to demonstrate their understanding of story elements such as plot, character, and theme. Dramatization can be done in a variety of ways, including pantomime, puppet shows, Reader's Theatre, or a formal play. Folktales, fables, short legends, and learning stories are especially good for dramatization because of their simple plots, straightforward characterization, and brevity. Figure 6.2 lists some stories that are particularly appropriate for dramatization with classes and small groups.

Typically, dramatizations begin with you reading the story to the children, usually more than once. After children have responded to the story's content, you can engage them in conversation about ways the story might be dramatized. This could be as simple as having a narrator read the text aloud while students pantomime the story. Or students could assume the roles of various characters and read their assigned parts aloud in a Reader's Theatre format. Puppets could be created, or a more formal play presented to an audience might be organized. Sometimes small groups will select a tale to perform for each other or another class. The particular form your drama takes will depend on the story structure, your purpose for using it, and the amount of time you wish to devote to the activity.

Puppetry

Puppets are a valuable tool for bringing stories to life in the living literature classroom. Children involved in using puppets develop a deeper understanding of plot structure, characterization, and theme as they plan their cooperative presentations. They also acquire learning skills as they negotiate a script with their peers. Using puppets give children a safe opportunity to speak out because they are concealed behind a stage. They are also a particularly effective tool for English learners, providing engaging contexts for trying out newly acquired language skills (Sierra, 1991).

Traditional literature with its predictable, action-oriented plots, one-dimensional characters, and simple

Figure 6.2
Traditional
Literature for
Dramatizing

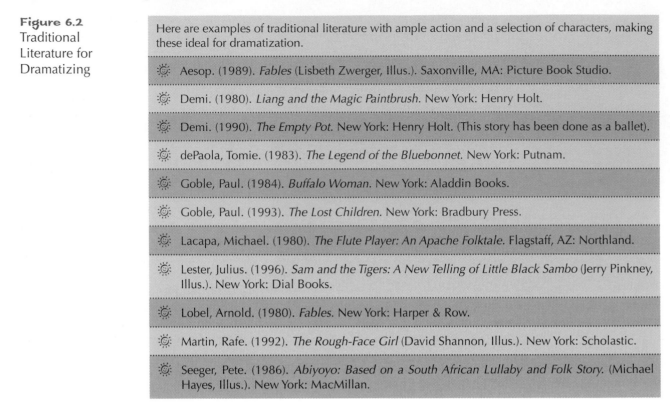

Here are examples of traditional literature with ample action and a selection of characters, making these ideal for dramatization.

☀ Aesop. (1989). *Fables* (Lisbeth Zwerger, Illus.). Saxonville, MA: Picture Book Studio.

☀ Demi. (1980). *Liang and the Magic Paintbrush.* New York: Henry Holt.

☀ Demi. (1990). *The Empty Pot.* New York: Henry Holt. (This story has been done as a ballet).

☀ dePaola, Tomie. (1983). *The Legend of the Bluebonnet.* New York: Putnam.

☀ Goble, Paul. (1984). *Buffalo Woman.* New York: Aladdin Books.

☀ Goble, Paul. (1993). *The Lost Children.* New York: Bradbury Press.

☀ Lacapa, Michael. (1980). *The Flute Player: An Apache Folktale.* Flagstaff, AZ: Northland.

☀ Lester, Julius. (1996). *Sam and the Tigers: A New Telling of Little Black Sambo* (Jerry Pinkney, Illus.). New York: Dial Books.

☀ Lobel, Arnold. (1980). *Fables.* New York: Harper & Row.

☀ Martin, Rafe. (1992). *The Rough-Face Girl* (David Shannon, Illus.). New York: Scholastic.

☀ Seeger, Pete. (1986). *Abiyoyo: Based on a South African Lullaby and Folk Story.* (Michael Hayes, Illus.). New York: MacMillan.

settings is a particularly good source for puppet shows. Selected stories should be short with clear, simple action. It helps to have just one or two lead characters to make it easier to manipulate the puppets. Settings and extra objects should also be simple. These elements add an appealing visual component; using too many of them, however, can be confusing to young puppeteers.

Children show their comprehension of "The Gingerbread Man" story by making puppets.

When analyzing a story for puppet performance, it helps to create a story analysis chart of characters, action, and necessary props so children focus on the main story elements and don't get sidetracked by extraneous details (Champlin & Renfro, 1985).

Students should next be encouraged to "play" their stories several times; this will set the story in their minds. Formal scripts aren't necessary and can actually inhibit the flow and spontaneity of the telling. Children then can add puppets, props, music, and other elements to what should now be a familiar story. Puppets can take many forms, from simple shadow and paper bag shapes to more elaborate rod puppets with movable parts.

Tech Note

The CD-ROM that accompanies this book features a sample story analysis chart children can use to plan their puppet plays.

Tech Note

The CD-ROM that accompanies this book features some suggestions for puppet formats as well as additional specific information on puppet making.

Tech Note

The CD-ROM that accompanies this book presents a model lesson on integrating traditional literature and science, using animal puppets and the book *Traveling to Tondo* (Aardema).

Tech Note

An adaptation of "The Old Man, His Son and the Donkey" for Reader's Theatre can be found on the CD-ROM that accompanies this book.

Reader's Theatre and Traditional Literature

Because traditional stories are often short and have active plots, they are well suited to Reader's Theatre, which is basically a dramatic reading of the story. Props and movement are limited in this activity. Usually the story will need to be adapted into a script before you use it for this activity. This typically involves deleting descriptive passages and words such as "said." The name of the character who is speaking is written at the beginning of their parts so actors can keep track. Often a narrator is added to read descriptions or to fill in events that would take too long for dialogue to reveal.

Writing and Traditional Literature

Writing in response to traditional literature can be a useful way to support students' understanding of these stories. However, we caution you to be careful about asking children to imitiate a particular form, creating their own "legend" or "folktale." For a story truly to be a legend, for example, it would need to have a kernel of truth that has been embellished in multiple tellings. Thus, a story made up from someone's imagination for a school assignment simply would not qualify as a legend. Instead, children could study the culture and traditional literature of a country first. Then they could write their own story that incorporates elements of that country's culture and literature, being careful not to term it as a valid form of traditional literature from that country. Or students could write in the manner of a particular form after becoming familiar with many examples of that form. That said, however, we suggest the following activities as possible writing responses to traditional literature.

"Fractured" Folktales

Many authors have rewritten traditional literature so they are set in contemporary times, gender roles are reversed, the point of view is shifted, the plot line is twisted to add humor, or other story elements are manipulated to pro-

duce a new story. Thus, for example, in Marilyn Tolhurst's *Somebody and the Three Blairs*, Baby Bear stealthily enters a human dwelling with hilarious results. Jon Scieszka changes the perspective of the Three Little Pigs to that of the wolf in *The True Story of the 3 Little Pigs! The Three Little Javelinas* (Lowell) is another transformation of this classic story. In Arthur Yorinks's *Ugh* and Babette Cole's *Prince Cinders*, the Cinderella character is male.

Older students who have extensive background with traditional literature enjoy writing "fractured" folktales. We suggest you begin this activity by reading together many examples of transformed stories, then compare them to the original stories on which they are based. Finally, children can write their own transformed or "fractured" tales. One group in a fifth-grade class, for example, transformed Aesop's "The Boy Who Cried Wolf" into "The Boy Who Called 9–1–1." Another group transformed *Little Red Riding Hood* to a big-city setting with a teenage girl named "Red" and an

"Cover" by Lane Smith, copyright © 1989 by Lane Smith, illustrations, from THE TRUE STORY OF THE 3 LITTLE PIGS! by Jon Scieszka, illustrated by Lane Smith. Used by permission of Viking Penguin, A Division of Penguin Young Readers Group, A Member of Penguin Group (USA) Inc., 345 Hudson Street, New York, NY 10014. All rights reserved.

Text Set   "Fractured" Folktales

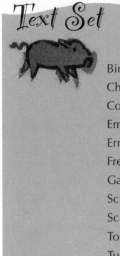

Birdseye, Tom. (2001). *Look Out Jack! The Giant Is Back.* New York: Holiday House.

Child, Lauren. (2000). *Beware of the Storybook Wolves.* New York: Levine.

Cole, Babette. (1987). *Prince Cinders.* New York: Putnam.

Emberley, Michael. (1990). *Ruby.* Boston: Little, Brown.

Ernst, Lisa. (1995). *Little Red Riding Hood.* New York: Simon & Schuster.

French, Fiona. (1986). *Snow White in New York.* Oxford: Oxford University Press.

Garner, James Finn. (1994). *Cinder-Elly.* New York: Viking.

Scieszka, Jon. (1989). *The True Story of the 3 Little Pigs!* New York: Viking.

Scieszka, Jon. (1991). *The Frog Prince Continued.* New York: Viking.

Tolhurst, Marilyn. (1991). *Somebody and the Three Blairs.* New York: Orchard Books.

Tunnell, Michael. (1993). *Beauty and the Beastley Children.* New York: Tambourine Books.

Figure 6.3 Ways to Transform Traditional Stories Into Modern Versions (Titles in parentheses are examples of published works.)

1. Change the style, from old-fashioned to modern language. (Jon Scieszka's *The True Story of the 3 Little Pigs!*)

2. Change or add to the details in the plot (Marilyn Tolhurst's *Somebody and the Three Blairs*).

3. Change a few of the main events in the plot (Stephen Kellogg's *Chicken Little*).

4. Keep a few of the main events, but change most of the plot (Jane Yolen's *Sleeping Ugly*).

5. Change the setting (time and place). If the setting is changed, there will probably need to be many more changes in characters and details (Fiona French's *Snow White in New York;* Arthur Yorinks's *Ugh*).

6. Change the point of view (Jon Scieszka's *The True Story of the 3 Little Pigs!,* told by the wolf).

7. Change the characters in the story by

   —changing their occupation (Stephanie Calmenson's *The Principal's New Clothes*)

   —changing their sex (Babette Cole's *Prince Cinders*)

   —reversing their roles in the story (*Somebody and the Three Blairs*)

8. Write a sequel to the original story (Scieszka's *The Frog Prince Continued*).

9. Keep the words of the original story, but change the illustrations (Anthony Browne's illustrated version of Jacob & Wilhelm Grimm's *Hansel and Gretel*).

antagonist named "Spike Wolf," a local juvenile delinquent. Figure 6.3 lists some suggestions for transforming a story,

Traditional Tale Newspaper

Have children brainstorm the sections in a newspaper: sports, society, news, editorials, obituaries, etc. Using folktales, tall tales, or other similar traditional stories, create a newspaper incorporating elements from those tales. For example, children might create a society column by Cinderella describing the ball, an obituary for the witch in Hansel and Gretel, or a sports article reporting on the race between the tortoise and the hare from Aesop's fables.

A useful way to promote this strategy is to have numerous newspaper models available. Using columns and features in real newspapers will help students think of ideas for their stories.

Using printshop software, students can transform their various articles on folktale characters into a realistic newspaper, even adding art and comics as desired. Some classes sell their completed papers to other students in the school.

Family Folklore Collections

Have children interview family members about stories that have been handed down. These can be written in the students' own words and bound into books. Then institute a Family Folklore day where parents and guardians are invited to the classroom for sharing.

Playwriting

Students can do minor revisions of traditional tales to make them suitable for puppet shows, radio plays, Reader's Theatre, or acting. This could be done with traditional or updated versions. The resulting productions can be shared with classes of younger students. The acts of rewriting and the repeated rereadings for rehearsal support literacy goals in increasing reading fluency.

Summary

Throughout this chapter, we have introduced the types, origins, features, and functions of traditional literature as a cultural phenomenon from all human cultures. We have established that traditional literature has a place in the curriculum as a genre of literature, and also as support for the study of other curricular areas. We have suggested ways to evaluate traditional literature for both cultural and literary purposes. We have also offered many teaching ideas to make using traditional literature in the classroom meaningful, exciting, and supportive of overall literacy goals.

Action Research for Teachers

Helping First/Second-Grade Children Appreciate the Literary Qualities of Folklore

Nancy Bryant
Highland Park Elementary

Kathy Havens
Windermere Elementary

Once upon a time, as first/second-grade teachers, we realized that children lacked experience with traditional literature. We focused our action research on children's written responses to prompts as they were immersed daily in folktales and their variants. We wanted to know what children would learn from participation in a yearlong experience with folktales, and if use of story elements in their writing would increase.

We each planned and implemented a 6-week folktale study where children were involved in numerous whole-group, small-group, and individual projects. Whole-group activities included class murals, mobiles, comparison charts, and drama. Children were also involved in cooking, letter writing, creating a museum, and arranging a folktale feast. Children were also engaged in individual book extension projects. We then continued reading folktales on a daily basis throughout the rest of the school year.

After we read many folktales aloud to the class, the children responded to the following prompt: "Can you write a story like this?" Some children drew pictures; many wrote words or a story; and for others, we took dictation. We collected four writing samples (September, November, January, and March) using the same writing prompt with all of the children in both classes; the September writing was a "pretest" to determine whether the unit had any effect on the children's understanding. We analyzed our writing samples by defining and charting the following story elements: title, opening, setting, vocabulary, refrains, characters (known or created), character develop-

ment, conflict, resolution, dialogue, magical elements, ending, retelling (memorized or varied), and constructed stories.

As we collected and examined the children's writing samples from the first semester, we saw very little growth in their use of story elements, even though they had been exposed daily to these elements. At this point, we decided to do some direct whole-group instruction of the story elements. For example, we asked children to locate the opening of a favorite tale. We then read these openings aloud and listed them on a chart, which was displayed and referred to for the rest of the year. We did similar lessons for settings, characters, endings, and story conflicts. We also generated a list of things children knew about folktales, including the theme of threes, happy endings, evil stepmothers, and magical objects.

After the direct instruction, many children began to incorporate the basic story elements in their writing such as title, opening, setting, characters, conflict, and resolution. In addition, children used many of the basic story elements in their independent daily writing such as journal writing and self-authored books, and even in the district writing assessment.

When planning for this research project, we thought that by the conclusion of the year, children would be able to construct their own folktales. In retrospect, we now believe that this may not have been a developmental possibility for first- and second-grade writers: Only a very few of the most capable children were able to attain this goal.

In summary, we believe our study contributed to children's writing more-developed stories. We wonder if these children would have made growth in their writing regardless of the study. Of course, the answer is yes, but would they have included

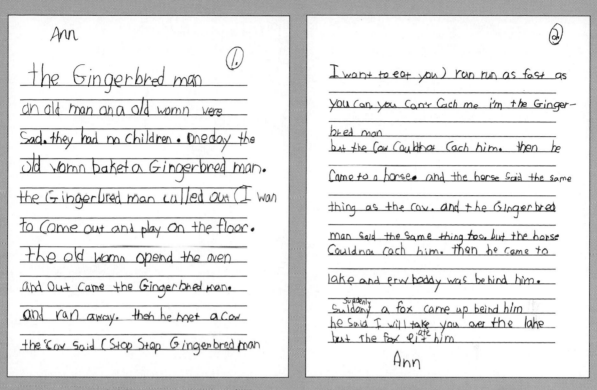

Figure 6.4 A Child's Use of Literary Elements From "The Gingerbread Man"

some of the elements found in folktales? We speculate our instruction made a difference.

As a result of our action research, we recommend that classroom teachers read folktales on a regular basis as part of their literacy programs. We also encourage direct instruction of story elements, because this resulted in children's writing more-developed stories. So, snip snap snout, this tale is told out!

Writing Sample

Figure 6.4 illustrates how one child (Ann) used literary elements from "The Gingerbread Man" to create her own rendition. Dialogue from the story and the sequential structure are two elements that Ann has internalized, then "borrowed" for her writing.

Chapter 7

PICTURE BOOKS

"Children's books are a short literary form like a sonnet. The soundness of their structure is therefore crucial—more important than in longer and more leisurely forms of writing." (Rosemary Wells, in Zinsser, 1990, p. 123)

Picture books are such a joy. Like all good literature, they take readers on safe adventures without ever having to leave their chairs. Picture books are, indeed, for all seasons, for all reasons, in all genres, and for all students. Today's picture books are found not only in the nursery but also on the shelves of middle school libraries and in classrooms at every grade level in between. Picture books cut across age boundaries—teachers will have no trouble finding appropriate titles for any age, for any aspect of the curriculum, or just for enjoyment. Using picture books is an experience we want all students to have as a way to live the joys of literature.

This chapter discusses important aspects of picture books, and it will also explore some of the many possibilities of sharing picture books with all students at all grade levels. Here are the questions we explore:

- What are picture books? What are their elements—how do we talk about the craft of the artist?

- How do we evaluate quality of the writing?

- What are some different kinds of picture books?

- What criteria do we use to make good selections? How do we use criteria when building a classroom collection of picture books?

- How do we help students talk about both the art and the content of picture books?

- What are good strategies for sharing picture books in classrooms that support curriculum, meet the needs of diverse learners, and promote critical thinking?

What Are Picture Books?

Picture books are the marriage of literature and fine arts into a unique literary form. In this form, the art extends and animates the story in ways that "vivify, quicken, and vitalize" (Sendak, 1988, p. 3) the experience of reading. To compare a picture book to a novel would be like comparing television to radio; they are different media that are experienced differently. Picture books are not

Writing for very young children is the most difficult discipline I know.

Rosemary Wells, picture book author, in Zinsser, 1990, p. 128.

In a thirty-two-page picture book, text and illustrations are shared, so space is limited. I like to keep the main text as short and accessible as possible, so as to not turn off a reluctant reader (like myself).

Aliki, 1996, p. 209

one genre. Rather, they are a form that cuts across all genres.

With few exceptions, picture books have 32 pages. These may include the title page, but endpapers are also added in hardcover books. Although the pages of a picture book are rarely numbered, they are generally the same length.

For all picture books, even in those intended for younger readers, there is an expectation that the books are well written with pleasing, literary language. Age is taken into account, but the writing is not simplistic, choppy, or condescending to children.

Authors take the art of writing these books seriously. "No kind of writing lodges itself so deeply in our memory, echoing there for the rest of our lives, as the books that we met in our childhood," William Zinsser explains; "when we grow up and read them to our own children, they are the oldest of old friends. Their spell is woven so simply and in so few words that anyone might think they were simple to write" (1990, p. 3).

Zinsser goes on to explain that "to enter and hold the mind of a child or a young person is one of the hardest of all writers' tasks" (1990, p. 3). If anyone thinks that writing children's books is child's play, we hope that idea has been put to rest.

The marriage of art and writing in a picture book means that the reader has the privilege of experiencing the creativity of two individuals (when the illustrator and the author are different people) or two aspects of one highly talented person's capabilities (when the artist and the author are the same person). The whole—the finished product—is far greater than the sum of its parts. The two forms—art and writing—have an effect on readers in ways that differ somewhat from reading novels, for example.

The process of producing a picture book begins with the text. After the text is approved for publication, it is sent to the artist, who must

Tech Note
Read more about Rosemary Wells on the CD-ROM that accompanies this book.

Tech Note
Find out more about Aliki on the CD-ROM that accompanies this book.

interpret the text in his or her own vision that will enhance and extend the words. Typically, the author does not know what the artist has done until the book is complete!

Because of the variety of good picture books available, you will find that different picture books are designed for different audiences. Whereas some are geared toward younger readers, others contain more sophisticated content and are intended for students in intermediate and middle grades. Some would even argue that there are picture books intended mostly for adults. Using picture books with older readers is discussed later in this chapter. Although they may have once been thought of as solely for younger children, this is no longer the case. Picture books are for *everybody*.

Picture Books Are a Form, Not a Genre

Picture books can be categorized into any genre. Although many are classified as fiction, they may be traditional literature, poetry, fantasy, science fiction, realistic fiction, and historical fiction.

Picture books that are considered fiction are designated as "juvenile fiction" on the title page verso (sometimes referred to as "verso" page) or copyright page. Which genre of fiction a picture book exemplifies is often a matter for teacher and librarians to determine, depending on the book's content. Understanding picture books makes more sense once we understand how they developed as a form.

How Picture Books Came to Be

The idea that pictures can illustrate a story predates the printing press (Townsend, 1983). Early humans left their picture stories on the walls of caves, many of which still survive. Some of these ancient pictures may have been writing systems with recurring symbols that were meaningful to the community that used them. Consequently, the idea of bringing text and pictures together is a quite natural union.

Randolph Caldecott, for whom the prestigious Caldecott Medal is named, is generally considered the father of the picture book (Marcus, 1998; Sendak, 1988). British-born Caldecott was a nineteenth-century English illustrator whose early books were lively and "set the standard that artists ever since have hoped to match" (Marcus, 1998, p. 4). Two of his works are considered the earliest picture books: *Sing a Song for Sixpence* and *Hey Diddle Diddle*. In these works, it is evident that Caldecott did not

> *A good picture book must ring with emotional content, so that children care about what's going on. Otherwise they will fall asleep.*
>
> *Rosemary Wells, in Zinsser, 1990, p. 129*

merely create illustrations to go along with the words; rather, there was an interpretation, a unique perspective that suggests the illustrations were orchestrated carefully. Sendak relates that "Caldecott is an illustrator, he is a songwriter, he is a choreographer, he is a stage manager, he is a decorator, he is a theater person; he's superb, simply" (1988, p. 24).

Some experts also consider the work of Beatrix Potter a strong influence on the history of the picture book, although the format of these little books from another century differ from picture books today. When Potter was doing her writing and illustrating at the end of the nineteenth century, publishing books solely for children was still most unusual.

At first glance, one might think the illustrations in *The Tale of Peter Rabbit*, first published in 1902, are a good complement to the story. Yet there are subtleties in the expressions on characters' faces that suggest feelings not communicated in the words. Sendak (1988) suggests that little birds in the pictures of Flopsy, Mopsy, and Cottontail are emotional mirrors to the actions in Potter's imaginative stories. All in all, Potter used art in the manner we have come to expect of good picture books. Her work helped build the form we know today.

According to Sendak, Frenchman Jean de Brunhoff "practically reinvented the illustrated book" (1988, p. 95). Between 1931 and 1939, de Brunhoff turned out a number of works, beginning with the familiar elephant Babar; these stories were created to amuse two children in the family. De Brunhoff came from a publishing family (both his brother and his brother-in-law were magazine editors), so he was no stranger to publishing. Furthermore, de Brunhoff's books exemplify for Sendak the "heart of [his] conception of what turns a picture book into a work of art. The graphics are tightly linked to the loose prose-poetry, remarkable for its ease of expression" (1988, p. 99). Sendak contends that it was this body of work that forever changed the nature of illustrated books.

Today's picture books have evolved and emerged over the decades from Potter's distinguished contributions. Many of today's picture books are expertly written and illustrated. There is a wealth of titles for a wide range of ages, and it is our important work as teachers and librarians to lead students to the best.

Tech Note
More about the history of children's literature is available on the CD-ROM that accompanies this book.

Elements of Picture Books

Picture books consist of literary texts and illustrations that have been strategically designed to be effective and attractive. They are assembled for publication in a complex and lengthy process that makes them more expensive than many other kinds of books. Each of these elements is presented and discussed in the section that follows.

Exploring the Art and Design of Picture Books

Illustrator Uri Shulevitz (1985) states that "the main function of illustration is to illuminate text, to throw light on words. In fact, illustration in medieval books is called *illumination* and the term *illustration* derives from the Latin verb meaning 'to light up,' to illuminate" (p. 120). In the next section of this chapter, we introduce you to the notion of learning to look at illustrations—to see in what ways they "light up" or illuminate the words. Learning to look more deeply and more thoroughly at how illustrators do this increases our appreciation and knowledge of how picture books work.

Lawrence Sipe (1998) states:

Every part of the picture book is meaningful, from front to back cover. If we simply begin to read where the story begins without examining its cover, dust jacket, endpages, title page, and other front matter, we miss much meaning. (p. 66)

We agree! There is so much to explore inside and on the outside of picture books. Each encounter with a picture book always reveals something new.

Just as we have specific terms to describe a story, a poem, or a book of nonfiction, we also have a specialized vocabulary for talking about picture books. The Terms for Teachers feature on p. 150 defines these. In addition, to introduce how to explore picture books deeply and carefully, we model a think-aloud of a book (a strategy we discussed in chapter 3). Then we describe three important aspects about illustrations: the visual or pictorial elements, the media, and the style of illustrations. Later in the chapter, we describe more ways that your students can grow in their appreciation and understanding about the graphic arts of the picture book.

Learning to Look: Outside and Inside Picture Books

Let's explore picture books by looking at one of our current favorites—Jennifer Armstrong's *Audubon: Painter of Birds in the Wild Frontier*, illustrated by Jos. A. Smith. We begin by examining it, like meeting a new person. What are our first impressions?

We share our impressions of *Audubon* through a think-aloud. John Stewig (1995) talks about the importance of *learning to look,* and he says that art and words interact with and enrich each other. He urges adults to become knowledgeable in order to help children appreciate the richness and creativity of picture books. We believe that learning to look at how words and art go together is critical for teachers as well as for students of all ages, and that through a think-aloud, we can model this process for students.

A Think-Aloud That Models How Effective Readers Explore a Book

First, we model activating prior knowledge. We already know some things about the time period in which John James Audubon was a painter—the early 1800s, when there was an expansive frontier to explore. We notice the size of the book—tall and large—that may reflect the grandness of the frontier.

We browse through the book and are awed by the spectacular title page with a portrait of Audubon and by the beautiful illustrations that grace subsequent pages. The illustrations look to be watercolor; we've seen many picture books where the illustrator has used watercolors. We recognize the qualities indicating that watercolor is the medium. Perhaps we'll learn more somewhere in the book about the medium the illustrator used. We'll look carefully to see if that information is included on the copyright page or elsewhere.

As we continue to browse through the book, we find notes from the author and the artist on the copyright page, which in this case is the very last page. We scan this page for interesting information and insights. We learn that this book is listed as juvenile literature and biography in the Library of Congress information. We also learn that Audubon lived from 1785 to 1851 and was a nineteenth-century painter and naturalist who became famous for his paintings of birds. We also find that the illustrator, Jos. A. Smith, dedicated this book to his father, who read him a biography of Audubon when he was a child with mumps. It was that book that made him want to be an artist! This is interesting information because it means that the illustrator had an early and deep appreciation for Audubon. There is a lot to learn from the copyright page that can contribute to our appreciation of this book.

We see that both the author and the illustrator discuss how difficult it was to re-create information when what is written about Audubon is not definitive. Author Jennifer Armstrong acknowledges that through research about Audubon, it is difficult to separate what's true from the more legendary aspects of the man. No one questions his contribution to natural history, however. Jos. A Smith also describes the challenges of illustrating this book. Because there are no photographs of Audubon or what he saw,

Terms for Teachers

Discourse of Picture Books

Artistic Design—An artist called a book designer is responsible for the artistic design of a picture book. Size, paper color and quality, font, style of endpapers, cover art, and so on, are all decisions related to artistic design.

Bleed—A picture or background that goes to the edge of a page, with no white space showing. A full bleed occurs when the picture or background extends on all four edges.

Challenge Page—In a predictable book or an early-reading book, this page, typically near the end of the story, contains more text than most other pages and presents some challenges to the reader in length and sometimes more vocabulary than in the rest of the book.

Cloth Binding—A rigid book cover (also called a hard cover) made of cardboard covered by cloth, special paper, or plastic; costs more but lasts longer than paperback binding.

Composition—The arrangement of elements on a page or in a photograph or other piece of art.

Copyright Page—This page, usually located on the reverse of the title page, contains the copyright, the name and address of the publisher, the book's ISBN number, genre, Library of Congress Cataloging-in-Publication Data, and more. Sometimes the author's birth year, the art medium, and the number of the book's edition and printing are listed.

Cover Art—The art, generally created by the book's illustrator, that has been selected for a book's cover. Of course, many books that are not picture books (including this one!) also have cover art. Cover art can help a book get the attention of readers and/or can foreshadow what the book is about.

Dedication Page—Many books have been dedicated to people, and this information is generally given on a page before or after the title page. Authors and illustrators both add their dedications.

Dummy—A mock-up of the finished book with cut-and-pasted text and sketches of the proposed pictures.

Dust Jacket—The removable protective paper cover on a hardcover book, containing some cover art, and additional information about the book, author, and illustrator on the flaps.

Endpapers—The paper on the inside front and back cover of a cloth-bound book. Sometimes the paper is plain, or it may be illustrated with images consistent with the book's illustrations. Endpapers strengthen the binding and hide the sewing or glued parts of the spine.

Genre—The category to which a book's content belongs, such as fiction, traditional literature, poetry, etc.

Illustrated Book, Illustrated Text—A book that contains illustrations, although the story can stand alone without the art.

Illustrator—The person or team who creates the art that goes into a book.

Medium—The art material used to create an illustration. Often the medium is mentioned on the copyright page. (Media commonly used in picture books are listed in the Terms for Teachers feature on page 156.)

Page Layout—The look of pages in a book—where the text and illustrations will be placed, font size, whether text will appear on each page or on alternating pages, etc. These decisions are made by book designers.

Paperback—A glued paper binding, without endpapers, which makes a book less expensive but also less durable.

Signature—A sheet of printed pages that when folded become part of a book or publication.

Thumbnail—A very small sample sketch, or a small version of a picture or photo; used for planning because many can be viewed at one time.

Title Page—The page after the cover and before the beginning of the story that contains the title and the names of the author, the illustrator, and usually the publisher as well.

Two/Three/Four Color Printing—Picture books are colorful; up to four colors of ink are used to obtain the desired results. The more colors, the more expensive the process and the higher the resulting cost of the book. The paper passes through the press once for each color family.

Visual Literacy—The way art or other graphics contribute to the understanding of the book, coupled with the ability of the reader to go back and forth between words and nontextual elements to gain meaning from both. Book artists understand how visual literacy works and thus plan illustrations features that extend and enhance meaning.

White Space—The area on a page not covered by print or illustrations.

Smith was forced to use his imagination to create his illustrations; he imagined what Audubon saw, and painted that.

Take the dust jacket off and spread it out flat. The front of the book jacket, which depicts Audubon on horseback, looks like it also is done in watercolors. Audubon is shown crossing a river while sketching what appears to be an eagle swooping down to the water to grab a fish. Other animals and birds depicted are indicative of the bountiful wildlife of the period. The back of the jacket shows an excited and somewhat bewildered Audubon, who looks like he has discovered masses of birds in flight. Under the dust jacket, the cover depicts the very same scenes (depending on the edition you have, of course).

The endpapers are a deep forest green, suggestive of the expansive forests of the early 1800s. It is a good color choice because it reflects the setting of the book.

The title page is impressive: The illustrator painted a portrait of Audubon at about waist level looking outward to readers. His pensive look makes him appear to be fascinated by what he observes in the distance. The illustrator may have tried to capture how Audubon must have looked as he was ready to sketch—pensive as he studied his subject.

We end the think-aloud here to say that the title page is an excellent entrée into this book. At this point, it would be interesting to invite students to comment on what they see in this illustration of Audubon and what predictions they make about the content of the book.

Visual Elements

Nothing about the art in picture books is random. Pictures are built on principles, and these principles influence a reader's response (Bang, 1991). The basic terms we use to describe the visual or pictorial elements in picture books are line, color, shape, texture, and design or composition. We define each term here and give examples from *Audubon* for each of them. We also offer examples from other picture books.

Line. Illustrators use line to define what they draw or paint. Lines show movement, shape, and texture, or they suggest emotion or mood. Lines can be of different widths and textures and can be placed horizontally or vertically on the page.

One picture from *Audubon* shows the setting after an earthquake hits; the illustrator has used diagonal lines effectively to show the movement of trees. He does this again to give the feeling of 9,000 swifts flying about. Jennifer Armstrong's choice of words nicely parallels the illustration when the birds are described as a "tornado" and as "twittering".

Jos. A. Smith, AUDUBON: PAINTER OF BIRDS IN THE WILD FRONTIER, by Jennifer Armstrong. Illustrated by Jos. A. Smith, 2003, Harry N. Abrams.

Illustrators use line to show action, movement, and more. In *The Grannyman*, Judith Byron Schachner uses curved, jagged, and straight lines to bring out the character of two cats—one old and stodgy and one young and playful.

In the picture-book biography, *You Forgot Your Skirt, Amelia Bloomer!*, by Shana Corey, illustrator Chesley McLaren uses lines in dashing, vibrant, curvy, flowing ways to capture the bold spirit of a woman who made wearing bloomers fashionable in the 1800s.

Color. Illustrators have choices regarding use of color or shades of black and white to reflect the plot or the topic of the book, to mirror the tone or mood of the characters, or to authentically represent cultural aspects and the setting of the book. Bright colors (red, orange, and yellow) make us feel warm and cozy, as in *Wild Child*, by Lynn Plourde and illustrated by Greg Couch. Couch's illustrations for this exquisite book about autumn are done with bright, fiery

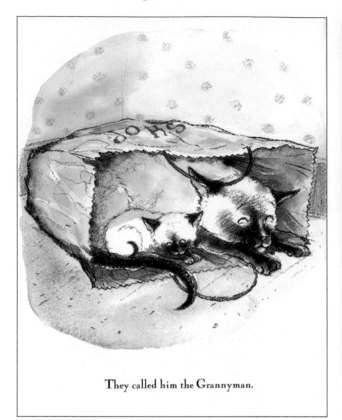

They called him the Grannyman.

From THE GRANNYMAN by Judith Byron Schachner, copyright © 1999 by Judith Byron Schachner. Used by permission of Dutton Children's Books, A Division of Penguin Young Readers Group, A Member of Penguin Group (USA) Inc., 345 Hudson Street, New York, NY 10014. All rights reserved.

Cover from SECTOR 7 by David Wiesner. Jacket illustrations copyright © 1999 by David Wiesner. Reprinted by permission of Clarion Books/Houghton Mifflin Company. All rights reserved.

reds, brilliant yellows, and oranges. Use of warm colors that are associated with agriculture is effective in *Harvesting Hope: The Story of Cesar Chavez*. On the other hand, paler, cool colors (green, blue, and violet) make us feel calm, quiet, and peaceful. Examples of these colors are found in David Wiesner's *Sector 7*—a wordless picture book that takes place in the evening.

Here are some basic words that help us talk about color. *Hue* is the color itself. *Primary colors* are red, blue, and yellow. These are the basic colors that can't be made by mixing colors. *Secondary colors*—orange, green, and purple—are created by mixing two primary colors. *Tertiary colors* are the ones between the primary and secondary colors, such as yellow-green and blue-violet. *Value* is how light or dark a color is, based on adding either black, to achieve a *shade*, or white, to create a *tint*. *Jumanji*, by Chris Van Allsburg, is an excellent example of how an illustrator uses light and dark for a three-

dimensional appearance. In this case, the illustrations are monochromatic—all one color.

Saturation indicates brightness or dullness in colors. Emotion and tone can be manipulated by how light or dark the colors are, as seen in *Molly Bannaky*, by Alice McGill and illustrated by Chris K. Soentpiet. Soentpiet's watercolor illustrations are outstanding in the way he uses light and color to focus attention on these historical characters and events.

In *Audubon*, illustrator Jos. A. Smith uses woodsy hues—secondary and tertiary colors—to reflect the wilderness setting as well as the dress of the day. Audubon himself is depicted in a brown coonskin hat with a visor, leggings, and a dark jacket. In the artist's note, Smith says that he used Audubon's self-portrait from his sketchbook and portraits done by his sons to help him accurately portray Audubon. Brighter colors are reserved for the accurate clothing of the Shawnee people depicted in the book.

In Barbara Cooney's *Miss Rumphius*, who lived by the sea, the colors used echo the New England seaside—lots of blues and greens and white—perfect for this delightful picture book.

Grace Lin evokes a warm, busy family atmosphere with primary and secondary colors in *Dim Sum for Everyone!*
From DIM SUM FOR EVERYONE! by Grace Lin, copyright © 2001 by Grace Lin. Used by permission of Alfred A. Knopf, an imprint of Random House Children's Books, a division of Random House, Inc.

Both setting and mood are superbly portrayed in *Virgie Goes to School With Us Boys*, by Elizabeth Fitzgerald Howard and illustrated by E. B.Lewis. Lewis's watercolors portray the post–Civil War South as Virgie, an African American girl, proves that she can go to school just like her brothers. The colors accurately depict the time and communicate a poverty-ridden and subdued postwar climate.

A loving, joyful mood is cast in *Just the Two of Us*, by Will Smith and illustrated by Kadir Nelson. The love of father and son is portrayed in subdued values. Character facial expressions grow brighter with each new step the son takes from birth to adolescence. Thus the art helps to communicate the subtleties in the story.

Shape.   Illustrators use intersecting lines to create shapes to depict mood or setting, or to represent cultures accurately. Shapes used in *Audubon* reflect little-explored, sparsely inhabited, and pristine forestlands. In one picture, the immense size of a tree occupying most of the page signals the enormity of the wilderness, and in others,

many birds suggests the density of the forests and landscape.

The framed illustrations that take on the feel and look of a theatre stage are just right for the mythical and fantastic plot in *Hey, Al*, by Arthur Yorinks and illustrated by Richard Egielski. Paul Goble also uses both line and shape effectively in *The Girl Who Loved Wild Horses*, a Native American folktale. In the herds of buffalo he paints, we have the repeating shapes of the massive buffalo bodies, and their running in diagonal lines shows action.

Texture.   When readers want to reach out and touch an illustration, the artist probably has used a combination of shape, line, and color to create a surface quality or texture that readers respond to. In *Audubon*, Jos. A. Smith depicts the grand size of a butternut tree, so large that 9,000 swifts call the inside of it home. He establishes the size of the tree by positioning Audubon in front of it and extending the tree beyond the top of the page.

Illustrators Cara Moser and Barry Moser use shape to effectively create a large, part fearsome but mostly lovable

Cover from MOLLY BANNAKY by Alice McGill, illustrations by Chris Soentpiet. Jacket art copyright © 1999 by Chris Soentpiet. Reprinted by permission of Houghton Mifflin Company. All rights reserved.

Fourth grader Tiara, interviewing illustrator Jerry Pinkney at the 1999 Virginia Hamilton Conference at Kent State University.

dog named Truman in *Sit, Truman*, by Dan Harper. Truman is so enormous that he almost jumps off the page. The soft brown watercolors and Truman's size invite a good-natured pat from readers. The same holds true for a smaller puppy named Hugs, who goes out one day to see how many kisses he can collect. In *Hugs and Kisses*, by Christophe Loupy and illustrated by Eve Tharlet, the little puppy, Hugs, is made soft and lovable by the illustrator's skillful use of brown tints and soft lines, creating a texture to touch.

Design or Composition.   An illustration comes together through the artist's successful use of line, color, shape, and texture. Norton and Norton (2003) say that "when an illustration has an overall unity, balance, and sense of rhythm, viewers experience aesthetic pleasure; when the design is weak, viewers often feel that they are looking at an incomplete, incoherent, or boring picture" (p. 122). Similarly, Uri Shulevitz (1985) says, "A picture should not be a puzzle. When a picture is unreadable, it defeats the purpose of illustration" (p. 121).

The design of an entire book comes together with some other important considerations. In *Audubon*, the design of the book, as already discussed, suits the content of the book. From the size to the cover, the quality of the pages, the artwork, and the text, all work in harmony in this book. This combination makes for a unified whole that is an aesthetically pleasing book to read.

The Three Questions: Based on a Story by Leo Tolstoy, written and illustrated by Jon J. Muth, balances each illustration with a distinctive layout that permits the eye to focus on the most important object or objects in the picture. This is also the case in *Home Run: The Story of Babe Ruth*, by Robert Burleigh and illustrated by Mike Wimmer. In this book, the right-hand pages are illustrated with larger-than-life characters done in oils. Many of the illustrations almost have the look and feel of photographs. These powerful illustrations, combined with text on the left-hand pages, honor Babe Ruth with legendary status.

Illustrator Molly Bang (2000) offers readers principles of design that make it fun to take another look at illustrations you know well and test out what she suggests. Figure 7.1 presents some common principles used in determining the composition or design of an illustration.

How Do We Determine What Media the Artist Used?

Medium is often very difficult to determine. A trend today is for picture books to provide information about the medium that was

Tech Note

Profiles of Jerry Pinkney, Nikki Grimes, Julius Lester, and Gloria Jean Pinkney, who were also interviewed by fourth grader Tiara, are on the CD-ROM that accompanies this book.

So the horse bent down
and gave him a big kiss.
Hugs closed his eyes and
smiled. He'd never ever had
a kiss from a horse!
It was a bit damp of course,
and sticky, but it was
quite warm.
Hugs thanked the horse
and went on.

From HUGS AND KISSES by Christophe Loupy and illustrations by Eve Tharlet. Copyright © 2001 by North-South Books Inc. Used by permission.

Figure 7.1 How Pictures Work

A skilled artist knows how illustrations work. Nothing about the art in picture books is random or done without thought. Pictures are built on principles, and these principles help influence reader response (Bang, 2000). They are used in determining the qualities and composition of a page, along with the use of sharp or curved lines, colors, angles, and positioning.

☀ What is most important in the picture is larger and nearer to the center of the page.

☀ Sharp, angular lines with points communicate strength and harshness, and rounded and curved lines communicate warmth and softness.

☀ Lighter background colors suggest safety, and dark and bold colors in the background suggest something scary or unknown.

☀ Objects vary in size to create the background and the foreground and to give a sense of depth.

☀ Diagonal lines suggest action or movement.

☀ Shapes leaning toward the protagonist can communicate the blocking of something, and shapes leaning away from the protagonist can signal something opening or moving forward.

☀ Horizontal lines and shapes create a sense of restfulness and calm.

☀ Vertical lines suggest height and energy.

☀ Including different colors or shapes can create contrasts that draw the viewer's attention.

Terms for Teachers

Media Used in Illustrations

Paints

Generally two kinds: translucent and transparent, such as watercolors, and opaque, such as tempera, gouache, and oils.

Acrylic—Plastic-based, synthetic paint that creates an opaque effect; dries faster than oils, and so the illustrator can repaint or rework the painting sooner.

Examples: *The Very First Thanksgiving Day,* by Rhonda Gowler Greene and illustrated by Susan Gaber; *Edward in the Jungle,* by David McPhail; *Grandfather Counts,* by Andrea Cheng and illustrated by Ange Zhang.

Gouache (pronounced *gwash*)—Water-based paint composed of powdered color mixed with chalk and looks like tempera.

Examples: *The Yellow House: Vincent van Gogh and Paul Gauguin Side by Side,* by Susan Goldman Rubin and illustrated by Jos. A. Smith (watercolor and gouache); *The Glorious Flight: Across the Channel with Louis Blériot,* by Alice and Martin Provensen; *The Trouble with Baby,* by Marisabina Russo.

Tempera—A quick-drying, bright paint that can also be diluted with water to create softer effects.

Example: *Where the Wild Things Are,* by Maurice Sendak.

Watercolor—A very popular medium of artists, made by mixing pigments with water.

Examples: *Miss Hunnicutt's Hat,* by Jeff Brumbeau and illustrated by Gail de Marcken; *All I See,* by Cynthia Rylant and illustrated by Peter Catalanotto.

Woodcut and Scratchboard

Scratchboard—Black ink is applied to a drawing board and a sharp tool is used to scratch through the surface when dry.

Examples: *The Ballad of Belle Dorcas,* by William H. Hooks and illustrated by Brian Pinkney; *Seven Candles for Kwanzaa,* by Andrea Davis Pinkney and illustrated by Brian Pinkney.

Woodcuts—An ancient form of illustration that could be used even in early printing presses. Cut marks are made with a sharp instrument into the surface of a block of wood, paint or ink is applied, and the block is pressed onto paper to duplicate.

Examples: *At Christmastime,* by Valerie Worth and illustrated by Antonio Frasconi; *A Story, a Story,* by Gail E. Haley; *Snowflake Bentley,* by Jacqueline Briggs Martin and illustrated by Mary Azarian; *When the Moon Is Full: A Lunar Year,* by Penny Pollock and illustrated by Mary Azarian; *Once a Mouse,* by Marcia Brown.

Other Construction Techniques

Collage—Artwork created by arranging combinations of materials such as cloth or paper on a flat surface.

Examples: *The Snowy Day,* by Ezra Jack Keats; *Smoky Night,* by Eve Bunting and illustrated by David Diaz; *The Very Hungry Caterpillar,* by Eric Carle; *Market Day,* by Lois Ehlert; *Steamboat! The Story of Captain Blanche Leathers,* by Judith Heide Gilliland and illustrated by Holly Meade; *Golem,* by David Wisniewski (cut-paper sculpture); *Where the Forest Meets the Sea,* by Jeannie Baker (collage construction or assemblage using a variety of actual materials); *Animals in Flight,* by Steve Jenkins and Robin Page (cut-paper collage; spot illustrations created in Adobe Illustrator); *Sleep, Sleep, Sleep: A Lullaby for Little Ones Around the World,* by Nancy Van Laan and illustrated by Holly Meade (artwork created with torn paper).

Computer-Generated Graphics—Artists create their work on the computer.

Examples: *Gus and Button,* by Saxton Freymann and Joost Elffers (photographs scanned and collaged on the computer). *Rolie Polie Olie,* by William Joyce; *Gluey: A Snail Tale,* by Vivian Walsh and illustrated by J. Otto Seibold (illustrations done in Adobe Illustrator).

Paper Engineering—The art of folding papers in ways to create pop-up or movable parts within a picture book.

Example: *Cookie Count: A Tasty Pop-Up,* by Robert Sabuda.

Crayon, Pencil, and Charcoal

Charcoal—

Example: *Olivia Saves the Circus,* by Ian Falconer (charcoal and gouache on paper).

Conté Pencil—A hard pencil that gives a charcoal effect

Examples: *Jumanji* and the sequel, *Zathura: A Space Adventure,* by Chris Van Allsburg.

Crayon—

Example: *Fish Is Fish,* by Leo Lionni

Pencil—

Examples: *The Cat's Purr,* by Ashley Bryan; *The Song and Dance Man,* by Karen Ackerman and illustrated by Stephen Gammell (colored pencil); *Hondo and Fabian,* by Peter McCarty (colored pencil); *Oh Yeah!,* by Tom Birdseye and illustrated by Ethan Long (colored pencil and acrylics); *Alphabeasts,* by Wallace Edwards (watercolor and colored pencil).

Terms for Teachers

Range of Styles of Illustrations in Picture Books

Cartoon Art—This style is simple, playful, and unrealistic or exaggerated. Cartoon style is particularly good for creating humor and satire.

Examples: *Giggle, Giggle, Quack* and *Click, Clack Moo: Cows That Type*, by Doreen Cronin and illustrated by Betsy Lewin; *Officer Buckle and Gloria*, by Peggy Rathmann.

Expressionistic Art—This style is used as a way for the artist to depict feelings and emotions. Objects and people do not have to be represented realistically, as they do in representational art.

Examples: *Hiroshima, No Pika*, by Toshi Maruki; *Sophie*, by Mem Fox and illustrated by Aminah Brenda Lynn Robinson; *Smoky Night*, by Eve Bunting and illustrated by David Diaz.

Impressionist Art—In this style, the artist is interested in the influence of light on color, and objects are not well defined. This artwork can look abstract.

Examples: *Mr. Rabbit and the Lovely Present*, by Charlotte Zolotow and illustrated by Maurice Sendak; *Say It!*, by Charlotte Zolotow and illustrated by James Stevenson.

Naive or Folk Art—This style is associated with self-taught artists who paint from their own experiences. Typically, there is a lot of detail associated with folk art and naive styles.

Examples: *Tar Beach*, by Faith Ringgold; *A Chair for My Mother*, by Vera Williams.

Realistic or Representational Art—This style mirrors what we see in real life. The artwork echoes situations and characters in a real or authentic way.

Examples: *To Climb a Waterfall*, by Jean Craighead George and illustrated by Thomas Locker; *Butterfly House*, by Eve Bunting and illustrated by Greg Shed; *I Have an Aunt on Marlborough Street*, by Kathryn Lasky and illustrated by Susan Guevara.

Surrealistic Art—In this style, things aren't what they seem. The artist plays with the viewer's perceptions, making the scene appear a little out of kilter. At the same time, the artist makes people and objects look real.

Examples: *Jumanji* and *The Mysteries of Harris Burdick*, by Chris Van Allsburg; *Tuesday* and *Free Fall*, by David Wiesner; *Changes*, by Anthony Browne.

---

used, typically on the copyright page. This is a welcome feature, and we would encourage more publishers to offer this information to their readers. As students become more thoughtful about and interested in illustrations in their favorite books, they are anxious to find specific information about them.

For example, interesting information about the woodcut prints appears on the copyright page of *Sally Goes to the Farm*, an oversized book about Sally, a black Labrador. In this book, she takes her first trip to the country. Writer and illustrator Stephen Huneck provides excellent, informative notes about his artwork for readers. He explains that to make a woodcut print, he begins with a crayon drawing in which he lays out shapes and colors. Next he carves each shape on a block of wood; when he has finished, he has a set of carved blocks, one for each color in the print. Then each block is inked with the appropriate color, and special acid-free paper is pressed onto the ink. The process is repeated for all the carved blocks. Finally, the finished print is hung up to dry.

An extra challenge for readers in determining the media used is that many artists combine media, called *mixed media*, to showcase their work. For example, in the Caldecott award–winning *Joseph Had a Little Overcoat*, illustrator Simms Taback used watercolors, collage, gouache, pencil, and ink. Aminah Brenda Lynn Robinson, the illustrator for the intriguing book *Sophie*, by Mem Fox, used acrylics, dyes, and house paint on rag cloth. This blend of paints and materials gives a very distinctive appearance that complements the story. The Terms for Teachers feature on this page describes media and artistic styles used in illustrations.

Exploring the Writing in Picture Books

Before you began this chapter, you may have assumed that writing a picture book is easier than writing a novel. Perhaps you haven't paid much attention to the writing in a picture book. However, the text of a picture book must be composed carefully to say a lot in a limited amount of space. Within this limitation, there is still an expectation of skilled, high-quality writing. The features we expect in a novel are largely the same for a picture book, whether it's a story, an informational book, or poetry. Some of the aspects of good writing are delineated here.

Characters

Let's start with a picture book that is narrative—one that tells a story. In good storytelling, we need characters. Characters are the heart and soul of fiction, and the same is true in a picture book. When readers become hooked on a particular picture book series with recurring characters, such as Norman Bridwell's giant red dog "Clifford" Tomie dePaola's "Stega Nona" and "Big Anthony," or Marc Brown's aardvark "Arthur," it's because they have formed strong attachments to the characters.

Not all characters that authors create show up again, of course. Usually the writer must develop the character to be appealing and believable in just one book. The art will play a key role here, but early on in a picture book, we begin to get to know a character. Just as in fiction, we learn about characters by what they say, what they do, and what others (sometimes the narrator) tell about them. As in all good writing, "show, don't tell" is still preferred. Rather than saying that a character is sad, a skilled writer might make the character cry, hide in closets, or miss a loved one—a way to show the character's sadness without saying it outright. Thus readers infer sadness as they transact with the story.

Plot

The plot is the sequence of events in a narrative, usually centered on a problem or an issue. Plots could involve a character struggling with issues of growing up, a mystery, or a character trying to get somewhere, accomplish a task, escape from something, change something, etc.

In picture books, plots are often simple and straightforward, without complexities or subplots. Typically the main character is about the age of the intended audience. Or a youthful narrator may tell a story about a person or an event. One useful idea to examine with students is "Who is telling the story?" In *Ira Sleeps Over* (Waber), the storyteller is Ira, the young boy about to go on his first sleepover. In *Visiting Day* (Woodson), the little girl tells the story about her regular trips to visit her Daddy in prison.

Often the plot unfolds from the narration of a third party, the implied or anonymous storyteller. In *Harvesting Hope: The Story of Cesar Chavez* (Krull), the story unfolds from the anonymous storyteller. In Falconer's *Olivia Saves the Circus*, again the anonymous storyteller relates Olivia's adventures in her imagined world. Readers feel that they are peeking in on Olivia's world. This is another popular way to relate a story's plot.

Setting

Because of the limited space of the picture book, setting needs to be established within the first few pages. This is especially important when the setting is critical to the plot (such as when the weather or the environment is the crux of the story). For example, in Byrd Baylor's *The Desert Is Theirs*, the setting is critical to the story because Baylor is describing the life and beliefs of the Tohono O'odham indigenous people—also called the desert people—in the Arizona Sonoran desert. In Thomas Locker's retelling of *The Boy Who Held Back the Sea*, the setting (the dike that holds back the sea in Holland is breaking and is threatening floods) becomes the crux of the plot with a boy trying to save his village and his people.

Of course, setting is greatly enhanced and enriched by illustrations that extend the reader's understanding of the story. For Baylor's book, artist Peter Parnall has painted wistful watercolors in the hues of the desert. For Locker, the Dutch/Flemish style of oils give a feeling of old Holland and the art of the Dutch Masters, such as Rembrandt. But language also contributes enormously to the setting in a good book.

Well-Written Prose

Good writing has appealing words and sentences. Bill Martin Jr., longtime author and educator, loved to talk about the sounds of language. He wanted children to fall in love with that sound. Good writing is smooth and connected, or sometimes staccato, or jumpy, for effect—just as in a good novel. In Martin and Archambault's *White Dynamite and Curly Kid*, the writers use a staccato effect in the prose to enhance the rodeo feeling, much like a jump-rope rhyme. They write, "Oh! He's outa the chute! Gone plumb dumb wild! KAN-sas, TEX-as, U-tah, Maine. That bull's pitchin' with all his might . . . twenty four tons a' White Dynamite!"

Another feature of well-developed prose is repetition. Repetition is a key aspect of much oral storytelling and appropriately sometimes finds its way into written prose. In Cynthia Rylant's sentimental journey back to *When I Was Young in the Mountains*, each page begins "When I was young in the mountains," and then expresses a different part of rural Appalachian life. The repetition feels soothing, like a recurring, familiar melody.

Repetition is handled more subtly in describing Gloria Houston's *My Great-Aunt Arizona*. Based on Houston's real-life great-aunt and longtime school teacher, Arizona, this story takes readers through one woman's lifetime. Several times throughout the story, Houston repeats a simple description of Arizona's clothing—her dresses, petticoats, shoes, and apron. This phrase is repeated as Arizona ages, which suggests a constancy and steadfastness of the character and her impact on the author.

Well-developed, readable, appealing language is an expectation in all writing, including nonfiction. In good nonfiction writing, we look for aspects such as well-organized writing, clarity and coherence, good explication of ideas, use of figurative language, appropriate tone, and emotional involvement or voice (McClure, 2003). In *Gorilla Walk*, by Ted and Betsy Lewin, the description of heading into gorilla territory is everything we want to see in good writing. The Lewins describe the giant tree ferns as "cat claws" and vines as "ropelike." Or consider how the writing in Doreen Rappaport's *No More! Stories and Songs of Slave Resistance* builds suspense and tension. She describes how a character is suddenly and cautiously aware that an overseeing sailor had forgotten to reshackle him and others. As he realizes the opportunity that has been afforded them, amidst their disbelief of such good luck, they quickly make a plan. Rappaport's choice of words communicates the disbelief, the tension, and the excitement.

Figurative Language

Language that is not literal is called *figurative*. If we say, "The finger that just got caught in the door bled and hurt badly," then we are using literal language—telling it like it is. If we say, "The finger that just got caught in the door felt like a nonstop, pulsing jackhammer, spraying and spitting blood all over," then we are speaking of the same event using comparisons. This is *metaphoric language*. The explicit comparison of the injured finger to a pulsing jackhammer is one type of metaphoric language called a *simile*. Similes are common and effective in good writing. The more subtle comparison of the blood spitting—because blood can't really spit—to an action of a person or animal is a *metaphor*. Both similes and metaphors are examples of metaphoric language.

Skilled writers of picture books use metaphoric language adeptly. In *The Butterfly*, set in occupied World War II Europe, Patricia Polacco writes of "The tall shining boots of marching Nazi soldiers. Their heels clicked like gunshots along the cobblestone path." Not only does the author use a simile here, but the comparison is one consistent with the wartime tenor of the story.

Writer Pegi Deitz Shea uses much figurative language in *The Whispering Cloth*. This tale is of Hmong families in a refugee camp trying to earn enough money for a ticket to America. The main character, Mai, is trying to picture her deceased parents. The clever choice of words—saying that smells *bombarded* and a story was *erupting*—hints at the tragic way her parents died trying to escape. Because smells don't bombard and stories don't actually erupt, the subtle comparison of the effect of the smells to bombing is effective. Metaphoric language is an important part of good writing.

Leads

Writers know that the opening line or lines of a book are critical. After all, the reader's first impression often determines whether he or she wants to turn the page. Leads can also set a mood or tone, and foreshadow events in the story. In *The Klondike Cat* (Lawson), the story opens, "The news spread like flames in a summer wind." The powerful simile in this lead suggests what will happen next (news will arrive) and sets the tone for a very literary storytelling.

Mary Bahr begins her story *My Brother Loved Snowflakes* with "Snowflakes liked my brother, Willie. And why not? Nobody cared about them the way he did." This language suggests a story about a character's relationship to and adventures with snow. Even the title helps foreshadow coming events.

Dialogue

Some picture books use dialogue—talk between characters—as a writing technique. Much can be communicated about characters by the way they talk and what they say. In *Ira Says Goodbye* (Waber), we revisit best friends as they face separation when Reggie's family is moving. " 'Isn't it terrible?' I said. 'Isn't it terrific?' he said. I looked at Reggie. 'Did you just say terrific?' 'Uh-huh,' said Reggie. 'Did you just say Uh-huh?' I said. 'Uh-huh,' said Reggie." In this brief exchange, readers understand that Ira feels let down, even betrayed, because Reggie does not express being upset about moving away. Dialogue is an effective writing tool for developing characters in stories.

Understatement

Sometimes a difficult choice in writing is deciding when you have said too much, and when you've said not enough. Experienced authors have learned this balance—that you don't need to say everything, and that sometimes *less* is *more*. Good writers trust their readers to make the connection and fill in between the lines as needed.

Judith Hendershot's *In Coal Country* tells of her early life in a company mining town. When the story finally gets to the long-awaited Christmas day off from the grueling schedule, one very simple line says much: "No whistle called Papa to the mine." This statement suggests to the reader the rarity of times the family could be together to enjoy each other, how that whistle controlled daily life, and the relief of not having it this one precious day.

In Patricia Polacco's *The Keeping Quilt*, short statements are filled with many ramifications about change. As the story goes through multiple generations of marriages and family, Polacco writes about how at first, men and women did not mingle at weddings. By the next generation, men and women mingle but do not dance together. By the most recent generation, men and women dance together. These brief statements say little and much at the same time, because they clue the reader to the overwhelming cultural changes that occurred in her community in those time periods. These understatements trust readers to infer, think, and develop insights.

Voice

One intangible feature of experienced writing is called *voice*. A writer's voice is the signature style—the sum total of all aspects of his or her style. Some writers have more recognizable voices than others. In the same way that we come to know the artistic style of illustrators, we also come to know the writing style of many writers. For example, Byrd Baylor has a consistently soft, poetic voice in her books, which is soft and poetic in titles such as *I'm in Charge of Celebrations*, *The Way to Start a Day*, *When Clay Sings*, *Hawk, I'm Your Brother*, and *Your Own Best Secret Place*.

Some authors have adopted a writing voice that sounds like that of a child. Bernard Waber does this adeptly in *Ira Sleeps Over* when the pesky sister talks with a whiny, sing-song voice: "How will you feel sleeping without your teddy bear for the very first time? Hmmmmmmmm?"

Judith Viorst similarly has created the point of view of her mischievous young son, Alexander, in several books whose titles include his name—*Alexander and the Terrible, Horrible, No Good, Very Bad Day* and *Alexander, Who Used to Be Rich Last Sunday*. Even the titles sound like something children would say. In *Alexander, Who's Not (Do You Hear Me? I Mean It!) Going to Move*, main character Alexander tells brother Nick he has a "puke-face." This and other childlike prose helps readers easily identify with characters who think and talk as they often do.

Good Writing in Nonfiction

Much is addressed in this book about high expectations for nonfiction writing. We all have encountered nonfiction that was dry, boring, unattractive, and extremely unpleasant to read. Without repeating any information here, it is simply important to note that nonfiction is now better written and the writing quality is more highly valued. Good organization of information, attractive graphics, access features, and other expectations are presented in chapter 9.

What Makes Poor Writing?

In books for young people, there are certain features that cause experts in children's literature to rate them poorly. First of all, text that is written "down" (sometimes called "dumbed down") with simplistic, short, choppy sentences and with a very limited vocabulary, is *not* considered skilled writing. Often people believe that this kind of writing is better suited to younger, less developed readers. Even if this is true, the developing reader is unlikely to fall in love with the book, learn new words, or experience models of good writing.

Some basal reader companies feature books with limited vocabulary and stilted, contrived texts. Sometimes getting in a certain word or word pattern is valued over literary quality and reader interest. Some of these stories have lines similar to "Don has a cap for a pen," "The watch will scratch the witch," or "Mat is a cat with a hat."

We have never seen such writing cause a child to fall in love with books or reading. In fact, the 5-year-old son of a teacher friend of ours, who had been raised on many good books, saw such a reading book for the first time at his mother's school. "Do your students *like* this book, Mommy?" the youngster queried. His teacher-mother explained that the book was used for reading instruction, to which her 5-year-old said, "Why don't they just read Judith Viorst or something?" (personal communication, May, 1989). This literate 5-year-old shares our views about good literary quality in books for children.

Another writing feature we take issue with in youth literature today is didacticism. Didactic writing is preachy, telling young people explicitly what is right or wrong. Although good writing contains myriad lessons about life, few people want lessons to hit them over the head.

Forms of Picture Books

Picture books come in a variety of forms. Some, such as board books and first books for babies, are not relevant to the K–8 focus of this book. However, a number of others are.

Alphabet Books

An alphabet book uses letters of the alphabet to carry a theme through the book. Some alphabet books are nonfiction as well, because they communicate information about a place, an event, or an idea. For example, *L is for Lobster* (Reynolds) is a book about the state of Maine.

Concept Books

A nonfiction book covering one concept or idea is called a concept book. For example, Tana Hoban's *Circles, Triangles, and Squares* is devoted to shapes. Concept books are discussed in more depth in chapter 9, "Nonfiction."

Pop-Up Books

Pop-up books make use of paper engineering: Stiff pages open to create scenes or have characters stand up as the reader opens the pages all the way. For the 100th anniversary of the classic *The Wonderful Wizard of Oz*, by L. Frank Baum, artist Robert Sabuda produced a commemorative pop-up book that includes all the original text but also depicts all the major scenes from the book, such as the Kansas tornado popping up in the first page spread. More typically, though, pop-up books contain limited text and are geared toward younger readers.

Interactive Books

These books also contain some engineering, but are less complex than pop-up books. They invite readers to lift, open, flip, pull, or do something with flaps of paper that stick out from the page. Eric Hill's Spot books, which fea-ture the adventures of a dog named Spot, are interactive books. Eric Carle's books, such as *The Very Busy Spider*, give readers something to touch (the emerging web, done in relief) or something to hear, as in *The Very Quiet Cricket*, where a sound chip is embedded into the binding.

Wordless Picture Books

Wordless picture books contain primarily art, although some may have a few words. The detail in the art does tell a story, however. One child we know calls these books "do it yourself stories." For example, Tomie dePaola's classic *Pancakes for Breakfast* tells a simple story of an older woman going through the process of making pancakes, starting with having the idea of how nice they would be for breakfast. David Wiesner's *Tuesday* depicts a story that can be considered fantasy; the illustrations portraying a night when frogs fly through the air.

Predictable Patterned Language Books

These are picture books written with predictable language and repeating patterns. Predictability can be the result of obvious patterns, use of rhyme, or text that closely follows illustrations. These books play a critical role in early

Meet... Tomie de Paola

Author and illustrator of *Strega Nona; Now One Foot, Now the Other; Nana Upstairs & Nana Downstairs; The Clown of God; Bill and Pete; Tom; The Art Lesson; The Legend of the Bluebonnet; Strega Nona Meets Her Match*. Tomie has authored and/or illustrated more than 200 titles.

Tomie's life is detailed in some of his titles, such as *The Art Lesson, Watch Out for the Chicken Feet in Your Soup, Tom, Nana Upstairs & Nana Downstairs, Oliver Button Is a Sissy*, and others. He decided early on he would become a real artist like his uncles, and thought crayons and other art supplies were the best presents a boy could get from his parents. He drew not only on paper, but also on his bedsheets and the walls of his bedroom under the wallpaper. He also loved books and reading, and waited with bated breath for the first day of school to learn to read. He claims he was extremely disappointed when his kindergarten teacher told him they would not be learning to read until first grade. He initially tried to leave school that day, saying he would "be back next year." Somehow, he was convinced to stay in kindergarten in spite of his concerns about having to wait so long for learning to read.

All of his family members appear in various books he has written and/or illustrated. He feels he owes much to many of them, but especially his mother who read to him so often.

"My motto is, if you can read, you can learn everything about anything and anything about everything. Also, there is nothing wrong with reading purely for pleasure. You have to fall in love with books." Mr. dePaola lives in New Hampshire but grew up in Meriden, Connecticut.

reading, because their predictability helps ensure reader success and helps students understand how language works. The writing is appealing because of its rhythm. Patterned, predictable books are essential in shared reading (see chapter 11). Classic patterned books include *Brown Bear, Brown Bear, What Do You See?* (Martin) and *The Very Hungry Caterpillar* (Carle). More predictable titles are listed in chapter 11.

> All really good picture books are written to be read five hundred times.
>
> Rosemary Wells, author, in Zinsser, 1990, p. 131

design. But we also look to reader responses to signal that a particular book is a winner. Students are not shy about expressing their favorites. If experts love a book but children don't pick it up, then we have to wonder what it lacks. Naturally, different books appeal to different people, and preferences change with age and life experience. Taking all these points into account, teachers and students can learn to evaluate picture books.

Choosing Quality Picture Books

In choosing quality picture books, we look for all the features discussed so far—exciting art, good writing, attractive

Evaluating Picture Books

The Guidelines for Choosing Literature feature on this page lists criteria for evaluating picture books. However, student response to the books and their popularity with children are also considerations.

Guidelines for Choosing Literature

Evaluating Picture Books

- ☀ The art in the book must be extremely well executed in its medium. Evaluating art, of course, requires some knowledge about the medium being used.

- ☀ The art must enhance and extend the story, incorporating "visual literacy" (see Terms for Teachers p. 150). There should be "flow and harmony" (B. Elleman, personal communication, May, 2002) between pictures and text. The art should add something in terms of interpretation of the text rather than merely illustrating what the words say.

- ☀ Setting is established through the artwork when text is limited, and should be done quickly in the earliest pictures.

- ☀ Subject matter should be appropriate to the ages and interests of the children for whom the book is intended.

- ☀ Language style should be smooth, fluid, and readable by youngsters. Words should not necessarily be limited to ones children might know (because that often makes the writing dull), but writers consider their choice of words in view of the child audience. Bill Martin refers to this as the "sounds of language," and those sounds should be pleasing.

- ☀ Accuracy and currency are important, especially for nonfiction picture books. Information presented in words and illustrations should be accurate and up-to-date.

- ☀ Good picture books that depict nonmainstream cultural groups have accurate, nonstereotyping images and accurate depictions of the cultural group in terms of setting and objects that appear in the language and illustrations. Peoples and their lives should be depicted with respect.

- ☀ Children's responses to a picture book are the final evaluation. A book that no child wants to read will not be successful.

Expert evaluation is based on the criteria that have been developed over the years by the Caldecott Medal Committees, because the Caldecott Medal is the most prestigious award in the United States that is given to a picture book. Information about that award follows.

Awards for Excellence in Picture Books

The Caldecott Medal

This award, named for book pioneer Randolph Caldecott, is the highest award a picture book can receive. The Medal is awarded annually to one American picture book, but Honor books may also be chosen. This award is for the art in the book, but the book as a whole is taken into account. The Caldecott Medal and other awards are important in the writing and publishing field, because books that win awards are likely to stay in print and to sell well.

The 15 members of the Caldecott Committee, which chooses the Medal winners, are all members of the American Library Association and include school librarians and public librarians. These individuals have interests and knowledge of books and book art as well. (Barbara Elleman, former member of the Caldecott Committee; personal communication, May, 2002).

The 15 members of the committee serve 1-year terms, and they meet three times during the year. The chair of the committee is elected by ALSC (Association of Library Service to Children); 7 members are appointed, and another 7 are elected, with consideration for balance of gender and ethnicities represented.

Members of the committee may not solicit titles from publishers, nor may they discuss the books they are considering with other members of the committee until the deliberations meeting. Caldecott Honor books are discussed separately from the Medal nominees.

The Caldecott Committee looks for books in which the art is excellently executed, where there is a flow or harmony between pictures and text, where the stories can't stand alone apart from the illustrations, and where the illustrator's interpretation has made a contribution to the overall work.

Other Picture Book Awards

Other awards for picture books are also worth noting. The New York Times Choice of Best Illustrated Children's Books of the Year is given for excellence in illustration. Another award, the Charlotte Zolotow Award, started in 1998, honors a picture book for excellence in writing. This award is named for well-known author and editor Charlotte Zolotow. The Laura Ingalls Wilder Award is given to an author or an illustrator whose books have made a substantial and lasting contribution to literature for children. This award, given every 5 years, was established in 1954. The Ezra Jack Keats Award, given biennially, honors the late Ezra Jack Keats and is given to promising new artists and writers. This award is sponsored by the Ezra Jack Keats Foundation.

All the awards described are determined by experts in the field. Other children's choice awards are voted on by readers themselves. The Arizona Young Reader's Award, for example, given biennially, is sponsored jointly by the two largest universities in the state— The University of Arizona and Arizona State. Often state library associations run reader's choice awards.

Tech Note

See the CD-ROM that accompanies this book for a complete listing of these awards and all winners.

Building a Classroom Library

As you read this book and learn how to select good books for children, you know that you want quality literature available for your students. Often we tell teachers to start with books that have won awards—not only the awards given by experts that we have mentioned, but also those given by readers, such as the Arizona Young Reader's Award and the Georgia Book Award.

Another way to build a classroom collection is to identify good titles through resources such as this book and book clubs. Arrow Book Club, Trumpet Book Club, and the Scholastic Book Club are all avenues for purchasing less-expensive editions of books. Teachers who distribute book club materials and organize ordering for students get bonus books for their classrooms. Many classroom collections are built or sustained by these book clubs.

Picture book collections should include some of the following:

- Picture books that have won awards.
- Other titles by award-winning authors or illustrators.
- Picture books by authors who are minorities, especially but certainly not limited to the cultures represented in your community. Collections should reflect our global community.
- Picture books that support content-area study for science, social studies, math, health, and language arts.
- Books on audiocassettes are a great addition to every classroom listening center.

- Picture books that span all genres—poetry, nonfiction, and fiction.
- Picture books that are pertinent to your state, region, and local history.
- Picture books that have been featured on public television on programs such as *Reading Rainbow*.
- Picture books displayed as "best picks" by local librarians and booksellers.

Special Considerations for Young Children

Picture books are the backbone of primary classrooms, which serve students from age 4 through third grade (8- to 9-year-olds, most typically). They are used most often in the following ways.

Reading Aloud

Conscientious teachers do their best to ensure that children are read to at least once per day. Reading aloud to children is the most important foundation of literacy: It develops needed skills related to beginning reading and to continued reading development. This is so important that we devote an entire chapter of this book (chapter 10) to reading aloud.

> We should not underestimate what children are capable of when they talk about picture books; even young readers can be very sophisticated as literary critics of picture books.
>
> *Lawrence Sipe, 1998, p. 67*

Content-Area Learning

Picture books contain rich content to enhance not only literature learning, but also social studies, math, science, health—all subject areas can be taught using picture books. Content-area learning is described in depth in chapter 9, "Nonfiction."

Independent Reading

In independent reading, students read alone, usually in self-selected books. Much is known about the value of independent reading in school and how the time students spend reading correlates with academic success. We discuss these issues and pertinent research in chapter 12, "Independent Reading."

Shared and Guided Reading

Shared reading involves using authentic texts, such as picture books, with a group in an instructional context. Shared reading is essential in earliest reading instruction and continues in classrooms that use effective practices. Guided reading also uses books and other materials, with small target groups, and explicit teaching about language conventions (see chapter 11).

Picture Books and Their Role in Comprehension

The basis of reading comprehension is that developing readers learn to interpret words, creating pictures in their minds. This "imaging" is one of the foundations of comprehension. Picture books play an important role, then, in developing comprehension.

In a sense, picture books do for developing readers what readers must eventually do for themselves—create relevant images about the text. In the same way an illustrator interprets text through visuals, readers interpret text with mental images. In cases where these images do not occur for readers, then comprehension is poor and readers are "at risk."

Graham (1990) believes that the contribution of illustrations to reading development has been seriously underestimated. Picturing what one is reading is a fundamental aspect of learning to read with comprehension. Mental images stimulated by illustrations and text are carriers of information to the brain, and are integrated with a person's senses. Consequently, the reader imagines what things look like, feel like, and sound like and how they smell, because the illustrations generate these reactions. In this process, book language becomes meaningful and vivid. Pictures play a big part of this process when the artist's detail suggests sensory images.

Picture Books in Intermediate and Middle School Classrooms

Many of us grew up seeing picture books in the part of the library designated for younger readers. Their cataloging still uses the letter *E* in the Dewey Decimal system, which originally stood for "Easy." However, not all picture books are "Easy," so media specialists introduced the term "Everybody" to replace "Easy." Now many teachers and librarians call picture books "Everybody books." We agree.

Certainly many picture books are targeted for the youngest readers. However, just as many are not. Because picture books are the marriage of literature and art and because their form is unique, they appeal to a wide audience, including adults. The skillful illustrations, the literary language, and the choices of content all make picture books a resource and a source of pleasurable reading.

In intermediate and middle school classrooms, picture books serve a variety of purposes. First of all, they can be a wonderful introduction to content. Quality nonfiction books (see chapter 9) are sources of good information with accompanying graphics. These books support content-area instruction in many ways.

Second, picture books often contain the same literary devices used in more sophisticated and complex literature. Consequently, picture books can be used for teaching about topics such as bias, alliteration, irony, and flashbacks. Encountering these devices in picture books is more evident and obvious than in longer works of fiction (see chapter 14 for specifics on this issue).

For example, Jennifer Estabrook, an eighth-grade English teacher, uses the picture book *Rosie's Walk* (Hutchins) to teach her students irony. "They could see that it was an example of irony when one would expect the fox to get the hen. After that, they saw irony everywhere" (personal communication, October, 1999). On another occasion, she read aloud *Terrible Things*, by Eve Bunting, and asked students to relate it to the Holocaust;

this book is a good example of allegory. She initially was concerned that they would find the book too juvenile, but they did not. One of the questions she had them consider was why the author would tell the story of the Holocaust in a picture book.

Third, many picture books on the market today either are too sophisticated for younger readers and require the experience and maturity of older readers, or they are written in such a way that they can be appreciated on multiple levels. Moviemakers know that parents take children to see their popular movies; embedded in the movies for children are subtleties for the adults in the audience to keep them entertained as well. Picture books are like this. People get different things out of a book based on what they bring to the reading experience.

Last, picture books belong in the intermediate and middle school program because they are literature, and because they are beautiful. To deny picture books to older students is to deny them access to a wonderful source of aesthetic pleasure.

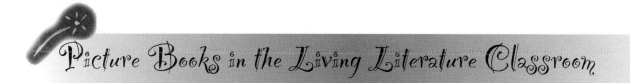

Picture Books in the Living Literature Classroom

In this section, we look at many ways to use picture books in classrooms. These include ways to select the books, talk about them, and use them in teaching. All the strategies presented are suitable for students at varied levels, unless a strategy specifically states otherwise. Different ages and kinds of learners are accommodated with the complexity of the titles used and with the varied expectations for activities and assignments.

Special education students may be readers who struggle. These strategies address multiple intelligences and use modes of learning that are successful for a wide range of students. Everything we present here is equally appropriate for special education students. These students just require more detailed instruction, may need these tasks divided into several steps, and may take more time to finish when a product is the result.

Often when we present these ways of using books in our classes or in workshops, teachers ask, "How do we assess these things?" The way you assess depends on your goals for your students. Some assessment is accomplished through observation of the process and thoughtful considerations of the products: Did I get what I expected when I asked students to do this? If not, what could I have

done better to make it happen? Did I provide a clear model of what I expected?

Teacher-created rubrics are one popular way to assess and evaluate. On such a rubric, teachers list what elements they expect and how each element will be evaluated in an assignment or lesson. Sharing this rubric in advance helps students better understand expectations.

Other popular means of assessment are peer assessment and self-assessment. Simple feedback forms or journals where students express what they believe they learned and how they could improve are revealing, and often candid. Peer assessments of other students' work may or may not corroborate what self-assessment suggests. Also, keep in mind that not everything needs to be assessed; some activities should be for practice, for enjoyment, and for building values and habits about literacy learning.

Webbing Books

Webbing is a strategy that teachers use to aid in planning curriculum around the use of books and stories. Often done with colleagues, webs help teachers think about how to integrate literature and aspects of the curriculum.

Webbing can be done in a number of ways. Here we explain two—one web done by story themes, and the other done by subject areas.

When webbing by theme, one writes the book or story title in the middle of a piece of paper. Arranged around the center are the principal or key themes in the book. From there, lesson ideas are appended. Consider an example with Jeanette Winter's book *Follow the Drinking Gourd*, shown in Figure 7.2. In this story, a character named Peg Leg Joe travels around Southern plantations as a handyman doing odd jobs, but with a mission to teach slaves a spiritual-sounding song, "Follow the Drinking Gourd." Imbedded in the words of the song are directions about how to escape using the Underground Railroad. Then, the book follows one family's escape using the words.

Picture a figure emerging such as the one shown in Figure 7.2. The key ideas in this book are the Underground Railroad, the North Star in the constellation "Little Dipper," the song itself, and the sequence of the escape. The

Figure 7.2   Webbing by Theme

From FOLLOW THE DRINKING GOURD by Jeanette Winter, copyright © 1988 by Jeanette Winter. Used by permission of Alfred A. Knopf, an imprint of Random House Children's Books, a division of Random House, Inc.

theme of the song might be developed to include a study of other spirituals, especially African American ones; students might locate the music to this song, collect several recordings and listen to them, and even consider playing the recordings in their music classes.

The Underground Railroad theme might be embellished by studying why the Quakers took such risks to help slaves escape; some key abolitionists; the routes used between the Southern states and Canada; and how long these journeys would take. To learn more about the escape, students might understand how families needed to obtain drugs to keep babies and small children asleep during the journey; how escaping slaves were able to travel only at night, and then only when the moon helped them see; and how slaves had to be wary of those tracking them with bloodhounds.

This web can be made more detailed with discussion of constellations that navigators used, including Ursa Ma-jor, the "drinking gourd," and Ursa Minor, which contains the North Star. Other ideas related to navigation could be added.

At this point, teachers who are webbing books or stories are brainstorming specific ideas and concepts they would like to teach with the book. For example, they may decide to teach about escapes using Virginia Hamilton's narratives by former slaves in *The People Could Fly,* or reading to students *Long Journey Home* (Lester), which also details a slave's escape.

Another way to web a book is around subject areas. This helps teachers ensure that they have included aspects from different content areas as they plan. Webbing *Follow the Drinking Gourd* from subjects might look like Figure 7.3. The figure is divided by subjects, and ideas for teaching in each are offered. For example, one might include math by calculating the distances and time it took to travel. Using maps of the eastern United States would be helpful.

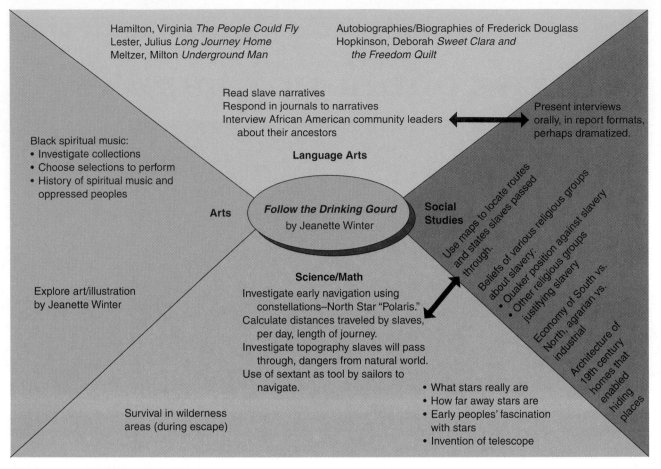

Hamilton, Virginia *The People Could Fly*
Lester, Julius *Long Journey Home*
Meltzer, Milton *Underground Man*

Autobiographies/Biographies of Frederick Douglass
Hopkinson, Deborah *Sweet Clara and
the Freedom Quilt*

Read slave narratives
Respond in journals to narratives
Interview African American community leaders
about their ancestors

Present interviews
orally, in report formats,
perhaps dramatized.

Language Arts

Black spiritual music:
• Investigate collections
• Choose selections to perform
• History of spiritual music and
oppressed peoples

Arts

Follow the Drinking Gourd
by Jeanette Winter

**Social
Studies**

Use maps to locate routes
and states slaves passed
through.
Beliefs of various religious groups
about slavery:
 • Quaker position against slavery
 • Other religious groups
 justifying slavery
Economy of South vs.
North, agrarian vs.
industrial
Architecture of
19th century
homes that
enabled
hiding
places

Explore art/illustration
by Jeanette Winter

Science/Math
Investigate early navigation using
constellations—North Star "Polaris."
Calculate distances traveled by slaves,
per day, length of journey.
Investigate topography slaves will pass
through, dangers from natural world.
Use of sextant as tool by sailors to
navigate.

• What stars really are
• How far away stars are
• Early peoples' fascination
with stars
• Invention of telescope

Survival in wilderness
areas (during escape)

Figure 7.3   Webbing by Subject Area

Teaching with Picture Books

When we share picture books with students, we obviously want to stimulate powerful thinking and good discussion about books as well as to develop critical-thinking abilities, promote deeper understanding of the stories, and help our students become better readers. Design questions about the art and the text that genuinely interest or puzzle you as a reader. Ask questions that also invite varied responses instead of one correct answer. Modeling these kinds of questions will help students learn to ask them on their own as they work with each other in literature circles (see chapter 13). In Figure 7.4, we suggest questions that apply not only to picture books but also others. Some are more appropriate when students are farther along in a book or have finished reading the book.

Through the first section of this chapter, you learned about how to discuss the art and writing of picture books; apply this learning to discussing books with your students.

Getting Students Talking About the Art in Picture Books

Earlier in this chapter, you learned about the art in picture books. Students of all ages can learn about these types of media, how pictures work, and how to consider the role of illustrations in books they read.

Some years ago, two art teachers in our literature class taught us that we can ask some of the same questions about illustrations that we do about text. For example, we often ask students to write what a story they've read means to them, to tell us how a story makes them feel, something interesting they noticed about the story, or what they are reminded of. These questions can also be good ones for looking at art.

1. What interesting thing did you notice about this book?

2. Is there a character you plan to remember all your life? Why?

3. How does this book make you feel?

4. What does this book remind you of in your own life experience?

5. Does anything in this book remind you of another book you've read? movie you've seen? television show?

6. How did the author help you get to know the main character in this book?

7. Why do you think the author wrote this book?

8. If you could change the ending of this book, what would you do differently?

9. Is there a sentence in this book that you think is particularly well-written language?

10. Can you tell when and where this book takes place?

11. What have the illustrator and the author done to establish the setting?

12. What have you learned from this book that you would like to share?

Figure 7.4 Good Questions for Picture Books

One way to get students talking more about books, and especially about the artwork, is to develop thought-provoking questions specific to art. In Figure 7.5 we offer some ideas.

Using Wordless Picture Books

It once was thought that wordless picture books were only for young children or for those who could not yet read, but this is not the case. Wordless picture books are complete stories communicated through elaborate and detailed illustrations. These skillful works of art can be used in a number of ways.

☺ Teachers can use wordless picture books to have developing readers generate oral texts. The pictures afford opportunities for oral expression with an individual student or a small group of students. Students can practice storybook-type language they have heard in stories read to them. When teachers hear children using storybook language, such as "Once upon a time," it is a clue that they are internalizing the language that belongs to books, a skill acquired from hours of being read to. A child's developing "concept of story" is indicative of emerging understandings that are part of overall literacy development (Applebee, 1978).

☺ For developing writers, even in intermediate and middle school grades, teachers have students write the texts they believe suit wordless books. This strategy allows students to write text and use storybook language without the burden of creating a story from scratch. Wordless picture books also can be enjoyed just for the beautiful art form that they are. These "do it yourself books" are fun. Some students say they like them because they can create a slightly different story each time they "read" them.

Picture Books to Teach Critical Literacy and Higher-Level Thinking

Critical literacy involves using books, especially fiction, to raise issues that require students to ponder aspects of life. Many authors address issues of social justice, ethics, civil rights, and human rights in their books. Through books, then, teachers can initiate deeper discussions, encourage cultural thinking, and perhaps even shape attitudes. (In chapter 8, "The Fiction Family," we discuss critical literacy in more depth.) Because picture books are short, they can be read and discussed in one or two lessons.

For example, one of our graduate students put together a text set of books for his fifth-grade class dealing with westward expansion and Native Americans, but ones

Figure 7.5 Good Questions for Talking About Art

1. How did the illustrations at the beginning of the book make you feel? What about other parts of the book?

2. How has the illustrator used size and placement of objects to make you notice something important?

3. Does the format of the book enhance the story? Why or why not? (Look for kinds of paper, colors of paper, page borders, writing and pictures together on the page or on different pages.)

4. Is there a sense of motion in some of the illustrations? Explain which objects have motion and how this affects response to the story.

5. What sort of colors and coloring did the illustrator choose for this story? Why do you think these are a good choice?

6. How would you describe the pictures in this book to someone who has never seen it?

7. Do the illustrations remind you of a place you know?

8. What is similar about the illustrator's style throughout this book?

9. If you could step into one of the illustrations, which one would you choose? Why?

10. What in the illustrations helps you know the setting of the story?

11. What do the illustrations tell us that the words do not?

12. How are these illustrations like or different from those in other books you have read recently? Compare these illustrations with those of another illustrator. Do you have a preference?

13. Look at the first and last illustrations in the book. Is there anything special about these, and are they different from those in the rest of the book? If so, why do you think they are different?

14. What would it be like to read this book without illustrations?

15. What do the illustrations remind you of?

that express the native point of view. This teacher realized that westward expansion is rarely taught this way, and he wanted his unit and the discussions to be provocative.

They were. The fifth graders began to view this part of history from a totally different perspective, even drawing parallels to international issues in the former Yugoslavia and to other instances of tragic ethnic cleansing.

What had inspired this fifth-grade teacher was a chapter in a teacher researcher book (Patterson, Santa, Short, & Smith, 1993) describing a third-grade teacher in a critical-literacy discussion group on the topic of war. Using a text set of picture books that dealt with sensitive issues, and with parental permission, this teacher had her students read and respond to books such as *Faithful Elephants* (Tsuchiya), *Rose Blanche* (Innocenti), *My Hi-*

roshima (1990), and *Hiroshima No Pika* (1980). These picture books, intended for more mature readers, gave students a far different view about war than any social studies textbook could. One boy expressed in his journal at the end of the project that he had decided not to play any more war games at home—he had realized that war was not a game and not something to be taken lightly.

Picture Books and Character Education

Teachers find picture books to be good sources of material for developing character education. Whether character education, once called values clarification, belongs in the

Text Set — *Westward Expansion From a Native Standpoint*

Bruchac, Joseph. (2000). *Crazy Horse's Vision.* New York: Lee & Low.

Erdrich, Louise. (1999). *The Birchbark House.* New York: Hyperion.

Harrell, Beatrice Orcutt. (1999). *Longwalker's Journey.* New York: Dial Books.

Penman, Sarah. (2000). *Honor the Grandmothers: Dakota and Lakota Women Tell Their Stories.* St. Paul, MN: Minnesota Historical Society Press.

Tohe, Laura. (1999). *No Parole Today.* Albuquerque, NM: West End Press.

Teacher Resources:

Rethinking Columbus, published by *Rethinking Schools Magazine.* http://www.rethinkingschools.org/publication/columbus/columbus.shtml

http://www.oyate.org - website run by Native American women about children's books with Native themes.

Video: Dances With Wolves. (1990). Directed by Kevin Costner, screenplay by Michael Blake.

school has often been questioned—some believe it is the purview of homes and religious groups to handle this aspect of development. Nonetheless, in a landmark study, educator John Goodlad (1984) asked 27,000 teachers, students, and parents what they wanted from schools. Outcomes of this study showed strong sentiments that most people do want more than academics in their schools, including attention to positive behavior development. People want schools to pay attention to vocational and social issues as well as to traditional academic ones.

Character education is a way to address social development. Through books, one can teach about caring, compassion, honesty, responsibility, forgiveness, and much more. Susan Hall (2000) has detailed the character traits that can be taught and books that can support the development of various traits. A few of these traits are presented in Figure 7.6 along with names of books for each purpose. These can be used in classroom discussions, especially around areas of need and concern, as well as for understanding the meanings of these concepts. School counselors may also make use of books dealing with character education.

Picture Books as Writing Models

Picture books make great models for teaching writing. First of all, some picture books are based on personal narrative. Although they are classified as fiction, stories such as Patricia Polacco's *Thank You, Mr. Falker* are based on the author's life. Stories such as these and many others can be models for students to think about stories that can come from their own lives. Using picture books as models in personal narrative is discussed in chapter 14, "Students as Authors."

Picture books are also useful in teaching literary devices such as irony, alliteration, and metaphors. These also are described in chapter 14, along with other ways to use books to support students' continued writing growth.

Innovations on Books for Group Writing

Many books lend themselves to being rewritten. The original book serves as a model for a new book to which everyone in the class makes a contribution.

These innovations, sometimes called parodies, or *copy changes,* can be done in a number of ways. With youngest readers, the teacher may compose much of the text but have students help produce the book, illustrating the pages and writing text neatly onto the pages. At other times, students each produce their own page independently.

Some book parodies have a content focus. In one multiage primary class, the topic in science was the sea. Using *The Napping House* (Wood & Wood) as a model, students developed pages of "The Napping Sea" and suspended them from clotheslines all across the room. Reading these pages was both a lesson for the entire class and a free-time choice activity when pairs of students would take a pointer and read the clotheslines together.

Another content focus we have seen used Bernard Most's *If the Dinosaurs Came Back.* Although this book is fiction, each picture of a dinosaur is a real depiction of these extinct giants. The second-grade students completed

Figure 7.6
Character Traits and
Picture Books That
Exemplify Them

Cooperation
Cooper, Helen. (1998). *Pumpkin Soup*. New York: Farrar, Straus & Giroux.
Doyle, Malachy. (1999). *Jody's Beams* (Judith Allibone, Illus.). Cambridge, MA: Candlewick Press.
Gibbons, Faye. (1996). *Mountain Wedding* (Ted Rand, Illus.). New York: Morrow.
Courage
Aardema, Verna. (1991). *Borreguita and the Coyote* (Petra Mathers, Illus.). New York: Knopf.
Atkins, Jeannine. (1999). *Mary Anning and the Sea Dragon* (Michael Dooling, Illus.). New York: Farrar, Straus & Giroux.
Empathy
Ackerman, Karen. (1988). *Song and Dance Man* (Stephen Gammell, Illus.). New York: Knopf.
Bruchac, Joseph. (1994). *The Great Ball Game: A Muskogee Story* (Susan L. Roth, Illus.). New York: Dial Books.
Honesty
Duncan, Alice Faye. (1999). *Miss Viola and Uncle Ed Lee* (Catherine Stock, Illus.). New York: Atheneum.
Ernst, Lisa Campbell. (1989). *When Bluebell Sang*. New York: Bradbury Press.
Gill, Janet. (1999). *Basket Weaver and Catches Many Mice* (Yangsook Choi, Illus.). New York: Knopf.
Responsibility
Brown, Margaret Wise. (1998). *The Little Scarecrow Boy* (David Diaz, Illus.). New York: HarperCollins.
Schertle, Alice. (1995). *Down the Road* (E. B. Lewis, Illus.). New York: Browndeer Press.

one page on the dinosaur of his or her choice (pictures had to be accurate) and decided what use the dinosaur could have in today's world (the use was humorous).

Sometimes book parodies have just a writing focus to support developing literacy. Many teachers use predictable, patterned language books such as Martin's *Brown Bear, Brown Bear, What Do You See?* and *Polar Bear, Polar Bear, What Do You Hear?* to create group books that classes read over and over, and never seem to tire of. The text set on p. 173 lists picture books that are suitable for this activity.

More Strategies With Books

Sketch-to-Stretch

Developed at Indiana University and researched by Marjorie Siegel (1984), sketch-to-stretch is a literature-based strategy that is easy to implement, has many uses, and is a useful strategy for students of all ages and abilities. Very simply, af-

ter students have read a book or heard a book read aloud, they individually draw what the story means to them. The deliberately vague instructions are intended to give students opportunities to express themselves and to encourage independent thinking.

Often, teachers follow this up with having students discuss their drawings in a sharing session. The students' talk is a useful informal assessment for teachers to determine whether they comprehended the story. Some students draw something from the story, which indicates the presence of literal comprehension. Other students go beyond the text in their drawing, making connections to their own experience, which is indicative of higher-level thinking—a most desirable outcome.

One book that has been widely used to research this strategy is the Caldecott Medal book *Sylvester and the Magic Pebble* (Steig) (Leland & Harste, 1994). In this picture book, an ordinary family of donkeys loses their beloved son, Sylvester, when the son discovers a magic pebble and uses it foolishly. Because most readers can re-

Text Set

Some Picture Books for Innovations

Aardema, Verna. (1991). *Traveling to Tondo*. New York: Knopf.

Brown, Margaret Wise. (1949). *The Important Book*. New York: Harper.

Calmenson, Stephanie. (1989). *The Principal's New Clothes*. New York: Scholastic.

Charlip, Remy. (1964). *Fortunately*. New York: Scholastic.

Martin, Bill. (1983). *Brown Bear, Brown Bear, What Do You See?* New York: Holt.

Martin, Bill. (1991). *Polar Bear, Polar Bear, What Do You Hear?* New York: Holt.

Mayer, Mercer. (1973). *What Do You Do With a Kangaroo?* New York: Scholastic.

Most, Bernard. (1978). *If the Dinosaurs Came Back*. New York: Harcourt Brace.

Rylant, Cynthia. (1982). *When I Was Young in the Mountains*. New York: Dutton.

Viorst, Judith. (1972). *Alexander and the Terrible, Horrible, No Good, Very Bad Day*. New York: Atheneum.

Wood, Don, & Wood, Audrey. (1984). *The Napping House*. San Diego: Harcourt Brace.

Zolotow, Charlotte. (1965). *Someday*. New York: Harper & Row.

late to family issues, this selection produces interesting drawings from students.

Some students draw their families and express their gratitude for being together. Other students draw something more directly related to the story, such as depicting Sylvester's parents as extremely sad. Some use this story to think about the loss of a loved one, and make a drawing related to that loss.

Using E-Mail and Chat Rooms for Book Talk

Just about every child wants to use e-mail. Because it involves students in writing and reading, using e-mail reinforces basic instructional goals and supplies an authentic writing audience.

Teachers have devised clever uses for e-mail to promote book talk. Some teachers pair their students with undergraduate students at a university—those who plan to become teachers. The university students and the children agree to read the same books and then talk about those books on-line. The university students use their new skills to ask good questions and to stimulate student thinking.

In another variation using the Internet, teachers seek e-mail pals for their students in another English-speaking country or elsewhere in the United States. Again, students agree to read certain books at the same pace. Then, they e-mail each other about their responses to the books, use instant messaging to talk in real time (if time zones permit it during school hours), or converse in chat rooms set up for this purpose.

Like all Internet use, teachers should monitor students using e-mails or instant messaging. Some teachers have all e-mails printed so they can see how students are talking about the books. Technical support staff can assist teachers in monitoring student efforts and restricting unauthorized uses of the Internet.

Books and Media

Some classes delve into the world of media along with their use of literature. We have seen classes and groups of students create movies or filmstrips based on their book. One group re-created *Bill and Pete Go Down the Nile* (dePaola) by using stuffed toys of a bird and a crocodile and putting them against various backdrops to film their own little movie.

Some middle schoolers we know have used computer software for writing plays based on their book. These sorts of software provide characters to choose from, voices, props, settings, and other tools. The computer will run the student-written play once it is written and configured. Of course, students can also write plays the old-fashioned way with paper and pencils.

Book Boxes

These are cardboard boxes, either reused from a store or made from school supplies, that are small enough to fit on a tabletop. Each of the sides is decorated with scenes or objects related to the story the students have read. Students can also collect props that can be kept in the box to tell the story.

Accordion Books

Sometimes instead of making a traditional book, children enjoy folding a long piece of paper like an accordion and creating scenes on each frame or page to go along with what they have read. These could be made from a variety of materials, such as construction paper, card stock, and butcher paper. The stiffer papers enable the books to stand up nicely to be displayed.

Performing With Picture Books

Picture books afford many classroom opportunities for drama. Drama is an underutilized aspect of reading programs, but important in a living literature classroom. Following are some ways of dramatizing with picture books; others are presented in chapters throughout the book.

Picture Books as Plays

Bill Martin Jr. is an advocate of producing picture books as plays in classrooms. Adapting the text of a book simply for acting out can be memorable in addition to supporting academic goals for literacy learning. Books as plays can be done simply with minimal planning, or in more complex ways requiring rehearsal, props, and scenery (personal communication, July, 1987).

Performing Martin and Archambault's *Barn Dance!* is an example of how you can keep the experience relatively simple. In *Barn Dance!*, a boy on a farm goes to bed at night, but is drawn to noises in the barn, where he ends up joining all the barnyard animals in a lovely hoedown. The skinny boy is the only human character, but students can also play the old dog, the owl, the scarecrow, the other musicians, and the rest of the animals square dancing. Because the story is told by a third-person narrator, one student can practice reading the script and narrate the dramatization; other students can act out what the narrator is reading. The narrator can also pause in places for animals to repeat short lines in the text, and when the text calls for music for dancing. The addition of some country music, a few props such as Western-style hats, scarves, and perhaps animal masks can make the drama a little more exciting, but is purely optional.

"Where does one get such props?" you may be wondering. Typically, teachers are good at finding and saving things. In this case, we recommend you collect old hats from friends and family and other such items as Halloween masks, scarves, bandanas, shawls, aprons, a sheet or blanket, and inexpensive costume jewelry, and store everything in a big basket or tub. Let students explore what the tub has to offer that can help them feel more "in character."

Puppetry

Almost any story that students can act out can also be performed with puppets. Puppets made from socks, brown paper bags, and other materials can simulate storybook characters for acting. Some students prefer puppetry to acting out on their own because they can feel anonymous. There are specific examples of puppetry in chapters throughout the book.

Process Drama

Process drama is a simulation of a book, scene, or issue. Whereas acting out books as plays follows the text, process drama has opportunities for students to go beyond the text. Not limited to teaching literature, process drama can be used in a variety of ways in other content areas. For the purposes of literature teaching, however, our comments are limited to using books.

Process drama can be a lesson in which the teacher or students select a key scene from a story; the scene needs to involve issues, dilemmas, choices, or complex human interactions. Students are assigned to be characters in the story, and perhaps also implied ones, such as people in the town or in the setting.

Two suitable picture books for process drama are *Sweet Clara and the Freedom Quilt* (Hopkinson) and *Follow the Drinking Gourd* (Winter). Both stories are historical fiction in which slaves must decide whether to risk an escape. In *Sweet Clara*, the slaves use a map in the form of a quilt that Clara has constructed from knowledge gained by carriage-driving slaves. Local slaves study it to understand the lay of the land and know how to proceed through the Underground Railroad system. As described earlier in *Follow the Drinking Gourd*, slaves are taught a song by an abolitionist plantation worker who travels from place to place; embedded in the song are the directions to the Ohio River and freedom.

Twenty-first-century students rarely understand the gravity of the decisions slaves had to make when they considered life-threatening choices. Teachers can help them empathize with these dilemmas by assigning classmates to be the characters in the story, as well as other assorted slaves from the plantations. After assigning various characters who have different personalities (cautious, cantankerous, strong leadership, etc.), teachers give students 5–10 minutes to improvise conversations the slaves may have had. In living through the eyes of literature characters, students can better understand the complexities and emotions of early plantation life.

Process drama can be used with any age group, but it is especially successful with older students who need relevancy in their learning. Teachers gain insights into student thinking and learning and can use this information to inform further instruction.

Summary

In this chapter, we learned that picture books are a specialized form, a marriage of fine arts and writing. With practice, we can learn to look critically at both the art and the writing of picture books, and teach our students to ask good questions about both. We can apply this knowledge when choosing high-quality books for our collections, and we can use these books in a variety of ways in classrooms, including to teach writing, as vehicles for character education, to support reading comprehension or content-area learning, and for the sheer pleasure of these gems of the literary world.

Action Research for Teachers

What Effects Will the Use of Picture Books Have on Eighth-Grade Writing and Attitudes Toward Picture Books?

Claudia Kozel
Suburban Middle School

Claudia loves picture books, and she sees their potential for older readers. She wanted a way to teach eighth graders to appreciate these works as well as to make them useful in the middle school curriculum. She designed her passion for picture books into her action research study with 30 honors English students who included 6 English learners. She selected books that were personal narrative models for writing, because narrative writing is a curriculum goal.

First, Claudia developed a simple survey to discover student knowledge and attitudes about picture books. Not surprisingly, most students reported that picture books are for little children or people who cannot read very well. Next, Claudia selected an array of picture books that she knew to be personal narrative, such as *Tom* (dePaola) and

Thank You, Mr. Falker (Polacco). She taught mini-lessons about writing based on Noden's *Image Grammar* (1999) using the picture books as models. By the end of the study, each eighth grader was to write a picture book based on personal narrative. Additionally, Claudia maintained a researcher log. She had student artifacts to analyze, and she repeated the survey about picture books at the end of the study.

By the end of the study, 20 out of 30 students reported that they would likely choose to read picture books again, no longer considering them babyish books. Some respondents stated that they would read picture books to younger siblings and while baby-sitting. Claudia felt her study validated her belief that picture books have a place in middle school classrooms, in appreciation of literature, and in writing instruction.

8

THE FICTION FAMILY
Realistic Fiction, Historical Fiction, Fantasy, and Science Fiction

"Fiction for the young, no less than fiction for the more mature, must first of all be good fiction—the exploration in narrative form of human experience. Fiction is not primarily about problems or ideas or values, but about people. People, of course, have problems and ideas and values, but they are first of all mortal flesh living in a specific place at a specific time. The writer of fiction is not a teacher or preacher or psychologist or sociologist, but a storyteller." (Katherine Paterson, 1982, p. 140)

our fifth-grade girls opted to read *The Lottery Rose* (Hunt) together in a literature group. Over several weeks of talking together and writing in their literature response journals, they'd become attached to the main character, Georgie, an abused child who is placed in foster care. Once there, he tries to find a home for his only possession: a rosebush he'd won in a convenience store lottery.

On one particular Friday, the girls finished the book and asked to be excused from recess. They gathered in a corner of the classroom with their reading response journals. Soon the teacher noticed that the girls were crying on their journals. Later, as she read their entries, she discovered that this group had made powerful emotional connections to the book.

Marissa wrote, "Robin died. I had a deep feeling inside that something bad was going to happen." Sarah wrote, "Robin died. Robin died. I can't believe it. Robin died." Barbara wrote, "I don't know how Irene Hunt could write such a sad story." Allison wrote, "Today Robin died and my emotions and feelings are so mixed up."

Marissa went on to say, "I knew it was going to be touching, that is why I chose it. The author's words just brought sudden tears from me." Sarah added, "When Georgie sacrificed his rosebush for Robin, it made me think hard. If only there were more people in the world that could change. Turn from being bad to a thoughtful, loving child. Even though Robin died, he'll always be a part of me forever." Barbara concluded, "Georgie giving his rosebush away really got to me . . . sorry but I can't write any more today."

Literature, particularly fiction, can make us cry, laugh, and feel compelled to change our lives. Author Russell Freedman expressed these sentiments perfectly when he said, "Reading a good book is like making a lifelong friend. That book will live in your memory forever" (personal communication, September, 1999). This ability to transform us is the power of good fiction.

The teacher of reading has two jobs: The first is to teach students to read, and the second is to teach students to *want* to read. Teaching reading is as much about creating lifelong readers as it is about creating competent readers. Here is where fiction comes in. To the best of our knowledge, no one we know has ever fallen in love with worksheets, basal readers, or programmed reading materials out of a box. However, people do fall in love with books and stories.

For many of us, falling in love with literature occurs in fiction. It is in fictional stories that people are so real to us, where we bring our own life to the experience of reading. Or as one of the girls who read *Lottery Rose* said, "Robin will always be within me and a part of me." Fiction often creates intense responses that lead to a lifelong passion for reading.

Sheila Cochrane, fourth-grade teacher, discusses fiction with a small group.

This chapter introduces you to the genre of fiction. In this chapter, we answer the following questions:

- ☀️ What is fiction? How does fiction differ from other genres?

- ☀️ What are the most common types of fiction written for children?

- ☀️ What are the literary elements of fiction?

- ☀️ What selection criteria can teachers use to find the best, most memorable fiction for use in their classrooms?

- ☀️ How can teachers support affective, emotional responses to fiction as well as help children appreciate what authors do to craft a piece of fiction that will evoke a personal response?

What Is Fiction?

Fiction is experience in narrative. It provides a window into what makes us human. Fiction does not mean a story is "fake" or "untrue"; rather, fiction can illuminate truth, making us reconsider what we perceive as reality. Author Madeleine L'Engle calls fiction "a vehicle for truth," and says that "truth and story are what connect human beings to each other" (Schmidt, 1991, p. 11).

The Children's Literature Dictionary (Latrobe, Brodie, & White, 2002) defines fiction as "imaginary narrative created by an author, not a record of fact. The narrative may be a novel, short story, drama or a narrative poem. All fiction is imaginative, but the work's genre determines how true to real life the work must be to be plausible" (71–72).

The things I write for children are the issues I care about and are important in my life and that I want to talk about—identity, a search for home, responsibility, "who am I" and "what does it mean to be human in the world?"

Karen Cushman, author, in McKindley, 1998, p. 8

Types of Fiction Used With Children

Several genres of fiction are used with children: contemporary realistic fiction, historical fiction, fantasy, and science fiction. They have many elements in common, but they also have distinct qualities that differentiate them.

Contemporary Realistic Fiction

The genre of contemporary realistic fiction includes stories about animals and people that could actually exist along with events that could actually happen in today's world or in the recent past. Even if the story seems unbe-lievable, think about whether it could actually happen to someone in today's world as we know it. If so, then it is contemporary realistic fiction. An important value of contemporary realistic fiction is that it offers readers a window into the human condition through reading about how characters cope with issues and challenges in their lives.

Reading interest inventories indicate that contemporary realistic fiction is the most popular literary genre, particularly among intermediate and middle school students (Monson & Sebesta, 1991). You can probably guess why this is true: Students love to read about other children like themselves who are going through life circumstances that are similar to what they're experiencing. Do you remember reading every Judy Blume book you could find? Her books *Are You There God? It's Me, Margaret, Then Again, Maybe I Won't*, and *Blubber* are still popular with students. Blume doesn't hold back on the range of topics she discusses, from being too fat to experiencing sex for the first time to questioning one's religion. That's what children love about her work and the books of others who write in this genre.

Historical Fiction

Books of historical fiction are also about people and events that could actually happen, but these stories take place in the past, which is usually defined as the time up to and including the Vietnam War era in the 1960s. Writers of historical fiction take on the difficult task of piecing together the puzzle of reality in a different time. Through them, we experience authentic voices of the past; we learn how people felt, cared, believed, valued, laughed, and cried. Although the characters are generally fictionalized to varying degrees, the setting is an actual time in the past, and the details of dialogue, actions, beliefs, foods, and daily activities must be consistent with the time period, given what we know about the historical era. Minor characters may be based on real people who lived in the times of the story. Often settings are also actual places.

Those who write historical fiction love and respect history. Accurate details are an important aspect of the writer's craft in historical fiction; authors usually do extensive research to acquire the details needed to enrich the story. They must be careful not to include any anachronisms—objects, references, or speech patterns that weren't yet in use during the historical era of a book.

Through historical fiction, students can vicariously live the issues, actions, and emotions of people in previous generations. They can begin to understand the course of human events and timeless universal truths. Lessons learned through historical fiction complement content-area studies, adding an affective dimension that is infinitely more touching, memorable, and comprehensible than lessons that are devoid of emotions. So, for example, we could read a textbook pas-

> The knowledge base a writer must form in order to write one book about another time, the culture of that time, the behaviors of the people of that time, and the language of that time is equal to and sometimes surpasses the research involved in a graduate degree from a university. I have done both, and the degrees involve less work.
>
> *Gloria Houston, author; personal communication, September, 1999*

sage about the Southern region of the United States in the 1930s, a time when most African Americans in that region were sharecroppers. We might find the information interesting, but we would likely fail to understand what that experience was really like. Through the artistry of Mildred Taylor in *Roll of Thunder,*

Hear My Cry, however, we can feel the rage of Cassie and her brothers, all African American children, when the school bus full of white children not only passes them by, but splashes their new back-to-school clothes with mud in a deliberate act of humiliation. Historical fiction supplies the humanity in history, teaching lessons and providing insights that textbooks cannot do alone.

James Lincoln Collier, author of several popular historical fiction novels, including, *My Brother Sam Is Dead*, *Jump Ship to Freedom*, and *The Clock*, describes his purpose in writing historical fiction in the following way:

> When I write, I try deliberately to catch readers up in my story, to make them feel things, and in the end, if I am very lucky, to change their internal landscape a little by showing them a new way of looking at the world.
>
> *(C. Collier, 1999, p. 9)*

It is this emphasis on teaching about "the ideals and values that have been important in shaping the course of history" (C. Collier, 1999, p. 3) that makes historical fiction such an important genre.

Fantasy

A fictional work is categorized as fantasy when it contains elements that are not considered possible in our world. These could be such disparate components as talking animals, ghosts, transformations, immortal beings, or the presence of magic. The story might otherwise be totally believable, but the addition of just one magical element categorizes it as fantasy.

Fantasy is an excellent genre to use with students because it explores possibilities limited only by the imagination. In the fantasy world of a book, we can do anything, see anything, be anything: We can tesseract with Mrs. Whatsit, raise a baby dragon in the country of Pern, step through the wardrobe into Narnia, and board the Hogwarts train from Platform 9-3/4.

Stretching the imagination through literature has wonderful psychological rewards, extending the boundaries of what we perceive as reality. Many scientists will tell you that as children, they were fantasy and science

Cover by Max Ginsburg, from ROLL OF THUNDER, HEAR MY CRY by Mildred D. Taylor, copyright © 1991 by Max Ginsburg, cover illustration. Used by permission of Puffin Books, A Division of Penguin Young Readers Group, A Member of Penguin Group (USA) Inc., 345 Hudson Street, New York, NY 10014. All rights reserved.

Older students discuss one of the criteria for fantasy.

oceans. Science fiction presents a view of the world that one day might be possible, given what we know about science and technology. Writers of this genre have a tough assignment: They must speculate about future technology and advances in human knowledge while writing a plausible story. Thus, they must create detailed descriptions of scientific inventions such as robots, computers, and spaceships so that readers believe in them. However, these scientific facts shouldn't override the plot, and all details must be logically consistent. They also must introduce ethical or societal implications of these future inventions.

Elements of Fiction

We feel strongly that children's personal interpretations and opinions are valid responses to books. However, we also think they can expand their responses and become more deeply engaged if they know what experienced readers think about when responding to a book. The elements readers typically consider when evaluating fiction are characterization, plot, theme, setting, style, and point of view. Although we examine each of these elements individually, in reality, skilled authors weave them together to create a cohesive whole.

Characterization

Characterization is the heart of fiction. Good fiction writers create credible, multidimensional characters that ring true with readers, and with whom readers can journey through the reading experience. Think back to the books that have been the most memorable to you: We suspect that in most cases, the first and most indelible memories have to do with characters.

The main character of the story is termed the *protagonist*. This is the person around whom the story revolves; the problems or situations facing this person drive the plot. Thus, for example, Marty, in Phyllis Reynolds Naylor's popular novel *Shiloh*, is the person whose conflicted thoughts about stealing an abused dog are clearly evident to the reader. We learn about other characters as the story unfolds, but it is Marty and his dilemma that we focus upon. Similarly, we empathize and celebrate family life on the prairie with Laura in *Little House on the Prairie* (Wilder), and we agonize with Meg in Madeleine L'Engle's *A Wrinkle in Time* as she travels through time and space to find her missing father. These characters are all protagonists in their respective stories.

fiction readers; considering new possibilities in fantasy led them to think creatively and to push the limits of scientific truth. Fantasy takes us out of our everyday world, helping us to consider new possibilities.

Fantasy also can take children within themselves, showing them universal human truths they need to understand to become competent adults, truths such as the importance of loyalty, how to bravely face incredible danger, or stay true to yourself when tempted by false promises. Fantasy shows students that such knowledge is not gained easily, but often evolves through struggles with external forces as well as with oneself. Far from being divorced from reality, fantasy actually sheds light on what is true and gets at the heart of what it means to be human.

Science Fiction

A story is considered science fiction when the elements are based on reasonable scientific theory, that is, not yet possible according to what we currently know. In science fiction, someone may travel forward or backward in time, visit a neighboring planet, or encounter mysteries in the depths of the

> *Fantasy helps one of our deepest needs, the need to make sense out of the world, the need to make sense out of our lives . . . Fantasy touches our deepest feelings and in so doing it speaks to the best and most hopeful parts of ourselves. It can help us learn the most fundamental skill of all: how to be human.*
>
> Lloyd Alexander, fantasy writer; personal communication, September, 1999

Cover, from SAVING SHILOH by Phyllis Reynolds Naylor. Cover copyright © 1997 by Barry Moser. Used by permission of Barry Moser.

even if the main character is an animal (remember Winnie-the-Pooh, from A. A. Milne's classic book, or Babe, from Dick King-Smith's *Babe, the Gallant Pig*). Authors work diligently to reveal their characters. Readers come to know these characters by what they say or think, what they do, and what others say about them; so an author might describe a character's thoughts, create dialogue with other characters, portray the thoughts others have about the character, or show the character in action.

Christopher Paul Curtis uses all these techniques to make his character Buddy come alive in *Bud, Not Buddy*. Because the story is written in the first person, readers come to know Bud's thoughts and feelings intimately: his

From BUD, NOT BUDDY (JACKET COVER) by Christopher Paul Curtis, copyright. Used by permission of Random House Children's Books, a division of Random House, Inc.

Many stories also feature an *antagonist*; this character is the foil for the protagonist. Sometimes the antagonist attempts to stop what the main character wants to accomplish or is on the opposing side of a controversy. That character might have another point of view or could invoke a dilemma through which we get to know the main character. For example, Harry Potter, in the series by J. K. Rowling, must endure the bullying of fellow student Draco Malfoy as well as constant clashes with the evil Voldemort. Stanley Yelnats, in Louis Sachar's *Holes*, must contend with the evil Warden in order to survive the endless hole digging he is forced to endure at Camp Green Lake. Karen Cushman's Birdy, in *Catherine, Called Birdy*, is a young medieval English girl who must battle her parents to avoid marrying an elderly man.

In good fiction, main characters are highly developed. Through the course of the story, readers come to know their gifts as well as their flaws and struggles. This is true longing for a father and a permanent home; his famous "Rules for Having a Funner Life and Making a Better Liar Out of Yourself" that guide his actions; and his fear of vampires. Readers understand why he travels on foot from Detroit to Flint, Michigan, and why he is cautious around people he doesn't know well. They also see him through the eyes of members of the Dusky Devastators of the Depression, a jazz band he connects with, who alternately tease and comfort him as he searches for his identity.

Christopher Paul Curtis takes the crafting of his characters very seriously. Although he writes historical fiction, he says he doesn't "want to whack [children] over the head with history. That's a good way to lose them" (Canton, 2001, p. 33). Rather, he says, "They get to know the characters first. They get to know Bud, his life in the orphanage; they know what kind of kid he is . . . my hope is that it triggers them into asking lots of questions" (p. 33).

Some characters grow across multiple books, becoming increasingly real and memorable to readers; J. K. Rowling's Harry Potter is one example of this. When we meet Harry, he is a frightened, downtrodden 11-year-old boy, unaware of his heritage or his powers. As the series progresses, he becomes increasingly more daring as well as comfortable with the many challenges he faces. Similarly, we meet Beverly Cleary's Ramona as the pesky younger sister to Beezus in *Beezus and Ramona*. Eventually Ramona stars in her own books, and readers come to love this active, challenging child to whom they can easily relate.

This close attention to creating fully developed characters helps authors maintain consistency as a story evolves. They must be sure that everything each character says or does is consistent with prior thoughts and actions. The character's behavior should also be congruent with his or her age and the cultural context of the story; a character can't suddenly develop magical powers when faced with an evil dragon, for example, when there has been no previous reference to such powers.

Plot

Plot is another important element of fiction. The plan of action, how the events unfold, how the central conflict is resolved, and what characters do are all aspects of plot. Some authors outline plot details in advance, just as they might sketch out characters. J. K. Rowling, for example, stated she had all seven books in the Harry Potter series mapped out before she began writing the first volume (Gray, 1999). Others claim almost divine intervention, that parts of the story write themselves, as if the characters "take over" and drive the story.

A well-constructed plot develops logically, with events evolving plausibly from what has previously occurred. The story usually features some sort of conflict in which the main characters struggle with a problem or overcome some obstacle. Children's literature stories typically feature four main types of conflict: (a) person against person, (b) person against society, (c) person against nature, and (d) person against self (Lukens, 1999; Norton & Norton, 2003). Some stories focus on one conflict, whereas others have layers of conflict or several conflicts that evolve as the story progresses.

Good plots are not predictable. Rather, authors strive to make their plots believable, yet fresh and original. For example, in *Crispin: The Cross of Lead*, author Avi crafts an intriguing mystery set in medieval times. Crispin is left to fend for himself after his mother dies. To complicate matters, he is falsely accused of murder and must run for his life. His many adventures and his final decision keep readers intrigued. As one child said about Crispin's adventures, "What I enjoyed most is that there was nothing predictable about the story. I was always surprised."

Plots in children's books tend to be linear, with identifiable beginnings, middles, and ends. Younger children typically find flashbacks; multiple, interwoven plot lines; or other more complex plot structures difficult to follow. Often the story focuses on one main struggle or pivotal event. For example, in *The Watsons Go to Birmingham— 1963* (Curtis), the story revolves around a trip taken by an African American family. In *Stone Fox* (Gardiner), a boy's quest to win a dogsled race and earn money to save the family home is the focus of the story.

Some children's books, particularly those for more mature readers, feature complex or multiple plots. In *Roll of Thunder, Hear My Cry* (Taylor), Cassie's actions clearly are the focus, but nearly every other character also faces a private struggle that is developed through the book. Cassie's mother clashes with the school board; her father constantly worries about having sufficient money to keep their land; and her brother faces confrontations with another boy who is determined to get him into trouble.

Some books are characterized by multiple plots. For example, in *Holes* (Sachar), Stanley's plight of digging holes day after day at Camp Green Lake is intertwined with an equally engaging plot about how Camp Green Lake came to be. The popularity of this book attests to the author's skill in developing these subplots so children can follow them.

Children also tend to enjoy plots that feature lots of action with minimal dialogue or description. The cliffhangers at the end of chapters along with breathtaking action that characterize Avi's *Beyond the Western Sea*, an exciting story of three children emigrating from Ireland to America, keep children's interests. Gary Paulsen's *Hatchet* also features riveting action when the main character, Brian, faces one challenge after another as he struggles to survive in the Canadian wilderness. Paulsen reveals Brian's thoughts to his readers, but the emphasis is always on the plot: what happens next.

Theme

Theme is the underlying meaning of the story: what the author wants us to learn about life or society. This concept might best be understood by thinking about how themes evolve in music. When we watch a movie with a theme song (think *Gone With the Wind* or *Titanic*), the increasingly familiar melody surfaces time and again as the movie progresses; that horizontal thread of melody becomes the theme. Themes in literature work the same way: Connecting threads of ideas resurface through the characters and their actions as the story unfolds.

Themes in books for young children are frequently based on situations, problems, and emotions close to children's own experiences. For example, the theme of *Frog and Toad Are Friends*, by Arnold Lobel, is the importance of friendship. In contrast, themes in books for older readers often focus on the journey to adulthood and the consequences of one's choices (Norton & Norton, 2003). Linda Sue Park's *A Single Shard*, a story about a young orphan boy in twelfth-century Korea who wants desperately to be a potter, is a good example of this. Although the story is set in medieval Korea, we quickly come to realize that the book focuses on themes important to all people of all times, such as pride in honest effort, loyalty, the importance of kindness, and the value of accumulated wisdom for solving life's problems.

Sometimes themes are directly stated, but in other books, readers must think critically in order to discern the meaning the author is trying to convey. Writers must be careful that their theme does not override the story so that the message becomes too didactic or preachy.

Many well-written books feature multiple themes or themes that function at several layers of meaning. Gary Paulsen's *Hatchet* has a theme of person versus the environment. However, this experience changes Brian from an indulged boy to one who is independent and responsible. Because the experience has forever changed Brian, this is also a coming-of-age story.

Figure 8.1 lists some common themes found in children's books, along with suggested books that feature each theme.

Setting

Setting is both where and when a story takes place. Settings can be real places within a real time period, invented places within real time, or invented places in time that is manipulated. Setting is typically a more important quality in fiction than in other genres. If Meg hadn't been in an alien world searching for her father, she would never have discovered the concept of *A Wrinkle in Time* (L'Engle); if Jethro hadn't lived in a border state prior to the Civil War, then it would have been unrealistic for his brothers to have divided loyalties in *Across Five Aprils* (Hunt). Jonas,

Cover, from A SINGLE SHARD by Linda Sue Park. Jacket and case cover copyright © 2001 by Jean and Mou-sien Tseng. Reprinted by permission of Clarion Books/Houghton Mifflin Company. All rights reserved.

in Lois Lowry's *The Giver*, ran away because he felt trapped by the unfeeling, protective society in which he lived. Because setting and plot often support each other, understanding time and place in a story contributes to appreciation of the events.

Authors create a vivid, believable setting in several ways. First, all elements of the setting need to be consistent. This is particularly important when the setting is a historical era or an invented world, such as the realm of Narnia in *The Lion, the Witch and the Wardrobe* (Lewis) or Revolutionary War–era Boston in *Johnny Tremain* (Forbes). If we are going to believe that the Meeker family, from *My Brother Sam Is Dead* (Collier & Collier), exists in Revolutionary War–era America, then they must be described as wearing clothes, eating foods, and living in dwellings consistent with that era. If the Gryffindor

Figure 8.1
Common Themes
In Fiction

Theme	Sample Books Featuring the Theme
☀ Conflict: Person vs. Environment (physical and cultural)	*Hatchet*—Gary Paulsen *Where the Lilies Bloom*—Vera Cleaver & Bill Cleaver *Island of the Blue Dolphins*—Scott O'Dell *Monkey Island*—Paula Fox *The Giver*—Lois Lowry *My Daniel*—Pam Conrad *Shabanu: Daughter of the Wind*—Suzanne Fisher Staples
☀ Conflict: Person vs. Self	*Joey Pigza Swallowed the Key*—Jack Gantos *The Language of Goldfish*—Zibby O'Neal *Wizard of Earthsea*—Ursula Le Guin *Maniac Magee*—Jerry Spinelli *Lord of the Deep*—Graham Salisbury *What Hearts*—Bruce Brooks
☀ Coming of Age: Self-acceptance, Morality, Ability to Face Problems and Responsibilities; Awareness of One's Destiny	*Tuck Everlasting*—Natalie Babbitt *When Zachary Beaver Came to Town*—Kimberly Willis Holt *Dicey's Song*—Cynthia Voigt *The Summer of the Swans*—Betsy Byars *Holes*—Louis Sachar *The Birchbark House*—Louise Erdrich *The Lost Years of Merlin*—T. A. Barron *The Golden Compass*—Philip Pullman
☀ Search for Freedom	*North to Freedom*—Anne Holm *The Clay Marble*—Mingfong Ho *The Year of Impossible Goodbyes*—Sook Nyul Choi *Jip: His Story*—Katherine Paterson *Tonight, by Sea*—Frances Temple *Parvana's Journey*—Deborah Ellis *Red Midnight*—Ben Michael
☀ Loyalty and Honor	*My Brother Sam Is Dead*—James Collier & Christopher Collier *Charlotte's Web*—E. B. White *Roll of Thunder, Hear My Cry*—Mildred Taylor *Number the Stars*—Lois Lowry *On My Honor*—Marion Dane Bauer
☀ Conflict: Good Versus Evil	*A Wrinkle in Time*—Madeleine L'Engle *The Lion, the Witch and the Wardrobe*—C. S. Lewis *The Dark Is Rising*—Susan Cooper *Harry Potter and the Sorcerer's Stone*—J. K. Rowling
☀ Personal and Social Responsibility	*The Great Gilly Hopkins*—Katherine Paterson *A Single Shard*—Linda S. Park *The Other Side of Truth*—Beverley Naidoo *Lyddie*—Katherine Paterson *Among the Hidden*—Margaret Peterson Haddix

(continues)

Theme	Sample Books Featuring the Theme
☼ Getting Along With Others: Friendships, Family Conflicts; Accepting Differences	*The Hundred Dresses*—Eleanor Estes *Walk Two Moons*—Sharon Creech *The Goats*—Brock Cole *My Louisiana Sky*—Kimberly Willis Holt *Toning the Sweep*—Angela Johnson *The Sign of the Beaver*—Elizabeth George Speare
☼ Quests and Adventures	*The Black Cauldron*—Lloyd Alexander *A Girl Named Disaster*—Nancy Farmer *Park's Quest*—Katherine Paterson *James and the Giant Peach*—Roald Dahl *The Blue Sword*—Robin McKinley

Figure 8.1
(continued)

Tower in the Harry Potter series requires a password for entry, that must happen every time a character attempts to go into the tower.

Setting is also developed through the use of details and rich descriptions. Whether it's the hum of wind, the roar of the ocean, the thundering of trains, or the smell of a prairie fire, authors choose words and images to evoke the senses and make the story come alive.

Describing the setting is an art in fiction writing: Too much description becomes tedious, leaves nothing to the reader's imagination, and makes for boring writing, but too little description fails to engage the reader. Readers need enough to help them connect with the story; then they can use their imaginations to fill in the rest.

Style

Children's books need more than plot, theme, character, and setting; they need language to knit these elements together. This is the function of style. Authors use language to compose a story using their own distinct voice.

Style is a writer's creative use of words, sentence structures, and literary devices to give a story a unique voice for readers. Style is not a mechanical literary device that follows a prescribed blueprint. Rather, the style an author uses to craft a story must fit the plot, characters, and cultural milieu. Most important, the style must make the story come alive. Just as composers blend tone and rhythm to create a symphony, authors imaginatively fuse elements of language into a compelling voice for their story. It is the style—the rhythm of the sentences, the vivid descriptions, the fresh imagery—that subtly affects a reader's response.

> The rhythm, the flow, the pace, the syllables, and the words that make up the sentences are part of a kind of music that I listen for. There is a judgment that the inner ear makes as I go along. It says yes, that's good, or no, no good, and I don't question it. It comes from someplace where (if it's a good day) the mind and heart and ear are in balance. I have learned to trust it.
>
> William Hooks, author; personal communication, September, 1999

Even the youngest children can appreciate finely crafted language that resonates in the ear and mind.

Some fiction writers use a fluid, poetic style in which the language is rhythmical and at times alliterative; Patricia MacLachlan, who writes both contemporary realistic and historical fiction, is particularly known for this style. Read aloud the following passage from MacLachlan's *Sarah, Plain and Tall*, the story of a young woman who travels from Maine to the western prairie in the 1800s as a mail-order bride.

> Autumn will come, then winter cold with a wind that blows like the wind off the sea in Maine. There will be nests of curls to look for, and dried flowers all winter long. When there are storms, Papa will stretch a rope from the door to the barn so we will not be lost when we feed the sheep and the cows and Jack and Old Bess. And Sarah's chickens, if they are living in the house. There will be Sarah's sea, blue and gray and green, hanging on the wall. And songs, old and new. And Seal with yellow eyes. And there will be Sarah, plain and tall. (p. 58)

The descriptive words and varied sentence structure create a compelling rhythm that conveys perfectly the feel of endless space and sky.

In contrast, some writers use a more abrupt, choppy style. For example, Gary Paulsen uses this technique very effectively in *Hatchet*, where his main character's thoughts are focused on the pain of his parents' divorce.

Fiction writers often use figurative language to develop style in their work. Skilled writers invent fresh comparisons that make their work distinctive while developing setting, plot, and characters. In *Walk Two Moons*, Sharon

Jacket art Copyright © 1985 by Marcia Sewall. Jacket Copyright © 1985 by HarperCollins Publishers Inc.

A student creates a dust jacket as an extension to Gary Paulsen's *Hatchet*.

Creech has her main character use similes that fit the story's Appalachian context and the young girl's personal background. For example, she compares the trouble her eccentric grandparents inevitably get into when they drive a car to a young filly that inevitably follows a mare. Children typically do not like stories with too much description or "flowery language." However, they can learn to appreciate how figurative language adds to the flavor of a story.

Point of View

The perspective from which a story is told is its *point of view*. The omniscient, all-knowing, storyteller's voice is a point of view often used in fiction. When the author uses this voice, the thoughts and feelings of several, or even all, characters can be revealed. *The Lion, the Witch and the Wardrobe* (Lewis) and *Charlotte's Web* (White) are both told from this perspective.

A limited third-person point of view focuses on the perspective of one character; the story is still told in the third person, but the reader knows the story only through the filter of one character's perspective. *Bridge to Terabithia*, by Katherine Paterson, is told from that point of view. Jerry Spinelli uses this point of view to begin *Wringer* in the following way:

> He did not want to be a Wringer. This was one of the first things he had learned about himself. He could not have said exactly when he learned it, but it was very early. And more than early, it was deep inside. In the stomach, like hunger. (p. 1)

First-person narrative (using "I," "me," etc.) is a popular point of view in children's books, particularly in fiction. This perspective provides a sense of immediacy and intimacy that often draws readers into the story. You may remember Judy Blume's *Are You There God? It's Me, Margaret*. This book is still popular with girls because of its cozy first-person perspective that draws readers in.

> Are you there God? It's me, Margaret. We're moving today. I'm so scared God. I've never lived anywhere but here. Suppose I hate my new school? Suppose everybody there hates me? Please help me God. Don't let New Jersey be too horrible. Thank you.

Some writers transcend the first-person point of view by shifting perspective from one character to another as the story progresses to create a revolving first-person perspective. Paul Fleischman does this in *Bull Run*, a novel about the first battle of the Civil War. The perspectives of 16 people affected by the battle—some Southern, some Northern, observers, fighters, men, women—are presented in various vignettes. The reader comes to see the horrors of war. In *Maggie's Door*, by Patricia Reilly Giff, two characters, one female (Nory) and one male (Sean), recount their experiences traveling from Ireland to America during the Irish potato famine.

The plot structure, how an author chooses to reveal character, and the intended message help authors determine which point of view they will employ; these decisions, in turn, influence readers' responses

Language really is a dance for me. I long ago decided that I would do anything possible to make a story work right — including sometimes getting fast and loose with grammar. Story is all, and language is a tool to make the story work right.

Gary Paulsen, author, in McClure & Kristo, 1996, p. 27

to the story. When we evaluate fiction, then, we need to determine who is telling the story and whether this is an effective point of view.

Adults use some additional terms to discuss various aspects of fiction. The Terms for Teachers feature that follows lists and defines some of these terms.

Terms for Teachers

Discourse of Fiction

Anthropomorphism—Attribution of human traits to animals, who then talk and may display other human behaviors.

Aside—Narration directed to the reader that the characters are not privy to, often in a different voice or style to distinguish it.

Characters—The people or animals in stories.

Cliché—An overused expression that has lost any impact or freshness.

Cliffhanger—An event in the plot partially told at the end of a chapter or section to make the reader want to read on.

Climax—The point in the plot where something is solved, uncovered, accomplished, or achieved.

Conflict Resolution—Following the climax, events coming together toward the end of the story.

Deconstruction—The act and art of dissecting a text to look critically at the author's purposes, biases, implied assumptions, worldview, and subtle use of language.

Didactic—Text that explicitly preaches or teaches, generally in a moralistic sense; the lesson presented takes precedence over literary quality.

Flashback—Interruption of the time sequence of the plot by an event from the past.

Flat Character—A static character in a story. Little growth or change occurs in the character's personality.

Foreshadow—To hint, sometimes very subtly, of things to come later in the plot.

Form—The manner in which a work is presented, such as in a novel, a poem, or a picture book.

Genre—The category of text by type, such as fiction, nonfiction, poetry.

Imagery—Mental pictures created with words.

Intertextuality—Reference in one text to something readers may know from another text; calling a person a "wolf in sheep's clothing" refers to the folktale "The Boy Who Cried Wolf."

Irony—A subtle twist in the plot that results in the opposite of what was expected.

Main Plot—The larger event(s) driving the progress of the story.

Major Characters—People or animals with major roles in fiction.

Minor Characters—Characters appearing once or occasionally in a story.

Omniscient Narrator—The narrator who is not also a character in the story.

Personification—Attribution of human traits to inanimate objects, such as a train engine that talks.

Plot—The events of a story.

Round Character—A character who changes and grows in a story.

Subplots—Less central events that offer complexity, such as a struggle by a minor character within the story, or a dilemma that plagues the main character from time to time.

Suspense—The presence of unsolved dilemmas or events that don't quite make sense, or the holding back of explanations to encourage readers to continue. Especially popular in mysteries.

Symbolism—Technique of using a motif or object to represent something else.

Transfiguration—Transformation of people in a story into animals, or vice versa.

Voice—A recognizable trait in an author's writing that is the sum total of style, point of view, etc.

Guidelines for Selecting High-Quality Fiction

How do you determine high-quality fiction so that you can be sure your students grow as critical readers? The Guidelines for Choosing Literature feature on p. 189 has criteria to help you select books for your classroom.

Awards for Excellence in Fiction

A good way to determine excellence in fiction is to examine award-winning books. Similar in prestige to the Newbery Medal, the National Book Award for Young People's Literature is presented yearly by the National Book Foundation to recognize the outstanding contribution to children's literature. Although the committee considers books of all genres, the vast majority of the winners thus far have been works of fiction.

Tech Note
Access the Companion Website for complete lists of winners for all awards discussed in this chapter.

Some awards are given for specific genres. For example, the Scott O'Dell Historical Fiction Award goes each year to a meritorious book for children or young adults published in the previous year. Author Scott O'Dell established this award to encourage other writers to focus on historical fiction.

The Jefferson Cup honors a distinguished biography, historical fiction, or American history book for young people. Fiction winners of this award include such diverse titles as *Storm Warriors*, by Elisa Carbone, *Preacher's Boy*, by Katherine Paterson, *Soldier's Heart*, by Gary Paulsen, *The Ornament Tree*, by Jean Thesman, *Shades of Gray*, by Carolyn Reeder, *After the Dancing Days*, by Margaret Rostkowski, and *Sarah, Plain and Tall*, by Patricia MacLachlan.

Several awards are given to books with a specific focus. The Edgars, named after Edgar Allan Poe, are given by the Mystery Writers of America in various categories, including juvenile fiction. The Josette Frank Award is given annually to honor books of literary merit in which children or young people deal in a positive or realistic way with difficulties in their world while growing emotionally and morally.

The Jane Addams Book Award, presented annually since 1953 by the Women's International League for Peace and Freedom, is given to the children's book that most effectively promotes the cause of peace, social justice, and world community. Beginning in 1993, a picture-book category was added. Although books from all genres are considered, works of fiction dominate the list of winners.

Building a Classroom Library

Because fiction is so popular with children, books from this genre will likely be the backbone of your collection. You should definitely include a large number of books from contemporary realistic fiction, historical fiction, and fantasy. Science fiction tends to be somewhat less popular; however, some science fiction should be included, particularly if you work with middle-grade students. Have books from a variety of reading levels to accommodate the likely range of readers in your classroom.

When considering specific titles, start with those you love and find irresistible; your enthusiasm for these personal favorites will likely kindle enthusiasm in your students. Include books you know through experience or from research that children tend to enjoy. The studies on children's reading preferences (noted in chapter 3) are a good place to find fiction titles that appeal to a wide audience. Children's Choice awards, such as those sponsored by the International Reading Association and many states, also provide insights into titles children have voted as "not to be missed." Although these awards are not always given to fiction, award programs in which children select the winners most frequently honor this genre. Additionally, you can encourage your own students to select books for the collection. They can establish a "recommendation center" in the classroom library where they feature books they've enjoyed and recommend to friends. They can put self-stick notes inside the cover, detailing what is so inviting about the book. In some classrooms, the inside covers of the most popular books are blanketed with notes!

Once your basic fiction collection is gathered, it is helpful to organize the books so your students can easily access titles. Have special sections for horse stories, mysteries, those "guaranteed to make you laugh," or those "just like the Harry Potter series." A section for "hot" new books, such as the latest Lemony Snicket or Gary Paulsen title, could entice children to dive right in. Organize sections by theme, nonfiction matched with related fiction, or fictional books paired with poetry that relates to a particular book's theme or characters. Books you have read aloud, along with their sequels, might form another section; this would particularly help your less able readers easily find books for which they have sufficient background to read successfully.

Some teachers have students help organize the collection at the beginning of the year. This is a great way to help your students become familiar with the collection and to suggest ways to organize the books that will be meaningful to them. Additionally, this activity is a great

Guidelines for Choosing Literature

Evaluating Fiction for Children

Characterization

☼ Are the characters true to life? Do they seem plausible? Are their actions consistent with their age and cultural background?

☼ Are the main characters multidimensional? Do they have both strengths and weaknesses?

☼ Do any of the characters grow and change? Are the reasons for their actions clear?

Plot

☼ Does the book tell a good story?

☼ Is the story line developmentally appropriate for the intended audience? (Are the events understandable and interesting to the children who will read it?)

☼ Is the plot original, yet believable?

☼ Does the story unfold logically?

☼ Does the climax seem possible?

☼ Are controversial issues presented openly and honestly?

Setting

☼ Does the author make the setting seem real?

☼ Is the setting appropriate for the story?

☼ Does the author transport readers to the setting so that they feel a part of it?

Theme

☼ Is the theme developmentally appropriate and of interest to the book's intended audience?

☼ Does the theme emerge naturally from story events, or does it override the story?

☼ Has the author talked down to children or become too didactic in conveying the theme?

☼ Is the theme relevant for today's children?

☼ Will the theme help readers grow and change?

Style

☼ Is the style appropriate for the book's intended audience?

☼ Is this author's use of devices such as figurative language fresh yet understandable to the book's intended audience?

☼ Is the dialogue suited to the characters? Do they sound like real people?

(continues)

Evaluating Fiction for Children (continued)

Point of View

- ☀ Is the point of view appropriate for the story?
- ☀ In a book written in first person, do readers get a sense of how other characters think and feel?
- ☀ In a book written in third person, do readers get a good sense of how several characters think and feel?

Additional Considerations for Contemporary Realistic Fiction

- ☀ Does the book honestly show contemporary life—the joys as well as the challenges—for readers?
- ☀ Is the story enduring? Does it have relevance beyond its contemporary setting?
- ☀ Is violence or other negative behavior shown to have consequences?

Additional Considerations for Historical Fiction

- ☀ Are fact and fiction integrated so that the facts don't overwhelm the story?
- ☀ Are the details of setting, events, and characterization consistent with the historical era of the story?
- ☀ Does the dialogue convey a sense of the historical era without seeming stilted or being difficult to understand?
- ☀ Does the story accurately reflect the cultural values and norms of the era without condoning outdated stereotypes of race or gender?
- ☀ Does the theme provide insights about the past? Does the theme provide insights for contemporary life?
- ☀ Is the conflict well defined and appropriate for the historical era of the book?
- ☀ Are the perspectives of minorities and women from that era accurately portrayed?

Additional Considerations for Fantasy

- ☀ Has the author made the story believable? How?
- ☀ Is the setting believable? How has the author created a setting that is believable to readers?
- ☀ Are the fantasy elements logical and consistent with the story?
- ☀ Is the plot original?

Additional Considerations for Science Fiction

- ☀ Does the author base the concepts in the book on facts?
- ☀ Does the author remain consistent with established scientific knowledge while pushing the boundaries of what we accept as "fact" or "truth"?
- ☀ Does the author explore how future possibilities have implications for contemporary society?

evaluation tool as you observe the criteria they use to sort the books into categories.

Most important, be choosy about the fiction titles you have available for children; they will find the Walt Disney cartoon versions of the classics and Captain Underpants books on their own. The books in your collection should be well written, with believable, interesting characters who are approximately the same age as your students, and thought-provoking themes with which they can identify. This will help them become lifelong lovers of fiction.

Special Considerations for Young Children

Many teachers of young children find it useful to organize books by reading levels, to make it easier for children to find "just-right" books for independent reading. Often, they use colored stickers on the spine of the book or place books at a similar level together in a basket. However, be careful that children don't get stuck thinking they can read only books at a particular level. Encourage them to stretch themselves and to read titles that might be challenging, but also interesting to them.

Classroom libraries for young children should also include many transitional chapter books, particularly those that are part of a series. Featuring transitional books such as the Cam Jansen mysteries or Magic Tree House books in a special section will help children who are just moving into chapter books find some that are interesting and that they can read successfully. Figure 8.3 on p. 201 presents a helpful list of transitional and series books that will guide you in selecting appropriate titles for your collection.

Special Considerations for Older Students

Students' tastes in fiction become more specialized and diversified as they grow older and become more proficient readers. Thus, your collection will need to include more titles as well as a larger number of titles representing different genres, authors, and themes in order to meet their needs.

Categorizing Fiction

Children's literature professionals group fiction in many ways: for example, by content, theme, historical era, and use of a particular literary device. The dilemma is that books usually fit into more than one category; a family story, for example, might also be a survival story or a mystery. Children often come up with their own viable ways to categorize books, thus offering yet another perspective on categories.

In this chapter, we have organized books for each genre of fiction in the ways we think will be most useful for discussion as well as most meaningful for teachers. Thus, for contemporary realistic fiction, books are organized by theme; historical fiction books are organized by historical era; and fantasy/science fiction books are organized by content. Appendix A at the end of this book lists categories of fiction and sample titles for each; the titles listed are annotated on the CD-ROM that accompanies this book.

Contemporary Realistic Fiction

Contemporary realistic fiction is the fictional genre most popular with children; thus these stories are often the backbone of a living literature book collection. We have organized this category thematically because we have found that teachers frequently create theme studies with realistic fiction.

Peer Relationships

Children of all ages are concerned about interacting appropriately with a wide variety of people. Books that explore peer relationships reflect the issues children encounter in their own lives. Schools, camps, and neighborhoods are the settings for many of these stories. The Newbery-winning *Bridge to Terabithia*, by Katherine Paterson, is a classic book in this category. This story revolves around the friendship between 10-year-olds Jess and Leslie, children from different backgrounds who both feel isolated from their families. They create a secret retreat, dubbed Terabithia, and develop a strong friendship in the process.

Family Relationships

Stories that explore the relationships among siblings as well as between children and adult family members are also popular in realistic fiction. Many of these portray a relatively happy child with loving parents, doing normal daily activities such as bedtime rituals, preparing meals, and playing together. Lois Lowry's Anastasia Krupnik series is an excellent example of these books, as are Beverly Cleary's Ramona books. *The Mouse Rap*, by Walter Dean Myers, and *Yang the Youngest and His Terrible Ear* (Yamioka), along with its sequels, are examples that feature multicultural families.

In other stories, the family experiences problems such as divorce, sibling rivalry, adoption, and poverty or is portrayed as unconventional. Not all children live in safe, nuclear families, and they need to see themselves depicted in the books they read. In *My Louisiana Sky*, by Kimberly Willis Holt, for example, Tiger Ann Parker must contend

Text Set   *Selected Works by Katherine Paterson*

Novels
The Master Puppeteer. (1975). Crowell.
The Great Gilly Hopkins. (1978). Crowell.
Jacob Have I Loved. (1980). HarperCollins.
Come Sing, Jimmy Jo. (1985). Dutton.
Bridge to Terabithia. (1987). Crowell.
Park's Quest. (1989). Dutton.
Lyddie. (1991). Putnam.
Flip-Flop Girl. (1994). Dutton.
Jip: His Story. (1996). Puffin.
Preacher's Boy. (1999). Clarion.
The Same Stuff as Stars. (2002). Clarion.

Picture Books
The Sign of the Chrysanthemum. (1973). Crowell.
Rebels of the Heavenly Kingdom. (1983). Dutton.
The Tale of the Mandarin Ducks. (1990). Lodestar.
The Smallest Cow in the World. (1991). HarperCollins.
Celia and the Sweet, Sweet Water. (1998). Clarion.
Parzival: The Quest of the Grail Knight. (1998). Lodestar.
The Wide-Awake Princess. (2000). Clarion.

Short Novel
The King's Equal. (1992). HarperCollins.

Nonfiction
Images of God (with John Paterson). (1998). Clarion.

For Teachers: Essays and Commentaries
Gates of Excellence: On Reading and Writing Books for Children.
  (1981). Elsevier.
A Sense of Wonder: On Reading and Writing Books for Children.
  (1995). Plume.
The Invisible Child: On Reading and Writing Books for Children.
  (2001). Dutton.

with parents who are developmentally handicapped. In *Waiting to Disappear*, by April Fritz Floyd, 13-year-old Elizabeth Mullins's mother suffers a mental breakdown. Typically the situations are resolved positively, or the authors provide a sense of hope that things will improve. *A Step From Heaven* (Nu), *Jazmin's Notebook* (Grimes), *Shabanu: Daughter of the Wind* (Staples), and *Lord of the Deep* (Salisbury) portray diverse families who are struggling with these same issues.

Interactions with extended family members such as grandparents, cousins, aunts, uncles, and foster parents are often a significant part of children's lives. In children's literature, these adult characters are often unconventional in their behavior. Sometimes the extended family member raises the child, as in *Journey* and *Arthur, For the Very First Time*, by Patricia MacLachlan, *Walk Two Moons*, by Sharon Creech, and *Missing May*, by Cynthia Rylant. In *Miracle's Boys*, by Jacqueline Woodson, it is the oldest brother who raises his siblings after both parents die. In other books, the older adult is portrayed as a mentor who offers important guidance and support. For example, in *Maniac Magee* (Spinelli), Maniac gets love and a positive perspective from Grayson, an aging zoo worker who finds the boy in the buffalo pen at the zoo.

Animal Stories

Animal stories are classified as realistic fiction if the animal characters act according to their true nature and are not anthropomorphized. The animal characters play a featured role; however, the human character typically changes as a result of interacting with the animal. You may be familiar with some of the classics in this category, such as *The Incredible Journey* (Burnford) and *Where the Red Fern Grows* (Rawls). These books are still popular with children because of their powerful stories and strong depictions of animal characters.

Several recent realistic animal books have captured the hearts of children. The Newbery Medal winner *Shiloh* (Naylor), along with its sequels *Shiloh Season* and *Saving Shiloh*, tells the poignant story of an abused dog and the boy who rescues him. *Because of Winn-Dixie* (DiCamillo) tells of a stray dog that is found and becomes the beloved friend and companion to a young girl. *Zulu Dog*, by Anton Ferreira, takes place in South Africa just after apartheid is abolished.

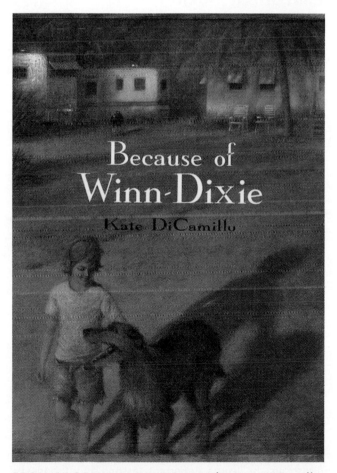

BECAUSE OF WINN-DIXIE © 2000 by Kate DiCamillo. Reproduced by permission of the publisher Candlewick Press, Inc., Cambridge, MA.

Adventure and Survival Stories

Children, particularly middle schoolers, enjoy reading about others their age who use determination and ingenuity to endure incredible challenges and survive on their own. Main characters in these stories typically succeed and grow toward maturity as they tackle challenging situations. Classic titles in this category include O'Dell's *Island of the Blue Dolphins*, *Call It Courage* (Sperry), George's *My Side of the Mountain* (and its sequels), and *Julie of the Wolves* (and its sequels).

Gary Paulsen is a contemporary writer whose exciting adventure stories capture even the most reluctant readers. *Hatchet* and the sequels *The River*, *Brian's Winter*, and *Brian's Return* depict a young boy surviving alone in the Canadian wilderness with increasing satisfaction and competence. Paulsen's *The Voyage of the Frog* is a survival story that takes place at sea.

Although the setting for many survival stories is in the wilderness or some remote place, these books can also be set in an urban environment. Paula Fox's *Monkey Island*, about a young boy living with a group of homeless people in New York City, is an excellent example of this. *From the Mixed-Up Files of Mrs. Basil E. Frankweiler* (Konigsburg) features two young children who have run away from home and who live in the Metropolitan Museum of Art. *Slake's Limbo*, by Felice Holman, tells of a 13-year old, pursued by gangs, who hides in the New York subway system for 121 days.

Sometimes the conflict and survival occur within the character's own mind or arise from a physical infirmity. The Joey Pigza books, by Jack Gantos, depict a boy with attention deficit hyperactivity disorder who cannot control his behavior.

Humorous Stories

Children love to read about characters like themselves who encounter humorous situations and predicaments. Although many of the titles we've already discussed fall into this category, humorous books are so popular with students that they deserve separate mention. Beverly Cleary's Ramona books are classics, as are Judy Blume's stories of Peter and his younger brother, Fudge, in *Tales of a Fourth Grade Nothing* and *Superfudge*.

Mysteries

Many students enjoy reading mysteries because of the suspense and the opportunity to become a part of solving the puzzle. Mysteries have won more state children's choice awards than any other genre, suggesting that mysteries truly are favorites of children (Tomlinson & Lynch-Brown, 2002, p. 140). The Encyclopedia Brown series, by

Donald Sobol, is a classic mystery series that is still popular with today's children, particularly with 8- to 10-year-olds. The books feature a young boy who is the only person to pay close attention to clues that solve crimes in his town. Laurence Yep's mysteries, *The Case of the Lion Dance* and *The Case of the Firecrackers*, are exciting stories that also offer readers a glimpse into Asian American life. A complex mystery that keeps children guessing right up to the end is Ellen Raskin's *The Westing Game*.

Sports

Sports stories depict the enjoyment as well as hard work that children go through playing sports, focusing on both teamwork and individual striving for excellence. Unfortunately, many sports books are not particularly well written, so children will need to select carefully from what is available.

Matt Christopher is one of sports literature's most prolific writers. His stories feature both team and individual sports; the main character, typically a male, overcomes some difficulty or challenge so he can be accepted as part of a team.

Romance

Stories about how to attract the opposite sex and falling in love are particularly popular with upper elementary and middle school girls. Well-written books include Zibby Oneal's *In Summer Light, Philip Hall Likes Me. I Reckon Maybe.* (Greene), and *Unclaimed Treasures* (MacLachlan). The better romance stories feature a heroine with a multifaceted personality who grows and changes as the story develops.

School Stories

Virtually all children go to school, so they can easily relate to stories about various aspects of school life, including first-day jitters, embarrassing moments, and eccentric teachers. Books about school life can be found for children at all age and interest levels, making these books particularly appropriate for motivating reluctant readers. The best books in this category corroborate the common experiences of school life, showing characters who may experience problems or obstacles that they overcome through their own initiative or with the assistance of sympathetic teachers or peers. For example, *Beyond Mayfield*, by Vaunda Nelson, explores racism in school. The story, which takes place in the 1960s, explores an incident when an African American student is falsely accused by her teacher of stealing a pen. Many of the popular series books also fit into the category of school stories.

Coming of Age

As children grow into adulthood, they begin learning that choices have consequences and that they need to accept responsibility for their actions. Sometimes this means standing up for what you believe in, making difficult choices, or facing defining moments. Many books of contemporary realistic fiction focus on the process of becoming a mature person who grows emotionally as the story unfolds. Often, an event precipitates this growth, and the main character must work through issues related to this event. Beverley Naidoo's *The Other Side of Truth* tells the story of 12-year-old Jade who, along with her younger brother, is sent from Nigeria to an uncle in London after her mother is murdered and her father faces imprisonment for criticizing the Nigerian government. Jade must use her wit and determination to help the two of them survive.

Historical Fiction

One way to categorize historical fiction is to examine common topics or themes. The text sets in this chapter, in Appendix A, and on the Companion Website show you historical fiction organized from this perspective. Another way to organize this genre is by historical era.

Twelfth- to Sixteenth-Century History

Historical fiction about the earliest times is usually set in Europe or Asia. Many of the stories feature young women who overcome some sort of oppression or young men who must seek their identity. Karen Cushman's *Catherine, Called Birdy, The Midwife's Apprentice*, and *Matilda Bone* depict three young women in medieval England who fight against the restrictions of their times to grow into self-understanding. The hero of Avi's *Crispin: The Cross of Lead* is a medieval child with no family—or so it seems. However, when he discovers his true identity, he is put in terrible danger, and he has one close escape after another as he attempts to elude those who wish to steal his birthright.

Stories about life in Asian cultures, although less numerous, also provide a fascinating glimpse into these people's lives. Linda Sue Park's *A Single Shard*, set in twelfth-century Korea, tells the story of Tree-Ear, a young orphan who becomes apprenticed to a master ceramicist. Gradually he wins his master's trust and is allowed to deliver a pot to the king's emissary. Although his journey is disastrous, he learns important lessons about honesty, loyalty, determination, and beauty.

Early America (Sixteenth–Eighteenth Centuries)

Several writers of children's historical fiction have chronicled early American life, from the perspective of both European settlers and native peoples. The lives of native peoples, in particular, have been much more positively portrayed in contemporary books than they were in the past.

The Salem witchcraft trials are a popular topic from early American history for children's historical fiction. Elizabeth George Speare's *The Witch of Blackbird Pond* is an appealing book for older readers. Flamboyant Kit Tyler, who has moved to Massachusetts from Barbados, is accused of witchcraft; the result is a terrifying trial. Other stories focus on early settlers. For example, Speare's *The Sign of the Beaver* is a complex book for older readers that explores the relationship between Matt, a young white boy living alone on the Massachusetts frontier, and Attean, grandson of the chief of a Native American tribe. Avi's *The True Confessions of Charlotte Doyle* is an exciting story of a young girl traveling alone from England to America who becomes involved in a mutiny.

The Revolutionary War era has inspired many excellent books for children. Most are from the perspective of the American patriots, but some explore important issues affecting both sides of issues such as divided loyalties, treachery, the treatment of minorities, and the ravages of war. You may have read *Johnny Tremain* (Forbes), about a young silversmith's apprentice who joins the patriots' cause. Although this is a lengthy book, we've had middle-grade readers, particularly boys, successfully read it. Other titles present multiple perspectives on this historical era and explore complex issues, making them well suited for generating thoughtful discussions about diverse viewpoints surrounding the war. For example, *My Brother Sam Is Dead* (Collier & Collier) depicts a Tory family who has one son fighting for the patriot cause. Told through the eyes of the younger brother, the story shows the heartbreaks and injustices that come from war, no matter where one's loyalties lie. *The Fighting Ground* (Avi) and *Sarah Bishop* (O'Dell) also present more critical views of war. *Jump Ship to Freedom* (Collier & Collier) and *Hang a Thousand Trees With Ribbons* (Rinaldi) show the war from the African American perspective.

Westward Expansion (Nineteenth Century)

Stories about westward expansion before and after the Civil War are among the most popular in children's historical fiction. Common themes in these books include the quest for land and self-determination, conflicts between cultures (particularly Native American and settlers), and families working together to make a life for themselves. Some depict the experience in relatively positive terms, such as the Little House books, by Laura Ingalls Wilder, or *Our Only May Amelia*, by Jennifer Holm, which describes the life of a young girl who is the only young female in a family of seven brothers as well as in her entire Finnish-American community. *Sarah, Plain and Tall*, by Patricia MacLachlan, is one of the best-known stories depicting a prairie family living later in the nineteenth century; this loving family experiences some hardships, but on the whole, lives a quiet, contented life. In contrast, Pam Conrad's *Prairie Songs*, Ann Turner's *Grasshopper Summer*, and Kathryn Lasky's *Beyond the Divide* are excellent stories for mature readers that explore the more difficult facets of life for settlers.

Other books tell of the dying culture of North America's native peoples as European settlers moved west. Scott O'Dell's *Sing Down the Moon* and Harrell's *Longwalker's Journey* provide an insider's perspective as the southeastern native tribes were forced toward Oklahoma on the horrific "Longwalk." Young readers can also experience the story of *Sacajewea* (Bruchac), which is told in a native storytelling style, using both Sacajewea's and William Clark's perspectives.

Civil War Era (Nineteenth Century)

The American Civil War is another nineteenth-century historical event that has been well chronicled in fiction for young people. Many books use incidents from the war as a backdrop for their stories. *Across Five Aprils* (Hunt) is a classic story for older readers that tells of members of a family living in the border state of Illinois who are torn apart by loyalties to both the North and the South. *Shades of Gray* (Reeder) depicts an orphan Southern boy who must live with an uncle who is a conscientious objector.

Other books recount the early slave experiences of African Americans in America. James's *Ajeemah and His Son* and Hansen's *The Captive* show the lives of slaves before their capture along with the horror that follows. Gary Paulsen's *Nightjohn* is a realistic, emotional account of one slave who, although brutalized, persists in teaching other slaves to read. The book is narrated by Sarny, one of the other slaves on the plantation, who becomes the focus of *Sarny: A Life Remembered*, a later book by Paulsen.

Nineteenth Century: Industrialization and Immigration

America changed dramatically in the nineteenth century as industrialization spread and immigrants arrived from many countries. The advent of the industrial revolution brought with it deplorable working conditions in factories. *Lyddie* (Paterson) tells the story of a young farm girl who goes to Lowell, Massachusetts, to work in a textile mill. However, she finds dangerous working conditions, uncaring supervisors, and the beginnings of the labor movement.

Millions of immigrants also came to America looking for economic opportunity and freedom. *Beyond the Western Sea* (Avi) and its sequels are adventurous stories of three Irish children determined to immigrate to America. *Nory Ryan's Song* (Giff) is a more poignant story of one girl's life during the Irish potato famine that ends with her opportunity to emigrate. *Esperanza Rising* (Ryan) is the story of a young, pampered Mexican girl who flees with her mother to the United States after her father dies. They are forced to live in poverty, and Esperanza learns to become independent. In addition to showing readers a historical era, these books are also survival stories because the characters frequently struggle against societal restrictions or face inner conflicts.

Twentieth Century: War and the Great Depression

The Great Depression was a defining time in American history. Many children's books explore the hardships people experienced during this very difficult period. Mildred Taylor's *Roll of Thunder, Hear My Cry* depicts the life of a close-knit African American family in Mississippi during the 1930s; the racism they experience is countered by a loving environment that helps them survive. Taylor has written equally powerful sequels and prequels (books detailing the earlier lives of certain characters) in *The Well, Song of the Trees, Let the Circle Be Unbroken, The Friendship*, and *The Land*. Karen Hesse's *Out of the Dust* tells of one girl's life during the Oklahoma Dust Bowl era. Written in a poetic free-verse style, this novel depicts the psychological pain young Billie Jo must endure as she copes with her mother's death in a fire Billie Jo caused as well as with her father's resulting isolation. Played against the constant presence of dust that sneaks through every crack and pore, the novel has a realism that makes it unforgettable to readers. Christopher Paul Curtis's Bud in *Bud, Not Buddy* lives in Michigan in the 1930s; although the focus of this book is Bud's search for his identity, events and people of the Depression are important components of the story.

World War II is another popular topic in children's historical fiction. Books about the Holocaust, children living their daily lives on the homefront in America, and European resistance to the German occupation help children understand multiple perspectives on this defining event of the twentieth century. Books about the war in Europe, particularly the Holocaust, are particularly numerous. A few stories, such as Esther Hautzig's *The Endless Steppe* and Jane Yolen's *The Devil's Arithmetic* recount harrowing experiences in concentration camps. Most, however, detail children who are hidden or who escape. Many are fictionalized accounts of true experiences. For example, Lois Lowry's *Number the Stars* tells the exciting story of Anne Marie, a child living in Denmark during the German occupation, who helps sneak a Jewish family out of the country.

Books about America during this era focus on the effects of war on children. Among the best known are *Stepping on the Cracks* and its sequels, by Mary Downing Hahn. These books depict American children going about their everyday lives with the war as a backdrop and daily reminder.

The internment of Japanese Americans during World War II, particularly after the bombing of Pearl Harbor, is a less well known aspect of American history. Several children's books have been written to help children understand this era. *Journey to Topaz* (Uchida) is a fictionalized account of the experiences endured by the author's family who were placed at Topaz, an internment center in Utah. *Journey Home* (Uchida) tells of the family's release, after which they find more distrust when they return home. Graham Salisbury's *Under the Blood-Red Sun* shows how Japanese Americans in Hawaii were treated at this time.

Twentieth Century: Civil Rights and Social Unrest

Problems with racism and segregation simmered throughout the twentieth century and exploded as the Civil Rights movement of the 1960s. Several excellent children's books chronicle this tumultuous time in American history. For example, Christopher Paul Curtis uses both humor and pathos to relate the experiences of 10-year-old Kenny as he and his family drive from Detroit to Birmingham, Alabama, in *The Watsons Go to Birmingham—1963*.

Fantasy

Fantasy is generally categorized by the fantasy elements featured in the book. These elements can range from a ghost appearing in an otherwise realistic story, to one character possessing special, magical qualities, to completely imagined worlds with their own culture, language, and settings, all described down to the last detail. To guide your decisions as to which books will be most suitable for your students, we use some of the most common elements as the basis for our categories. We have also organized our categories according to the complexity of the fantasy.

Text Set — The Holocaust Through Fiction, Biography, and Memoir

Adler, David A. (1995). *Child of the Warsaw Ghetto*. New York: Holiday House.

Bachrach, Susan. (1999). *Tell Them We Remember: The Story of the Holocaust*. Boston: Little Brown.

Bawden, Nina. (1973). *Carrie's War*. Philadelphia: Lippincott.

Bernbaum, Israel. (1985). *My Brother's Keeper: The Holocaust Through the Eyes of an Artist*. New York: Putnam.

Choi, Sook Nyul. (1991). *The Year of Impossible Goodbyes*. Houghton Mifflin.

Houston, Gloria. (1992). *But No Candy* (Lloyd Bloom, Illus.). New York: Philomel.

Kerr, Judith. (1997). *When Hitler Stole Pink Rabbit*. New York: Putnam & Grosset Group.

Lakin, Patricia. (1994). *Don't Forget* (Ted Rand, Illus.). New York: Tambourine Books.

Lobel, Anita. (1998). *No Pretty Pictures: A Child of War*. New York: Greenwillow Books.

Lowry, Lois. (1990). *Number the Stars*. Boston: Houghton Mifflin.

McDonough, Yona Zeldis. (1997). *Anne Frank* (Malcah Zeldis, Illus.). New York: Henry Holt.

McSwigan, Marie. (1986). *Snow Treasure*. New York: Scholastic.

Meltzer, Milton. (1976). *Never to Forget: The Jews of the Holocaust*. New York: Harper.

Nieuwsma, Milton J. (1998). *Kinderlanger: An Oral History of Young Holocaust Survivors*. New York: Holiday House.

Orlev, Uri. (1984). *The Island on Bird Street*. Boston: Houghton Mifflin.

Park, Linda Sue. (2002). *When My Name Was Kioko*. New York: Clarion Books.

Rol, Ruud van der, & Verhoeven, Rian. (1993). *Anne Frank Beyond the Diary: A Photographic Remembrance*. New York: Viking.

Russ, Joanna. (1972). *The Upstairs Room*. New York: HarperCollins.

Sim, Dorrith M. (1996). *In My Pocket*. (Gerald Fitzgerald, Illus.). New York: Harcourt Brace.

Valovkova, Hana. (1993). *I Never Saw Another Butterfly: Children's Drawings and Poems from Terezin Concentration Camp 1942–1944*. New York: Schocken Books.

Yolen, Jane. (1998). *The Devil's Arithmetic*. New York: Viking.

Toys and Animals

Stories about animals and toys that talk are among the best-loved fantasy and are excellent stories for introducing young children to this genre. A. A. Milne's *Winnie-the-Pooh*, Kenneth Grahame's *The Wind in the Willows*, Margery Williams's *The Velveteen Rabbit*, and Michael Bond's *Paddington Bear* are classics that are still cherished by today's children. The timeless tale of *Charlotte's Web* (White) also falls into this category. At the start of this story, readers believe the book will be about an ordinary farm. However, when Fern's pet runt pig, Wilbur, begins conversing with a spider named Charlotte, the fantasy elements take over the plot, and the relationships among the animal characters become the focus.

Time-Shift Fantasy

In some stories, characters move between the present and the past or the future. These stories challenge our assumptions about time, suggesting that time may be more fluid and manipulable than we commonly think. One of the most popular time-shift fantasies is Natalie Babbitt's *Tuck Everlasting*. In this intriguing and beautifully written story, young Winnie discovers a family who cannot die because they have drunk from a magical spring that gives everlasting life (although most characters in time-shift fantasy jump ahead or back in time, the characters in *Tuck Everlasting* are eternally trapped in the present). Soon Winnie must make an important decision: Should she drink the water and become immortal or live her natural

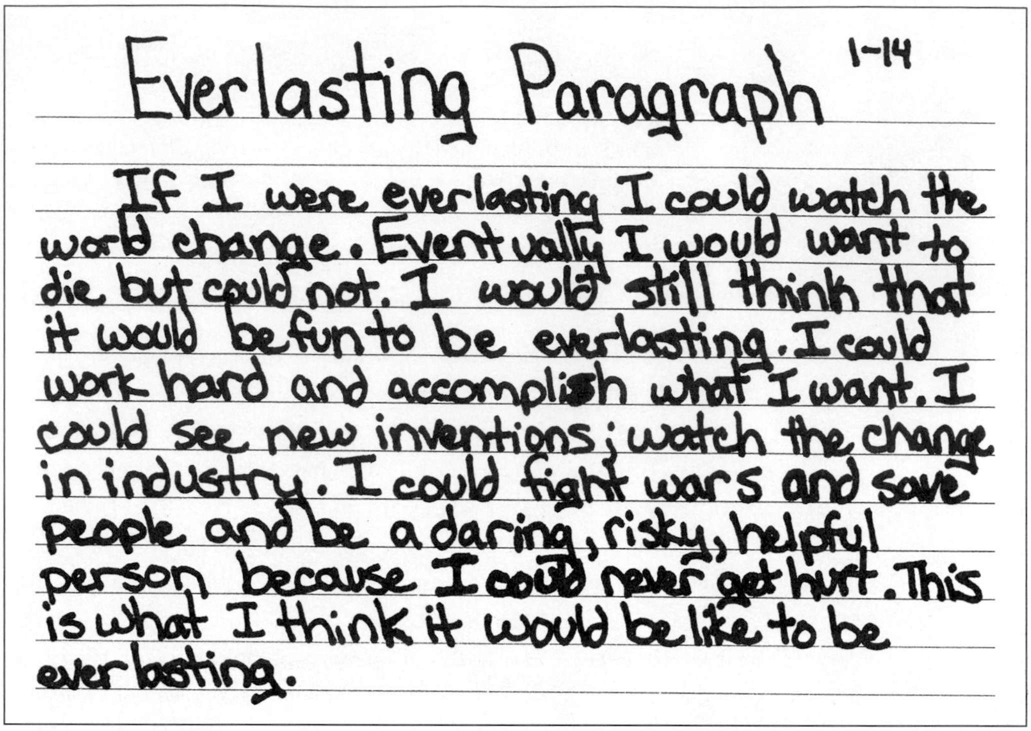

Figure 8.2 One Fifth-Grade Student Responds to the Central Theme of *Tuck Everlasting*

> # Everlasting Paragraph   1-14
>
> If I were everlasting I could watch the world change. Eventually I would want to die but could not. I would still think that it would be fun to be everlasting. I could work hard and accomplish what I want. I could see new inventions; watch the change in industry. I could fight wars and save people and be a daring, risky, helpful person because I could never get hurt. This is what I think it would be like to be everlasting.

life cycle? Her choice leads to much debate among readers of this story, making it an excellent book for introducing middle-grade students to fantasy. Figure 8.2 shows one student's response to *Tuck Everlasting*.

Often time shifts are linked to a common object or place that appears in both times. For example, C. S. Lewis's children in *The Lion, the Witch and the Wardrobe* travel in and out of Narnia through the back of a wardrobe. In *King of Shadows* (Cooper), aspiring actor Nat Fields is transported back to Shakespeare's time while performing at a replica of the Globe Theatre.

Ghosts and the Supernatural

Students enjoy the shivers they get from reading stories about ghosts and supernatural occurrences. There are many formulaic books of this type that are full of spooky houses, blood, fast-paced events, and improbable plot twists. However, there also are many well-written books, with unpredictable plots and fully developed characters that deserve attention from young readers. For example, Pam Conrad's *Stonewords* features Zoe, a young girl who encounters a ghost from the past; Zoe tries to avert the disaster that caused her friend's death. Mary Downing Hahn's *Wait Till Helen Comes* tells of a child who died in a fire who returns as a ghost that lures children to their deaths so she has companions.

Other books introduce children to fairies, elves, or other supernatural elements, often related to a specific culture. *A Stranger Came Ashore* (Hunter) is based on Shetland Island legends of selkies, seals who took on human shapes and caused mischief. *The Folk Keeper* (Billingsley) tells of Corenna, an orphan with special powers to tame the "folk," who cause havoc for humans. Eventually she comes to understand her connection to the sea and the selkies.

Stories Based on Folklore

Several authors have expanded stories from traditional literature into full-length fantasy novels. For example, Gail Carson Levine explores the question of why Cinderella meekly obeyed her stepmother in *Ella Enchanted*. In Levine's version of the classic tale, Ella is under a spell and must find her true self before being released from the curse. McKinley's *Beauty* and *Rose Daughter* go beyond the traditional tale of "Beauty and the Beast" to explore the complex relationship between a young girl and her seemingly abhorrent suitor; each looks at the psychological aspects of the traditional folktale to discover the motivations behind the actions of one-dimensional characters.

Crazy Characters and Unusual Worlds

Students particularly enjoy fantasy that features eccentric characters, such as *Pippi Longstocking* (Lindgren), Willie Wonka in *Charlie and the Chocolate Factory* (Dahl), *Mary Poppins* (Travers), and the diverse personalities Dorothy encounters in *The Wonderful Wizard of Oz* (Baum). Sometimes unusual things happen, such as a peach tree producing giant fruit in *James and the Giant Peach* (Dahl); or miniature people creating their own tiny world, as in *The Borrowers* (Norton) and its sequels. Eve Ibbotson's *Island of the Aunts* features three elderly aunts who, recognizing their mortality, must kidnap three neglected children to carry on the tasks of caring for the magical creatures they've rescued over the years.

Heroic Fantasy

Sometimes termed "high fantasy," these stories usually involve courageous young protagonists who search for their identity as they battle self-doubt along with some sort of external evil that threatens them. Frequently, the main character has a quest to fulfill, or that individual must face challenges that can be completed only through

Jacket art by Mike Wimmer, copyright © 2000 by Mike Wimmer, jacket art, from THE WINGS OF MERLIN by Thomas A. Barron. Used by permission of Philomel Books, A division of Penguin Young Readers Group, A Member of Penguin Group (USA) Inc., 345 Hudson St., New York, NY 10014. All rights reserved.

a combination of physical prowess and inner strength. Although some of these stories feature humor, the tone is typically serious as characters battle evil, pursue dangerous quests, and agonize over difficult decisions. *Harry Potter and the Sorcerer's Stone* (Rowling), along with its sequels, is an example of this type of fantasy. Harry Potter wrestles with discovering who he really is while battling the evil Voldemort, who is determined to destroy him. Taren, in the Prydain Chronicles, by Lloyd Alexander, confronts evil and discovers important values such as honor, sacrifice, and courage as he journeys with his faithful companions. Younger readers, particularly girls, enjoy Tamora Pierce's Circle of Magic books, which typically feature adolescent girls in the 12- to 14-year-old age group who face obstacles as they complete a quest or noble task.

Many books in this category are set in imaginary worlds and use ancient epics or legends as the basis of their stories. J. R. R. Tolkien does this in his Lord of the Rings series. T. A. Barron uses the legends surrounding Merlin from King Arthur tales for *The Lost Years of Merlin* and its sequels. Philip Pullman created complex, gripping stories in the His Dark Materials trilogy. Inspired by Milton's *Paradise Lost*, Pullman explores issues of spirituality, loss of innocence, the concept of duality in personality, and the nature of good and evil in *The Golden Compass*, *The Subtle Knife*, and *The Amber Spyglass*.

Science Fiction

Science fiction fantasies share many of the qualities of heroic fantasies, but the quests and struggles for survival are typically played out in a futuristic world, one in which there may be interaction between earthlings and visitors from other planets (Woolsey, 2003). One of the most popular and enduring books of science fiction for children is Madeleine L'Engle's *A Wrinkle in Time*. Twelve-year-old Meg must travel through time and space, battling evil and conformity, to rescue her scientist father who is being held captive on the evil planet Camazotz.

Other stories remain firmly set on earth but raise interesting questions about the organization of society or how the world might look following war or ecological devastation. Lois Lowry presents a future that seems calm and safe in *The Giver*: violence, dissension, and happiness have been eradicated, and history, knowledge, and emotions are carefully controlled. In the beginning of the story, the world of the protagonist, Jonas, seems neat, tidy . . . idyllic. As readers explore it further, they discover the roles into which people have been systematically slotted. However, Jonas, who has been selected to receive the community's memories, soon comes to realize that this is a sterile existence, one devoid of all color, joy, love, and pain. Adolescents who read this book typically become

Meet... Madeleine L'Engle

Author of *A Wrinkle in Time; A Wind in the Door; A Swiftly Tilting Planet; An Acceptable Time; Meet the Austins; The Moon by Night; Many Waters; A Ring of Endless Light; The Crosswicks Journals; The Arm of the Starfish;* and others.

Ms. L'Engle, born in New York City, got off to a slow start as a writer when her work broke the traditions of the times and publishers initially didn't know it would sell. *A Wrinkle in Time* was rejected by over 20 publishers before it was finally bought, and it went on to win the 1962 Newbery Medal. Ms. L'Engle broke with tradition when her protagonist was female, and there were no female protagonists in science fiction. As Madeleine says, "I'm a female. Why would I give all the best ideas to a male?"

Another taboo Madeleine broke in the Young Adults publishing industry was mixing science fiction with fantasy. The publishers said it couldn't be done. Ms. L'Engle asked, "Why not? We live in a fantasy universe, and subatomic particles and quantum mechanics are even more fantastic than the macrocosm. Often the only way to look clearly at this extraordinary universe is through fantasy, fairy tale, myth."

Madeleine L'Engle believes she is "lucky enough to be able to spend her life doing what she loves." Writing, for her, is about "trying to make sense of life." She has been making "sense of life" prolifically, with over forty volumes of plays, poems, essays, and novels for children and adults. She lives in New York City and serves as writer-in-residence at the Cathedral of St. John the Divine in New York.

Tech Note
You can access additional interviews with authors on the CD-ROM that accompanies this book.

---

deeply involved with Jonas and the choices he makes; they also argue, often passionately, about the ending. Lowry's *Gathering Blue* is more a companion book than a sequel. It explores a future society that is pastoral but that lacks kindness and compassion. Lowry's *Messenger* brings the trilogy to a harrowing conclusion.

Series Books

Once children read a book they like, they commonly ask, "Do you have another one just like it?" Child readers, like adult readers, get hooked on an author's style, they get acquainted with characters, or they learn about the historical era in which the story takes place. Books such as the Harry Potter series, Ramona stories, and the Little House on the Prairie are good examples.

Other books become popular through word of mouth. Thus, you might have many students reading books from the Baby-Sitters Club, Goosebumps, Choose Your Own Adventure, or Anamorphs series. These books are often formulaic, with little change in plot structure or characterization. R. L. Stine, creator of the Goosebumps series, acknowledges this and says, "Nobody learns and nobody grows. Mostly, they're just running" (Greenlee, Monson, & Taylor, 1996). However, series books line the shelves of children's bookstores and are found heading the national best-seller lists. They are also the most common purchases from children's book clubs (Strickland, Walmsey, Bronley, & Weiss, 1994).

A survey of teachers by Brooks, Waterman, and Allington (2003) discerned children's favorite series books. The Arthur series, by Marc Brown, was ranked first, followed by R. L. Stine's Goosebumps series, Chandler's The Box Car Children, Martin's Baby-Sitters Club books, the Pleasant Company's American Girl series, and Norman Bridwell's Clifford, the Big Red Dog. Some differences in preference were based on gender (girls, for example, liked American Girl and Baby-Sitters Club books, whereas these books appealed to few boys).

Many features of series books that are typically criticized (plot predictability, one-dimensional characters) are what young readers like about them. The use of continuing characters, stable settings, and predictable plots allows readers to build substantial background knowledge, aiding comprehension (Brooks, Waterman, & Allington, 2003). Perhaps their greatest contribution, however, is how they help young readers discover pleasure in reading (Lukens, 1999).

These books seem to have a special magic for middle-grade readers. However, research has found that children view these as the fast food of the literary world: fun to read but not a substitute for reading the better literary fare their teachers recommend (Greenlee et al., 1996). There are several series that we recommend. Our suggestions include books from all fiction genres so that you have a wide variety of books to give to your students who want more of the same. Figure 8.3 lists some series we've found are popular with children, but that also tend to be well written.

Tech Note
The CD-ROM that accompanies this book features lists of titles in each series.

Figure 8.3
Recommended Series Books Popular With Students

Primary Grades	
Series Name	*Author*
Miss Nelson	Harry Allard
Arthur	Marc Brown
Pee Wee Scouts	Judy Delton
Polk Street School	Patricia Reilly Giff
Aldo Applesauce	Joanna Hurwitz
Einstein Anderson	Seymour Simon
The Boxcar Children	Gertrude Chandler Warner
Magic Tree House	Mary Pope Osborne
Cam Jansen	David Adler
Amber Brown	Paula Danziger
Junie B. Jones	Barbara Park
Horrible Harry	Suzy Kline
Ramona Quimby	Beverly Cleary
Ralph S. Mouse	Beverly Cleary
Amelia Bedelia	Peggy Parish
Nate the Great	Marjorie Weinman Sharmat
Henry and Mudge	Cynthia Rylant
Clifford the Big Red Dog	Norman Bridwell
Hobie Hanson	Jamie Gilson
Owen Foote	Stephanie Greene
Judy Moody	Megan McDonald
Gus and Grandpa	Claudia Mills

Intermediate Grades	
Series Name	*Author*
Dynamite Dinah	Claudia Mills
Encyclopedia Brown	Donald Sobol
Lemony Snicket	Lemony Snicket
Circle of Magic	Tamora Pierce
Anastasia	Lois Lowry
Tillerman Family	Cynthia Voigt
Spike It! and others	Matt Christopher
Wayside School	Louis Sachar
Sammy Keyes	Wendelin Van Draanen
Bingo Brown	Betsy Byars
The Blossom Family	Betsy Byars
Jack on the Tracks and others	Jack Gantos
Mitsy of Chincoteague	Marguerite Henry
Sebastian Barth	James Howe
Alice	Phyllis Reynolds Naylor
Soup	Robert Newton Peck
Libby on Wednesday and others	Zilpha Keatley Snyder

Fiction in the Living Literature Classroom

How do we help children thoughtfully find all these wonderful books? And how do we help them respond to what they read so that literature becomes an essential part of their lives? Ann Cameron, a noted fiction writer, says the following about bringing children and books together:

> When we help children participate in the stories they read, we're helping them to heal themselves and grow as human beings, to understand the world as it is, and to imagine a better world. If we encourage children to express what they think and feel and to write down the worlds they can imagine, their language will show us wonders.
>
> (McClure & Kristo, 1996, p. 230)

This section shows you how to help your students connect with books, going beyond dioramas and book reports to interacting with books in ways that make them think and question. We begin by discussing issues of censorship, because works of fiction are questioned and ultimately banned more than those of any other genres. Next, we discuss the concept of critical literacy because helping children think critically about books can transform and elevate their responses. Finally, we present some classroom-tested ideas that we've found work well in stimulating children to return to books for a more thoughtful look.

Censorship

Not everyone believes that children should read books that feature topics such as drugs, treachery, sexuality, or death. Many react as one male student did in Professor Christine Leland's class at Indiana University when she introduced books on controversial topics. This student condemned *White Wash* (Shange), about a young brown-skinned girl who is walking home from school when she is suddenly surrounded by a gang who throws white paint on her, as a book that "belonged in the trash" because it was about a "nasty" subject. He further stated that children were better off with stories about good deeds and happy endings (Lewison, Leland, Flint, & Moller, 2002, p. 221).

Many adults would agree with this opinion. These people believe it's important to protect children from influences they perceive as evil or harmful. However, the issue becomes complicated because what is considered "harmful" depends on one's perspective. Many people don't want children exposed to racist or sexist stereotypes

and might censor books on this basis. Others fear books that feature characters questioning God, government, or parents. However, teachers have a responsibility to provide children with high-quality literature that challenges them to explore different ideas. We must also help them critically examine these ideas so they will be able to think for themselves, developing judgment, imagination, and a sense of responsibility (McClure, 1995, p. 5).

Yet, we cannot deny the very real concerns of parents as to the values they wish to instill in their own children. Many reasonable, intelligent adults believe some young children aren't ready for the graphic sex described in Judy Blume's *Forever* or the alternative lifestyle portrayed in *Heather Has Two Mommies*, by Lesléa Newman. It's healthy if parents and their children confront controversial issues together rather than deny their existence.

Teachers have important decisions to make when selecting fiction for use in their classrooms. What books are the best selections for reading aloud? independent reading choices? literature circles? Following are some questions you can ask yourself when selecting books for use in your classroom.

- Is the book appropriate for reading aloud to the class? Some books containing sensitive material might not make good read-alouds, but they may be suitable for students to read alone.
- Is it a good literature circle book? Books with issues are good fodder for discussion, but consider the age of the class and the sophistication needed for the particular issues. Sometimes certain issues are better suited to more mature students.
- Should it be placed in the classroom library for independent reading so individuals have access to it?
- Should it not be included in your classroom library?

In part, these questions can be addressed by examining the selection criteria we outlined previously in this chapter. At the same time, what needs to be considered is how much realism is sufficient to help children respond thoughtfully to the themes and issues presented in a

Tech Note

Visit the Companion Website to link to the American Library Association at ala.org. There you can read the Freedom to Read paper on the relationship between democracy and freedom in print.

Tech Note

Using the Companion Website, you can link to the website of the National Council of Teachers of English to access their book-selection criteria and for ideas for handling book challenges.

book. These questions can guide your thinking as you make purposeful decisions about the books you will use with your students. Additionally, the Committee on the Right to Read of the National Council of Teachers of English has developed a set of criteria to help teachers make these decisions.

You also need to know how to respond if a parent or community member challenges a book you're using. Censorship is unpredictable; teachers are often surprised when parents object to a book. This can sometimes lead to a panicked response: To avoid publicity, some teachers stop using a particular book. It is better to be prepared, so that small incidents don't escalate into confrontations.

One of the best ways to avoid problems is to be proactive. If you communicate with parents about the books you're using, why you think they are good, and what you plan to discuss, you will find most parents will understand a book's value. They are also more apt to realize that children have unique, diverse responses to books and often focus on quite different aspects of stories than adults might expect. For example when a parent challenged the presence of Mary Raynor's *Mr. and Mrs. Pig's Evening Out* in a Maryland school library, the librarian urged her to read the book aloud to her child. The parent, who had been concerned that her child would never trust babysitters again after reading the book, discovered her child found it hilarious that the pig parents failed to notice the babysitter was a wolf (O'Neal, 1990).

Some teachers write rationales, explaining why they have decided to use certain books. Donelson (1975, p. 4) suggests that a basic rationale should include the answers to at least five questions.

1. Why would the teacher consider using this book with a specific class?
2. What particular objectives—literary, psychological, or pedagogical—does the teacher have for using the book?
3. How will the book be used to meet these objectives?
4. What problems of style, tone, theme, language, or other possible grounds for censorship exist in the book, and how will the teacher plan to meet those problems?
5. How will the students of a class be different because of their reading of the book?

Other teachers have meetings during which parents actually read and discuss books their children will read. Sometimes they share children's written responses to these books. Besides corroborating that writing is required, these responses can provide compelling evidence that students are not concentrating on the prurient aspects of the books, but rather on literary qualities and personal meaning.

Despite your best efforts to educate the public, challenges can occur. Therefore, teachers and librarians should be prepared. Establishing some formal procedures for when books are questioned can defuse a difficult situation. Guidelines for responding to complaints should be clear and should describe explicitly the steps in the review process, the people responsible for each step, and the appeal procedure. Ideally, guidelines should encourage resolution of complaints at the most direct point: first the teacher or librarian, then the principal. The school board should be the last resort. Requiring that parents talk directly to the person using the book often helps them see the professional as dedicated and caring, with a good sense of the educational validity for using the book in question. The person or group making the complaint should detail in writing exactly what aspects of a book they find objectionable (citing specific page numbers). Once the paperwork is complete, a committee can meet to discuss the complaint.

Challenges to the book you use must be treated with respect. A reasoned, thoughtful response can usually defuse most situations. But be prepared to have your statements taken out of context, misconstrued, or even twisted to support a censor's agenda. Sometimes, particularly if the objection comes from an organized group, emotionally laden language or subtle pressure will be used. For example, officials in one Ohio school system were asked for the names of teachers using objectionable materials so they could be the focus of prayers by a group identifying themselves as "Prayer Warriors for Children" (personal communication, December, 1993). Difficult as it may be, you must remain professional with both adults and children in these situations. Professional organizations such as People for the American Way, National Coalition Against Censorship, American Library Association, and National Council of Teachers of English also provide active support for professionals who are facing prolonged battles over censorship.

Critical Literacy

Rather than prohibiting children from reading controversial books, we suggest you use books for critical analysis. Termed "critical literacy," this practice encourages students to explore issues requiring critical questioning of social institutions, inequities, and the status quo. The most helpful books for this purpose are often works of fiction (although some books in other genres can be effective). To be truly literate and to function effectively in the twenty-first century, children must be able to do more than read and respond superficially to text; they also need to understand how language works, how to find and question the cultural story being told, and how to act on their new awareness. Using books that stimulate discussions of critical literacy helps children read many other materials more critically, and leads to stimulating, lively class discussions. For teachers, it helps us move away from a curriculum that values consensus and conformity toward one that is more accepting of diversity. Lewison, Leland, et al. (2002) suggest that "taking the plunge" into what one might term "dangerous territory" is the right thing to do. "Is there danger in bringing these controversial discourses into schools?" they ask. "Yes—but there might well be more danger in leaving them outside the classroom door" (p. 224).

Teacher Linda Christensen phrases this as wanting her students "to be outraged when they encounter texts, museums, commercials, classes, and rules that hide or disguise a social reality that glorifies one race, one culture, one social class, one gender, or one language, without acknowledging the historical context that gave it dominance" (Christensen, 1999, pp. 209–210). She contends that critical literacy is "embedded in students' lives just as deeply as the students' lives are embedded in this society" (p. 213), and she wants them to question it all.

Critical literacy has four components, according to Lewison, Flint, and Van Sluys (2002). First is teaching and learning that "disrupts the commonplace": in other words, challenging students to look at everyday life with a new lens by problematizing all subjects of study. Second, critical literacy investigates multiple viewpoints to discern and listen to diverse perspectives, especially those ordinarily less dominant or less heard. Third, critical literacy classroom discussions focus on sociopolitical issues, studying the power relationships within political systems. But conversation is not enough. Fourth, children need to be invited to take action; to think about how they will position themselves in the world on particular issues. This often includes changing what they say as well as how they will act (Lewison, Flint, & Van Sluys, 2002, pp. 382–384).

Good Critical Questioning

Following are some questions that are helpful for developing critical literacy skills in children. Not all questions apply to all texts. However, they are general enough to be applicable for many different genres and themes. In the issue or situation being discussed:

- ☺ What assumptions are being made?
- ☺ What are my feelings in this matter?
- ☺ What are the cultural and historical contexts?
- ☺ What is valued?
- ☺ What forces are supportive and resistant to change?
- ☺ What are the long-term issues, and how do these fit with short-term issues and goals?
- ☺ What are the consequences of change, and for whom?
- ☺ What is my personal response to these questions?

The "critical literacy" text on p. 205 lists titles that will generate interesting discussions on issues of social justice, equity, and power.

> **Tech Note**
> So that these questions make more sense to you, go to the CD-ROM that accompanies this book, where we have an example of using critical questioning with *Molly Bannaky* (McGill, 1999, illustrated by Soentpiet), a historical fiction book based on a true story. This discussion focuses on critical issues of social class, gender, and race, so it's a good example.

Author/Illustrator Studies

One way to help students connect with living authors is through young author's conferences, daylong gatherings of children who share their original writings with each other. Another popular strategy we discuss here is called author study, whereby an entire class, a group, or an individual researches the life and work of an author.

> *Social issues books can enrich our understanding of history and life by giving voice to those who have traditionally been silenced or marginalized. They make visible the social systems that attempt to maintain economic inequities.*
>
> Lewison, Leland, Flint, & Moller, 2002, p. 215

Learning about the person's life is key in making him or her real for the students. They may discover, for example, how much work writing is, that sometimes even established authors still get rejection slips, and that getting started in the writing field is often difficult. Media specialists and educational magazines can steer students and teachers to information about authors. Additionally, many authors have websites that provide more information on their work.

Another part of an author study is to read more than one work by the author. This way, a student gains

Text Set

Critical Literacy

Browne, Anthony. (1998). *Voices in the Park*. New York: DK Publishing.

Bunting, Eve. (1991). *Fly Away Home* (Ronald Himler, Illus.). New York: Clarion Books.

Bunting, Eve. (1998). *So Far From the Sea*. New York: Clarion Books.

Fenner, Carol. (1991). *Randall's Wall*. New York: Simon & Schuster.

Fenner, Carol. (1995). *Yolonda's Genius*. New York: McElderry.

Gardiner, John Reynolds. (1980). *Stone Fox*. New York: HarperCollins.

Hesse, Karen. (1998). *Just Juice*. New York: Scholastic.

Hesse, Karen. (2001). *Witness*. New York: Scholastic.

Ikeda, Daisaku. (1992). *Over the Deep Blue Sea*. New York: Knopf.

Konigsburg, E. L. (2000). *Silent to the Bone*. New York: Atheneum.

Lester, Julius. (1998). *From Slave Ship to Freedom Road* (Rod Brown, Illus.). New York: Puffin Books.

Spinelli, Jerry. (1990). *Maniac Magee*. Boston: Little, Brown.

Spinelli, Jerry. (2000). *Stargirl*. New York: Knopf.

Taylor, Mildred D. (1976). *Roll of Thunder, Hear My Cry*. New York: Penguin.

Wiles, Deborah. (2001). *Freedom Summer* (Jerome Lagarrigue, Illus.). New York: Atheneum.

Tech Note
Access the author study of Jean Craighead George located in chapter 8 on the CD-ROM that accompanies this book.

insights into the commonalities or scope of an author's writing and/or illustrating. Generally this study culminates in a display about the author, a poster, an oral presentation, or some other creative project.

Drama and Fiction

Children respond naturally to stories, especially fiction, through drama. You have probably seen children spontaneously act out stories that have been read to them or that they've read themselves. Sometimes they replay a plot, or they might focus on a particular character and begin assuming that character's attitudes, dress, or language patterns while they play. Teachers can capitalize on this tendency and use drama to help children explore and respond to what they've read.

One of the easiest ways to do this is to organize opportunities for role-playing characters, reliving pivotal points in the plot, or exploring alternative possibilities for plot development after children have shared their initial responses to a story. To encourage role-playing, it helps first to have the whole group build a sense of a character by considering questions such as the following:

☺ What would you look like if you were this character?
☺ How would this character move? sound?
☺ How would this character act in response to other characters he/she might encounter?

Several children could then become that character. The rest of the group could discuss the differences in each person's interpretation. Once several characters are developed, the group can play a scene from the story. One scene could be presented several times by different groups, with discussion following each presentation that focuses on how children interpreted their character.

When dramatizing plot, students should be involved in selecting the particular aspects of the plot to re-create—typically, parts with action and dialogue. After developing characters, you next need to help the students develop the selected scene. Questions such as the following are helpful with this process:

☺ What happens in this scene?
☺ What are the most important events/interactions in this scene?
☺ What is the mood of this scene?
☺ How should dialogue be incorporated?
☺ Is a narrator necessary to "fill in the gaps"?

As with characterization, several groups could dramatize the same scene, with discussion afterward about how each group interpreted it. Eventually, several scenes could be developed to be presented in sequence.

A variation of this activity, which is particularly appropriate for older children, is to dramatize alternative plots. They could consider, for example, what might have happened if a character had made a different choice at a pivotal moment in the book. This activity can lead to interesting dramatizations and stimulating discussions.

Other Ways to Use Drama With Fiction

The following are some additional ways drama can be used to support children's response to fiction.

- In pairs, children can review books in the tradition of movie critics, perhaps calling the review "At the Bookshelves." Each person, in turn, gives an honest opinion of the book. They can discuss setting, characters, plot, and theme—but they don't give away the ending. They can provide a "thumbs up, thumbs down" evaluation at the conclusion of their presentation.
- Have children put a character on trial. One student can be the attorney for the defense, and another can be prosecutor. Children should prepare their case on paper, giving arguments for their point of view and supporting them with facts from the book.
- Create a script for some part of the book, which is then acted out. Or students can record the script to become a radio show.
- Create a talk show: Assign one student to be the host; the "guests" on the show are the book characters, and the topic for discussion is a problem in the book. One variation is the retrospective view, where the "guests" are the characters grown up, years later, looking back on the problem. Videotaping this "talk show" can lend extra credibility to the activity.
- Children can create a Reader's Theatre script for a book. To rewrite the script, students must reread portions of text, write dialogue consistent with their characters, and rehearse their work. Performing requires few props other than a background such as a sheet, moveable chalkboard, or other available structure.
- Children can create character monologues. Each student who has read the book selects a character and dresses as that person, creates a mask to represent the character, or draws a poster-portrait as if it were framed to hang on the wall. Then, each student writes

a one-page monologue from the character's perspective, introducing the character and his or her perspective on something in the book. After sufficient rehearsing, students perform their monologues.

Strategies for Before, During, and After Reading

In chapter 3, we discussed the importance of supporting students' comprehension through activities before, during, and after reading. Here we show how these concepts apply to the reading of fiction.

Prereading Discussions and Activities

Teachers are generally poised to have students complete activities after reading a book. However, if the material in a book is challenging to readers for any reason, especially reasons having to do with readers' schemata, then it is logical to develop students' experiential background prior to the reading.

One easy activity to do before students read a book is to lead a discussion. Finding out what students already know about the topic and posing questions to see if they understand important concepts can help steer the discussion toward activating or building schemata, as discussed in chapter 3. For example, suppose students are about to read Gary Paulsen's survival story *Hatchet*. Discussions can begin with finding out which students have experience in the woods, perhaps through camping or scouting. Then the teachers can ask students what they would do if they found themselves alone in the woods: How would they provide their needed food, shelter, and warmth? After they've considered these issues, students are prepared to empathize with Brian in the novel. They will better appreciate his struggles and his achievements, and their comprehension of the story will be enhanced.

The key here is to ask yourself several questions before beginning a novel with a group of students:

- What knowledge do students likely already have?
- What concepts will arise in the book for which students may need additional experience to enhance their understanding?
- How can I prepare students for enjoyable and effective reading?

Sometimes, it makes sense to take multiple days to prepare for the reading of a new book; this is time well spent.

Here are some specific activities that will also enhance reading when done prior to reading a book.

Anticipation Guides

Developed by Readence, Bean, and Baldwin (1981), an anticipation guide is a list of statements with which students are asked to either agree or disagree. When there is a strong element of values in the book to be read, this tool can be especially helpful. For example, for the popular *Tuck Everlasting* (Babbitt), students might be asked whether they would like to live forever; whether there is ever an appropriate time to disobey your parents; and whether people have the right to sell a product, even if the product is harmful or fake. Students can brainstorm answers to such questions on their own, then meet in small groups to discuss them. The ensuing discussions prepare them for the issues in the book.

Word Sorts

In this activity, the teacher lists on the board a variety of words that appear in the book, or writes words on individual word cards. In small groups, students sort the words into several groups, labeling each group in ways that make sense to them. Students often come up with numerous ways to sort the words, and think of a wide variety of labels. This strategy gives them both experience recognizing key words and the opportunity to talk about those words and use them in meaningful ways prior to reading.

Questionnaires

A technique proposed by Reasoner (1976), questionnaires work well when there are issues, values, or controversy in the book to be read. Teachers construct a list of questions about controversial issues that could arise in the book and that should stimulate students to think and discuss in advance. For example, students might be preparing to read *Scorpions*, by Walter Dean Myers. In this novel, peer pressure and insufficient parental supervision (because a single mother needs to work long hours) drive a character to join a violent gang. Teachers might design a questionnaire that asks for student opinions about gangs, about how easily they believe they would succumb to peer pressure in a variety of instances, how it feels to belong to a special group, and so on. As with the anticipation guide, the object is to raise awareness, expand knowledge of relevant concepts, and develop understanding of vocabulary before reading the novel.

Activities During Reading

Sometimes it may be appropriate to teach students strategies to use between chapters or sections while reading a more challenging book. These should be used only when needed, so as to minimize interference with the enjoyment of a book.

Character Webs

Character webs (also called character maps) can help students sort out people in their novel, especially when keeping track of them may present some challenges (Yopp & Yopp, 2001). These can be implemented in numerous ways. Students draw a web figure on paper, which begins with the protagonist in the middle of the paper. As characters are introduced in the story, students write their names on the paper or poster and add details about them (appearance, job, role) as the story builds. The web is expanded as new characters appear, or as readers get to know characters better.

Character webs also can center only on the protagonist. As readers get to know that character in more depth, they add more information. In this case, the emerging web would have circles or key words that describe traits or roles of that character.

Character Perspective Charts

This strategy (Yopp & Yopp, 2001) is especially well suited to a book that has two fairly important characters, such as *Bridge to Terabithia* (Paterson) or *The Pain and the Great One* (Blume). Students construct a two-column chart, and write the name of each of the two main characters at the top. Listing topics such as setting, problem, goals, attempts to resolve problem, attempts to reach goal, outcomes, and theme, students then write information about these topics from the perspective of the two characters. For example, in *The Pain and the Great One*, the "Great One," the older sister, would consider the problem to be her little brother, who is spoiled. The "Pain," who is the younger brother, would consider the problem to be that his big sister is "stuck up." This strategy is very conducive to small groups or pairs so that discussion about these elements enriches the lesson.

Double-Entry Journals

Some teachers have had great success with double-entry journals, especially for readers who struggle with comprehension. Folding the pages of journal notebooks in half lengthwise, students label one side "Summary" and the other side "Responses." Students summarize the day's reading in the first column. In the second column, they write how they feel about what happened, or what questions they have. Teachers like this strategy because the journals are a good comprehension check and can be used for assessment.

Postreading Activities

Writing Prequels and Sequels

Many students are familiar with books that have sequels. Individually, in pairs, or in small groups, they can write either the sequel to a book (following the story) or a prequel (the story prior to the current book). These can be presented in numerous ways—as little novels, as picture books, or in another media such as video.

Chapter 4 provides a list of excellent book extension ideas. These also are appropriate ways to support children's responses after reading a fictional story.

Connecting Poetry and Fiction

Finding poetry that relates to fiction can also help children extend their understanding of theme, character, or setting. For example, after students read Gary Paulsen's *Hatchet*, librarian Karen Hildebrand (personal communication, June, 1999) selected the poems "In the Middle" and "Long Ago Days," from Myra Cohn Livingston's *There Was a Place and Other Poems*, to reflect Brian's feelings about his parents' divorce; "I Am Young," from Jo Carson's *Stories I Ain't Told Nobody Yet*; Sarett's "The Loon," from Burton E. Stevenson's *Home Book of Modern Verse*; and "Stars," from Livingston's *Sky Songs*, to describe Brian's feelings of loneliness after the crash; and Arnold Adoff's *Tornado!* to give students a heightened perspective of Brian's experience with a tornado. She then encouraged them to find published poems or write their own to reflect their responses to Paulsen's book. Their choices ranged from Carl Sandburg's "Lost," in *Rainbows Are Made*, compiled by Lee Bennett Hopkins, to Shel Silverstein's "Forgotten Language," in *Where the Sidewalk Ends*. Some of the students wrote their own poems, such as the one in Figure 8.4.

Hatchet

The hatchet is everything
The food, the shelter, the protector.
It is life.

Only the hatchet can cut the fine wood
Only the hatchet may help me from death to life.

The woods are lonely, cold and hungry
Only the hatchet to keep me alive within.

by Brian, Grade 8
Teacher/Librarian Karen Hildebrand
Willis Middle School, Delaware, Ohio

Figure 8.4   An Eighth Grader's Response to *Hatchet*

Comparing Points of View

Students can expand their understanding of an issue or event by exploring different perspectives on historical and contemporary events. Sometimes varying points of view are explored in the same story, as in *The Sign of the Beaver*, by Elizabeth George Speare (which shows a Native American and a pioneer boy interacting on the frontier in Massachusetts), *Nothing But the Truth*, by Avi, *Bull Run*, by Paul Fleischman, or *Morning Girl*, by Michael Dorris (which reveals the thinking of two Taino children who encounter Christopher Columbus). At other times, this study involves reading several books. For example, children could read books about the westward movement from the perspective of white settlers. They could then read stories about the perspective of Native Americans, such as *Legend Days*, by Jamake Highwater, or *Only Earth and Sky Last Forever*, by Nathaniel Benchley. Or they could read many of the traditionally popular books about the American Revolution, then contrast the ideas presented in them by reading books that describe the very different experiences of women and minorities (particularly African Americans) during this time. Some books for this purpose include *Patriots in Petticoats* (Clyne), *War Comes to Willy Freeman* (Collier & Collier), *Amos Fortune, Free Man* (Yates), *Letters From a Slave Girl* (Lyons), and *Or Give Me Death* (Rinaldi).

Time Lines

Students can create a time line of events in a novel. Or they can create an individual time line for the life of one character. This activity does not need to be limited to historical fiction; time lines can easily be created for events or characters in other forms of fiction as well. Major events in the book can be charted chronologically, and children can create drawings to illustrate the selected events. If the book is a historical fiction story, older children can compare the time line they create from the story with a time line of major historical events of the era in which the story is set. This is an excellent way for students to see how context shapes the events in a story.

Creating a Newspaper

After students read a book, they can create a fictional newspaper that features elements typically found in a regular newspaper:

- ☺ *Masthead*—The name of the newspaper should reflect some aspect of the story as well as the setting or historical era (if the book is historical fiction).
- ☺ *Lead story*—An account of one exciting scene in the book.
- ☺ *Book review*—A short summary of the novel; includes a recommendation.

- *Editorial*—A reader's opinion on a moral or social issue that was important to the book. Or commentary could focus on how the main character solved a major problem in the story. In the case of historical fiction, this could be a significant issue from the time period.
- *Additional features*—Advice columns, comics, classified ads, obituaries, advertisements, etc. Features should relate to the story or historical era.

Students can create the newspaper with word-processing software; Figure 8.5 is an example of such a paper. If they are responding to a historical fiction book, they can use various print and electronic resources to research the historical era in which the story takes place. This activity teaches students to summarize, organize, analyze, and synthesize their ideas so they fit with appropriate sections of the paper. They also revise and edit their writing as the project develops. (This project is adapted from eighth-grade teacher Marianne Rossi's "Historical Fiction Newspaper Project," regional winner of the 2002 International Reading Association's Award for Reading and Technology.)

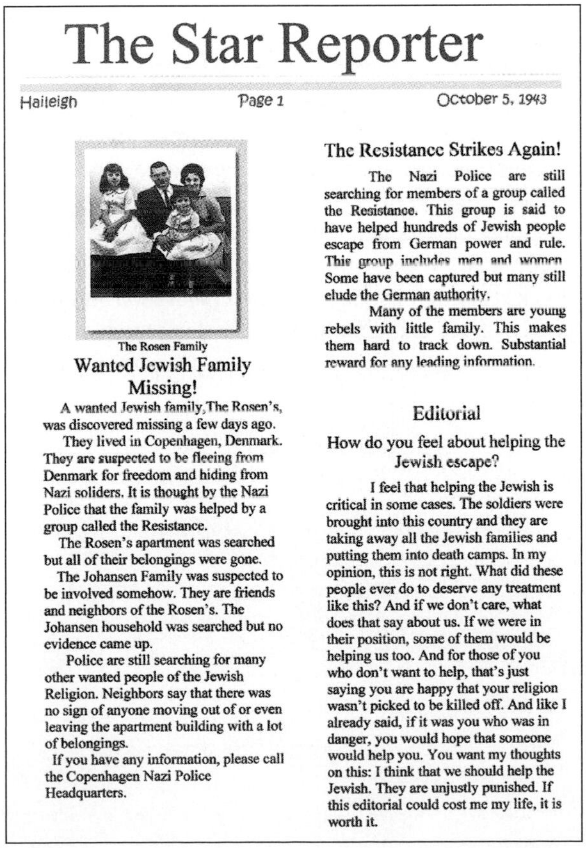

The Star Reporter

Haileigh Page 1 October 5, 1943

The Rosen Family

Wanted Jewish Family Missing!

A wanted Jewish family,The Rosen's, was discovered missing a few days ago.

They lived in Copenhagen, Denmark. They are suspected to be fleeing from Denmark for freedom and hiding from Nazi soliders. It is thought by the Nazi Police that the family was helped by a group called the Resistance.

The Rosen's apartment was searched but all of their belongings were gone.

The Johansen Family was suspected to be involved somehow. They are friends and neighbors of the Rosen's. The Johansen household was searched but no evidence came up.

Police are still searching for many other wanted people of the Jewish Religion. Neighbors say that there was no sign of anyone moving out of or even leaving the apartment building with a lot of belongings.

If you have any information, please call the Copenhagen Nazi Police Headquarters.

The Resistance Strikes Again!

The Nazi Police are still searching for members of a group called the Resistance. This group is said to have helped hundreds of Jewish people escape from German power and rule. This group includes men and women. Some have been captured but many still elude the German authority.

Many of the members are young rebels with little family. This makes them hard to track down. Substantial reward for any leading information.

Editorial

How do you feel about helping the Jewish escape?

I feel that helping the Jewish is critical in some cases. The soldiers were brought into this country and they are taking away all the Jewish families and putting them into death camps. In my opinion, this is not right. What did these people ever do to deserve any treatment like this? And if we don't care, what does that say about us. If we were in their position, some of them would be helping us too. And for those of you who don't want to help, that's just saying you are happy that your religion wasn't picked to be killed off. And like I already said, if it was you who was in danger, you would hope that someone would help you. You want my thoughts on this: I think that we should help the Jewish. They are unjustly punished. If this editorial could cost me my life, it is worth it.

Figure 8.5 One Child's Response to Lois Lowry's *Number the Stars*

Writing Letters and Diary Entries

Writing letters to characters in a novel is an excellent way to help children focus on character traits, point of view, plot, and theme. Because letters are a form of communication used throughout history, this type of response works particularly well for historical fiction. Writing letters allows children to focus on specific aspects of a story and communicate a personal response. Following are some possible activities.

- As yourself, write a letter recommending the book to a friend or relative. Send the letter.
- As yourself, write a letter to a character, telling what you learned about life from him or her, offering advice to the character, or describing the feelings the story aroused in you.
- As a character in the story, write to another character, providing advice, reflecting on past actions, or telling why you admire that character.
- As the main character, write a letter to the reader in which you reveal your innermost thoughts.

Figure 8.6 shows a letter a student wrote for *Letters From Rifka* (Hesse), in which she takes the perspective of one character to communicate with Rifka, the main character.

Diary entries are another form of writing that can help children think more deeply about a book. As with letters, diaries have long been a way for people to record their personal thoughts and emotions. One useful activity is for readers to keep a diary as if they are the main character in a story. After reading each chapter of a book, children can be challenged to

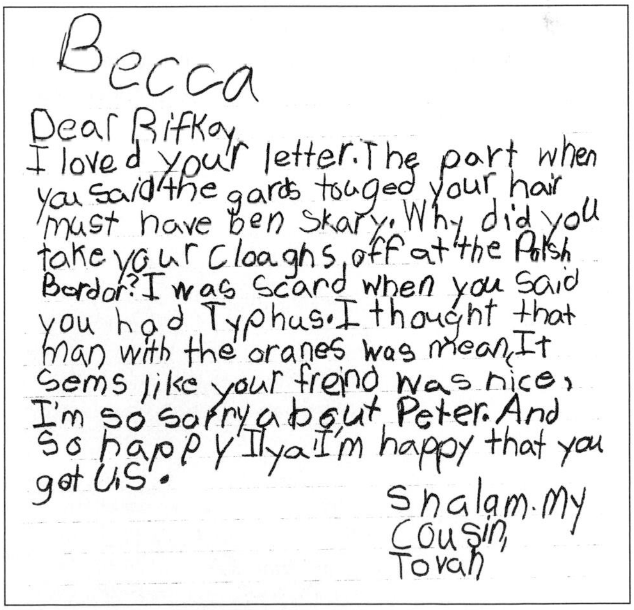

Becca

Dear Rifka,
I loved your letter. The part when you said the gards touged your hair must have ben skary. Why did you take your cloaghs off at the Polsh Bordor? I was scard when you said you had Typhus. I thought that man with the oranes was mean. It sems like your frend was nice, I'm so sorry about Peter. And so happy Ilya I'm happy that you got us.

Shalom. My Cousin,
Tovah

Figure 8.6 A Student Letter Written From the Perspective of a Character in *Letters From Rifka*

"stay in character" as they respond to chapter events using that character's perspective, language, history, etc.

These writings can be evaluated by having buddies exchange their diaries. After reading each other's entries, they can respond to the following questions:

- Do the entries/letters seem believable?
- Do the entries/letters seem accurate (i.e., do they reflect the character, setting, and time period of the book)?
- Are the entries/letters complete? Did the writer do a good job of assuming the persona of the character?
- What is your overall impression of the entry or letter?

Artifact Collections

Students can gather artifacts (sometimes termed "jack-draws," a modification of "jackdaws," crowlike birds that collect brightly colored objects in their nests) that represent significant aspects of a book. These can represent characters, themes, settings, or plot elements. For example, if readers are doing an artifact collection for Taylor's *Roll of Thunder, Hear My Cry*, they can bring in a battered book to represent the materials the mother had to use in her teaching career, a bag of dirt to reflect the book's theme of holding on to the land, or a rope and matches to reflect the climax of the story. Or for a more contemporary story such as *Pictures of Hollis Woods* (Giff), children can create a gallery of family pictures to symbolize Hollis and her desire for a family, or draw pictures expressing particular emotions that characterize the personalities of the main characters.

Media Presentations

Students can create a number of types of media presentations based on their book: a slide show on the computer; a PowerPoint presentation; a presentation using moviemaking software; a video recording of a scene from the book; or writing a play based on a scene using computer playwriting software where students select background sounds and voices and then write dialogue in the software. Students can also create slides for a filmstrip (see your school media specialist for places that make filmstrips) or a photo essay based on the book. They can also create storyboards or gameboards.

Storyboards

After students read a novel, they divide 12" × 18" construction paper into eight rectangles. They outline each box with a black felt marker. Set up criteria such as the following for each box:

- Title
- Main character
- Setting (time and place)
- Situation or conditions before conflict occurred
- Antagonist/problem
- Conflict
- Resolution
- Denouement

Encourage students to put both text and illustrations in the boxes.

Literature-Based Board Games

Students of many ages enjoy playing board games. When games that look and act like board games are connected with literature and are a supportive reading strategy, students don't really know they are working—they think they are just playing a game. When children create game boards based on a story, they must repeatedly return to the book to check story details, quotes from characters, and the like. Figure 8.7 gives the directions for making such a game.

Figure 8.7
Literature-Based
Board Games

Purpose: To create a venue for readers to practice texts in an enjoyable manner and to use semantic (context) strategies during reading.

Topic: Any good story of sufficient length, folktale, or picture book. Adjust this strategy to different age groups and reading abilities with the difficulty of the story or book chosen. It can be adapted for early readers (use shorter, predictable books) and intermediate/middle school readers (use longer stories, adult short stories, longer folktales, or chapters from novels). This activity makes an excellent learning center or learning station.

Materials:

File folders or poster board
Index cards or other tag board in at least three colors
Envelopes or small plastic bags
Game tokens, buttons, or bottle caps
Laminating material
Scissors or paper cutter
Markers, pens, or crayons

Figure 8.7
(continued)

Design a game board on poster board or a file folder (the latter is easier to store). Use three colors of tag board, create 7–12 spaces of each, and arrange them on the board, alternating colors in some pattern (blue, pink, and yellow, for example), from a starting space to a finish space. Decorate the board as desired, and laminate for long-term use.

Select text from the story and use it to create the following three kinds of activities. Assign each activity to a color used on the game board.

1. *Vocabulary Cards*—Choose a phrase or sentence from the story. Write it (or type, or word-process) on the card, underlining a challenging or interesting word that students may not know. The directions can state that when players land on the (pink) spaces on the board, they are to pick up a (pink) card, read the card to other players, and explain the meaning of the underlined word. Prepare about 1½ times as many cards as there are spaces of that color on the game board.

2. *Cloze Cards*—Again, write a phrase or sentence from the text, on the (blue) card, but leave a blank for one key word in the sentence. Players who land on a (blue) space pick a (blue) card, read it to the other players, and guess a word that makes sense in the blank. The response is correct if the other players agree. If there is disagreement, players must look back in the book to find the text. Prepare about 1½ times as many cards as there are spaces of that color on the game board.

3. *Sentence Sets*—Write a phrase or sentence from the text on the (yellow) card, which has been cut into a strip. Change the beginning capital letter to lowercase (unless the first word is a proper noun) and omit the ending punctuation, but preserve other punctuation and the proper nouns. Cut the sentence apart into two, three, four, or sometimes five pieces (for added challenge), and place the pieces in an envelope. Cut most sentences into two or three pieces; cut one or two sentences into four pieces and one into five. When players land on a (yellow) space, they choose an envelope containing the pieces of one sentence, read the pieces, and construct a meaningful sentence. Other players must agree the sentence is reasonable, if not identical to the original. Be careful not to make too many sets of five, and never cut sentences apart into individual words (or else it is too hard even for the teachers!). Prepare about 1½ times as many sentences as there are spaces of that color on the board.

   Prepare directions for the game for two to four players. All players must read the book together each time the game is played. Consider having the game end when everyone arrives at the finish. Use a die or old spinner, or make a die from a piece of sponge.

ESL Adaptation: Because English learners have a limited vocabulary, omit the vocabulary cards. Use just two activities instead: the cloze cards and the sentence sets.

Middle School Adaptation: Older students still like games. Consider making a game for a novel they are reading together. Prepare one set of cards for a middle chapter or two, and perhaps another for when they have completed the book.

Early Reader Adaptation: Early readers may need the book or story read to them. Another person, such as a more proficient reader, can read the cards to them. They can do the rest fairly well.

Hints: Be sure to code sentence pieces placed in envelopes so they can be easily reunited and put away at the end of play. A letter or number code works well. A generic game board could be used for more than one game. Store game parts in plastic bags, envelopes, or portfolios.

Assessment: Students need practice that is not evaluated. Playing games like this is a form of practice. It is an opportunity for kid watching, (Goodman, 1978) however, to observe reading strengths and needs and use of cooperative skills with classmates.

Summary

This chapter has shown you many exciting books you can share with children in the genre of fiction. We defined fiction in general, then we delineated the types of fiction: contemporary realistic fiction, historical fiction, fantasy, and science fiction. We described the literary elements people generally use to talk about fiction as well as important criteria you should consider in selecting fiction for use in your classroom. Important issues relevant to the study of fiction, including censorship and critical literacy, were addressed. Finally, we offered a wealth of teaching ideas that support children's response to fiction. With these tools in hand, you will be able to spark a love for this genre in your students.

Action Research for Teachers

Historical Fiction in the ESL Classroom

Brenda Custodio
Hilltonia Middle School

Literature-based instruction in mainstream classrooms is finally becoming the norm, but in English as a Second Language circles, it is still innovative and new. Moving away from grammar-based textbooks and oral drills has been a slow process. Methods courses today are finally stressing that teachers need to develop all aspects of communication using "authentic" materials in a natural approach.

For ESL students in the United States, authentic materials come from the literature that is being read and enjoyed by their American classmates. Novels, plays, and poems introduce these students to the lifestyles and culture. Students are assisted in cultural adjustment at the same time that they are practicing and improving their English skills.

As an ESL teacher at Hilltonia Middle School in Columbus, Ohio, I used children's and young adult literature for many years. Because our curriculum included an introduction to American history, government, and culture, I decided to focus on historical fiction because it would allow students to acquire knowledge of these areas in an interesting format. I had the same students for the 3 years that they are in middle school, so I was able to divide American history into three segments and cover one part each year. The first year, we began with pre-Columbian America and concluded with the American Revolution and the Constitution. The second year, we read novels on slavery, the Civil War, the Westward movement, and immigration. The third year began with the early 1900s and brought the students to modern America.

I believe that using historical fiction in this setting meets several needs simultaneously. It

- introduces ESL students to popular children's and young-adult novels;
- integrates oral and written language skills;
- helps children experience the past vicariously, encouraging them to think about as well as feel what life was like in another time and place;
- provides information on the background of current American society;
- develops a sense of the role various cultures have played in U.S. history;
- serves as a bridge to mainstream language arts and social studies subjects, preparing students for the tasks those disciplines require;
- gives opportunities for critical thinking and for using higher-level thinking skills such as synthesis, correlation, and comparison;
- incorporates many disciplines (geography, history, economy, art, music, reading, language arts, etc.) in an interesting and informative format;
- is applicable in a multiage, multilevel classroom because students are engaged in many projects and in cooperative groups.

Each spring, all ESL students in Columbus are given a placement test to see if their English level has improved and whether they are prepared to exit the program. I used the reading comprehension, oral reading, and word recognition sections of this assessment to determine how much their literacy skills had increased during their stay at Hilltonia. I compiled results only for my 10 eighth graders because they had been involved in the program for 3 years and should have demonstrated the most change. All had made good progress of at least a grade level in their reading and English skills.

I believe that the most exciting statistic is that no student was performing at middle school level at the end of sixth grade, but by the end of eighth grade, half of the students were finally performing at this level. Although the progress of these students was not outstanding, it was steady and encouraging.

I also asked each student to complete a reading interest survey and to participate in an oral review of the program. Students answered several questions about their reading preferences, their impressions of themselves as readers, and their evaluation of the ESL program at Hilltonia (see p. 214). The survey included some surprising information, but most was what I expected.

I was pleasantly surprised that the students read as much out of class as they say they do, and they seem to have gotten more out of the novels than sometimes I felt they did. Obviously many of the students still think of a good reader as just someone with good skills, but not all of them felt that way. I try to emphasize comprehension above skill mastery, but old impressions die hard.

I believe that the data given here support my premise that historical fiction is a viable tool for teaching ESL in a literature-based classroom.

Number of years in the U.S. (Answers ranged from 2–15 years)

Native Country

5	3	1	1
Cambodia	Laos	Mexico	Dominican Republic

Do you consider yourself a good reader?

5	5
Yes	No

Do you go to the library at least once a month?

5	5
Yes	No

Do you think novels are a good way to learn ESL?

5	5
Yes	No

Do you think the books you have read in ESL have helped your reading skill or speed?

10	0
Yes	No

Would you use the same class design if you were the teacher? (historical fiction)

8	1
Yes	No

What types of reading do you do outside of school?

2	7	1	3
Novels	Magazines	Poems	Newspapers

In your opinion, what is a good reader?

Reads fast, no repetition, knows the words, sounds out words, someone who likes to read, knows the hard words and what they read about, someone who reads and learns at the same time, someone who reads at home, at school, and in the bathroom!

What part of reading do you like the best?

You know something is going to be wrong, adventure, when I read I can imagine, easy words, war and culture, people react to situation, fight or problem, it's just amazing how authors write about, poems

How many books did you read for pleasure in the past year?

(1)	(4)	(3)
None	From 1–4	More than 4

Novels are supposed to help you learn about life. Tell me about one thing you read in our novels that has helped you in your life.

How people live in other places.

It can tell you how to fit in at school as a foreigner

Learn about how it is in war

To not be so harmful or evil

I want to get better in everything I can, like in *New Kids in Town*

Stay away from gangs

Civil War

Alexis Stigge's Multiage Intermediate Class

Alexis teaches 10 to 13 year olds in a self-contained classroom, team-teaching themed units with two other multiage intermediate teachers. Together, they plan one overarching theme for the year and, as part of this theme, they develop many smaller units, so much of their teaching is contextualized.

This year, their overarching theme is "Human Cultures." Alexis and her colleagues have narrowed their focus for the next 6 weeks to "Ancient Cultures," and more specifically to ancient Greece, ancient China, and ancient Egypt. Alexis's room becomes ancient Greece, and the other two classrooms focus on China and Egypt. Students choose to specialize in one of the three cultures during their daily 9:00–11:00 integrated learning block.

Classroom Environment

Entering the ancient Greece room, you can't help but bump into white cardstock Greek columns and other architectural "wonders" students have jointly constructed in the course of their study.

You'll also find a computer station, bookcases holding the classroom library, and shelves that display every book related to ancient Greece that the class has pulled from the school media center. These include fiction, nonfiction, magazines, and picture books—or as students in Alexis's class call them, "everybody books."

Most wall space is used to display student work, but one bulletin board is set aside for management items such as classroom jobs, schedules, and a calendar. Students apply for these "jobs" and are "paid" on the 15th of the month as part of their mathematics learning. Jobs include botanist, custodian, librarian, teacher assistant, announcer, and window washer. Students apply for positions, specifying the desired job and explaining why they would be a good candidate. Once a month, those who have completed their jobs successfully are paid with a special lunchtime in the classroom, including cartoon watching and a snack that Alexis provides.

Tech Note

For a great text set of picture books for intermediate readers, go to the CD-ROM that accompanies this book.

Reading Workshop

Alexis reads aloud to the class daily. She believes in the power of reading aloud to students at all grade levels, and is convinced that there are some challenging and exciting picture books that students at this level just shouldn't miss. Her students agree!

Some of these readings are related to ancient Greece, such as Greek myths. Alexis uses the myths for read-aloud, for literature study, and for reading-related direct instruction.

Students also read independently for 30 minutes most days, often getting together into groups to share what they have been reading. More purposeful, small-group reading instruction takes place as well. For 6-week periods, groups focus their literary study on a single element, such as *characterization*. During this period, all minilessons, as well as much of the discussion and activities, will center on *characterization*.

> The great advantage of using "everybody books" in the classroom for this age is that you can provide an understandable text for all reading levels, and the students feel empowered to share their knowledge and thoughts. Students frequently scrutinize illustrations to see if the clothes are accurate, or the food, the weapons, maybe the columns on the temple, or they recognize Greek gods in the scenes. It is a delightful, relaxing, but educational tool that all students, regardless of their reading level, look forward to using.
>
> *Alexis Stigge*

Text Set

Ancient Greece for Intermediate Grades

Aliki. (1994). *The Gods and Goddesses of Olympus.* New York: HarperCollins

Barth, Edna. (1976). *Cupid and Psyche: A Love Story.* New York: Seabury Press.

Briquebec, John. (1990). *The Ancient World: From the Earliest Civilizations to the Roman Empire.* New York: Warwick.

Coolidge, Olivia. (1962). *Men of Athens.* Boston: Houghton Mifflin.

Cooney, Caroline. (2002). *Goddess of Yesterday.* New York: Delacorte.

Fisher, Leonard. (1984). *The Olympians: Great Gods and Goddesses of Ancient Greece.* New York: Holiday House.

Glubok, Shirley. (1976). *Olympic Games in Ancient Greece.* New York: Harper & Row.

Haviland, Virginia. (1996). *Favorite Fairy Tales Told in Greece.* New York: Beech Tree.

Krull, Kathleen. (1999). *They Saw the Future: Oracles, Psychics, Scientists, Great Thinkers, and Pretty Good Guessers.* New York: Atheneum.

Lasker, Joe. (1983). *The Great Alexander the Great.* New York: Viking.

Low, Alice. (1985). *The Macmillan Book of Greek Gods.* New York: Macmillan.

Manna, Anthony. (1997). *Mr. Semolina-Semolinus: A Greek Folktale.* New York: Atheneum.

Marshall, Laura. (1992). *The Girl Who Changed Her Fate.* New York: Atheneum.

Orgel, Doris. (1999). *We Goddesses: Athena, Aphrodite, Hera.* New York: Dorling-Kindersley.

Philip, Neil. (1994). *King Midas.* Boston: Little, Brown.

Rockwell, Anne. (1969). *Temple on a Hill: The Building of the Parthenon.* New York: Atheneum.

Waldherr, Kris. (1993). *Persephone and the Pomegranate: A Myth from Greece.* New York: Dial.

Woodford, Susan. (1981). *Parthenon.* New York: Cambridge University Press.

Writing Workshop

In addition to the writing they will be doing about their ancient culture topic, students work on their personal self-selected writing. Various students are in different stages of their work, but everyone is working on something of their choosing. At times, journals are used as learning logs where students make daily entries about something they have learned in their unit. This strategy not only makes use of writing to enhance learning, but also allows Alexis to assess what students are getting from lessons.

This informal assessment helps Alexis develop minilessons throughout the month. Minilessons might target descriptive writing, using quotation marks, comma use, or any common errors the students' writing reveals.

Choice

During the 9:00–11:00 block, students move to the classroom and theme of their choice, where they have made a 6-week commitment and negotiated a work contract. Each student selects a focus topic within the culture chosen, such as citizenship, weapons, games, government structures, clothing, architecture, music and drama, or economics.

Students follow their work contracts to execute each investigation. Contract components include writing, both fiction and nonfiction; a model made to scale; and a game, puzzle, or quiz that can be shared with the class. Students in Alexis's room make choices within established guidelines. She encourages students to take risks with their learning and to push and challenge themselves as readers and writers; her expectations are high but not unrealistic.

Multiage Components

Because Alexis's class is multiage, you may wonder how she meets the needs of all her learners. Alexis states that she forgets who is in what grade, and that for the way she teaches, multiage is very compatible. All students must be doing their best work at all times, and youngsters push one another to grow and develop, no matter where they are on various learning continua. Everyone sticks to a contract on an ancient culture and participates in reading and writing workshop, and in all content areas.

Math and Science

Time each afternoon is set aside for math and science. Alexis works closely with her colleagues to plan learning experiences that connect with other content areas, helping students deepen their understanding and make connections across the different areas. She wants learning to be as seamless for students as possible.

The ancient cultures theme allows for a natural focus on a "Money" unit. Students have great fun with a mini-Olympics, connecting ancient Greece with a "Mathematical Measurement" unit, and the class spends a good deal of the ancient Greece focus studying geometry. Alexis and her students also find creative ways to link the science units "Mysterious Powders" and "Levers and Pulleys" with the "Ancient Cultures" theme.

How Is Literature Alive in This Multiage Classroom?

Alexis loves literature and wants to continue the kinds of experiences her students have enjoyed at the elementary level; too often when students reach the intermediate grades and middle level, they leave exciting and enriching experiences with literature behind. She builds on students' engagement with literature by

* reading aloud to students of all ages

* helping students find a wide variety of challenging and engaging books, including appropriate picture books

* encouraging collaboration and student support to help one another grow and learn

* allowing students to make choices within established guidelines

* holding high but reasonable expectations for every student in her class

* linking literacy activities with content-area development

NONFICTION

"Nonfiction is the currency with which public policies and legislation are made, societal needs are discussed, cultural aesthetics are defined, life lessons are conveyed, historical narratives are transmitted and matters of war and peace are decided. Nonfiction is about life itself, and that is why I am passionate about it." (Penny Colman, nonfiction author; personal communication, September, 1999)

Consider the following scene: The place is a steamy classroom on a very humid summer morning. The classroom is a reading/writing clinic for low-achieveing readers, ages 8 to 12. What is unusual about this scene, however, is that all the children are engrossed in their learning. For the past 3 weeks, they have been actively engaged in exploring nonfiction literature.

What has made the difference? Their teacher, Judy Bouchard, has been sharing nonfiction books during the daily shared reading time. Many of these books feature beautiful photographs, clear captions, excellent maps and diagrams, and compelling writing. Each student has also been involved in researching his or her own "burning question." Once students explore their topics, they create their own nonfiction books, which they proudly share with each other.

Judy strongly believes in including many nonfiction books in her classroom, then showing children explicitly how this genre works. She says, "These books act as mentors for my students as they work on creating their own nonfiction. They give students so many options to consider as they write, like choosing the best organizational scheme for their book, how visuals and diagrams should be used, how to write content in engaging ways, and how to design the book visually so as to engage readers. All my kids can do this because they are interested in their topics and have a deep understanding of how nonfiction works."

Nonfiction writing is everywhere. Think about how many times you refer to or read factual material throughout the day: articles in the newspaper, a reference book, a repair manual, a cookbook, a map, the Internet, spam, etc. We live in a world saturated with nonfiction material!

We know, too, that boys and girls of all ages are drawn to nonfiction (Pappas, 1991). Indeed, many children cut their literary teeth on nonfiction through small board books that teach concepts such as letters, numbers, and simple vocabulary. Preschool and primary school children are captivated by this genre as well. To test this, arrange a table of nonfiction selections and see how quickly children flock to them. One of us had the experience of going to a public library to gather picture books for one of her classes. As she was busily pulling books off the shelves, she suddenly realized her pile was getting smaller rather than larger. Then she noticed a group of preschoolers who were sitting near her, all excitedly examining the brightly colored nonfiction books she'd selected, including *Truck*, by Donald Crews, and *Drive a Tractor*, by Lara Holtz.

Above all, a good science book is imbued with passion for science and nature, and invites readers to engage with, imagine and experience science in ways they may never have thought of before.

Ford, 2002, p. 271.

Teachers find that their students flock to visually appealing, interesting nonfiction books such as *I Love Guinea Pigs* by Dick King-Smith. I LOVE GUINEA PIGS Text © 1994 by Foxbusters Ltd. Illustrations © 1994 by Anita Jeram. Reproduced by permission of the publisher Candlewick Press, Inc., Cambridge MA, on behalf of Walker Books, Ltd., London.

Teachers who use nonfiction as supplements or alternatives to textbooks in science and social studies find that their students become much more enthusiastic about the content. And when teachers involve students in personal inquiries, helping them develop questions to explore through using nonfiction books, they find children's engagement as well as knowledge soars. This is the power of nonfiction.

Over the last decade, nonfiction for children has gained tremendous respect. We now have books for students in which authors must meet the same high standards as those writing for adults. They share their research process, document their sources, and tell readers when they don't have the answers and need to speculate. They write with clarity, freshness, and accuracy. They don't talk down to children, but approach them respectfully, as fellow inquirers.

This chapter introduces you to the fascinating genre of nonfiction. Specifically, we address the following questions:

- What is nonfiction? How does it differ from other genres?

- What are some specific types of nonfiction?

- How can teachers determine the best books in this genre?

- How can you develop your own passion for and commitment to nonfiction?

- What are some strategies for helping children discover this genre and how to use it?

- How can teachers support children's effective use of nonfiction for exploring research topics?

- How can teachers support students' understanding of nonfiction through drama?

What Is Nonfiction?

On the face of it, the term *nonfiction* seems odd. No other genre is defined through negation. The term is even stranger when you realize we're defining the factual, the actual, things that really happen, with an explicit disclaimer that assures the reader we didn't make it up.

Nonfiction literature encompasses nonfiction or informational books as well as biographies. Good nonfiction books are those that spark wonder as well as joy in learning. These are the books we go to for answering specific questions, for finding information about a particular person or topic, or for simply browsing because the book's content or layout has attracted us. Essentially, these books, sometimes termed "the literature of fact" (Cullinan & Person, 2001), contain factual information about anything and everything: "real objects, phenomena, events, people, animals and plants" (Latrobe, Brodie, & White, 2002, p. 96). The Terms for Teachers feature below lists words that are useful for discussing and understanding nonfiction.

It isn't always easy to determine if a book is nonfiction. We suggest you look at a few books to see if you can tell the difference. Consider the following questions: What made you think the book was nonfiction? Does it have an illustrator or photographer? Are acknowledgments included? Does it have an index or table of contents? Browse through the book. What other evidence can you find to suggest this is a nonfiction book?

A quick (although not always foolproof) way to discern whether a book is nonfiction is to look at the copyright page (see description in chapter 7). This is the page usually found on the reverse of the title page, although sometimes the information from a copyright page is placed at the back of the book. This page typically contains the Library of Congress Cataloging in Publication Data, including the ISBN number (a unique number assigned to every published book to allow for ease of ordering from any vendor), the copyright date,

Terms for Teachers

Discourse of Nonfiction

Access Features—These features help readers understand and locate information. Examples include: table of contents, glossary, index, sidebars, bulleted lists, headings, bibliographies, prefaces, and epilogues.

Nonfiction—Books in which the writing is factual.

Organizational Structures—Organization is determined by such aspects as the topic, scope and depth of information, and purpose of the book. Examples of ways authors organize their writing include: sequenced structures, enumerative, compare-contrast, chronological, cause-effect, question-and-answer, and narrative.

Sidebars—These features present information set off from the text, typically in a box. They often provide summaries or additional information for readers.

Types of Nonfiction Books—The purpose and depth and scope of a topic influence the type of book a nonfiction author chooses to write. Examples of types: concept books; informational picture storybooks; photographic essays; survey books; specialized books; journals, diaries, sketchbooks, and documents; life-cycle books; activity/craft; experiment and how-to books; identification books/field guides; reference books; and biographies.

Visual Information—These supportive features help readers further comprehend the text. Examples include: dust jacket, layout and design of the book, photographs, illustrations, captions and labels, time lines, diagrams, maps, and endpapers or endpages.

For Bob Marstall, a fine artist and a good
companion in both civilized and wild places.
— L. P.

For Patricia Lee Lewis—poet, writer, teacher,
traveler, and friend—whose Texas-flavored
blend of grace and grit inspires me, and whose
encouragement and advice steadies me.
— B. M.

Acknowledgments

The author wishes to thank Dr. Kevin McGowan, Cornell Vertebrate Collections, Cornell University; and Dr. Donald F. Caccamise, Professor and Head, Department of Fishery and Wildlife Sciences, New Mexico State University, for their valuable assistance.

The artist wishes to thank Barbara Scully of *The Whistling Crow* in Shelburne Falls, Massachusetts, and Mark Kelly of *Wild Encounters* in Hopkinton, Massachusetts,—licensed "crow rehabbers" who helped greatly in his search for flight-challenged crows to use as models. Special thanks to Diane De Groat for permission to photograph her three stuffed crows; to John Zokowski of *Butler-Dearden Paper Service*, and to Barbara De Vitto of *Hunt Photo and Video* of Melrose, Massachusetts, for introducing him to the Hahnemuhle line of "digital fine-art" papers.

Artist's Note

The art for this book was prepared by using my computer and an Epson Stylus Color 1520 inkjet printer to transfer my pencil drawings onto a Hahnemuhle digitally prepared watercolor paper ("Wm. Turner," 190g), which was then coated with two layers of acrylic matte medium and painted with oils in the usual way.

Text copyright © 2002 by Laurence Pringle
Illustrations copyright © 2002 by Bob Marstall
All rights reserved

Published by Boyds Mills Press, Inc.
A Highlights Company
815 Church Street
Honesdale, Pennsylvania 18431
Printed in China
Visit our Web site at www.boydsmillspress.com

Publisher Cataloging-in-Publication Data

Pringle, Laurence.
  Crows! : strange and wonderful / by Laurence Pringle : illustrated by Bob Marstall. —1st ed.
[32] p. : col. ill. ;   cm.
Summary: An introduction to the life and behavior of crows.
ISBN 1-56397-899-7
1. Crows—Juvenile literature. (1. Crows.) I. Marstall, Bob. II. Title.
598.964 21   CIP   QL696.P2367 2002
2001092591

First edition, 2002
The text of this book is set in 15-point Clearface regular.

10 9 8 7 6 5 4 3 2 1

Figure 9.1   Copyright Page From *Crows! Strange and Wonderful*

and a summary of the book. Subject headings are usually indicated. These might be your first clues as to whether the book is nonfiction. Look closely at the area where the ISBN is located. If you see the term "juvenile literature," it is likely that the book is nonfiction. Biographies, on the other hand, are clearly labeled. Some copyright pages list "juvenile nonfiction and fiction"; this might indicate a blend of historical nonfiction and fiction, indicating that the author made up some of the information. Figure 9.1 shows the copyright page from *Crows! Strange and Wonderful*, by Laurence Pringle. See also the cover of the book on p. 224.

The designation of "juvenile literature" is important information because some books look like nonfiction but may, in fact, be a blended book or "faction" (Avery, 1998): a book that fuses fact with fiction. Many people mistake these books for nonfiction. For example, *The Bracelet* (Uchida), which describes the experiences of a young American-Japanese girl in World War II who is sent to an internment camp, *Mary McLean and the St. Patrick's Day Parade* (Kroll), and *Katie's Trunk* (Turner), which describes the story of a Loyalist girl during the American Revolution who must protect her home against patriots, are books that are often confused. All of these are true stories to which the authors have added fictional details to move the story along, to introduce important facts, or to make the narrative more dramatic.

Myrna Zarnowski (1995) cautions teachers about using informational storybooks that blend fact and fiction. She states, "Social issues—those we face today and those others faced in the past—are hard enough to understand. We should not make these issues even harder by providing young readers with books that contain a murky mix of fact

Illustrations copyright © 2002 by Bob Marstall, from *Crows! Strange and Wonderful,* written by Laurence Pringle, illustrated by Bob Marstall. Published by Boyds Mills Press, Inc. Reprinted by permission.

and fiction. Instead, we can seek out reading material that shows how historians and social scientists think and write. Quality nonfiction does this" (p. 194).

Dorothy Leal (1995), in contrast, found that informational storybooks with a scientific focus "may indeed be a useful tool for learning science because it may make science information more memorable" (p. 199). She believes informational storybooks can be used to engage student interest "as a doorway to a deeper processing of information that comes with expository [nonfiction] text" (p. 199).

We think informational picture storybooks have a place in your classroom because they can interest children in exploring more about a topic. However, check the copyright page, and work with children to understand that parts of the book may be fictional.

Elements of Nonfiction

Nonfiction writers use various writing tools to create books that are factual yet interesting to read. Some of these tools are similar to those used by writers of fiction, poetry, and traditional literature; others are unique to the nonfiction genre. The following are the most common elements that nonfiction writers use.

Format

A book's format is how it works as a whole. Format includes the size and shape, endpapers or endpages, and typeface.

Size and Shape

Recent nonfiction books are much more visual than ever before. Design teams often take special care to create books of distinctive shapes and sizes to mirror the information they contain. For example, look at *Leonardo's Horse,* written by Jean Fritz and illustrated by Judson Talbott. The book's dome-shaped top reflects the narrative, which tells of a bronze horse da Vinci wanted to create. Although he failed, his dream was realized through the

From LEONARDO'S HORSE by Jean Fritz, illustrated by Hudson Talbott, copyright © 2001 by Hudson Talbott, illustrations. Used by permission of G. P. Putnam's Sons, A Division of Penguin Young Readers Group, A Member of Penguin Group (USA) Inc., 345 Hudson Street, New York, NY 10014. All rights reserved.

talented work of Charles Dent and Nina Akamu. The bronze statue they created was so huge it took a dome-shaped gallery to produce it.

The Dinosaurs of Waterhouse Hawkins (Kerley) stands 12¼ inches tall and is 9¼ inches wide. These dimensions enable Selznick's dinosaurs to dominate the double-page spread and tower above all things, thus enriching the printed text (Kerper, 2003).

Book Covers and Endpapers

We can tell a good deal about a book from its cover. Many of today's nonfiction books feature enticing covers that draw readers in. Endpapers or endpages also often provide visual clues to the book's content. For example, in *Leonardo's Horse*, the endpapers are bronze. In *The Dinosaurs of Waterhouse Hawkins*, the endpapers include a dinner invitation and a menu. In *B. Franklin, Printer*, by David Adler, the endpapers feature Franklin's maritime ideas as sent to his friend Alphonsus LeRoy in Paris.

Typeface and Distinctive Markings

Often designers choose certain typefaces to enhance the appearance of a book. For example, in *B. Franklin, Printer*, the typeface looks old-fashioned. The copyright page of the book states this is the Caslon Antique font, a typeface frequently used by Franklin himself.

Every chapter of this book also begins with an interesting symbol or ornament. Again, the copyright page states these are from books printed and sold by Franklin. Features like these give evidence of the scholarship and research that went into creating the book.

Two books that incorporate several of these elements to create distinctive formats are *Woody Guthrie: Poet of the People*, by Bonnie Christensen, and *Hurricane!*, by Cynthia Pratt Nicolson. The Woody Guthrie book is designed so the lyrics of "This Land Is Your Land" grace the top of each page in swirling script. In *Hurricane!*, every page is loaded with photographs, sidebars, experiments to try, and diagrams. Many of these features are placed at an angle to give the appearance of heavy winds knocking objects off the page.

Robert Sabuda uses incredible paper engineering to create two pop-up books: *Young Naturalist Pop-Up Handbook: Beetles* and *Young Naturalist Pop-Up Handbook: Butterflies*, written by Matthew Reinhart. The pop-up insects in each are intricately detailed, and pull-out tabs are packed with additional visual information. Each book is packaged in a box with a museum-quality paper model of the insect. All of these features provide readers with a unique, engaging format that irresistibly draws them into the books.

Visual Information

Illustrations and other visual material are an increasingly vital aspect of nonfiction books. Today's books are filled with extraordinary photographs and illustrations so that they look almost like "coffee table" books. These books are also rich in content, with the visual information clarifying and expanding readers' understanding of the topic. Visual features might expand an explanation, show additional details, provide more information, or make an abstract idea more concrete. For example, in *Rome: In Spectacular Cross-Section*, by Andrew Solway, Stephen Biesty, the illustrator, used oversized, full-color cross-sectional drawings to show what it was like in Rome in 128 A.D. Most of the text is in the form of labels for the pictures on each massive two-page spread, creating a book that conveys information in a highly visual way.

Nonfiction books now feature illustrations in a variety of media. Gone are the days of only black-and-white sketches. Today's books feature illustrations from full-color photographs to detailed colored drawings, to intricate computer imagery. For example, Walter Wick's award-winning photographs in *A Drop of Water* draw the reader's eye to the intricacies of one magnified drop of water in different settings. Charles Micucci created detailed drawings to document a year in a beehive in *The Life and Times of the Honeybee*.

Diagrams, maps, tables, captions, and time lines are visual features that are important to nonfiction. Sometimes these are central to the book, as in *Mosque, Building Big, Castle, Pyramid, Mill, Underground*, and *The Way Things Work*, all by David Macaulay. In other books, such as *Brooklyn Bridge*, by Lynn Curlee, diagrams clarify and enhance the text.

Captions are the explanatory information accompanying illustrations, photographs, diagrams, and maps. Good captions are clearly written and either elaborate on the running text or provide new information. Sometimes captions describe two visuals. In this case, words such as "left" and "below," signaling directionality, should be clearly indicated. Readers often skip over captions, considering them unimportant. When this happens, they usually miss important information not found elsewhere in the text. Books that have particularly clear captions include *One World, Many Religions: The Way We Worship*, by Mary Pope Osborne, *Behind the Mask: The Life of Queen Elizabeth I*, by Jane Resh Thomas, and *Discovering the Inca Ice Maiden: My Adventures on Ampato*, by Johan Reinhard.

Labels work like captions but are short and concise and are placed near the object being labeled. For example, Laurence Pringle's *Crows! Strange and Wonderful* features a two-page spread of different kinds of crows that are clearly labeled. A diagram of a fin whale is clearly labeled in *Do Whales Have Belly Buttons? Questions and Answers About Whales and Dolphins*, by Melvin and Gilda Berger.

Maps are another form of visual information found in nonfiction across several content areas. Some maps orient readers to the content of a book. For example, in both *Asteroid Impact* (Henderson) and *Gorilla Walk* (Lewin & Lewin), readers are greeted with a map at the beginning which sets the stage for the content that follows. Some maps record movement, such as those in *Animals on the Trail with Lewis and Clark* (Patent), showing how animal life changed as the journey progressed, and *The Cod's Tale* (Kurlansky), showing the shipping routes for cod, rum, molasses, and slaves.

In contrast, time lines depict the passage of time. *The Cod's Tale* features an interesting example of this. This time line, located on many of the book's pages, documents historical milestones while the text discusses the importance of cod from early times to the present. A different kind of time line, a family tree, is on the endpapers of *Jack: The Early Years of John F. Kennedy* (Cooper).

Access Features

Access features help readers acquire information about the content of the book. The table of contents, glossary, bibliographies of books for further reading, author/illustrator notes, preface, afterword, sidebars, and index are all examples of access features. Not every nonfiction book includes these but when they're missing, experienced readers are sometimes at a loss as to how they can locate specific information.

Contemporary nonfiction for children contains an increasing number of these features. In *Popcorn!*, for example, author Elaine Landau includes a list of additional web-based resources and sprinkles sidebars of interesting additional facts throughout the text. *The Environment: Saving the Planet*, by Harlow and Morgan, includes a table of contents, a page called "About the Book" that describes each major section of the table of contents, and a bulleted list entitled "Remember: Be a Smart Scientist" that lists instructions for doing experiments and keeping records. Each page of this book is packed with additional visual information including sidebars, diagrams, and directions for experiments. These

From THE MAGIC SCHOOL BUS IN THE TIME OF THE DINOSAURS by Joanna Cole, illustrated by Bruce Degen. Text copyright © 1994 by Joanna Cole, illustrations copyright © 1994 by Bruce Degen. Reprinted by permission of Scholastic Inc. The Magic School Bus is a registered trademark of Scholastic Inc.

elements work together to help readers fully appreciate and access all the rich information in a nonfiction book.

Highly visual nonfiction entices readers. However, some of today's nonfiction books are crowded with visuals, which may make it difficult to access the information or even know where to start reading. Skilled authors help readers navigate the text. For example, the *Magic School Bus* books, by Joanna Cole and illustrated by Bruce Degen, offer readers a varied mix of interesting, stimulating information with illustrations that crowd every inch of the page. Although this format engages children, it can be overwhelming, and sometimes children need assistance discerning how to read these entertaining, informative books. Fortunately for the *Magic School Bus* books, Cole and Degen carefully orchestrate text and illustrations so that all information is interrelated; it doesn't matter what you read first, because the concept is mentioned elsewhere on the page. Each piece of information reinforces another (Bamford & Kristo, 2003, p. 284).

An Extraordinary Life: The Story of a Monarch Butterfly, by Laurence Pringle with paintings by Bob Marstall, is an excellent example of text and illustrative material working together to create an award-winning nonfiction book. Note the detail and clarity of description in the sample page from this book.

Accuracy

Accuracy is one of the most important elements of a nonfiction book. Children often use a library book as their sole source of information on a topic of interest. That book has to be accurate, because children have limited access to corroborating or contradictory evidence (Ford, 2002, p. 266).

How do readers know authors are providing the best and most current information on a topic? One way is to examine the author's credentials, usually found on the jacket flap, in the introduction, or on the "About the Author" page at the back of the book. If the book is written by someone who is not a recognized expert, it helps to see if the author consulted experts and has cited them. Sometimes a special section in the front or back matter will describe the author's research process, or the copyright page may include acknowledgments and a list of sources the author consulted. Readers can also check the copyright, because older books might have out-of-date facts. Verifying all these details will help ensure the author has the credentials to write accurately on the topic. Once students get a feel for authors' work, they can trust what these writers produce. Authors such as Jim Murphy, Penny Colman, Russell Freedman, Jean Fritz, James Cross Giblin, Laurence Pringle, and Patricia Lauber do impeccable research and have thus won the respect of readers.

From AN EXTRAORDINARY LIFE: THE STORY OF A MONARCH BUTTERFLY by Laurence Pringle, illustrated by Bob Marstall. Published by Orchard Books/Scholastic Inc. Text copyright © 1997 by Laurence Pringle, illustrations copyright © 1997 by Bob Marstall. Reprinted by permission.

Questionable explanations can also be checked against other books on the same topic, the Internet, and local adult authorities. Additionally, teachers should be alert to language and images that play into children's misconceptions. For example, as Ford (2002) points out, a diagram with colored layers representing layers of the earth may make sense to adults. However, children may perceive these same layers simply as paint stripes (p. 266).

Another aspect of accuracy, particularly for science books, is whether the author has used anthropomorphism—the attribution of human feelings and behavior to animals, plants, or inanimate objects. Authors must be very careful to avoid this as they write or they risk creating an inaccurate portrayal of scientific phenomena.

The Amazing Life of Benjamin Franklin, by James Cross Giblin and illustrated by Michael Dooling, is a picture book biography that has extensive back matter related to accuracy, including detailed source notes from

Meet... Penny Colman

Author of *Girls: A History of Growing Up Female in America; Corpses, Coffins, and Crypts: A History of Burial; Rosie the Riveter: Women Working on the Home Front in World War II;* and *Madam C. J. Walker: Building a Business Empire.*

"I have a passion for women's history that is apparent in all my work, even in my books that do not appear to focus on women." Ms. Colman was influenced by "growing up in an artistic and intellectually intense family where our interests ranged from the arts, to politics, to science, to one year raising exotic chickens."

Ms. Colman would like teachers and other readers to remember that "nonfiction is literature, too. Good non-fiction is important and powerful because it deals with real stories about real events, real things, and of course, real people. Reading good nonfiction is a good way to learn to write good nonfiction.

"Being a writer means thinking deeply, feeling acutely, and rewriting endlessly until finally, your words and sentences and paragraphs are completely clear, coherent, and compelling."

Penny Colman makes her home in Englewood, New Jersey.

Giblin and an artist's note. The back matter also includes a time line of important events in Franklin's life and other interesting historical materials that add to a reader's sense that Giblin has thoroughly researched his topic.

Style

Writing style in nonfiction, as in fiction, is that elusive quality that draws readers into a book and makes it memorable for them. Imagination; imagery; vivid, rhythmic language; and interesting descriptions are just as important in a book of biography or science as they are in fiction. Many nonfiction writers carefully document facts and present their ideas coherently, but if they present those facts in a boring, dry fashion, it is unlikely they will ignite readers' enthusiasm or passion for their subject.

For example, Robert Burleigh introduces *Chocolate: Riches From the Rainforest* in the following way: "Chocolate. It is that dark, pleasantly bittersweet, creamy, luscious, mouth-watering, impossible-to-forget taste. Mmm" (unpaged). After reading that lead, don't you just want to eat a piece of chocolate right now? This kind of vivid language makes you want to read (and eat!) more.

Aspects of style that good nonfiction writers pay attention to include the following.

> When I work on a nonfiction book for children, I've found that there is no such thing as overdoing research. After I've completed my first draft, I have the text checked by scientists familiar with the subject.
>
> Bruce McMillan, author, 1993, p. 99.

> Establishing my first paragraph is essential. It introduces the subject, provides the flavor and sets the mood . . . It is the anchor to which the second and subsequent paragraphs will link . . . I write in longhand, over and over, changing words and phrasing, until the Great Breakthrough comes when words begin to flow, towed out on a thread of thought.
>
> Aliki, author, in McClure & Kristo, 1996, p. 211.

Leads and Conclusions

Writers of nonfiction often wish to engage their readers immediately. They do this in several ways: they pose a question that is then answered in subsequent text, make provocative statements, or use a poem or song to set the context. Some create intriguing chapter titles to generate interest. Nonfiction writers also often craft chapter conclusions to provide an effective transition to the next chapter, compelling the reader to continue. Or they might create a conclusion to the book that leaves the reader satisfied or wanting to know more. Nonfiction writer Debbie Miller does this effectively as she concludes *River of Life*, a book about an Alaskan river that sustains the many plants and animals living in and near it.

Snowflakes blow and swirl once again, wrapping the mountains in sparkling layers of white. A sheet of winter ice tucks in the whispering river. Many birds fly south, raven stays. Grizzly bear hibernates, moose survives the cold. The earth and all its living things will be patient until the sun melts the snow and the river rushes to the sea once again." (p. 28)

The rhythmic description of a world going to sleep gives the reader a satisfying sense that life will continue when spring arrives.

Language: Sentence Structure and Vocabulary

Even in nonfiction, graceful, elegant language is an important aspect of the writing. Writers use varied sentence lengths; alliteration; precise, vivid verbs; and colorful descriptions to make their writing resonate in the mind and the ear. Reread the passage from *River of Life*; notice how Miller repeats the sound of *s* to give a hushed, still quality to her words. She also varies sentence lengths to establish a rhythm that slows the pace and adds to the quiet feeling. Phrases such as "ice tucks in the whispering river" and "the river rushes to the sea" create vivid pictures in a reader's mind.

Nonfiction writers also need to carefully introduce specialized and technical vocabulary so that it is memorable yet understandable. New words must be introduced, precisely defined, and then embedded in context so readers remember them. Sometimes these words are italicized to alert readers to pay attention. Sometimes synonyms are used to clarify meaning. Or a visual such as a diagram or photograph helps extend the meaning.

Figurative Language

Nonfiction writers sometimes use analogies or figurative language as a stylistic device to make their meaning clear as well as memorable to readers. Freeman (1994) discovered that writers of selected Orbis Pictis Nonfiction Award–winning books were much more likely to use familiar comparisons as well as extended or clustered analogies, adding to the quality of the writing. For example, Collard uses simile effectively in *The Forest in the Clouds* when he describes how "the tropical trade winds blow, sucking up moisture like dry thirsty lungs" (unpaged). Cynthia Rylant embeds metaphors within the poetic rhythm of her words in *Appalachia: The Voices of Sleeping Birds* when she describes night in the following way:

Night in these houses is thick, the mountains wear heavy shawls of fog and giant moths flap at the porch lights while cars cut through the dark billows like burrowing moles. (p. 13)

The metaphors resonate in the mind and paint a vivid picture of this landscape.

Clarity

A clear, lucid, cohesive text is a particularly important aspect of style in nonfiction. Without clarity, a nonfiction book will fail in its main purpose to inform readers. So authors must carefully order their ideas and support them with explanations and examples. They must include important information without overwhelming readers. Organizational structure, language, and content should work together so that writers create an easily understandable context for their information.

Organization

Nonfiction writing can be organized in various ways. Determining the structure used for a book is a critically important decision for nonfiction writers because structure supports a reader's comprehension of the information (Salesi, 1992). Text structures and patterns should evolve naturally from the content as well as from the author's purpose for writing. Figure 9.2 features the most typical structures used in nonfiction along with examples. Although we have described these organizational features separately, you should know that authors often embed one structure within another.

Categorizing Nonfiction by Form

With so many nonfiction books available, it is important that you become aware of the different types. The more knowledgeable you are about what is available, the better able you will be to help students select just the right books to explore a topic and to select books yourself to support your curriculum. You will also be able to find books that show your students how authors think and write about a field of study. This, in turn, will influence the kind of writing your students do about that topic.

Different types of nonfiction serve different purposes. For example, an alphabet book on birds is written in a unique style and presents limited

> The challenge of writing nonfiction is to achieve a message that is correct, clear and concise. Added to that is the quest to reach the soul of one's voice. Facts without emotion—without playfulness, humor or harmony—are as colorless as a weather report. If I manage to do this, I do so with pain, because rewriting is what I do most.
>
> *Aliki, author, 1996, p. 209*

Figure 9.2
Organizational
Structures of
Nonfiction

Structure	Examples
Sequenced—Information is presented in a particular order—usually numerically or alphabetically as in counting and alphabet books, but this structure can also be used in other books where the order of elements is important.	Alphabet Books—*Firefighter A to Z*, by Chris L. Demarest; *Girls A to Z*, by Eve Bunting; *The Young Adventurer's Guide to Everest: From Avalanche to Zopkio*, by Jonathan Chester.
	Counting Books—*Fish Counting*, by Arthur David Zoller; *The Crayon Counting Book*, by Pam Muñoz Ryan and Jerry Pallotta
	Other Sequenced Structures—*Kidtopia: 'Round the Country and Back Through Time in 60 Projects*, by Roberta Gould; *Magnetism*, by John Farndon
Enumerative—A main idea is presented and then subtopics that relate to it follow, or the book begins with a simple aspect of the topic and moves to more complex concepts. This structure is also used when the author includes an introduction to set the stage for examples of the topic. Survey or "all about" books are typically organized enumeratively.	*People Around the World*, by Antony Mason; *Safely to Shore: America's Lighthouses*, by Iris Van Rynbach
Compare-Contrast—Information is put side by side to examine it for similarities and differences.	*Did You Hear That? Animals with Super Hearing*, by Caroline Arnold; *Hey, Daddy! Animal Fathers and Their Babies*, by Mary Batten; *Beaks!*, by Sneed B. Collard III; *The News About Dinosaurs*, by Patricia Lauber
Chronological—This structure is used to denote the passage of time. A chronological structure could note a historical event or the passage of a person's life in a biography.	*A Picture Book of Lewis and Clark*, by David A. Adler; *Down a Sunny Dirt Road: An Autobiography*, by Stan & Jan Berenstain; *My Season With Penguins: An Antarctic Journal*, by Sophie Webb
Cause-Effect—This structure shows how one thing has an effect or influence on something else. Cause-effect is often embedded within another structure.	*Ice Age Mammoth: Will This Ancient Giant Come Back to Life?*, by Barbara Hehner; *What a Great Idea! Inventions That Changed the World*, by Stephen Tomecek
Question-and-Answer—This structure consists of questions and responses to questions about a particular topic. Typically, each page of a book with this structure contains a question, with its answer on the same page or close to it.	*How Do Frogs Swallow With Their Eyes?*, by Melvin and Gilda Berger; *Question Time: Explore and Discover Birds*, by Angela Wilkes
Narrative—A common organizational structure in nonfiction, in which story or fictional elements are woven with factual information.	*Ms. Frizzle's Adventures: Medieval Castle*, by Joanna Cole; *A Dragon in the Sky: The Story of a Green Darner Dragonfly*, by Laurence Pringle

information on the topic. In contrast, a reference or even a survey book will offer a more comprehensive treatment of the topic. *Depth* and *scope* are two terms used to indicate how a topic is covered: Depth indicates how far into a topic the author goes, and scope indicates how wide a lens the author uses to write about a topic. It is important to have books with both depth and scope for students to use. The text set on page 232 lists several types of nonfiction books that focus on the topic of birds.

Each type of nonfiction is described here in more depth. Appendix B at the end of this book lists recommended exemplary books in each category.

Concept Books

Concept books typically are a child's first taste of nonfiction. They usually focus on a specific topic such as learning colors, opposites, shapes, pairs, or animals. These books build children's understanding of a concept and the language associated with it as well as help them make generalizations about the world. Concept books also often explore more complex ideas for young children such as telling time, classifying objects, or how to do basic tasks. They have minimal text and usually have photographs to clearly depict the concept. Often they have durable plastic covers so even babies and young toddlers can safely handle them. Some concept books are designed for older children. Books of this type might depict aspects of a culture, such as the homes people live in around the world or the ways common children's games such as hopscotch, dominoes, and jacks are played. Or they might explore an advanced concept such as ecology.

Alphabet and counting books are specialized types of concept books. However, not all alphabet and counting books are nonfiction. You should carefully check the content or look on the copyright page to see if it meets the criteria for nonfiction. (See Guidelines for Choosing Literature on p. 237) Both alphabet and counting books are typically sequentially organized. An alphabet book usually provides brief information about a set of vocabulary words associated with a specific subject such as dinosaurs, birds, the Middle Ages, and so on. Sometimes the alphabet itself is the concept being taught; when this is the case, the book typically features alphabet letters along with pictures of items that start with each letter. The most useful books feature both upper- and lowercase forms of each letter and use corresponding objects that clearly illustrate the letter.

Alphabet books are not necessarily for the very young. Some use sophisticated formats to convey advanced concepts such as historical eras or scientific classification. Two that older children will appreciate are *Q is for Quark: A Science Alphabet Book* (Schwartz) and *The Queen's Progress: An Elizabethan Alphabet* (Mannis).

Counting books use a numerical sequence to present facts. Often a theme will guide the content; thus, children might be asked to count animals or items in photographs of city scenes. Examples of thematic counting books include *Emeka's Gift: An African Counting Story* (Onyefulu) and *My Arctic 1, 2, 3*, by Michael Kusugak.

As with alphabet books, the concept of number sometimes is the focus of the book. When this is the case, the objects to be counted should be very clear. *Counting Is for the Birds* (Mazzola) and *Count!* by Denise Fleming are excellent examples of this category of counting books.

Informational Picture Storybooks

Nonfiction books of this type have a strong narrative or story line working in tandem with the illustrations. Factual information is interspersed throughout the story. However, as we discussed previously, it isn't easy to differentiate between fact and fiction in these books. Teachers must be careful to show children the differences. It helps when authors include an explanation of what is factual in an introduction or in the book's back matter. For example, *Christmas in the Big House, Christmas in the Quarters* (McKissack & McKissack) compares and contrasts how Christmas was celebrated by plantation owners and their slaves in Virginia just before the Civil War. Historically accurate facts and details are intermingled with stories of fictional characters to create a fascinating glimpse of this era.

Photographic Essays

These books provide an insider's look into another culture or life. Photos are used to document the topic. Often these books evoke an emotional response because they are so personal and immediate. However, books illustrated with photographs are not necessarily photographic essays. Typically, in a photo essay, readers go on-site with the writer and the photographer. The purpose may be to visit another culture, to travel the wilderness with a wolf pack, or to spend a day with a physically challenged child. An excellent example of a photo essay is *Celebrating a Quinceañera: A Latina's 15th Birthday Celebration*, by Diane Hoyt-Goldsmith and with photographs by Lawrence Migdale. A *Quinceañera* is an important event, combining the religious and cultural rituals of the Mexican American culture with a grand, festive celebration of the transition from childhood to adulthood. Goldsmith's lively writing combined with Migdale's stunning photographs bring the celebration to life.

Survey Books

Many nonfiction books are survey books. These focus on a main topic such as the Civil War or marine animals, providing an introduction, then a discussion of subtopics that

Text Set

Different Types of Nonfiction on One Topic (Birds)

Armstrong, Jennifer. (2003). *Audubon: Painter of Birds in the Wild Frontier* (Jos. A. Smith, Illus.). New York: Abrams. (Biography)

Kalman, Bobbie, & Smithyman, Kathryn. (2002). *The Life Cycle of a Bird.* New York: Crabtree. (Life-cycle book)

León, Vicki. (1995). *Parrots, Macaws & Cockatoos.* Glenview, IL: Silver Burdett. (Identification book)

Pringle, Laurence. (2002). *Crows! Strange and Wonderful.* Honesdale, PA: Boyds Mills Press. (Survey)

Swinburne, Stephen R. (1998). *In Good Hands: Behind the Scenes at a Center for Orphaned and Injured Birds.* San Francisco: Sierra Club Books for Children. (Photographic essay)

Weidensaul, Scott. (1998). *National Audubon Society First Field Guide to Birds.* New York: Scholastic. (Field guide)

Gibbons introduces young readers to a host of topics about chickens, from egg and embryo formation to hatching and growing. From CHICKS & CHICKENS by Gail Gibbons. Copyright © 2003 by Holiday House. Reprinted by permission.

Students create dioramas or shadow boxes depicting McKissack and McKissack's *Christmas in the Big House, Christmas in the Quarters.*

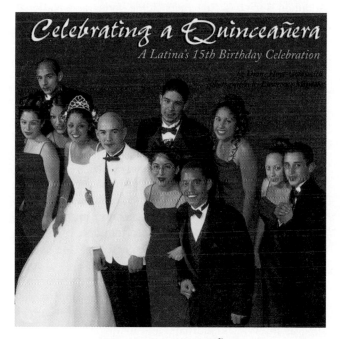

From CELEBRATING A QUINCEAÑERA: A LATINA'S 15TH BIRTHDAY CELEBRATION, written by Diane Hoyt-Goldsmith, photographs by Lawrence Migdale. Copyright © 2002 by Holiday House. Reprinted by permission.

extends the reader's understanding. Bamford and Kristo (2000) suggest readers "think about these as 'all about books,' but not necessarily as in-depth presentations" (p. 27). Breadth of coverage rather than depth is the focus. Often authors of survey books adopt a particular perspective or stance to make coverage of a broad topic more manageable. For example, they might focus on everyday life to present Roman history, as in *Rome: In Spectacular Cross-Section* (Solway, 2002), or explore the characteristics of many kinds of sharks, as depicted in *All About Sharks*, by Jim Arnosky.

Specialized Books

Nonfiction books of this type are designed to provide information about a limited topic or a specific aspect of a broader subject. They are resources for students with special interests and are likely to be used for intensive rather than extensive study. Many are written in an engaging writing style that keeps readers engrossed while providing fascinating facts that feed their curiosity. These books are more specialized than ever, focusing on unusual topics that intrigue children. For example, *The Great Fire*, by Jim Murphy, weaves personal accounts from actual survivors with documented historical accounts to create a riveting narrative of the 1871 fire that transformed Chicago into a smoldering wasteland. Patricia Lauber's *What You Never Knew About Tubs, Toilets and Showers* explores how people used these conveniences through history.

Journals, Diaries, Sketchbooks, and Documents

Some authors use sketchbooks, journals, or other original documents as the basis for nonfiction books. Virginia Wright-Frierson uses this format for her beautifully illustrated, informative descriptions of different ecosystems in *A Desert Scrapbook, An Island Scrapbook*, and *A North*

American Rainforest Scrapbook. Each presents drawings labeled "finds," maps, entries from an observation notebook, and detailed watercolor illustrations to help children visualize the areas.

Some authors incorporate primary sources such as archival documents, photographs, newspapers, diaries, interviews, letters, and eyewitness accounts. These historical documents are integrated with text or in some cases are the main thrust of the book. For example, *Dog of Discovery: A Newfoundland's Adventures With Lewis and Clark* (Pringle) includes entries from Lewis and Clark's actual journals. In *Tell All the Children Our Story: Memories and Mementos of Being Young and Black in America*, Tonya Bolden uses both primary and secondary sources to describe the black experience in America throughout history. Milton Meltzer uses letters, diaries, memoirs, interviews, ballads, and newspaper articles to depict life during the Civil War in *Voices From the Civil War: A Documentary History of the Great American Conflict*.

Life-Cycle Books

Children are fascinated by plants and animals, so life-cycle books are often popular with them. These books typically explain the events of a plant or animal's life from birth to death or the events of one year. Often these books show dramatic struggles with predators or other enemies, making them exciting for young readers. For example, *A Dragon in the Sky: The Story of a Green Darner Dragonfly* (Pringle) tracks the life of a green darner dragonfly in a western New York swamp that migrates hundreds of miles to a pond in Florida. Each stage of its development, along with the threats it continually faces, is carefully chronicled. In another example, Wendy Pfeffer uses informative, poetic text, complemented by three-dimensional paper sculptures, to present the life cycle of a tree in *A Log's Life*.

Activity/Craft, Experiment, and How-to Books

These nonfiction books acquaint children with ways to become actively involved in their own learning, whether it be completing a science experiment, baking fudge brownies, planting a window garden, knitting a hat, drawing a horse, or coping with divorce. This type of nonfiction is designed for readers to thumb through rather than read cover to cover. They are also good resources for iden-

> The Great Fire had been headline news across the country when it happened, but its importance in our nation's history has faded over time. Few history texts even bother to mention it these days, and I doubted that it was part of many school curriculums outside the state of Illinois. I worried that teachers and librarians around the country might find the subject matter too specialized or too local in nature to warrant inclusion in their collections. My job, then, was to pull out other themes that might broaden the book's appeal.
>
> Jim Murphy, author, 2001, p. 96.

tifying project ideas, as well as for fostering hobbies and helping children realize that reading can lead to interesting pursuits. Books such as *Checkmate at Chess City* (Harper), *Crafts to Make in the Winter* (Ross), and *The Best Birthday Parties Ever! A Kid's Do-It-Yourself Guide* (Ross) are excellent examples of this type of book.

Identification Books/Field Guides

The purpose of this type of nonfiction book is to name and identify all examples of a specific class or group of living things. More complex than a concept book, these books usually identify an example of a category along with specific descriptive information. Several publishers have excellent field guide series such as the National Audubon Society's *First Field Guide* series and National Geographic's *My First Pocket Guide* series.

Reference Books

In this type of nonfiction, readers will find factual information in a succinct format. Books such as dictionaries, atlases, almanacs, fact books, and encyclopedias are considered reference books.

Biographies

A biography is the story of a person's life or some portion of it. In the past, biographies often included exaggerations or inaccuracies so as to make the person seem perfect. Biographies of famous leaders, in particular, sometimes left readers with a distorted view of an individual rather than an accurate perspective on the person and the times. Few biographies explored the lives of common, everyday people. In contrast, contemporary biographers are concerned with portraying the subject of a biography with integrity. Excerpts from primary sources such as interviews, journals, and diaries are often integrated into the text for authenticity. An introduction disclosing the author's challenges in locating information or finding unbiased opinions might also be included. Bibliographies of books for further reading and an afterword describing the author's research process are often an additional feature. All these elements give readers a more balanced, accurate portrayal of people who are the subjects of biographies.

An important issue in biography writing is how much content can be fictionalized. How much can authors conjecture, based on the facts, and how much

Text Set

Abraham Lincoln Biographies

Adler, David. (1989). *A Picture Book of Abraham Lincoln*. New York: Scholastic.

Borden, Louise. (1999). *A. Lincoln and Me*. New York: Scholastic.

Brenner, Martha. (1994). *Abe Lincoln's Hat*. New York: Scholastic, Inc.

D'Aulaire, Ingrid. (1987). *Abraham Lincoln*. New York: Bantam Doubleday Dell.

Freedman, Russell. (1989). *Lincoln: A Photobiography*. New York: Houghton Mifflin.

Fritz, Jean. (1993). *Just a Few Words, Mr. Lincoln: The Story of the Gettysburg Address*. (Charles Robinson, Illus.). New York: Putnam.

Gross, Ruth Belov. (1973). *True Stories About Abraham Lincoln*. New York: Scholastic.

McGovern, Ann. (1992). *. . . .If You Grew Up With Abraham Lincoln*. (Brinton Turkle, Illus.). New York: Scholastic.

must they adhere to what is part of the documented record? Jean Fritz, noted for her lively biographies of America's Founding Fathers, has the following opinion on this issue:

> Once a biographer has collected the facts, it is not a matter of coaxing up a story; it is a question of perceiving the story line that is already there . . . I need as much evidence as I can get, for I do not invent. *(in Giblin, 2000, p. 418)*

In his Newbery acceptance speech for *Lincoln: A Photobiography*, Russell Freedman took an even stronger stand in favor of sticking to the facts and avoiding any sort of dramatization. Referring specifically to Lincoln, Freedman asserted, "It certainly wasn't necessary to embellish the events of [Lincoln's] life with imaginary scenes and dialogue, Lincoln didn't need a speech writer in his own time, and he doesn't need one now" (Giblin, 2000, p. 418).

So biographers have a difficult task: They must make their subject come alive, but do so in a way that reflects the documented actions, speech patterns, and actual

In discussing the importance of exact dialogue in biographies, Jean Fritz says, "But I won't omit words because they may be strange to a young reader. In my research on Paul Revere, for instance, I had discovered Paul's own account of his midnight ride. He reported verbatim the talk between him and the British soldiers who stopped him. One soldier said, "Sir, may I crave your name?" Well, I relish that eighteenth-century use of the word "crave," and I wasn't going to take it out. I thought children could surely figure out its meaning from the context.

Jean Fritz, in Zinsser, 1990, p. 27

I think it's important for teachers to have biographies in the classroom that relate to children's lives—especially now. Really remarkable stories about people who achieved—like Jackie Robinson, for instance, who I know at one time ran with the gang, but then someone spoke to him about making something of himself and he was really impressed by that and it changed his life. There are a lot of stories like that about people who have overcome a lot of difficulties in their lives and gone on to achieve.

Gloria Jean Pinkney, author; personal communication, September, 1999

events of that person's life. Depending on the completeness of the historical record, this can be a formidable task.

Biographies come in several forms, including the following.

Simplified Biographies.

These biographies are usually in picture-book format. Simplified biographies are intended primarily for young students as an introduction to a person's life. Because they provide only basic information, they can easily avoid more complicated issues. Examples include *America's Champion Swimmer: Gertrude Ederle* (Adler) and *Rosa Parks* (Greenfield). One biography written in an interesting format is *The Pot That Juan Built*. In this book, author Nancy Andrews-Goebel combines a cumulative rhyme with factual information about Juan Quezada, a famous Mexican potter.

Picture-Book Biographies.

These are brief presentations in which illustrations are an important element in describing a person's life. A picture-book biography may be of an entire life or a particular part of a person's life, or it may present an overview of the highlights of one life. Jean Fritz is particularly well known for her engaging picture-book accounts of famous people that present their very human, often humorous, side. Her books such as *Why Don't You Get a Horse, Sam Adams?*, *And Then What Happened, Paul Revere?*, and *The Great Little Madison* help children see these figures as real people.

Partial Biographies. As the name implies, this type of biography is limited to describing a portion of a person's life. For example, in *Dragon Bones and Dinosaur Eggs: A Photobiography of Explorer Roy Chapman Andrews*, author Ann Bausum focuses on five of Andrews's fossil-hunting trips to the Gobi Desert. In *A Special Fate: Chiune Sugihara, Hero of the Holocaust*, author Alison Leslie Gold describes the specific, important work that Chiune Sugihara, a Japanese diplomat, did to help save the lives of Jews in Lithuania during World War II.

Complete Biographies. A complete biography spans a person's life and usually captures in some depth the critical and significant aspects of that life. For example, Russell Freedman's biography *Babe Didrikson Zaharias: The Making of a Champion* details Babe's early childhood, her various athletic endeavors, her personal life, and her death at a relatively young age.

Collective Biographies. These biographies are themed collections composed of brief biographies of several people. Examples include Krull's *Lives of the Presidents: Fame, Shame (and What the Neighbors Thought)* and *Lives of Extraordinary Women: Rulers, Rebels (and What the Neighbors Thought)*, *Let It Shine: Stories of Black Women Freedom Fighters* (Pinkney), and *Ten Kings and the Worlds They Ruled* (Meltzer).

Autobiographies and Memoirs. This type of nonfiction is written by the person who is the subject of the book. Many children's authors, such as Tomie dePaola, have written their own stories. One notable autobiography for children is *Leon's Story*, by Leon Tillage. This is the story of a sharecropper's son who grew up in the South during the Depression and worked as a janitor in a Baltimore school. *Red Scarf Girl*, by Ji-li Jiang, recounts the memoirs of the author, who grew up in China during the Cultural Revolution. *Through My Eyes*, by Ruby Bridges, describes her experience as the first African American child to integrate the New Orleans schools in the 1960s.

Selecting High-Quality Nonfiction

What are the best examples of this genre that you should consider as you select nonfiction books to support the exploration of topics in your curriculum or in children's independent research? We believe there are several specific criteria you should use. The Guidelines for Choosing Literature feature on p. 237 lists the issues we think are important for determining the quality of nonfiction books. Two excellent resources for finding good nonfiction to use with children are *Making Facts Come Alive: Choosing and Using Quality Nonfiction Literature, K–8* (2003), by Rosemary A. Bamford and Janice V. Kristo, and *The Best in Children's Nonfiction: Reading, Writing, and Teaching Orbis Pictus Award Books* (2001), edited by Myra Zarnoski, Richard M. Kerper, and Julie M. Jensen.

Awards for Nonfiction Literature

Nonfiction is gaining in prestige. As a result, several awards have been created to showcase the best work in this category. For example, the National Council of Teachers of English established the Orbis Pictus Award for Outstanding Nonfiction for Children to promote and recognize excellence in nonfiction writing.

The Robert F. Silbert Informational Book Award, established by the American Library Association, is presented annually to the author of the most distinguished informational book published in the previous year. Because the award was established in 2001, only a few books have won it thus far: *Sir Walter Ralegh and the Quest for El Dorado* (Aronson), *Black Potatoes: The Story of the Great Irish Potato Famine* (Bartoletti), and *The Life and Death of Adolf Hitler* (Giblin). Additionally, the Boston Globe Horn Book Award has a nonfiction category.

Tech Note

Access the Companion Website for a list of winners and honor books of this award, or go to www.ncte.org/elem/awards/orbispictus.

Tech Note

Go to the Companion Website for more information on the Silbert Award, Washington Post–Children's Book Guild Nonfiction Award, Orbis Pictus, and the Straus Award. Links to sites featuring winners and honor books can be made from the Website. The CD-ROM that accompanies this book also lists winners of these awards.

Guidelines for Choosing Literature

Evaluating Nonfiction

Accuracy

- ☀ Is the information accurate and up-to-date?
- ☀ Are different points of view acknowledged (where appropriate)?
- ☀ Are sources and facts documented?
- ☀ Is the essential information related to that topic included?
- ☀ Is the author qualified to write on the topic?
- ☀ Is the author an acknowledged expert on the topic?
- ☀ Has the author clearly distinguished between fact and conjecture?

Content

- ☀ Is the scope of the book appropriate for its intended audience?
- ☀ Is the subject adequately covered without overwhelming readers with information?
- ☀ If the book requires children to follow directions, are they clear, with easy-to-find materials? Are the projects age-appropriate?

Style

- ☀ Is the information clear?
- ☀ Does the style draw readers into the book and stimulate their interest?
- ☀ Has the writer used clear examples, with comparisons within the experience of the intended audience?
- ☀ Is the language fresh, vivid, and interesting?
- ☀ Is technical vocabulary presented clearly and memorably?

Organization

- ☀ Is the information structured clearly?
- ☀ Is the organizational scheme well suited to the content?
- ☀ Are the access features informative and easy to use?

Illustrations and Format

- ☀ Do illustrations complement the text, clarifying and/or extending the reader's understanding?
- ☀ Are illustrations appropriate for the content?
- ☀ Are diagrams, maps, time lines, and other visual information clear, informative, and visually appealing?
- ☀ Are captions or other labels for illustrations clear and informative?
- ☀ Does the book design reflect the content and draw readers into the book?

The Washington Post–Children's Book Guild Nonfiction Award honors an author or author-illustrator whose body of work has contributed significantly to the quality of nonfiction for children; criteria such as clarity, accuracy, reader appeal, and engaging presentation likely to challenge and stimulate young readers are considered. The Flora Stieglitz Straus Award for Nonfiction has a slightly different focus. Given by the Bank Street College of Education, it honors a nonfiction book that advances humanitarian ideals and serves as an inspiration for young people.

Building a Classroom Nonfiction Library

It is critically important that you make careful decisions about the nonfiction titles you will select for your classroom and school library collections. You want to make sure children have the best, most up-to-date thinking about a topic. When you share nonfiction books with your students or have them available for research, you are essentially inviting those authors into your classroom. The authors act as guides, helping children learn about new topics or giving them new information on a topic of which they might already possess some knowledge. What children read about a topic contributes to much of their knowledge. When a book presents misconceptions or inaccuracies or when it fictionalizes information, children tend to remember this inaccurate information (Barman, 2000; Owens, 1999; Zarnowski, 1995), so it is imperative that teachers choose the best books to enhance their students' learning.

We are fortunate to live during a time when there are many excellent nonfiction books available for an incredible diversity of topics and ages. But along with this abundance is the need to be thoughtful and discriminating in your choices. You should never be able to say that your collection is complete; this is more true for nonfiction than for any other genre. There will always be a new title to add as well as a need to replace old or inaccurate books. It's much better to have fewer nonfiction books you know well and can skillfully use than to have many books that fill shelves but provide inaccurate information or present facts in unappealing, dull ways. So beware of the lure of inexpensive garage sale books and well-intended donations from parents or community members. You might want to save a few outdated titles on some specific topics to show how knowledge changes over time or for evaluation activities where you help children compare several books to judge the quality of information presented. Otherwise, outdated books should be pulled from your collection.

Resist the temptation as well to select books that fit your curriculum but for which you have no information as to their excellence. Read reviews in professional references such as *Hornbook* or *Book Links*, and *Adventuring With Books: A Booklist for Pre-K–Grade 6* (McClure & Kristo, 2002). Also consult booklists such as *Outstanding Science Trade Books for Children* (published in the March issue of *Science and Children*) and *Notable Trade Books in the Social Studies* (published in the June issue of *Social Education*). The winners of awards described in this chapter also are good resources.

As you select books, look for balance in terms of topic, curriculum, and student interests. Build text sets that represent a range of types, styles, formats, organizational structures, content, and formats. Be sure you have addressed topics across many content areas, including science, social studies, mathematics, and the arts.

Additionally, you should include books in your collection that are for pure enjoyment. Much of today's nonfiction is too beautifully designed not to savor it. Who knows? That sampling and savoring may open the door to new learning.

Part of third-grade teacher Shelly Moody's nonfiction library.

Nonfiction in the Living Literature Classroom

This section provides you with teaching ideas for making nonfiction an enjoyable, integral part of your curriculum. How often you use nonfiction with children, along with your own enthusiasm for the genre, will influence your students' enthusiastic use of these books. We hope you learn how to open children's minds to all the wonders of the world through nonfiction books.

Not every educator or parent is as excited about nonfiction literature as we are. Some do not consider nonfiction worthy of being called literature. Author and critic Betty Carter (2000) describes how some adults view these books:

> Children tell me over and over that nonfiction reading isn't considered real reading by many parents, teachers and librarians. They confess they like particular books but can't check them out because they have to get "something to read" instead. That "something to read" is invariably fiction. (p. 703).

Adults have traditionally embraced story, that is, fiction, as a vehicle for imparting information because they believed it was easier to understand than other forms of writing. Although many young children are first exposed to books through nonfiction concept books, the emphasis soon moves to hearing fictional stories read aloud. As they enter formal schooling, stories form the basis for early book experiences. Children become accustomed to the structure of fiction and the language used to talk about it. They have significantly less experience with nonfiction and the discourse associated with it.

Children's literature professionals have also traditionally not given nonfiction the recognition it deserves. Awards such as the Newbery Medal have typically gone to fiction. In fact, since 1922, the only nonfiction winners of the Newbery have been a few biographies: *Daniel Boone*, by James Daughtery, *Carry On, Mr. Bowditch*, by Jean Lee Latham, and *Lincoln: A Photobiography*, by Russell Freedman. A few Honor books are from this category as well. And only recently have the special awards for nonfiction been established.

Nonfiction and Boys

The tendency to undervalue nonfiction is particularly a problem for boys. Many boys are reluctant readers—they are disengaged from reading and spend less time reading (Barrs, 1993; Robinson & Weintraub, 1973). However, recent research has investigated the kinds of reading

boys do enjoy and discovered they prefer nonfiction, particularly books with eyecatching visuals (Smith & Wilhelm, 2002). According to Smith and Wilhelm, this is because nonfiction texts connect more directly to readers' lives. Seeing oneself and one's concerns in a text are significant factors in boys' engagement with a book and in their ability to achieve a reading "flow" or total immersion in reading. This kind of immersion is the most basic facet of engaged reading (Smith & Wilhelm, 2002). We must be sure we provide for our male students by giving them lots of high-quality, visually appealing nonfiction literature.

Becoming Committed to Using Nonfiction

Before you can effectively support children's selection and use of good nonfiction, you need to know and love it yourself. You probably know much more about fiction than nonfiction. We suspect that when you were a child, the books read aloud to you and that you read independently—Nancy Drew, the Goosebumps titles, and other series books—were primarily fiction. When you did read nonfiction, it may well have been biographies. Frankly, what was available in the past was rather dull, with few color illustrations and dry, stilted text, broken up with only a few visuals. It's important that you examine the wonderful, inspiring, and exciting nonfiction now available for students. Studying how nonfiction is organized, how it differs from fiction, and what the various kinds are will be a valuable learning experience for you.

Once you become intrigued by nonfiction, you can be the teacher who ignites a passion for learning through nonfiction. You do this by having excellent nonfiction books readily available, helping children become aware of the genre through a variety of shared classroom activities, and planning classroom inquiry so that children explore nonfiction thoroughly. We strongly believe teachers should present nonfiction in the primary grades and build on this early exposure by teaching more advanced concepts in later grades. There is no need to wait until the higher grades to share nonfiction aloud, to invite discoveries about it, and to show children how to read and write it.

Reading Aloud Nonfiction

Nonfiction, regrettably, is usually not the first genre teachers think of when planning what to share for reading aloud. The choice is usually fiction. Yet we know children love nonfiction and would undoubtedly enjoy hearing it read aloud.

There are many benefits to including this genre in some of your read-aloud sessions. For one thing, it develops students' awareness of how expository text sounds. When they hear how well-written nonfiction sounds, they will be more successful when they read this genre themselves. Additionally, read-aloud sessions provide an excellent opportunity to show students the elements and structure of nonfiction. You can point out access features, show how visuals support content, and study the use of organizational devices such as subheadings during read-aloud time. You can also introduce children to nonfiction authors, pointing out their writing style as well as how they structure information and how they select the information they present. Ultimately, reading aloud equalizes the learning potential. All students can learn new content even if they aren't proficient readers.

It isn't always effective or advisable to read aloud an entire nonfiction book in one session, especially if concepts and vocabulary are new to students. Try reading aloud excerpts of books, such as chapters, to interest them in hearing more. In fact, this might be your purpose for reading aloud: sharing just enough so that children will be motivated to read the book independently. Be aware, however, that sharing only excerpts may interrupt the flow. Students could walk away from the read-aloud session disengaged and missing important understandings (Wilson, 2001). Thus, you will sometimes want to read books in their entirety, stopping to discuss the content, answering student questions, and helping them form their own questions before you share another section of text.

Invite conversation before reading to tap prior experience and build background knowledge. This will significantly increase comprehension as well as their engagement with the book. One way to do this is activate as many of the senses as possible. For example, use maps, photographs, posters, recordings, foods, discussions, and related books. Read author notes aloud to give students a sense of the book's content; biographer Jean Fritz, for example, frequently shares interesting tidbits of her research or fascinating facts about the person who is the subject of her book. This information can entice readers to hear more.

Figure 9.3 features a list of nonfiction books we've found that work well as read-alouds. You might be surprised to see some of the books we suggest, such as "best" lists, almanacs, and trivia books; these are popular choices for sharing (Vardell, 1998). Children find these books very intriguing, and sharing them often results in interesting discussions.

Teaching Students About the Genre of Nonfiction

The most basic but necessary things you can do with nonfiction are show students how it is structured and explain how to evaluate its quality and usefulness to the reader. Many teachers use their read-aloud or shared reading sessions for this purpose: During these times, they deliberately and explicitly point out how a book is structured, how the visual information supports the content, how the author has used language to enhance the meaning, or how the author has documented the research process. They also can use the following activities to help students become familiar with the features of nonfiction.

Nonfiction Scavenger Hunts

Grade 5 teacher Judy Bouchard frequently uses "Nonfiction Features Scavenger Hunts" to teach her students about this genre. For the introductory hunt, Judy displays many nonfiction titles along with some fiction titles (to see if her students can discriminate between fiction and nonfiction). She asks students to select at least two nonfiction books from the assortment and tell why they think the books are excellent. Judy uses their choices and justifications as baseline data to determine her students' knowledge of nonfiction.

Subsequent hunts challenge children to find various nonfiction text features such as sidebars, glossaries, captions, and indexes. Once found, the example of each feature is shared with the larger group. When Judy hears comments such as "Let's check out this book before we choose it for our hunt" and "You have to look on the copyright page to see how old the information is in this book," she feels confident her students are learning how to use this genre.

Teacher Shelly Moody does a similar activity with her third graders; her main purpose is to help them become more familiar with the terminology used to describe book parts. Shelly gives each student a nonfiction book. She also has a high-quality nonfiction book that contains most of the features that students will identify during the lesson; one that works particularly well for this purpose is *Whales: Killer Whales, Blue Whales and More*, by Deborah Hodge. She places a list of the features the group will be searching for on the overhead; each student also has a copy of this list. See Figure 9.4 for an example of such a list. After she names and explains each feature, she shows the group that feature

Figure 9.3 Good Nonfiction Read-Alouds

Biography

Adler, David A. (2000). *America's Champion Swimmer: Gertrude Ederle* (Terry Widener, Illus.). New York: Harcourt.

Blumberg, Rhoda (2001). *Shipwrecked! The True Adventures of a Japanese boy.* New York: HarperCollins.

Bridges, Ruby. (1999). *Through My Eyes.* New York: Scholastic.

Brown, Don. (2003). *Mack Made Movies.* New York: Roaring Brook.

Christensen, Bonnie. (2003). *The Daring Nellie Bly: America's Star Reporter.* New York: Knopf.

Corey, Shana. (2000). *You Forgot Your Skirt, Amelia Bloomer!* (Chesley McLaren, Illus.). New York: Scholastic.

Freedman, Russell. (1997). *Eleanor Roosevelt: A Life of Discovery.* Boston: Houghton Mifflin.

Ganci, Chris. (2003). *Chief: The Life of Peter J. Ganci, a New York City Firefighter.* New York: Orchard Books.

Krull, Kathleen. (2000). *Lives of Extraordinary Women: Rulers, Rebels (and What the Neighbors Thought)* (Kathryn Hewitt, Illus.). New York: Harcourt.

Pinkney, Andrea Davis. (2000). *Let It Shine: Stories of Black Women Freedom Fighters* (Stephen Alcorn, Illus.). New York: Harcourt.

Rappaport, Doreen. (2001). *Martin's Big Words: The Life of Dr. Martin Luther King, Jr.* (Bryan Collier, Illus.). New York: Scholastic.

Rockwell, Anne. (2000). *Only Passing Through: The Story of Sojourner Truth* (R. Gregory Christie, Illus.). New York: Knopf.

Rubin, Susan Goldman. (2001). *The Yellow House: Vincent van Gogh and Paul Gauguin Side by Side* (Jos. A. Smith, Illus.). New York: Abrams.

Tallchief, Maria, with Rosemary Wells. (1999). *Tallchief: America's Prima Ballerina* (Gary Kelley, Illus.). New York: Viking.

Wolf, Bernard. (2003). *Coming to America: A Muslim Family's Story.* New York: Lee & Low.

Books About Animals

Brandenburg, Jim (1993). *To the Top of the World: Adventures With Arctic Wolves.* New York: Walker.

Collard, Sneed B. (1997). *Animal Dads* (Steve Jenkins, Illus.). New York: Houghton Mifflin.

Dewey, Jennifer Owings. (1994). *Wildlife Rescue: The Work of Dr. Kathleen Ramsay* (Don MacCarter, Photog.). Honesdale, PA: Boyds Mills Press.

George, Jean Craighead. (2000). *How to Talk to Your Cat* (Paul Meisel, Illus.). New York: HarperCollins.

Lyon, George Ella. (2003). *Mother to Tigers* (Peter Catalanotto, Illus.). New York: Atheneum.

Markle, Sandra. (2001). *Growing up Wild: Wolves.* New York: Atheneum.

Montgomery, Sy. (2001). *The Man-Eating Tigers of Sundarbans* (Eleanor Briggs, Photog.). New York: Houghton Mifflin.

Swanson, Diane. (1995). *Coyotes in the Crosswalk: True Tales of the Animal Life in the Wilds of the City!* (Douglas Penhale, Illus.). New York: Voyageur.

Natural Phenomena and Weather

Harrison, David L. (2002). *Volcanoes: Nature's Incredible Fireworks* (Cheryl Nathan, Illus.). Honesdale, PA: Boyds Mills.

Lauber, Patricia. (1996). *Hurricanes: Earth's Mightiest Storms.* New York: Scholastic.

(continues)

Figure 9.3
(continued)

Trivia and Fun Facts

Ash, Russell. (2002). *The Top 10 of Everything.* New York: DK Publishing.
Editors of Sports Illustrated for Kids. (2003). *Sports Illustrated for Kids Year in Sports 2004.* New York: Scholastic.
Morse, Jenifer Corr. (2003). *Scholastic Book of World Records 2004.* New York: Scholastic.
Young, Mark C. (2002). *The Guinness Book of World Records.* New York: Bantam.

Historical Nonfiction

Armstrong, Jennifer. (1998). *Shipwreck at the Bottom of the World: The Extraordinary True Story of Shackleton and the Endurance.* New York: Crown.
Bartoletti, Susan Campbell. (2001). *Black Potatoes: The Story of the Great Irish Famine, 1845–1850.* New York: Houghton Mifflin.
Colman, Penny. (1995). *Rosie the Riveter: Women Working on the Home Front in World War II.* New York: Crown.
Colman, Penny. (2002). *Where the Action Was: Women War Correspondents in World War II.* New York: Crown.
Fritz, Jean. (2001). *Leonardo's Horse* (Hudson Talbott, Illus.). New York: Putnam.
Greenstein, Elaine. (2003). *Ice-Cream Cones for Sale!* New York: Scholastic.
Kurlansky, Mark. (2001). *The Cod's Tale* (S. D. Schindler, Illus.). New York: Putnam.
Martin, Jacqueline Briggs. (2001). *The Lamp, the Ice, and the Boat Called Fish* (Beth Krommes, Illus.). New York: Houghton Mifflin.
McKissack, Patricia C., & McKissack, Frederick L. (2003). *Days of Jubilee: The End of Slavery in the United States.* New York: Scholastic.
Murphy, Jim. (2000). *Blizzard!: The Storm That Changed America.* New York: Scholastic.
Peterson, Cris. (1999). *Century Farm: One Hundred Years on a Family Farm.* Honesdale, PA: Boyds Mills Press.
Smith, David J. (2002). *If the World Were a Village: A Book About the World's People* (Shelagh Armstrong, Illus.). New York: Kids Can Press.
Solheim, James. (1998). *It's Disgusting and We Ate It: True Food Facts From Around the World and Throughout History!* (Eric Brace, Illus.). New York: Simon & Schuster.
Stanley, Jerry. (1992). *Children of the Dust Bowl: The True Story of the School at Weedpatch Camp.* New York: Crown.
Warren, Andrea. (2001). *We Rode the Orphan Trains.* New York: Houghton Mifflin.

Science and Discoveries

Bial, Raymond. (2000). *A Handful of Dirt.* New York: Walker.
Branley, Franklyn M. (2000). *The International Space Station (Let's Read and Find Out Science)* (True Kelly, Illus.). New York: HarperCollins.
Pringle, Laurence. (1997). *An Extraordinary Life: The Story of a Monarch Butterfly* (Bob Marstall, Illus.). New York: Orchard Books.
Pringle, Laurence. (2001). *A Dragon in the Sky: The Story of a Green Darner Dragonfly* (Bob Marstall, Illus.). New York: Orchard Books.
Reinhard, Johan. (1998). *Discovering the Inca Ice Maiden: My Adventures on Ampato.* Washington, DC: National Geographic Society.
Relf, Pat. (2000). *A Dinosaur Named Sue: The Story of the Colossal Fossil, the World's Most Complete T. Rex.* New York: Scholastic.
Webb, Sophie. (2000). *My Season With Penguins: An Antarctic Journal.* New York: Houghton Mifflin.

Figure 9.4
Nonfiction Feature
Search

Name _____

Nonfiction Feature Search

TITLES				
End Pages				
Title Page				
Copyright Page				
Dedication				
Copyright Date				
Table of Contents				
Headings				
Bold Print				
Glossary				
Index				
Introduction				
Author Notes				
About the Author				
Appendices				
Sidebars				
Inset (text box)				
Bullets				
Captions				
Photographs				
Labels				
Diagrams				
Maps				
Question Format				
Bibliography				

Source: Shelly Moody, personal communication, 2002

in her book. Then the students search for it in their own books. They place a check mark in the box next to the name of the feature if a book has it. "It is powerful for students to feel like knowledgeable critics of nonfiction," says Shelly. "Many even comment on what the author could have included to make the book more accessible to students."

Feature Booklets

Another way to help children become aware of nonfiction elements is to create feature booklets. This activity is adapted from Harvey's (1998) convention/purpose two-column notes idea. Students identify a particular nonfiction feature or convention in one column on their chart, then they state how it's used in the other column (p. 133). These booklets reinforce the learning of different conventions and also serve as a reference when students try using them in

Tech Note

The CD-ROM that accompanies this book features a description of a "think-aloud" session led by teacher Judy Bouchard in which she teaches her students how to access the information in nonfiction books.

their own writing. Figures 9.5 and 9.6 show examples made by fourth-grade students.

Helping Children Evaluate Nonfiction

It's useful to have children judge the quality of the books they use. This can be done by creating several kinds of charts.

Evaluation Charts

Create a chart divided into sections for each aspect of evaluating nonfiction: accuracy, visual features, style, and organization. For the nonfiction books you read aloud, your class can complete the chart following the reading. The chart can then become a reference for students as they select their own nonfiction books. This activity helps children feel like your partner in selecting books for sharing. It also increases their ability to use the language associated with the nonfiction genre.

First-grade teacher Tracy Hallee adapted this idea for her primary students. The group first created a list of what to look for in good nonfiction books. The children then created shadow boxes and written descriptions about animals. Their projects had to meet standards they had identified in the listing activity.

This activity can also be adapted for examining different types of nonfiction. The chart could be organized by the types of books you share with students, such as "biographies" or "life cycle" books. As you read a book, you note it on the chart, along with comments on the kind of information found in that book. Over time, the chart should reflect the different kinds of information found in various types of books. Children can then use this knowledge to make informed choices when researching their own topics.

Figure 9.6   Definition and Example of a Sidebar in a Fourth Grader's Feature Booklet

> Side Bar Page
>
> A side bar is a box that has extra imformation usally found on the side of page.
>
> Did you know that humming birds can fly backwards

> Table Of Contants
>
> Captions 1
> Diagrams 2
> About The Author 3
> Maps 4
> Graphs 5
> Glossary 6
> Dedication Page 7
> Side Bar 8
> Introduction 9
> Bibliography 10
> Acknowledgments 11
> Table of Contents 12
> Picture Credits 13
>
> A table of contents is a page that tells what is on what page.

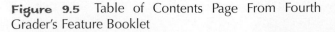

Figure 9.5   Table of Contents Page From Fourth Grader's Feature Booklet

Comparing Information in Nonfiction

Different types of nonfiction books and multiple books on the same topic provide varied perspectives. Children can examine various books, then analyze how the information complements, or in some cases contradicts, itself. For example, several biographies on one person could be collected. Design a chart to help students compare and contrast the information available about that person's life. Use questions such as the following:

- To what extent did you find conflicting information?
- How can you sort out the conflicts?
- What kind of information did you find in each book?
- What do the authors say about their credentials and the research process?

This idea can be adapted to other types of books on the same topic. For example, if students are investigating whaling, they can read *Whaling Days*, by Carol Carrick, along with Jim Murphy's *Gone A-Whaling: The Lure of the Sea and the Hunt for the Great Whale* and chart how the information in each book complements the other.

You can also have students find a fiction and a nonfiction book on the same topic. After reading them, they can create a Venn diagram that contrasts what can be learned about the topic from each type of book. Students can also consider how fiction and nonfiction differ.

Additionally, students can closely examine and evaluate the visual information in nonfiction books on the same topic. For example, you could have them compare the simple drawings of Gail Gibbons in *The Moon Book* with Seymour Simon's photographs in *The Moon*. What does the visual information in each book convey? What is the effect on the reader of each kind of information?

Helping Children Unearth Nonfiction Treasures

Browsing

Many children are overwhelmed by the number of books that can be found on a topic. They just don't know where to start or how to quickly peruse what's available before selecting a few books to meet their needs. Browsing is an effective way to help students examine the classroom collection of nonfiction books or a collection on a specific topic (Chambers, 1996b). Take nonfiction books off the shelves and display them on tables; approximately 10 to 15 minutes once or twice a week is a reasonable time for general browsing. Encourage students to share "new finds" with each other and chat about what they find.

Browsing can also be done in more structured ways. In this kind of browsing, students look for specific nonfiction titles or information. One way to do this is through nonfiction telegrams. To create a telegram, the teacher writes a message that requires the recipient to locate a particular book or specific information. Figure 9.7 shows sample nonfiction telegrams. Each telegram is written on a sheet of paper that is then folded and placed in a box. All books students will use to respond to the telegrams should be displayed on tables. Each student or pair chooses a telegram, reads the message, and browses the choices to the appropriate book. When everyone is finished, the telegrams and related books are shared.

Once children become acquainted with nonfiction telegrams, they can create their own. This is an excellent activity for getting them to look more closely at books. It is also a valuable assessment tool because you can design questions about specific aspects of nonfiction such as glossaries or sidebars.

Structured browsing can also be related to a specific unit such as insects or the westward movement. Opportunities to browse nonfiction books on a specific topic will help students bring more to the subsequent class discussions on that topic. To help structure their search, have them divide a notebook page into three columns. In the first column, they record the book title. In the second column, they record what they are learning about the topic as they browse through that book. In the third column, they should jot down questions about the information they find. Browsing also provides students with background to apply to K-W-L activities.

Nonfiction Book Pass

This activity enables students to see many nonfiction titles in a brief time (Wilhelm, Baker, & Dube, 2001). The teacher gives each student a list of all the titles being used in this activity and one book to browse through. Students then quickly record an assessment of their book in words or by using a symbol (smiling, neutral, or frowning face), indicating whether they would like to spend more time with that particular book. After a few minutes, the teacher calls "Book Pass," and students pass their book along to the next person. Following the activity, students are given time to read the books that caught their eye.

Nonfiction on Display

Encourage browsing by creating a "showcase collection" of nonfiction on a specific topic or type of nonfiction book. Invite students to browse through the display as part of their independent reading time. Students also can create their own displays; this provides yet another opportunity for them to browse through the nonfiction collection.

Read Around the Room

Fifth-grade teacher Mary Smith has a useful book browsing idea she calls "Read Around the Room." She invites parents,

Figure 9.7
Nonfiction Literary
Telegrams

—In this book, the author used interviews with family members and childhood memoirs to write about the true story of Grace McCance Snyder. (Answer—*Pioneer Girl: Growing Up on the Prairie*, by Andrea Warren)

—Learn about what it was like to survive in the most brutal conditions. (Answer—*Black Whiteness*, by Robert Burleigh)

—Learn what a "misery whip" is in this book. (Answer—*SmokeJumpers One to Ten*, by Chris L. Demarest)

—In the United States, there are only two spiders that can bite you. Find out what they are in this book. (Answer—*Spinning Spiders*, by Melvin Berger)

—The French sculptor Frédéric-Auguste Bartholdi offered a very special gift to the United States. Find out what it is in this book. (Answer—*Looking at Liberty*, by Harvey Stevenson)

—Find out about the longest blizzard in American history in this book. (Answer—*America's Great Disasters*, by Martin W. Sandler)

—Find out how two creative people make choices that result in a completed book. (Answer—*What Do Illustrators Do?*, by Eileen Christelow)

—This is the account of how people who lived in poverty survived a disastrous event in history. (Answer—*Black Potatoes: The Story of the Great Irish Famine, 1845–1850*, by Susan Campbell Bartoletti)

—This book contains a cutaway of the New York Public Library. (Answer—*Small Worlds: Maps and Mapmaking*, by Karen Romano Young)

—Learn how the word "cranberry" got its name in this book. (Answer—*The Berry Book*, by Gail Gibbons)

grandparents, community members, university students, and the principal to bring in five of their favorite nonfiction books to share with her students. Each visitor meets with a small group of students for 10 to 15 minutes. When Mary gives the signal, the children rotate to another group. Mary believes this activity helps spark student interest in nonfiction and shows them that reading is a lifelong pursuit.

Using Nonfiction to Support Exploration of Independent Research Topics

One of the most frequent assignments emerging from a unit or inquiry project is "the report." You probably remember doing this in school. And you probably did what we did. We came up with a topic, or one was assigned to us. We went to the only resource we knew—the encyclopedia—and copied or paraphrased the information we

found there. We made a nice-looking cover for the report and called it done.

Children today have so many more wonderful resources to choose from. However, this abundance can be overwhelming. Teachers must show them how to discover, organize, and then respond to the information they need to explore a topic. When this topic is self-selected, students are particularly motivated to dig deeply and to stay engaged for an extended time.

The following are some recommended procedures for helping children conduct their own research.

1. *Identifying a topic.* Students need to identify what they want to explore. This might be a topic entirely of their own choosing or one within a larger unit of study that is part of the curriculum. Sometimes it helps if students leaf through several books, then brainstorm possible topics of interest. Picture books are a good resource for this stage of the research process because they often present essential information in a format that is easy to access. You might also read aloud from a selection of books; this can generate questions and stimulate your students to learn more.

2. *Identifying specific questions to investigate.* Once children select a general topic, they need to identify specific questions to which they want to find answers. A primary reason for writing nonfiction is to answer questions: the ones that inspire, intrigue, fascinate, and drive us to learn. Students can write each question on a separate sheet of paper, leaving most of the paper blank for later data collecting. Or they can create a web of their topic before writing questions.

3. *Researching the topic.* Students next need to gather and read sources on their topic. They should be encouraged to consult various sources as well as types of nonfiction, from survey books to alphabet books to reference books. The use of primary sources such as letters, speeches, and diaries should also be encouraged. Students should be nudged just to read initially, without taking notes or, as indicated in Lucy Calkins's *Lessons From a Child* (1983), "The next thing we do is we read until our heads are full" (p. 162). As Calkins suggests from her research, we, too, have found that it is helpful to have students first read easier books on a topic to develop a background of information, and then tackle the more advanced books. It's a good idea to show students that some nonfiction books should be read carefully and sequentially whereas others can be skimmed, with certain sections read more thoroughly.

We'd like to offer one caution in this research process: The Internet is a seductive research tool for students. However, it's essential that you use it selectively and never let it be the only reference resource. Writer and book reviewer Betty Carter (2000) suggests that much of what nonfiction books offer youngsters can't be replicated. "At present," she contends, "outstanding nonfiction books repeatedly surpass other sources in the kinds of cognitive challenges they offer. But for these kinds of works to survive, adults who select books for and share books with children must recognize their strengths, encourage their continual publication, and acknowledge their place in the development of lifetime readers" (p. 697).

4. *Recording information.* Even first graders can record the information they've gathered through reading. Primary children can write simple answers to questions they've generated or draw pictures, and older students can write key facts or ideas on note cards, respond in

> It is 3 p.m. and I am picking up my son, Fraser, from school. Waiting for Fraser, I am ready to ask him the usual question. "So what did you do at school today?" and expect the usual reply, "Nothing," even though I know his day has been packed full of exciting adventures that I will eventually hear about later that evening. Today, however, is different. Before I even have the opportunity to greet him, Fraser runs up to me with an enthusiasm akin to a child's first visit to Disneyland. "Papa," he shouts, "We're doing nonfiction writing, and I'm doing dogs, and Sharon lets me. I have to go and get some books and find out about them. I love dogs. Can you believe it? Dogs. My favorite!"
>
> Tony Stead, educator and writer, 2002, p. 3.

learning logs, or write answers to questions. Two-column notes are another good strategy: Children divide a paper in half and put notes about a topic on one side and a response to the information on the other side. Figure 9.8 lists suggestions for two-column notes. Children also can be encouraged to create diagrams, cross-sections, time lines, or other visuals as they research to solidify their understandings.

5. *Teaching your topic.* Once children have completed their research, it's helpful if they "teach" their topic to someone else. This helps them organize what they've learned so they communicate their understandings in their own language.

6. *Refining understandings.* Once children have taught their topic to a small group, they can return to their references to fill in any gaps or correct misunderstandings. Then the information must be organized and presented in some way. Children must decide which facts and concepts are the most important. If they have discovered contradictory evidence, they must resolve that problem. They must then decide the format they think will best suit their information. The process for doing that is the topic of the next section.

Children as Nonfiction Authors

Once children have researched their topic, they need some way to present what they've learned. Through immersing students in nonfiction as well as teaching them how the genre is structured, you can help children write excellent nonfiction of their own. The more you draw children's attention to the different types of nonfiction, the kinds of information included in each, and how authors convey their content, the more you'll see these features incorporated in their writing. This is the concept of "intertextuality" at work; intertextuality means that what we read, talk about, and experience influences our writing (Tierney & Shanahan, 1996). Kristo and Bamford (2004) state that "you want students at any age, then, to be able to do these things—point out that aspect or feature, name it, describe how to use it, read and understand it, and use it in their writing" (p. 99).

So as you share nonfiction with children, you should discuss not only the content but also how the text and the visuals are crafted. To help you do this, create a mentor text set (Anderson, 2000) of high-quality nonfiction books that are excellent examples of what you want to

Figure 9.8 Two-Column Notes

The two-column note is a T-chart with two headings. Two-column notes are especially useful, because they are so adaptable. Headings are limited only by the imagination. Individually or as a group, children can complete the information and use it as the basis for a discussion or further exploration of a topic. The following are some suggested headings:

- ☼ What I know/What I wonder about
- ☼ Questions about the topic/Answers I discovered
- ☼ Opinion/Proof
- ☼ Facts/Questions (while reading, jot down facts on one side and questions about those facts on the other)
- ☼ Direct quote/Personal response to quote
- ☼ Notes/Responses (students take notes on one side, and record personal responses to those notes on the other)
- ☼ What's interesting/What's important (helps students begin to read more critically)
- ☼ Questions/Answers
- ☼ What the text is about/What it makes me think about
- ☼ Topic/Details (helps students organize information about a topic)

teach children about nonfiction writing. You will probably want to include examples of how authors explain their research process. Others might be clear examples of diagrams, flowcharts, time lines, and other visuals; good uses of access features such as glossaries, sidebars, and tables of contents; and examples of varied writing styles and organizational formats. These books will serve as your premier teaching collection and should always be available to repeatedly show good examples. You can also create text sets of a range of books on a specific topic you are studying. This will let students see the many possible ways authors present information on a topic.

Once you have developed a mentor text set, you can begin teaching children how nonfiction books are crafted. For example, showing them an alphabet book, a survey book, and an informational picture book on the same topic will help them understand there is a range of possible ways they can organize and present their own research. Creating journal entries, "how-to" books, and newspaper articles are other viable ways to present information. You can also help children understand how nonfiction authors use visuals such as diagrams, maps, flow charts, and cross-sections; they will then discover when and how to use visuals in their own writing. It is also helpful to show both simple and complex visuals so children understand the role of both in conveying information.

Take a careful look at the writing in Figures 9.9 and 9.10, done by third graders. What does it tell you about these students' knowledge of nonfiction conventions? It is evident these students have a thorough knowledge of different kinds of nonfiction as well as an awareness of many tools that nonfiction writers use to make their books lively and informative.

Snapshot Vignettes

This idea helps students who are overwhelmed by the task of documenting biographical information. Have them select the five to seven significant events in the life of their subject and visualize how each event might look. They can then draw each event as a detailed snapshot, adding a descriptive caption about what is happening in the picture. The pictures and captions should then be arranged chronologically. The children can then write a summary of the person's life, using the snapshots as a guide. They also can consider how the events in the snapshots evolved and how the person responded to each event.

Cereal Box Projects

To show students how to convey information in a concise way, sixth-grade teacher Kathy Jesenovich has her stu-

Text Set

Sample Nonfiction Mentor Text Set

This mentor text set includes aspects and features of science-oriented nonfiction books, appropriate for a range of ages, that contain clear examples of a range of nonfiction features. Each title is followed by a brief description of its excellent qualities.

- Bird, Betting, & Short, Joan. (1997). *Insects*. Greenvale, NY: Mondo. (Table of contents using a main heading and subheadings, diagrams, cross-sections, flow charts, photographs, and captions.)

- Gibbons, Gail. (2003). *Horses!* New York: Holiday House. (Diagrams, use of labels, summary chart, combination of visuals and text on each page presented in an organized way.)

- Lauber, Patricia. (1993). *Volcano: The Eruption and Healing of Mount St. Helens*. New York: Aladdin Books. (Narrative and more personal style of writing to use in contrast with the Seymour Simon book.)

- Simon, Seymour. (1988). *Volcanoes*. New York: Morrow. (Factual style of writing.)

- Swanson, Diane. (1991). *Safari Beneath the Sea: The Wonder World of the North Pacific Coast*. San Francisco: Sierra Club Books for Children. (Straightforward and interesting table of contents; excellent overall organization; every aspect of this book is consistently presented through each chapter, such as the same number of subheadings, sidebars, photographs, and captions.)

Sixth graders in Kathleen Miller's class write alphabet books on nonfiction topics such as math.

dents create cereal box displays. Although Kathy does this with social studies reports, the idea can easily be adapted to other content areas by changing the specific types of information.

In this project, students display the results of their research for a particular topic by placing information on and inside a cereal box. For example, Kathy has her social studies students put a map and pictures of an African country they've researched on the front panel; facts about the country's religion, language, currency, resources, climate, etc., on one side; several paragraphs of general information on another side; bibliography on the bottom; and three activities (crossword puzzle, game, etc.) that help others learn about the country inside the box.

Tech Note

See the CD-ROM that accompanies this book for more complete directions for making cereal box displays.

Using Graphic Organizers With Nonfiction

Graphic organizers are useful tools for documenting information gathered through reading nonfiction books. Organizing what was learned in a visual display helps children

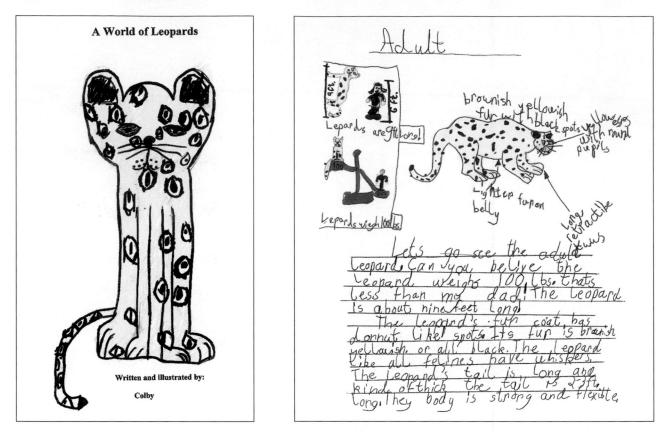

Figure 9.9   Example of Nonfiction Writing by a Third Grader

Figure 9.10   Third Grader's Nonfictional Writing

comprehend and retain what they read. Children can also clarify their understandings as they frequently return to a book while completing the chart. Following are some graphic organizers that work particularly well for nonfiction.

KWL Charts

Students divide a paper into three sections with a heading at the top of each section: "What I Know About the Topic," "What I Want to Find Out," and "What I Learned About the Topic." Before reading, they complete the first two sections; after reading, they complete the third one. A fourth column can ask students to list their sources of information. KWL charts often are more successful when students first have an opportunity to browse books about a topic, particularly if they are unfamiliar with it. KWL charts often are initially done as a teacher-led activity, then children do them on their own as they become accustomed to the format.

Comparison Charts

These work well for showing the ways several books vary. Possible topics for comparison charts are comments from a discussion about several books on a topic written in different styles (e.g., narrative versus a more typical expository style); thoughts on what one can learn from fiction, nonfiction, or poetry written on a topic; and how one author's voice and style can be traced across multiple books. For example, many of the short novels in Mary Pope Osborne's *Magic Tree House* series, in which a group of children travel back in time to different historical eras, have a nonfiction companion book that provides information on the era the children visit. Because these books are intended for primary-age readers, comparing the novel and its companion volume would give young children an early start in analyzing the differences between fiction and nonfiction. If two books are being compared, a Venn diagram is effective for showing similarities and differences on a selected book feature.

Group Summary Charts

Creating group summary charts helps children organize and review information they've acquired from reading. To do this, the children (whole class or small groups) should establish a purpose for reading. Divide a chart into four or five parts and label them with each general category of information you plan to look for in the book. For example, if the group is reading books about animals, they might want to discover information about "homes," "food," "physical appearance," and "interesting facts." After reading, children volunteer information for each category. As you record their comments, it's helpful also to encourage discussion. A final group summary is then produced using the information on the chart.

Semantic Mapping

Semantic mapping encourages vocabulary and concept development by graphically displaying words in categories, showing how they are related. After reading the passage, the group selects a word that represents the major theme or subject of the book or a section of the book. This is written in the middle of the chart. The children then brainstorm as many words as they can that relate to the selected word. Children can be encouraged to return to the text for ideas. As they think of words, they can begin putting them in categories. The categories are refined and new words added as the discussion continues. Children's ideas are recorded on a chart in webbing format. After the map is completed, new information can be added as additional books are read on the topic. Different colored markers can be used to indicate which information has been added.

Time Lines

Time lines work well for organizing events of a person's life following the reading of a biography, a life-cycle book in science, the development of a historical era, or the evolution of a scientific theory, to name a few examples. Using long, horizontal paper, children or the teacher draw a horizontal line across the middle; events are added at various intervals along the line to mark significant events. Younger children often use pictures or drawings to mark the events.

This idea can be adapted to study the genre of nonfiction and how the ideas in the books on one topic have evolved. The teacher or students can find all the books on one topic. Then they can design a time line chart to show how the books have changed through the years. Categories for comparison might include visual material, writing style, and content. With biographies, children could document how the information about that person changed across several books.

Supporting Response to Nonfiction With Drama

Many teachers don't typically think about using drama to support children's responses to nonfiction. However, drama can be an excellent strategy for helping children think more deeply about books in this genre. Many of the drama strategies we've already discussed can be easily adapted for use with nonfiction. Reader's Theatre, for example, is particularly useful. We've found books with dialogue, such as *The Magic School Bus* series, or books like those organized in a question-answer format, work well. Once the book or a section of it has been rewritten into a script, a small group can present the book to the class. Figure 9.11 lists some nonfiction books that we've found work well for Reader's Theatre. Following are some additional ideas for using drama with nonfiction.

Personal Interviews

This idea works particularly well in conjunction with reading biographies. Children can "become" a person they've read about, complete with props and costumes; they are then videotaped giving a personal interview. This idea can also be adapted to focus on a specific scientific, historical, or mathematical topic. In this case, children become "experts" on the topic and are videotaped as they provide information.

Meeting of the Minds

In this activity for middle grades, children become famous people they've read about. Small groups then conduct a discussion on a topic of mutual interest to the

Figure 9.11
Nonfiction Books
That Are Suitable
for Reader's
Theatre

The Magic School Bus Series	Joanna Cole and Bruce Degen
The Popcorn Book	Tomie dePaola
Leaf Jumpers	Carole Gerber
John Muir and Stickeen: An Alaskan Adventure	Elizabeth Koehler-Pentacoff
Harvesting Hope: The Story of Cesar Chavez	Kathleen Krull
The Boy on Fairfield Street: How Ted Geisel Grew Up to Become Dr. Suess	Kathleen Krull
The News About Dinosaurs	Patricia Lauber
The Yellow House: Vincent van Gogh and Paul Gauguin Side by Side	Susan Goldman Rubin
Mr. Lincoln's Whiskers	Karen B. Winnick

group. For example, students who read biographies of political figures might be grouped to discuss the influence of their person on history. Or those who read biographies of artists might discuss how their art differs. It seems to work best if the teacher facilitates the discussion, asking students to comment on how their subject's life evolved, how that person overcame obstacles, the need for risk taking and other issues, as well as talking about a common experience.

If students have difficulty with this discussion, they can first work in pairs to compare the characteristics of their subjects. They can also role-play scenes from the lives of their characters or hold mock press conferences to practice and refine their characterizations.

Summary

Nonfiction has now taken its rightful place as a viable genre of children's literature. We have many books on virtually every conceivable topic for all ages. Some of the most beautifully designed, well-written books now available for children are nonfiction. This high quality is the result of extensive research and collaboration among all the members of the production team, from authors and illustrators to editors and designers. We believe that as the market grows, there will be continued emphasis on producing the best nonfiction for our students.

This chapter showed you the importance of using nonfiction in your classroom. We defined nonfiction and described some of the major types: concept books, informational picture storybooks, photographic essays, survey books, specialized books, journals, diaries, sketchbooks, life-cycle books, activity books, field guides, reference books, and biographies. We also discussed the tools authors use to create high-quality nonfiction, including format, accuracy, visual information, access features, style, and organizational structure. We shared many exemplary nonfiction titles, along with criteria for determining excellence in this genre. Finally, we presented a wealth of ideas for using nonfiction with students.

Action Research for Teachers

Middle School, Nonfiction Writing Through Alphabet Books

Kathleen M. Miller
Brimfield Middle School

Kathleen wanted to find out if she could enhance her middle school students' interests and knowledge about nonfiction by having them create some of their own nonfiction texts using an alphabet-book format. During her 8-week study, Kathleen began surveying her students about their attitudes toward social studies and nonfiction writing. She then paired students to design, write, illustrate, and bind nonfiction books, which they would then read to third graders. She maintained a researcher log in which she recorded her observations, comments from students, and other reflections about the process.

Once the books were completed, students not only had planned and executed their books, but they had learned a great deal about the features of good nonfiction writing and graphics; they became more critical consumers of books and more appreciative of the kind of work that goes into a quality book. They were also gratified by the reactions of the younger students to their work.

Kathleen now uses this project regularly in her classroom and has expanded it into math and science as well. Having students write nonfiction accomplishes writing goals, research goals, and content-related goals. A photo of one of Kathleen's student's books is shown on page 249.

Part III

Literature for Teaching Reading and Writing

A Seed of Creativity

1. Get a seed of creativity.
2. Plant it in the soil of emotion.
3. Water it with the water of feelings.
4. Wait two of the longest days of your life.
5. Watch it bloom with love.

"A Seed of Creativity"
by Jeffrey Pritt
Grade 3
Used by permission

READING ALOUD:
Bringing Literature Alive
for All Ages

"To me, the best part of school was when the teachers read aloud to us. I think I have learned many of life's important lessons through literature." (Cynthia DeFelice, author; personal communication, September, 1999).

hat are your memories of having someone read aloud to you? Was it a bedtime tradition that you remember fondly? Maybe you recall an older sibling, your mother, your father, or another relative sitting with you and sharing a book aloud, bringing the print on the pages alive. Or perhaps you remember a teacher sharing a favorite book or a brand new one.

In this chapter, we address the following questions:

☀ Why is hearing literature read aloud key in the literacy growth and development of children?

☀ What are ways to select the best books to read aloud? What are techniques for reading aloud effectively?

☀ How can teachers help students enjoy and learn about books through read-alouds?

Now a word from your authors! Jan, Wendy, and Amy begin this chapter by sharing some read-aloud memories of their own.

Jan's story When I went to school in the 1950s and 1960s, I don't recall teachers reading aloud to me. They may have, but I don't remember. What does come to mind, from way before formal schooling began, are the sweet, happy memories of my very old Lithuanian grandmother.

Grammy couldn't read much English, but nonetheless she shared favorite Mother Goose rhymes and stories from a tattered antique anthology of tales and stories. How did she do this not being able to read English? Grammy knew her tales; she had internalized the rhythms and cadence of English, and relied on the illustrations to tell the stories while keeping the book open and the pages turned.

At that moment, I was forever enthralled with the beauty and sound of language. I didn't care if every word spoken by Grammy was actually on the page, but was instead warmed and comforted by her storybook words that kept me returning to books for a lifetime.

Wendy's story Like Jan, I also don't have any memories of being read to in school. Although my mother maintains she did read to me, I also have no memories of this. Personally, I fell in love with listening to stories read aloud on National Public Radio, in Maine, when I heard Madeleine L'Engle's *A Wrinkle in Time* read on a children's literature program. It was while I was teaching sixth grade that I started reading regularly to my class.

What I would like to share, however, is that every year I taught sixth grade, I read *Where the Red Fern Grows*, by Wilson Rawls, to my class. This classic is a tear-jerker if you love animals, as I do. Maybe it's the same for people no matter what their interests, but I can tell you what happened when I read this to my class.

First of all, you could hear a pin drop. Every single student, from the avid readers to the most reluctant ones, was rapt with the story, every day after lunch. They lobbied to hear more of it sooner, with pleas of "Please read one more chapter today!"

The funny thing, though, is that the last three chapters of this book are so sad that I could not get through reading them aloud without crying. I am not talking wet eyes, I am talking serious crying. So, I did something unusual: I went home and read the last three chapters into my tape recorder, where I could keep tissues in one hand, and pause the tape often to blow my nose.

So, I played these chapters for the class on tape. There was not a dry eye in the room. Surely not mine, but at least we could all cry together and I could get through the tape with just a mild dabbing of my eyes.

My students are all grown up now, but I am confident they haven't forgotten this book. Truly, you tend to remember books you have cried over!

Amy's story In contrast to Jan and Wendy, I have good memories of being read aloud to at David Fairchild Elementary in Miami, Florida. I particularly remember the chapter books selected by my fifth-grade teacher, Mr. Bockting. "Mr. B." was one of those teachers with "personality." He taught his classes all the rousing patriotic songs he knew, including the Air Force and Army Academy anthems; he taught Spanish by having students read favorite stories such as "The Three Bears"; and he read aloud every day from stories that featured children going on exciting adventures.

I particularly remember his reading aloud *The Lion's Paw*, by Robb White. This book is a wonderful adventure story featuring three runaway children and their sailboat, which takes place on the waters surrounding South Florida and the Keys. The story is unpredictable and exciting at every turn, and I remember waiting breathlessly each day to see what further adventures and challenges awaited the children.

Mr. Bockting also read aloud Marie McSwigan's *Snow Treasure*, which takes place in Norway during World War II. In this book, a group of children hide their country's gold from the Nazis by sledding past the German guards and building snowmen over sets of gold bullion bars. I particularly remember one scene in which a Nazi soldier starts to kick over a snowman, thus exposing the bars. Fortunately, another child throws a snowball at him, diverting his attention and saving the day. I was a wreck, worrying about whether the children's plan would be exposed!

Mr. Bockting taught me that reading books aloud can entertain, enthrall, and captivate children. He opened a whole new world of books and experiences to me and developed a love for adventure stories that I still possess.

Bringing literature alive for children by sharing books aloud is one of the most satisfying and pleasurable aspects of teaching. Your experiences with hearing books read aloud may have been when you were very young or in the primary grades; those years are critical for children to experience books. However, hearing a good book read aloud is something we never outgrow. Reading aloud needs to happen for every student—gifted, at-risk, and everyone in between, at all grade levels. It's that important.

In this chapter, teachers from several grade levels share their thoughts on reading aloud and how they make this time one of the cornerstones of their literacy programs. Their ideas for infusing read-alouds into the curriculum will provide you with an awareness of how teachers make decisions about planning for sharing books aloud at different grade levels and for a variety of purposes.

> *Reading aloud is a great way to get kids into books— I remember absolutely loving it when the teacher read aloud when I was a kid. I was completely lost in the story.*
>
> *William Sleator, author; personal communication, September, 1999*

> *Tracy Hallee, a first-grade teacher, says that it's vitally important for her students to enjoy reading and that sharing lots of different kinds of books makes that happen. Reading aloud several books by the same author or illustrator helps her students begin to make comparisons between books, as well as build an awareness of book language and how it changes across genres—from poetry to nonfiction.*

> *Children who don't have reading aloud experiences with their parents on a regular basis are missing out on one of childhood's most important experiences.*
>
> *Rosemary Wells, writer and illustrator, in Marcus, 2002, p. 211*

Why Is Reading Aloud So Essential?

Author and teacher Will Hobbs says it best:

> *Read alouds are pure magic when you pick a book that really works and read it dramatically for the whole class. To my mind, a teacher who shies away from reading aloud to the entire class misses the finest opportunity for actually teaching that language arts classes provide. Kids need to hear the written word read dramatically to develop and to continually improve their inward ear, so that as they turn to their own silent reading, they will model the expression you used. (personal communication, September, 1999)*

Some children have not had to wait for formal schooling or even preschool to hear good books read aloud; their parents and family members have believed in the value of sharing books aloud with their children from the time they were infants or even before they are born. Hearing books read aloud is one of the earliest and most beloved memories many children have, and it is where the seeds are planted for developing a love for reading.

Jim Trelease, the author of *The Read Aloud Handbook* (2000), the best-selling guide to children's books, says this about reading aloud:

> *Along with everything else, reading to students can be considered "seed money" in reaching tomorrow's parents. The student who never sees or hears an adult reading aloud for pleasure is unlikely to grow up and read to children. Reading aloud to the student, however, improves the chances the listener will someday read to his or her child and thus strengthens the possibility of future education being a true partnership between parent–teacher and classroom–teacher. (pp. 236–237)*

A read-aloud in a first-grade classroom.

Tech Note

Learn more about what authors say about the influence of early home experiences with read-alouds on the CD-ROM that accompanies this book.

Becoming a Nation of Readers (Anderson, Hiebert, Scott, & Wilkinson, 1985), a report of the National Institute of Education, states that "the single most important activity for building the knowledge required for eventual success in reading is reading aloud to children" (p. 23). In fact, the merits of reading aloud to children have been evident in the professional literature for decades.

According to Galda, Ash, and Cullinan (2000), "Since the beginning of the 20th century, both theorists and practitioners have argued that reading to children helps prepare them for literacy and to develop literacy skills, develops interest in reading, promotes language development, increases reading achievement, positively influences their writing, and provides opportunities for social interaction" (p. 371).

Oralia Garza de Cortés served as president of RE-FORMA, which advocates for library and information services to Latinos and the Spanish speaking. She co-founded the Pura Belpré Award (recognizing Latino authors and illustrators whose work celebrates and honors the Latino culture). Oralia Garza de Cortés (2001) has a very important message about the research in support of early literacy practices, particularly read-alouds.

But what about children from families not well versed in the ways of middle-class America? Children whose parents the message has failed to reach? Unschooled, non-reading parents too poor or too tired from two, perhaps even three part-time jobs, with barely enough time to spend in a quality way with their children, let alone devote the necessary time to such a noble effort? And what about recent immigrants, those who may not have previously heard these messages, or who may not understand the message because the messenger has failed to communicate it in language they understand? Are we to dismiss these as anomalies or exceptions to a literate culture? Or will libraries face up to their responsibility to serve the new, changing face of America? Judging from the latest projected US Census figures, however, we cannot easily dismiss these populations, particularly since many states are expected to undergo massive transformations from majority to "minority-majority" states by 2040 and 2050. (p. 153)

Studies have pointed to the importance of reading aloud before children enter school as a way to build an interest in reading and to develop early literacy skills (Bagh-

ban, 1984; Clark, 1976; Doake, 1985; Durkin, 1966; Teale, 1981). Researchers (e.g., Britton, 1970; Elley, 1989; Mendoza, 1985; Meyer & Rice, 1984; Steffensen, Joag-Dev, & Anderson, 1979; Wells, 1986) indicate that reading aloud is effective in developing and supporting many aspects of literacy, including the following:

- interest in reading
- language development
- building vocabulary
- developing listening comprehension
- understanding different kinds of sentence structures
- learning how language is used in books
- developing a sense of story—the way a story works—such as that there is often a beginning, a middle, and an end
- fostering an awareness of the world and building background knowledge contributing to the comprehension of other texts

Why Reading Aloud to Older Students Is Critical

A sixth-grade teacher says, "I'd like to read aloud to my students during their literacy block, but there just isn't time. Anyway, they're old enough to read for themselves. They don't need me reading to them." This teacher's statements about reading aloud, unfortunately, are heard too often. The thought of reading aloud to older students sounds juvenile and without purpose because older students can read on their own. The same thoughts permeate down to the intermediate grades, even to grade 4. Some parents and teachers think that reading aloud is a detriment to children who already know how to read. In other words, why read to children who already know how to read? That is a misconception about the power and reasons behind reading aloud. Nothing could be further from the truth! Those who support using literature for instruction say that reading aloud is a key feature of such programs (Galda & Cullinan, 2001; Huck, Hepler, Hickman, & Kiefer, 2001). Some mistakenly believe that reading aloud is best suited for preschool children and for the primary grades. However, English author and Hans Christian Andersen Award winner Aidan Chambers (1996b) says this:

Reading aloud to children is essential in helping them become readers. And it is a mistake to suppose that reading aloud is only needed in the early stages (the period people tend to call "learning to read"). In fact it has such value, and learning to read is such a long-term process, and the bit we call "learning" such a small part of it, that reading aloud is necessary all through the school years. (p. 49)

One benefit of reading aloud is increased listening comprehension, which is an excellent goal for reading aloud at every grade level—even through high school. One big payoff here is the introduction of all the new vocabulary words that will be encountered. As Jim Trelease (2000) comments, "The listening vocabulary is that reservoir of words that feeds the reading vocabulary pool" (pp. 238–239).

When reading aloud to older students, consider choosing books that will challenge and interest them but that are still within reach of their understanding. These kinds of books present many exciting teaching and discussion opportunities. Reading aloud also brings one text, whether it is a poem, a historical fiction story, or nonfiction, alive for a whole class. Making thoughtful decisions as a class about what books to read aloud across a year in middle school, for example, can go a long way to building class unity and establishing a learning community. Many teachers discover that these common experiences can be drawn upon throughout the school year for lessons and discussions.

Check back at the list of what reading aloud can do for students and their growth as literacy learners. Make reading aloud so important that you have to find room in the schedule for it. As an intermediate or middle-level teacher who shares the joys of literature aloud with students, you'll be the teacher students remember with fondness as the one who read aloud to them!

Guidelines for Effective Read-Alouds

Choosing Books to Read Aloud

Librarian and teacher Judy Freeman (1995) makes these comments about choosing books to share aloud with children:

> As an adult reader of children's books, I have quirky tastes and will try out any type of book. I can suspend disbelief with the best of them. What's hard is figuring out which books will send kids reeling. Adults tend to read books with a critical standard so high that we sometimes overestimate a book's child appeal without considering its true audience. (p. 4)

Tech Note

See the CD-ROM that accompanies this book for a treasury of great books for read-alouds appropriate for kindergarten through grade 8.

See Figure 10.1 for Judy Freeman's ways to identify good books for sharing aloud. Also see Figure 10.2 for sources of good books for reading aloud. In addition, use the Guidelines for Choosing Literature features in the genre chapters in this book as guides for finding good read-aloud choices.

Figure 10.1 How to Recognize Books that Work Well for Read-Alouds

More Books Kids Will Sit Still For: A Read-Aloud Guide (1995), by Judy Freeman, is a wonderful collection of chapters about maximizing the read-aloud experience as well as a compendium of annotated read-aloud lists for preschool through grade 6. In it, she lists "50 Ways to Recognize a Read-Aloud." Here are several that are just too good not to share with you.

"The story surprises us with the unexpected because it's unlike anything else we've ever read" (p. 8).

"It lets us in on personal secrets about the author or the characters so we feel as if we really know them" (p. 9).

"There is at least one memorable scene that you remember long after the book is finished" (p. 11).

"The special experience of hearing this book read aloud causes children to want to continue reading on their own" (p. 14).

"The story introduces people to other races, cultures, and communities, and encourages children to make connections to their own lives and broaden their own views of the world" (p. 15).

"It has the power to perplex children and challenges them to think deeply and analyze a situation" (p. 21).

Brown, J. E., & Stephens, E. C. (Eds.). (2003). *Your reading: An annotated booklist for middle school and junior high* (11th ed.). Urbana: IL: National Council of Teachers of English.

Cooper-Mullin, A., & Coyle Marmaduke, J. (1998). *Once upon a heroine: 450 books for girls to love.* Lincolnwood, IL: Contemporary Books.

Freeman, J. (1995). *More books kids will sit still for: A read-aloud guide.* Providence, RI: R. R. Bowker.

McClure, A., & Kristo, J. V. (2002). *Adventuring with books: A booklist for pre-K–grade 6* (13th ed.). Urbana, IL: National Council of Teachers of English.

Odean, K. (1997). *Great books for girls.* New York: Ballantine Books.

Odean, K. (1998). *Great books for boys.* New York: Ballantine Books.

Trelease, J. (Ed.). (1992). *Hey! Listen to this: Stories to read aloud.* New York: Viking.

Trelease, J. (Ed.). (1993). *Read all about it! Great read-aloud stories, poems, and newspaper pieces for preteens and teens.* New York: Pengiun Books.

Trelease, J. (2001). *The read-aloud handbook* (5th ed.). New York: Penguin Books.

Yokota, J. (2001). *Kaleidoscope: A multicultural booklist for grades K–8* (3rd ed.). Urbana, IL: National Council of Teachers of English.

See reviews of good books in these journals:

Book Links

Journal of Children's Literature

The Dragonlode

The Reading Teacher

Language Arts

The Horn Book Magazine

☼ Go on-line to locate booksellers who help readers find titles similar to ones they really liked.

☼ Check out the children's literature websites on the CD-ROM that accompanies this book.

Figure 10.2
Sources of Great Books for Read-Alouds

Know Your Selections

Familiarize yourself with the book you've chosen to read aloud, and know the reasons why you want to share it. Don't be caught off guard. Read the book beforehand even though it may be highly recommended in reviews or by colleagues. Make sure the book is right for you and for your students in terms of content and reasons why you want to share it. Choose books that you love and enjoy for a host of reasons. Share those reasons with students; you'll be reflecting your ideas about why reading is a positive experience for you.

For example, you might say, "I know how much we all enjoyed Cynthia Rylant's book *The Relatives Came*, when relatives came visiting one summer and seemed to stay for weeks. I remember how much we laughed at the illustrations by Stephen Gammell of all the people in the house talking and laughing and eating up a storm! Remember

Cynthia Rylant's words: 'It was different, going to sleep with all that new breathing in the house' (unpaged). We talked about how we all have our own relatives and friends visit and all the fun we have sharing stories. So, I think you'll enjoy Patricia Polacco's book *When Lightning Comes in a Jar*. It's about a family reunion. Let's see what you think about this book."

Third-grade teacher Mary Seward says, "I really believe it's important for children to be read stories that they would not otherwise be able to read. They learn so much about how a story works and about characters in stories. And best of all, they *love* it!" She notes that some of the books she shares aloud are for fluent independent readers, but when she reads them aloud, all children benefit from getting to know books that they might not be able to read on their own.

Mary also comments that "*I Have a Dream: The Story of Martin Luther King*, by Margaret Davidson, aligns with my

Tech Note

See the CD-ROM that accompanies this book for multigrade primary teacher Sue Pidhurney's Surefire Read Aloud Hits.

curriculum, and *Where the Red Fern Grows*, by Wilson Rawls, is my absolute favorite. The children in third grade love it. They could read it on their own, but to listen to—it's the *best*! The children laugh uproariously when I read *The BFG*, by Roald Dahl and *Sideways Stories from Wayside School*, by Louis Sachar."

Note that on Mary Seward's list, there are several classics. Don't forget about these, but also make it a goal to plan out the read-aloud banquet throughout the year with "must have" selections. These can be the titles that you don't want to miss sharing aloud with your students. You'll want to strike a balance across the year with newer titles and ones that have endured over time, plus books that represent a sampling from all the genres.

Leading Students to What's Good

Reading aloud is one of the most effective ways for introducing a wide array of genres to children. We all have our favorites; you may realize that you never share a certain

The Relatives Came

Story by CYNTHIA RYLANT   Illustrated by STEPHEN GAMMELL

Reprinted with the permission of Atheneum Books for Young Readers, an imprint of Simon & Schuster Children's Publishing Division from THE RELATIVES CAME by Cynthia Rylant, illustrated by Stephen Gammell. Illustrations copyright © 1985 Stephen Gammell.

Cover from WHEN LIGHTNING COMES IN A JAR by Patricia Polacco, copyright © 2002 by Babushka, Inc. Used by permission of Philomel Books, A Division of Penguin Young Readers Group, A Member of Penguin Group (USA) Inc., 345 Hudson Street, New York, NY 10014. All rights reserved.

kind of book because you don't care for that genre. However, remember that your students' favorite genres might be different from yours.

Judy Freeman (1995) shares this sound advice:

If we want to eliminate categories from our adult reading, fine; but to skip any genre while selecting books for our students to read is to deny them our expertise. We are duty bound to learn to appreciate all types of children's books if we expect to tap into and nurture our children's tastes. (p. 4)

Make it a professional goal to sample titles from genres that aren't appealing to you. Talk to colleagues and scan reviews of books to find titles that you'd like to read for yourself. It's critical that students get to sample from the wide range of children's literature available today— picture books, international and multicultural titles, contemporary fiction, modern fantasy, science fiction, poetry, nonfiction (including biography), traditional literature, and historical fiction. Think about the books you share every year: Are they ones that children hear again at different grade levels? How can you expand and revise your list to include balance?

Consider reading aloud Newbery Medal and Honor titles or other award-winning books; award winners often challenge even the best readers in your class in terms of story structure, topics, and vocabulary. Design opportunities to support or scaffold children's understandings of these more complex works by sharing challenging titles aloud. Adults play a critical role in shaping students as readers, because they are the ones who will share books that can fuel students' imaginations and ignite a love of reading.

What We Learn When Things Go Wrong: Read-Aloud Choices That Don't Always Hit the Mark

Here's an anecdote about the day a read-aloud went all wrong in a fifth-grade class (Kristo, 1996):

> One day I began reading a chapter book loaded with descriptions, metaphors, and allegory. The literature reviews agreed that my choice was a good one. But if this book was supposed to be so good, why wasn't anyone listening? Finally, after three days of watching my students squirm in their seats, I bravely put the book down on my desk and said, "Okay, talk to me about this squirming."
>
> What did I learn from this teaching experience? Since I was trying to create an atmosphere of a book-loving culture in my classroom, I needed to do more talking with my students about books and about what adults do who love books. We don't always finish every book we start, and we don't always continue with a book that we don't like. The book we don't care for is likely to be the one that will stay on the table and go unread; the one we have good intentions to finish but just never manage to do that.
>
> We needed to talk about all kinds of responses to books; that it was okay to be bored by a book. Our conversation that day led to me actually talking about the kinds of books I like to read—nonfiction, historical fiction, poetry, and all kinds of picture books. I told my students that I have an alphabet book collection and one of wordless picture books. I think that you could have heard a pin drop in that room—everyone was so enthralled to hear "the teacher" talking so personally about her own favorite kinds of books. (p. 127)

Involve students in read-aloud decisions, particularly if one of the purposes is enjoyment of literature. Choose three to five titles that you think they'll enjoy and prepare a brief book talk about each. You may introduce the book by sharing a story or related incident about it or even bring in a prop and query children about it and how it

might relate to the book. Or you could simply give a synopsis of each book—just enough to whet the appetite. Then allow students to vote for their preferences in priority order. For young children, the titles can be listed on one side of the paper and a selection of faces—from smiling to sad—on the other side. This gives students a voice in the selection of a book that may be a chapter book and one that they will be sitting through for many days.

Another idea is to give students an interest inventory at the beginning of the year and another one mid-year as a way to informally assess interest: Include questions about the kinds of books they like to hear read aloud, topics they want to know more about, and what they like to read. Also include a listing of genres of books. For example, you might have a pie diagram evenly divided labeling major genres as well as subgenres, such as mysteries. Ask students to color in the slices of the pie they are most familiar with as readers. The pie diagram and their responses to the questions will give you a good idea at a glance of the kinds of reading your children have done and will make clear the types of books you may want to introduce during the year.

Sometimes readers get stuck in a reading rut by choosing one kind of book to read all the time. Students may become experts about a kind of book—horse stories, for example, or dinosaur books, or books written by one author. They can be designated as class experts and do some projects making use of their expertise, such as designing a class display and an author information board. But there's always room to grow as readers, and reading aloud can be the vehicle for helping children explore authors and genres they may never have considered. That is reason enough to read aloud to *all* ages.

Students learn to trust your judgment about books; this will carry over from books you read aloud to those you suggest for their independent reading. When you choose a book that students don't care for, admit it and discuss why it was a flop. There are important lessons here about the range of responses readers have to books.

See Figure 10.3 for a sampling from "One Hundred Books That Shaped the Century" created by four children's literature experts—Karen Breen, Ellen Fader, Kathleen Odean, and Zena Sutherland. This is another great source for sharing aloud books that have withstood the test of time.

Planning Your Read-Aloud

As you think about choosing a book, you should also be thinking about how you want to share it and why. Write notes, a lesson plan, or record on self-stick notes aspects about the book or how you want to share it and then attach them to the book.

Figure 10.3 A Sampling From the "One Hundred Books That Shaped the Century"

The books listed here were unanimous choices. See the entire list created by Karen Breen, Ellen Fader, Kathleen Odean, and Zena Sutherland in "One Hundred Books That Shaped the Century," *School Library Journal*, January 2000, 46(1), 50–58. P = Primary (K–2), I = Intermediate (grades 3–5), M = Middle (grades 6–8).

Tuck Everlasting, by Natalie Babbitt (I/M)

Madeline, by Ludwig Bemelmans (P)

Are You There God? It's Me, Margaret, by Judy Blume (M)

Goodnight Moon, by Margaret Wise Brown (P)

The Chocolate War, by Robert Cormier (M)

Harriet the Spy, by Louise Fitzhugh (I)

Anne Frank: The Diary of a Young Girl, by Anne Frank (M)

Lincoln: A Photobiography, by Russell Freedman (I/M)

Julie of the Wolves, by Jean Craighead George (I/M)

The Snowy Day, by Ezra Jack Keats (P)

From the Mixed-Up Files of Mrs. Basil E. Frankweiler, by E. L. Konigsburg (I)

A Wrinkle in Time, by Madeleine L'Engle (I/M)

The Lion, the Witch and the Wardrobe, by C. S. Lewis (I/M)

Frog and Toad Are Friends, by Arnold Lobel (P)

Sarah, Plain and Tall, by Patricia MacLachlan (I)

Winnie-the-Pooh, by A. A. Milne (P)

Island of the Blue Dolphins, by Scott O'Dell (I)

Bridge to Terabithia, by Katherine Paterson (I)

The Tale of Peter Rabbit, by Beatrix Potter (P)

Where the Wild Things Are, by Maurice Sendak (P)

The Cat in the Hat, by Dr. Seuss (P)

Charlotte's Web, by E. B. White (I)

Little House in the Big Woods, by Laura Ingalls Wilder (I)

When you begin a new book, don't hurry into it; spend time on the cover or the dust jacket discussing the title, the author, and the illustrator. See if the end pages hold something special for readers to notice.

This is a good opportunity to help students make connections with other books they've read by the same author. They may be familiar with the illustrator, or the topic might connect in some way with previous learning. Also reinforce the discourse or language of books. Use technical book vocabulary, such as *book jacket, cover, author, illustrator, genre, title page,* and *endpapers*. It's never too early to begin using the proper terms associated with

☼ Campbell. R. (2001). *Read-alouds with young children*. Newark, DE: International Reading Association.

☼ Post, A. D., Scott, M., & Theberge, M. (2000). *Celebrating children's choices: 25 years of children's favorite books*. Newark: DE: International Reading Association.

☼ Tiedt, I. M. (2000). *Teaching with picture books in the middle school*. Newark, DE: International Reading Association.

☼ Yopp, R. H., & Yopp, H. K. (2001). *Literature-based reading activities* (3rd ed.). Boston: Allyn & Bacon.

Figure 10.4
Excellent Resources to Invite Student Involvement During Read-Alouds

books; besides, young children love to learn new vocabulary. The understandings you establish early on about books will build a good foundation for your students' future interactions with books.

Plan ways to introduce the book by tapping knowledge students already have about the topic. Have other information available to help establish background information, such as maps, related books, photos, or a prop. Sometimes key objects will stimulate student interest in wanting to hear a story or book shared as well as provide basic understandings about the story line or topic of the book. For example, if you share a biography about Abraham Lincoln with children who are just learning about him, how would you introduce the book? How would you do this with older students who have some previous understandings?

Some publishers also prepare activity guides for their books. Go on line to see what publishers may have available. Here is a note of caution, though. These guides are sometimes good starting places, but you know your students best, so plan accordingly. Some books even include a discussion guide at the end, such as *Ghost Wings*, by Barbara Joosse, a heartwarming story set in Mexico during the time of the monarch butterflies' annual migration.

Invite interaction throughout the read-aloud, stopping to ask for comments or to ask a question. Think through where you might stop in a chapter book for the daily reading. You don't necessarily have to stop at the end of a chapter; instead, end at a cliff-hanging moment in the action to interest students to hearing more the next day. See Figure 10.4 for resources that will help in designing student involvement during read-alouds.

After reading aloud, discuss the book and, depending on purposes, suggest additional ways to respond. Research done by Hoffman, Roser, and Battle (1993) indicates that all too often, children aren't asked to discuss or respond in any significant way to what they've heard read aloud. It's important to invite some kind of response after

every read-aloud session. It might be simply a question that asks about reactions to the book or ways to help students make connections to what they know or other books they've read; or a response could include writing, artwork, and dramatic engagements that invite students back into the book. See the genre chapters for more ideas as well as the chapters on comprehension and response to literature.

Creating the Setting for Reading Aloud

Seat students in the best possible way for them to enjoy and benefit from hearing the book read aloud. Primary students often seat themselves around you on the floor while you sit in a comfortable chair, such as a rocker; older students may stay at their desks or tables. Sharing a picture book means that you have to be able to show

Children enjoy a read-aloud from an animated, enthusiastic teacher.

Meet... Jon Scieszka

Author of *The True Story of the 3 Little Pigs!; The Stinky Cheese Man; Math Curse; Squids;* and others.

I'm the second oldest and very nicest of six boys, born in Flint, Michigan. I have written 4,876 books. I've read 783,893,001 others. I've climbed Mt. Everest backwards and blindfolded in my bathrobe. And I also tend to make up a lot of stories. So I think I've found the perfect job for me—being a writer who makes up stories!

I've been influenced by reading *Go, Dog, Go* over and over at an early age, watching too many cartoons, reading everything from Sluggo comics and *MAD* magazine to Nietzsche and Cervantes, and wrestling with my brothers.

The best literature is all about life. The characters in kids' literature may happen to be a pair of hippos, a frog, or a pig and a spider; but their stories are the essence of being human. With my stories, I always hope to entertain my readers and get them to see some of themselves as they laugh.

If you want to be a writer, you have to be a reader. That's the fun part. The hard part about being a writer is the simple act of making yourself sit down and write, write, write (then you have to make yourself read what you've written and throw most of it away, but that's too depressing to even start to get into . . .). Not everyone is, or should be, a writer. Just like not everyone is, or should be, a plumber. But if you want to be a writer, there is only one way to do it. And it's so simple that it doesn't even sound like it can be true: If you want to be a writer, you have to sit down and write.

I started writing (and keep writing) because I get such a kick out of all the things a string of words can conjure into being—humor, sadness, happiness, craziness, thought, nonsense. It really is some kind of magic."

---

the illustrations to everyone. Remember to move around so that everyone can see the illustrations or to provide some dramatic flair.

Animating the Read-Aloud

Maintain some eye contact with your audience, if it is culturally appropriate to do so. Engage your listeners by drawing them into the book. It might be difficult to do when reading a chapter book, but you should know the story well enough to lift your eyes off the pages to engage with your audience of eager listeners. When reading aloud a picture book, decide whether you will hold it so that everyone can see the illustrations as you read it or whether you will read and then show the illustrations. Sometimes this is a matter of style, but at other times, your purposes will dictate what you do.

According to Chambers (1996b):

All writing is a kind of a playscript. To enjoy a story or a poem you have to know how to convert print into the

Here are third-grade teacher Mary Seward's tips for effective read-alouds:

- ☺ *Start with short stories and as listening abilities increase, move to full-length novels.*
- ☺ *Read books that you have read and loved.*
- ☺ *Read stories about both genders.*
- ☺ *Read humorous stories and poems—children love to laugh!*
- ☺ *Stories about animals are always a hit.*

movement of action, the sound of characters thinking and talking, while giving every scene, every sequence, the right pace (slow or fast or a silent pause) that will turn printed information into vivid drama. (p. 50)

Use appropriate gestures, voice, props, etc., to make the story or poem meaningful and engaging to students. Chambers's quote invites us to think about how to make a story, a poem, a nonfiction book, or a biography come alive for children. This is difficult, if not impossible, to do if the book is unfamiliar to you. For example, when you read a book aloud, you might decide to change your voice for certain characters because this really makes the story come alive. If you aren't familiar with the book, you won't know when to change your voice according to how a character might talk.

Don't be afraid to try different ways to share books authentically and sincerely. Build your repertoire of techniques. Your students will love you for it, and it will make lasting impressions about the magic of bringing words on a page to life.

Teachers often dramatize a read-aloud by effectively changing their voices and by using gestures.

Pacing

Pace yourself so that you aren't reading too fast or too slowly. If you're unsure about how you sound, then tape-record your voice to play back later and assess. You'll develop your voice for sharing books aloud. Take pride in that.

Increase the time you read aloud daily. However, keep in mind that you might also be reading aloud several times a day for other purposes—as a way to introduce a new unit in science or social studies, as part of a minilesson, as an ongoing read-aloud of a chapter book, etc.

The Listening Center

Listening centers are easy to create in classrooms for all ages. All they require are one audiotape recorder and several sets of headphones to be used at once. Students respond well to taped stories and poems read aloud. This builds their capacity for listening as well as their listening vocabulary and comprehension. The activity requires little planning (once you have a repertoire of tapes). Assessment and follow-up may be planned, but often the listening center is used for practice and the pleasure of hearing literature read aloud.

Many libraries now carry audio books for all ages and are available for classroom use. Also, some teachers record stories and poems for students to use at a listening center or as a whole class. Or they may solicit the help of friends with interesting reading voices to make tapes (retirement communities can be great sources of volunteer help for this and other classroom needs). It's an excellent experience for students to hear different voices, from a variety of places and ethnic backgrounds, as it broadens their experiences with language.

Reading Aloud and Its Place in Instruction

In this section, we discuss times when reading aloud is meant to be fun and serendipitous, and times when teachers may want to tap its potential for focused instruction and the development of reading skills.

Reading Aloud for Pleasure

Because reading aloud is so beneficial, there should be times—lots of them—when you and your students enjoy books read aloud simply for the pure pleasure of it. Always having an instructional agenda can have a negative effect, killing the love of listening, or making it too serious. Reading books together is also a bonding and intimate act, as you experience the joys and sorrows of a story together. These experiences have a place in classrooms and show that one of the values of literature is that it has the potential to affect us emotionally.

Also plan for ways to share literature when children are ready to go home, when they are restless or before an assembly, right after recess, or while waiting to go to lunch. Have several short-story and poetry anthologies bookmarked with selections you know and can share on the spot.

Reading Aloud to Make Connections With the Curriculum

Reading aloud to students is so important that it deserves the same careful planning that we put into designing a reading workshop or a math or science lesson. We highly recommend a planned read-aloud at least once a day at all grade levels, but in early primary classrooms, teachers usually read aloud several times daily. Reading aloud can lead to rich learning opportunities. As you plan, think seriously about how you can incorporate reading aloud into your curriculum.

The research of Meyer, Wardrop, Stahl, and Linn (1994) proposes that the quality of the read-aloud makes a difference. It is not simply a silver bullet that, once in place, literacy development will happen. Kamil, Mosenthal, Pearson, and Barr (2000) investigated this and discovered that some adult interactive behaviors influence the qualitative aspects of read-aloud activities. In other words, it is helpful when adults incorporate questioning, scaffolding, dialogue and responses, praise or positive feedback, offering or extending information, clarifying information, restating information, directing discussion, sharing personal reactions, and relating concepts to life experiences. These terms show that reading aloud is not a decoration or frill but can be at the heart of a well-orchestrated and planned lesson. Vacca, Vacca, and Gove (2000) remind us how serious and how central reading aloud is in classrooms, and how it "needs to be incorporated into all aspects of the curriculum" (p. 371). The delight of a book read aloud, though, shouldn't be lost within a lesson.

Enjoyment of literature is key, but ways to learn more about it can flow naturally from carefully thinking through the purpose and intent of the read-aloud. First-grade teacher Tracy Hallee engages her young listeners as a result of hearing high-quality read-alouds. Tracy's read-alouds are designed for children to discuss aspects of the plot, characters, and illustrations as well as to experiment with a range of drama activities.

Tracy suggests that read-alouds are effective when books are chosen thoughtfully with your students' interests taken into account and your purposes are clear in your mind; it is essential to read the book yourself before reading it to the class. Effective read-alouds (especially picture storybooks) are explored together from end page to end page. Before reading the book aloud, Tracy sometimes does a book talk or takes a book walk where she invites her students to make predictions about the text. This activity taps their prior knowledge.

Tracy stops often to ask children about what they are thinking and feeling, or to share connections they are making with the text. She says, "This is where I explicitly share what I am thinking as a reader, so that I can show my students how engaged readers think about what they are reading. Many times during a rereading, I will take the opportunity to talk about what good writers do. Meaningful literature is our best example for children when we are looking at our own writing. If we are working on the concept of leads or thinking about our word choice, we look to see how other writers do it. It is amazing and rewarding to watch children 'try out' or explore an author's style and in turn view themselves as accomplished authors."

Tracy plans for ways to engage children before, during, and after reading aloud. There is a call to integrate more

opportunities for students to interact during read-alouds (Deford, 2001; Fountas & Pinnell, 2001; Kristo, 1993). These are sometimes called *interactive read-alouds* (Deford, 2001; Fountas & Pinnell, 2001). Deford (2001) says this about interactive read-alouds: "It is intended to suggest that during read aloud there should be intentional, ongoing invitations to students to actively respond and interact within the oral reading of a story" (p. 133).

Think of times when you wanted to complete a story you were reading aloud and thus saved student questions and discussions until you had finished reading the book. Deford (2001) says that this pattern of first the adult reading and then the student asking for permission to speak is common practice. However, encouraging questions and discussion during read-alouds makes students become more active learners. While hearing a poem, story, or nonfiction selection read aloud, students are encouraged to ask and answer questions as part of the read-aloud experience. These interactions during read-alouds strongly scaffold or support student learning.

Read-alouds serve a variety of instructional purposes, such as discussing the illustrations in picture books; using them as the central component in minilessons to teach various aspects of writing; experiencing response to literature through art, writing, and dramatic engagements; teaching new concepts and understandings in content areas such as math, science, social studies, and fine arts; and increasing students' ways of comprehending text. Use think-aloud strategies to help students learn how to comprehend text. Think-alouds are described in earlier chapters.

Tech Note

Sample lessons that teacher and writer Jill Ostrow designed for incorporating comprehension strategies through read-alouds are available on the CD-ROM that accompanies this book.

Summary

Read-aloud guru Jim Trelease (2000) laments that even though we have children who dutifully read in school, we still aren't producing students who see reading as a life-long pleasure outside school. He says, "[T]he missing ingredient is reading aloud to children" (p. 240).

In this chapter, we explained how critical sharing books aloud is to the literacy development of all students, regardless of age. We also discussed ways to plan and design read-alouds and how they can be used effectively for instructional purposes or purely for enjoyment.

Action Research for Teachers

The Effects of Reader's Theatre on Comprehension and Fluency

Rita K. Jeffries
Fifth Grade—Urban

Rita's concern was a lack of enthusiasm for reading, as well as weaker skills in comprehension and fluency, in her inner-city classroom. She thought perhaps dramatizing reading, using Reader's Theatre, would be motivating and would provide an avenue for increasing needed skills. Prior to her study, Rita collected baseline data on her students by administering a reading attitude survey to each student, and also taking a reading sample and analyzing it using *The Reading Miscue Inventory* (Goodman, Watson, & Burke, 1987). She used these same instruments for a posttest at the end of her study, and she maintained a researcher log throughout. Rita collected the same data for comparison from another fifth-grade class not involved in Reader's Theatre.

Rita obtained scripts for Reader's Theatre wherever possible; some she located from children's literature resource books with help from a media specialist. She gave students choices in the scripts they would use. Although some students were initially reluctant to perform in front of their peers, this quickly passed, and enthusiasm for this project ran high.

Rita found the students in the group using Reader's Theatre began to show progress in comprehension and fluency, even in a 7-week study. Moreover, they liked using dramatization and were eager to do it often. She concluded that Reader's Theatre is a useful strategy that should be an ongoing part of her reading program.

Tracy Hallee's First Grade

Enter this first-grade classroom and you will feel the buzz of student activity. Students may be involved in a dramatic enactment based on a piece of literature. Perhaps they're working in small groups, listening to teacher Tracy Hallee read aloud, or sharing poems they wrote themselves.

Creating an Effective Primary Classroom Literacy Environment

This positive place that warmly welcomes readers and writers is the result of Tracy's sincere joy in bringing children and books together. It's not only the collection of high-quality children's literature accessible to her students, but also her understanding about the ways children learn and grow as readers and writers that lead her practice.

A classroom meeting space is designated in the back area of the classroom. This is where the day begins and ends, and where the class gathers for activities such as read-alouds, minilessons to learn new strategies in reading and writing, and participating in dramatic events.

Reading and Writing to Learn About the World

Tracy's first graders soak up nonfiction books, especially those with photographs of everything from animals to birds, dinosaurs to reptiles. Tracy chooses nonfiction books for some of her read-alouds because the language is beautifully crafted; she also uses them to teach specific aspects about how nonfiction works, or because the book is connected with the content she is teaching.

For example, Tracy chooses *Animals in Flight* (Jenkins & Page) to share aloud because of the animal unit the class is working on. As she opens the book and starts to flip the pages, the children notice that the artwork is similar to another book Tracy has shared with them: *What Do You Do When Something Wants to Eat You?* (Jenkins). The children have a spirited conversation about the similarities in the cut-paper collages. Tracy is thrilled that they recalled the earlier book and suggests that they design a class chart of similarities between the two books, as they also record important facts they're learning about animals. This chart will expand with the information from additional read-alouds on animals that she has planned.

Helpful Nonfiction has...

- glossary- a mini-dictionary that tells you what the special **bold** words mean
- side bar- extra information the author adds near the main text
- table of contents- tells you what information is covered in the book and what pages you'll find it on
- photographs- they make it more real-life
- index- we can find specific in kind of details and the page number
- page numbers- you know what page to look on
- labels- so you know what you're looking at
- maps- you could see where things are

But first, she asks children to listen carefully to how the authors begin this book. The children listen with rapt attention as Tracy reads with grand expression, making the words lift off the pages! She prepares the students to hear more of the book by asking them to focus on the questions on this first page. "How do they do it? When, and why, did they take to the air?" She wants the children to notice if and how the authors will answer these questions as she reads more of the book.

Nearby in the classroom is a chart with bulleted information about what to look for in good nonfiction: a glossary, sidebars, a table of contents, and so on. She wants to teach her students about how these authors include interesting and important information about animals in flight in both strategically placed sidebars and captions.

Tracy is gradually leading her students into their own nonfiction writing by reading good selections of nonfiction books on the topic under study. By using high-quality nonfiction books for read-alouds and shared reading and later for guided reading and independent reading experiences, she will also be helping students understand how nonfiction as a genre works, and how writers, illustrators, and photographers craft well-written and well-designed nonfiction. She will help them create their own toolboxes of strategies to use in their writing of nonfiction.

Reading Aloud

Read-aloud time is one of Tracy's favorite parts of the day. One of Tracy's goals is to help children increase their listening comprehension, and a successful way of doing this is by inviting children to react to some simple but powerful questions. She relies on the important work of English author Aidan Chambers (1996), who developed questions that tap into what readers first notice about a book, what puzzles them, and what patterns they find (p. 92). Tracy often replaces questioning with, "Tell me more about what you're thinking." Chambers says "it suggests a desire for collaboration, indicating that the teacher really does want to know what the reader thinks, and that it anticipates conversational dialogue rather than an interrogation" (p. 42).

Tracy's read-alouds are interactive—she expects students to converse with her throughout the story, rather than waiting until the story is finished. Today, Tracy invites children to talk about the parts they like, as well as what they are puzzled about, from *The Other Side* (Woodson), a book about two neighbor children, one black and the other white, separated by a fence between their two houses. Students scramble to share their viewpoints about fairness and the courage to do what's right.

Lin-Sue says that at first she wondered why Clover, the African American girl in the story, didn't go right over to see Annie, the white girl. She said maybe Clover's mother was mean, but just "an inch of mean," "because, after all, her mother must have had it in her heart enough to finally let her play with that white girl."

Dramatic Enactments

Students in Tracy's class often move from hearing a book read aloud, to discussion, and then to dramatization. Sometimes students will re-create a favorite scene with puppets. Children also love creating phone conversations with one another as they take on the roles of characters. For *The Other Side*, one child becomes Clover and the other becomes Annie. Tracy encourages children to focus their conversations by starting with a line from the book.

Another dramatic strategy that works well is "Mantle of the Stranger" (Wilhelm, 2002a). In this strategy, Tracy can act as the uninformed person, or stranger, who pretends not to know the story. Her job is to find out what's going on in the story and why. Everyone is subject to being on the "hot seat," where they are questioned about the characters and their actions. The students find it fun to try to enlighten Ms. Hallee about the events and characters in the book.

Symbolic Story Representation

Jamie, Will, and Marty are called to the story table, where the children will engage in what's called *symbolic story representation*, a strategy in which readers manipulate symbols or cut-outs from the book to describe where they see themselves in the world of the story. Today, children in this group will become part of the story world of *From Far Away*, by Robert Munsch, a story about a young girl from another country adjusting to school. The children huddle around cut-outs of characters and scenery from the book. Marty, standing near the cut-outs, volunteers to be first to talk about the story. Marty picks up a figure from the story and says that she has a connection from her own life. She remembers, like the character in the story, being afraid of trying new things for the first time. Tracy asks Marty if she'd like to say anything to the characters. Then Tracy and the other children continue to discuss the book and Marty's connections to the story.

How Is Literature Alive and Well in This Primary Classroom?

Tracy's students are immersed in literature throughout the day. Tracy is strategic about how she plans to incorporate children's books. She wants to help children uncover new meanings and learn how to make thoughtful and insightful connections to their own lives, as well as to the world and to other books (Keene & Zimmermann, 1997). She selects from a host of ways:

- ☀ sharing a book aloud

- ☀ providing opportunities for children to look more closely at a book

- ☀ stimulating talk about the book

- ☀ encouraging dramatization

- ☀ suggesting other ways to respond through writing and drawing

- ☀ teaching students how to enter the world of a story through symbolic story representation

Chapter

11

SHARED AND GUIDED READING

"Just as the children learn to say nursery rhymes by hearing them said aloud, so they can learn whole units of meaning once they have heard the sounds of the sentences 'ringing in their ears'." (Bill Martin Jr., in Martin & Brogan, 1966, p. 2)

his chapter shows how you can use literature with students to help them become literate while also loving literature. Specifically, we discuss the following questions:

☼ What is shared reading?

☼ What is guided reading?

We define each approach, describe the critical aspects you need to be able to implement them, and show you sample lessons to help you link practice with theory.

Enter Judy Shaal and Pat Ivory's busy kindergarten, and you will find yourself immersed in literacy. As soon as the children arrive, they find a book in the classroom library, sit down, and start reading. Soon the room is full of talk as children read aloud to themselves or share favorite pictures and aspects of stories with friends. Today, after the usual lunch count, attendance tally, and other routine tasks, Pat begins the day by reading aloud. She reads *Click, Clack, Moo: Cows That Type*, by Doreen Cronin, a delightfully humorous picture book in which the cows go on strike until the farmer supplies them with electric blankets. The concepts explored in the book are sophisticated, but Pat's enthusiastic manner and the interactive comments she intersperses throughout the reading hold the children's attention. She also answers any questions they have about the meaning.

Judy then takes over for shared reading time. After reminding the children about the farm poem they read the preceding week, she asks them to help her read a riddle about something on the farm.

Farm Riddle
"Moo, Moo, Moo!"
It's morning on the farm.
Who's that waking up
Inside the big red barn?

She tells the children they need to look carefully at the clues left by the words to discover what the poem is talking about. They read the poem together again, while Alexis uses a pointer to mark each word as it's read. "What time of day is it? Who should be waking up? What animal is this book talking about?" Judy asks the children. Alexis then picks the picture card of a cow from a series of cards depicting various farm animals. "How do you know that card says 'a cow'?" Judy asks Alexis. "Because it starts like Cameron's name," she replies, pointing to the pocket chart containing cards with each child's name printed on them. Judy then asks various children to point out words they know in the poem and to look for the same

words in other print around the room. They then read "Farm Riddle" one more time, again pointing to each word as it is read. "Tomorrow, we will read another farm riddle," Judy tells the children. "Who do you think will be waking up next?"

The group turns next to a shared reading of *Mrs. Wishy Washy* (Cowley), the focus book for the week. Pointing to each word, she progresses through the book, stopping to draw children's attention to certain words or humorous pictures. Whenever Mrs. Wishy Washy talks, Judy reads the part expressively, clearly showing Mrs. Wishy Washy's annoyance with all those animals who refuse to take a bath. One child asks which animals are girls and which are boys, because she noticed that different pronouns were used to refer to different animals. Judy quickly turns back to that page and points to *he* and *she* to show the children how the pronouns referring to the animals changed. "Where did all the animals go?" she asks. "Away," reply the children while Judy points to the word "away" in the text. "I have a question for you," she tells the children next. "How do you know what animal they're talking about in the parts 'away went the cow,' 'away went the duck,' 'away went the pig'?" Various children tell her "because it starts like Cody," "I looked at the first letter," "the cow's the first animal in the picture so I knew the first animal word was cow," and so on. "So, you used two things to help you," replies Judy. "You used the first letter of the word and the picture. That's great! That's what good readers do!" They continue through the book, discovering words they know, counting the number of letters in some words and the number of words on a page, discussing the comical plot, and predicting what will happen next.

Occasionally Judy changes to Spanish to help Kellyn, her Latino child, participate in the activity: "Que es palabra?" (What is this word?) and "Que quantos palabras?" (How many words) she asks, and Kellyn points out the book parts.

Soon it is snack time. While Judy passes out the juice and crackers, Pat leads the group in singing the snack song. As she points to each word, the children sing:

It is time for us to have our snack
Please sit down and hands in your lap
Wait 'til everyone has their food.
Then eat your snack;
Yum, yum, it's good.

The children discuss a few of the words, then move to their seats to eat.

Following snack, many of the children meet with Judy and Pat for guided reading groups. When not working with the teachers, they do activities at their seats or at learning centers. This week's centers include arranging sentence strips in a pocket chart to re-create a familiar poem, categorizing magnetic alphabet letters on a large board, reading books from their individual book bin, painting a farm mural, and journal writing.

Judy's children are immersed in literature; it permeates everything they do. They read books, poems, songs, lunch menus, classroom charts. They write stories, captions, poems, reports, letters, signs. They are enthusiastic lovers of literature and are firmly convinced they are readers and writers. Is this really possible with children as young as 5? We say a resounding "yes"!

Shared Reading

Shared reading, especially with very young children, is a joyous, collaborative activity in which students and teachers read carefully selected texts, usually in enlarged format. Although shared reading provides a good deal of scaffolding or instructional support from the teacher, the student's role is to be an apprentice in the learning process. The expectation in shared instruction is for the students to be problem solvers as they and the teacher work together to learn more about a specific text.

Because shared reading has its roots in work with young children, this chapter focuses attention on using this approach with that age group. However, shared instruction is appropriate for all age students, if the intent of the instruction is to study and learn from a text together (Kristo & Bamford, 2004; Parkes, 2000).

During shared reading lessons with young readers, the teacher and a group of children sit close together to read and reread in unison. Preparing an enlarged version on an overhead transparency makes sense so that everyone can benefit and participate in the lesson. Sometimes teachers read the more difficult parts alone, inviting the children to join in on the more predictable segments. Each student is encouraged to participate at his/her developmental level. Thus, some children might be confidently saying each word whereas others might chime in on repeated sections or stay silent through the entire reading.

Shared reading has two important purposes. First, it gives young children an enjoyable literacy experience so that they grow to love stories and become fascinated with the sounds of book language. Second, shared read-

ing lessons systematically show how print works so children can become independent readers and writers. Thus, a shared reading experience doesn't stop with one reading; on the contrary, the group reads and rereads the text, delving into explorations of language, meaning, and print. We explore each of these purposes in more depth.

Providing an Enjoyable Experience With Books

Shared reading builds on the child's early read-aloud experiences, particularly with bedtime stories. Based on research by Don Holdaway (1979), it is designed to emulate the pleasurable experience that often occurs one-on-one or in a small group with an enthusiastic adult. Parents and caregivers snuggle children on their laps and draw them into the world of books through spirited readings and discussions about what is read. They create opportunities for children to participate and often redirect the activity based on their responses. Children's favorites are the basis for rereadings, which are always different because young readers make new connections between the story and their experience, experiment with different aspects of language, discover new aspects of story or illustration that had previously been unnoticed, and make connections to other books (Martinez & Roser, 1985; Parkes, 2000; Sulzby, 1985). Soon they are carrying the book around and offering to read it to you. You've probably had that experience. You might have been amazed at how closely these young readers replicated the text, even when the book was held upside-down! These pleasurable experiences with books make children feel confident that they too can become readers and writers.

Showing Children How Print Works

Shared reading offers many opportunities to focus on print and discover how it works to create a meaningful text. When children are provided with whole, predictable texts and have opportunities to explicitly examine how print works, they can use their knowledge of the English language (syntactic information), their understanding of how stories and poems are typically structured (semantic information), and their sense of how alphabetic symbols relate to sounds (phonological information) to take on reading behaviors for themselves. Repeated assisted readings of literature in which children

> I love the way a young child, just learning language, rolls a word around her tongue, and if she likes the sound of it, may chant it over and over.
>
> Nancy White Carlstrom, author, in McClure & Kristo, 1996, p. 237

can use all the cueing systems—syntactic, semantic, and graphophonic—help them effectively and efficiently orchestrate these systems to read.

Thus, in shared reading sessions, teachers call attention to letter–sound relationships and other features of print. They model the problem-solving strategies good readers use and how to anticipate words in texts by considering what makes sense, what sounds right, and what looks right when a reader closely examines the print. They help children become aware of print conventions: that reading goes from left to right (directionality); where the front and back of the book are; the role of punctuation; what a word is; and the language we use to talk about reading and writing. They also discuss how stories are structured, how fiction differs from nonfiction, and how both differ from poetry.

Critical Elements of Shared Reading

Teachers must think about several important elements when they begin implementing shared reading in their classrooms. These include

- establishing a comfortable environment;
- selecting a variety of enlarged, predictable texts;
- ensuring all children have opportunities to actively participate;
- providing opportunities to reread favorite books;
- focusing on text features and reading strategies.

We look at each of these elements in detail.

Establishing a Comfortable Environment

To help ensure a successful shared reading experience, you should try to replicate the intimacy and joy of the bedtime read-aloud experience. Thus, a carpeted area where the whole class can comfortably sit together and clearly see the text is important. You need to be seated so that everyone can see you and positioned so that you can reach the text. However, you should be sitting low enough to maintain eye contact, encourage interaction, and project enthusiasm. Many teachers sit on a rocking chair and prop the text on an easel or chart stand.

Selecting a Variety of Enlarged, Predictable Texts

You also need a carefully chosen collection of materials for reading, including stories, songs, poems, nonfiction, and writings created by the children. Many teachers find that predictable books are useful for this activity, particularly if

they are working with beginning readers, because these texts seem to provide the most support for encouraging child participation in shared reading. Predictable titles typically have one or more of the following qualities:

- repetition (of words, lines, phrases)
- rhyming
- a familiar sequence (months, days of the week, etc.)

Other excellent texts might not necessarily be predictable but could contain at least some of the following features, making them appropriate for shared reading sessions:

- Strong story lines that are grounded in everyday experiences familiar to children.
- Factual texts that use simple, clean writing and organization along with supportive illustrations.
- Lively, rhythmical language.
- Illustrations that support the text and occasionally extend it.
- Humor.
- Simple, active plot.
- Memorable characters with whom children can identify.
- Satisfying endings. (Parkes, 2000)

Examine books carefully before you use them. Even though a book may be in enlarged format, that doesn't mean it is appropriate for shared reading lessons. Some lovely illustrated books have been enlarged, but they are not predictable or engaging enough to support the development of reading and writing through shared reading.

The text set on p. 278 lists predictable books suitable for shared reading. Figure 11.1 presents Judy Shaal's top ten big books for shared reading.

Tech Note

Insights about writing shared reading materials from Brenda Parkes, staff developer and author of shared reading books and the teacher resource *Read It Again! Revisiting Shared Reading* (2000), are available on the CD-ROM that accompanies this book.

Texts don't need to be restricted to books: You can use songs and poems, for example, that have been copied onto chart paper or tag board strips arranged on a pocket chart. Of course, these should feature the same predictable and/or engaging qualities as books. The children's own writings can also be used. Mainly, text used for shared reading should have sufficient substance to sustain scrutiny and many rereadings.

Enlarged texts also don't have to be commercially purchased. You can create your own. For example, you can write out the text of a story and have children create their own versions of the illustrations, or you can make overhead

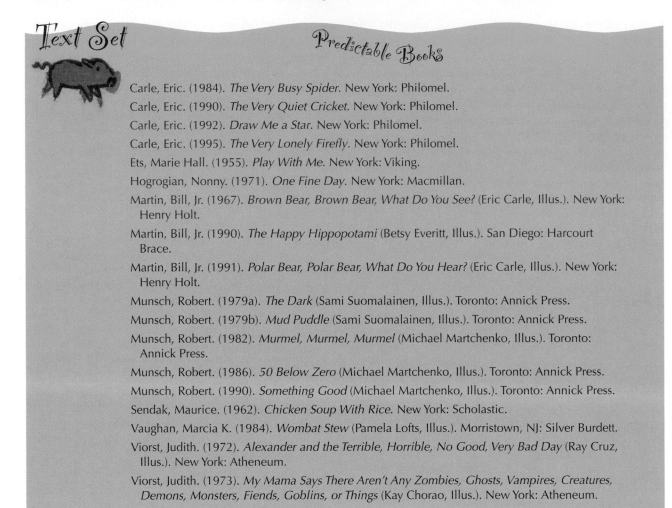

Text Set

Predictable Books

Carle, Eric. (1984). *The Very Busy Spider*. New York: Philomel.

Carle, Eric. (1990). *The Very Quiet Cricket*. New York: Philomel.

Carle, Eric. (1992). *Draw Me a Star*. New York: Philomel.

Carle, Eric. (1995). *The Very Lonely Firefly*. New York: Philomel.

Ets, Marie Hall. (1955). *Play With Me*. New York: Viking.

Hogrogian, Nonny. (1971). *One Fine Day*. New York: Macmillan.

Martin, Bill, Jr. (1967). *Brown Bear, Brown Bear, What Do You See?* (Eric Carle, Illus.). New York: Henry Holt.

Martin, Bill, Jr. (1990). *The Happy Hippopotami* (Betsy Everitt, Illus.). San Diego: Harcourt Brace.

Martin, Bill, Jr. (1991). *Polar Bear, Polar Bear, What Do You Hear?* (Eric Carle, Illus.). New York: Henry Holt.

Munsch, Robert. (1979a). *The Dark* (Sami Suomalainen, Illus.). Toronto: Annick Press.

Munsch, Robert. (1979b). *Mud Puddle* (Sami Suomalainen, Illus.). Toronto: Annick Press.

Munsch, Robert. (1982). *Murmel, Murmel, Murmel* (Michael Martchenko, Illus.). Toronto: Annick Press.

Munsch, Robert. (1986). *50 Below Zero* (Michael Martchenko, Illus.). Toronto: Annick Press.

Munsch, Robert. (1990). *Something Good* (Michael Martchenko, Illus.). Toronto: Annick Press.

Sendak, Maurice. (1962). *Chicken Soup With Rice*. New York: Scholastic.

Vaughan, Marcia K. (1984). *Wombat Stew* (Pamela Lofts, Illus.). Morristown, NJ: Silver Burdett.

Viorst, Judith. (1972). *Alexander and the Terrible, Horrible, No Good, Very Bad Day* (Ray Cruz, Illus.). New York: Atheneum.

Viorst, Judith. (1973). *My Mama Says There Aren't Any Zombies, Ghosts, Vampires, Creatures, Demons, Monsters, Fiends, Goblins, or Things* (Kay Chorao, Illus.). New York: Atheneum.

transparencies because children's attention is then focused on the text as it appears on the overhead projector. Also, short texts can be copied onto sentence strips.

Opportunities and Invitations to Participate

Texts and activities used for shared reading should delight children and encourage them to participate in the readings. However, this participation shouldn't interrupt the flow of the story. Rather, you should think about ways to subtly and naturally invite children in. Engage the group in honest dialogue where you share ideas, listen to different ideas, and debate differences in opinion. Asking children to predict what might happen next and suggesting they contribute a rhyming word to complete a line, join in on a repeating phrase, or comment briefly on illustrations are all good ways to do this. As a result, children become

involved in the reading and begin discovering how to do it independently.

Opportunities to Reread

Providing opportunities to reread books is an important part of the shared reading experience. With each reading, children confirm what they know about the book in particular and about print in general. They then use that knowledge to support deeper explorations of the text (Parkes, 2000). These understandings are deepened when they examine books more closely on their own. And they do this at their own level: Some might read the entire text confidently, whereas others may be able to join in on a repetitive or memorable part of the text. Still others might listen as a friend reads the story aloud.

Thus, copies of favorite shared reading books and poems should be available for browsing in the classroom li-

Title	Publisher/Author	Correlating Theme
Mrs. Wishy Washy	The Wright Group	Farm Animals
The Farm Concert	The Wright Group	Farm Animals
Buttons, Buttons	Creative Teaching Press	Colors
I See Patterns	Creative Teaching Press	Counting
I Can Read	Creative Teaching Press	Alphabet
In a Dark, Dark Wood	The Wright Group	Fall/Halloween
Rosie's Walk	Pat Hutchins	Weather/Concepts
Sleepy Bear	Lydia Dabcovich	Winter/Bears
Mouse Mess	Linnea Riley	Food/Harvest/Thanksgiving
Guess How Much I Love You	Sam McBratney	Friends/Family/Valentines

Figure 11.1   Top Ten Favorite Shared Reading Big Books, Contributed by Judy Shaal

brary and in activity centers. For example, a favorite poem can be written on sentence strips and made available for children to assemble in a pocket chart. A pointer can be placed in the library next to a collection of enlarged books for use in small-group peer-led rereadings. Audiotapes of favorite books can be made to encourage rereadings. Extra copies of books can be clipped onto skirt hangers or stored in plastic tubs for easy retrieval by children.

Focusing on Text Features and Reading Strategies

As students become confident with a shared reading text, they can pay closer attention to print and how it works. They can begin studying various features of print such as sight words, letter–sound relationships, directionality, and punctuation. Just be careful to drill these elements in a way that encourages children's interest in the story. The teaching should be done in an informal, conversational way within the context of the whole text. Following are some good activities for this purpose.

- *Write words and phrases from the story on charts or white boards*–These can then be used for studying letter–sound patterns and for further writings in response to the story (Combs, 2002). This also helps with one-to-one matching. For this purpose, the strip is held directly beneath the matching line of print, and children point to each word in the text and on the strip.
- *Identify high-frequency "sight words"*–Cover words with colored highlighter tape, circle with Wikki-Stix,

re-create with magnetic letters, and match words on cards to the words in the text. Word cards using words from the story can be sorted by theme, phonetic elements, or other categories the children create. Add to the class word wall those words that become very familiar to the group.

- *Identify rhyming words*–Cover with similarly colored highlighter tape, re-create with magnetic letters, or circle with Wikki-Stix. Then children can build new words with magnetic letters that aurally match the ones in the text. Or they can use name cards to find classmates' names that rhyme with the target words.
- *Mask portions of text*–(with self-stick notes, sliders, correction tape) to support children's developing use of context and how it works with initial consonants and consonant combinations. Typically, teachers mask all but the beginning letter of a word, then ask children to guess it based on what makes sense as well as on the beginning letter. The word is then revealed and meaning is confirmed.
- *Practice using all sources of information to discern meaning*–Ask children to predict what will come next in the story, guess how to say particular words, and use what they see as clues on the book's cover to guess meaning. Then challenge them to justify their answer by examining all the clues in both text and illustrations.

Activities can be done in both large and small groups, although small groups are probably better because they allow for more participation and encourage attentive behavior from children. Strategies should be carefully selected, based on what children already know about print and what they are ready to learn.

Many engaging activities can support children's developing sense of how print works. The following are some concepts that teachers can demonstrate through activities associated with shared reading.

- ☺ *Print carries a message*–Although young children often rely on illustrations to guide their reading, print is ultimately what carries the message. Children need to understand this fundamental concept.
- ☺ *Book knowledge*–Show children the front and back of the book, explain concepts of author and title, show how to hold a book and turn the pages.
- ☺ *Concepts of print*–These include directionality, concept of letter, word, and punctuation.
- ☺ *High-frequency words*–Good readers recognize words automatically; committing many words to memory contributes to fluency and comprehension. Children who participate in repeated readings of predictable books learn more sight vocabulary than they do in more conventional texts such as basal readers (Bridge, Winograd, & Haley, 1983).
- ☺ *Phonological awareness*–This is the ability to break words into component sounds. Aspects include rhyming, syllable onsets and rimes, identifying phonemes (the smallest units of speech sounds). Activities often involve pointing out words that sound or are spelled alike.
- ☺ *Letter–sound relationships*–This skill involves making connections between letters and their corresponding sounds. Explore letter–sound relationships by pointing to words with particular letters and sounds, circling target letters or words beginning with target letters, listing all the words in the text featuring particular letters, finding names of classmates that begin with target letters, etc.
- ☺ *Context*–Good readers use an understanding of context along with their knowledge of letters and sounds to anticipate what words will be in the text.
- ☺ *Using all sources of information to discern meaning*–Good readers efficiently use and integrate all the sources of information available to them, including semantic, syntactic, and graphophonetic cues.

Tech Note

Bobbie Fisher, kindergarten teacher and expert on shared reading, describes her role in the classroom from her book, *Joyful Learning: A Whole Language Kindergarten* (1991), on the CD-ROM that accompanies this book.

Typical Shared Reading Lessons

When planning a shared reading lesson, you must first consider the developmental needs of your students. What literacy skills do they know and use with confidence? What new understandings do they need so that they grow as readers and writers? Which of these new understandings are they ready to take on?

Then you must consider your school district and state curriculum guidelines. The standards for Judy Shaal's district and state (Judy is the teacher featured in the vignette at the beginning of the chapter), for example, require her to focus on helping children develop a repertoire of sight words, identify beginning sounds, acquire the ability to use beginning sounds and context to predict, identify story structure, and develop self-monitoring strategies. She knows her children aren't all ready for every standard. However, she selects competencies that many of her children are ready to learn, while understanding that some will need many more experiences before they are ready to use them.

Finally, you must consider the text. What patterns do you see that will support children's reading? What high-frequency words can be emphasized so they become sight words? What is the text structure? Do children need help to understand that structure? Does the structure exemplify a particular type of text so that children can apply their sense of it to new texts they encounter?

Critical Components of a Typical Shared Reading Lesson Series

Most shared reading lessons last several days (typically a week) and include the following segments.

First Reading. Children become familiar with the story line and language patterns of the text during the first reading of a story. Sometimes they just listen as the teacher points to the text and reads aloud; however, they are encouraged to participate whenever they can. So you might ask them for predictions about what might happen next or invite them to join in on a repetitive refrain or supply a highly predictable word. Often the talk is very conversational, as if you are browsing together through the book. Just be sure to emphasize the text by reading distinctly and pointing to each word.

Some teachers use various strategies to heighten interest or show children how to use preliminary information to guess what the book might be about before the first reading. They might cover up part of the title or write only the first letter of the words in the title on the chalkboard or white board. They then invite the children to guess the title using illustrations and information from the print as it is

An easel where a teacher launches shared reading in a primary class.

Tech Note

You'll find author profiles of two popular authors for young children—Robert Munsch and Pat Hutchins—on the CD-ROM that accompanies this book.

sufficient support to make meaning in the story. Others believe it takes away the drama inherent in seeing the story unfold for the first time and also limits the work the children must do to make meaning for themselves. We believe the structure of the story and the developmental level of your students should determine whether you do a "picture walk" before a first reading.

At the conclusion of the first reading, you can ask children to share something they noticed about the book that they are going to look for next time. These comments can help you determine what the children notice and what interests them. They can set the stage for the next day's rereading.

Shared Rereadings. Repeated readings of a text help children become more confident in their knowledge of how text works while building fluency. It also supports more extensive explorations of text features you think the children are ready to experience.

The strategies and activities you use during rereadings are based on the children's readiness to attend to the print as well as what you think might help them extend

Cover from BROWN BEAR, BROWN BEAR, WHAT DO YOU SEE? written by Bill Martin Jr. Illustrated by Eric Carle. Illustrations copyright ©1992 by Eric Carle. Reprinted by permission of Henry Holt and Company, LLC.

gradually revealed. Or a "Storybook Plan" (Fisher & Medvic, 2000, p. 74) can be used: This activity provides a structure for helping children use the information on the cover, such as illustration details, title, and author, to predict what the book will be about. The predictions from the plan are then modified after reading the book.

Figure 11.2 presents a typical lesson plan for shared reading for a first-grade class at the beginning of the year.

There is some debate as to whether you should take a "picture walk" through the text before reading. Proponents of this activity believe it helps children become familiar with the language and the story line so they have

Figure 11.2 A First-Grade Shared Reading Lesson Plan

This lesson plan shows how shared reading might evolve over 5 days.

Text: *Brown Bear, Brown Bear, What Do You See?* (1983), by Bill Martin Jr. and illustrated by Eric Carle

Grade Level: Kindergarten/first grade (depending on children's development)

Day One—Introducing the Book

- Share "Teddy Bear, Teddy Bear" (from *Play Rhymes,* compiled by Marc Brown) in enlarged format on chart paper. Read the poem with the children several times and then add motions. Cover up the rhyming words with self-stick notes, and then have the children guess the masked words. Reveal words and write each set of rhyming words on the white board. Ask the children to tell what they notice about the words. Have them look for the word *bear* in the poem and match the word card with the word in the text. Discuss how the poem and book you are about to read are both about bears.

- Present *Brown Bear, Brown Bear, What Do You See?* Before you discuss the cover and the title, cover all but the *b* in each occurrence of the word *bear* in the title with a self-stick note. Ask students to guess what the masked word is by using the picture and beginning sound. Uncover the word and confirm the guess. Ask students to predict what the book will be about. Discuss any other books they know by Bill Martin Jr. and illustrator Eric Carle.

- Do a first reading of the story: As you read, point to each word with a pointer. Children join in as they are able. Before each page, ask them to predict what will happen next, such as who the bear will encounter next.

- Tell children you will read the book again tomorrow. Ask them what they will particularly look for in the next reading. Suggest they find the word *bear* in the story and circle it with Wikki Stix. Discuss the beginning sound of *bear* and other words that begin with the same letter and sound. Find the word *bear* around the room, or find other words beginning with *b,* including the children's names.

Day Two—Rereading the Story and Word Study

- Reread "Teddy Bear, Teddy Bear." Identify the word *bear* in the poem and cover with highlighter tape. Highlight rhyming words as children identify them again.

- Introduce the story again. Ask children what they plan to notice in today's reading. Read the story, pointing to each word in the text. Ask children to read along with you. Also ask them to make predictions and to recall the sequence of events from the previous day's reading.

- Have children match words and sentences on cards to those in the story. Use a framer to isolate the study high-frequency words such as *see, me,* and names of colors.

- Return to the text and have children point out various features such as rhyming words (*see* and *me*), color words, beginning sounds such as *b, s,* and *m.* Use self-stick notes to cover up words except the beginning letter and have children guess the masked word. Uncover the word and confirm their guesses. Ask them how they figured out the word.

- Discuss the story structure of this book, which is a "list-sequence" pattern. Make a list of story events on a white board or on chart paper. Review the sequence with the group.

- Close with an additional reading and acting out of "Teddy Bear, Teddy Bear."

Day Three—Group Rereading of Story, Word Work, Partner Reading

- Read and act out Jane Yolen's "Sleep, Little Bear Sleep," from Goldstein's *Bear in Mind: A Book of Bear Poems* (in enlarged format). Find target sight words in the poem such as *bear* and *me* and circle them with Wikki Stix. Make each word with magnetic letters. Show how *sleep* is like and different from *me* and *see.* Make similar and/or other rhyming words with magnetic letters.

- Reread the story, pointing to words. By now, most children should be confident with it.

- Do word work similar to that done on Day Two.

Figure 11.2
(continued)

Day Three—(continued)

☀ Provide a set of small word cards from the story. Have partners identify and hold up various sight words. Use the cards to (a) re-create sentences from the story and (b) create new sentences. Share their sentences with the group. (This activity could be made easier by having pairs of children manipulate sentences from the story on large strips.)

☀ Pair children up and have them read small copies of the books together.

☀ Put extra sentence strips and word cards in the Pocket Chart Center so children can re-create the story during independent work time.

Day Four—Reading, Retelling, and Word Work

☀ Read and act out *We're Going on a Bear Hunt,* retold by Michael Rosen, in enlarged format. Find sight words, consonants, etc., that were previously identified from the *Brown Bear* story in the chant. Use self-stick notes to mask significant words or sections of the chant and have children guess what the masked text segment is.

☀ Reread the story chorally. Children should be taking the lead now, requiring little teacher support. Encourage children to offer comments as to favorite parts, favorite characters, etc.

☀ Using stick puppets, have children act out the story, or select children to take on roles of various characters and do a drama of the story. Put puppets in the Storytelling Center for later independent retelling.

☀ Create a chart of special words the group wants to remember from the story (i.e., high-frequency words that have become sight words). Write these words on a group chart or on the class word wall.

Day Five—Extension Activities and Review of the Week's Work

☀ Let children decide which poems or songs they want to read one more time.

☀ Reread the book one more time, possibly letting children take turns pointing to the words.

☀ Find new words on the word wall that were added this week.

☀ Write a class text that builds on the story by emulating its structure, theme, vocabulary, and so on.

Tech Note
You can view a student-created book called *Yellow Lion, Yellow Lion* on the CD-ROM that accompanies this book.

their literacy skills. You can select from the following activities, depending on what you want children to learn about literacy.

◎ *Use cloze procedures*–Hesitate before a word you think children should know. Ask them to supply the word, then discuss how they figured it out.

◎ *Plan participatory activities*–Ask children to clap the rhythm of a repetitive chant, read character dialogue together, sing a verse from a song or chant, repeat lines you read, and so on.

◎ *Reread specific parts*–Identify particularly memorable aspects of the story such as a repeating phrase, some character dialogue, or interesting words and read to find those items.

◎ *Point out text features*–Encourage children to find particular words, letters, punctuation marks, etc., that you think they are ready to notice.

In addition to many varied texts in enlarged format, certain tools and materials will help you implement the components of a shared or guided reading lesson. Most are available at a teacher or office-supply store. Figure 11.3 lists these items.

Focusing on Literary Elements in Both Fiction and Nonfiction. Children also need to have experience with exploring how authors develop characters, structure plots, and craft language to create an engaging and memorable story. This helps them begin to think like authors and illustrators. Thus, they can discuss how authors develop characters through discussions during and after reading. They can also do various extension activities such as writing thought bubbles for characters, creating new dialogue, making character description webs, or creating props and costumes for dramatizations (Parkes, 2000). Activities such as storyboards, diagrams, and story maps can help children explore plot.

Meet... Bill Martin Jr.

Author of *Brown Bear, Brown Bear, What Do You See? (with Eric Carle); Listen to the Rain* (with John Archambault); *Barn Dance!; The Ghost-Eye Tree; Knots on a Counting Rope* (with John Archambault); *Chicka Chicka Boom Boom; The Happy Hippopotami; The Magic Pumpkin* (with John Archambault); *Old Devil Wind;* and many more.

"It was my inability to read which had a tumultuous negative influence on my ability to write. But I remember when I wrote my first book, I just sat down and wrote. I wasn't afraid, I just wrote it and made a few changes. The success of the book (*The Little Squeegy Bug*) hooked me.

"Language is learned in the sentence form, not word by word, by word. Children can learn to read sentences as easily as they can learn to read the word or the letter. All day long, for various pruposes, children should be introduced to various stories and poems and songs. And children listening to a teacher tell a story, book, or song are in the process of language learning.

"Writing is important because it records events that soon transpire and they are only told in the reading of a book. That is what makes stories so important. My greatest joy in life is coming to the place where a manuscript is finished. It is like getting a monkey off my back, releasing a burden that has been like a puzzle to me. And then I can delight as an illustrator brings my story to life."

Bill Martin Jr. is originally from Kansas, and made his home in Texas until his death in 2004.

A word wall helps first graders learn new words.

☼ Easel: Place enlarged text on this. Some have built-in storage for big books and a combination magnetic/dry-erase board on the front for word work.

☼ Pointer: Long enough so you can point to the text yet not obscure it.

☼ Colored translucent highlighter tape: Used to cover print you want to highlight so as to focus children's attention on those elements.

☼ Wikki-Stix: Thin, pliable, colored strips that can be manipulated to form circles or underlines to highlight words or other aspects of text. They can be reused, and they stick to any surface.

☼ Self-stick notes: Different sizes and colors can be used to mask various aspects of text or cover text so new stories can be created. Darker colors mask better than lighter colors.

☼ Word, phrase, and sentence cards: Written on oak-tag or cardboard.

☼ Correction tape: Used to mask or cover up aspects of text for rewriting. The tape is placed over existing print. New text suggested by the children is written on the tape.

☼ Magnetic letters and board: Used extensively in word work. It is best to have several sets, particularly of lowercase letters.

☼ Sliding masks: Devices used to isolate words, word parts, letters, or phrases for closer observation. Features a cut-out section covered with a piece that slides out to reveal a letter, word, etc., in the text.

☼ Whiteboard: Useful for supporting discussion of text features. Simply write the feature on the board, then wipe off later.

☼ Pocket chart and sentence strips: Used to exhibit enlarged version of a relatively short text or for follow-up activities where children rebuild previously read text. Features slots to hold sentence strips that can be moved. Sentence strips may have lines for writing or may be blank.

☼ Clear plastic nametag holders and blank index cards: For making nametags to identify characters during role-playing or other drama activities.

Figure 11.3 A Teacher's Tool Box for Shared Reading and Guided Reading

Nonfiction texts feature unique elements that you can explore with students, including indexes, glossaries, specialized language, and visual features such as diagrams, captions, and labels. Activities in which students create charts that sort and classify information from a text, practice using indexes or tables of contents, use pronunciation guides, or replicate a particular style of diagram will help them discover how authors use these elements to convey information.

Extending Shared Reading. Children should also have many opportunities to retell and respond to a shared reading text. These activities can be done in large or small groups or as independent projects. Retelling encourages children to reconstruct the meaning, and responding encourages them to consider their personal reactions and how those shape what they take away from text. Both are important for literacy development. Following are some suggested activities for extending children's responses to

a shared reading text; they are intended as catalysts to help you think of new possibilities to fit particular texts.

☺ Retell through puppet shows, creative drama, flannel boards, storyboards (series of pictures from significant aspects of the story; sometimes these stories are written down for later independent reading).

☺ Create new versions of the story (termed "text innovations") by adding more verses or characters, changing the story line, adding new adventures, adding dialogue, etc. These are often done as shared or interactive writing but could also be done as independent writing. The text innovations can be made into individual books or a new class shared reading book.

☺ Cut apart text and illustrations for pocket chart activities. Mount illustrations in a pocket chart. Ask children to match text with the illustrations; ask

Third-grade teacher Shelly Moody works with students following a shared reading lesson.

them to re-create the sequence of the story and tell it to a partner.

- Write responses to the story in individual journals.
- Create tape recordings of the story. These can be placed in an area along with copies of the book for rereadings.
- Artistic extensions might include making new illustrations for the story, a mural or story map of events, paintings, collages, and mobiles.
- Read new books that feature similar sight words, language patterns, or story structures.

Shared reading gives children an initial sense of how reading goes. It provides an excellent foundation for the more independent strategies developed in guided reading.

Guided Reading

As children become aware of how print works through shared reading, read-alouds, and many informal encounters with books, they need opportunities to use and extend their understandings through daily practice. You know yourself that you can't get really good at playing a musical instrument or a sport without focused, hard work; the same is true for reading.

Following a ten-year research project studying exemplary elementary teachers and their teaching of reading, Richard Allington (2002) concluded: "It is the high accuracy, fluent and easily comprehended reading that provides the opportunities to integrate complex skills and strategies into an automatic, independent reading process" (p. 743).

Guided reading provides the opportunity for this practice to occur in a supportive context. In guided reading, teachers show students the "tricks of the trade," then provide focused support to help them become independent readers and writers.

In contrast to shared reading, where teachers read texts with children in a large-group setting, guided reading is done with small groups of students who use similar reading strategies and are able to read the same levels of text with teacher support (Fountas & Pinnell, 1996, p. 2). As with shared reading instruction, guided reading lessons are appropriate for students of all ages.

The text is one that students can read with the strategies they currently use but also has opportunities for them to learn something new. Teachers then provide guidance as they help their students use what they know to understand the text. They also demonstrate new strategies children can use. The focus is on constructing meaning while using problem-solving strategies to figure out words readers don't know, contending with increasingly complex sentence structures and comprehending new concepts or ideas (Fountas & Pinnell, 1996, p. 2). The goal is to help children learn how to use reading strategies easily and independently, which makes guided reading the "heart of a balanced literacy program" (Fountas & Pinnell, 1996, p. 1).

Critical Elements of Guided Reading

As in shared reading, there are several elements teachers must consider when implementing guided reading in their classrooms.

Grouping

Successful guided reading lessons involve carefully selected, small groups of children who are at approximately the same developmental reading level and can therefore benefit from reading the same text. These groups should be viewed as temporary and fluid. Children who are reading texts that are too easy will not improve; conversely, if a child is attempting to read a text that is too difficult, he or she will become discouraged. You should continually monitor children's work in these groups and as they demonstrate their ability to use new skills and strategies, groups should be reconfigured to reflect these changes. Using running records, along with your daily observations of children's work during all literacy activities, will give you information on how to structure your guided reading groups.

> In order to support growing readers, we need to respect them. It is my job to educate students by giving them what they need to accept challenges and become independent. It's the foundation of who I am as an educator.
>
> Jill Ostrow, educator; personal communication, September, 1999

Selecting Texts

This is critical: A good text for guided reading should support children's use of the skills and strategies they know and can use easily. However, it should also provide a few challenges that will help them grow as readers. This is the instructional level, meaning that children should be able to accurately read 90%–95% of the text and comprehend 75%–90% of the ideas independently (Burns, 1998).

In addition to considering your students' developmental reading level, you must also consider how the characteristics of the text itself will provide support or pose challenges for your students (Fountas & Pinnell, 1999). However, no single characteristic determines whether a book is "easy" or "difficult." For example, a text with one line of print may seem easy, but closer examination may reveal that it includes many difficult, technical, or unfamiliar words, making it more challenging to read. Conversely, a text may have more print on each page but be repetitive, use high-frequency words, and feature a familiar story, making it easy to read. You must look at multiple aspects of texts to find those that are "just right" for your guided reading groups. The following are some qualities to consider:

- *Text length*–Length includes consideration of number of pages, number of words, and number of lines on each page. Children should begin with short, simple texts, then progress to longer texts with more print on each page.
- *Illustrations*–Books for beginners should have attractive, clear illustrations that will engage children. They should also provide valuable information as to the story's meaning so readers can use this information strategically. Visuals in nonfiction texts are particularly important for supporting the acquisition of meaning from text. More proficient readers rely less on visual information (except in nonfiction) and can handle fewer illustrations as well as pictures that provide less obvious clues to meaning.
- *Size and layout of print*–Large, clear print with distinctive spaces between words and lines is easiest to read. More proficient readers can read increasingly smaller print and contend with print that features unconventional layout.
- *Punctuation*–Texts with basic punctuation such as periods and question marks are easier to read than those that use a range of punctuation marks.
- *Content*–Themes, ideas, and concepts that are familiar to young readers and closer to their experience are easier to read. More complex content, with abstract ideas, multiple themes, and subjects more removed from daily experience, makes a book more difficult.
- *Text structure and genre*–Texts with simple ideas and few characters are typically easier than those with intricate story structures, featuring characters that change and develop. Nonfiction texts with simple, obvious organizational patterns (chronological, for example) are easier than those that use more complex or embedded patterns, such as cause and effect. Additionally, nonfiction text structure is often more challenging because children may not have much prior experience with this genre or may be unfamiliar with the topic.
- *Language structure*–Sentence structures that closely match those of the child's are easiest to read. Simple sentences, often one or two on a page, are usually good for beginning guided reading texts. Longer, embedded sentences and texts organized into paragraphs, sections, and chapters are appropriate for more advanced readers.

⊛ *Predictability*–Predictability is characterized by repeated language patterns, rhythm, and rhyme. Predictable books provide excellent support for beginning guided reading groups. As children become more proficient and are able to rely on their abilities to integrate all the cueing systems, text predictability becomes less important.

⊛ *Vocabulary*–The easiest texts feature a limited set of high-interest, high-frequency words that are familiar to children. These words generally can be easily solved based on the children's repertoire of reading strategies. More difficult texts feature a range of vocabulary, including multisyllabic words and those not generally found in oral language, such as specialized or technical terms. Words in texts for beginners should be within their experience, but more advanced readers can expand their knowledge through exposure to more advanced vocabulary in a text.

⊛ *Relation to curriculum*–Books that focus on topics related to children's ongoing studies in your classroom will be easier to read because children will have developed background knowledge that they can link to the vocabulary, ideas, and concepts in the text.

Many publishers of books for guided reading provide ratings of their books' difficulty levels. They can help you get a rough gauge of how you might use a particular book. However, trust your instincts: you know your children. Over time, as you acquire many books and use them with children, you will be able to select books accurately and efficiently for use with your students.

Sample Guided Reading Lesson

Figure 11.4 features a sample guided reading lesson of *Wishy Washy Day*, by Joy Cowley, for a group of first graders. It will give you a sense of how a guided reading lesson might proceed.

Critical Elements in a Guided Reading Lesson

Guided reading lessons typically consist of several key elements:

Figure 11.4
Sample Guided
Reading Lesson

☼ **Book Introduction**

Write "Wishy Washy Day" on the white board. Have children frame "Wishy Washy Day" on the cover. Have children discuss other stories they've read about Mrs. Wishy Washy and her animals. Have them look at the cover and predict from the cover and their experience: "What do you think a wishy washy day is? What might happen to Mrs. Wishy Washy's animals on a wishy washy day?" Take a "picture walk" through the first part of the story (up to p. 13). Discuss where each animal hides; emphasize that the dog hides in a "shed" if you think children might not know what that is. Make the word *instead* with magnetic letters on the magnetic/white board. Show that *in* is a word they know and that they can use this information to figure out the word *instead*. Suggest they read to find out what happens on wishy washy day.

☼ **Reading of the Story**

Children move apart and read the story independently. Listen in on various readers and make notes on self-stick notes of strategies they are using as well as any problems they encounter. Listen carefully to the reading of one child selected for that day.

☼ **Postreading—Discussion and Teaching Points**

Hold a quick discussion of the story. Hopefully, children will offer responses and opinions, but if not, you may need to ask some questions such as "What happened when Mrs. Wishy Washy tried to wash the animals?" "How do you feel when you have to go in the tub for a scrub?" Suggest that children dictate all the animals in the story and where they tried to hide. Write their ideas on the white board and discuss how this is a "list-sequence" story structure.

Ask if any words gave the children trouble. (If they don't bring up problems, take the lead.) Use magnetic letters and the white board to write the sentence with the target word missing (except for the beginning letter). Review the strategy of using beginning letter and surrounding words to determine what the word is.

Suggest that the students make a "step book" of the story by writing a sentence on each page of the book, then illustrating it. This task can be made easier by having children glue strips with sentences already written on them onto the step book pages. They return to their seats to work independently.

- Book introductions, in which teachers help children notice the unique features or "tricky" aspects that might cause difficulty for them.
- Reading of the text by the students while the teacher listens and occasionally provides quick, focused assistance when necessary.
- Follow-up discussion of the text and one or two carefully selected teaching points the teacher thinks will contribute to the group's growth as readers.
- Activities in which students do additional independent work with a text.

Book Introductions. Texts used in guided reading sessions should be introduced so that you help children successfully access the text, yet leave room for independent problem solving. Introductions should be brief; what you discuss depends on both the story and your students' needs. Your students' background knowledge, the literary knowledge they possess, and the features of the text all affect how you structure a book introduction. Noted researcher Marie Clay (1991) summarizes the purpose of the book introduction in the following way:

> This is not a case of telling the children what to expect. It is a process of drawing children into the activity before passing control to the children and pushing them gently towards problem solving the whole first reading of the story for themselves. (p. 265)

The amount of support provided in an introduction depends on your knowledge of the text—either fiction or nonfiction—and the abilities of your readers. You need to think carefully about your introduction so that it flows like a conversation in which you provide support and promote accessibility but leave room for independent work. Thus, you might do some of the following things:

- Explain ideas and concepts that are important in the text but that might be unfamiliar to the children.
- Call attention to vocabulary that students might not know but that is essential to understanding the text.
- Help children become familiar with language patterns and structures that are critical to the text.
- Draw attention to the text structure, helping children understand how to use these structures to gain meaning.
- Examine unusual text layouts that might be difficult to follow.
- Discuss aspects of character, plot, or theme that the children might find difficult, or features of nonfiction that might be challenging.

Guided Reading of the Text. Following the introduction, have the students read the text independently. There is some debate as to whether this reading should be done aloud or silently. Of course, the ultimate goal is independent silent reading. However, beginning readers typically read aloud to themselves. This is recommended for beginners, because it enables the teacher to hear how each student is processing the text. Additionally, when children read aloud quietly, you can "listen in" and intervene if needed. Any assistance you provide should be brief, focused, and designed to help the child use what he or she knows to work through difficulties to be able to continue reading.

During this time, teachers also observe what students are doing as they read: how they are using their knowledge of print to gain meaning, what they need to know to be more successful, and how fluent their reading is. Many teachers make informal observations on children's progress or jot down notes on specific items they think should be brought to children's attention following the reading. They also do more formal monitoring through running records or completion of literacy checklists.

Discussion and Teaching Points. After the students read the text, you can bring the group back together for a brief discussion of the plot, theme, or character development if the text is a story, or ask appropriate questions if the text is nonfiction. Students should also be encouraged to share their personal responses to the story. These discussions may also include revisiting the story to support an opinion or reread a specific part.

You can then base one or two teaching points on what you observed about the strategies the children used or struggled with. This is a great opportunity to help children move forward in their understanding about how print works. However, be cautious: you should choose only one or two items you think children need but also are ready for. A teaching point for a beginning reader might be how to use illustrations to confirm meaning or how to guess what a critical word in the story might be. More able readers might need help with analyzing word structure, identifying cause and effect in plots, coordinating visual cues with meaning and language structures, or understanding features of nonfiction. Advanced readers may need assistance with understanding complex themes, unusual text structures, or episodic plots, as well as more complex aspects of nonfiction writing or visual information. In all instances, the emphasis should be on what children can learn from the teaching point that they can then apply to other texts. Your teaching should be brief but very focused and clear.

Extensions. Following the teaching points, students typically return to their seats for independent work. This can take many forms. For example, they can reread familiar books from previous guided reading lessons that are placed in their group's book box in the library area. Or they might work at learning centers located around the room. These centers include carefully planned activities that help children apply what they know to familiar or new texts, including listening to books on tape, creating art projects in response to a story, pocket chart reading, letter or word games and sorting activities, creative writing, and the like. Still other students might be sitting at tables or desks working on journals, independent response projects, or similar activities.

Figure 11.5 lists resource books on specific ideas for managing independent work while you are teaching.

> *Activities must set up children for success so they see themselves as independent readers—the ultimate goal of guided reading.*
>
> Ford & Optiz, 2002, p. 717

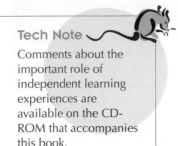

Tech Note

Comments about the important role of independent learning experiences are available on the CD-ROM that accompanies this book.

Summary

In this chapter, we discussed shared and guided approaches to reading instruction. In shared instruction, the students and the teacher work together to study and learn from text. Either a big book or an enlarged text on an overhead is used so that all students can easily see and focus on the text. This is an excellent approach to use when students are learning new aspects about text—whether it is fiction or nonfiction.

We also described guided reading, a small-group instructional approach where each student is reading the same text. The teacher provides support while learners take over and show what they can do as they read fiction or nonfiction texts. This is a good opportunity for the teacher to observe and learn what students are able to do, thus informing his or her next instructional steps. Both shared and guided reading approaches are appropriate for all age groups.

Figure 11.5
Resource Books for Independent Activities During Guided Reading

Burch, M. M., & Beech, L. (2001). *Instant file-folder games for reading.* New York: Scholastic.

Diffily, D., Donaldson, E., & Sassman, C. (2001). *The Scholastic book of early childhood learning centers (grades preK–K).* New York: Scholastic.

Feldman, J. R. (1997). *Wonderful rooms where children can bloom! Over 500 innovative ideas and activities for your child-centered classroom.* Peterborough, N.H.: Crystal Springs Books.

Finney, S. (2000). *Keep the rest of the class reading while you teach small groups (grades 3–6).* New York: Scholastic.

Finney, S. (2003). *Independent reading activities that keep kids learning . . . while you teach small groups (grades 3–6).* New York: Scholastic.

Helm, J. H., & Katz, L. (2001). *Young investigators: The project approach in the early years.* New York: Teachers College Press.

Isbell, R., & Exelby, B. (2001). *Early learning environments that work.* Beltsville, MD: Gryphon House.

Marriott, D., & Kupperstein, J. (1997). *What are the other kids doing while you teach small groups?* Cypress, CA: Creative Teaching Press.

Nations, S., & Alonso, M. (2001). *Primary literacy centers: Making reading and writing stick.* Gainesville, FL: Maupin House.

Neuman, S. B., Copple, C., & Bredenkamp, S. (2000). *Learning to read and write: Developmentally appropriate practices for young children.* Washington, DC: NAEYC.

Optiz, M. (1994). *Learning centers (grades K–4).* New York: Scholastic.

Vergeront, J. (1987). *Places and spaces for preschool and primary (indoors).* Washington, DC, NAEYC.

Action Research for Teachers

Can Using Music With Shared Reading Enhance Literacy Skills in Kindergarten?

Natalie Chappie & Rachel Fleischaker
Kindergarten, Canton, Ohio, City Schools

Natalie, a kindergarten teacher, and Rachel, a music teacher, collaborated on this study, each using their talents to see if they could make a difference with Natalie's inner-city 5- and 6-year-olds. The teachers each kept a researcher log. They administered a popular "concepts about print" test to each student (Goodman & Altwerger, 1981), as well as part of the Elementary Reading Attitude Survey (McKenna & Kear, 1990) and a sight word vocabulary test that they administered at three intervals during their yearlong study. They collected writing samples from each student on a regular basis, sent home parent surveys at the beginning and end of the study, and videotaped or audiotaped some of the shared book experiences using music.

Throughout the year, the teachers introduced books with text that could be sung or songs that could be printed and made into books or wall charts with their students. They introduced a new book or song weekly. Many of the selections coincided with other concepts in the curriculum, such as colors or letter names.

Each Monday, the new text was introduced. On Tuesdays, Wednesdays, and Thursdays, activities such as dramatizing the texts were used, and on Fridays, writing was used as a way to extend appreciation of the texts.

The teachers examined all their data and analyzed the six most at-risk students in more depth. These students all made great progress according to the results of the "concepts about print" test, as well as in their attitudes toward reading. The writing samples were the most revealing, showing impressive signs of improvement. Children showed progress on all measures. The teachers concluded that their study gathered lots of good evidence about how children successfully progressed. The students responded positively to the lessons involving music and seemed to be engaged in their learning. Natalie believed that this group of students made more progress than previous ones did with a more traditional early reading program. Both teachers want to continue their collaborative efforts in teaching and designing action research projects.

Chapter 12

INDEPENDENT READING

"Those of us who are committed readers know what it's like to be hooked on a book. I spend some days at work in my office, which happens to be in my home. There's many a day I want to leave my desk and lie on my bed to continue whichever novel I am reading at the moment. It's such a wicked thought! But it's that feeling of being drawn into the book or pulled along by a book, of not wanting to put a book down, of reading until I A.M. in the morning when I have an early start on the following day . . . it's that feeling that I want to pass on to my students when I'm teaching literature. If I can develop this, then I know the children will be lifelong readers." (Australian educator Lorraine Wilson, 2002, p. 147)

In this chapter, we describe independent reading, an approach that provides the important opportunity for students to select books on their own, read them, respond to them, and talk to others about what they have read. Specifically, we address the following questions:

- What is independent reading?

- What are the critical elements for implementing independent reading?

- How is independent reading organized?

What Is Independent Reading?

From the first day of school, we want all children to have a desire to read and engage with books. Even kindergartners can browse through books, using pictures to "tell" a story or point to words they know. Although at times we will guide their selections by designating a "poetry day" or "nonfiction week," we expect children to grow into becoming self-sufficient in choosing books they can read and will enjoy. This gives them the opportunity to apply what they know about literacy to books that are personally interesting to them. We hope that reading many books independently will help them become more fluent readers and will build confidence in their abilities to successfully handle increasingly complex texts (Clay, 1991; Morrow, 1985). Beck and McKeown (1991) also report that vocabulary growth after the second grade is influenced by the amount of time children spend reading independently.

You can make independent reading—also termed "individualized reading" or "reading workshop"—an important focus of your total reading program. This is not a different teaching method; rather, it is a different way to organize and structure reading instruction (Holdaway, 1980). Students spend the majority of their time reading and responding at their own pace to self-selected books. The teacher periodically gathers students into large and small groups for brief lessons on reading strategies, booksharing sessions, or response

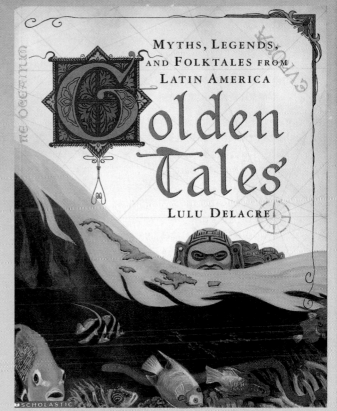

From GOLDEN TALES: MYTHS, LEGENDS, AND FOLKTALES FROM LATIN AMERICA by Lulu Delacre. Published by Scholastic Press/Scholastic Inc. Copyright © 1996 by Lulu Delacre. Reprinted by permission.

Books and especially good literature are the keys to success in life. The more you read, the broader your horizons become, and your insight about life grows.

Lulu Delacre, author; personal communication, September, 1999

My kids are on fire with books!

Tracy Hallee, grade 1 teacher who uses children's literature as the focus of her reading program.

activities. The teacher also meets periodically with students to assess their progress and guide further reading. Typically, upper- and middle-grade teachers use this approach because their students are more independent readers. It is easily modified to fit the restricted time schedules that characterize upper grades. However, primary teachers also can successfully implement independent reading time, although they generally must provide extra support with book selection and spend more time on teaching reading strategies.

Critical Elements of Independent Reading

Just as they do in shared and guided reading, teachers must think about important elements when they begin implementing independent reading in their classrooms:

- ☺ organizing a classroom library;
- ☺ helping students select books;
- ☺ helping students keep track of what they read;
- ☺ providing time for reading;
- ☺ providing opportunities for book sharing;
- ☺ providing opportunities to respond to books;
- ☺ ensuring one-on-one time with each student;
- ☺ focusing on reading strategies.

Let's look at each of these in more detail.

Organizing a Classroom Library

Classrooms need to have a library with a wide range of books representing diverse topics, genres, and levels so students have enough choices to select from. Along with classic, notable works of fiction, nonfiction, and poetry, you should include series books, joke and riddle books, children's magazines, craft books, and other "popular" literature to meet the wide tastes of all students. Typically, at least 10 books per child is a good starting point, but more is better. Where do you find these books, particularly if you're a beginning teacher? Libraries are a good resource. You can also obtain inexpensive paperback books from children's book clubs such as Scholastic and Trumpet. PTA groups and parents can be asked to donate money or books.

Storing and displaying books are critical to helping children access books that are engaging, but also at their independent level. Teachers Karen Szymusiak and Franki Sibberson (2001; Sibberson & Szymusiak, 2003) studied how bookstores displayed and marketed books as they designed their classroom libraries to foster children's easy access to books. Using baskets to sort books helps ensure the covers face out for easy browsing (an important marketing technique). Baskets also allow for organizing books into categories that intrigue children. For example, they suggest organizing series books and books by favorite authors into their own categories. Books that have been introduced in class, sequels, or books on similar topics to read-alouds can also be put in special baskets. Thus, children might browse through and select a book

from the Gary Paulsen basket because he's become a favorite author. The same basket might include some Will Hobbs books because Hobbs writes adventure stories similar to Paulsen's. Teachers of younger students might create a basket of alphabet books or predictable texts. Franki and Karen have a separate area in their libraries for nonfiction that is sorted by topic. Poetry has its own area and is separated into baskets by poet, topic, and other inviting ways. You can invite your children to sort and categorize the books themselves for the classroom library. It's fascinating to observe what categories are interesting and meaningful to them.

Tech Note
Find what English author and educator Aidan Chambers says about displaying books on the CD-ROM that accompanies this book.

Helping Students Select Books

Children need to be shown how to find books that are not too difficult or too easy, but "just right" for them. Adults usually read the back cover, preview chapter titles, and skim through the pages before selecting a book. We should encourage students to do the same—briefly dip into a book to see if it is interesting or appropriate. They can also try out a book to determine if it is at a comfortable reading level. If they read a few pages and there are too many unfamiliar words or reading feels frustrating, the book may be too difficult. However, always remember that if children are highly motivated to read a particular book, you should encourage them to do so. That high level of interest will often carry them through difficulties, and the challenge will help them grow as readers.

Are Prescribed Book Lists a Good Idea?

Whether to have prescribed, required book lists for each grade level is an issue that isn't easily answered. For us, more questions than simple answers emerge.

- ☺ Who will design the list? Is this individual or committee very familiar with teaching literature, as well as with evaluating and selecting appropriate books?
- ☺ What is the purpose of the list? Why is it needed?
- ☺ What are the short-term and long-term goals for such a list? In what ways will it improve students' literacy education?
- ☺ How will the list be used? Will it open doors or close

> *Books on display speak for themselves. . . . All in all, good displays take relatively little time and effort to set up compared with the value of their effect.*
>
> Aidan Chambers, 1996b, p. 20

them? Is the intent of the list to be helpful or to exercise control?

☺ What books will be excluded? To what extent will multicultural literature be represented?

☺ Who will keep the list updated so that new books are added every year? Any list needs to be updated annually because of the great number of new titles available.

We don't think a required book list for reading aloud or for independent reading is inherently a bad idea. However, even an idea that starts off with the best intentions can quickly fall apart when restrictions are established that prohibit students from accessing books. Here are possible concerns about imposing a required book list:

1. Does the list mean that no student can independently read a book that is on a required list of read-aloud selections? Do we really want to discourage students from reading on their own?

2. Can a teacher at one grade level use a book for sharing aloud that is required at another grade? Would we say that good literature should not be read twice? Many who reread favorite books contend that each new reading is a different experience. Teacher Sharon Taberski (2000) says, "Rereading is a powerful strategy. It allows young readers to read a text with more support the second and third time, and to work out different problems with each rereading" (p. 150). Older readers also discover new things when they read a book more than once. Chambers (1996a) says, "Books that are worth bothering with at all are worth (may demand) rereading" (p. 66).

3. Where does student choice enter into the equation? Student choice is a critical component of establishing lifelong readers.

4. Are children hearing only a limited selection of books with some of the same titles repeated year after year? How does this broaden their reading horizons?

Creating required, prescribed reading lists, though often well-intentioned, is sometimes fraught with problems that in the long run may work counter to our long-term goals of creating lifelong independent readers. A suggested list might better serve your goals.

Helping Students Keep Track of What They Read

Students who read books they have selected themselves are more likely to find books they love and ultimately become passionate about reading. Middle school teacher Nancie Atwell (1998) says it well:

The ability to read for pleasure and personal meaning . . . is not a gift or a talent. It comes with the ability to choose, books to choose among, time to read and a teacher who is a reader . . . selecting one's books and reading them in school is not a luxury. It is the wellspring of student literacy and literacy appreciation. (p. 34)

If children have the opportunity to find and read books they love, they will find pleasure and satisfaction in reading.

It's important for students to keep track of what they read. Students can use a notebook or create their own folder to list each book they read. Chambers calls these *reading diaries*, a special place to record their reading selections (1996b). Chambers says:

If reading doesn't affect our lives, doesn't change us or influence our behavior, it is no more than a pass-time entertainment, and hardly worth all the fuss we make of it. But if reading books affects our lives emotionally, intellectually, ethically, and in all sorts of other ways, as I believe it does, then it matters which books we put into our heads. And if it matters what we put into our heads, it also matters that we remember what those books were. (p. 39)

Students should indicate the titles, authors, and genres of books in their reading diaries. This record of their reading histories can travel with the children to subsequent grades, giving teachers at the next grade levels a good idea of the extent of reading each child has done as well as the titles and types of books read.

Depending on your purposes, it is also a wise idea to help children maintain a balance in the types of books they select to read. Teachers can create a visual, such as a pie chart divided according to genres. As children read a number of books from each genre, that slice of the pie is colored. This kind of record-keeping system gives students an excellent visual representation of their preferred genres. It also shows teachers what genres need to be introduced through minilessons, for example, to help children expand their literary horizons.

Providing Time for Reading

You need to ensure that students have regular and sufficient time for independent reading. Thus, you need to set aside a specific time each day for this purpose. The amount of time allotted to this activity increases throughout the year until younger children build up to 15 or 20 minutes; more experienced readers can maintain their attention for 30 minutes or more. During this time—sometimes called "Sustained Silent Reading" (SSR) or "Drop Everything and Read" (DEAR)—children are expected to read without interruption, usually to themselves. Some teachers allow partner reading or book sharing during this time, particularly in classrooms with younger children. The idea is to have sustained, focused contact with books.

The teacher's role varies during this time. Some read silently along with their students. Others like to spend the time observing and talking with children, finding answers to questions such as, "Are they making appropriate book choices for their developmental level?" "What books do they find interesting?" "How are they thinking through plot, character development, and other literary elements?" "What do they do when faced with a word they don't know?" Information from these observations can inform teaching; it's a luxury to make them in uninterrupted fashion.

Providing Opportunities for Book Sharing

Many students become excited about a book or poem they've read and want to share it with the class. These spontaneous, enthusiastic presentations are an excellent way to stimulate reading and expand children's choices: Peer recommendations are powerful. Thus, it's a good idea to schedule regular opportunities at the end of independent reading time for this purpose.

Book Bistro

Developed by Wendy C. Kasten and former middle school ESL teacher Lori Krug Wilfong, Book Bistro is a way to encourage and monitor independent reading in grades 3–8.

The notion is that readers can linger over good books, talking and enjoying an atmosphere that could include soft music, maybe refreshments, just as in your favorite bookstore or coffee shop.

On the fourth Friday of each month (or whatever time works), students bring in a book that they are reading independently. Two days before the Book Bistro, students describe their book on a 3 × 5-inch index card (title, genre, two-sentence plot summary). Teachers use the cards to place students into groups of five according to the type of book they have read, or however the teacher wishes to create the groups (the teacher assigns each group a number). At the beginning of the Bistro, students answer two questions pertaining to their books, choosing from a menu of six questions. These questions are open-ended and will not give away too much of the plot or ending. Examples of these questions follow:

1. What do your classmates need to know about your book that would interest them in reading it?
2. What touched you about this book?
3. Would you want to keep this book in your personal library? Why or why not?

Students were told to bring a favorite book to an outdoor book sharing discussion between fifth graders at Davey Elementary and Kent State students. Zane is giving a book talk on his recent favorite.

Fourth-grade students read independently.

4. Does this book remind you of anything you have learned or talked about in school?
5. Does this book lend itself to being made into a movie? Why or why not?
6. How does this book relate to your life?

Before the first Book Bistro, the teacher models a good book talk using these six questions as a guide. It is also a good idea to have a group of five students model the Book Bistro for the entire class to discuss what to look for in their own groups.

After students have selected their guiding questions, the predetermined groups get together, sitting in a circle or around a table (an overhead showing the group assignments would expedite this process). The teacher gives everyone two peer evaluations, explaining that each student will evaluate the person on his or her right and left, based on the questions on the evaluation. Students talk briefly about their books, possibly using an egg timer to signal when time is up. When one reader's time is up, the next student gives a short talk. Teachers might choose to add time for open discussion as needed. After all students have had a turn, they take 5 minutes to fill out their two evaluations. Besides the name of the evaluator, the person being evaluated, and the title of that person's book, the evaluation consists of three questions and looks like the form shown in Figure 12.1.

> *I just know when I arrive at school and one of the older boys wants to stop me and talk about his current novel—"Have you read the next chapter, Lorraine? What did you think. . . ?"—that something is right about our school literature program.*
>
> *Australian educator Lorraine Wilson, 2002, p. 148*

When students finish this activity, the teacher has concrete evidence of the type and depth of independent reading students are engaging in. These forms are typically included in student evaluation files.

Providing Opportunities to Respond to Books

Educators Jeffrey D. Wilhelm, Tanya N. Baker, and Julie Dube (2001) make these comments about what good reading is all about:

> *Good reading is more than a reconstruction of the author's meanings. Readers must relate what they read to what they already know. They must evaluate the new knowledge in terms of the old and the old in terms of the new. They must see and hear and move about in a story world that they create with the text. They must select and organize and make appropriate additions and be prepared to go beyond what the writer is telling them. They must be ready to create meaning, and this meaning is visual, auditory, physical, intellectual, and affective. (p. 34)*

Students need opportunities to respond to books they've selected. However, we offer a word of caution: Be sure the response activities don't take precedence over reading. Keeping this in mind, there are many ways you can encourage children to respond critically and aesthetically to books. For example, teacher Nancie Atwell uses "dialogue

---

PEER EVALUATION

Person you are evaluating: _____

Title of this person's book: _____

Your name: _____

Circle the number that best fits your answer.

1. Would you read this book after hearing about it?

1	2	3	4	5
Never	Unlikely	Neutral	Maybe	Definitely

2. How well prepared was this person?

1	2	3	4	5
Not prepared		Somewhat prepared		Very Prepared

3. In a few short sentences, describe how well your group worked today. What could be done next time to make it better? (Use the back of this paper for your answer.)

Figure 12.1
Sample Peer Evaluation Form

Meet... Judy Blume

Author of *Iggie's House; Blubber; Are You There God? It's Me, Margaret; Deenie; It's Not the End of the World; Starring Sally J. Freedman as Herself; Tiger Eyes; Forever; Tales of a Fourth Grade Nothing; Superfudge;* and others.

"Many of my books are set in New Jersey, because that's where I was born and raised. When I was growing up, I dreamed of becoming a cowgirl, a detective, a spy, a great actress, or a ballerina. Not a dentist like my father, or a homemaker like my mother—certainly not a writer, although I always loved to read. I didn't know anything about writers. It never occurred to me they were regular people and that I could grow up to become one, even though I loved to make up stories inside my head.

When I grew up, my need for story telling didn't go away. So when my own two children started preschool, I began to write and I've been writing ever since! My characters live inside my head for a long time before I actually start to write a book about them. They become so real to me I talk about them at the dinner table as if they are real. Some people consider this weird. But my family understands.

A lot of readers ask me for "writing tips." I wish it were that easy! There are no hard fast rules for writing, and no secret tricks, because what works for one person doesn't always work for another. Everybody is different. That's the key to the whole business of writing—your individuality."

Ms. Blume now maintains a home in New York City and in Key West, Florida. Her website is http://www.judyblume.com.

---

journals" in which children write letters to peers or to her, reflecting on their books. These letters can be about virtually anything, including how children felt when they read the book, what they liked or didn't like about the author's writing, and what the book reminded them of. Other teachers provide some structure for journal entries with prompts or questions to which students can respond (Atwell, 1998). Figure 12.2 features ideas for journal prompts.

First-grade teacher Sharon Taberski (2000) uses a "Response Sheet," with space at the top for children to draw a picture and lines at the bottom for them to record the title, author's name, and a few sentences about the book. Eventually her children move to using Response Notebooks, which are composition-style books for recording their responses to books they read.

Students can also respond in ways other than writing. For example, they can create puppet shows, plays, choral readings, radio broadcasts, and other dramatic productions. Those reading books with similar themes or topics can hold discussions. Students also can create weavings, murals, cartoons, collages, constructions, and other art projects.

Ensuring One-on-One Time With Each Student

Because students are reading books independently, teachers need time to personally monitor each student's progress and provide guidance if necessary. This is done through regularly scheduled individual conferences. Conference time is not usually a time for teaching (although quick strategy teaching can be done if the need arises); this is the teacher's time to learn about what students are doing with their books. Typically, conferences last 10–15 minutes and are scheduled with each child on a regular basis. During the conference, teachers might have children share their personal responses to the book, read aloud a passage they've prepared, and share their response logs. They might ask children some questions about their books, make suggestions for selecting future books, or investigate what reading strategies their students are using.

Teachers usually keep detailed notes on their conferences. Some have forms with specific categories of information that they look for and comment on; others use a more open-ended system in which they record general comments and observations.

Figure 12.2
Prompts and Tips
for Literature
Response Journals

Ways to Help Students Get Started in Their Journals:

Not all prompts work at all times. Students can keep a written record handy of the following questions to use when they need help stimulating their thinking.

1. How does today's reading make you feel?

2. What is something interesting you noticed about what you read?

3. What does today's reading remind you of?

4. Why do you think the author wrote this book?

5. What did you read today that got you thinking in a different way?

6. If the author, poet, or illustrator could visit with you, what would you ask that person about what you read, and why?

7. What do you think happened before the first chapter of the book?

8. What do you think happened after the last chapter of the book?

9. If you could become one of the characters in the book, who would it be, and why?

10. Write a letter to one of the characters in the book.

11. What would you tell a friend about this book?

Tips About Journal Writing:

- Journal entries help us get to know our students better, both personally and academically. At first, some students may summarize when they begin writing journal entries. Or when reading something culturally unfamiliar or different, their responses may look less sophisticated. These things are normal.

- Developing good journal writers takes time. Invite students to share their journals during discussions as a way to show a variety of ways to respond.

- In assessing journals, look for effort, thoughtfulness, and evidence of critical thinking.

- Journal entries can be focused at times to accomplish instructional goals, such as writing to a specific prompt, practicing summarizing skills, or retelling.

- Summarizing is a different skill than retelling. Summarizing requires condensing the information but usually maintaining the important points, whereas retelling is a reiteration of the main information.

Focusing on Reading Strategies

As with shared and guided reading, teachers using the workshop approach need to show children effective strategies for gaining meaning with text. This is usually done with whole-class minilessons in which children focus on some important aspect of reading and then practice implementing it. Sometimes teachers organize a temporary small group for a skill or strategy that only a few children need to practice. Examining the books students are reading along with observations of their interactions with those books provides teachers with ideas for minilesson topics.

How Is Independent Reading Organized?

Because independent reading is a management system, we can't present a model lesson. However, we can show you how to organize your classroom and what events should occur to ensure that your students are learning to live and love literature.

Opening Activities

This time is devoted to helping children focus on what will be expected of them during independent reading time. They can sign up for individual conferences or a turn to share. Some teachers take 5–10 minutes for a "Status of the Class" check (Atwell, 1998), during which they quickly note the progress of students' reading from the previous day and help them set goals for the current day's reading. This information might be recorded as numbers of pages or as a general summary each student provides.

Daily Teacher Read-Aloud

This component should not be neglected or omitted, even if time is short. Read-alouds help you introduce different genres, develop awareness of literary devices, and model strategies that good readers use (Robb, 2000). See chapter 10 for details about reading aloud.

Minilessons

This is your time for direct teaching. For approximately 10–20 minutes, you demonstrate reading strategies, concepts, and techniques and give information you think students need to be good readers or to participate efficiently in the workshop. Nancie Atwell (1998) suggests using four categories of minilessons: procedural (workshop rules and routines), issues of literary crafting (what authors consider when they write), conventions of written language (grammar, rules of punctuation, etc.), and reading strategies. Following the lesson, many teachers provide some form of guided practice in which students apply what they've learned to a text they're currently reading.

Quiet Reading Time

During this time (30–45 minutes), students read silently on their own. They usually keep a record of what they've read in a simple response log, where they note the author and title of the book along with some comments. How-

ever, distractions and assignments are kept to a minimum so that children stay focused on their reading. Some teachers also let students use this time for journal writing, independent research, and other quiet projects; some also hold individual conferences during this time. However, the emphasis should be on reading.

Activity Time

Approximately 25–30 minutes should be allotted to various independent activities (Holdaway, 1980). Some students choose to quietly continue reading or writing. Others work on book responses or learning-center tasks, or they meet in small groups for book discussions or strategy lessons. This is typically the time when individual conferences are held.

Closing Session

In the last 10–15 minutes of independent reading, the group comes together for sharing and debriefing. At this time, students present responses to books they've read, enthusiastically share their favorite book or poem, or participate in a quick lesson on a topic you believe will benefit them all. Former middle-grade teacher Laura Robb (2000) has a Reader's Chair to spotlight students as they present book talks in which they make personal connections to the story as well as observations about the writer's literary techniques. This is also the time when you discuss any organizational or behavioral concerns with the group, brainstorming strategies for resolving them.

Using independent reading can support your students' growth as readers and writers. Letting them choose books that are personally satisfying and engaging, coupled with activities that help them deepen their appreciation for and understanding of the book, can help children become enthusiastic members of the literacy club.

> *Books were always the present I liked best. Who knew what wonders lay between its covers—what magic, what astounding information, what tales of high adventures, what strange people and places?*
>
> *Patricia Lauber, personal communication, September, 1999*

Summary

In this chapter, we learned about independent reading as an approach that encourages students to select their own books for reading. Teachers guide and support using this approach by helping students make good decisions about what books to read and how to keep records of what they read, and by conferencing with students about their progress. After reading a book independently, students respond in myriad ways reflecting their understanding of the book.

Action Research for Teachers

The Effect of Sustained Silent Reading on Fluency

Michael J. Lewis
Northeast Ohio Urban District

The purpose of Michael's 8-week research project was to determine if the implementation of two weekly, 15-minute periods of sustained silent reading would improve student attitudes toward reading and would increase reading fluency and reading rate. For the reading sessions, eight urban, at-risk adolescents were allowed to bring in reading materials of their own choosing. Most selected current magazines, but others chose paperback novels.

The results of informal interest and attitude surveys showed that 88% of the students improved their attitude toward reading. Administration of a popular published informal reading inventory showed that six out of eight, or 75% of the students, improved in reading rate.

Chapter 13

LITERATURE CIRCLES

"I believe literature can be the validation of a child's experiences and a bridge to understanding other peoples and cultures. It can serve as a catalyst for meaningful discussions that might foster respect among the multiethnic student body of today's schools." (Lulu Delacre, author; personal communication, September, 1999)

ne of the most exciting things happening in reading and literature instruction today is that students of all ages are experiencing reading and enjoying books together in literature circles. In this chapter, we discuss the following questions:

- ☼ What are literature circles?

- ☼ Why are literature circles an important component in literacy programs?

- ☼ How can teachers implement, manage, and assess literature circles?

- ☼ How can teachers adapt literature circles to accommodate learners who are different?

- ☼ What does research say about literature circles?

What Are Literature Circles?

Literature circles are a literature-based teaching approach that can constitute an important part of a comprehensive literacy program in K–8 classrooms. Literature circles typically are composed of four or five students of mixed abilities. These groups read a novel, picture book, or nonfiction title in common. Depending on the size of the class, then, there may be five circles reading concurrently in the classroom.

One way to organize and conduct literature circles is to have student-led groups engage in four processes together. First, students read the book on their own, in pairs, or aloud together, depending on the book and the ability levels of the students. Second, students respond to their reading on an ongoing basis by writing in their journals. Third, circles meet regularly to discuss the reading most recently completed. And last, at the end of the book, each circle designs a creative presentation that communicates what the story meant to them. Or if students read nonfiction, they share responses that reflect the content of the book. Depending on purpose, each group should give just enough of an advertisement or book talk about what they read to interest others in wanting to read it.

Why Literature Circles?

The definition of literacy has changed over time. At one time, being literate meant having the ability to sign one's name and recognize it in print. Later it came to mean a very basic ability to read and function in everyday life with not only signing one's name, but also reading signs, labels, directions, public notices, and the like. Today, we all have far higher expectations of literacy and what it means to be literate. In today's classrooms, our challenge is not only to teach children how to read but also to help them enjoy reading. We want our students to experience what happens to us when we enjoy reading—that feeling of falling into a book and into the depths of a story world, of savoring over and over again the talents of a poet, or of becoming so engrossed in a nonfiction book that we lose track of the time.

The question, then, becomes: How do we teach children to prize and value reading? The answer lies in having them fall in love with books, words, the sounds of language, stories, and information—all valuable aspects that books offer. Ultimately, we want our students to view reading and writing as meaningful, pleasurable experiences that they will seek to repeat on their own again and again.

One way we know that hooks readers into reading is to have memorable experiences in school around books. One of these is the sustained engagement with a book that we read and share with others. This approach is often called literature circles.

Literature circles provide a venue for students to read high-quality books and to share those books with interested others. Reading books together is memorable and intimate. It affords opportunities for sharing and listening as well as reading. Having time to discuss a book gives students opportunities to hear multiple perspectives and to express personal views. These are real discussions—where students take the lead to converse about a book rather than those where teachers do all or nearly all of the talking. Teachers, in fact, are not always present, nor are they participating, in circle discussions. We say more about this later when we describe the teacher's role in literature circles.

Designing a presentation at the end of the book provides students with lasting memories about both the book and the experience of talking and working together. The amount of work that goes into these presentations is a feast of talk and even argument about the content—a reading teacher's dream of having students so engaged in the process!

Implementing Literature Circles

In this section, we describe ways to implement literature circles in a classroom of intermediate-aged learners between 10 and 14 years old. Later in this chapter, we present variations on literature circles for students who are younger, less proficient readers. Although we describe some of our favorite ways of doing literature circles, there are many variations to this approach to suit differing needs. Some of these are presented later in the chapter.

Selecting Books

The task of selecting books for literature circles seems daunting to some teachers at first. But everyone can implement literature circles even if current knowledge of books is somewhat lacking, because teachers can consult resources such as this book, librarians, media specialists, booksellers, and colleagues who know books. See the Tech Notes for resources located in your school or public libraries. These references will offer book lists organized by age, topic, and content themes.

Tech Note

Find titles of award-winning books as excellent choices for use in literature circles on the CD-ROM that accompanies this book. Also available are lists of recommended literature circle titles for grades 2–8, as well as professional sources to help you locate good titles.

Selecting Nonfiction for Literature Circles

The standard fare for literature circle reading is fiction, but nonfiction can be used as well. Nonfiction makes particularly good sense to parallel a unit in social studies or science. For example, groups might read a biography that corresponds with a time period being studied in history. Many biographies are in picture-book format, such as those by David Adler (picture-book biographies for young children, although some titles are very appropriate for older students) and by Diane Stanley, which are picture-book biographies appropriate for intermediate and middle-level students. Historical nonfiction might also be chosen, some of which is found in picture-book format. The same applies in science: Excellent titles in picture-book format could be used to dovetail units in science. See chapter 9 for sample titles.

We do recommend that you not mix nonfiction titles with fiction for literature circles unless students are clearly aware of the differences between fiction and nonfiction. For example, it would be confusing to mix historical nonfiction books and historical fiction without thoroughly discussing the differences between the in-

formation in both, because even older students may confuse fact and fiction.

You might also find pertinent pieces for nonfiction literature circles using *Cobblestone Magazine* (ages 8–14) and *Appleseeds* (primary grades) focusing on American history and social studies. See *Ranger Rick* (ages 6–12) and *Science World* (grades 7–10) for science materials.

Fiction is very popular for literature circles, so the remainder of the chapter focuses on using that genre for implementing literature circles. However, if you choose nonfiction titles, make sure that students have some basic understandings about the content and about any unfamiliar features of nonfiction (see chapter 9). Using nonfiction for literature circles will be worth the "front loading" or teaching that you do when you see that students are excited to talk about topics they know something about and are enthusiastic about sharing their understandings and discoveries with each other (Kristo & Bamford, 2004).

Tech Note

Available on the CD-ROM that accompanies this book is information about children's magazines and professional resources to use when planning nonfiction for literature circles.

Implementing Literature Circles Using Fiction

Nominate about six to eight quality novels appropriate to the age group you are teaching and the size of the class. These novels can all be related to one theme, such as the environment, different kinds of families, and people from different cultures, or all novels can be by the same author. Others might simply be great novels that you are fairly certain will appeal to the ages and stages of your students. Keep in mind that you will not want more than five students in any group; limiting group size helps ensure active participation.

Here's an example. Let's say your theme is people from different backgrounds and cultures as part of a study of tolerance and acceptance. The books you nominate are *Dragonwings*, by Laurence Yep, *Roll of Thunder, Hear My Cry*, by Mildred Taylor, *The House on Mango Street*, by Sandra Cisneros, *Walk Two Moons*, by Sharon Creech, *The Talking Earth*, by Jean Craighead George, *Flip-Flop Girl*, by Katherine Paterson, *Cousins*, by Virginia Hamilton,

> I tried an experiment with the literature circle groups. In one group I put all the quiet girls. I was amazed and pleased at how much more they participated in the discussion than they usually do!
>
> Candis Penley, grade 3 teacher; personal communication, November, 2001

Meet... Katherine Paterson

Author of *Bridge to Terabithia; The Great Gilly Hopkins; Jip: His Story; The Master Puppeteer; The Sign of the Chyrsanthemum; Park's Quest; Lyddie; Jacob Have I Loved; Flip-Flop Girl; Come Sing, Jimmy Jo; Preacher's Boy; The Same Stuff as Stars;* and many others.

"I was read to from birth. I can't remember when I couldn't read or when I didn't love books. Of course, your whole life and everything it touches make you the writer you are."

Paterson would like to remind teachers that "a book is a private contract between a writer and a reader. Don't try to force another reader to share your contract. And, above all, don't kill the joy."

When asked what other messages she would like to give to young readers, she replied, "I get to write the books. I don't think I'm entitled to more messages. But if they want to write, I suggest they read as widely and as intensively as possible. I do believe that reading makes writers who and what they are. I would love for young readers to know what books can give them that other media cannot. But this, I think, they must learn by experience, not by preaching."

Ms. Paterson is a former teacher and missionary. She lives in Vermont. She admits there is some of her in all her books, but especially in *Come Sing, Jimmy Jo.*

---

and *Walk Two Moons*, by Sharon Creech. Read the books you want to use to be certain they are appropriate for your class, and to have meaningful interactions about those books with students.

Multiple copies of the chosen books are preferable, so every reader has a copy. When resources are limited, two students can share a copy, because much of reading can be done at school. We know one teacher in a poorly funded school who implemented literature circles with only single copies of each novel. Readers passed around the copies during literature circle reading time. Their listening skills improved greatly because listening was crucial to participating in the group.

Tech Note

A text set of novels with a historical theme is available on the CD-ROM that accompanies this book.

Organizing the Class Into Groups

As you consider titles to present, it is important that you have read the books you've chosen. Some teachers begin by doing their reading and planning during a school vacation. Prepare a "book talk" to introduce each book briefly to the class. In a book talk, you interest the students in the book by briefly presenting some highlights, and some aspect you think will attract attention without giving the story away. You might also read a short excerpt from the book.

When you give your book talks, you can invite students who have already read these books to help or to share comments and opinions. Next, have students consider their first, second, and third choices of books they would like to read. Reading ability is not particularly relevant at this juncture.

Listing the books on a chalkboard or white board, ask students each to vote three times. Tally their votes and see which books become the most desired. Select the most popular books, considering your class size and, again, not having more than five persons per group. Erase titles with the fewest votes. Generally, that means about five titles will remain.

Once you have the final list of titles, ask students now to vote only once. Make it clear from the start that not everyone can get his or her first choice every time you do literature circles. Let students know that titles are always available for later use, and also for independent reading.

The way the final groups fall out is critical to the success of literature circles. Look over the emerging groups by what title they indicated as their first choice. Adjust groups that are too large or too small, or that contain

Cover from THE SAME STUFF AS STARS by Katherine Paterson. Jacket illustrations copyright © 2002 by Jim Burke. Reprinted by permission of Clarion Books/Houghton Mifflin Company. All rights reserved.

incompatible students. Consider requesting that some students join a group with their second or third choice of books.

Lorraine Wilson (2002) says:

Of course, in school when a group is to read the same title, not every child in the group gets his first choice each time, but the group titles can be selected by the group rather than the teacher. Some teachers doubt children's capacity to select their literature titles. I think trust is an issue here. Children will not select titles that are too easy for them or from which they will gain nothing, whether it be for enjoyment or further understanding of the ideas. If through our whole-class demonstrations we are introducing a variety of genres and authors, children will not continue reading the same material, choice after choice after choice. (p. 150)

Make certain each group has a strong reader. Because these are heterogeneous groups, the strength of the more proficient readers will assist in the development of others. Having readers of mixed abilities will actually help the groups as they proceed. We hope it will become evident in the sections that follow that the heterogeneous nature of the groups is a strength of the approach.

Determine the schedule for your groups, and set up the first meeting during reading workshop time or at another time of the day. Groups typically meet at the same time. Decide how many times per week your schedule will permit. Before groups are launched, discuss the guidelines, procedures, and rules for how to work as an effective and on-task group with members contributing.

The Role of the Teacher

Literature circles are not traditional reading groups. The role of the teacher is not to run the groups, correct miscues (deviating from the text in some way by omitting a word, repeating, not knowing a word, etc.), or supply challenging words the group is having difficulty decoding. Whereas reading groups are often grouped by ability and are teacher-led sessions, these are not.

Your role as a teacher here is as facilitator. Some groups will thrive early on and need little attention; other groups will find portions of their work in literature circles difficult or challenging. In these cases, teachers sometimes join a group for a little while. Some groups need reminders about skills for being a cooperative group, such as taking turns, being a good listener, and not monopolizing the conversation. Groups that have difficulty with an unfamiliar genre or the language used in the book may benefit from having you join the group for 15–20 minutes to read aloud the opening section to launch the group's work. This may also enable the readers to "get an ear" for the author's style.

If all groups are meeting concurrently and each student is meaningfully engaged, you will have an opportunity to observe all the circles in action. This time also affords you the flexibility to float from group to group as needed. Once groups are going well (and not all groups go well in the beginning), permit yourself the luxury of sitting near enough to a group to hear what is going on without interrupting. Listening to the talk in the group will give you insights as to how groups are functioning. Some teachers use a tape

I have three literature circle groups on different books. I sit on the periphery and pretty much stay out of the discussion unless they have a question about procedures.

Candis Penley, grade 3 teacher; personal communication, November, 2001

recorder to record group conversations so they can listen to them later to learn if groups are on task and how they are discussing the book.

Reading Together

One good way to conduct literature circles is to have a great deal of the reading is done in school and can be done as a shared experience. In some literature circles, students take turns with reading portions of the book as negotiated by the group. For example, some groups choose to take turns by pages or sections. Others take turns by days, having one reader per day. Not everyone needs to read aloud if, for example, a student is extremely reluctant to do so or if members of the group can read the book independently; some students have had negative experiences reading aloud in front of others and feel humiliated when making miscues.

This process occurs daily in some classrooms for up to 45 minutes. Other classes have schedules that permit circles to meet only a few times per week. Meeting several times a week, though, is critical: Too much time between readings is difficult on readers because of a lack of continuity.

To ensure that reading aloud is a positive experience, teachers generally set some guidelines. Let group members know that everyone makes miscues at times—even teachers. Second, we don't recommend forcing anyone to read aloud who is truly uncomfortable with it. Third, be sure members understand that they shouldn't immediately prompt their classmate when that person is reading aloud and stops momentarily to take a breath or to hesitate. Instead, establish guidelines so that they do not prompt, but supply the needed word only when the reader has had some time to think. Readers need chances to go back to the beginning of the sentence or phrase, and to try again to get the needed word, perhaps with the support of context and visual information. Only when all else fails, or when the reader requests help, should group members step in.

Obviously, respect is a key in any group. Because most members will choose to read aloud sometimes, they will want to practice treating others as they wish to be treated. Taking time to discuss and model respect will assist groups in becoming successful at working together.

When reading certain books, group members may struggle with a character's name. All readers do this at times when they encounter a name from a different country or culture; this is a good strug-

We're going to have literature circles for Warton and the King of the Skies. *I am interested in how they will interact in the groups in this round. Because of the many challenging personalities in my class, this time I will design the groups.*

Candis Penley, grade 3 teacher; personal communication, November, 2001

gle for readers to have. Members can suggest and negotiate a common pronunciation for each troubling word.

Reading aloud enables a number of skills to develop as well as an opportunity to nurture reading skills. Struggling readers hear models of good, fluent reading that is often lacking in more traditional reading programs and approaches. Not all reading is done aloud all the time. Sometimes portions are read outside the circle, silently, or with buddies.

Everyone in the group learns new vocabulary as newer words arise that some members of the group know and others do not. Teachers find that difficult words in the text may be known by some member of the circle. This helps with the group's independence from teacher intervention. Students will ask other students what a word means when they might not ask a teacher. Peers helping peers enables everyone to gain more than when students read alone.

Listening skills also develop during literature circles. At times, it is even prudent to remove multiple copies of the book to require students to listen carefully. Listening is a neglected skill in many reading/writing classrooms. Teachers all want students to develop good listening skills, but don't always know of good ways to accomplish that. Literature circles are one effective way to teach students to listen.

Veterans of literature circles have shared with us that the act of reading a book aloud feels comforting and even intimate. The time becomes valued, even precious, to some readers. Sometimes sharing in a group helps selected students respect each other. The members of the group may act differently in the literature circle than in other learning activities, which gives students an opportunity to know their classmates better.

Literature Response Journals

A rich aspect of literature circles is the use of the journals for responding to literature. After groups have read aloud for a period of time, group members retreat to the privacy of their journals for a little writing. Typically this is done immediately following time for reading while thoughts about the reading are fresh.

Although reading may be a wonderful process as a private act, interacting with others about what we read also is a compelling and rewarding process.

Kasten, 1997, p. 99

Literature responses are supposed to be open-ended, with no specific prompts. Expectations can be explained in a few different ways. For example, some teachers tell students to write whatever they are thinking. This may be difficult at first, because many students have come to expect that teachers are seeking "right answers," and here there are none. Students writing in this way will choose to summarize, comment, or make connections as they see fit.

Not all teachers are able to get response journals off the ground in this way. For some, posting a list of generic questions in the room helps students think about how to get started in their journals. Here are three helpful questions based on the work of Borders and Naylor (1993):

☺   What do you notice about today's reading?
☺   How does today's reading make you feel?
☺   What does today's reading remind you of?

Students select a question that makes sense to them that day. Not all questions work all the time; the second question, for example, may not apply if readers have just started a new book and nothing very important has happened yet.

Of course, there are questions that do not always provoke the kind of responses you might expect from readers. For example, a common question is "What is your favorite part of the story?" This question is sometimes difficult to respond to, because readers may not be able to identify only one favorite part. Even some adult readers have trouble answering this question. In fact, in one adult class, we asked teachers to identify one favorite book they had read. We asked, "What was your favorite part?"

This question caused some in the group to giggle. They were frustrated with the question (although it is one that we have asked of students). Teachers maintained that when they loved a book, "all of it" was their favorite part. However, some students will enjoy responding about a favorite part, and others will want to talk about the most exciting, the scariest, or the most memorable parts. Let the story or the content guide your questions.

Getting journaling going can be difficult for a while; students trained in other ways to do school may be reluctant to write their real feelings. Creating a safe place to let them take risks is a challenge for the teacher of literature. Another idea to consider is "fishbowling," which is a process conducted by one group in front of the class. In this case, one group has a literature discussion while the others watch, listen, and learn. This is an effective technique when a group understands the point of journaling. Ask the writer's permission to share these with the class, perhaps anonymously if needed.

One teacher we worked with decided to assess student writing based on effort. Giving his fifth graders a score of 1–10 based on the thoughtfulness and effort in

their responses, regardless of content, proved very successful. Students took journaling more seriously, and as the year progressed, these points were no longer needed to get good responses.

Students who are least comfortable with a text or with the journaling process often begin with summaries of their reading in their journals. This is a good start, but we want our students to do more than that—we want them to show they understand and connect what they read with their personal lives, with other books they've read, and with what they know or have experienced in the world (Keene & Zimmerman, 1997). Minilessons can be an effective way for teachers to model higher levels of response. Before too long, students begin to take some risks by making predictions in their journals, questioning a character's decisions, and even questioning the author. These are deeper kinds of written responses and go far beyond summaries.

As students grow, they also start to make connections in their journals, such as comments that the story reminds them of another story, of a television program, or of something from their own experiences. These too are highly valued responses, because they demonstrate evidence of critical thinking in the sense that students understand the text and can apply their reading elsewhere. More details about literature response are offered in chapter 4.

Discussions

Almasi and Gambrell (1997) say, "Participation in peer discussions improves students' ability to monitor their understanding about text, to verbalize their thoughts, to consider alternative perspectives, and to assume responsibility for their own learning" (p. 152). The types of discussion that are nurtured through this approach are authentic conversations. In literature circles, we are working toward lively, genuine exchanges of ideas and experiences, or what Peterson and Eeds (1990) call *grand conversations*.

Ardith Davis Cole (2003) offers excellent suggestions for beginning literature discussions slowly and thoughtfully. One is to model what she wonders about and questions, not only about what she reads, but about the world around her. Building on the work of Wheatley (2002), Cole says that this develops a spirit of curiosity, which is the "foundation of a good conversation" (p. 22). As part of her read-aloud sessions, Cole models the kinds of things she wonders about as she reads and then has students pair up to share what they wonder about from the book being read aloud. Experiences such as these help to establish the kinds of conversations we want students to have in larger literature discussion groups.

Weslandia is a good choice for inviting stimulating discussions and a variety of responses from a wide range of ages. WESLANDIA Text © 1999 by Paul Fleischman. Illustrations © 1999 by Kevin Hawkes. Reproduced by permission of the publisher Candlewick Press, Inc., Cambridge, Ma.

Wonderful and exciting conversations also begin with response journals. Students can elect to share their entries or talk about what they wrote. Ultimately, we want this sharing of entries to spark a lively discussion—one student chaining on another's interesting connection, reminding someone else of another thing to share, and so on.

Getting these discussions going may be difficult at first, because many students have had few experiences where they are asked to discuss their opinions and experiences freely—especially in school. As mentioned earlier, some teachers have "fishbowled" a group who is discussing more effectively than others in front of the class as a model. This process can show reticent stu-

> *I begin each year modeling the literature circle process with a book I share with the class. My aim is to model grand conversations with books on a regular basis.*
>
> Judy Bouchard, grade 5 teacher; personal communication, November, 2002

dents that they are being encouraged to build a good conversation. Too often, students still think there is one right way to do this, and they are reluctant to take risks. Getting past this point can be frustrating.

One primary teacher, Ms. Farinacci, was having trouble getting her class discussions off the ground. Children in her second grade simply read their journal entry and went on to the next person. Once all four or five students had shared their writing, they announced to their teacher that they were done!

At the point when a group understood the notion of talking with each other and truly sharing ideas, Ms. Farinacci "fishbowled" that group in the center of her room with others looking on. Soon the groups were chattering away more productively. In fact, within a few weeks, they became annoyed with her when it was time to stop, informing her they still had "so much to talk about."

Presentations

Presentations are the "icing on the cake" of literature circles, because they bring together the group lived experience of literature circles and leave all members of the class with a sense of something worthwhile about the book. After reading the book, a group makes a presentation to the class that shows what the book has meant to them. These presentations are generally limited to 10 minutes and shouldn't give away the story.

The content of a presentation is negotiated and typically uses drama, music, technology, arts and crafts, and even dance to communicate something significant about the book. From a teaching perspective, we recommend that groups consider ways all members can be involved, no matter what their contributions may be.

Most groups require several planning times before the day of the presentations. Don't think of this planning time as wasted time. The conversations and the arguments that one can overhear when readers are planning their presentations are rich with the kind of literary talk teachers savor. For example, students might argue about how a character should talk or dress, what parts of the book are better to act out, what happened to whom, which character should be the narrator, and many more wonderful worries. Students are strengthening their comprehension of the plot, characters, and setting while they are rereading sections of the book to find dialogue or check facts.

Some teachers plan a certain day where all groups present and turn it into a small festival, to which other classes are invited. Other teachers schedule various presentations at the end of several consecutive days, at the beginning of reading workshop time, or right after lunch or recess. Some videotape the presentations to share with families on "Back to School Night" or at other events. However they are managed, presentations honor both the books and the readers' transactions with them.

The possibilities for presentation ideas are endless, but here are some examples (many of these are explained more fully in other chapters):

1. Readers select one to three brief key scenes from the book and act them out, generally with some basic props.
2. Readers decide how a movie trailer would look if the book were a movie. Using a school camcorder, they stage and film the enticing clip that will motivate viewers to want to read the book.
3. The group can designate students to play key characters. One student can be the talk show host who interviews the characters as if they were real people.
4. Students prepare a PowerPoint or other computer presentation that can include text, photos, or perhaps audio or video clips along with narration.

Older students create a chapter-by-chapter depiction as they read E. B. White's *Charlotte's Web*.

5. Using mural-type paper, the group draws key scenes from the book and shares a narration about their work with the class.

6. Each reader prepares a poster or picture from the story and creates an accompanying monologue.

7. Group members compose a song, poem, or rap that highlights the book, which they perform for the class. Performances can incorporate instruments, percussion, or background sound from a tape or CD.

8. The group designs and builds a diorama in a cardboard box, or builds a scene from the book using a palette from an old box. Group members explain to the class the significance the scene plays in the book, and why they selected it.

9. Students simulate a popular game show, such as "Who Wants to Be a Millionaire?" or "Jeopardy," using characters from the book and talk/questions related to the story.

10. Students create a newsletter or newspaper based on the book using desktop publishing, with headline stories about major events in the book, editorials by minor characters, and even sports stories, classified ads, advice columns, and comics related to the book. These newspapers are shared and perhaps distributed as part of the presentation.

Providing opportunities for creative students to excel in their contribution to the group at this point is especially important: Often the struggling readers have gifts that are not evident during other aspects of literature circles. Presentations afford an opportunity to tap other intelligences and talents that are underutilized in some classrooms.

Variations on Literature Circles

Although many literature-circle enthusiasts agree that literature circles should be heterogeneous, student led, and used with high-quality literature (Daniels, 2002; Gambrell & Almasi, 1996; Hill, Johnson, & Noe, 1995; Kasten, 1995; McMahon & Raphael, 1997), there are various ways to accomplish the goals of literature circles. Some models, such as the one presented here, allow for a fair amount of teacher variation; other models provide a more structured approach.

Daniels (2002) presents a version that some teachers prefer to use as a starting place for discussions. Each member of the literature circle has a designated role within the group and a guide sheet for that role. Roles include the

> *I have seen the beauty of kids engaged in grand conversations, and it is truly remarkable.*
>
> *Judy Bouchard, grade 5 teacher; personal communication, November, 2002*

connector, the questioner, the literary luminary, and the illustrator, and so on. (p. 103). These roles define what members do following their reading. One advantage of this strategy is that the role sheets document the work and the progress of the group and can often be a part of the assessment and evaluation of the group. One concern is that the role sheets may take the place of lively conversations about the books. Teachers have to work diligently with students to use the role sheets effectively and/or to gradually ease students away from too much dependence on them.

McMahon and Raphael (1997) call their version of literature circles "book clubs," which is an appealing name to students. An entire class may read the same book, sometimes beginning with the teacher reading part of it aloud. Some silent reading, some whole-class discussion, and small-group discussions vary the way the strategy proceeds on a particular day.

Written personal responses are still essentials of this program. Open-ended "think sheets" prompt students to think about literature in various ways. These sheets are not predetermined questions but rather contain a prompt to have students think about a certain topic or theme in the selection and respond to it, and to suggest in writing, in advance of discussion time, something they'd like to bring up for discussion.

Research on Literature Circles

Both university researchers and classroom teachers have researched literature circles to determine whether students become better readers, whether they improve attitudes about reading, and whether the format promotes higher-level thinking skills. Kasten (1995; 1997) studied the talk in literature circles of both children in elementary classrooms and adults in graduate reading classes. The nature of the talk was similar for adult students and children. Both kinds of readers spent time during discussions checking their comprehension of the text; this often took the form of verifying details, keeping characters straight, and reviewing who did what in the plot. Other conversations centered on valuing and judging what was read and were related to character actions, alternatives to character's actions, and possible outcomes. Also see the work by these researchers on literature circles: Almasi, 1995; Eeds and Wells, 1989; Gambrell, 1996; Goatley, Brock, and Raphael, 1995; Goatley and Raphael, 1992; Hill, Noe, and King, 2003.

Literature Circles and Special Needs Learners

Things were extremely busy in the classroom as Eddy, Jesse, and Hank were placing chairs, getting a video cam ready, and directing people into their places. Jesse had been designated by his classmates as the talk show host. Eddy was going to play Peter Hatcher from Judy Blume's *Tales of a Fourth Grade Nothing.* Hank would be the baby, "Fudge," in the story.

One of their three teachers in this classroom (designated for behaviorally disordered children) would be doing the filming. Lights, camera, action! Jesse was shy at first, but he had prepared a long list of detailed questions to ask his guests, the characters from the popular Blume novel. He went through his slightly rehearsed part, quizzing his guests about the story, their motives, and their opinions. He took his role as talk show host seriously. All the while Hank, in one of the chairs on the "set" of the show, kept falling out of his chair. The "show" ran almost an hour with the students in character before a camera.

Afterward, the teacher asked Hank why he kept falling out of his chair. He responded that he'd thought a lot about the character "Fudge" in the story and was quite certain that it is the way "Fudge" would have behaved.

None of these special needs boys liked reading before they began reading this book. Now they couldn't wait to start the sequel, *Superfudge.* This was the first time the group had done literature circles.

This anecdote is an authentic scene from a special education classroom where the 12 students were labeled as severely behaviorally disturbed. These particular children came from all over the district and were unable to function at all in typical classrooms. Until the teachers started literature circles using the novel by Judy Blume, they had made no attempt to have the students work together, because the students' volatile behaviors often caused trouble when they were grouped. However, the act of being in this group with a book they enjoyed was sufficiently motivating for the students to control their behavior in order to participate.

In our collective experiences, we have seen literature circles implemented in middle school and secondary special education classes with a variety of learner needs. Adept teachers knowing the strengths and needs of their students were able to successfully implement literature circles. In some cases, teachers had to remain present, although in the background, during student meeting times. Another teacher structured the time with specific limits for each part of the strategy for students unable to regulate their own groups.

We also have seen severely struggling readers in a regular classroom participate fully in literature circles. These students struggled but were intelligent children. A fifth grader, for example, who was not yet able to independently read books read by most first graders still participated fully while his group read Gary Paulsen's *Hatchet.* This youngster could not read *Hatchet* on his own, but he could listen well and did so throughout the process. He could use a journal to record his thoughts in words and pictures. Once discussion time began, he didn't look any different from any other learner. In fact, he had much to contribute with a personal love of nature and experience with family camping.

Nearly all special education students and struggling readers can become participants in literature circles. With appropriate adaptations, increased directions, and supervision, most can be successful and enjoy the fruits of reading high-quality literature and contributing to literary conversations. For these types of learners, making the effort to adapt literature circles is crucial to letting them try. Rarely do struggling learners get to experience learning strategies that appeal to their age and their intellect, rather than simply their reading level. It's important to remember that struggling readers and even many special education students need high-quality literature and chances to think critically. They are not necessarily less intelligent; they are simply different in some way.

Literature Circles in Primary Grades

A kindergarten teacher taught us how to adapt literature circles for 5- to 7-year-olds. She was certain her students could interact with quality literature and make good conversation about texts—even if they could not all read the books yet. Consequently, she would do book talks at the beginning of the week, and her students would sign up for a group based on a title of choice (or second or third choice). The teacher arranged for the students to have the book read to them at least twice during the week. Sometimes the books were read aloud to the entire class. At other times, older students from other classes or occasionally volunteers would read the stories to the children.

Tech Note

A text set of picture books for primary-grade literature circles is available on the CD-ROM that accompanies this book.

Literature response journals look somewhat different at the kindergarten level. Kindergarten students are in varying stages of early literacy: Some can write sentences, others can write only words, and some communicate best in pictures. Students respond in their own way, often with a combination of words and pictures. This teacher's students completed their journals before Friday, when discussion groups were scheduled to meet.

The kindergartners were in no way disadvantaged during discussions because they were younger and not yet independent readers. They had lots to say. In fact, they were not shy about offering opinions, having had less time to learn the limits of school talk. They had "grand conversations."

Later we witnessed a first-grade group that had been brought to a professional conference to demonstrate their literature circle skills before other teachers. They launched right into a discussion in front of strangers, complete with making judgments about the characters, talking about the plot, and noting connections to other books they read. It was exciting to see how literature circles can be adapted for nearly all classroom grades and settings.

Cultural Considerations

When classrooms have students from diverse cultures, teachers may need to consider student background in planning for literature circles. First of all, students react and respond to literature based on their cultural background. Imagine how differently a Caucasian girl and a Native American girl react to a book involving westward expansion, or how a Jewish child might react to books on the Holocaust. The content of books can be highly personal to some cultures, and sometimes even offensive. Teachers of children from diverse cultures may want to consult an authority on literature selections for the culture, including source books and websites.

Tech Note

See the CD-ROM that accompanies this book for help in finding quality titles on Native American culture.

Another consideration in grouping would be whether to have mixed-gender groups. Some teachers with immigrant students from Middle Eastern countries have found that girls don't speak up in the presence of boys from the same culture. In such cases, having some all-girl groups might be appropriate.

Historical fiction will present many challenges to students from foreign countries, as well as some from certain subcultures within the United States. Different cultural groups view history differently, such as Native American children whose families have lived in the area of the U.S. since before there was a United States. Native Hawaiian children may also view the role of Hawaii in American history from a different perspective. Areas of Alaska identify more strongly with Russian history than with American history (Oleska, 1994).

What is important to consider here is that students may have different perspectives on history and may have little or no background in history that other students take for granted. Having little background before reading a book influences how someone comprehends it. Teachers can help provide scaffolding and support to readers by discussing the targeted historical era and sharing nonfiction books and other materials about the events or people before tackling a novel.

Assessing Literature Circles

Literature circles can be assessed in numerous ways. Some teachers have students fill out self-assessment sheets about their role in the group, and about how classmates contributed. These sheets enable teachers to credit groups for their process of conducting the strategy and working together cooperatively. Figure 13.1 shows a sample self-assessment sheet.

Other teachers use response journals for evaluation. Students might receive points for their efforts, as described earlier. Journal responses give clues to teachers about students' developing responses to literature (see chapter 4 on response for more details).

As with most journaling, it is counterproductive to assign letter grades to response journals based on content, mechanics, or punctuation. These journals are first-draft writing; first drafts are never intended for a wide audience, and in the real world of writing are not evaluated. First-draft writing isn't supposed to be perfect. Response journals need to be safe places where students take risks sharing ideas and connections.

A form to evaluate student presentations could include the following criteria: how well members cooperated with each other, how prepared the group was (e.g., Did they rehearse?), to what extent the group stayed within time guidelines, and whether they involved all group members. Teachers might require each group to use technology in some way, or to incorporate something else relevant to classroom goals in their work. Figure 13.2 gives examples of items to evaluate in literature circle presentations that can be adapted to suit different classroom goals.

Figure 13.1
Student Self-Assessment Form
for Literature Circles

My name is _____ Today's date _____

The book we finished is _____

The author is _____

The other people in my circle are:

_____   _____

_____   _____

Here's what I think about my contribution to my circle:

_____

_____

Next time, I think I should do better on:

_____

_____

Someone in my group I would like to compliment is _____

because _____

_____

_____

I have concerns about this in our group:

_____

_____

Answer either a or b below.

a. I like working in literature circles because _____

    _____

b. I don't enjoy working in literature circles because _____

    _____

The teacher could help me do my best work in literature circles by _____

_____

Figure 13.2
Sample Items for
Evaluating
Literature Circle
Presentations

☼ The presenters shared the title and the author of the book.

☼ The group presentation ran smoothly and showed good planning and effort.

☼ Each presenter was given a turn to share with the class what he or she had done and/or his or her reactions to the book.

☼ The presenters and their project showed effort and understanding of the book.

☼ The presenters shared insights about the book.

☼ The presenters were able to field questions about the book from the audience.

☼ The presenters shared just enough about the book to whet the appetite of others to want to read it.

Practices in assessment and evaluation for reporting student progress vary greatly. Where specific grades are required, parts of literature circles can be evaluated as needed. Teachers will need to adapt ways of evaluating and assessing to meet local demands and requirements. What we assess in this practice, as with any others, should reflect what we value in our children's education.

those we teach. Even our youngest and least proficient readers can participate. Literature circles engage readers in deep and meaningful ways with high-quality trade books. Peer-led groups are inclined toward deeper and more personally relevant discussions than typically happen in more traditional reading and literature instruction. The process and outcomes of literature circles are consistent with effective practices in literacy.

Summary

Literature circles are an important part of the living literature classroom, no matter what the ages and abilities of

Action Research for Teachers

The Implementation of Literature Circles in the Middle School Classroom

Dana McCluggage-Perkins
Sixth Grade, Urban, Barberton, Ohio

Dana implemented literature circles in her sixth-grade, urban middle school class. She wanted to investigate whether she would uncover evidence of higher-level thinking skills and if her students were progressing toward state proficiency objectives using this approach. Dana collected data through student surveys and student journals, and through analyzing their discussions in their literature circles. She also kept a researcher's log.

Dana learned that literature circles appeal to the emotional needs of middle school students and offer many benefits to a reading program. She found that students enjoyed reading and talking

about what they read and were enthusiastic about their learning. She also found that the process of doing literature circles addressed various levels of learning as well as the state proficiency objectives. Most of all, Dana found that literature circles allowed students to take ownership of and responsibility for their learning. Students began to acknowledge that people have different opinions, ideas, and feelings; they valued the choice and voice literature circles gave them in the classroom. She also found evidence of higher levels of thinking in her analysis of the students' journals and discussions. All in all, 80% of students rated their literature circle experiences very highly.

Students as Authors:
Literature and the Writing Process

"If you like to write, chances are it's because you love reading. You've realized that good writing is much more than avoiding mistakes in spelling, sentence construction, punctuation, and so on. Good writing engages the reader's intelligence and imagination." (Will Hobbs, author; personal communication, September, 1999)

I n this chapter, we discuss how the writing process is part of the living literature classroom and present the basics of organizing a writer's workshop. Specifically, we discuss the following questions:

- ☀ What are the connections between reading and writing?

- ☀ What is the writing process?

- ☀ Why do teachers need to model the writing process?

- ☀ What does a writing workshop look like? How do teachers manage and assess writing?

- ☀ How do teachers use children's books to teach writing?

- ☀ How does classroom publishing work, and how do teachers organize young author's conferences?

Learning to Write by Reading

Throughout this book, the authors and illustrators who share their views have made an important point again and again: We all learn to write through reading. First of all, we fall in love with the art of writing when we hear the language of books from those who read aloud to us and then read the books we love on our own. We learned what makes a good story and how good language sounds. And we found in these books the models we emulate in our own writing. Our authors made some other points about writing, too. For example, they taught us that writing is often hard work—with lots of drafts and much revision. Writing takes years of practice, just as any craft or art does, such as playing a musical instrument or becoming a good swimmer or artist.

While we are teaching children to write and are studying the craft of writing through the children's books we share, we also need to remember to communicate that writing, like all life skills, is a continuous learning process, a lifelong one. As children's author Will Hobbs recounts at the be-

ginning of this chapter, writing is more than the act of getting sentences grammatically correct or even getting all the words spelled correctly. Rather, it is getting our story, our poem, or our information in the best form so that it says what we want to say effectively.

Teachers as Writing Models

Because the craft of writing is a lifelong learning process, even the best-planned classroom writing program will die a certain death if the teacher doesn't see him- or herself as a writer. If we wish to teach students to write but they never see us practicing the craft ourselves, then the need for this thing we call writing is less believable and less credible. If we have not struggled with our own writing or experienced success and all the hard work it involves, then we cannot understand what happens to our students.

This is quite a challenge. Many educators today did not have the benefit of teachers who were experienced in teaching writing. Fortunately, there is help for teachers who are apprehensive about teaching writing. There are many professional resources available, and most colleges and universities offer courses in the teaching of writing.

Every minute you spend reading is a minute spent learning to write. And it's painless. As you read, you absorb the sounds and rhythms of words, the accents and flow of language.

Alice Schertle, author/poet; personal communication, September, 1999

Writers hard at work.

One such opportunity is the National Writing Project. Based in California, the writing project now has sites all over the country. Through the NWP website, teachers can locate sources for such a summer writing experience. In this case, teachers are interviewed as part of the application process. Teachers who are writing project alums take credit for helping to shape the future of writing instruction in the schools where they teach. By whatever means, all teachers need support to know how to teach and manage a writing program.

The Writing Process in the Living Literature Classroom

The writing process centers on what students think and do as they write. The five aspects of the writing process are prewriting, drafting, revising, editing, and publishing; see Figure 14.1 for a list of the key features of each. It's important to note that the labeled and numbered stages are a convenient way to describe the process. Writers don't necessarily move through the stages in order; rather, the process of writing involves recurring cycles (Tompkins, 2003).

Developing a comprehensive and effective writing program is an important part of any living literature classroom. Melding the writing program with children's books is an important part of any literature-rich classroom; after all, good children's literature gives us the best models for fiction, nonfiction, poetry, picture books, and even specialized books such as alphabet books. As you have heard from the voices of authors and illustrators, we learn to write by reading (Wood, 1999). In our literature collections are the best possible tools for our writing programs as well.

Figure 14.1
Key Features of the Writing Process

Prewriting
- ☼ Write on topics based on personal choice.
- ☼ Engage in rehearsal activities before writing.
- ☼ Identify the audience for the writing.
- ☼ Identify the function of the writing activity.
- ☼ Choose an appropriate form for the writing based on audience and function.

Drafting
- ☼ Write a rough draft.
- ☼ Emphasize content rather than mechanics.

Revising
- ☼ Reread the writing.
- ☼ Share writing in writing groups.
- ☼ Participate constructively in discussions about classmates' writing.
- ☼ Make changes in the composition to reflect the reactions and comments of both teacher and classmates.
- ☼ Between the first and final drafts, sometimes make substantive rather than minor changes.

Editing
- ☼ Proofread the composition.
- ☼ Help proofread classmates' compositions.
- ☼ Identify and correct mechanical errors.
- ☼ Meet with the teacher for a final editing.

Publishing
- ☼ Publish writing in an appropriate form.
- ☼ Share the finished writing with an appropriate audience.

Source: Adapted from Tompkins, 2003, p. 48.

The Writer's Workshop in the Living Literature Classroom

The term *writer's workshop* was coined by Maine teacher Nancie Atwell (1987) to reflect the busy and engaging nature of a comprehensive writing curriculum. A writer's workshop has several components: self-selected writing, minilessons, conferences, group sharing, and editing conferences.

Self-Selected Writing

Typically, each student in a classroom has a writing file or folder kept somewhere in the room, which contains multiple pieces of writing in various stages of the writing process. Or students can keep a writer's notebook. Writer Ralph Fletcher (1996) says, "A writer's notebook gives you a place to live like a writer, not just in school during writing time, but wherever you are, at any time of day" (p. 3). Start-

ing with self-selected topics is important: Students learn best when they write on topics and themes they care about. This teaches developing writers that they have a voice, that writing comes from their own ideas, and that topics for writing are not something that the teacher "gives" them. Of course, there are times when writing prompts are appropriate or when a specific topic or assignment is given. In writer's workshop, however, students learn to find topics that they care about and become invested in writing about.

One of the best ways to help students think about topics and stories to write is through children's literature. Many authors write from their own experiences; knowing this can help students think about potential topics, as well. As a result, students may try their hand at writing personal narratives, a good genre for beginning writers. Personal narrative is described in more detail later in this chapter.

> *Children should know that authors get discouraged, too, that sometimes we lose our confidence. That we get back manuscripts with red squiggles, bristling with post-its in the margins asking questions.*
>
> Ann Turner, author; personal communication, September, 1999

> *When I'm starting a new story, it takes a lot of faith. If you just keep working, you'll reach a point when the story starts coming to life. That's what the writer lives for!*
>
> Will Hobbs, author; personal communication, September, 1999

Meet... Will Hobbs

Author of *Bearstone; Beardance; Change in Latitudes; Downriver; The Big Wander; Kokopelli's Flute; Beardream; River Thunder; Far North; Ghost Canoe; The Maze; Howling Hill; Jason's Gold;* and others.

"My life and my writing are both intertwined with wilderness. My feelings for the wild grew from my 3rd, 4th, and 5th grade years in Alaska. When we moved to California, I spent a lot of time exploring the hills and hiking the Sierras. I've been backpacking and running rivers ever since, mostly in the Four Corners states close to my home in Durango, Colorado.

I was a reading and English teacher for seventeen years, mostly at the 7th grade level in Durango. I'd always wanted to write, simply because I loved reading, and finally got serious about it. Being a teacher, it was a natural fit for me to write for kids. It was just as natural for me to have the stories take place in wilderness settings. Whether I'm writing realistic fiction, a mystery, fantasy, or historical adventures, my books to date have been set in wild places I love.

I grew up in a home with books, but it was a teacher reading aloud at school who set the hook for good. After that I became an avid independent reader and found my own way to the library. The books I enjoyed are still a part of me. Though fiction is my first love, I read lots of nonfiction, especially when it comes to researching my novels. I continue to be interested in the interaction of people and place."

Mr. Hobbs was born in Pittsburgh, Pennsylvania, but lives in Durango, Colorado.

Minilessons

Another aspect of the writer's workshop is the "minilesson." These focused skill-building opportunities, proposed by Lucy Calkins (1986), are short lessons for the whole class, a small group of students, or even an individual writer on some aspect of writing.

What to teach in minilessons depends on the current needs of the writers in the classroom. Usually the lessons fall into one of several categories: skills and strategies, the craft of writing, and management aspects of the writer's workshop (Hindley, 1996). For example, if a teacher notices that several students are attempting to

Tech Note
See the CD-ROM that accompanies this book to learn what author Ann Turner says about "how stories choose her," what Pat Hutchins says influences her writing, and what motivates author William Sleator to write.

include dialogue in their writing, a 10-minute minilesson about using dialogue and quotation marks can be planned. Or if several writers are using too many run-on sentences, a minilesson on avoiding run-on sentences might be well timed. Other minilessons might involve how to use a writer's notebook, what students can do to get ready for an editing conference, strategies they can use if they can't come up with a topic, and how to use effective descriptions in their writing.

Teachers often use children's literature as the tool for teaching a minilesson. Using literature as a model, one can teach just about all the literary and writing techniques that need to be addressed. Ideas are presented throughout this chapter for how to do that effectively.

Tech Note
Good advice for writers from author Will Hobbs is available on the CD-ROM that accompanies this book.

Conferences About Content

For any writer, the most important aspect of writing is the content. Putting thoughts on paper and getting the language the way the writer wants it are the goals of the writing conference.

Writing conferences can be either planned or serendipitous. Generally, the student writer begins by reading aloud the piece in question. This serves two purposes: The author hears the sound of the language he or she has written,

and the teacher or older peer hears what has been written so far.

Writing conferences usually are short, and they focus on one logical aspect of the writer's need. However, after listening to the piece, teachers should respond first with a positive and specific comment about the student's writing. Building on student strengths is important for developing writers. These comments should be sincere and can be kept simple, such as saying how effective the beginning of the piece is, pointing out a vivid phrase, responding to something humorous by laughing, or pointing out what is funny.

Students will respond well to comments that are specific about their writing. Such comments demonstrate a genuine interest on the teacher's part, and they show the teacher was listening; "I think your setting is so scary," "What a great opening line," and "You have left me in suspense" are all comments that encourage writers to continue. Very general praise such as "It's good" or "I like it" will quickly stagnate young writers, because these comments sound like those you might say to anyone.

The next part of these short conferences is raising questions with the writer. Again, these need to be specific to the piece: "Is this character you call your friend a girl or a boy?" "What does this house that you mention look like?" "Where does this story take place?" "What are you going to write next?" Raising questions helps writers understand how an audience perceives their writing and what might not be well understood. Answering these questions will help a writer think about possibilities for revision.

> *I tell children, when I go and talk in classrooms, that each one of them has a story to tell. Each one has experienced change, loss, joy, growth, and moments of inspiration.*
>
> *Ann Turner, author; personal communication, September, 1999*

Group Sharing—Author's Chair

One of us visited a multiage primary classroom one day when 6-year-old Jesse, a Hispanic bilingual migrant child, came up with a simple booklet clutched to his chest. "Can I read you my story?" He had already read this story to his teacher, a student teacher, the janitor, the principal, the computer teacher, the school nurse, and anyone else willing to stand still and listen. Jesse was still an emergent reader, but he had dictated a story about elephants to his teacher, after they had read books about elephants and studied them. His little book, only six pages long, was bound with staples and a construction-paper cover which he had illustrated. All day long, he carried his book to his chest. He took it to lunch, out to recess, to physical education, and when he went to see his Title I teacher.

A few weeks later, near the end of the school year, Jesse's teacher held a ceremony: She had made each child a medal hanging on colorful ribbon, and she invited parents to the event. She had the school principal award the medals. Each child got one, no matter where he or she was in writing development. The medal said "The Club of Writers." Every child was admitted to the club, reminiscent of writer Frank Smith's notion of the importance of every child being a member of the literacy club (Smith, 1988).

Classmates are a good source of feedback for developing writers. Consequently, group sharing is an important part of the writer's workshop. Some teachers call this sharing time "Author's Chair," and even have a specially designated chair in the room where student authors sit to share their writing. One writer with a draft or a finished piece volunteers to read his or her work aloud, and the rest of the class gathers nearby to listen.

The class is taught ways to respond appropriately, starting with what they liked about the person's writing. The young author seated in the special chair calls on those with their hands up, which students enjoy very much. Then they also call on those who have a question they'd like to pose to the writer. Just as in conferences with the teacher, these questions can motivate the writer to make revisions. Classmates may also suggest ideas for further writing. Often the child in the author's chair selects the next person to sit in this designated chair of honor.

In a typical classroom with a well-developed writer's workshop, an author's chair with group sharing occurs a few times a week, usually for 10–20 minutes as schedules permit. Obviously, the teacher decides how the procedure runs, tailoring it to particular class needs.

Editing Conferences

The writing conferences between teachers and students described earlier focus on issues such as spelling or punctuation. Content issues should all be resolved as much as needed before editing conferences take place. Generally, the teacher runs editing conferences, but sometimes in multiage classrooms or in situations where some students have become good editors, classmates provide some of the conferencing.

Grade 3 Maine teacher Jody Workman holds a group writing conference.

One teacher we know designates committees in his fifth-grade class to handle much of the editing concerns. For example, he organizes spelling and punctuation committees. Nearly completed pieces of writing that are scheduled for publication can be routed through the needed committees. These committee members become responsible for signing off that the pieces have been checked and edited before being returned to the author. These committees become very adept at editing. Eventually, the teacher rearranges the committee members to help students become versatile and well practiced in many areas of editing.

Managing the Writing Classroom

All practicing teachers will tell you that managing the reading and writing classroom presents challenges. Working out a suitable system takes time but is extremely important to the success of the program and especially for assessment purposes (Fletcher & Portalupi, 2001; Wood & Laminack, 2001).

First of all, most writing workshop classrooms store student writing in individual file folders of some sort. Folders with pockets help keep materials secure. Storing the folders in a box, crate, or drawer easily accessible to all students is generally preferable to having students keep them in their desks, cubbies, or lockers where they can easily become lost. These folders hold multiple drafts of ongoing writing. They also may store samples of writing done

Students sometimes draw in their writer's notebooks as a prewriting strategy.

earlier in the school year, so that there is always an array of writing from each student.

Alternatively, many teachers have children use writer's notebooks, as previously mentioned. Notebooks maintain a continuity and organization for the drafts. Most teachers advise not sending pieces home until the end of the year (or keeping photocopies). When writing from an entire year is available, teachers gain a developmental perspective on the student writers' changes over the year.

Teachers need management strategies for keeping track of writers' progress. Some teachers develop a three-ring notebook with a divider for each student. Designing a half-page form that expedites note taking a teacher might wish to do after conferencing with each student. For example, a place on the form might be for recording the title of the piece or the genre of writing, with space after to write the essence of what was discussed at the writing conference, such as content ideas, suggestions for revising, the writer's comments about the piece, and potential minilessons, such as using commas, ways to help the writer with leads, or using more descriptive writing.

Getting in the habit of taking brief notes like this is helpful in planning future minilessons with individuals, small groups, or the whole class. Once the teacher notices that several students struggle with how to end their stories, for example, he or she might plan a minilesson on this aspect. These same notes inform teachers about how to describe to parents or caregivers what children are doing in their writing, and are helpful for completing report cards or progress reports.

Student self-assessment is another important part of managing the writing classroom. After modeling, teachers ask students to talk about their own goals for writing in general or for a particular piece that they're working on. These comments, too, can be recorded in the teacher's notebook. Even first graders, when given encouragement, can describe what they need to do with their own writing. The teacher can model age-appropriate goal statements, such as wanting to write a poem or remembering to start each sentence with a capital letter. Self-assessment opportunities need to be regularly scheduled into workshop time.

One teacher we know writes notes on large index cards for each student in the class; these are stored in a card file where they are easy to retrieve. Another teacher makes notes on sticky labels, which she always has available on a clipboard. At the end of the day or week, she places these labels on a file folder prepared for each student in the class. Lots of address-size sticky labels can fit on one file folder.

Of course, it is challenging to meet with students as often as teachers might like to. If you remember that writing conferences are extremely brief, making the most of them with a good management system helps things run more smoothly. See ideas for kinds of conference in Tompkins, *Teaching Writing: Balancing Process and Product* (2004), and Anderson, *How's It Going? A Practical Guide to Conferring With Student Writers* (2000), among others.

Atwell (1998) mentions that she learns where students are in their writing by having a large classroom meeting. Class members prepare to state where they are in their writing and whether they need a conference, while she takes notes (taking notes about where students are in their writing is often called status-of-the-class record keeping [Atwell, 1998]). This format enables her to realize all at once how students are doing with assignments or with their own writing, and how much time will be needed to meet any desired deadlines (such as a school publication or a back-to-school night display).

Figure 14.2 lists some writing do's and don'ts to guide teachers toward effective practices in writer's workshop.

Assessing and Evaluating Writing

Assessing implies that someone (teacher, student writer) is discerning the strengths and needs of the writer or of a piece of writing. Conversely, evaluating means making a judgment about the writing, perhaps for a progress report.

Writing Do's	Writing Don'ts
☼ Enable students to find personally meaningful topics.	☼ Have narrow, restricted topics.
☼ Nurture conferences between teacher and student and among students.	☼ Use red pens to correct pieces or write vague comments on papers. Students don't attend to or benefit from these.
☼ Recognize that some pieces and writers need more time than do others.	☼ Constrain writing with very limited time expectations.
☼ Provide ample paper.	☼ Constrain writing with a limited amount of space.
☼ Demonstrate to students that sometimes writers abandon pieces they do not like; some writing can be for practice and needs no evaluation.	☼ Think every piece of writing needs to be completed or evaluated.
☼ Give one or two constructive suggestions, depending on the ability of the writer.	☼ Offer too many ideas for revising writing. Too much may overwhelm the writer.
☼ Make suggestions but retain the writer as the owner of his or her own piece.	☼ Take over revisions of a child's work. Too much interference takes away writer ownership.
☼ Nurture a peer-helping climate where students can help each other, where possible, or wait until later to edit for spelling and punctuation.	☼ Require students to look up words in a dictionary or word bank during drafting. This gets in the way of the process and takes too much writing time.
☼ Develop multiple ways to share, display, and publish student writing.	☼ Be the only audience for student writing.
☼ Make use of integrating language arts, such as teaching spelling and grammar in the context of the writing process.	☼ Separate the teaching of writing, reading, and spelling.

Figure 14.2   Writing Do's and Don'ts

	Plot/Events	Characterization	Setting	Holistic Quality
1.	Events disorganized, out of sequence. No coherence among events. Events don't logically contribute to the message overall. Some events may even be difficult to understand separately.	Character/s inappropriate to the piece. Character/s may be mentioned, but the piece is written from the vantage point of writer as character without separation of self from character/s. No distinction between major and minor character/s.	It is not clear where the action takes place nor does it seem in any way to interact with what happens.	Piece is not semantically integrated; there is little intra-sentence coherence and almost no intersentence coherence. The piece is more a collection of sentences, clauses and/or phrases than a coherent piece of discourse. No overall purpose or audience is evident.
2.	Some events logically contribute to or are out of sequence. Events are not explained fully. Usually one sentence suffices. It is apparent that the writer is constructing the events as she/he goes along without thought of the whole. There are few cohesive ties, and some are ambiguous.	Character/s appropriate but somewhat ambiguous. Emphasis is more on plot than character. It is usually clear what happens but not necessarily to whom or by whom. Cohesive problems occur that add to the ambiguity, yet there is an attempt to tell about someone other than the writer/self.	Setting is mentioned. It is clear where the action happens, but it is given no real role in the action. There is almost no description provided, usually a label.	There is evidence that the writer is attempting to order events, introduce and/or label character/s, and/or to direct a message of some kind for a purpose. There is rudimentary evidence of a conflict and some type of resolution or an indication of related events occurring across a time frame. Setting may be identified but it will not be developed.
3.	Most events contribute logically to the whole and are sequenced appropriately. Story flows without major interruptions from inappropriate or irrelevant information, yet some events have little detail. Often whole events are described with one sentence.	Character/s appropriate and clearly identified. There is an attempt here to provide information about how the character/s felt as well as what she/he thought and did. There may be a distinction between major and minor characters.	Where the action takes place contributes to the piece as a whole. The writer makes an attempt to describe setting and its effect on the action and/or the character/s in the piece, but setting is not fully developed.	The piece has a beginning, a middle, and an end with related events and/or character/s operating in some time frame. Setting is revealed where appropriate and its effect on character/s noted. Some details of the events are provided with appropriate mood and tone. A sense of coherence is evident, which indicates that the whole is greater than the sum of the parts.
4.	Events contribute logically and sequentially to an ordered whole. It is apparent that the writer has constructed each event to fit systematically within the whole and has provided detailed relevant information about each event. The writer controls and directs the events rather than merely reporting them. The writer demonstrates many varied uses of cohesive ties.	All characters are well defined and elaborated. The writer demonstrates control of character development and distinguishes clearly between characters. Some are definitely major and some minor.	The writer describes setting fully and also clearly indicates what effect it has on the character/s and events.	The piece is obviously the result of an integration of purpose, audience, voice, and controlled syntax. The events flow logically from one to another with purpose and/or message clearly evidenced. Character/s and/or ideas are well developed, and all conflicts are resolved. There is a sense of the writer in control of the tools for conveying a purpose to an audience of some kind.

Figure 14.3 Semantic Analysis of Children's Writing—Narrative
From Goodman & Wilde, 1992.

Self-Assessment

First of all, many researchers and theorists believe that all assessment should include an element of self-assessment. In addition to students assessing their writing for their own purposes, they need to be involved with self-assessment and self-evaluation as part of the reporting system and to learn how to describe their progress to their families. Articulating what they believe was done well and identifying what needs improvement are important ways for developing writers to take responsibility for their own learning.

One way to help students do this is to ask them to rank order their work for a period of time, from the piece they perceive as best to the one they consider needs the most work; students also are expected to defend their ratings with insights about their work. Another useful self-assessment strategy is for students to rank order their work according to how they believe their teacher would do it and why.

Rubrics

Probably the most popular way teachers assess and evaluate student writing is by creating a rubric that is relevant to the assignment or type of writing. Rubrics generally have four to five levels that discern the features sought in the writing. Rubrics can focus on content issues, as well as other aspects of the writing such as spelling and word usage. Figure 14.3 describes a rubric used for assessing the developing semantic elements of a story, covering plot, characters, setting, and a holistic score. This rubric can be utilized with all four categories, which would yield more assessment information, or with just the holistic category, which might be a grade on the final piece. This rubric (useful for all levels) was first used in an Arizona writing study (Goodman & Wilde, 1992) on the Tohono Indian Reservation (1981–1983).

Tech Note
A book list to support teachers in their teaching of writing, including assessment and evaluation, can be found on the Companion Website.

Traits

A powerful way to look at teaching and assessing writing is the 6 + 1 traits of writing model (Culham, 2003). The traits are: ideas, organization, voice, word choice, sentence fluency, conventions, and presentation. These traits represent the characteristics of good writing. Learning about them gives teachers a common vocabulary for describing qualities of writing and for assessing writing.

Using Books to Teach Writing

In this section, we describe specific ways to use children's literature not only to support the comprehensive writing program, but to be at the very heart of a workshop. After all, we've been saying that to learn to write, we need to read.

Teaching About Genres

Throughout this book, you have learned to identify literary genres, such as contemporary fiction, poetry, and traditional literature. We also have explored how picture books cut across all genres—nonfiction, fiction, fantasy, biography, and poetry. It makes good sense, then, to share examples of fine children's books to teach about writing different genres and how to use literary devices.

Personal Narrative

In a personal narrative, we write about the people and events that we care about and those things that have shaped our personalities. Students in K–8 classrooms are often tested on their ability to write personal narrative; we also suggested earlier that personal narrative is a good way to get writer's workshop off the ground.

Personal narrative is mostly true writing that is developed around a person, event, or memory. Something about the person, event, or memory is critical or personally significant, or perhaps it represents a turning point or a lesson in our lives. Sometimes we fictionalize aspects of it to make the story more readable, such as compressing the time in which the event happened, or adding our current insights into the event.

One popular example of a personal narrative is Tomie dePaola's *Nana Upstairs & Nana Downstairs.* Clearly, this story is an actual family memory for Tomie, and what happens in the story is accurate. Another example is Patricia Polacco's *Thank You, Mr. Falker,* a memory of Patricia's struggles with reading and school (a favorite with reading teachers!). The dust jacket flap of *Aunt Flossie's Hats (and Crab Cakes Later),* by Elizabeth Howard, explains that the inspiration for the story was the author's real Aunt Flossie from Baltimore.

Personal narratives demonstrate that great stories often are real ones from our own lives, and sometimes the events are fairly ordinary. Such books can help students think about their own personal stories. Reading these aloud to students, followed by discussion of "What did this story make you think about?" can motivate writers to discover their own stories. Sharing books that are personal narratives is a terrific way to generate writing topics. The text set on page 326 lists personal narrative titles to consider as examples.

Text Set   Children's Books Using a Personal Narrative Style

Caines, Jeannette. (1982). *Just Us Women* (Pat Cummings, Illus.). New York: Harper & Row.

Chocolate, Debbi. (1998). *The Piano Man* (Eric Velasquez, Illus.). New York: Walker.

dePaola, Tomie. (1974). *Watch Out for the Chicken Feet in Your Soup*. Englewood Cliffs, NJ: Prentice Hall.

dePaola, Tomie. (1979). *Oliver Button Is a Sissy*. New York: Harcourt Brace.

dePaola, Tomie. (1981). *Now One Foot, Now the Other*. New York: Putnam.

dePaola, Tomie. (1993). *Tom*. New York: Putnam.

dePaola, Tomie. (1997a). *Nana Upstairs & Nana Downstairs*. New York: Putnam.

dePaola, Tomie. (1997b). *The Art Lesson*. New York: Putnam.

Dragonwagon, Crescent. (1984). *Jemima Remembers* (Troy Howell, Illus.). New York: Macmillan.

Hendershot, Judith. (1987). *In Coal Country* (Thomas B. Allen, Illus.). New York: Knopf.

Howard, Elizabeth Fitzgerald. (2001). *Aunt Flossie's Hats (and Crab Cakes Later)* (James Ransome, Illus.). New York: Clarion.

Polacco, Patricia. (1988). *Rechenka's Eggs*. New York: Philomel.

Polacco, Patricia. (1992). *Chicken Sunday*. New York: Philomel.

Polacco, Patricia. (1998). *Thank You, Mr. Falker*. New York: Philomel.

Rylant, Cynthia. (1982). *When I Was Young in the Mountains* (Diane Goode, Illus.). New York: Dutton.

Williams, Vera B. (1982). *A Chair for My Mother*. New York: Greenwillow.

Brainstorming enables students to capture their ideas after sharing a personal narrative. Students can offer stories about what the book makes them think about and then list them on a chart or chalkboard, or even in individual student notebooks for future writing ideas. Hearing the thoughts of classmates helps students to think about their own story ideas.

Other Genres

Teachers can teach any literary genre by using examples of children's literature (Tompkins, 2004; Wood; 1999). For example, if your goal is to teach nonfiction or expository writing, select a text set of high-quality nonfiction books. Then, using the guidelines in chapter 9, teach students to evaluate nonfiction appropriately. Use good examples of nonfiction writing from these books as models for students to try in their own writing.

Multigenre Writing

Students can learn multiple genres of writing when they study topics that relate to good literature. Instead of traditional reports, students can write an array of written documents that connect with a novel or picture book. For

example, Grierson (2002) describes how a student who had read Yolen's *The Devil's Arithmetic* found additional research on the Holocaust, and then created different kinds of writing that helped her reflect on her reading.

Students sometimes fill old suitcases or shoe boxes with "memorabilia" of an era—except that students actually create the items. The items can include newspaper clippings from the era, letters and postcards from a character, passports or visas, and even old-looking brochures or advertisements. Multigenre writing is especially effective with historical fiction or historical children's books.

Literary Devices

Children's books, particularly picture books, are an excellent source for teaching students about literary devices, such as flashbacks, foreshadowing, imagery, irony, and symbolism. For example, flashbacks are devices where a story generally begins in the present and then goes back to an earlier part of a character's life. Barbara Cooney's *Miss Rumphius* is a good example of this. Teach about the use of flashback in a minilesson and then encourage students to try this device in their writing or to record it in a writer's notebook or folder, along with an example, to use in future writing.

Another device is foreshadowing—dropping a hint early in a story that something is going to happen. Harry Allard uses foreshadowing in *Miss Nelson Has a Field Day*; as do Eve Bunting, in *The Man Who Could Call Down Owls*, and Tedd Arnold, in *No Jumping on the Bed*. Again, using the books as models, the teacher reads one or more examples of the writing during a minilesson and then invites students to draw generalizations about using such a device.

Figure 14.4 lists some popular literary devices and a sampler of books to teach each one. More extensive lists of these resources are available in teacher resource books (Hall, 1990, 1994, 2002; Kurstedt & Koutras, 2000).

Writing Techniques

Picture books and novels are equally good for teaching students more effective writing techniques. The advantages of picture books are that entire books can easily be read as part of lessons and that they are closer in length to what students ultimately will write. Novels have

Hyperbole—Exaggeration in literature

Bauer, Caroline (1984). *Too Many Books.*

Baylor, Byrd. (1982). *The Best Town in the World.*

Stolz, Mary. (1988). *Storm in the Night.*

Imagery—Language that summons up vivid mental images.

Adoff, Arnold. (1988). *Flamboyan.*

Bunting, Eve. (1982). *Ghost's Hour, Spook's Hour.*

Martin, Jacqueline Briggs. (1998). *Snowflake Bentley.*

Inference—A reader draws logical conclusions when limited facts are available, but clues or hints are presented.

Aliki. (1983). *Use Your Head, Dear*

Bang, Molly. (1983). *Dawn.*

Flournoy, Valerie. (1985). *The Patchwork Quilt.*

Irony—A twist in the way things turn out, something unpredictable; a contrast between what appears to be true and the reality.

Baylor, Byrd. (1994). *The Table Where Rich People Sit.*

Goode, Diane. (1988). *I Hear a Noise.*

Graham, Bob. (1988). *Crusher Is Coming!*

Personification—Objects take on the characteristics of people.

Goble, Paul. (1987). *Death of the Iron Horse.*

McKissack, Patricia. (1986). *Flossie and the Fox.*

Turner, Ann (2000). *Secrets from the Dollhouse.*

Symbolism—An element or detail in the story is symbolic of something else, such as hope, courage, or strength.

Ikeda, Daisaku. (1992). *The Cherry Tree.*

Berger, Barbara Helen. (1986). *When the Sun Rose.*

Heine, Helme. (1985). *The Pearl.*

Figure 14.4
Teaching Literary Devices Using Children's Books

Adapted from Hall, 2002.

wonderful models as well, but they require a bit more planning, finding passages that illustrate what we want to teach, and putting these passages on an overhead, on the class computer system, or even on a handout for students.

Metaphor

Writer Harry Noden (1999) suggests that we mine good literature for examples of beautiful metaphoric language, much as how we would explore fine art at a museum for examples of artistic techniques. One exercise Noden suggests is for students to search favorite books for metaphors and to make a list of those that are especially appealing.

In one of our classes, students recorded favorite metaphoric language on a piece of drawing paper, and then we posted the papers on the chalkboard, as we would display drawings. Students wandered through the "gallery" of language examples, noting and appreciating the cleverness in them, sharing why certain ones were favorites (see chapter 8 for more about metaphor and simile in fiction).

Leads

Leads are the way a writer begins a story or piece. They are important because they influence the reader, especially as to whether to continue reading.

One of us visited third-grade teacher Danielle Gruhler's writing classroom when she was teaching a lesson on leads. Her students gathered on old but comfortable furniture in the "living room" of her classroom. Danielle had an array of Patricia Polacco's picture books, ones that her students were already familiar with. Together they examined Polacco's leads, reading them aloud, savoring the language and beautiful writing of each of them. Here are some examples:

- ☺ "She was the last of her kind. A creature of legends." (*Babushka Baba Yaga*)
- ☺ "It wasn't that Natasha was a truly naughty child." (*Babushka's Doll*)
- ☺ "On sultry summer days at my grandma's farm in Michigan, the air gets damp and heavy." (*Thunder Cake*)

Talking about leads such as these, students had the opportunity to react, to share how the language made them feel, to identify how a lead can create suspense or anticipation or present a mood.

As a next step, teachers can talk about different kinds of leads—how questions, a quotation, an anecdote, among others, can work as a "hook" to engage readers (Freeman, 2001). Picture books and novels can both be excellent sources of leads for students to discover and study. The same sort of lesson can also apply to teaching endings of books.

Point of View

An important skill for all students is to recognize when discourse, or writing, is written from a specific point of view. In both picture books and novels, this may be made obvious or explicit. In nonfiction literature, biases and points of view may be more subtle. Learning to identify point of view is part of becoming a critical reader.

Certain picture books make point of view obvious. For example, Jon Scieszka had fun with taking the wolf's point of view instead of the pigs' in *The True Story of the 3 Little Pigs!* Similarly, *The Three Little Wolves and the Big Bad Pig* (Trivizas) spoofs the common folktale, but raises the serious issue that texts are written with a point of view that may or may not be easily discernible.

Some other books also make points of view explicit. Judy Blume's *The Pain and the Great One* offers the opposing viewpoints of an older sister and a younger brother. The design of this book is unique in that you actually turn it upside down and backward to get an entirely new text, as if the book is wholly different.

Another way to explore point of view uses folk or fairy tales, but changes the characters or their gender. Thus, "Cinderella" might become "Cinder-fella" and have a pauper boy vie for the chance to be chosen by a lovely princess at a ball. Goldilocks might become the one whose home has been violated by three bears. The possibilities for learning and humor are considerable.

From THE PAIN AND THE GREAT ONE by Judy Blume. Copyright © 1985 by Random House, Inc. Reprinted by permission.

Classroom Publishing

There is nothing quite so motivating to an emerging writer as seeing his or her writing in print and in book form, and then having other people read it. A book of one's own, that looks like a "real" book, is a powerful message about having a voice and a chance to be heard. Invite students to explore books such as *How a Book Is Published* (Kalman, 1995) to learn the steps in publishing a book.

Not everything should be published, of course. But for the work that represents a student's best or favorite work, the act of putting it into publication gives it credibility as a worthwhile piece of writing. Everyone in a classroom should experience being published from time to time.

Teachers have different ways of organizing publishing. Sometimes the school has a publishing center in an old closet or in the media center, so that materials such as colored paper, wallpaper, glues, long staplers, and even bookbinding machines are all readily available in one place. Other teachers have a publishing center in their classroom. Still others have parent or other school volunteers who take care of classroom-based publishing.

Planning the published book is important. Students can decide how much text from their piece of writing should go on each page. All good picture books deserve graphics. Students may color, paint, photograph, or create their art in ways that professional illustrators do, as we discussed in chapter 7, "Picture Books."

Not all writers are good illustrators. Just as professional authors do, a student author may need to collaborate with another student as illustrator. These can be good partnerships that make the most of each child's expertise.

However classroom publishing is organized, this important part of the writing process should not be omitted. Student work can be displayed in the classroom or media center. Other students will be excited to read the works of their peers (Kasten, 1991). These works are also highly motivating for others in the class or school.

> *If you want to be a writer, you must agree to two things: First you must be a reader; and second you must be a re-writer!*
>
> J. Patrick Lewis, author/poet; personal communication, September, 1999

> *Like most good things, [writing] requires work. What lifts competent, utilitarian language into the realm of art, of poetry, is craft.*
>
> Alice Schertle, author/poet; personal communication, September, 1999

An array of student-published books on display and ready for the classroom library.

Young Author's Conferences

Young author's conferences are events planned so that student writers can showcase their writing, and additionally meet an author and/or illustrator of children's books. These events can be sponsored within a school, a district, a library, or even a college or university in conjunction with local schools. Typically, students attending the event share a piece they have written and "published" (in their school using a bookbinding machine or perhaps bound by hand in some way). Equally important is the opportunity to meet and interact with an author/illustrator.

These events have many benefits. For example, students gain a better understanding of the writing process when they hear a professional talk about the trials and the joys of writing. Students learn that writing is a lifelong learning process and is hard work. Another important lesson they learn from writers is that good stories can be ordinary everyday events in someone's life.

Attending a young author's conference also helps students understand that writers are real, living people, just like themselves. One young boy asked Tomie dePaola during a question-and-answer session, "Why are you still alive?" Clearly this child still believed that authors are people who died long ago.

Students who have attended such an event treasure the memories of their special day. Often, they experience a renewed interest in writing and in the work of the author they met. One second-grade teacher who had five very reluctant writers in her class reported one such benefit the day Verna Aardema visited their south Florida school. Verna Aardema is the author of books such as *The Lonely Lioness and the Ostrich Chicks* and *Misoso: Once Upon a Time Tales From Africa.* These five boys were so moved by Verna's wonderful storytelling of her traditional tales that they returned to their classroom that day determined to write stories. Although it wasn't officially writing time, their teacher let them sit and write all afternoon.

Planning a young author's conference requires considerable work (Freeman & Kasten, 1990; Goodman, Cox, Milz, & Haussler, 1977; Kasten, 1987), but the results last years and years in the memories of the lucky children who see reading and writing as something within their reach.

Summary

Today, many classrooms have a comprehensive writing program in place that emphasizes writing as a *process*. Much has been written on the benefits of a process approach, and how to manage and evaluate a good writer's workshop. Children's literature plays an important role in the writing process because good books are good writing models and excellent "instigators" for writing ideas. Student writing needs to be promoted through using authentic writing audiences, such as other peers, and through classroom-based publishing of students' best works. Students can discover in a good writing classroom that they, too, are writers who have something to say to the world.

Action Research for Teachers

Can Using Wordless Picture Books Improve Student Skills and Attitudes in Writing?

Julie Denges

Fourth Grade, Suburban, Northeast Ohio

Because Julie's students would be tested in a statewide mandated test on narrative writing skills, Julie wondered if using wordless picture books as writing prompts would help her students improve in both their skills and attitudes toward writing.

Before she began, she designed an eight-question interest survey about student experiences and attitudes toward writing. She planned to administer the survey to her fourth graders as well as to students in another teacher's class. She also re-administered the survey at the end of her 8-week study. Julie maintained a daily researcher log, and analyzed student writing with a 4-point rubric she created with test expectations in mind. She implemented her program idea with her class, whereas the other teacher's class received traditional writing instruction.

For her program, Julie had students work in pairs to create a story map based on wordless picture books. She taught a number of minilessons on characters and setting using the wordless picture books as the impetus. Students then co-wrote stories based on the books. Julie taught writing conventions in the context of the writing pieces. By the time she introduced a second set of books, students generated their story maps and wrote independently. Each student completed two to three pieces of work in the 8-week period.

Julie found that her strategy stimulated valuable dialogue among students about their stories as they discussed ideas. More than half of the students believed they had improved in their writing as a result of this strategy. Working together was also a valuable part of the strategy, especially as students became increasingly interested in each other's writing and read each other's work more regularly. One unexpected outcome was how many parents commented on this and on their student's improved attitudes toward writing during the parent–teacher conferences. Julie's class did show more improvement on the writing rubric than the students in the other fourth grade class. Julie attributes some of the success in her writing program to the inspiration of the books, the handling of writing mechanics within context, and the collaboration of peers.

Appendix A

Categories of Fiction

Contemporary Realistic Fiction

Peer Relationships

The Cybil War   Betsy Byars
A View From Saturday   E. L. Konigsburg
The Egypt Game   Zilpha Snyder
Bluish   Virginia Hamilton
All Alone in the Universe   Lynne Rae Perkins
The Friends   Kazumi Yumoto
I Hadn't Meant to Tell You This   Jacqueline Woodson

The Sisterhood of the Traveling Pants   Ann Brashares
Blubber   Judy Blume
The Goats   Brock Cole
Harriet the Spy   Louise Fitzhugh
Bridge to Terabithia   Katherine Paterson
Wringer   Jerry Spinelli

Family Relationships

Time Pieces   Virginia Hamilton
Baseball in April and Other Stories   Gary Soto
Child of the Owl   Laurence Yep
Salsa Stories   Lulu Delacre
Eagle Song   Joseph Bruchac
The Heart of a Chief   Joseph Bruchac
Destiny   Vicki Grove
Memories of Summer   Ruth White
Jacob Have I Loved   Katherine Paterson
Homecoming   Cynthia Viogt
Dicey's Song   Cynthia Voigt
Year of the Sawdust Man   Alice La Faye
The Color of My Words   Lynn Joseph
Belle Prater's Boy   Ruth White
Dear Mr. Henshaw   Beverly Cleary
Ruby Holler   Sharon Creech
Saffy's Angel   Hilary McKay
Arthur, For the Very First Time   Patricia MacLachlan
Heaven   Angela Johnson
Pictures of Hollis Woods   Patricia Reilly Giff
The House of Wings   Betsy Byars

Homecoming   Cynthia Voigt
The Most Beautiful Place in the World   Ann Cameron
Everything on a Waffle   Patsy Horvath
The Graduation of Jake Moon   Barbara Park
Alida's Song   Gary Paulsen
Over the Water   Maude Casey
Dancing in Cadillac Light   Kimberly Willis Holt
Toning the Sweep   Angela Johnson
Maniac Magee   Jerry Spinelli
The Same Stuff as Stars   Katherine Paterson
Miracle's Boys   Jacqueline Woodson
My Louisiana Sky   Kimberly Willis Holt
Waiting to Disappear   April Young Fritz
A Step From Heaven   Ann Nu
Jazmin's Notebook   Nikki Grimes
Shabanu: Daughter of the Wind   Suzanne Fisher Staples
Lord of the Deep   Graham Salisbury
Journey   Patricia MacLachlan
Walk Two Moons   Sharon Creech
Missing May   Cynthia Rylant

Animal Stories

King of the Wind   Marguerite Henry
Old Yeller   Fred Gipson
Incident at Hawk's Hill   Alan Eckert
Shiloh   Phyllis Reynolds Naylor
Shiloh Season   Phyllis Reynolds Naylor

Saving Shiloh   Phyllis Reynolds Naylor
Because of Winn-Dixie   Kate DiCamillo
Zulu Dog   Anton Ferreira
The Incredible Journey   Sheila Burnford
Where the Red Fern Grows   Wilson Rawls

Adventure and Survival Stories

Island of the Blue Dolphins   Scott O'Dell
Call It Courage   Armstrong Sperry
My Side of the Mountain (and sequels)
    Jean Craighead George
Julie of the Wolves (and sequels)   Jean Craighead George
Hatchet (and sequels)   Gary Paulsen
Voyage of the Frog   Gary Paulsen
The Breadwinner   Deborah Ellis
Parvana's Journey   Deborah Ellis
Tonight by Sea   Frances Temple
Red Midnight   Ben Mikaelsen
A Stone in My Hand   Cathryn Clinton
Where the Lilies Bloom   Vera Cleaver & Bill Cleaver

Monkey Island   Paula Fox
From the Mixed-Up Files of Mrs. Basil E. Frankweiler
    E. L. Konigsburg
Slake's Limbo   Felice Holman
The Joey Pigza series   Jack Gantos
A Corner of the Universe   Ann Martin
Tiger's Fall   Molly Bang
Mine For Keeps   Jean Little
The Summer of the Swans   Betsy Byars
The Language of Goldfish   Zibby Oneal
Freak the Mighty   Rodman Philbrick
Crazy Lady   Jane Conly

Humorous Stories

Wayside School stories   Louis Sachar
Holes   Louis Sachar
How to Eat Fried Worms   Anne Rockwell
Skinnybones   Barbara Park

The Best Christmas Pageant Ever   Anne Robinson
Harris and Me   Gary Paulsen
The Exiles   Hilary McKay

Mystery Stories (see also series books listed in Figure 8.3; many series books are mysteries)

Encyclopedia Brown   Donald Sobol
The Case of the Lion Dance   Laurence Yep

The Case of the Firecrackers   Laurence Yep
The Westing Game   Ellen Raskin

Sports Stories

Thank You, Jackie Robinson   Miriam Cohen
The Moves Make the Man   Bruce Brooks
Iron Man   Chris Crutcher

The Heart of a Champion   Carl Deuker
The Contender   Robert Lipsyte

Romance Stories

In Summer Light   Zibby Oneal
Philip Hall Likes Me. I Reckon Maybe.   Bette Greene

Unclaimed Treasures   Patricia MacLachlan

School Stories (see also series books listed in Figure 8.3)

Ramona's World   Beverly Cleary
Beyond Mayfield   Vaunda Nelson
You're a Brave Man, Julius Zimmerman   Claudia Mills
Lizzie at Last   Claudia Mills

Flying Solo   Ralph Fletcher
Nothing But the Truth   Avi
Flour Babies   Anne Fine
Darnell Rock Reporting   Walter Dean Myers

Coming-of-Age Stories

On My Honor   Marion Dane Bauer
Missing May   Cynthia Rylant
A Summer to Die   Lois Lowry
One-Eyed Cat   Paula Fox

Make Lemonade   Virginia Euwer Wolff
Lord of the Deep   Graham Salisbury
The Other Side of Truth   Beverley Naidoo

Historical Fiction

Twelfth- to Sixteenth-Century History

A Proud Taste for Scarlet and Miniver   E. L. Konigsburg
The Queen's Fool   Jane Yolen
The Shakespeare Stealer   Gary Blackwood
The Playmaker   J. B. Cheaney
The True Prince   J. B. Cheaney
The Master Puppeteer   Katherine Paterson

The Kite Rider   Geraldine McCaughrean
Crispin: The Cross of Lead   Avi
A Single Shard   Linda Sue Park
The Midwife's Apprentice   Karen Cushman
Matilda Bone   Karen Cushman
Catherine, Called Birdy   Karen Cushman

Early American

Birchbark House   Louise Erdrich
Sweetgrass   Jan Hudson
Morning Girl   Michael Dorris
Beyond the Burning Time   Kathryn Lasky
Tituba of Salem Village   Ann Petry
A Lion to Guard Us   Clyde Bulla
The Cabin Faced West   Jean Fritz
The Courage of Sarah Noble   Alice Dalgliesh
My Brother Sam Is Dead   James Collier &
     Christopher Collier

Jump Ship to Freedom   James Collier &
     Christopher Collier
The Fighting Ground   Avi
Sarah Bishop   Scott O'Dell
Island of the Blue Dolphins   Scott O'Dell
The Witch of Blackbird Pond   Elizabeth George Speare
The Sign of the Beaver   Elizabeth George Speare
Guests   Michael Dorris

Westward Expansion (Nineteenth/Twentieth Century)

Caddie Woodlawn   Carol Ryrie Brink
The Ballad of Lucy Whipple   Karen Cushman
Destination Gold   Julie Lawson
Little House on the Prairie (and sequels)
     Laura Ingalls Wilder
Our Only May Amelia   Jennifer Holm
Prairie Songs   Pam Conrad

Grasshopper Summer   Ann Turner
Beyond the Divide   Kathryn Lasky
Sarah, Plain and Tall   Patricia MacLachlan
Skylark   Patricia MacLachlan
Sing Down the Moon   Scott O'Dell
Longwalker's Journey   Beatrice Harrell
Sacajawea   Joseph Bruchac

Civil War Era

Charley Skedaddle   Patricia Beatty
Thunder at Gettysburg   Patricia Lee Gauch
Bull Run   Paul Fleischman
Rifles for Watie   Harold Keith
Letters From a Slave Girl   Mary Lyons
Jip: His Story   Katherine Paterson
Stealing South: A Story of the Underground Railroad
     Katherine Ayres

Trouble Don't Last   Shelley Pearsall
Shades of Gray   Carolyn Reeder
Across Five Aprils   Irene Hunt
Ajeemah and His Son   James Berry
The River Between Us   Richard Peck
Nightjohn   Gary Paulsen
Sarny   Gary Paulsen

Nineteenth Century: Industrialization and Immigration

Fair Weather   Richard Peck
Maggie's Door and *Nory Ryan's Song*   Patricia Reilly Giff
Dragon's Gate   Laurence Yep
Lyddie   Katherine Paterson

Letters From Rifka   Karen Hesse
Esperanza Rising   Pam Muñoz Ryan
Beyond the Western Sea series   Avi

Twentieth Century: War and the Great Depression

Sounder   William Armstrong
Treasures in the Dust   Tracey Porter
Nowhere to Call Home   Cynthia DeFelice
When Hitler Stole Pink Rabbit   Judith Kerr
The Island on Bird Street   Uri Orlev
The Upstairs Room   Johanna Reiss
So Far From the Bamboo Grove   Yoko Kawashima
   Watkins
Year of Impossible Goodbyes   Sook Nyul Choi
When My Name Was Keoko   Linda Sue Park
Lily's Crossing   Patricia Reilly Giff

The Art of Keeping Cool   Janet Taylor Lisle
Summer of My German Soldier   Bette Green
Bud, Not Buddy   Christopher Paul Curtis
Roll of Thunder, Hear My Cry (and sequels)   Mildred
   Taylor
Out of the Dust   Karen Hesse
Journey to Topaz and *Journey Home*   Yoshiko Uchida
The Endless Steppe   Esther Hautzig
The Devil's Arithmetic   Jane Yolen
Number the Stars   Lois Lowry
Under the Blood-Red Sun   Graham Salisbury

Twentieth Century: Civil Rights and Social Unrest

The $66 Summer   John Armistead
Dancing in Cadillac Light   Kimberly Willis Holt
Walking to the Bus Rider Blues   Harriette Robinet
Mississippi Trial, 1955   Chris Crowe

The Red Rose Box   Brenda Woods
The Watsons Go to Birmingham—1966   Christopher
   Paul Curtis

Fantasy

Toys and Animals

Pigs Might Fly   Dick King-Smith
Babe, the Gallant Pig   Dick King-Smith
Mrs. Frisby and the Rats of NIMH   Robert O'Brien
Stuart Little   E. B. White
The Mennyms   Sylvia Waugh
Bunnicula: A Rabbit-Tale of Mystery   Deborah Howe
   & James Howe
The Mouse and the Motorcycle   Beverly Cleary
Watership Down   Richard Adams

Redwall series   Brian Jacques
The Castle in the Attic   Elizabeth Winthrop
The Indian in the Cupboard   Lynn Reid Banks
The Wind in the Willows   Kenneth Grahame
Winnie-the-Pooh   A. A. Milne
The Velveteen Rabbit   Marjorie Williams
A Bear Called Paddington   Michael Bond
Charlotte's Web   E. B. White

Time-Shift Fantasy

Tom's Midnight Garden   Phillippa Pearce
Fog Magic   Julia Sauer
The Root Cellar   Janet Lunn

King of Shadows   Susan Cooper
The Lion, the Witch and the Wardrobe   C. S. Lewis

Ghosts and the Supernatural

Sweet Whispers, Brother Rush   Virginia Hamilton
The Thief Lord   Cornelia Funke
Ghosts in the Gallery   Barbara Wallace
The Ghost Comes Calling   Betty Ren Wright

The Folk Keeper   Franny Billingsley
The Mermaid Summer   Mollie Hunter
Stonewords   Pam Conrad
Wait Till Helen Comes   Mary Downing Hahn

Stories Based on Folklore

Zel   Donna Jo Napoli
The Magic Circle   Donna Jo Napoli
Spinners   Donna Jo Napoli
Straw Into Gold   Gary Schmidt

Shadow Spinner   Susan Fletcher
Ella Enchanted   Gail Carson Levine
Beauty   Robin McKinley
Rose Daughter   Robin McKinley

Crazy Characters and Unusual Worlds

Island of the Aunts   Eva Ibbotson
James and the Giant Peach   Roald Dahl
Mary Poppins   P. L. Travers
The Wonderful Wizard of Oz   L. Frank Baum
Pippi Longstocking   Astrid Lindgren

Charlie and the Chocolate Factory   Roald Dahl
Inkheart   Cornelia Funke
The Littles   John Peterson
The Borrowers   Mary Norton

Heroic Fantasy

Blue Sword   Robin McKinley
Hero and the Crown   Robin McKinley
The Dark Is Rising (and sequels)   Susan Cooper
Heartlight   T. A. Barron
A Wizard of Earthsea   Ursula Le Guin
Harry Potter and the Sorcerer's Stone (and sequels)
    J. K. Rowling

The Prydain Chronicles series   Lloyd Alexander
The Lost Years of Merlin (and sequels)   T. A. Barron
Lord of the Rings   J. R. R. Tolkien
His Dark Materials trilogy   Philip Pullman

Science Fiction

Settings Outside Our World

Dragonsong   Anne McCaffrey
The Wonderful Flight to the Mushroom Planet
    Eleanor Cameron

The Green Book   Jill Paton Walsh
A Wrinkle in Time   Madeleine L'Engle

Settings Within Our World

Hidden Children (and sequels)   Jane Marks
The Ear, the Eye and the Arm   Nancy Farmer
The House of the Scorpion   Nancy Farmer
The White Mountains (and sequels)   John Christopher
Z for Zachariah   Robert O'Brien

The Last Book in the Universe   Rodman Philbrick
The City of Ember   Jeanne DuPrau
Enchantress From the Stars   Sylvia Engdahl
The Giver   Lois Lowry
Gathering Blue   Lois Lowry

Appendix B

Categories of Nonfiction

Concept Books

The Boat Alphabet Book   Jerry Pallotta
Let's Dance   George Ancona
My Arctic 1, 2, 3   Michael Kusugak
Pizza Counting   Christine Dobson
The M and M's Brand Counting Book   Barbara McGrath
1, 2, 3: What Do You See?   Arlene Alda
Turtle Island ABC: A Gathering of Native American
     Symbols   Gerald Hausman

Color Zoo   Lois Ehlert
Go, Go, Go! Kids on the Move   Stephen Swinburne
The Queen's Progress: An Elizabethan Alphabet   Celeste
     Mannis
Q Is for Quark: A Science Alphabet Book   David
     Schwartz

Photographic Essays

Iditarod Dream: Dusty and His Sled Dogs Compete in
     Alaska's Jr. Iditarod   Ted Wood
Tierra del Fuego: A Journey to the End of the Earth
     Peter Lourie
Coming to America: A Muslim Family's Story
     Bernard Wolf

Celebrating Ramadan   Diane Hoyt-Goldsmith
Celebrating a Quinceañera: A Latina's 15th Birthday
     Celebration   Diane Hoyt-Goldsmith
Crocodiles and Alligators   Seymour Simon
People Around the World   Anthony Mason

Survey Books

Secrets of the Deep Revealed   Frances Dipper
Birds: Nature's Magnificent Flying Machines
     Caroline Arnold
The Berry Book   Gail Gibbons
Fields of Fury: The American Civil War
     James M. McPherson

All About Sharks   Jim Arnosky
Crocodiles and Alligators   Seymour Simon
The Kingfisher Young People's Book of Living Worlds
     Clive Gifford & Jerry Cadle
Rome: In Spectacular Cross-Section   Andrew Solway

Documents, Albums, Journals, and Diaries

Tell All the Children Our Story: Memories and Mementoes
     of Being Young and Black in America   Tonya Bolden
Cowboy: An Album   Linda Granfield
Dog of Discovery: A Newfoundland's Adventures With
     Lewis and Clark   Laurence Pringle
Where the Action Was: Women War Correspondents in
     World War II   Penny Colman
Freedom Roads: Searching for the Underground Railroad
     Joyce Hansen & Gary McGowan

A Desert Scrapbook   Virginia Wright-Frierson
An Island Scrapbook   Virginia Wright-Frierson
North American Rainforest Scrapbook
     Virginia Wright-Frierson
Voices From the Civil War: A Documentary History of the
     Great American Conflict   Milton Meltzer

Specialized

Blizzard: The Storm That Changed America   Jim Murphy
Inside the Alamo   Jim Murphy
The Great Fire   Jim Murphy
Kids on Strike   Susan Campbell Bartoletti
Black Potatoes   Susan Campbell Bartoletti
The Encyclopedia of Preserved People: Pickled, Frozen, and Mummified Corpses From Around the World   Natalie Jane Prior

Children of the Dust Bowl: The True Story of the School at Weedpatch Camp   Jerry Stanley
Toilets Toasters & Telephones: The How and Why of Everyday Objects   Susan Goldman Rubin
How Henry Ford Built a Legend   David Weitzman
Chocolate: Riches From the Rainforest   Robert Burleigh
What You Never Knew About Tubs, Toilets, & Showers   Patricia Lauber

Identification/Field Guides

Safely to Shore: America's Lighthouses   Iris Van Rynbach
The Look-It-Up Book of the 50 States   Bill Gutman
Rain Forest Babies   Kathy Darling
First Field Guides, by National Audubon Society and Scholastic, such as *Rocks and Minerals*   Edward Riciutti

National Geographic Society "My First Pocket Guide" Series, *such as Stars and Planets*   John O'Byrne
Reptiles   John Behler

Life-Cycle Books

Come to the Ocean's Edge: A Nature Cycle Book   Laurence Pringle
Volcanoes: Nature's Incredible Fireworks   David L. Harrison
The Life and Times of the Ant   Charles Micucci
The Life and Times of the Peanut   Charles Micucci

From Seed to Plant   Gail Gibbons
Apples   Ken Robbins
A Dragon in the Sky: The Story of a Green Darner Dragonfly   Lawrence Pringle
Red-Eyed Tree Frog   Joy Cowley
A Log's Life   Wendy Pfeffer

Reference Books

Amazing Dinosaurs: The Fiercest, the Tallest, the Toughest, the Smallest   Dougal Dixon
Scholastic Dinosaurs A to Z: The Ultimate Dinosaur Encyclopedia   Don Lessem
Gods, Goddesses and Monsters: A Book of World Mythology   Sheila Keenan
The Kingfisher Children's Illustrated Dictionary and Thesaurus   Heather Couper & Nigel Henbest

Space Encyclopedia   Heather Couper & Nigel Henbest
My First Book of Biographies: Great Men and Women Every Child Should Know   Jean Marzollo
Dinosaurs to Dodos: An Encyclopedia of Extinct Animals   Don Lessem
Scholastic Student Thesaurus   John Bollard
Scholastic Book of World Records   Jenifer Corr Morse

Information Picture Storybooks

The Magic School Bus books, such as *The Magic School Bus Explores the Senses*   Joanna Cole
Ship   David Macaulay
Nobody Particular   Molly Bang

In the Heart of the Village: The World of the Indian Banyan Tree   Barbara Bash
Christmas in the Big House, Christmas in the Quarters   Patricia McKissack & Fredrick McKissack

Experiment and Activity Books; Craft and How-To Books

The Kids Can Press Jumbo Cookbook   Judi Gillies & Jennifer Glossop
Kidtopia: 'Round the Country and Back Through Time in 60 Projects   Roberta Gould
How Science Works: Discover the Science Behind Planes, Boats, Rockets, Cars, Trucks   Jim Pipe and Mark Jackson

Checkmate at Chess City   Piers Harper
Crafts to Make in the Winter   Kathy Ross
The Best Birthday Parties Ever: A Kid's Do-It-Yourself Guide   Kathy Ross
How to Make Super Pop-Ups   Joan Irvine

Picture-Book Biographies

America's Champion Swimmer: Gertrude Ederle
  David Adler
The Life and Death of Adolf Hitler   James Cross Giblin
The Amazing Life of Benjamin Franklin
  James Cross Giblin
Why Don't You Get a Horse, Sam Adams?
And Then What Happened, Paul Revere?   Jean Fritz
The Great Little Madison,   Jean Fritz
What's the Big Idea, Ben Franklin?   Jean Fritz

Only Passing Through: The Story of Sojourner Truth
  Anne Rockwell
Hatshepsut, His Majesty, Herself   Catherine Andronik
Leonardo da Vinci   Diane Stanley
Michelangelo   Diane Stanley
Woody Guthrie: Poet of the People   Bonnie Christensen
The Man Who Made Time Travel   Kathryn Lasky
Tallchief: America's Prima Ballerina   Maria Tallchief

Partial Biographies

A Special Fate: Chiune Sugihara, Hero of the Holocaust
  Alison Leslie Gold

*Dragon Bones and Dinosaur Eggs: A Photobiography of
  Explorer Roy Chapman Andrews*   Ann Bausum

Complete Biographies

Ida B. Wells: Mother of the Civil Rights Movement
  Dennis Brindell Fradin & Judith Bloom Fradin
Babe Didrikson Zaharias: The Making of a Champion
  Russell Freedman
Behind the Mask: The Life of Queen Elizabeth I
  Jane Resh Thomas

Malcolm X: A Fire Burning Brightly   Walter Dean Myers
B. Franklin, Printer   David Adler
*There Ain't Nobody That Can Sing Like Me: The Life of
  Woody Guthrie*   Anne Neimark

Collective Biographies

*How They Got Over: African Americans and the Call of
  the Sea*   Eloise Greenfield
*Lives of the Presidents: Fame, Shame (and What the
  Neighbors Thought)*   Kathleen Krull

*Lives of Extraordinary Women: Rulers, Rebels (and What
  the Neighbors Thought)*   Kathleen Krull
Ten Kings and the Worlds They Ruled   Milton Meltzer

Autobiographies and Memoirs

King of the Mild Frontier: An Ill-Advised Autobiography
  Chris Crutcher
Leon's Story   Leon Tillage

Red Scarf Girl: A Memoir of the Cultural Revolution
  Ji-li Jiang
Through My Eyes   Ruby Bridges

Children's Book References

Aardema, Verna. (1975). *Why mosquitoes buzz in people's ears* (Leo Dillon & Diane Dillon, Illus.). New York: Dial Books.

Aardema, Verna. (1977). *Who's in rabbit's house?* (Leo Dillon & Diane Dillon, Illus.). New York: Dial Books.

Aardema, Verna. (1979). *Riddle of the drum* (Tony Chen, Illus.). New York: Four Winds Press.

Aardema, Verna. (1981). *Bringing the rain to Kapiti Plain* (Beatriz Vidal, Illus.). New York: Dial Books.

Aardema, Verna. (1982). *What's so funny, Ketu?* (Marc Brown, Illus.). New York: Dial Books.

Aardema, Verna. (1988). *Princess Gorilla and a new kind of water* (Victoria Chess, Illus.). New York: Dial Books.

Aardema, Verna. (1989). *Rabbit makes a monkey of lion* (Jerry Pinkney, Illus.). New York: Dial Books.

Aardema, Verna. (1991a). *Pedro and the Padre* (Friso Henstra, Illus.). New York: Dial Books.

Aardema, Verna. (1991b). *Traveling to Tondo*. New York: Knopf.

Aardema, Verna. (1994). *Misoso: Once upon a time tales from Africa*. New York: Knopf.

Aardema, Verna. (1995). *How the ostrich got a long neck* (Marcia Brown, Illus.). New York: Scholastic.

Aardema, Verna. (1996). *The lonely lioness and the ostrich chicks*. New York: Knopf.

Ackerman, Karen (1988). *Song and dance man*. New York: Knopf.

Ackerman, Karen. (1991). *The leaves in October*. New York: Dell.

Ackerman, Karen. (1994). *The night crossing* (Elizabeth Sayles, Illus.). New York: Knopf.

Adams, Richard. (1996). *Watership down*. New York: Scribner.

Adler, David. (1989). *A picture book of Abraham Lincoln*. New York: Scholastic.

Adler, David A. (1995). *Child of the Warsaw ghetto*. New York: Holiday House.

Adler, David A. (2000). *America's champion swimmer: Gertrude Ederle* (Terry Widener, Illus.). New York: Harcourt.

Adler, David A. (2001). *B. Franklin, printer*. New York: Holiday House.

Adler, David A. (2003). *A picture book of Lewis and Clark* (Ronald Himler, Illus.). New York: Holiday House.

Adoff, Arnold. (1977). *Tornado! Poems* (Ronald Himler, Illus.). New York: Delacorte.

Adoff, Arnold. (1979). *Eats*. New York: Lothrop, Lee & Shepard.

Adoff, Arnold. (1986). *Sports pages*. New York: Lippincott.

Adoff, Arnold. (1989). *Chocolate dreams: Poems*. New York: Lothrop, Lee & Shepard.

Adoff, Arnold. (1991). *In for winter, out for spring*. San Diego: Harcourt Brace.

Adoff, Arnold. (1995a). *Slow dance heart break blues* (William Cotton, Illus.). New York: HarperCollins.

Adoff, Arnold. (1995b). *Street music: City poems* (Karen Barbour, Illus.). New York: HarperCollins.

Adoff, Arnold. (1996). *I am the darker brother* (Benny Andrews, Illus.). New York: Simon & Schuster.

Adoff, Arnold. (1997). *Love letters* (Lisa Desimini, Illus.). New York: The Blue Sky Press.

Adoff, Arnold. (2000a). *The basket counts* (Michael Weaver, Illus.). New York: Simon & Schuster.

Adoff, Arnold. (2000b). *Touch the poem* (Lisa Desimini, Illus.). New York: Scholastic.

Adoff, Arnold. (2002). *Black is brown is tan*. New York: HarperCollins.

Aesop. (1989). *Fables* (Lisbeth Zwerger, Illus.). Saxonville, MA: Picture Book Studio.

Agard, John, & Nichols, Grace (Eds.). (1994). *A Caribbean dozen: Poems from Caribbean poets*. Cambridge, MA: Candlewick Press.

Agard, John, & Nichols, Grace. (1994). *No hickory, no dickory, no dock: Caribbean nursery rhymes*. Cambridge, MA: Candlewick Press.

Agard, John, & Nichols, Grace. (2003). *Under the moon & over the sea: Caribbean nursery rhymes*. Cambridge, MA: Candlewick Press.

Ahlberg, Janet, & Ahlberg, Allan. (1986). *The jolly postman or other people's letters*. Boston: Little, Brown.

Ahlberg, Janet, & Ahlberg, Allan. (1999). *Each peach pear plum*. London: Viking.

Alarcón, Francisco X. (1997). *Laughing tomatoes and other spring poems*. San Francisco: Children's Book Press.

Alarcón, Francisco X. (1998). *From the belly button of the moon and other summer poems*. San Francisco: Children's Book Press.

Alarcón, Francisco X. (2001). *Iguanas in the snow and other winter poems*. San Francisco: Children's Book Press.

Alcott, Louisa May. (1868/1950). *Little women*. Boston: Roberts Brothers.

Alda, Arlene. (1998). *Arlene Alda's 1 2 3: What do you see?* Berkeley, CA: Tricycle Press.

Alexander, Lloyd. (1965). *The black cauldron*. New York: Holt, Rinehart and Winston.

Alexander, Lloyd. (1968). *The high king*. New York: Dell.

Alexander, Martha G. (1981). *Move over, twerp*. New York: Dial Books.

Aliki. (1962). *My five senses*. New York: Crowell.

Aliki. (1979a). *Manners*. New York: Crowell.

Aliki. (1979b). *Mummies made in Egypt*. New York: HarperCollins.

Aliki. (1981). *Digging up dinosaurs*. New York: Crowell.

Aliki. (1983). *A medieval feast*. New York: Crowell.

Aliki. (1984). *Feelings*. New York: Greenwillow.

Aliki. (1987). *Welcome little baby*. New York: Greenwillow.

Aliki. (1988). *A weed is a flower—The life of George Washington Carver*. New York: Simon & Schuster.

Aliki. (1993). *My visit to the aquarium*. New York: HarperCollins.

Aliki. (1999). *William Shakespeare and the Globe*. New York: Harper-Collins.

Allard, Harry. (1977). *Miss Nelson is missing!* (James Marshall, Illus.). Boston: Houghton Mifflin.

Allard, Harry, & Marshall, James. (1985). *Miss Nelson has a field day*. Boston: Houghton Mifflin.

Allen, Judy. (1992). *Whale*. Cambridge, MA: Candlewick Press.

Amato, Carol A. (1995). *Young readers' series—To be a WOLF* (David Wenzel, Illus.). New York: Barron's Educational Series.

American Girl. (Eds.). (2002). *Yikes! A smart girl's guide to surviving tricky, sticky, icky situations* (Bonnie Timmons, Illus.). Middleton, WI: Pleasant Company.

Ancona, George. (1976). *And what do you do?: A book about people and their work*. New York: Dutton.

Ancona, George. (1982). *Bananas: From Manolo to Margie*. New York: Clarion Books.

Ancona, George. (1989). *The American family farm: A photo essay*. San Diego: Harcourt Brace.

Ancona, George. (1991). *The aquarium book*. New York: Clarion Books.

Ancona, George. (1998). *Barrio: Jose's neighborhood*. San Diego: Harcourt Brace Jovanovich.

Ancona, George. (1999). *Carnaval*. San Diego: Harcourt Brace.

Ancona, George. (2001). *Let's dance*. New York: Lodestar Books.

Anderson, Laurie Halse. (2000). *Fever 1793*. New York: Aladdin Books.

Anderson, Rachel. (1993). *Bus people*. New York: Henry Holt.

Andrews, Jan. (1985). *Very last first time*. New York: McElderry.

Andrews-Goebel, Nancy. (2002). *The pot that Juan built* (David Diaz, Illus.). New York: Lee & Low.

Andronik, Catherine. (2001). *Hatshepsut, his majesty, herself*. New York: Atheneum.

Anholtz, Laurence. (1994). *Camille and the sunflowers*. New York: Barron's Educational Series.

Anholtz, Laurence. (1996). *Degas and the little dancer*. London: Frances Lincoln.

Ardagh, Philip. (1999). *The hieroglyphs handbook*. New York: Scholastic.

Argueta, Jorge. (2001). *A movie in my pillow*. San Francisco: Children's Book Press.

Armistead, John. (2000). *The $66 summer*. Minneapolis: Milkweed.

Armstrong, Jennifer. (1997). *Lili the brave*. New York: Random House.

Armstrong, Jennifer. (1998). *Shipwreck at the bottom of the world: The extraordinary true story of Shackleton and the Endurance*. New York: Crown.

Armstrong, Jennifer. (2003). *Audubon: Painter of birds in the wild frontier* (Jos. A. Smith, Illus.). New York: Abrams.

Armstrong, William H. (1972). *Sounder*. New York: Scholastic.

Arnold, Caroline. (1983). *Pets without homes* (Richard Hewett, Illus.). New York: Clarion Books.

Arnold, Caroline. (1993). *Cats* (Richard Hewett, Illus.). Minneapolis: Carolrhoda.

Arnold, Caroline. (1994a). *Sea lion* (Richard Hewett, Illus.). New York: Morrow.

Arnold, Caroline. (1994b). *Watching desert wildlife* (Arthur Arnold, Illus.). Minneapolis: Carolrhoda.

Arnold, Caroline. (1996). *Stories in stone* (Richard Hewett, Illus.). New York: Clarion Books.

Arnold, Caroline. (1997a). *African animals*. New York: Morrow.

Arnold, Caroline. (1997b). *Hawk highway in the sky* (Robert Kruidenier, Illus.). San Diego: Harcourt Brace.

Arnold, Caroline. (1999a). *Baby whale rescue* (Richard Hewett, Illus.). New York: Troll.

Arnold, Caroline. (1999b). *Playtime for zoo animals* (Richard Hewett, Illus.). New York: Lerner.

Arnold, Caroline. (2001). *Did you hear that? Animals with super hearing* (Cathy Trachok, Illus.). Watertown, MA: Charlesbridge.

Arnold, Caroline. (2003). *Birds: Nature's magnificent flying machines* (Patricia J. Wynne, Illus.). Watertown, MA: Charlesbridge.

Arnold, Tedd. (1987). *No jumping on the bed*. New York: Dial Books.

Arnosky, Jim. (2003). *All about sharks*. New York: Scholastic.

Aronson, Marc. (2000). *Sir Walter Ralegh and the quest for El Dorado*. New York: Clarion Books.

Asch, Frank. (1998). *Cactus poems*. San Diego: Harcourt.

Ash, Russell. (2002). *The top 10 of everything*. New York: DK Publishing.

Ashabranner, Brent. (1998). *Always remember: The story of the Vietnam Veterans Memorial* (Jennifer Ashabranner, Photog.). New York: Putnam.

Attenborough, Elizabeth. (2001). *Poetry by heart: A child's book of poems to remember*. New York: Scholastic.

Atwater, Richard, & Atwater, Florence. (1938/1986). *Mr. Popper's penguins*. Boston: Little, Brown.

Avi. (1984). *The fighting ground*. New York: Lippincott.

Avi. (1990). *The true confessions of Charlotte Doyle*. New York: Orchard Books.

Avi. (1991a). *Nothing but the truth: A documentary novel*. New York: Orchard Books.

Avi. (1991b). *Windcatcher*. New York: Avon.

Avi. (1994). *The barn*. New York: Orchard Books.

Avi. (1996). *Beyond the western sea*. New York: Orchard Books.

Avi. (1998). *Poppy and Rye*. New York: Avon.

Avi. (2002). *Crispin: The cross of lead*. New York: Hyperion Books.

Ayres, Katherine. (2002). *Stealing south: A story of the Underground Railroad*. New York: Yearling.

Babbitt, Natalie. (1975). *Tuck everlasting*. New York: Farrar, Straus & Giroux.

Bahr, Mary. (1992). *The memory box* (David Cunningham, Illus.). Morton Grove, IL: Albert Whitman.

Bahr, Mary. (2002). *My brother loved snowflakes: The story of Wilson A. Bentley, the snowflake man* (Laura Jacobsen, Illus.). Honesdale, PA: Boyds Mills Press.

Baird, Audrey B. (2001). *Storm coming!* Honesdale, PA: Boyds Mills Press.

Baird, Audrey B. (2002). *A cold snap: Frosty poems*. Honesdale, PA: Boyds Mills Press.

Baker, Jeannie. (1987). *Where the forest meets the sea*. New York: Greenwillow.

Bang, Molly. (1988). *Delphine*. New York: Morrow.

Bang, Molly. (1999). *When Sophie gets angry—Really, really angry. . .* New York: Blue Sky/Scholastic.

Bang, Molly. (2001a). *Nobody particular: One woman's fight to save the bays*. New York: Henry Holt.

Bang, Molly. (2001b). *Tiger's fall*. New York: Henry Holt.

Banish, Roslyn. (1992). *A forever family*. New York: HarperCollins.

Banks, Lynne Reid. (1981). *The Indian in the cupboard*. New York: Doubleday.

Barrett, Mary Brigid. (1994). *Sing to the stars* (Sandra Speidel, Illus.). New York: Little, Brown.

Barron, T. A. (1991). *Heartlight*. New York: Philomel.

Barron, T. A. (1996). *The lost years of Merlin*. New York: Philomel.

Barron, T. A. (1998). *The fires of Merlin*. New York: Philomel.

Barron, T. A. (2000). *The seven songs of Merlin*. Minneapolis: Sagebrush.

Bartoletti, Susan Campbell. (1999). *Kids on strike*. Boston: Houghton Mifflin.

Bartoletti, Susan Campbell. (2001). *Black potatoes: The story of the Great Irish Famine, 1845–1850*. Boston: Houghton Mifflin.

Barton, Bob, & Booth, David. (1995). *Mother Goose goes to school: More than 100 rhymes and activities*. Markham, ON: Pembroke.

Base, Graeme. (1993). *The eleventh hour: A curious mystery*. New York: Abrams.

Bash, Barbara. (1996). *In the heart of the village: The world of the Indian banyan tree*. San Francisco: Sierra Club Books.

Batten, Mary. (1998). *All aboard reading—Baby wolf* (JoEllen McAllister Stammen, Illus.). New York: Grosset & Dunlap.

Batten, Mary. (2002). *Hey, daddy! Animal fathers and their babies* (Higgins Bond, Illus.). Atlanta: Peachtree.

Bauer, Marion Dane. (1986). *On my honor*. New York: Clarion Books.

Bauer, Marion Dane. (1996). *When I go camping with Grandma* (Allen Garns, Illus.). New York: Troll.

Bauer, Marion Dane. (1997a). *Allison's puppy* (Laurie Spencer, Illus.). New York: Hyperion Books.

Bauer, Marion Dane. (1997b). *If you were born a kitten* (JoEllen McAllister Stammen, Illus.). New York: Simon & Schuster.

Bauer, Marion Dane. (1997c). *Turtle dreams* (Diane Dawson Hearn, Illus.). New York: Holiday House.

Bauer, Marion Dane. (1998a). *Bear's hiccups* (Diane Dawson Hearn, Illus.). New York: Holiday House.

Bauer, Marion Dane. (1998b). *Christmas in the forest* (Diane Dawson Hearn, Illus.). New York: Holiday House.

Bauer, Marion Dane. (1999a). *An early winter*. Boston: Houghton Mifflin.

Bauer, Marion Dane. (1999b). *Sleep, little one, sleep* (JoEllen McAllister Stammen, Illus.). New York: Simon & Schuster.

Baum, L. Frank. (1900). *The wonderful wizard of Oz*. New York: Dover.

Bausum, Ann. (2000). *Dragon bones and dinosaur eggs: A photobiography of explorer Roy Chapman Andrews* (photographs from the American Museum of Natural History). Washington, DC: National Geographic Society.

Baylor, Byrd. (1977). *When clay sings* (Tom Bahti, Illus.). New York: Scribner.

Baylor, Byrd. (1975). *The desert is theirs* (Peter Parnall, Illus.). New York: Scribner.

Baylor, Byrd. (1976). *Hawk, I'm your brother* (Peter Parnall, Illus.). New York: Scribner.

Baylor, Byrd. (1979). *Your own best secret place* (Peter Parnall, Illus.). New York: Scribner.

Baylor, Byrd. (1981). *Desert voices*. New York: Atheneum.

Baylor, Byrd. (1986). *I'm in charge of celebrations* (Peter Parnall, Illus.). Boston: Houghton Mifflin.

Baylor, Byrd. (1991). *Everybody needs a rock*. New York: Atheneum.

Baylor, Byrd. (1994). *The table where rich people sit* (Peter Parnall, Illus.). New York: Scribner.

Baylor, Byrd, & Parnall, Peter. (1978). *The other way to listen*. New York: Scribner.

Beatty, Patricia. (1997). *Charley Skedaddle*. Minneapolis: Sagebrush.

Beeler, Janet Shaw. (2002). *Changes for Kaya*. New York: Pleasant Company.

Behler, John. (1999). *Reptiles*. New York: Scholastic.

Bellairs, John. (1996). *The mummy, the will, and the crypt* (Edward Gorey, Illus.). New York: Penguin.

Belting, Natalie. (1992). *Moon was tired of walking on air* (Will Hillenbrand, Illus.). Boston: Houghton Mifflin.

Bemelmans, Ludwig. (1939/1962). *Madeline*. New York: Viking.

Benchley, Nathaniel. (1974). *Only earth and sky last forever*. New York: HarperTrophy.

Benton, Barbara. (1985). *Ellis Island: A pictorial history*. New York: Fact on File.

Berenstain, Stan, & Berenstain, Jan. (2002). *Down a sunny dirt road: An autobiography*. New York: Random House.

Berger, Melvin. (2003). *Spinning spiders* (S.D. Schindler, Illus.). New York: HarperCollins.

Berger, Melvin, & Berger, Gilda. (1993). *Where did your family come from? A book about immigrants* (Robert Quackenbush, Illus.). New York: Ideals.

Berger, Melvin, & Berger, Gilda. (1995). *Water, water everywhere*. Philadelphia: Chelsea House.

Berger, Melvin, & Berger, Gilda. (1999). *Do whales have belly buttons? Questions and answers about whales and dolphins*. New York: Scholastic.

Berger, Melvin, & Berger, Gilda. (2001). *Why do wolves howl? Questions and answers about wolves* (Roberto Osti, Illus.). New York: Scholastic.

Berger, Melvin, & Berger, Gilda. (2003). *How do frogs swallow with their eyes?* (Karen Carr, Illus.). New York: Scholastic.

Bergman, Thomas. (1990). *Going places: Children living with cerebral palsy*. Milwaukee: Gareth Stevens.

Bernbaum, Israel. (1985). *My brother's keeper*. New York: Putnam.

Berndt, Catherine. (1987). *Pheasant and kingfisher* (Raymond Meeks, Illus.). New South Wales, Australia: Ashton Scholastic.

Berry, James. (1991). *Ajeemah and his son*. New York: HarperCollins.

Bial, Raymond. (1999). *The Underground Railroad*. Boston: Houghton Mifflin.

Bial, Raymond. (2000). *A handful of dirt*. New York: Walker.

Bierhorst, John. (1992). *Lightning inside you and other Native American riddles*. New York: Morrow.

Bierhorst, John. (1994). *On the road of stars: Native American night poems and sleep charms*. New York: Simon & Schuster.

Bierhorst, John. (1998). *In the trail of the wind: American Indian poems and ritual orations*. New York: Farrar, Straus & Giroux.

Birdseye, Tom. (1993). *Just call me stupid*. New York: Holiday House.

Birdseye, Tom. (2003). *Oh Yeah!* (Ethan Long, Illus.). New York: Holiday House.

Bitton-Jackson, Livia. (1997). *I have lived a thousand years: Growing up in the Holocaust*. New York: Simon & Schuster.

Bjork, Christina. (1985). *Linnea in Monet's garden* (Lena Anderson, Illus.). New York: Farrar, Straus & Giroux.

Blackwood, Gary. (2000). *The Shakespeare stealer*. New York: Puffin Books.

Blake, Robert J. (1999). *Yudonsi*. New York: Philomel.

Blos, Joan W. (1979). *A gathering of days: A New England girl's journal, 1830–1832*. New York: Scribner.

Blumberg, Rhoda. (2001). *Shipwrecked! The true adventures of a Japanese boy*. New York: HarperCollins.

Blume, Judy. (1970a). *Are you there God? It's me, Margaret*. New York: Bradbury Press.

Blume, Judy. (1970b). *Iggie's house*. Englewood Cliffs, NJ: Bradbury Press.

Blume, Judy. (1971). *Then again, maybe I won't*. New York: Bradbury Press.

Blume, Judy. (1972a). *It's not the end of the world*. New York: Bantam.

Blume, Judy. (1972b). *Tales of a fourth grade nothing*. New York: Yearling Books.

Blume, Judy. (1973). *Deenie*. New York: Dell.

Blume, Judy. (1974a). *Blubber*. New York: Bradbury Press.

Blume, Judy. (1974b). *The pain and the great one* (Irene Trivas, Illus.). Scarsdale, NY: Bradbury Press.

Blume, Judy. (1975). *Forever*. Scarsdale, NY: Bradbury Press.

Blume, Judy. (1977). *Starring Sally J. Freedman as herself*. Scarsdale, NY: Bradbury Press.

Blume, Judy. (1980). *Superfudge*. New York: Dutton.

Blume, Judy. (1981). *Tiger eyes*. New York: Dell.

Blume, Judy. (1993). *Here's to you, Rachel Robinson*. New York: Orchard.

Blyton, Enid. (1996). *The naughtiest girl in the school*. London: Penguin.

Bodecker, N. M. (1998). *Hurry, hurry, Mary dear*. New York: McElderry.

Bolden, Tonya. (2001). *Tell all the children our story: Memories and mementoes of being young and black in America*. New York: Abrams.

Bollard, John. (2002). *Scholastic student thesaurus*. New York: Scholastic.

Bolotin, Norman, & Herb, Angela. (1995). *For home and country, a Civil War scrapbook*. New York: Lodestar Books.

Bolton, Lesley. (2002). *The everything classical mythology book: Greek and Roman gods, goddesses, heroes and monsters from Aries to Zeus*. Avon, MA: Adams Media.

Bond, Michael. (1972). *Paddington Bear*. New York: Random House.

Bond, Michael. (1998). *A bear called Paddington* (Peggy Fortnum, Illus.). Boston: Houghton Mifflin.

Booth, David. (Sel.). (1990). *'Til all the stars have fallen: A collection of poems for children* (Kady MacDonald Denton, Illus.). New York: Viking.

Borden, Louise, & Lewin, Ted. (1999). *A. Lincoln and me*. New York: Scholastic.

Brandenburg, Jim. (1993). *To the top of the world: Adventures with Arctic wolves*. New York: Walker.

Branley, Franklyn M. (2000). *The international space station* (Let's read and find out science) (True Kelly, Illus.). New York: HarperCollins.

Brashares, Ann. (2003). *The sisterhood of the traveling pants*. New York: Delacorte.

Brenner, Barbara. (Sel.). (2000). *Voices: Poetry and art from around the world*. Washington, DC: National Geographic Society.

Brenner, Martha. (1994). *Abe Lincoln's hat*. New York: Scholastic.

Brett, Jan. (1999). *Gingerbread baby*. New York: Putnam.

Bridges, Ruby. (1999). *Through my eyes*. New York: Scholastic.

Bridwell, Norman. (1963). *Clifford, the big red dog*. New York: Scholastic.

Bridwell, Norman. (1966). *Clifford takes a trip*. New York: Scholastic.

Bridwell, Norman. (1985). *Clifford and the grouchy neighbors*. New York: Scholastic.

Bridwell, Norman. (1987). *Clifford's manners*. New York: Scholastic.

Bridwell, Norman. (1992). *Clifford counts bubbles*. New York: Scholastic.

Bridwell, Norman. (1999). *Clifford grows up*. New York: Scholastic.

Brill, Marlene Targ. (1993). *Allen Jay and the Underground Railroad* (Janice L. Porter, Illus.). Los Angeles: Lerner.

Brink, Carol Ryrie. (2003). *Caddie Woodlawn*. Waterville, ME: Thorndike Press.

Brooks, Bruce. (1984). *The moves make the man*. New York: Harper & Row.

Brooks, Bruce. (1990). *Everywhere*. New York: HarperCollins.

Brooks, Bruce. (1992). *What hearts*. New York: HarperCollins.

Brooks, Gwendolyn. (1956). *Bronzeville boys and girls*. New York: Harper & Row.

Brooks, Martha. (1997). *Bone dance*. New York: Orchard Books.

Brooks, Walter R. (2001). *Freddy the detective* (Kurt Wiese, Illus.). New York: Penguin.

Broome, Errol. (1993). *Dear Mr. Sprouts*. New York: Knopf.

Brown, Don. (2003). *Mack made movies*. New York: Roaring Brook.

Brown, Jeff. (1992). *Flat Stanley*. New York: HarperTrophy.

Brown, Marc. (1987). *Play rhymes*. Dutton.

Brown, Marc. (1989). *Teddy bear, teddy bear*. New York: Dutton.

Brown, Marcia. (1961). *Once a mouse*. New York: Scribner.

Brown, Margaret Wise. (1947). *Goodnight moon* (Clement Hurd, Illus.). New York: HarperCollins.

Brown, Margaret Wise. (1949). *The important book*. New York: HarperTrophy.

Brown, Tricia. (1984). *Someone special just like you*. New York: Holt, Rinehart and Winston.

Browne, Anthony. (1990). *Changes*. New York: Knopf.

Browne, Anthony. (1998). *Voices in the park*. New York: DK Publishing.

Bruchac, Joseph. (1983a). *Breaking silence: An anthology of contemporary Asian-American poets*. New York: Greenfield Review Press.

Bruchac, Joseph. (1983b). *Songs from this Earth on Turtle's back*. New York: Greenfield Review Press.

Bruchac, Joseph. (1991). *Keepers of the Earth* (John Kahionhes Fadden, Illus.). Golden, CO: Fulcrum.

Bruchac, Joseph. (1992). *Thirteen moons on a turtle's back: A Native American year of moons*. New York: Philomel.

Bruchac, Joseph. (1994). *Returning the gift: Poetry and prose from the first North American's native writers festival*. Tucson: University of Arizona Press.

Bruchac, Joseph. (1997). *Eagle song*. New York: Dial Books.

Bruchac, Joseph. (1998). *The heart of a chief*. New York: Dial Books.

Bruchac, Joseph. (1999a). *Between earth and sky: Legends of Native American sacred places* (Thomas Locker, Illus.). San Diego: Harcourt.

Bruchac, Joseph. (1999b). *Pushing up the sky* (Teresa Flavin, Illus.). New York: Dial Books.

Bruchac, Joseph. (2000a). *Crazy Horse's vision* (S. D. Nelson, Illus.). New York: Lee & Low.

Bruchac, Joseph. (2000b). *Sacajawea*. New York: Harcourt.

Bruchac, Joseph. (2000c). *Squanto's journey*. New York: Harcourt.

Brumbeau, Jeff. (2003). *Miss Hunnicutt's hat* (Gail de Marcken, Illus.). New York: Orchard Books.

Bryan, Ashley. (1971). *The ox of the wonderful horns and other African folktales*. New York: Atheneum.

Bryan, Ashley. (1977). *The dancing granny*. New York: Atheneum.

Bryan, Ashley. (1985). *The cat's purr*. New York: Atheneum.

Bryan, Ashley. (1986). *Lion and the ostrich chicks and other African folk tales*. New York: Atheneum.

Bryan, Ashley. (1989). *Turtle knows your name*. New York: Atheneum.

Bryan, Ashley. (1991). *All night, all day: A child's first book of African American spirituals*. New York: Atheneum.

Bryan, Ashley. (1992). *Sing to the sun*. New York: HarperCollins.

Bryan, Ashley. (1998). *Ashley Bryan's African tales, uh-huh*. New York: Atheneum.

Bryan, Ashley. (2003). *Beautiful blackbird*. New York: Atheneum.

Bryant, Sally Smith. (1997). *Here's Juggins* (Lynne M. Beach, Illus.). Unity, ME: North Country Press.

Buck, Pearl S. (1948/1986). *The big wave*. New York: HarperTrophy.

Bulla, Clyde R. (1956). *The sword in the tree*. New York: Crowell.

Bulla, Clyde R. (1981). *A lion to guard us*. New York: HarperCollins.

Bulla, Clyde R. (1987). *The chalk box* (Thomas Ellen, Illus.). New York: Random House.

Bunting, Eve. (1980). *Terrible things: An allegory of the Holocaust* (Stephen Gammell, Illus.). New York: Harper & Row.

Bunting, Eve. (1984). *The man who could call down owls* (Charles Mikolaycak, Illus.). New York: Macmillan.

Bunting, Eve. (1989). *The Wednesday surprise* (Donald Carrick, Illus.). New York: Clarion Books.

Bunting, Eve. (1990). *The wall* (Robert Himler, Illus.). New York: Trumpet Club.

Bunting, Eve. (1991). *Fly away home*. New York: Clarion Books.

Bunting, Eve. (1994). *A day's work* (Robert Himler, Illus.). New York: Clarion Books.

Bunting, Eve. (1994a). *Smoky night* (David Diaz, Illus.). San Diego: Harcourt Brace.

Bunting, Eve. (1994b). *Sunshine home* (Diane de Groat, Illus.). New York: Clarion Books.

Bunting, Eve. (1996). *S.O.S. Titanic*. San Diego: Harcourt Brace.

Bunting, E. (1998). *So far from the sea*. New York: Clarion Books.

Bunting, Eve. (1999). *Butterfly house* (Greg Shed, Illus.). New York: Scholastic.

Bunting, Eve. (2002). *Girls A to Z* (Suzanne Bloom, Illus.). Honesdale, PA: Boyds Mills Press.

Burg, Brad. (2002). *Outside the lines: Poetry at play* (Rebecca Gibbon, Illus.). New York: Putnam.

Burleigh, Robert. (1998). *Black whiteness: Admiral Byrd alone in the Antarctic* (Walter Lyon Krudop, Illus.). New York: Atheneum.

Burleigh, Robert. (1998). *Home run: The story of Babe Ruth* (Mike Wimmer, Illus.). New York: Harcourt.

Burleigh, Robert. (2002). *Chocolate: Riches from the rainforest*. New York: Abrams.

Burnett, Frances Hodgson. (1911). *The secret garden*. New York: Stokes.

Burnford, Sheila. (1961). *The incredible journey*. Boston: Little, Brown.

Byars, Betsy. (1970). *The summer of the swans*. New York: Viking.

Byars, Betsy. (1981). *The Cybil war*. New York: Viking.

Byars, Betsy. (1982). *The house of wings*. Minneapolis: Sagebrush.

Byars, Betsy. (1988). *The burning questions of Bingo Brown*. New York: Viking.

Byars, Betsy. (1990). *Bingo Brown, Gypsy lover*. New York: Viking.

Caduto, Michael, & Bruchac, Joseph. (1989). *Keepers of the Earth*. Golden, CO: Fulcrum.

Caldecott, Randolph. (1882). *Hey Diddle Diddle and Baby Bunting*. London: Routledge.

Calhoun, Mary. (1983). *Big sixteen* (Trina Schart Hyman, Illus.). New York: Morrow.

Calmenson, Stephanie. (1989). *The principal's new clothes*. New York: Scholastic.

Cameron, Ann. (1981). *The stories Julian tells*. New York: Knopf.

Cameron, Ann. (1986). *More stories Julian tells*. New York: Knopf.

Cameron, Ann. (1988). *The most beautiful place in the world*. New York: Knopf.

Cameron, Ann. (1990). *Julian, dream doctor* (Ann Strugnell, Illus.). New York: Random House.

Cameron, Ann. (1995). *The stories Huey tells*. New York: Knopf.

Cameron, Eleanor. (1992). *The wonderful flight to the mushroom planet*. Boston: Little, Brown.

Campbell, Eric. (1991). *A place of lions*. San Diego: Harcourt Brace.

Carbone, Elisa. (2001). *Storm warriors*. New York: Knopf.

Carle, Eric. (1969). *The very hungry caterpillar*. New York: Philomel.

Carle, Eric. (1984). *The very busy spider*. New York: Philomel.

Carle, Eric. (1990). *The very quiet cricket*. New York: Philomel.

Carle, Eric. (1992). *Draw me a star*. New York: Philomel.

Carle, Eric. (1995). *The very lonely firefly*. New York: Philomel.

Carlson, Lori M. (1994). *Cool salsa: Bilingual poems on growing up Latino in the United States*. New York: Henry Holt.

Carlson, Lori M. (1998). *Sol a sol: Bilingual poems* (Emily Lisker, Illus.). New York: Henry Holt.

Carlson, Nathalie Savage. (1958). *The family under the bridge* (Garth Williams, Illus.). New York: Scholastic.

Carlstrom, Nancy White. (1998). *Midnight dance of the snowshoe hare: Poems of Alaska*. New York: Philomel.

Carrick, Carol. (1985). *Stay away from Simon* (Donald Carrick, Illus.). New York: Clarion Books.

Carrick, Carol. (1993). *Whaling days* (David Frampton, Illus.). New York: Clarion Books.

Carroll, Lewis. (1865). *Alice's adventures in Wonderland*. London: Macmillan.

Carroll, Lewis. (1985). *Alice's adventures under ground*. London: Pavillon.

Carroll, Lewis. (1987.). *Alice through the looking glass*. London: Macmillan.

Carson, Jo. (1989). *Stories I ain't told nobody yet: Selections from the people pieces*. New York: Orchard Books.

Carter, Alden R. (1999). *Dustin's big school day*. Morton Grove, IL: Whitman.

Carter, Anne. (1991). *Birds, beasts and fishes: A selection of animal poems*. New York: Atheneum.

Casey, Maude. (1996). *Over the water*. New York: Puffin Books.

Cassedy, Sylvia. (1993). *Zoomrimes: Poems about things that go*. New York: HarperCollins.

Castaneda, Omar S. (1991). *Among the volcanoes*. New York: Dell.

Castle, Caroline. (1993). *Grandpa Baxter and the photographs* (Peter Bowman, Illus.). New York: Orchard Books.

Catling, Patrick Skene. (1979). *The chocolate touch* (Margot Apple, Illus.). New York: Morrow.

Chaconas, Dori. (2002). *On a wintry morning*. New York: Puffin Books.

Chaikin, Miriam. (2002). *Don't step on the sky: A handful of haiku* (Hiroe Nakata, Illus.). New York: Henry Holt.

Chandra, Deborah. (1990). *Balloons and other poems* (Leslie Bowman, Illus.). New York: Farrar, Straus & Giroux.

Chandra, Deborah. (1993). *Rich lizard and other poems* (Leslie Bowman, Illus.). New York: Farrar, Straus & Giroux.

Chang, Ina. (1991). *A separate battle: Women and the Civil War*. New York: Lodestar Books.

Charlip, Remy. (1993). *Fortunately, unfortunately*. New York: Scott, Foresman.

Cheaney, J. B. (2002). *The playmaker*. New York: Yearling.

Cheaney, J. B. (2004). *The true prince*. Minneapolis: Sagebrush.

Chekhov, Anton. (1994). *Kashtanka* (Gennady Spirin, Illus.). New York: Harcourt Brace.

Cheng, Andrea. (2000). *Grandfather counts* (Ange Zhang, Illus.). New York: Lee & Low.

Cherry, Lynne. (1982). *The armadillo from Amarillo*. San Diego: Harcourt Brace.

Cherry, Lynne. (1992). *A river ran wild: An environmental story*. New York: Harcourt Brace.

Cherry, Lynne. (1995). *The dragon and the unicorn*. San Diego: Harcourt Brace.

Cherry, Lynne. (1997). *Flute's journey*. New York: Scholastic.

Cherry, Lynne. (1998). *The Shaman's apprentice*. San Diego: Harcourt Brace.

Cherry, Lynne. (2000). *The great kapok tree: A tale of the Amazon rain forest*. San Diego: Harcourt Brace.

Chester, Jonathan. (2002). *The young adventurer's guide to Everest: From avalanche to Zopkio*. New York: Tricycle Press.

Chesterman, Charles W. (1978). *The Audubon Society field guide to North American rocks and minerals*. New York: Knopf.

Childress, Alice. (1973). *A hero ain't nothin' but a sandwich*. New York: Coward-McCann.

Chocolate, Debbi. (1998). *The piano man* (Eric Velasquez, Illus.). New York: Walker.

Choi, Sook Nyul. (1991). *Year of impossible goodbyes*. Boston: Houghton Mifflin.

Christelow, Eileen. (1999). *What do illustrators do?* New York: Clarion Books.

Christensen, Bonnie. (2001). *Woody Guthrie: Poet of the people*. New York: Knopf.

Christensen, Bonnie. (2003). *The Daring Nellie Bly: America's star reporter*. New York: Knopf.

Christopher, John. (1967). *City of gold and lead*. New York: Macmillan.

Christopher, John. (2003a). *The pool of fire*. New York: Simon Pulse.

Christopher, John. (2003b). *The white mountains*. New York: Simon Pulse.

Christopher, John. (2003c). *When the tripods came*. New York: Simon Pulse.

Christopher, Matt. (1992). *Return of the homerun kid*. Boston: Little, Brown.

Christopher, Matt. (1999). *The Captain contest*. Boston: Little, Brown.

Christopher, Matt. (1999). *Spike it!* Boston: Little, Brown.

Ciardi, John. (1991). *The hopeful trout and other limericks* (Susan Meddaugh, Illus.). Boston: Houghton Mifflin.

Cisneros, Sandra. (1985). *The house on Mango Street*. Houston: Arte Publico Press.

Clark, Ann Nolan. (1991). *In my mother's house*. New York: Viking.

Clark, Margaret Goff. (1991). *Freedom crossing*. New York: Scholastic.

Clarke, Arthur C. (1966). Space pet. In M. Gartier (Ed.), *The magic word* (pp. 138–140). New York: Macmillan.

Cleary, Beverly. (1950). *Henry Huggins*. New York: Morrow.

Cleary, Beverly. (1952). *Henry and Beezus*. New York: Morrow.

Cleary, Beverly. (1955). *Beezus and Ramona*. New York: Morrow.

Cleary, Beverly. (1976). *The mouse and the motorcycle*. New York: Morrow.

Cleary, Beverly. (1981). *Ramona Quimby Age 8*. New York: Morrow.

Cleary, Beverly. (1990a). *Ramona the pest* (Louis Darling, Illus.). Santa Barbara, CA: Cornerstone Books.

Cleary, Beverly. (1990b). *Socks*. New York: Dell.

Cleary, Beverly. (1992). *Ribsy* (Louis Darling, Illus.). New York: HarperCollins.

Cleary, Beverly. (1999). *Ramona's world*. New York: Morrow.

Cleary, Beverly. (2000). *Dear Mr. Henshaw*. New York: HarperTrophy.

Cleaver, Vera, & Cleaver, Bill. (1969). *Where the lilies bloom* (Jim Spanfeller, Illus.). Philadelphia: Lippincott.

Clements, Andrew. (1996). *Frindle* (Brian Selznik, Illus.). New York: Simon & Schuster.

Clinton, Catherine. (Sel.). (1998). *I, too, sing America: Three centuries of African-American poetry* (Stephen Alcorn, Illus.). Boston: Houghton Mifflin.

Clinton, Catherine. (2000). *The black soldier: 1492 to the present*. Boston: Houghton Mifflin.

Clinton, Catherine. (2002). *A stone in my hand*. Cambridge, MA: Candlewick Press.

Coerr, Eleanor, & Himler, Ronald. (1999). *Sadako and the thousand paper cranes*. New York: Penguin.

Cofer, Judith Ortiz. (1995). *An island like you: Stories of the barrio*. New York: Orchard Books.

Cohen, Barbara. (1974). *Thank you, Jackie Robinson* (Richard Cuffar, Illus.). New York: Lothrop, Lee & Shepard.

Cohen, Barbara. (1999). *Molly's pilgrim*. New York: Scholastic.

Cohen, Miriam. (1972). *Lost in the museum* (Lillian Hoban, Illus.). New York: Dell.

Cohen, Miriam. (1977). *When will I read?* (Lillian Hoban, Illus.). New York: Greenwillow.

Cohen, Miriam. (1980). *First grade takes a test* (Lillian Hoban, Illus.). New York: Greenwillow.

Cohen, Miriam. (1993). *Second grade friends* (Diane Palmisciano, Illus.). New York: Scholastic.

Cohen, Miriam. (1998). *Down in the subway* (Melanie Hope Greenberg, Illus.). New York: DK Pub.

Cohen, Miriam. (1999). *Mimmy and Sophie* (Thomas F. Yezerski, Illus.). New York: Farrar, Straus & Giroux.

Cohn, Amy. (1993). *From sea to shining sea: A treasury of American folklore and folksongs* (various artists, Illus.). New York: Scholastic.

Cole, Babette. (1988). *Prince Cinders*. New York: Putnam.

Cole, Brock. (1987). *The goats*. New York: Farrar, Straus & Giroux.

Cole, Joanna. (Sel.). (1984). *A new treasury of children's poetry: Old favorites and new discoveries* (Judith Gwyn Brown, Illus.). Garden City, NY: Doubleday.

Cole, Joanna. (1996). *The magic school inside a hurricane*. New York: Scholastic.

Cole, Joanna. (1997). *The magic school bus goes upstream*. New York: Scholastic.

Cole, Joanna. (1999). *The magic school bus explores the senses* (Bruce Degen, Illus.). New York: Scholastic.

Cole, Joanna. (2001). *Ms. Frizzle's adventures: Ancient Egypt* (Bruce Degen, Illus.). New York: Scholastic.

Cole, Joanna. (2003). *Ms. Frizzle's adventures: Medieval castle* (Bruce Degen, Illus.). New York: Scholastic.

Cole, Joanna, & Calmenson, Stephanie. (Sels.). (1990). *Miss Mary Mack and other children's street rhymes* (Alan Tiegreen, Illus.). New York: Morrow.

Cole, Sheila. (2002). *The canyon*. New York: HarperCollins.

Cole, William. (1966). *Oh what nonsense*. New York: Viking.

Cole, William. (1981). *Poem stew*. Philadelphia: Lippincott.

Colgin, Mary L. (1982). *One potato, two potato, three potato, four: 165 chants for children*. Mt Rainier, MD: Gryphon House.

Collard, Sneed B. (1997). *Animal dads* (Steve Jenkins, Illus.). Boston: Houghton Mifflin.

Collard, Sneed B. (2000). *Acting for nature: What young people around the world have done to protect the environment* (Carl Dennis Buell, Illus.). New York: Heyday Books.

Collard, Sneed B. (2000). *The forest in the clouds* (Michael Rothman, Illus.). Boston: Charlesbridge.

Collard, Sneed B. (2002). *Beaks!* Boston: Charlesbridge.

Collier, Christopher, & Collier, James Lincoln. (1987). *Decision in Philadelphia: The Constitutional Convention of 1787*. New York: Random House.

Collier, James Lincoln. (2000). *A century of immigration*. New York: Marshall Cavendish.

Collier, James Lincoln, & Collier, Christopher. (1974). *My brother Sam is dead*. New York: Macmillan.

Collier, James Lincoln, & Collier, Christopher. (1978). *The winter hero*. New York: Scholastic.

Collier, James Lincoln, & Collier, Christopher. (1981). *Jump ship to freedom*. New York: Dell.

Collier, James Lincoln, & Collier, Christopher. (1983). *War comes to Willy Freeman*. New York: Delacorte.

Collier, James Lincoln, & Collier, Christopher. (1985). *The bloody country*. New York: Scholastic.

Collier, James Lincoln, & Collier, Christopher. (1994a). *The clock* (Kelly Maddox, Illus.). New York: Dell.

Collier, James Lincoln, & Collier, Christopher. (1994b). *With every drop of blood*. New York: Dell.

Collier, James Lincoln, & Collier, Christopher. (2001). *Who is Carrie?* New York: Random House.

Colman, Penny. (1994). *Madam C. J. Walker: Building a business empire.* Brookfield, CT: Millbrook Press.

Colman, Penny. (1995). *Rosie the riveter: Women working on the home front in World War II.* New York: Crown.

Colman, Penny. (1997). *Corpses, coffins and crypts: A history of burial.* New York: Henry Holt.

Colman, Penny. (2000). *Girls: A history of growing up female in America.* New York: Scholastic.

Colman, Penny. (2002). *Where the action was: Women war correspondents in World War II.* New York: Crown.

Cone, Molly. (1992). *Come back, salmon: How a group of dedicated kids adopted Pigeon Creek and brought it back to life* (Sidnee Wheelwright, Photog.). San Francisco: Sierra Club.

Conly, Jane Leslie. (1993). *Crazy lady.* New York: HarperCollins.

Conrad, Pam. (1985.). *Prairie songs.* New York: Harper & Row.

Conrad, Pam. (1989). *My Daniel.* New York: Harper & Row.

Conrad, Pam. (1990). *Stonewords: A ghost story.* New York: Harper & Row.

Cooney, Barbara. (1982). *Miss Rumphius.* New York: Viking.

Cooper, Floyd. (1996). *Mandela: From the life of the South African statesman.* New York: Philomel.

Cooper, Ilene. (2003). *Jack: The early years of John F. Kennedy.* New York: Dutton.

Cooper, Susan. (1970). *Dawn of fear.* New York: Harcourt Brace.

Cooper, Susan. (1973). *The dark is rising* (Alan E. Cober, Illus.). New York: Atheneum.

Cooper, Susan. (1977). *Silver on the tree.* New York: McElderry.

Cooper, Susan. (1986). *The grey king.* New York: Aladdin Books.

Cooper, Susan. (1993). *Danny and the kings* (Jos. A. Smith, Illus.). New York: McElderry.

Cooper, Susan. (2000a). *Greenwitch.* New York: Simon & Schuster.

Cooper, Susan. (2000b). *King of shadows.* New York: McElderry.

Cooper, Susan.(2002). *Green boy.* New York: McElderry.

Cooper, Susan. (2004). *Over sea, under stone.* New York: Aladdin Books.

Corey, Shana. (2000). *You forgot your skirt, Amelia Bloomer!* (Chesley McLaren, Illus.). New York: Scholastic.

Couper, Heather, & Henbest, Nigel. (1999a). *The Kingfisher children's illustrated dictionary and thesaurus.* Boston: Houghton Mifflin.

Couper, Heather, & Henbest, Nigel. (1999b). *Space encyclopedia.* New York: DK Publishing.

Cormier, Robert. (1974). *The chocolate war.* New York: Knopf.

Cormier, Robert. (1977). *I am the cheese.* New York: Pantheon.

Cowen-Fletcher, Jane. (1994). *It takes a village.* New York: Scholastic.

Cowley, Joy. (1993). *Wishy-washy day* (Elizabeth Fuller, Illus.). Bothell, WA: The Wright Group.

Cowley, Joy. (1999a). *Mrs. Wishy-Washy* (Elizabeth Fuller, Illus.). New York: Philomel.

Cowley, Joy. (1999b). *Red-eyed tree frog.* New York: Scholastic.

Creech, Sharon. (1994). *Walk two moons.* New York: HarperCollins.

Creech, Sharon. (1995). *Absolutely normal chaos.* New York: HarperCollins.

Creech, Sharon. (1996). *Pleasing the ghost* (Stacey Schuett, Illus.). New York: HarperCollins.

Creech, Sharon. (1997). *Chasing redbird.* New York: HarperCollins.

Creech, Sharon. (1998). *Bloomability.* New York: HarperCollins.

Creech, Sharon. (2000a). *Fishing in the air* (Chris Raschka, Illus.). New York: Joanna Cotler Books.

Creech, Sharon. (2000b). *The wanderer.* New York: HarperCollins.

Creech, Sharon. (2001). *Love that dog.* New York: HarperCollins.

Creech, Sharon. (2004). *Ruby Holler.* Minneapolis: Sagebrush.

Crewe, Sabrina. (1997). *The spider* (Colin Newman, Illus.). Austin, TX: Raintree Steck-Vaughn.

Crews, Donald. (1985). *Truck.* New York: Puffin Books.

Crist-Evans, Craig. (1999). *Moon over Tennessee: A boy's Civil War journal* (wood engravings by Bonnie Christensen). Boston: Houghton Mifflin.

Cronin, Doreen. (2000). *Click, clack, moo: Cows that type* (Betsy Lewin, Illus.). New York: Simon & Schuster.

Cronin, Doreen. (2002). *Giggle, giggle, quack* (Betsy Lewin, Illus.). New York: Simon & Schuster.

Crowe, Chris. (2003). *Mississippi trial, 1955.* Minneapolis: Sagebrush.

Crutcher, Chris. (1993). *Staying fat for Sarah Byrnes.* New York: Greenwillow.

Crutcher, Chris. (1995). *Ironman.* New York: Greenwillow.

Crutcher, Chris. (2003). *King of the mild frontier: An ill-advised autobiography.* New York: Greenwillow.

Cullinan, Bernice E. (1996). *A jar of tiny stars: Poems by NCTE award-winning poets.* Honesdale, PA: Wordsong, Boyds Mills Press.

Cullinan, Bernice E. (Ed.). (2002). *I heard a bluebird sing* (Jennifer Emery, Illus.). Honesdale, PA: Boyds Mills Press.

Curlee, Lynn. (2001). *The Brooklyn Bridge.* New York: Atheneum.

Curtis, Christopher Paul. (1995). *The Watsons go to Birmingham—1965.* New York: Delacorte.

Curtis, Christopher Paul. (1999). *Bud, Not Buddy.* New York: Delacorte.

Cushman, Karen. (1994). *Catherine, called Birdy.* New York: Clarion Books.

Cushman, Karen. (1995). *The midwife's apprentice.* New York: Clarion Books.

Cushman, Karen. (1996). *The ballad of Lucy Whipple.* New York: Clarion Books.

Cushman, Karen. (2002). *Matilda Bone.* New York: Clarion Books.

Dahl, Michael. (2002). *The coral coffin.* New York: Pocket Books.

Dahl, Roald. (1961). *James and the giant peach.* New York: Knopf.

Dahl, Roald. (1982). *The BFG* (Quentin Blake, Illus.). New York: Farrar, Straus & Giroux.

Dahl, Roald. (1984). *Boy.* New York: Penguin.

Dahl, Roald. (1988a). *Charlie and the chocolate factory.* New York: Puffin Books.

Dahl, Roald. (1988b). *Matilda.* New York: Viking.

Dakos, Kalli. (1990). *If you're not here, please raise your hand* (G. Brian Karas, Illus.). New York: Four Winds Press.

Dalgliesh, Alice. (1954). *The courage of Sarah Noble.* New York: Scribner.

Danziger, Paula. (1986). *This place has no atmosphere.* New York: Delacorte Press.

Danziger, Paula. (1996). *Amber Brown wants extra credit* (Tony Ross, Illus.). New York: Putnam.

Darling, Kathy. (1996). *Rain forest babies* (Tara Darling, Photog.). New York: Walker.

Daugherty, James. (1939). *Daniel Boone.* New York: Viking.

D'Aulaire, Ingrid. (1987). *Abraham Lincoln.* New York: Dell.

Davidson, Margaret. (1986). *I have a dream: The story of Martin Luther King.* New York: Scholastic.

Davies, Nicola. (2001). *Big blue whale* (Nick Maland, Illus.). New York: Candlewick Press.

Dawood, N. J. (1996). *Aladdin and other tales from the Arabian Nights.* London: Puffin Books.

de Angeli, Marguerite. (1949). *The door in the wall.* Garden City, NY: Doubleday.

de Angeli, Marguerite. (1954). *The book of nursery & Mother Goose rhymes.* New York: Doubleday.

DeArmond, Dale. (1990). *The boy who found the light: Eskimo folktales.* San Francisco: Sierra Club Books.

DeFelice, Cynthia. (1988). *The strange night writing of Jessamine Colter*. New York: Farrar, Straus & Giroux.

DeFelice, Cynthia. (1989). *The dancing skeleton* (Robert Andrew Parker, Illus.). New York: Macmillan.

DeFelice, Cynthia. (1991). *Weasel*. New York: Avon.

DeFelice, Cynthia. (1992). *Devil's bridge*. New York: Macmillan.

DeFelice, Cynthia. (1993). *The light on Hogback Hill*. New York: Macmillan.

DeFelice, Cynthia. (1994). *Lostman's river*. New York: Macmillan.

DeFelice, Cynthia. (1995). *Three perfect peaches* (Irene Trivas, Illus.). New York: Orchard Books.

DeFelice, Cynthia. (1996a). *The apprenticeship of Lucas Whittaker*. New York: Farrar, Straus & Giroux.

DeFelice, Cynthia. (1996b). *Casey in the bath* (Chris L. Demarest, Illus.). New York: Farrar, Straus & Giroux.

DeFelice, Cynthia. (1997). *Willy's silly grandma* (Shelley Jackson, Illus.). New York: Orchard Books.

DeFelice, Cynthia. (1998). *The ghost of Fossil Glen*. New York: Farrar, Straus & Giroux.

DeFelice, Cynthia. (1999). *Nowhere to call home*. New York: Farrar, Straus & Giroux.

Defoe, Daniel. (1843). *The life and adventures of Robinson Crusoe*. New Haven, CT: S. Barcock.

DeJong, Meindert. (1956). *The house of sixty fathers*. New York: Harper.

Delacre, Lulu. (1989). *Arroz con leche: Popular songs and rhymes from Latin America*. New York: Scholastic.

Delacre, Lulu. (1993). *Vejigantes masquerader*. New York: Scholastic.

Delacre, Lulu. (1996). *Golden tales: Myths, legends, and folktales from Latin America*. New York: Scholastic.

Delacre, Lulu. (2000). *Salsa stories*. New York: Scholastic.

Delafosse, Claude, Fuhr, Ute, & Sautai, Raoul. (1993). *Whales*. New York: Scholastic.

Demarest, Chris L. (2000). *Firefighter A to Z*. New York: Simon & Schuster.

Demarest, Chris L. (2002). *Smokejumpers one to ten*. New York: McElderry.

Demi. (1979a). *Bong Nam and the pheasants*. New York: Prentice Hall.

Demi. (1979b). *Under the shade of the mulberry tree*. New York: Prentice Hall.

Demi. (1980). *Liang and the magic paintbrush*. New York: Henry Holt.

Demi. (1990). *The empty pot*. New York: Henry Holt.

Demi. (1993). *Demi's secret garden*. New York: Holt.

Demi. (1995). *The stonecutter*. New York: Crown.

dePaola, Tomie. (1973/1987). *Nana upstairs & Nana downstairs*. New York: Puffin Books.

dePaola, Tomie. (1978a). *Bill and Pete*. New York: Putnam.

dePaola, Tomie. (1978b). *Clown of God*. San Diego: Harcourt Brace.

dePaola, Tomie. (1978c). *Pancakes for breakfast*. New York: Harcourt Brace.

dePaola, Tomie. (1978d). *The popcorn book*. New York: Holiday House.

dePaola, Tomie. (1979a). *Oliver Button is a sissy*. San Diego: Harcourt Brace.

dePaola, Tomie. (1979b). *Strega Nona*. New York: Simon & Schuster.

dePaola, Tomie. (1981). *Now one foot, now the other*. New York: Putnam.

dePaola, Tomie. (1983). *The legend of the bluebonnet: An old tale of Texas*. New York: Putnam.

dePaola, Tomie. (1985). *Mother Goose*. New York: Putnam.

dePaola, Tomie. (1988). *Tomie dePaola's book of poems*. New York: Putnam.

dePaola, Tomie. (1995). *The unicorn and the moon*. Parsippany, NJ: Silver Press.

dePaola, Tomie. (1996a). *Bill and Pete go down the Nile*. New York: Paperstar.

dePaola, Tomie. (1996b). *Strega Nona meets her match*. New York: Putnam.

dePaola, Tomie. (1997). *The art lesson*. New York: Putnam.

de Regniers, Beatrice Schenk, Moore, Eva, White, Mary Michaels, & Carr, Jan. (1988). *Sing a song of popcorn* (various artists, Illus.). New York: Scholastic.

Deuker, Carl. (1994). *The heart of a champion*. New York: HarperTrophy.

Dewey, Jennifer Owings. (1994). *Wildlife rescue: The work of Dr. Kathleen Ramsay* (Don MacCarter, Photog.). Honesdale, PA: Boyds Mills Press.

De Zutter, Hank. (1993). *Who says a dog goes bow-wow?* (Suse MacDonald, Illus.). New York: Dell.

DiCamillo, Kate. (2000). *Because of Winn-Dixie*. New York: Candlewick Press.

Dickens, Charles. (1990). *A Christmas carol*. Mankato, MN: Creative Education.

Dionetti, Michelle. (1996). *Painting the wind* (Kevin Hawkes, Illus.). Boston: Little, Brown.

di Pasquale, Emanuel. (2003). *Cartwheel to the moon: My Sicilian childhood*. Chicago: Cricket Books.

Dipper, Frances. (2003). *Secrets of the deep revealed*. New York: DK Publishing.

DiSalvo-Ryan, DyAnne. (1991). *Uncle Willie and the soup kitchen*. New York: Morrow.

Dixon, Dougal. (2000). *Dougal Dixon's amazing dinosaurs: The fiercest, the tallest, the toughest, the smallest*. Honesdale, PA: Boyds Mills Press.

Dobson, Christina. (2003). *Pizza counting* (Matthew Holmes, Illus.). Boston: Charlesbridge.

Doherty, Berlie. (1994). *Slake's limbo*. New York: Scholastic.

Dorris, Michael. (1992). *Morning girl*. New York: Hyperion Books.

Dorris, Michael. (1996). *Sees Behind Trees*. New York: Hyperion Books.

Dorris, Michael. (1999). *Guests*. New York: Hyperion Books.

Dorros, Arthur. (1990). *Rain forest secrets*. New York: Scholastic.

Dosier, Susan. (2000). *Civil War cooking: The Union*. Los Angeles: Blue Earth Books.

Dotlich, Rebecca Kai. (1998). *Lemonade sun: And other summer poems* (Jan Spivey Gilchrist, Illus.). Honesdale, PA: Boyds Mills Press.

Dotlich, Rebecca Kai. (2002). *A family like yours*. Honesdale, PA: Boyds Mills Press.

Doubilet, Anne, & Doubilet, David. (1991). *Under the sea from A to Z*. New York: Crown.

Dragonwagon, Crescent. (1984). *Jemima remembers*. New York: Atheneum.

Draper, Sharon. (1994). *Tears of a tiger*. New York: Simon & Schuster.

Droll, Virginia. (1994). *Beginnings: How families come to be* (Stacy Schuett, Illus.). Morton Grove, IL: Albert Whitman.

Dunbar, Paul Laurence. (1999). *Jump back, Honey: Poems*. New York: Jump at the Sun.

Duncan, Lois. (1973). *I know what you did last summer*. Boston: Little, Brown.

Duncan, Lois. (1989). *Don't look behind you*. New York: Dell.

Duncan, Lois. (1990). *Stranger with my face*. New York: Dell.

Dunn, Sonja. (1987). *Butterscotch dreams: Chants for fun and learning*. Portsmouth, NH: Heinemann.

Dunning, Stephen. (1976). *Reflections on a gift of watermelon pickle and other modern verse*. New York: HarperCollins.

DuPrau, Jeanne. (2003). *The city of Ember*. New York: Random House.

Dyer, Jane. (1998). *Animal crackers*. Boston: Little, Brown.

Eckert, Allan W. (1971). *Incident at Hawk's Hill*. Boston: Little, Brown.

Edwards, Wallace. (2002). *Alphabeasts*. Toronto, ON: Kids Can Press.

Ehlert, Lois. (1989). *Color zoo*. New York: HarperCollins.

Ehlert, Lois. (2000). *Market day: A story told with folk art*. New York: Harcourt.

Ellis, Deborah. (2001). *The breadwinner*. Toronto, ON: Groundwood Books.

Ellis, Deborah. (2002). *Parvana's journey*. Toronto, ON: Groundwood Books.

Elsom, Derek. (1997). *Weather explained: A beginner's guide to the elements*. New York: Henry Holt.

Engdahl, Sylvia. (2001). *Enchantress from the stars*. New York: Walker.

Erdoes, Richard, & Ortiz, Alfonso. (1985). *American Indian myths and legends*. New York: Pantheon.

Erdrich, Louise. (1999). *The birchbark house*. New York: Hyperion Books.

Ernst, Lisa Campbell. (1983). *Sam Johnson and the blue ribbon quilt*. New York: Mulberry.

Esbensen, Barbara J. (1987). *Words with wrinkled knees*. New York: Crowell.

Esbensen, Barbara J. (1992). *Who shrank my grandmother's house?* New York: HarperCollins.

Esbensen, Barbara J. (1994). *Baby whales drink milk* (Lambert Daus, Illus.). New York: Troll.

Esbensen, Barbara J. (1995). *Dance with me*. New York: Harper.

Esbensen, Barbara J. (1996). *Echoes for the eye: Poems to celebrate patterns in nature* (Helen K. Davie, Illus.). New York: HarperCollins.

Estes, Eleanor. (1944). *The hundred dresses*. New York: Harcourt Brace.

Ets, Marie Hall. (1955). *Play with me*. New York: Puffin Books.

Evans, Richard Paul. (2000). *The spyglass* (Jonathan Linton, Illus.). New York: Simon & Schuster.

Falconer, Ian. (2001). *Olivia saves the circus*. New York: Atheneum.

Farmer, Nancy. (1994). *The ear, the eye and the arm*. New York: Orchard Books.

Farmer, Nancy. (1998). *A girl named Disaster*. New York: Orchard Books.

Farmer, Nancy (2002). *The house of the scorpion*. New York: Atheneum.

Farndon, John. (2002). *Magnetism*. Windsor, Ontario: Benchmark.

Faust, Drew Gilpin. (1997). *Mothers of invention: Women of the slave-holding South in the American Civil War*. New York: Vintage Books.

Feelings, Tom. (1993). *Soul looks back in wonder*. New York: Dial Books.

Fenner, Carol. (1978). *The skates of Uncle Richard* (Ati Forberg, Illus.). New York: Knopf.

Fenner, Carol. (1991). *Randall's wall*. New York: Simon & Schuster.

Fenner, Carol. (1995). *Yolonda's genius*. New York: McElderry.

Ferreira, Anton. (2002). *Zulu dog*. New York: Farrar, Straus & Giroux.

Ferris, Helen. (Ed.). (1957). *Favorite poems, old and new* (Leonard Weisgard, Illus.). Garden City, NY: Doubleday.

Fine, Anne. (1995). *Flour babies*. Minneapolis: Sagebrush.

Fisher, Aileen. (1965). *In the woods, in the meadow, in the sky*. New York: Scribner.

Fisher, Aileen L. (1971). *Feathered ones and furry*. New York: Crowell.

Fisher, Aileen. (1980). *Out in the dark and daylight*. New York: HarperCollins.

Fitzhugh, Louise. (1964). *Harriet the spy*. New York: Harper.

Fleischman, Paul. (1988). *Joyful noise: Poems for two voices*. New York: Harper.

Fleischman, Paul. (1993). *Bull run*. New York: HarperCollins.

Fleischman, Paul. (1998). *Whirligig*. New York: Henry Holt.

Fleischman, Paul. (2000). *Big talk: Poems for four voices* (Beppe Giacobbe, Illus.). Cambridge, MA: Candlewick Press.

Fleming, Denise. (1992). *Count!* New York: Henry Holt.

Fletcher, Ralph. (1996). *Buried alive: The elements of love* (Andrew Moore, Illus.). New York: Atheneum.

Fletcher, Ralph. (1997a). *Ordinary things: Poems from a walk in early spring*. New York, Atheneum.

Fletcher, Ralph. (1997b). *Twilight comes twice*. Boston: Houghton Mifflin.

Fletcher, Ralph. (1998). *Flying solo*. New York: Clarion Books.

Fletcher, Ralph. (1999). *Relatively speaking: Poems about family*. New York: Orchard Books.

Fletcher, Susan. (1998). *Shadow spinner*. New York: Atheneum.

Florian, Douglas. (1994). *Beast feast*. San Diego: Harcourt.

Florian, Douglas. (1996). *On the wing*. San Diego: Harcourt.

Florian, Douglas. (1997). *In the swim: Poems and paintings*. San Diego: Harcourt.

Florian, Douglas. (1998). *Insectlopedia*. San Diego: Harcourt.

Florian, Douglas. (1999). *Winter eyes*. New York: Greenwillow.

Florian, Douglas. (2000). *Mammalabilia*. San Diego: Harcourt.

Florian, Douglas. (2001). *Lizards, frogs and polliwogs: Poems and paintings*. San Diego: Harcourt Brace.

Florian, Douglas. (2002). *Summersaults: Poems and paintings*. New York: Greenwillow.

Florian, Douglas. (2003). *Bow wow, meow meow*. San Diego: Harcourt Brace.

Flournoy, Valerie. (1985). *The patchwork quilt* (Jerry Pinkney, Illus.). New York: Dial Books.

Forbes, Ester. (1960). *Johnny Tremain*. Boston: Houghton Mifflin.

Forey, Pamela. (1987). *An instant guide to butterflies*. New York: Bonanza Books.

Forstchen, William R. (2001). *We look like men of war*. New York: Tom Doherty Associates.

Foster, John. (2001). *Pet poems* (Korky Paul, Illus.). Oxford, UK: Oxford University Press.

Fowler, Allan. (1996). *Spiders are not insects*. New York: Scholastic.

Fox, Mem. (1985). *Wilfrid Gordon McDonald Partridge*. New York: Kane Miller.

Fox, Mem. (1988). *Koala Lou*. San Diego: Harcourt Brace.

Fox, Mem. (1994). *Sophie* (Aminah Brenda Lynn Robinson, Illus.). San Diego: Harcourt Brace.

Fox, Mem. (1996). *Feathers & fools*. San Diego: Harcourt Brace.

Fox, Paula. (1973). *The slave dancer*. New York: Dell.

Fox, Paula. (1984). *One-eyed cat*. New York: Simon & Schuster.

Fox, Paula. (1991). *Monkey Island*. New York: Orchard Books.

Fradin, Dennis Brindell, & Fradin, Judith Bloom. (2000). *Ida B. Wells: Mother of the civil rights movement*. New York: Clarion Books.

Frank, Anne. (1952). *Anne Frank: The diary of a young girl*. Garden City, NY: Doubleday.

Franklin, Kristine L. (1992). *The old, old man and the very little boy* (Teresa D. Shaffer, Illus.). New York: Atheneum.

Freedman, Russell. (1980). *Immigrant kids*. New York: Dutton.

Freedman, Russell. (1989). *Lincoln: A photobiography*. Boston: Houghton Mifflin.

Freedman, Russell. (1994a). *Kids at work: Lewis Hine and the crusade against child labor*. New York: Clarion Books.

Freedman, Russell. (1994b). *The Wright brothers: How they invented the airplane*. New York: Holiday House.

Freedman, Russell. (1997a). *Eleanor Roosevelt: A life of discovery*. Boston: Houghton Mifflin.

Freedman, Russell. (1997b). *The life and death of Crazy Horse* (Amos Bad Bull, Illus.). New York: Holiday House.

Freedman, Russell. (1997c). *Out of darkness: The story of Louis Braille* (Kate Kiesler, Illus.). Boston: Houghton Mifflin.

Freedman, Russell. (1998). *Martha Graham: A dancer's life*. Boston: Houghton Mifflin.

Freedman, Russell. (1999). *Babe Didrikson Zaharias: The making of a champion*. Boston: Houghton Mifflin.

Freeman, Don. (1968). *Corduroy*. New York: Viking.

French, Fiona. (1986). *Snow White in New York*. Oxford: Oxford University Press.

Freymann, Saxton, & Elffers, Joost. (2001). *Gus and Button*. New York: Levine/Scholastic.

Fritz, April Young. (2002). *Waiting to disappear*. New York: Hyperion Books.

Fritz, Jean. (1967). *Early thunder*. New York: Coward-McCann.

Fritz, Jean. (1969). *George Washington's breakfast* (Paul Galdone, Illus.). New York: Coward-McCann.

Fritz, Jean. (1973). *And then what happened, Paul Revere?* (Margot Tomes, Illus.). New York: Putnam.

Fritz, Jean. (1974). *Why don't you get a horse, Sam Adams?* (Trina Schart Hyman, Illus.). New York: Coward-McCann.

Fritz, Jean. (1976). *What's the big idea, Ben Franklin?* New York: Putnam.

Fritz, Jean. (1977). *Can't you make them behave, King George?* (Tomie dePaola, Illus.). New York: Coward-McCann.

Fritz, Jean. (1982). *Homesick: My own story*. New York: Yearling.

Fritz, Jean. (1989). *The great little Madison*. New York: Putnam.

Fritz, Jean. (1991). *Bully for you, Teddy Roosevelt* (Mike Wimmer, Illus.). New York: Putnam.

Fritz, Jean. (1993). *Just a few words, Mr. Lincoln: The story of the Gettysburg Address* (Charles Robinson, Illus.). New York: Putnam.

Fritz, Jean. (1995). *You want women to vote, Lizzie Stanton?* (DyAnne DiSalvo-Ryan, Illus.). New York: Putnam.

Fritz, Jean. (1999). *Why not, Lafayette?* (Ronald Himler, Illus.). New York: Putnam.

Fritz, Jean. (2001a). *The cabin faced west*. Minneapolis: Sagebrush.

Fritz, Jean. (2001b). *Leonardo's horse* (Hudson Talbott, Illus.). New York: Putnam.

Froman, Nan. (2001). *What's that bug?* (Julian Mulock, Illus.). Boston: Little, Brown.

Frost, Helen. (2000). *Caterpillars*. Mankato, MN: Pebble Books.

Frost, Robert. (1959). *You come too: Favorite poems for young readers*. New York: Scholastic.

Frost, Robert. (1978). *Stopping by woods on a snowy evening* (Susan Jeffers, Illus.). New York: Dutton.

Funke, Cornelia. (2002a). *Inkheart*. New York: Scholastic.

Funke, Cornelia. (2002b). *The thief lord*. New York: Scholastic.

Gaeddert, Louann. (1994). *Breaking free*. New York: Atheneum.

Galdone, Paul (1975a). *The frog prince* (adapted from the retelling by the Brothers Grimm). New York: McGraw-Hill.

Galdone, Paul. (1975b). *The gingerbread boy*. New York: Clarion Books.

Ganci, Chris. (2003). *Chief: The life of Peter J. Ganci, a New York City firefighter*. New York: Orchard Books.

Gantos, Jack. (1998). *Joey Pigza swallowed the key*. New York: Farrar, Straus & Giroux.

Gantos, Jack. (2002). *What would Joey do?* New York: Farrar, Straus & Giroux.

Gantos, Jack. (2000). *Joey Pigza loses control*. New York: Farrar, Straus & Giroux.

Gardiner, John Reynolds. (1980). *Stone fox*. New York: Crowell.

Garrison, Webb. (2000). *Brady's Civil War*. New York: Salamander Books.

Gartis, Howard. (1904). *The Bobbsey twins*. Rahway, NJ: Mershon.

Garza, Carmen Lomas. (1990). *Family pictures / Cuadros de familia*. New York: Children's Book Press.

Gauch, Patricia Lee. (2003). *Thunder at Gettysburg*. Honesdale, PA: Boyds Mills Press.

George, Jean Craighead. (1959). *My side of the mountain*. New York: Dutton.

George, Jean Craighead. (1962). *Summer of the falcon*. New York: Crowell.

George, Jean Craighead. (1972). *Julie of the wolves* (John Schoenherr, Illus.). New York: Harper & Row.

George, Jean Craighead. (1980). *The cry of the crow*. New York: Harper & Row.

George, Jean Craighead. (1983). *The talking earth*. New York: Harper & Row.

George, Jean Craighead. (1988). *One day in the woods* (Gary Allen, Illus.). New York: Crowell.

George, Jean Craighead. (1989). *Shark beneath the reef*. New York: Harper & Row.

George, Jean Craighead. (1990a). *On the far side of the mountain*. New York: Dutton.

George, Jean Craighead. (1990b). *One day in the tropical rain forest* (Gary Allen, Illus.). New York: Crowell.

George, Jean Craighead. (1994). *Julie*. New York: HarperCollins.

George, Jean Craighead. (1995a). *Everglades* (Wendell Minor, Illus.). New York: HarperCollins.

George, Jean Craighead. (1995b). *There's an owl in the shower* (Christine Herman Merrill, Illus.). New York: HarperCollins.

George, Jean Craighead. (1995c). *To climb a waterfall* (Thomas Locker, Illus.). New York: Philomel.

George, Jean Craighead. (1997a). *Arctic son* (Wendell Minor, Illus.). New York: Hyperion Books.

George, Jean Craighead. (1997b). *Julie's wolf pack*. New York: HarperCollins.

George, Jean Craighead. (1997c). *Look to the north: A wolf pup diary* (Lucia Washburn, Illus.). New York: HarperCollins.

George, Jean Craighead. (1998). *The gorilla gang* (Stacey Schuett, Illus.). New York: Disney Press.

George, Jean Craighead. (1999). *Frightful's mountain*. New York: Penguin.

George, Jean Craighead. (2000). *How to talk to your cat* (Paul Meisel, Illus.). New York: HarperCollins.

George, Kristine O'Connell. (1997). *The great frog race and other poems* (Kate Kiesler, Illus.). New York: Clarion Books.

George, Kristine O'Connell. (1998). *Old elm speaks: Tree poems*. New York: Clarion Books.

George, Kristine O'Connell. (1999). *Little dog poems* (June Otani, Illus.). New York: Clarion Books.

George, Kristine O'Connell. (2001). *Toasting marshmallows: Camping poems* (Kate Kiesler, Illus.). New York: Clarion Books.

George, Kristine O'Connell. (2002a). *Little dog and Duncan*. New York: Clarion Books.

George, Kristine O'Connell. (2002b). *Swimming upstream: Middle school poems*. New York: Clarion Books.

George, Twig C. (2000). *Jellies: The life of jellyfish*. Brookfield, CT: Millbrook Press.

Geras, Adele. (1990). *My grandmother's stories: A collection of Jewish folk tales* (Jael Jordan, Illus.). New York: Knopf.

Gerber, Carole. (2004). *Leaf jumpers* (Leslie Evans, Illus.). Watertown, MA: Charlesbridge.

Gerson, Mary-Joan. (1992). *Why the sky is far away: A Nigerian folktale* (Carla Golembe, Illus.). Orlando, FL: Harcourt Brace.

Gerstein, Mordicai. (1987). *The mountains of Tibet*. New York: Harper & Row.

Ghigna, Charles. (2003). *A fury of motion: Poems for boys*. Honesdale, PA: Boyds Mills Press.

Gibbons, Gail. (1985). *The milk makers*. New York: Macmillan.

Gibbons, Gail. (1990). *Beacons of light*. New York: Morrow.

Gibbons, Gail.(1991a). *From seed to plant*. Holiday House.

Gibbons, Gail. (1991b). *Whales*. New York: Holiday House.

Gibbons, Gail. (1992a). *The great St. Lawrence seaway*. New York: Morrow.

Gibbons, Gail. (1992b). *Monarch butterfly*. New York: Holiday House.

Gibbons, Gail. (1994a). *Christmas on an island*. New York: Morrow.

Gibbons, Gail. (1994b). *Nature's green umbrella*. New York: Morrow.

Gibbons, Gail. (1994c). *Wolves*. New York: Holiday House.

Gibbons, Gail. (1995). *Planet Earth, inside out*. New York: Morrow.

Gibbons, Gail. (1997a). *The honey makers*. New York: Morrow Junior Books.

Gibbons, Gail. (1997b). *The moon book*. New York: Holiday House.

Gibbons, Gail. (1998). *Soaring with the wind: The bald eagle*. New York: Morrow.

Gibbons, Gail. (1999a). *Bats*. New York: Holiday House.

Gibbons, Gail. (1999b). *Exploring the deep, dark sea*. Boston: Little, Brown.

Gibbons, Gail. (1999c). *Pigs pigs*. New York: Holiday House.

Gibbons, Gail. (1999d). *The pumpkin book*. New York: Holiday House.

Gibbons, Gail. (2000a). *Apples*. New York: Holiday House.

Gibbons, Gail. (2000b). *Rabbits, rabbits and more rabbits*. New York: Holiday House.

Gibbons, Gail. (2002). *The berry book*. New York: Holiday House.

Gibbons, Gail. (2003). *Chicks & chickens*. New York: Holiday House.

Giblin, James Cross. (1983). *Fireworks, picnics and flags: The story of the Fourth of July symbols* (Ursula Arndt, Illus.). New York: Clarion Books.

Giblin, James Cross. (1987). *From hand to mouth: How we invented knives, forks, spoons and chopsticks and the table manners to go with them*. New York: HarperCollins.

Giblin, James Cross. (1990). *The riddle of the Rosetta Stone: Key to ancient Egypt*. New York: HarperCollins.

Giblin, James Cross. (1991). *The truth about unicorns*. New York: HarperCollins.

Giblin, James Cross. (1992). *George Washington: A picture book biography*. New York: Scholastic.

Giblin, James Cross. (2000). *The amazing life of Benjamin Franklin* (Michael Dooling, Illus.). New York: Scholastic.

Giblin, James Cross. (2002). *The life and death of Adolf Hitler*. New York: Clarion Books.

Giff, Patricia Reilly. (1997). *Lily's crossing*. New York: Delacorte.

Giff, Patricia Reilly. (2000). *Nory Ryan's song*. New York: Scholastic.

Giff, Patricia Reilly. (2002). *Pictures of Hollis Woods*. New York: Random House.

Giff, Patricia Reilly. (2003). *Maggie's door*. New York: Wendy Lamb Books.

Gifford, Clive, & Cadle, Jerry. (2002). *The Kingfisher young people's book of living worlds*. London: Kingfisher.

Gillies, Judi, & Glossop, Jennifer. (2000). *The Kids Can Press jumbo cookbook* (Louise Phillips, Illus.). Tonawanda, NY: Kids Can Press.

Gilliland, Judith Heide. (2000). *Steamboat! The story of Captain Blanche Leathers* (Holly Meade, Illus.). New York: DK Publishing.

Ginsburg, Mirra. (1992). *Asleep, asleep* (Nancy Tafuri, Illus.). New York: Greenwillow.

Giovanni, Nikki. (1987). *Spin a soft black song: Poems for children* (George Martins, Illus.). New York: Farrar, Straus & Giroux.

Gipson, Fred. (1956). *Old Yeller*. New York: Harper.

Glaser, Isabel Joshlin. (1995). *Dreams of glory: Poems starring girls*. New York: Atheneum.

Glaser, Linda. (1998). *Spectacular spiders* (Gay Holland, Illus.). Brookfield, CT: Millbrook Press.

Goble, Paul. (1978). *The girl who loved wild horses*. New York: Bradbury Press.

Goble, Paul. (1984). *Buffalo woman*. New York: Aladdin Books.

Goble, Paul. (1991). *Iktomi and the buffalo skull*. New York: Orchard Books.

Goble, Paul. (1993). *The lost children*. New York: Bradbury Press.

Gold, Alison Leslie. (2000). *A special fate: Chiune Sugihara, hero of the Holocaust*. New York: Scholastic.

Goldstein, Bobbye. S. (Sel.). (1989). *Bear in mind: A book of bear poems* (William Pène du Bois, Illus.). New York: Viking.

Goldstein, Bobbye S. (Sel.). (1992). *Inner chimes: Poems on poetry* (Jane Zalben, Illus.). Honesdale, PA: Boyds Mills Press.

Golub, Matthew. (1998). *Cool melons—Turn to frogs!* (Kazuko G. Stone, Illus.). New York: Lee & Low.

Gonzalez, Lucia M. (1994). *The bossy gallito: A traditional Cuban folktale* (Lulu Delacre, Illus.). New York: Scholastic.

Gonzalez, Lucia M. (1997). *Señor Cat's romance and other favorite stories from Latin America* (Lulu Delacre, Illus.). New York: Scholastic.

Gordon, Melanie Apel. (1999). *Let's talk about deafness*. New York: PowerKids Press.

Gordon, Ruth. (1993). *Peeling the onion: An anthology of poems*. New York: HarperCollins.

Gordon, Ruth. (Sel). (1995). *Pierced by a ray of sun: Poems about the times we feel alone*. New York: HarperCollins.

Gordon, Shirley. (1980). *The boy who wanted a family* (Charles Robinson, Illus.). New York: Dell.

Gould, Deborah. (1987). *Grandpa's slide show* (Cheryl Harness, Illus.). New York: Lothrop, Lee & Shepard.

Gould, Roberta. (2000). *Kidtopia: 'Round the country and back through time in 60 projects*. New York: Tricycle Press.

Graham, Joan Bransfield. (1994). *Splish splash: Poems* (Steven Scott, Illus.). Boston: Houghton Mifflin.

Graham, Joan Bransfield. (1999). *Flicker flash* (Nancy Davis, Illus.). Boston: Houghton Mifflin.

Grahame, Kenneth. (1908). *The wind in the willows*. New York: Scribner.

Granfield, Linda. (1994). *Cowboy: An album*. New York: Ticknor & Fields.

Gray, Elizabeth Janet. (1942). *Adam of the road*. New York: Viking.

Greenberg, Jan. (2001). *Heart to heart: New poems inspired by 20th century art*. New York: Abrams.

Greenberg, Jan, & Jordan, Sandra. (2000). *Frank O. Gehry: Outside in*. New York: DK Ink.

Greene, Bette. (1973). *Summer of my German soldier*. New York: Dial Books.

Greene, Bette. (1998). *Philip Hall likes me. I reckon maybe.* (Charles Lilly, Illus.). New York: Dial Books.

Greene, Rhonda Gowler. (2002). *The very first Thanksgiving day* (Susan Gaber, Illus.). New York: Atheneum.

Greenfield, Eloise. (1978). *Honey, I love* (Leo Dillon & Diane Dillon, Illus.). New York: Crowell.

Greenfield, Eloise. (1984). *Me & Neesie*. New York: HarperCollins.

Greenfield, Eloise. (1988). *Nathaniel talking* (Jan Spivey Gilchrist, Illus.). New York: Black Butterfly.

Greenfield, Eloise. (1991a). *Night on Neighborhood Street* (Jan Spivey Gilchrist, Illus.). New York: Dial Books.

Greenfield, Eloise. (1991b). *Under the Sunday tree*. New York: HarperTrophy.

Greenfield, Eloise. (1995). *Rosa Parks* (Gil Ashby, Illus.). New York: HarperCollins.

Greenfield, Eloise. (1997). *For the love of the game*. New York: HarperCollins.

Greenfield, Eloise. (1999). *Grandmama's joy* (Carole Byard, Illus.). New York: Penguin.

Greenfield Eloise. (2002). *How they got over: African Americans and the call of the sea* (Jan Spivey Gilchrist, Illus.). Amistad/HarperCollins.

Greenfield, Eloise. (2003). *Honey, I love* (Jan Spivey Gilchrist, Illus.). New York: HarperCollins.

Greenstein, Elaine. (2003). *Ice-cream cones for sale!* New York: Scholastic.

Greenwald, Sheila. (1993). *My fabulous new life*. New York: Harcourt Brace.

Greenwood, Barbara. (1998). *The last safe house: A story of the Underground Railroad* (Heather Collins, Illus.). Buffalo, NY: Kids Can Press.

Greenwood, Elinor. (2001). *Rain forest: Open your eyes to a world of discovery*. New York: DK Publishing.

Gregory, Kristiana. (1992). *Earthquake at dawn*. New York: Harcourt Brace.

Griego, Margot. (1981). *Tortillitas para Mama and other nursery rhymes in Spanish and English*. New York: Holt, Rinehart and Winston.

Grifalconi, Ann. (1986). *The village of round and square houses*. Boston: Little, Brown.

Grimes, Nikki. (1994). *Meet Danitra Brown* (Floyd Cooper, Illus.). New York: Lothrop, Lee & Shepard.

Grimes, Nikki. (1998a). *A dime a dozen*. New York: Dial Books.

Grimes, Nikki. (1998b). *Jazmin's notebook*. New York: Dial Books.

Grimes, Nikki. (1999). *My man Blue: Poems*. New York: Dial Books.

Grimes, Nikki. (2001a). *A pocketful of poems* (Javaka Steptoe, Illus.). New York: Clarion Books.

Grimes, Nikki. (2001b). *Stepping out with Grandma Mac*. New York: Orchard Books.

Grimm, Brothers. (1983). *Little Red-Cap* (Lisbeth Zwerger, Illus., Elizabeth D. Crawford, Trans.). New York: Morrow.

Grimm, Jacob, & Grimm, Wilhelm. (1981). *Hansel and Gretel* (Anthony Browne, Illus.). London: J. MacRae.

Gross, Ruth Belov. (1973). *True stories about Abraham Lincoln*. New York: Scholastic.

Grove, Vicki. (2000). *Destiny*. New York: Putnam.

Guarino, Deborah. (1997). *Is your mama a llama?* New York: Scholastic.

Guback, Georgia (1994). *Luka's quilt*. New York: Greenwillow.

Gunning, Monica. (1993). *Not a copper penny in me house: Poems from the Caribbean*. Honesdale, PA: Wordsong.

Gunning, Monica. (1998). *Under the breadfruit tree: Island poems*. Honesdale, PA: Wordsong/Boyds Mills Press.

Gutman, Bill. (2002). *The look-it-up book of the 50 states* (Anne Wertheim, Illus.). New York: Random House.

Guy, Ginger Foglesong. (1991). *Black crow, black crow* (Nancy Winslow Parker, Illus.). New York: Greenwillow.

Haddix, Margaret Peterson. (1995). *Running out of time*. New York: Simon & Schuster.

Haddix, Margaret Peterson. (1998). *Among the hidden*. New York: Simon & Schuster.

Hahn, Mary Downing. (1986). *Wait till Helen comes: A ghost story*. New York: Clarion Books.

Hahn, Mary Downing. (1991). *Stepping on the cracks*. New York: Clarion Books.

Haley, Gail E. (1970). *A story, a story: An African tale*. New York: Atheneum.

Hall, Donald. (Ed.). (1985). The Oxford book of children's verse in America. New York: Oxford University Press.

Hall, Margaret. (2001). *Money*. Chicago: Heinemann Library.

Halliwell, Sarah. (1998). *Who and when? Impressionism and postimpressionism: Artists, writers and composers*. Austin, TX: Raintree Steck-Vaughn.

Hallworth, Grace. (1990). *Cric crac: A collection of West African stories* (Avril Turner, Illus.). Egmont, CO: Egmont Children's Books.

Halperin, Wendy Anderson. (1998). *Once upon a company*. New York: Orchard Books.

Hamilton, Kersten. (1997). *The butterfly book: A kid's guide to attracting, raising, and keeping butterflies*. Santa Fe, NM: John Muir.

Hamilton, Virginia. (1974). *M. C. Higgins, the great*. New York: Macmillan.

Hamilton, Virginia. (1983). *Sweet whispers, Brother Rush*. New York: Avon.

Hamilton, Virginia. (1984). *The house of Dies Drear*. Boston: Macmillan.

Hamilton, Virginia. (1985). *The people could fly: American black folktales* (Leo Dillon & Diane Dillon, Illus.). New York: Knopf.

Hamilton, Virginia. (1987). *The mystery of Drear House*. New York: Greenwillow.

Hamilton, Virginia. (1988). *In the beginning: Creation stories from around the world*. San Diego: Harcourt Brace.

Hamilton, Virginia. (1990a). *Cousins*. New York: Philomel.

Hamilton, Virginia. (1990b). *The dark way: Stories from the spirit world* (Lambert Davis, Illus.). San Diego: Harcourt Brace.

Hamilton, Virginia. (1990c). *Second cousins* (Lambert Davis, Illus.). San Diego: Harcourt Brace.

Hamilton, Virginia. (1993). *Many thousand gone* (Leo Dillon & Diane Dillon, Illus.). New York: Knopf.

Hamilton, Virginia. (1995a). *Her stories: African American folk tales, fairy tales and true tales*. New York: Blue Sky Press.

Hamilton, Virginia. (1995b). *Jaguarundi*. New York: Blue Sky Press.

Hamilton, Virginia. (1999). *Bluish*. New York: Blue Sky Press.

Hamilton, Virginia. (2002). *Time pieces*. New York: Blue Sky Press.

Hansen, Joyce. (1994). *The captive*. New York: Scholastic.

Hansen, Joyce, & McGowan, Gary. (2003). *Freedom roads: Searching for the Underground Railroad*. Chicago: Cricket Books.

Harlow, Rosie, & Morgan, Sally. (2001). *The environment: Saving the planet*. London: Kingfisher.

Harms, John. (2001). *The saving of ARMA armadillo* (Brian Nelson, Illus.). Boston: Frederick Press.

Harper, Dan. (2001). *Sit, Truman* (Cara Moser & Barry Moser, Illus.). New York: Harcourt.

Harper, Piers. (1999). *Checkmate at Chess City*. Cambridge, MA: Candlewick Press.

Harrell, Beatrice O. (1999). *Longwalker's journey: A novel of the Choctaw Trail of Tears*. New York: Dial.

Harrison, David. (2000). *Farmer's garden: Rhymes for two voices* (Arden Johnson-Petrov, Illus.). Honesdale, PA: Boyds Mills Press.

Harrison, David L. (2002). *Volcanoes: Nature's incredible fireworks* (Cheryl Nathan, Illus.). Honesdale, PA: Boyds Mills Press.

Harrison, Joanna. (1994). *Dear bear*. London: HarperCollins.

Hart, George. (1990). *Ancient Egypt*. New York: Knopf.

Harvey, Miles. (1998). *Look what came from Egypt*. New York: Watts.

Haslam, Andrew. (1997). *Make it work! Oceans*. Chicago: Two-Can.

Hausman, Gerald. (1994). *Turtle Island ABC: A gathering of Native American symbols* (Cara Moser & Barry Moser, Illus.). New York: HarperCollins.

Hautzig, Esther. (1968). *The endless steppe: Growing up in Siberia*. New York: HarperCollins.

Havill, Juanita. (1993). *Jamaica and Brianna* (Anne Sibley O'Brien, Illus.). Boston: Houghton Mifflin.

Heard, Georgia. (1992). *Creatures of earth, sea, and sky*. Honesdale, PA: Boyds Mills Press.

Hehner, Barbara. (2001). *Ice Age mammoth: Will this ancient giant come back to life?* New York: Crown.

Heide, Florence Parry, & Gilliland, Judith Heide. (1992). *Sami and the time of troubles*. New York: Clarion Books.

Hendershot, Judith. (1987). *In coal country* (Thomas B. Allen, Illus.). New York: Knopf.

Henderson, Douglas. (2000). *Asteroid impact*. New York: Dial Books.

Henkes, Kevin. (1988). *Chester's way*. New York: Greenwillow.

Henkes, Kevin. (1990). *Julius the baby of the world*. New York: Greenwillow.

Henkes, Kevin. (1991). *Chrysanthemum*. New York: Greenwillow.

Henkes, Kevin. (1993). *Words of stone*. New York: Puffin Books.

Henkes, Kevin. (1996). *Lilly's purple plastic purse*. New York: Greenwillow.

Henry, Marguerite. (1948). *King of the Wind*. Chicago: Rand McNally.

Hermes, Patricia. (1991). *Mama, let's dance*. Boston: Little, Brown.

Hesse, Karen. (1991). *Wish on a unicorn*. New York: Holt.

Hesse, Karen. (1992). *Letters from Rifka*. New York: Henry Holt.

Hesse, Karen. (1993a). *Lavender* (Andrew Glass, Illus.). New York: Holt.

Hesse, Karen. (1993b). *Lester's dog* (Nancy Carpenter, Illus.). New York: Crown.

Hesse, Karen. (1993c). *Poppy's chair* (Kay Life, Illus.). New York: Scholastic.

Hesse, Karen. (1994a). *Phoenix rising*. New York: Holt.

Hesse, Karen. (1994b). *Sable* (Marcia Sewall, Illus.). New York: Holt.

Hesse, Karen. (1995). *A time of angels*. New York: Hyperion Books.

Hesse, Karen. (1996). *The music of dolphins*. New York: Scholastic.

Hesse, Karen. (1997). *Out of the dust*. New York: Scholastic.

Hesse, Karen. (1998). *Just juice*. New York: Scholastic.

Hesse, Karen. (2001). *Witness*. New York: Scholastic.

Hickman, Janet. (1994). *Jericho*. New York: Greenwillow.

Highwater, Jamake. (1977). *Anpao: An American Indian odyssey*. Philadelphia: Lippincott.

Highwater, Jamake. (1984). *Legend days*. New York: Harper & Row.

Hill, David. (1994). *See ya', Simon*. New York: Dutton.

Hill, Eric. (1982). *Nursery rhyme peek-a-book*. Los Angeles: Price Stern Sloan.

Hill, Eric. (1998). *Go Spot!* New York: Putnam.

Hill, Kirkpatrick. (1990). *Toughboy and Sister*. New York: Puffin Books.

Hill, Kirkpatrick. (1993). *Winter camp*. New York: McElderry.

Hill, Kirkpatrick. (2000). *The year of Miss Agnes*. New York: Simon & Schuster.

Himmelman, John. (2002). *Pipaluk and the whales*. Washington, DC: National Geographic Society.

Hines, Anna Grossnickle. (2001). *Pieces: A year in poems and quilts*. New York: Greenwillow.

Hinton, S. E. (1967). *The outsiders*. New York: Viking.

Hirschfelder, Arlene, & Singer, Beverly R. (1992). *Rising voices: Writings of young Native Americans*. New York: Charles.

Hisock, Bruce. (1993). *The big storm*. New York: Macmillan.

Hittleman, Carol, & Hittleman, Daniel. (Eds.). (2002). *A grand celebration: Grandparents in poetry*. Honesdale, PA: Boyds Mills Press.

Ho, Minfong. (1991). *The clay marble*. New York: Farrar, Straus & Giroux.

Ho, Minfong. (1996) *Maples in the mist. Children's poems from the Tang Dynasty* (Jean Tseng & Mou sien Tseng, Illus.). New York: Lothrop, Lee & Shepard.

Ho, Minfong. (1997). *Brother Rabbit: A Cambodian tale*. New York: Lothrop, Lee & Shepard.

Hoban, Russell. (1964). *A baby sister for Frances*. New York: Harper & Row.

Hoban, Russell. (1969). *Best friends for Frances*. New York: Harper & Row.

Hoban, Tana. (1974). *Circles, triangles, and squares*. New York: Macmillan.

Hobbie, Holly. (1997). *Toot and Puddle*. Boston: Little, Brown.

Hobbs, Will. (1989). *Bearstone*. New York: Atheneum.

Hobbs, Will. (1992). *Changes in latitude*. New York: Morrow.

Hobbs, Will. (1993). *Beardance*. New York: Macmillan.

Hobbs, Will. (1994). *The big wander*. New York: Dell Books.

Hobbs, Will. (1996a). *Downriver*. New York: Dell.

Hobbs, Will. (1996b). *Far north*. New York: Morrow.

Hobbs, Will. (1997a). *Ghost canoe*. New York: Avon.

Hobbs, Will. (1997b). *Kokopelli's flute*. New York: HarperCollins.

Hobbs, Will. (1998). *Howling hill*. New York: Morrow.

Hobbs, Will. (1999a). *Jason's gold*. New York: Morrow.

Hobbs, Will. (1999b). *The maze*. New York: Morrow.

Hobbs, Will. (1999c). *River thunder*. New York: Dell.

Hobbs, Will. (2000). *Beardream*. New York: Aladdin Books.

Hobbs, Will. (2001). *Down the Yukon*. New York: Morrow.

Hoberman, Mary Ann. (1976). *Bugs!* New York: Viking.

Hoberman, Mary Ann. (1978). *A house is a house for me*. New York: Viking.

Hoberman, Mary Ann. (1981). *Yellow butter, purple jelly, red jam, black bread*. New York: Viking.

Hoberman, Mary Ann. (1991). *Fathers, mothers, sisters, brothers*. New York: Joy Street Books.

Hoberman, Mary Ann. (1994). *My song is beautiful: Poems and pictures in many voices*. Boston: Little, Brown.

Hoberman, Mary Ann. (1998). *The llama who had no pajama: 100 favorite poems* (Betty Fraser, Illus.). San Diego: Harcourt Brace.

Hodge, Deborah. (1993). *Whales: Killer whales, blue whales and more* (Pat Stephens, Illus.). Toronto, ON: Kids Can Press.

Hoffman, Mary. (1991). *Amazing Grace*. New York: Dial Books.

Hoffman, Mary. (1993). *Henry's baby* (Susan Winter, Illus.). New York: Dorling Kindersley.

Hogrogian, Nonny. (1971). *One fine day*. New York: Collier Books.

Holbrook, Sara. (1997a). *Am I naturally this crazy?* Honesdale, PA: Boyds Mills Press.

Holbrook, Sara. (1997b). *I never said I wasn't difficult*. Honesdale, PA: Boyds Mills Press.

Holbrook, Sara. (1998a). *The dog ate my homework*. Honesdale, PA: Boyds Mills Press.

Holbrook, Sara. (1998b). *Walking on the boundaries of change*. Honesdale, PA: Boyds Mills Press.

Hollyer, Belinda. (2003). *The kingfisher book of family poems*. Boston: Houghton Mifflin.

Holm, Anne. (1990). *North to freedom* (L. W. Kingsland, Trans.). San Diego: Harcourt Brace.

Holm, Jennifer L. (1999). *Our only May Amelia*. New York: HarperCollins.

Holman, Felice. (1974). *Slake's limbo*. New York: Scribner.

Holt, Kimberly Willis. (1998). *My Louisiana sky*. New York: Holt.

Holt, Kimberly Willis. (1999). *When Zachary Beaver came to town*. New York: Holt.

Holt, Kimberly Willis. (2001). *Dancing in Cadillac light*. New York: Putnam.

Holtwijz, Ineke. (1998). *Asphalt angels*. Arden, NC: Front Street Press.

Holtz, Lara (1999). *Drive a tractor*. New York: DK Publishing.

Homer. (1962). *The Iliad* (Richmond Lattimore, Trans., Leonard Baskin, Illus.). Chicago: University of Chicago Press.

Hooks, William, H. (1990). *The ballad of Belle Dorcas* (Brian Pinkney, Illus.). New York: Knopf.

Hoover, H. M. (1990). *Away is a strange place to be*. New York: Dutton.

Hopkins, Lee Bennett. (Sel.) (1982). *Rainbows are made: Poems by Carl Sandburg* (Fritz Eichenberg, Illus.). New York: Harcourt Brace.

Hopkins, Lee Bennett. (1984). *Surprises* (Megan Lloyd, Illus.). New York: Harper & Row.

Hopkins, Lee Bennett. (1987). *More surprises* (Megan Lloyd, Illus.). New York: Harper & Row.

Hopkins, Lee Bennett. (1989). *People from Mother Goose* (Kathryn Hewitt, Illus.). San Diego: Harcourt Brace.

Hopkins, Lee Bennett. (1991). *Side by side: Poems to read together* (Hilary Knight, Illus.). New York: Simon & Schuster.

Hopkins, Lee Bennett. (Sel.). (1992). *Questions: Poems* (Carolyn Croll, Illus.). New York: HarperCollins.

Hopkins, Lee Bennett. (Sel.) (1993). *Extra innings: Baseball poems* (Scott Medlock, Illus.). San Diego: Harcourt Brace.

Hopkins, Lee Bennett. (1994). *Hand in hand: An American history in poetry* (Peter Fiore, Illus.). New York: Simon & Schuster.

Hopkins, Lee Bennett. (Sel.). (1996a). *Opening days: Sports poems* (Scott Medlock, Illus.). San Diego: Harcourt Brace.

Hopkins, Lee Bennett. (Sel.). (1996b). *School supplies: A book of poems* (Renee Flower, Illus.). New York: Simon & Schuster.

Hopkins, Lee Bennett. (1997a). *Dinosaurs*. San Diego: Harcourt.

Hopkins, Lee Bennett. (Sel.). (1997b). *Song and dance: Poems* (Cheryl Munro Taylor, Illus.).New York: Simon & Schuster.

Hopkins, Lee Bennett. (1998). *Climb into my lap: Poems to read together* (Kathryn Brown, Illus.). New York: Simon & Schuster.

Hopkins, Lee Bennett. (1999a). *Spectacular science* (Virginia Halstead, Illus.). New York: Simon & Schuster.

Hopkins, Lee Bennett. (1999b). *Sports! Sports! Sports! A poetry collection* (Brian Floca, Illus.). New York: HarperCollins.

Hopkins, Lee Bennett. (2002). *Hoofbeats, claws & rippled fins: Creature poems*. New York: HarperCollins.

Hopkinson, Deborah. (1993). *Sweet Clara and the freedom quilt*. New York: Knopf.

Hopkinson, Deborah. (2001). *Under the quilt of night* (James Ransome, Illus.). New York: Atheneum.

Hopson, Darlene Powell, Hopson, Derek S., & Clavin, Thomas. (1996). *Juba this and juba that: 100 African-American games for children*. New York: Simon & Schuster.

Horenstein, Henry. (1994). *My mom's a vet*. New York: Candlewick Press.

Horowitz, Anthony. (2002). *Point blank*. New York: Penguin.

Hort, Lenny. (1996). *How many stars in the sky* (James Ransome, Illus.). New York: Morrow.

Horvath, Patsy. (2001). *Everything on a waffle*. New York: Farrar, Straus & Giroux.

Houston, Gloria. (1990). *Little Jim*. New York: Philomel.

Houston, Gloria. (1992a). *But no candy* (Lloyd Bloom, Illus.). New York: Philomel.

Houston, Gloria. (1992b). *My Great-Aunt Arizona* (Susan Condie Lamb, Illus.). New York: HarperCollins.

Houston, James. (1977). *Frozen fire*. New York: Aladdin Books.

Howard, Elizabeth Fitzgerald. (1991). *Aunt Flossie's hats (and crab cakes later)* (James Ransome, Illus.). New York: Clarion Books.

Howard, Elizabeth Fitzgerald. (2000). *Virgie goes to school with us boys* (E. B. Lewis, Illus.). New York: Simon & Schuster.

Howard, Jane R. (1985). *When I'm sleepy* (Lynne Cherry, Illus.). New York: Dutton.

Howe, Deborah, & Howe, James. (1999). *Bunnicula: A rabbit-tale of mystery* (Alan Daniel, Illus.). New York: Atheneum.

Hoyt-Goldsmith, Diane. (1998). *Celebrating Chinese New Year* (Lawrence Migdale, Photog.). New York: Holiday House.

Hoyt-Goldsmith, Diane. (2001). *Celebrating Ramadan* (Lawrence Migdale, Photog.). New York: Holiday House.

Hoyt-Goldsmith, Diane. (2002). *Celebrating a Quinceañera: A Latina's 15th birthday celebration* (Lawrence Migdale, Photog.). New York: Holiday House.

Huck, Charlotte. (1989). *Princess Furball* (Anita Lobel, Illus.). New York: Greenwillow.

Huck, Charlotte. (1993). *Secret places* (Lindsay Barrett George, Illus.). New York: Greenwillow.

Huck, Charlotte. (1995). *Toads and diamonds* (Anita Lobel, Illus.). New York: Greenwillow.

Huck, Charlotte. (1998). *Creepy countdown* (Jos. A. Smith, Illus.). New York: Greenwillow.

Hudson, Jan. (1999). *Sweetgrass*. New York: Puffin Books.

Hughes, Langston. (1994). *The dreamkeeper and other poems*. New York: Knopf.

Huneck, Stephen. (2002). *Sally goes to the farm*. New York: Abrams.

Hunt, H. Draper. (2000). *Dearest Father: The Civil War letters of Lt. Frank Dickerson, A son of Belfast, Maine*. Unity, ME: North County Press.

Hunt, Irene. (1964). *Across five Aprils*. Chicago: Follett.

Hunt, Irene. (1976). *The lottery rose*. New York: Scribner.

Hunter, Mollie. (1975). *A stranger came ashore: A story of suspense*. New York: Harper & Row.

Hunter, Mollie. (1990). *The mermaid summer*. New York: HarperTrophy.

Hurst, Margaret (2001). *Grannie and the jumbie: A Caribbean tale*. New York: HarperCollins.

Hutchins, Pat. (1968). *Rosie's walk*. New York: Collier Books.

Hutchins, Pat. (1971). *Titch*. New York: Macmillan.

Hutchins, Pat. (1978). *Happy birthday, Sam*. New York: Greenwillow.

Hutchins, Pat. (1985). *The very worst monster*. New York: Greenwillow.

Hutchins, Pat. (1986). *The doorbell rang*. New York: Greenwillow.

Hutchins, Pat. (1992). *Silly Billy*. New York: Greenwillow.

Hutchins, Pat. (1994a). *Little pink pig*. New York: Greenwillow.

Hutchins, Pat. (1994b). *Three-star Billy*. New York: Greenwillow.

Hutchins, Pat. (1997). *Shrinking mouse*. New York: Greenwillow.

Hutchins, Pat. (1999). *It's my birthday*. New York: Greenwillow.

Hyman, Trina Schart. (1980). *A little alphabet*. Boston: Little, Brown.

Hyman, Trina Schart. (1983a). *Little Red Riding Hood*, by the Brothers Grimm. New York: Holiday House.

Hyman, Trina Schart. (1983b). *Sleeping beauty*. Boston: Little, Brown.

Ibbotson, Eva. (2000). *Island of the aunts* (Kevin Hawkes, Illus.). New York: Dutton.

Ikeda, Daisaku. (1992a). *The cherry tree*. New York: Knopf.

Ikeda, Daisaku. (1992b). *Over the deep blue sea* (Brian Wildsmith, Illus.). New York: Knopf.

Innocenti, Roberto. (1985). *Rose Blanche*. Mankato, MN: Creative Education.

The intelligent reader. (1844). Springfield, MA: Merriam.

Irvine, Joan. (1992). *How to make super pop-ups* (Linda Hendry, Illus.). New York: Morrow.

Isaacs, Anne. (1994). *Swamp angel* (Paul O. Zelinsky, Illus.). New York: Penguin.

Isadora, Rachel. (1991). *At the crossroads*. New York: Scholastic.

Isom, Joan Shaddox. (1997). *The first starry night*. Dallas: Whispering Coyote Press.

Jacobs, William Jay. (1990). *Ellis Island: New hope in a new land*. New York: Scribner.

Jacques, Brian. (1987). *Redwall*. New York: Putnam.

Jacques, Brian. (1988). *Mossflower*. New York: Philomel.

Jacques, Brian. (1990). *Mattimeo*. New York: Philomel.

Jacques, Brian. (1992). *Mariel of Redwall*. New York: Philomel.

Jacques, Brian. (1993). *Salamandastron*. New York: Philomel.

Jacques, Brian. (1994). *Martin the warrior*. New York: Philomel.

Jacques, Brian. (1997). *The pearls of Lutra*. New York: Putnam.

Jacques, Brian. (1998a). *The long patrol*. New York: Putnam.

Jacques, Brian. (1998b). *Marlfox*. New York: Putnam.

Jacques, Brian. (2000a). *The great Redwall feast*. New York: Puffin Books.

Jacques, Brian. (2000b). *The legend of Luke*. New York: Philomel.

Jacques, Brian. (2000c). *Lord Brocktree*. New York: Random House.

Jacques, Brian. (2001). *Taggerung*. New York: Philomel.

Jacques, Brian. (2002). *Triss*. New York: Putnam.

Jacques, Brian. (2003). *Loamhedge*. New York: Philomel.

Jacques, Brian. (2004). *The bellmaker*. Minneapolis: Sagebrush.

James, Simon. (2000). *Days like this: A collection of small poems*. Cambridge, MA: Candlewick Press.

Janeczko, Paul B. (Sel.). (1988). *The music of what happens: Poems that tell stories*. New York: Orchard Books.

Janeczko, Paul B. (Sel.). (1990). *The place my words are looking for: What poets say about and through their work*. New York: Bradbury Press.

Janeczko, Paul B. (Sel.). (1991). *Preposterous: Poems of youth*. New York: Orchard Books.

Janeczko, Paul B. (Sel.). (1995). *Wherever home begins: 100 contemporary poems*. New York: Orchard Books.

Janeczko, Paul B. (1998). *That sweet diamond*. New York: Atheneum.

Janeczko, Paul B. (Sel.). (2000). *Stone bench in an empty park* (Henri Silberman, Photog.). New York: Orchard Books.

Janeczko, Paul B. (Sel.). (2002). *Seeing the blue between: Advice and inspiration for young poets*. Cambridge, MA: Candlewick Press.

Jenkins, Steve. (1997). *What do you do when something wants to eat you?* Boston: Houghton Mifflin.

Jenkins, Steve, & Page, Robin. (2001). *Animals in flight*. Boston: Houghton Mifflin.

Jenness, Aylette. (1990). *Families: A celebration of diversity, commitment, and love*. Boston: Houghton Mifflin.

Jiang, Ji-li. (1997). *Red scarf girl: A memoir of the cultural revolution*. New York: HarperCollins.

Johnson, Angela. (1989). *Tell me a story, Mama* (David Soman, Illus.). New York: Orchard Books.

Johnson, Angela. (1990). *Do like Kyla* (James Ransome, Illus.). New York: Orchard Books.

Johnson, Angela. (1992). *The leaving morning* (David Soman, Illus.). New York: Orchard Books.

Johnson, Angela. (1993a). *Julius* (Dav Pilkey, Illus.). New York: Orchard Books.

Johnson, Angela. (1993b). *Toning the sweep*. New York: Orchard Books.

Johnson, Angela. (1998). *Heaven*. New York: Simon & Schuster.

Johnson, Angela. (2001). *Running back to Ludie*. New York: Orchard Books.

Johnson, Sylvia, A. (1999). *Mapping the world*. New York: Atheneum.

Johnston, Tony. (1985). *The quilt story* (Tomie dePaola, Illus.). New York: Putnam.

Johnston, Tony. (1996a). *Once in the country: Poems of a farm*. New York: Putnam.

Johnston, Tony. (1996b). *The wagon* (James Ransome, Illus.). New York: Morrow.

Johnston, Tony. (1999). *An old shell: Poems of the Galapagos* (Tom Pohrt, Illus.). New York: Farrar, Straus & Giroux.

Johnston, Tony. (2000). *It's about dogs*. San Diego: Harcourt.

Johnston, Tony. (2001). *Cat, what is that?* New York: HarperCollins.

Joosse, Barbara M. (1983). *Spiders in the fruit cellar* (Kay Chorao, Illus.). New York: Knopf.

Joosse, Barbara M. (1991). *Mama, do you love me?* (Barbara Lavallee, Illus.). San Francisco: Chronicle Books.

Joosse, Barbara M. (2002). *Ghost wings* (Giselle Potter, Illus.). San Francisco: Chronicle Books.

Jordan, Martin, & Jordan, Tanis. (1993). *Jungle days, jungle nights*. New York: Kingfisher Books.

Joseph, Lynn. (2000). *The color of my words*. New York: HarperCollins.

Joyce, William. (1999). *Rolie Polie Olie*. New York: Laura Geringer.

Jukes, Mavis. (1983). *No one is going to Nashville* (Lloyd Bloom, Illus.). New York: Knopf.

Jukes, Mavis. (1985). *Blackberries in the dark* (Thomas B. Allen, Illus.). New York: Dell.

Jukes, Mavis. (1987). *Like Jake and me* (Lloyd Bloom, Illus.). New York: Knopf.

Kahl, Jonathan, D. (1998). *National Audubon Society: First field guide—Weather*. New York: Scholastic.

Kalman, Bobbie. (1984). *Butterflies and moths*. New York: Crabtree.

Kalman, Bobbie, & Schaub, Janine. (1992). *I am a part of nature*. New York: Crabtree.

Kalman, Bobbie, & Smithyman, Kathryn. (2002). *The life cycle of a bird*. New York: Crabtree.

Karlitz, Gail. (1999). *Growing money: A complete investing guide for kids*. New York: Price Stern Sloan.

Katcher, Philip. (1995). *American Civil War armies & volunteer militia*. London: Reed.

Katz, Bobbi. (2000). *We, the people* (Nina Crews, Illus.). New York: HarperCollins.

Keats, Ezra Jack. (1962). *The snowy day*. New York: Viking.

Keats, Ezra Jack. (1968). *A letter to Amy*. New York: HarperCollins.

Keats, Ezra Jack. (1991). *Regards to the man in the moon*. New York: Trumpet.

Keenan, Sheila. (2003). *Gods, goddesses, and monsters: A book of world mythology*. New York: Scholastic.

Keene, Carolyn. (2002). *The mystery of the mother wolf*. New York: Pocket Books.

Keith, Harold. (1987). *Rifles for Watie*. New York: HarperTrophy.

Kellogg, Steven. (1973). *The island of the Skog*. New York: Dial Books.

Kellogg, Steven. (Reteller). (1984). *Paul Bunyan: A tall tale*. New York: Morrow.

Kellogg, Steven. (Reteller). (1985). *Chicken little*. New York: Morrow.

Kelly, Eric Philbrook. (1966). *The trumpeter of Krakow*. New York: Macmillan.

Kennedy, X. J. (1983). *The Owlstone crown*. New York: Simon & Schuster.

Kennedy, X. J. (1984). *The boy who loved alligators*. New York: Atheneum.

Kennedy, X. J. (1990). *Fresh brats*. New York: McElderry.

Kennedy, X. J. (1991). *The kite that braved Old Orchard Beach*. New York: Simon & Schuster.

Kennedy, X. J. (1992). *The beasts of Bethlehem*. New York: Simon & Schuster.

Kennedy, X. J. (1993). *Drat these brats*. New York: Simon & Schuster.

Kennedy, X. J. (1995). *Brats*. New York: Simon & Schuster.

Kennedy, X. J. (1997a). *The eagle as wide as the world*. New York: Simon & Schuster.

Kennedy, X. J. (1997b). *Uncle Switch: Looney limericks* (John O'Brien, Illus.). New York: Simon & Schuster.

Kennedy, X. J. (1999). *Elympics* (Graham Percy, Illus.). New York: Putnam.

Kennedy, X. J. (2002a). *Elefantina's dream* (Graham Percy, Illus.). New York: Putnam.

Kennedy, X. J. (2002b). *Exploding gravy: Poems to make you laugh*. Boston: Little, Brown.

Kennedy, X. J., & Kennedy, Dorothy M. (Sels.). (1992). *Talking like the rain: A first book of poems* (Jane Dyer, Illus.). Boston: Little, Brown.

Kennedy, X. J., & Kennedy, Dorothy M. (1999). *Knock at a star* (Andrew Portwood & Karen Lee Baker, Illus.). Boston: Little, Brown.

Kerley, Barbara. (2001). *The dinosaurs of Waterhouse Hawkins: An illuminating history of Mr. Waterhouse Hawkins, artist and lecturer* (Brian Selznick, Illus.). New York: Scholastic.

Kerr, Judith. (1972). *When Hitler stole pink rabbit*. New York: Coward-McCann.

Kidd, Diana. (1991). *Onion tears* (Lucy Montgomery, Illus.). New York: Orchard Books.

Kiesler, Kate. (2002). *Wings on the wind: Bird poems*. New York: Clarion Books.

Kimmel, Eric. (1997). *Anansi and the talking melon* (Janet Stevens, Illus.). New York: Holiday House.

King, Bob. (1991). *Sitting on the farm* (Bill Slavin, Illus.). New York: Orchard Books.

The Kingfisher children's illustrated dictionary and thesaurus. (1997). New York: Kingfisher.

King-Smith, Dick. (1983). *The queen's nose* (Jill Bennet, Illus.). New York: Harper & Row.

King-Smith, Dick. (1984). *Harry's mad* (Jill Bennet, Illus.). New York: Crown.

King-Smith, Dick. (1987). *The sheep pig.* New York: Dell.

King-Smith, Dick. (1990). *Pigs might fly.* New York: Puffin Books.

King-Smith, Dick. (1993a). *Dodos are forever* (David Parkins, Illus.). New York: Chivers.

King-Smith, Dick. (1993b). *Lady Daisy* (Jan Naimo Jones, Illus.). New York: Delacorte.

King-Smith, Dick. (1999). *Godhangers* (Andrew Davidson, Illus.). New York: Crown.

King-Smith, Dick. (2000). *The crowstarver* (Peter Bailey, Illus.). New York: Crown.

King-Smith, Dick. (2001). *Babe, the gallant pig* (Mary Rayner, Illus.). New York: Dell.

Kinsey-Warnock, Natalie. (1989). *The Canada geese quilt* (Leslie W. Bowman, Illus.). New York: Dell.

Kite, Lorien. (1999). *A rain forest tree* (Peter Bull, Illus.). New York: Crabtree.

Knight, Tim. (2001). *Journey into the rain forest.* London: Oxford.

Koehler, Phoebe. (1990). *The day we met you.* New York: Aladdin Books.

Koehler-Pentacoff, Elizabeth. (2003). *John Muir and Stickeen: An Alaskan adventure* (Karl Swanson, Illus.). Brookfield, CT: Millbrook Press.

Koller, Jackie French. (1995). *A place to call home.* New York: Atheneum.

Konigsburg, E. L. (1967). *From the mixed-up files of Mrs. Basil E. Frankweiler.* New York: Atheneum.

Konigsburg, E. L. (1973). *A proud taste for scarlet and miniver.* New York: Atheneum.

Konigsburg, E. L. (1996). *The view from Saturday.* New York: Atheneum.

Konigsburg, E. L. (1998). *Throwing shadows.* New York: Simon & Schuster.

Krementz, Jill. (1992). *How it feels to live with a physical disability.* New York: Simon & Schuster.

Krisher, Trudy. (1994). *Spite fences.* New York: Delacorte.

Krishna, Dharma. (1998). *Ramayana: India's immortal tale of adventure, love and wisdom.* Los Angeles: Torchlight.

Kroll, Steven. (1991). *Mary McLean and the St. Patrick's Day parade* (Michael Dooling, Illus.). New York: Scholastic.

Krull, Kathleen. (1995a). *Lives of the artists: Masterpieces, messes (and what the neighbors thought)* (Kathryn Hewitt, Illus.). New York: Harcourt Brace.

Krull, Kathleen. (1995b). *V is for victory: America remembers World War II.* New York: Knopf.

Krull, Kathleen. (1998). *Lives of the presidents: Fame, shame (and what the neighbors thought)* (Kathryn Hewitt, Illus.). San Diego: Harcourt Brace.

Krull, Kathleen. (2000). *Lives of extraordinary women: Rulers, rebels (and what the neighbors thought)* (Kathryn Hewitt, Illus.). New York: Harcourt Brace.

Krull, Kathleen. (2003). *Harvesting hope: The story of Cesar Chavez* (Yuyi Morales, Illus.). San Diego: Harcourt Brace.

Krull, Kathleen. (2004). *The boy on Fairfield Street: How Ted Geisel grew up to become Dr. Seuss* (Steve Johnson & Lou Fancher, Illus.). New York: Random House.

Krumgold, Joseph. (1991). *. . . And now Miguel.* Boston: Houghton Mifflin.

Kuklin, Susan. (1986). *Thinking big.* New York: Lothrop, Lee & Shepard.

Kurlansky, Mark. (2001). *The cod's tale* (S. D. Schindler, Illus.). New York: Putnam.

Kurtz, Jane. (2000). *River friendly, river wild.* New York: Simon & Schuster.

Kuskin, Karla. (1958). *In the middle of the trees.* New York: Harper.

Kuskin, Karla. (1961). *The bear who saw the spring.* New York: HarperCollins.

Kuskin, Karla. (1975). *Near the window tree: Poems and notes.* New York: Harper & Row.

Kuskin, Karla. (1992). *Dogs and dragons, trees and dreams.* New York: HarperCollins.

Kusugak, Michael. (1996). *My Arctic 1, 2, 3.* Toronto, ON: Annick.

Lacapa, Michael. (1990). *The flute player: An Apache folktale.* Flagstaff, AZ: Northland.

La Faye, Alice. (1999). *Year of the sawdust man.* New York: Aladdin Books.

Lakin, Patricia. (1994). *Don't forget* (Ted Rand, Illus.). New York: Tambourine Books.

Lambert, David. (1994). *New view: Seas and oceans.* Austin, TX: Raintree Steck-Vaughn.

Landau, Elaine. (1996). *Tropical forest mammals.* New York: Children's Press.

Landau, Elaine. (2003). *Popcorn!* (Brian Lies, Illus.). Boston: Charlesbridge.

Langstaff, John M. (1989). *Oh, a-hunting we will go* (Nancy Winslow Parker, Illus.). Boston: Houghton Mifflin.

Lankford, Mary D. (1998). *Dominoes around the world* (Karen Dugan, Illus.). New York: Morrow.

Lansky, Bruce. (1991). *Kids pick the funniest poems.* Deep Haven, MN: Meadowbrook.

La Prise, Larry, Macak, Charles P., & Baker, Tafft. (1997). *The hokey-pokey* (Sheila Hamanaka, Illus.). New York: Simon & Schuster.

Larrick, Nancy. (Ed.). (1988). *Cats are cats* (Ed Young, Illus.). New York: Philomel.

Larrick, Nancy. (Ed.). (1990). *Mice are nice.* New York: Philomel.

Lasky, Kathryn. (1981). *The night journey.* New York: Warne.

Lasky, Kathryn. (1983). *Beyond the divide.* New York: Macmillan.

Lasky, Kathryn. (1992). *I have an aunt on Marlborough Street* (Susan Guevara, Illus.). New York: Macmillan.

Lasky, Kathryn. (1993). *Monarchs.* Singapore: Harcourt Brace.

Lasky, Kathryn. (1996). *Beyond the burning time.* New York: Scholastic.

Lasky, Kathryn. (2003). *The man who made time travel* (Kevin Hawkes, Illus.). New York: Farrar, Straus & Giroux.

Latham, Jean Lee. (1955). *Carry on, Mr. Bowditch* (John O'Hara Cosgrave, II, Illus.). Boston, Houghton Mifflin.

Lauber, Patricia. (1994). *The news about dinosaurs.* New York: Aladdin Books.

Lauber, Patricia. (1996a). *Flood: Wrestling with the Mississippi.* Washington, DC: National Geographic Society.

Lauber, Patricia. (1996b). *Hurricanes: Earth's mightiest storms.* New York: Scholastic.

Lauber, Patricia. (1998). *Painters of the caves.* Washington, DC: National Geographic Society.

Lauber, Patricia. (1999a). *The tiger has a toothache* (Mary Morgan, Illus.). Washington, DC: National Geographic Society.

Lauber, Patricia. (1999b). *What you never knew about fingers, forks and chopsticks* (John Manders, Illus.). New York: Simon & Schuster.

Lauber, Patricia. (2000a). *Purrfectly purrfect* (Betsy Lewin, Illus.). New York: HarperCollins.

Lauber, Patricia. (2000b). *The true-or-false book of horses* (Rosalyn Schanzer, Illus.). New York: HarperCollins.

Lauber, Patricia. (2001a). *The true-or-false book of cats* (Rosalyn Schanzer, Illus.). Washington, DC: National Geographic Society.

Lauber, Patricia. (2001b). *What you never knew about tubs, toilets & showers* (John Manders, Illus.). New York: Simon & Schuster.

Lawlor, Veronica, & Giuliani, Rudolph W. (1995). *I was dreaming to come to America: Memories from the Ellis Island oral history project*. New York: Viking.

Lawrence, Jacob. (1993a). *The great migration: An American story*. New York: HarperCollins.

Lawrence, Jacob. (1993b). *Harriet and the promised land*. New York: Aladdin Books.

Lawson, Julie. (2001). *Destination gold*. Custer, WA: Orca.

Lawson, Julie. (2002). *The Klondike cat* (Paul Mombourquette, Illus.). Toronto, ON: Kids Can Press.

Leacock, Elspeth, & Buckley, Susan. (2001). *Journeys in time: A new atlas of American history* (Rodica Prato, Illus.). Boston: Houghton Mifflin.

Lear, Edward. (1940). *The complete nonsense of Edward Lear*. Mineola, NY: Dover.

Lear, Edward. (1989). *The jumblies*. Putnam.

Lear, Edward. (1990). *Of pelicans and pussycats: Poems and limericks*. New York: Penguin.

Lee, Claudia. (2002). *Messengers of rain and other poems from Latin America*. Toronto, ON: Groundwood Books.

Lee, Dennis. (1974). *Alligator pie*. Toronto, ON: Macmillan.

Lee, Dennis. (1983). *Jelly belly*. Toronto, ON: Macmillan.

Lee, Dennis. (1992). *The ice cream store*. New York: Scholastic.

Lee, Dennis. (1997). *Dinosaur dinner (with a slice of alligator pie)*. New York: Knopf.

Lee, Francis. (1999). *When the rain sings: Poems by young Native Americans*. New York: Simon & Schuster.

Leedy, Loreen. (2002). *Follow the money*. New York: Holiday House.

Le Guin, Ursula K. (1968). *A wizard of Earthsea* (Ruth Robbins, Illus.). Berkeley, CA: Parnassus Press.

L'Engle, Madeleine. (1955). *The arm of the starfish*. New York: Ariel Books.

L'Engle, Madeleine. (1962). *A wrinkle in time*. New York: Yearling.

L'Engle, Madeleine. (1973). *The wind in the door*. New York: Farrar, Straus & Giroux.

L'Engle, Madeleine. (1978). *A swiftly tilting planet*. New York: Farrar, Straus & Giroux.

L'Engle, Madeleine. (1981a). *Meet the Austins*. New York: Dell.

L'Engle, Madeleine. (1981b). *The moon by night*. New York: Dell.

L'Engle, Madeleine. (1981c). *The ring of endless light*. New York: Dell.

L'Engle, Madeleine. (1989). *The Crosswicks journals*. San Francisco: Harper.

L'Engle, Madeleine. (1990). *An acceptable time*. New York: Dell.

L'Engle, Madeleine. (1998). *Many waters* (Peter Sís & Cliff Nelson, Illus.). New York: Dell.

León, Vicki. (1995). *Parrots, macaws & cockatoos*. Glenview, IL: Silver Burdett.

Lepthien, Emilie. (1989). *Monarch butterflies*. Chicago: Children's Press.

Lepthien, Emilie. (1996). *A true book of sea turtles*. New York: Children's Press.

Lessem, Don. (1999). *Dinosaurs to dodos: An encyclopedia of extinct animals*. New York: Scholastic.

Lessem, Don. (2003). *Scholastic dinosaurs A to Z: The ultimate dinosaur encyclopedia* (Jan Sovak, Illus.). New York: Scholastic.

Lester, Julius. (1968). *To be a slave* (Tom Feelings, Illus.). New York: Scholastic.

Lester, Julius. (1972). *Long journey home*. New York: Scholastic.

Lester, Julius. (1994). *John Henry* (Jerry Pinkney, Illus.). New York: Dial Books.

Lester, Julius. (1995). *Othello*. New York: Scholastic.

Lester, Julius. (1996). *Sam and the tigers: A new telling of the Little Black Sambo* (Jerry Pinkney, Illus.). New York: Dial Books.

Lester, Julius. (1998). *From slave ship to freedom road* (Rod Brown, Illus.). New York: Puffin Books.

Lester, Julius. (1999). *Uncle Remus* (Jerry Pinkney, Illus.). New York: Phyllis Fogelman Books.

Lester, Julius. (2000). *Pharaoh's daughter*. San Diego: Whistle/Harcourt.

LeTord, Bijou. (1995). *A blue butterfly: A story about Claude Monet*. New York: Bantam Doubleday.

Levine, Gail Carson. (1997). *Ella enchanted*. New York: HarperCollins.

Levine, Gail Carson. (1999). *Dave at night*. New York: HarperCollins.

Levine, Gail Carson. (2000). *The wish*. New York: HarperCollins.

Levinson, Riki. (1993). *Soon, Annala*. New York: Orchard Books.

Levy, Constance. (1991). *I'm going to pet a worm today* (Ronald Himler, Illus.). New York: McElderry.

Levy, Constance. (1994). *A tree place* (Robert Sabuda, Illus.). New York: McElderry.

Levy, Constance. (1996). *When whales exhale and other poems* (Judy Labrasca, Illus.). New York: Simon & Schuster.

Levy, Constance. (1998). *A crack in the clouds and other poems* (Robin Bell Corfield, Illus.). New York: McElderry.

Levy, Constance. (2002). *Splash! Poems of our watery world* (David Soman, Illus.). New York: Orchard Books.

Levy, Elizabeth. (1992). *Keep Ms. Sugarman in fourth grade* (Dave Henderson, Illus.). New York: HarperCollins.

Lewin, Ted. (1993). *Amazon boy*. New York: Macmillan.

Lewin, Ted, & Lewin, Betsy (1999). *Gorilla walk*. New York: Lothrop, Lee & Shepard.

Lewis, C. S. (1950). *The lion, the witch and the wardrobe* (Pauline Baynes, Illus.). New York: Collier.

Lewis, J. Patrick. (1988). *The tsar and the amazing cow*. New York: Dial Books.

Lewis, J. Patrick. (1991a). *Earth verses and water rhymes*. New York: Knopf.

Lewis, J. Patrick. (1991b). *Two legged, four legged, no-legged rhymes*. New York: Knopf.

Lewis, J. Patrick. (1992). *The moonbow and Mr. B. Bones*. New York: Knopf.

Lewis, J. Patrick. (1993). *One dog day*. New York: Simon & Schuster.

Lewis, J. Patrick. (1994a). *The fat cats at sea*. New York: Knopf.

Lewis, J. Patrick. (1994b). *A hippopotamusn't and other animal verses*. New York: Penguin.

Lewis, J. Patrick. (1994c). *July is a mad mosquito*. New York: Simon & Schuster.

Lewis, J. Patrick. (1995a). *Black swan/white crow*. New York: Atheneum.

Lewis, J. Patrick. (1995b). *Ridiculous Nicholas*. New York: Penguin.

Lewis, J. Patrick. (1996). *Riddle-icious* (Deborah Tilley, Illus.). New York: Knopf.

Lewis, J. Patrick. (1998). *Riddle-lightful: Oodles of little riddle-poems* (Debbie Tilley, Illus.). New York: Knopf.

Lewis, J. Patrick. (2001). *Good mousekeeping and other animal home poems*. New York: Atheneum.

Lewis, J. Patrick. (2002). *Doodle dandies: Poems that take shape*. New York: Aladdin Books.

Liatsos, Sandra. (1997). *Bicycle riding and other poems*. Honesdale, PA: Boyds Mills Press.

Lin, Grace. (2001). *Dim sum for everyone!* New York: Knopf.

Lindgren, Astrid. (1950). *Pippi Longstocking*. New York: Viking.

Lindsay, Vachel. (1984). The moon's the north wind's cookie. In J. Cole (Ed.), *A new treasury of children's poetry* (p. 186). New York: Morrow.

Ling, Mary. (1992). *See how they grow butterflies*. New York: Dorling Kindersley.

Lionni, Leo. (1960). *Inch by inch*. New York: Astor Honor.

Lionni, Leo. (1963). *Swimmy*. New York: Pantheon.

Lionni, Leo. (1967). *Frederick*. New York: Pantheon.

Lionni, Leo. (1970). *Fish is fish*. New York: Pantheon.

Lionni, Leo. (1987). *Alexander and the wind-up mouse*. New York: Knopf.

Lionni, Leo. (1988). *Six crows*. New York: Knopf.

Lipsyte, Robert. (1987). *The contender*. New York: HarperCollins.

Lisle, Janet Taylor. (1989). *Afternoon of the elves*. New York: Orchard Books.

Lisle, Janet Taylor. (1993). *Forest*. New York: Orchard Books.

Lisle, Janet Taylor. (2000). *The art of keeping cool*. New York: Atheneum.

Little, Jean. (1995). *Mine for keeps*. New York: Viking.

Littlesugar, Amy. (2001). *Freedom school, yes!* (Floyd Cooper, Illus.). New York: Philomel.

Livingston, Myra Cohn. (1968). *A time beyond us: A collection of poetry* (James J. Spanfeller, Illus.). New York: Harcourt.

Livingston, Myra Cohn. (1974). *The way things are, and other poems* (Jenni Oliver, Illus.). New York: Atheneum.

Livingston, Myra Cohn. (1978). *Lollygag of limericks* (Joseph Low, Illus.). New York: Macmillan.

Livingston, Myra Cohn. (1984a). *Sky songs* (Leonard Everett Fisher, Illus.). New York: Holiday House.

Livingston, Myra Cohn. (1984b). *A song I sang to you* (Margot Tomes, Illus.). San Diego: Harcourt Brace.

Livingston, Myra Cohn. (1985). *Celebrations*. New York: Holiday House.

Livingston, Myra Cohn. (1986a). *Earth songs*. New York: Holiday House.

Livingston, Myra Cohn. (1986b). *Sea songs*. New York: Holiday House.

Livingston, Myra Cohn. (1987a). *Cat poems*. New York: Holiday House.

Livingston, Myra Cohn. (1987b). *I like you, if you like me*. New York: McElderry.

Livingston, Myra Cohn. (1988a). *A circle of seasons*. New York: Holiday House.

Livingston, Myra Cohn. (1988b). *Poems for mothers*. New York: Holiday House.

Livingston, Myra Cohn. (1988c). *There was a place and other poems*. New York: McElderry.

Livingston, Myra Cohn. (1989). *Remembering and other poems*. New York: McElderry.

Livingston, Myra Cohn. (1990a). *Dog poems*. New York: Holiday House.

Livingston, Myra Cohn. (1990b). *If the owl calls again*. New York: McElderry.

Livingston, Myra Cohn. (1991). *Lots of limericks* (Rebecca Perry, Illus.). New York: McElderry.

Livingston, Myra Cohn. (1992). *If you ever meet a whale*. New York: Holiday House.

Livingston, Myra Cohn. (1997). *Cricket never does: A collection of haiku & tanka* (Kees De Kiefte, Illus.). New York: Simon & Schuster.

Livingston, Myra Cohn. (1999). *Poems for fathers*. New York: Holiday House.

Llamas, Andreu. (1997). *Spiders: The great spinners* (Gabriel Casadevall, Illus.). Milwaukee: Gareth Stevens.

Llewellyn, Claire. (1998). *What's for lunch? Potatoes*. Boston: Children's Press.

Lobel, Arnold. (1970). *Frog and Toad are friends*. New York: HarperCollins.

Lobel, Arnold. (1980). *Fables*. New York: Harper & Row.

Lobel, Arnold. (Ed.). (1986). *The Random House book of Mother Goose*. New York: Random House.

Lobel, Arnold. (1988). *Book of pigericks: Pig limericks*. New York: HarperCollins.

Locker, Thomas. (1991). *The boy who held back the sea*. New York: Penguin.

Locker, Thomas. (1994). *Family farm*. New York: Penguin.

Locker, Thomas. (2002). *Water dance*. San Diego: Harcourt.

Lofts, Pamela. (1987). *How the kangaroos got their tail: An aboriginal story*. Cambridge: Cambridge University Press.

Longfellow, Henry Wadsworth. (1996). *Paul Revere's ride* (Ted Rand, Illus.). New York: Penguin.

Lord, Bette Bao. (1984). *In the year of the boar and Jackie Robinson*. New York: Harper & Row.

Loupy, Christophe, & Tharlet, Eve. (2001). *Hugs and kisses*. New York: North-South Books.

Lourie, Peter. (2002). *Tierra del Fuego: A journey to the end of the earth*. Honesdale, PA: Boyds Mills Press.

Lowell, Susan. (1993). *I am Lavina Cumming*. Minneapolis: Milkweed.

Lowell, Susan. (2003). *The three little javelinas* (Jim Harris, Illus.). Flagstaff, AZ: Rising Moon Press.

Lowenstein, Frank. (1999). *Bugs*. New York: Black Dog and Leventhal.

Lowry, Lois. (1977). *A summer to die*. Boston: Houghton Mifflin.

Lowry, Lois. (1985). *Anastasia Krupnik*. Boston: Houghton Mifflin.

Lowry, Lois. (1989). *Number the stars*. Boston: Houghton Mifflin.

Lowry, Lois. (1993). *The giver*. Boston: Houghton Mifflin.

Lowry, Lois. (2000). *Gathering blue*. Boston: Houghton Mifflin.

Lum, Darrell. (1994). *The golden slipper: A Vietnamese legend* (Makiko Nagano, Illus.). New York: Troll.

Lunn, Janet. (1996). *The root cellar*. New York: Puffin Books.

Lupton, Hugh. (Ed.). (2000). *The songs of birds: Stories and poems from many cultures*. New York: Barefoot Books.

Lyon, George Ella. (2003). *Mother to tigers* (Peter Catalanotto, Illus.). New York: Atheneum.

Lyons, Dana. (2002). *The tree* (David Lane Danioth, Illus.). New York: Illumination Arts.

Lyons, Mary, E. (1992). *Letters from a slave girl: The story of Harriet Jacobs*. New York: Scribner.

Macaulay, David. (1975). *Pyramid*. New York: Trumpet.

Macaulay, David. (1976). *Underground*. Boston: Houghton Mifflin.

Macaulay, David. (1977). *Castle*. Boston: Houghton Mifflin.

Macaulay, David. (1983). *Mill*. Boston: Houghton Mifflin.

Macaulay, David. (1993). *Ship*. Boston: Houghton Mifflin.

Macaulay, David. (1999). *Building the book: Cathedral*. Boston: Houghton Mifflin.

Macaulay, David. (2000). *Building big*. Boston: Houghton Mifflin.

Macaulay, David. (2003). *Mosque*. Boston: Houghton Mifflin.

Macaulay, David, with Neil Ardley. (1998). *The new way things work*. Boston: Houghton Mifflin.

MacDonald, Suse. (1992). *Alphabatics*. New York: Simon & Schuster.

MacDonald, Suse. (1995). *Nanta's lion*. New York: Morrow.

MacDonald, Suse. (1997). *Peck, slither and slide*. New York: Gulliver Books.

MacDonald, Suse. (1998). *Sea shapes*. San Diego: Harcourt Brace.

MacDonald, Suse. (1999). *Elephants on board*. San Diego: Harcourt Brace.

MacDonald, Suse. (2000). *Look whooo's counting*. New York: Scholastic.

MacLachlan, Patricia. (1980). *Arthur, for the very first time*. New York: HarperCollins.

MacLachlan, Patricia. (1984). *Unclaimed treasures*. New York: Harper & Row.

MacLachlan, Patricia. (1985). *Sarah, plain and tall*. New York: HarperCollins.

MacLachlan, Patricia. (1991). *Journey*. New York: Delacorte.

MacLachlan, Patricia. (1993). *Baby*. New York: Delacorte.

MacLachlan, Patricia. (1994). *Skylark*. New York: HarperCollins.

MacLachlan, Patricia. (1995). *What you know first* (Barry Moser, Illus.). New York: HarperCollins.

Maestro, Betsy. (1993). *The story of money*. New York: Mulberry Books.

Magorian, Michelle. (1981). *Goodnight, Mr. Tom*. New York: HarperCollins.

Mahy, Margaret. (1969). *A lion in the meadow* (Jenny Williams, Illus.). London: Dent.

Mahy, Margaret. (1986). *The tricksters*. New York: McElderry.

Mahy, Margaret. (1987). *Memory*. New York: McElderry.

Mahy, Margaret. (1989). *The great white man-eating shark* (Jonathan Allen, Illus.). New York: Trumpet.

Mak, Kam. (2002). *My Chinatown: One year in poems*. New York: HarperCollins.

Mannis, Celeste Davidson. (2003). *The Queen's progress: An Elizabethan alphabet* (Bagram Ibatoulline, Illus.). New York: Viking.

Margolis, Richard J. (1984). *Secrets of a small brother*. New York: Atheneum.

Markle, Sandra. (2001). *Growing up wild: Wolves*. New York: Atheneum.

Marks, Jane. (1995). *The hidden children: The secret survivors of the Holocaust*. New York: Random House.

Marshall, James. (2001). *Merry Christmas space case*. New York: Scholastic.

Martell, Hazel. (1998). *The great pyramid*. Austin, TX: Raintree Steck-Vaughn.

Martin, Ann. (2002). *A corner of the universe*. New York: Scholastic.

Martin, Bill, Jr. (1967/1983). *Brown bear, brown bear, what do you see?* (Eric Carle, Illus.). New York: Henry Holt.

Martin, Bill, Jr. (1970a). *The happy hippopotami* (Betsy Everitt, Illus.). San Diego: Harcourt Brace.

Martin, Bill, Jr. (1970b). *Old devil wind* (Robert J. Lee, Illus.). New York: Holt, Rinehart and Winston.

Martin, Bill, Jr. (1989). *Chicka chicka boom boom* (Lois Ehlert, Illus.). New York: Simon & Schuster.

Martin, Bill, Jr. (1991). *Polar bear, polar bear, what do you hear?* (Eric Carle, Illus.). New York: Henry Holt.

Martin, Bill, Jr., & Archambault, John. (1985). *The ghost-eye tree* (Ted Rand, Illus.). New York: Holt, Rinehart and Winston.

Martin, Bill, Jr., & Archambault, John. (1986a). *Barn dance!* (Ted Rand, Illus.). New York: Henry Holt..

Martin, Bill, Jr., & Archambault, John. (1986b). *While Dynamite and Curly Kidd* (Ted Rand, Illus.). New York: Henry Holt.

Martin, Bill, Jr., & Archambault, John. (1987a). *Knots on a counting rope* (Ted Rand, Illus.). New York: Scholastic.

Martin, Bill, Jr., & Archambault, John. (1987b). *Listen to the rain* (James Endicott, Illus.). Allen, TX: DLM Teaching Resources.

Martin, Bill, Jr., & Archambault, John. (1989). *The magic pumpkin* (Robert J. Lee, Illus.). New York: Henry Holt.

Martin, Jacqueline Briggs. (1998). *Snowflake Bentley* (Mary Azarian, Illus.). Boston: Houghton Mifflin.

Martin, Jacqueline Briggs. (2001). *The lamp, the ice, and the boat called Fish* (Beth Krommes, Illus.). Boston: Houghton Mifflin.

Martin, Rafe. (1992). *The rough-face girl*. New York: Scholastic.

Maruki, Toshi. (1980). *Hiroshima No Pika*. New York: Lothrop, Lee & Shepard.

Marzollo, Jean. (1994). *My first book of biographies: Great men and women every child should know*. New York: Scholastic.

Marzollo, Jean. (1997). *I'm a caterpillar*. New York: Scholastic.

Marzollo, Jean. (2000). *I love you* (Suse MacDonald, Illus.). New York: Scholastic.

Marzollo, Jean, & Marzollo, Claudio. (1982). *Jed's junior space patrol* (David S. Rose, Illus.). New York: Scholastic.

Mason, Antony. (2002). *People around the world*. London: Kingfisher.

Matas, Carol. (1993). *Daniel's story*. New York: Scholastic.

Mathis, Sharon Bell. (1975). *The hundred penny box* (Leo Dillon & Diane Dillon, Illus.). New York: Puffin Books.

Mathis, Sharon Bell. (1991). *Red dog blue fly: Football poems*. New York: Viking.

Matthews, John. (Reteller). (2002). *The book of Arthur: Last tales from the Round Table*. London: Vega.

Mavor, Salley. (1997). *You and me: Poems of friendship*. New York: Orchard Books.

Max, Jill. (1997). *Spider spins a story: Fourteen legends from native America* (Benjamin Harjo, Illus.). Phoenix: Northland.

Mayer, Marianna. (2000). *Beauty and the beast* (Mercer Mayer, Illus.). New York: SeaStar Books.

Mayer, Mercer. (1973). *What do you do with a kangaroo?* New York: Four Winds Press.

Mayer, Mercer. (1984). *The sleeping beauty*. New York: Macmillan.

Mayer, Mercer. (1990). *There's a nightmare in my closet*. New York: Dial Books.

Mayer, Mercer. (1999). *Just me and my family*. New York: Golden Books.

Mazzola, Frank, Jr. (1997). *Counting is for the birds*. Boston: Charlesbridge.

McCaffrey, Anne. (1969). *The ship who sang*. New York: Ballantine Books.

McCaffrey, Anne. (1971). *Dragonquest*. New York: Ballantine Books.

McCaffrey, Anne. (1973). *To ride Pegasus*. New York: Ballantine Books.

McCaffrey, Anne. (1976). *Dragonsong*. New York: Atheneum.

McCaffrey, Anne. (1977). *Get off the unicorn*. New York: Ballantine Books.

McCaffrey, Anne. (1978a). *The dragonriders of Pern*. Garden City, NY: Nelson Doubleday.

McCaffrey, Anne. (1978b). *The white dragon*. New York: Ballantine Books.

McCaffrey, Anne. (1991). *Dragonflight*. New York: Ballantine Books.

McCaffrey, Anne. (1996). *Black horses for the king*. San Diego: Harcourt Brace.

McCaffrey, Anne. (2003). *On dragonwings*. San Francisco: Del Ray.

McCarty, Peter. (2002). *Hondo and Fabian*. New York: Henry Holt.

McCaughrean, Geraldine. (Reteller). (1993). *The Odyssey*. New York: Oxford University Press.

McCaughrean, Geraldine. (2002). *The kite rider*. New York: HarperCollins.

McClaren, Clemence. (2000). *Waiting for Odysseus*. New York: Atheneum.

McCloskey, Robert. (1952) *One morning in Maine*. New York: Viking.

McCloskey, Robert. (1957). *Time of wonder*. New York: Puffin Books.

McCord, David. (1956). *Far and few: Rhymes of the never was and always is*. Boston: Little, Brown.

McCord, David. (1977). *One at a time* (Henry B. Kane, Illus.). Boston: Little, Brown.

McCord, David. (1987). *The five owls* (Vol. 2). Boston: Little, Brown.

McCourt, Lisa. (1997). *The rainforest counts!* (Cheryl Nathan, Illus.). Mahwah, NJ: Troll.

McCully, Emily Arnold. (1992). *Mirette on the high wire*. New York: Putnam.

McDermott, Gerald. (1975). *The stonecutter: A Japanese folk tale*. New York: Viking.

McDonald, Megan. (1990). *Is this a house for Hermit Crab?* (S. D. Schindler, Illus.). New York: Orchard Books.

McDonough, Yona Zeldis. (1997). *Anne Frank* (Malcah Zeldis, Illus.). New York: Henry Holt.

McGill, Alice. (1999). *Molly Bannaky* (Chris K. Soentpiet, Illus.). Boston: Houghton Mifflin.

McGovern, Ann. (1965). *The Arrow book of poetry*. New York: Scholastic.

McGovern, Ann. (1992). *... If you grew up with Abraham Lincoln* (Brinton Turkle, Illus.). New York: Scholastic.

McGrath, Barbara Barbieri. (2002). *The M & M's brand counting book* (Roger Glass, Illus.). Boston: Charlesbridge.

McGrath, Susan. (1985). *Your world of pets*. Washington, DC: National Geographic Society.

McGuffey, W. H. (1879). *McGuffey's fifth eclectic reader*. New York: Signet.

McKay, Hilary. (1996). *The exiles*. New York: Aladdin Books.

McKay, Hilary. (2003). *Saffy's angel*. Minneapolis: Sagebrush.

McKinley, Robin. (1978). *Beauty: A retelling of the story of Beauty & the Beast*. New York: Harper & Row.

McKinley, Robin. (1982). *The blue sword*. New York: Greenwillow.

McKinley, Robin. (1984). *The hero and the crown*. New York: Greenwillow.

McKinley, Robin. (1997). *Rose daughter*. New York: Greenwillow.

McKissack, Patricia. (1988). *Mirandy & Brother Wind*. New York: Knopf.

McKissack, Patricia. (1998). *The dark thirty: Southern tales of the supernatural* (Brian Pinkney, Illus.). New York: Knopf.

McKissack, Patricia, & McKissack, Fredrick L. (1994). *Christmas in the big house, Christmas in the quarters* (John Thompson, Illus.). New York: Scholastic.

McKissack, Patricia, & McKissack, Fredrick L. (1998). *Let my people go* (James Ransome, Illus.). New York: Simon & Schuster.

McKissack, Patricia, & McKissack, Fredrick L. (2003). *Days of jubilee: The end of slavery in the United States*. New York: Scholastic.

McLerran, Alice. (1985). *The mountain that loved a bird* (Eric Carle, Illus.). Saxonville, MA: Picture Book Studio.

McMahon, Patricia. (1995). *Listen for the bus*. Honesdale, PA: Boyds Mills Press.

McMillan, Bruce. (1991). *The weather sky*. New York: HarperCollins.

McNaughton, Colin. (2001). *Who's been sleeping in my porridge?* Minneapolis: Sagebrush.

McPhail, David. (2002). *Edward in the jungle*. Boston: Little, Brown.

McPherson, James M. (2002). *Fields of fury: The American Civil War*. New York: Atheneum.

McSwigan, Marie. (1942). *Snow treasure* (Mary Reardon, Illus.). New York: Dutton.

Medina, Jane. (1999). *My name is Jorge: On both sides of the river*. Honesdale, PA: Wordsong/Boyds Mills Press.

Medina, Jane. (2004). *The dream on Blanca's wall: Poems in English and Spanish*. Honesdale, PA: Wordsong/Boyds Mills Press.

Medlock, Scott. (Ed.). (1996). *Opening days: Sports poems*. San Diego: Harcourt Brace.

Meltzer, Milton. (1946). *In their own words: A history of the American Negro*. New York: Crowell.

Meltzer, Milton. (1968). *Langston Hughes: A biography*. New York: Crowell.

Meltzer, Milton. (1972). *Hunted like a wolf: The story of the Seminole War*. New York: Farrar, Straus & Giroux.

Meltzer, Milton. (1983). *The terrorists*. New York: Harper & Row.

Meltzer, Milton. (1985a). *Ain't gonna study war no more: The story of America's peace-seekers*. New York: Harper & Row.

Meltzer, Milton. (1985b). *Mark Twain: A writer's life*. New York: Watts.

Meltzer, Milton. (1990a). *Ten kings and the worlds they ruled*. New York: HarperCollins.

Meltzer, Milton. (1990b). *Underground man*. New York: Harcourt.

Meltzer, Milton. (1993). *Slavery*. New York: DaCapo.

Meltzer, Milton. (2002). *Voices from the Civil War: A documentary history of the great American conflict*. New York: Orchard Books.

Mendez, Phil. (1989). *The black snowman* (Carole Byard, Illus.). New York: Scholastic.

Merriam, Eve. (1964). *It doesn't always have to rhyme*. New York: Atheneum.

Merriam, Eve. (1984). *Jamboree: Rhymes for all times* (Walter Gaffney-Kessell, Illus.). New York: Dell.

Merriam, Eve. (1985). *Blackberry ink*. New York: Morrow.

Merriam, Eve. (1986). *Fresh paint*. New York: Atheneum.

Merriam, Eve. (1988). *You be good & I'll be night*. New York: Morrow.

Merriam, Eve. (1989). *A poem for a pickle*. New York: Morrow.

Merriam, Eve. (1994). *Higgle wiggle: Happy rhymes*. Morrow.

Merriam, Eve. (1995). *Bam bam bam* (Dan Yaccarino, Illus.). New York: Holt.

Merrick, Patrick. (1997). *Caterpillars*. Clanhassen, MN: Child's World.

Merrill, Jean. (1992). *The girl who loved caterpillars: A twelfth century tale from Japan* (Floyd Cooper, Illus.). New York: Philomel.

Meyer, Carolyn. (1995). *Drummers of Jericho*. San Diego: Gulliver Books.

Meyer, Donald J. (Ed.) (1997). *Views from our shoes: Growing up with a brother or sister with special needs* (Gary Pillo, Illus.). Bethesda, MD: Woodbine House.

Michelson, Richard. (1996). *Animals that ought to be*. New York: Simon & Schuster.

Michelson, Richard, & Saunders, Dave. (2000). *Ten times better* (Leonard Baskin, Illus.). New York: Marshall Cavendish.

Micucci, Charles. (1992). *The life and times of the apple*. New York: Orchard Books.

Micucci, Charles. (1995). *The life and times of the honeybee*. New York: Ticknor & Fields.

Micucci, Charles. (2000). *The life and times of the peanut*. Boston: Houghton Mifflin.

Micucci, Charles. (2003). *The life and times of the ant*. Boston: Houghton Mifflin.

Mikaelsen, Ben. (1991). *Rescue Josh McGuire*. New York: Hyperion Books.

Mikaelsen, Ben. (2002). *Red midnight*. New York: HarperCollins.

Miles, Betty. (2000). *The real me*. New York: Knopf.

Miller, Debbie. S. (2000). *River of life* (Jon Van Zyle, Illus.). New York: Clarion Books.

Miller, Margaret. (1992). *Where does it go?* New York: Greenwillow.

Mills, Claudia. (1999). *You're a brave man, Julius Zimmerman*. New York: Farrar, Straus & Giroux.

Mills, Claudia. (2000). *Lizzie at last*. New York: Farrar, Straus & Giroux.

Mills, Lauren A. (1991). *The rag coat*. Boston: Little, Brown.

Milne, A. A. (1924). *When we were very young*. New York: Puffin Books.

Milne, A. A. (1926). *Winnie-the-Pooh*. New York: Puffin Books.

Milne, A. A. (1927). *Now we are six*. New York: Dutton.

Milne, A. A. (1928). *The house at Pooh Corner*. New York: Puffin Books.

Milne, A. A. (1989). *The world of Christopher Robin*. New York: Dutton.

Milton, John. (1974). *Asimov's annotated Paradise Lost*. New York, Doubleday.

Milton, Joyce. (1992). *Step into reading—Wild, wild WOLVES* (Larry Schwinger, Illus.). New York: Random House.

Mitchell, Adrian. (1989). *Strawberry drums: A book of poems with a beat for you and all your friends to keep*. New York: Delacorte.

Mitchell, Margaree King. (1997). *Uncle Jed's barbershop* (James Ransome, Illus.). New York: Simon & Schuster.

Mochizuki, Ken. (1993). *Baseball saved us* (Dom Lee, Illus.). New York: Lee & Low.

Mochizuki, Ken. (1997). *Passage to freedom: The Sugihara story* (Dom Lee, Illus.). New York: Lee & Low.

Mohr, Nicholasa. (1979). *Felita* (Ray Cruz, Illus.). New York: Dial Books.

Mohr, Nicholasa. (1986). *Going home*. New York: Dial Books.

Montgomery, Sy. (2001). *The man-eating tigers of Sundarbans* (Eleanor Briggs, Photog). Boston: Houghton Mifflin.

Moore, Clement C. (1847). *A visit from Saint Nicholas*. New York: Spalding & Shepard.

Moore, Lilian. (Sel.). (1992). *Sunflakes: Poems for children* (Jan Ormerod, Illus.). New York: Clarion Books.

Moore, Lilian. (1997). *Poems have roots: New poems*. New York: Atheneum.

Mora, Pat. (1993). *Nepantla: Essays from the land in the middle*. Albuquerque: University of New Mexico Press.

Mora, Pat. (1996). *Confetti: Poems for children* (Enrique Sanchez, Illus.). New York: Lee & Low.

Mora, Pat. (1997). *Tomás and the library lady* (Raul Colón, Illus.). New York: Dragon Fly.

Mora, Pat. (1999). *The rainbow tulip* (Elizabeth Sayles, Illus.). New York: Penguin.

Mora, Pat. (2000). *My own true name: New and selected poems for young adults* (Anthony Accardo, Illus.). Santa Fe, NM: Arte Publico Press.

Mora, Pat. (2001). *Love to mama: A tribute to mothers*. New York: Lee & Low.

Mora, Pat. (2002a). *House of houses*. Boston: Beacon Press.

Mora, Pat. (2002b). *This big sky* (Steve Jenkins, Illus.). New York: Scholastic.

Mori, Kyoko. (1993). *Shizuko's daughter*. New York: Holt.

Morimoto, Junko. (1990). *My Hiroshima*. New York: Viking.

Morley, Jacqueline. (2001). *How would you survive as an ancient Egyptian?* (John James, Illus.). New York: Watts.

Morpurgo, Michael. (1992). *Waiting for Anya*. New York: Viking.

Morrison, Lillian. (1977). *The sidewalk racer and other poems about sports and motion*. New York: Lothrop, Lee & Shepard.

Morrison, Lillian. (1988). *Rhythm road: Poems to move to*. New York: HarperCollins.

Morrison, Lillian. (1992a). *At the crack of the bat*. New York: Hyperion Books.

Morrison, Lillian. (1992b). *Whistling the morning in*. Honesdale, PA: Boyds Mills Press.

Morrison, Tony, with Slade Morrison. (1999). *The big box* (Giselle Potter, Illus.). New York: Jump at the Sun/Hyperion Books.

Morse, Jenifer Corr. (2003). *Scholastic book of world records 2004*. New York: Scholastic.

Moss, Jeffrey. (1989). *Butterfly jar*. New York: Bantam Books.

Moss, Marissa. (2001). *Oh boy, Amelia*. Middleton, WI: Pleasant Company.

Most, Bernard. (1978). *If the dinosaurs came back*. San Diego: Harcourt Brace.

Mowat, Farley. (1961). *Owls in the family*. Boston: Little, Brown.

Munsch, Robert. (1979). *The dark* (Sami Suomalainen, Illus.). Toronto, ON: Annick Press.

Munsch, Robert. (1980). *The paper bag princess* (Michael Martchenko, Illus.). Toronto, ON: Annick Press.

Munsch, Robert. (1982). *The mud puddle* (Sami Suomalainen, Illus.). Toronto, ON: Annick Press.

Munsch, Robert. (1983). *David's father* (Michael Martchenko, Illus.). Toronto, ON: Annick Press.

Munsch, Robert. (1984). *Millicent and the wind* (Suzanne Duranceau, Illus.). Toronto, ON: Annick Press.

Munsch, Robert. (1985). *Thomas' snowsuit* (Michael Martchenko, Illus.). Toronto, ON: Annick Press.

Munsch, Robert. (1986a). *The boy in the drawer* (Michael Martchenko, Illus.). Toronto, ON: Annick Press.

Munsch, Robert. (1986b). *50 below zero* (Michael Martchenko, Illus.). Toronto, ON: Annick Press.

Munsch, Robert. (1987). *I have to go* (Michael Martchenko, Illus.). Toronto, ON: Annick Press.

Munsch, Robert. (1988a). *Angela's airplane* (Michael Martchenko, Illus.). Toronto, ON: Annick Press.

Munsch, Robert. (1988b). *Moira's birthday* (Michael Martchenko, Illus.). Toronto, ON: Annick Press.

Munsch, Robert. (1990). *Something good* (Michael Martchenko, Illus.). Toronto, ON: Annick Press.

Munsch, Robert. (1991). *Love you forever* (Sheila McGraw, Illus.). Willowdale, ON: Firefly Books.

Munsch, Robert. (1992a). *Murmel, murmel, murmel* (Michael Martchenko, Illus.). Toronto, ON: Annick Press.

Munsch, Robert. (1992b). *Purple, green and yellow* (Helene Desputeaux, Illus.). Toronto, ON: Annick Press.

Munsch, Robert. (1995). *From far away* (Michael Martchenko, Illus.). Toronto, ON: Annick Press..

Munsch, Robert, Kusugak, Michael, & Krykorka, Vladyana. (1988). *A promise is a promise*. Toronto, ON: Annick Press.

Murphy, Jim. (1990). *The boys' war*. New York: Clarion Books.

Murphy, Jim. (1992). *The long road to Gettysburg*. New York: Clarion Books.

Murphy, Jim. (1993). *Across America on an emigrant train*. New York: Clarion Books.

Murphy, Jim. (1995). *The great fire*. New York: Scholastic.

Murphy, Jim. (1996). *The young patriot: The American Revolution as experienced by one boy*. New York: Clarion Books.

Murphy, Jim. (1998). *Gone a-whaling: The lure of the sea and the hunt for the great whale*. New York: Clarion Books.

Murphy, Jim. (2000). *Blizzard: The storm that changed America*. New York: Scholastic.

Murphy, Jim. (2003). *Inside the Alamo*. New York: Knopf.

Muth, Jon J. (2002). *The three questions: Based on a story by Leo Tolstoy*. New York: Scholastic.

Myers, Edward. (1994). *Climb or die*. New York: Hyperion Books.

Myers, Walter Dean. (1988). *Scorpions*. New York: Harper & Row.

Myers, Walter Dean. (1990). *The mouse rap*. New York: HarperCollins.

Myers, Walter Dean. (1993a). *Brown angels: An album of pictures and verse*. New York: HarperCollins.

Myers, Walter Dean. (1993b). *Malcolm X: By any means necessary*. New York: Scholastic.

Myers, Walter Dean. (1994). *Darnell Rock reporting*. New York: Delacorte.

Myers, Walter Dean. (1996). *Slam!* New York: Scholastic.

Myers, Walter Dean. (2000). *Malcolm X: A fire burning brightly* (Leonard Jenkins, Illus.). New York: HarperCollins.

Na, An. (2001). *A step from heaven*. Asheville, NC: Front Street.

Naidoo, Beverley. (1985). *Journey to Jo'burg* (Eric Velasquez, Illus.). New York: Lippincott.

Naidoo, Beverley. (1989). *Chain of fire* (Eric Velasquez, Illus.). New York: Lippincott.

Naidoo, Beverley. (1997). *No turning back: A novel of South Africa*. New York: Hyperion Books.

Naidoo, Beverley. (2001). *The other side of truth*. New York: HarperCollins.

Namioka, Lensey. (1992). *Yang the youngest and his terrible ear*. New York: Dell.

Napoli, Donna Jo. (1995). *The magic circle*. New York: Puffin Books.

Napoli, Donna Jo. (1996). *Zel*. New York: Dutton.

Napoli, Donna Jo. (2001). *Spinners*. New York: Puffin Books.

Naylor, Phyllis Reynolds. (1974). *An Amish family* (Georgia Armstrong, Illus.). Chicago: J. P. O'Hara.

Naylor, Phyllis Reynolds. (1980). *Shadows on the wall*. New York: Atheneum.

Naylor, Phyllis Reynolds. (1986). *The keeper*. New York: Atheneum.

Naylor, Phyllis Reynolds. (1987). *Beetles, lightly toasted*. New York: Atheneum.

Naylor, Phyllis Reynolds. (1991). *Shiloh*. New York: Atheneum.

Naylor, Phyllis Reynolds. (1992). *All but Alice*. New York: Atheneum.

Naylor, Phyllis Reynolds. (1994a). *Boys against girls*. New York: Delacorte.

Naylor, Phyllis Reynolds. (1994b). *The fear place*. New York: Atheneum.

Naylor, Phyllis Reynolds. (1996). *Shiloh season*. New York: Atheneum Books.

Naylor, Phyllis Reynolds. (1997). *Saving Shiloh*. New York: Atheneum.

Naylor, Phyllis Reynolds. (1998). *Achingly Alice*. New York: Atheneum.

Naylor, Phyllis Reynolds. (1999). *Sweet strawberries* (Rosalind Charney Kaye, Illus.). New York: Atheneum.

Naylor, Phyllis Reynolds. (2000). *A spy among the girls*. New York: Delacorte.

Neimark, Anne E. (2002). *The life of Woody Guthrie: There ain't nobody that can sing like me*. New York: Atheneum.

Nelson, Vaunda Micheaux. (1999). *Beyond Mayfield*. New York: Putnam.

Nerlove, Miriam. (1996). *Flowers on the wall*. New York: McElderry.

Newman, Lesléa. (1989). *Heather has two mommies* (Diana Souza, Illus.). Boston: Alyson Wonderland.

Newton, Laura. (1986). *Me and my aunts* (Robin Oz, Illus.). Niles, IL: Albert Whitman.

Nichol, Barbara. (1994). *Beethoven lives upstairs* (Scott Cameron, Illus.). New York: Orchard Books.

Nicholas, Christopher. (1999). *Know-it-alls: Wolves!* (Drew-Brook-Cormack, Illus.). New York: McClanahan.

Nichols, Judith. (2003). *The sun in me: Poems about the planet*. Cambridge, MA: Barefoot Books.

Nicolson, Cynthia Pratt. (2002). *Hurricane!* Toronto, ON: Kids Can Press.

Nims, Bonnie Larkin. (1992). *Just beyond reach and other riddle poems* (George Ancona, Photog.). New York: Scholastic.

Nixon, Joan Lowery. (1986). *The other side of dark*. New York: Delacorte.

Nixon, Joan Lowery. (1987). *A family apart*. New York: Bantam.

Noonuccal, Oodgeroo. (1990). *Australian legends and landscapes* (Reg Morrison, Photog.). Milsons Point, New South Wales: Random House.

North, Sterling. (1963). *Rascal: A memoir of a better era*. New York: Dutton.

Norton, Mary. (1953). *The borrowers* (Beth Krush & Joe Krush, Illus.). New York, Harcourt Brace.

Nu, Ann. (2003). *A step from heaven*. New York: Puffin Books.

Nye, Naomi Shihab. (Sel.). (1992). *This same sky: A collection of poems from around the world*. New York: Four Winds Press.

Nye, Naomi Shihab. (1994). *Sitti's secrets* (Nancy Carpenter, Illus.). New York: Four Winds Press.

Nye, Naomi Shihab. (Sel.). (1995). *The tree is older than you are: A bilingual gathering of poems & stories from Mexico with paintings by Mexican artists*. New York: Simon & Schuster.

Nye, Naomi Shihab. (1998). *The space between our footsteps: Poems and paintings from the Middle East*. New York: Simon & Schuster.

Nye, Naomi Shihab. (1999). *Habibi*. New York: Simon & Schuster.

Nye, Naomi Shihab. (2000). *Come with me: Poems for a journey*. New York: Greenwillow.

O'Brien, Robert. (1986a). *Mrs. Frisby and the rats of NIMH*. New York: Aladdin Books.

O'Brien, Robert. (1986b). *Z for Zachariah*. New York: Simon & Schuster.

O'Byrne, John. (2002). *My first pocket guide: Stars and planets*. Washington, DC: National Geographic Society.

Ochoa, Annette Piña, Franco, Betsy, & Gourdine, Traci L. (Eds.). (2003). *Night is gone, day is still coming: Stories and poems by American Indian teens and young adults*. Cambridge, MA: Candlewick Press.

O'Dell, Scott. (1960). *Island of the blue dolphins*. Boston: Houghton Mifflin.

O'Dell, Scott. (1976a). *Sing down the moon*. New York: Dell.

O'Dell, Scott. (1976b). *Zia*. New York: Dell.

O'Dell, Scott. (1980). *Sarah Bishop*. Boston: Houghton Mifflin.

O'Dell, Scott. (1986). *Streams to the river*. Boston: Houghton Mifflin.

O'Dell, Scott. (1987). *The serpent never sleeps*. Boston: Houghton Mifflin.

Okimoto, Jean D. (1990). *Take a chance, Gramps!* Boston: Little, Brown.

Oneal, Zibby. (1980). *The language of goldfish: A novel*. New York: Viking Press.

Oneal, Zibby. (1985). *In summer light*. New York: Viking.

Onyefulu, Ifeoma. (1995). *Emeka's gift: An African counting story*. New York: Cobblehill.

Opie, Iona. (Ed.). (1999). *Here comes Mother Goose* (Rosemary Wells, Illus.). Cambridge, MA: Candlewick Press.

Opie, Iona, & Opie, Peter. (1955). *The Oxford nursery rhyme book*. London: Oxford.

Oritz, Simon J. (1988). *The people shall continue*. San Francisco: Children's Book Press.

Orlev, Uri. (1984). *The island on Bird Street*. Boston: Houghton Mifflin.

Osborne, Mary Pope. (1991). *Favorite Greek myths* (Troy Howell, Illus.). New York: Scholastic.

Osborne, Mary Pope. (1996). *One world, many religions: The ways we worship*. New York: Knopf.

Osborne, Mary Pope. (1999). *Spider Kane and the mystery at Jumbo Nightcrawler's* (Victoria Chess, Illus.). New York: Knopf.

Osborne, Will, & Osborne, Mary Pope. (2001). *Rain forests: A nonfiction companion to* Afternoon on the Amazon. New York: Random House.

Osborne, Will, & Osborne, Mary Pope. (2002). *Titanic: A nonfiction companion to* Tonight on the Titanic. New York: Random House.

Otfinoski, Steve. (1996). *Money: Earning it, saving it, spending it, growing it, sharing it*. New York: Scholastic.

Otto, Carolyn B. (2001). *Scholastic science readers—Wolves*. New York: Scholastic.

Oughton, Jerrie. (1995). *Music from a place called Half Moon*. New York: Doubleday.

Pallotta, Jerry. (1998). *The boat alphabet book* (David Biedrzycki, Illus.). Boston: Charlesbridge.

Pallotta, Jerry. (2002). *The skull alphabet book* (Ralph Masiello, Illus.). Boston: Charlesbridge.

Panzer, Nora. (Ed.). (1994). *Celebrate America: In poetry and art*. New York: Hyperion Books.

Paolilli, Paul, & Brewer, Dan. (2003). *Silver seeds: A book of nature poems*. New York: Puffin Books.

Parish, Peggy. (1966). *Amelia Bedelia and the surprise shower*. New York: Harper & Row.

Park, Barbara. (1987). *The kid in the red jacket*. New York: Knopf.

Park, Barbara. (1995). *Mick Harte was here*. New York: Knopf.

Park, Barbara. (1997). *Skinnybones*. New York: Random House.

Park, Barbara. (2000). *The graduation of Jake Moon*. New York: Atheneum.

Park, Linda Sue. (2002). *A single shard*. New York: Clarion Books.

Park, Linda Sue. (2004). *When my name was Keoko*. Minneapolis: Sagebrush.

Parker, Nancy Wilson. (1995). *Money, money, money*. New York: HarperCollins.

Patent, Dorothy Hinshaw. (2002). *Animals on the trail with Lewis and Clark* (William Muñoz, Photog.). New York: Clarion Books.

Paterson, Katherine. (1973). *The sign of the chrysanthemum* (Peter Landa, Illus.). New York: Avon.

Paterson, Katherine. (1974). *Of nightingales that weep*. New York: Crowell.

Paterson, Katherine. (1975). *The master puppeteer*. New York: Crowell.

Paterson, Katherine. (1977). *Bridge to Terabithia*. New York: Crowell.

Paterson, Katherine. (1978). *The great Gilly Hopkins*. New York: Crowell.

Paterson, Katherine. (1980). *Jacob have I loved*. New York: HarperCollins.

Paterson, Katherine. (1985). *Come sing, Jimmy Jo*. New York: Dutton.

Paterson, Katherine. (1989). *Park's quest*. New York: Dutton.

Paterson, Katherine. (1991). *Lyddie*. New York: Lodestar.

Paterson, Katherine. (1994). *Flip-flop girl*. New York: Dutton.

Paterson, Katherine. (1996). *Jip: His story*. New York: Puffin Books.

Paterson, Katherine. (1999). *Preacher's boy*. New York: Clarion Books.

Paterson, Katherine. (2002). *The same stuff as stars*. New York: Clarion Books.

Patrick, Denise Lewis. (1998). *Red dancing shoes* (James Ransome, Illus.). New York: Morrow.

Patron, Susan. (1993). *Maybe yes, maybe no, maybe maybe*. New York: Orchard Books.

Paulsen, Gary. (1985). *Dogsong*. New York: Puffin Books.

Paulsen, Gary. (1987). *Hatchet*. New York: Bradbury Press.

Paulsen, Gary. (1989). *The voyage of the Frog*. New York: Bradbury Press.

Paulsen, Gary. (1991). *The river*. New York: Delacorte.

Paulsen, Gary. (1993). *Nightjohn*. New York: Delacorte.

Paulsen, Gary. (1995). *Harris and me*. New York: Yearling.

Paulsen, Gary. (1996). *Brian's winter*. New York: Delacorte.

Paulsen, Gary. (1998a). *Sarny: A life remembered*. New York: Delacorte.

Paulsen, Gary. (1998b). *Soldier's heart: Being the story of the enlistment and due service of the boy Charley Goddard in the First Minnesota Volunteers*. New York: Delacorte.

Paulsen, Gary. (1999a). *Alida's song*. New York: Delacorte.

Paulsen, Gary. (1999b). *Brian's return*. New York: Delacorte.

Paulsen, Gary. (1999c). *My life in dog years* (Ruth Wright Paulsen, Illus.). New York: Dell.

Pearsall, Shelly. (2002). *Trouble don't last*. New York: Random House.

Peck, Richard. (1998). *A long way from Chicago*. New York: Dial Books.

Peck, Richard. (2003a). *Fair weather*. New York: Puffin Books.

Peck, Richard. (2003b). *The river between us*. New York: Dial Books.

Peck, Robert N. (1972). *A day no pigs would die*. New York: Dell.

Peck, Robert N. (1989). *Arly*. New York: Walker.

Peek, Merle. (1985). *Mary wore her red dress, and Henry wore his green sneakers*. New York: Clarion Books.

Pellegrini, Nina. (1991). *Families are different*. New York: Holiday House.

Penman, Sarah. (2000). *Honor the grandmothers: Lakota and Dakota women tell their stories*. St. Paul, MN: Minnesota Historical Society Press.

Perkins, Lynne Rae. (1999). *All alone in the universe*. New York: Greenwillow.

Peterson, Cris, & Upitis, Alva. (1999). *Century farm: One hundred years on a family farm*. Honesdale, PA: Boyds Mills Press.

Peterson, John. (1992). *The Littles*. New York: Scholastic.

Petry, Ann. (1991). *Tituba of Salem Village*. New York: HarperCollins.

Petry, Ann Lane. (1995). *Harriet Tubman, conductor on the Underground Railroad*. New York: HarperCollins.

Pfeffer, Wendy. (1997). *A log's life*. New York: Simon & Schuster.

Philbrick, Rodman. (1993). *Freak the mighty*. New York: Scholastic.

Philbrick, Rodman. (2000). *The last book in the universe*. New York: Blue Sky Press.

Philip, Neil. (Sel.). (1995). *Singing America: Poems that define a nation* (Michael McCurdy, Illus.). New York: Viking.

Pilkey, Dav. (1994). *Dog breath!: The horrible trouble with Hally Tosis*. New York: Blue Sky Press.

Pinkney, Andrea Davis. (1993). *Seven candles for Kwanzaa* (Brian Pinkney, Illus.). New York: Dial Books.

Pinkney, Andrea Davis. (1996). *Bill Pickett: Rodeo-ridin' cowboy*. San Diego: Harcourt Brace.

Pinkney, Andrea Davis. (1998). *Duke Ellington: The piano prince and his orchestra* (Brian Pinkney, Illus.). New York: Scholastic.

Pinkney, Andrea Davis. (2000). *Let it shine: Stories of black women freedom fighters* (Stephen Alcorn, Illus.). New York: Harcourt.

Pinkney, Andrea Davis. (2001). *Mim's Christmas jam* (Brian Pinkney, Illus.). New York: Harcourt.

Pinkney, Gloria. (1992). *Back home* (Jerry Pinkney, Illus.). New York: Puffin Books.

Pipe, Jim, & Jackson, Mark. (Eds.). (2001) *How science works: Discover the science behind planes, boats, rockets, cars, trucks*. New York: Cooper Beech.

Plourde, Lynn. (1999). *Wild child* (Greg Couch, Illus.). New York: Simon & Schuster.

Polacco, Patricia. (1988a). *Boat ride with Lillian Two Blossom*. New York: Philomel.

Polacco, Patricia. (1988b). *The keeping quilt*. New York: Simon & Schuster.

Polacco, Patricia. (1990a). *Babushka's doll*. New York: Simon & Schuster.

Polacco, Patricia. (1990b). *Just plain fancy*. New York: Bantam.

Polacco, Patricia. (1990c). *Thunder cake*. New York: Philomel.

Polacco, Patricia. (1992a). *Chicken Sunday*. New York: Philomel.

Polacco, Patricia. (1992b). *Mrs. Katz and Tush*. New York: Dell.

Polacco, Patricia. (1992c). *Picnic at Mudsock Meadow*. New York: Putnam.

Polacco, Patricia. (1993). *Babushka Baba Yaga*. New York: Philomel.

Polacco, Patricia. (1994a). *My rotten redheaded older brother*. New York: Simon & Schuster.

Polacco, Patricia. (1994b). *Pink and Say*. New York: Philomel.

Polacco, Patricia. (1998) *Thank you, Mr. Falker*. New York: Philomel.

Polacco, Patricia. (2000). *The butterfly*. New York: Philomel.

Polacco, Patricia. (2002). *When lightning comes in a jar*. New York: Philomel.

Pollock, Penny. (2001). *When the moon is full: A lunar year* (Mary Azarian, Illus.). Boston: Little, Brown.

Porter, Tracey. (1999). *Treasures in the dust*. New York: HarperTrophy.

Potter, Beatrix. (1900). *The tale of Peter Rabbit*. London: Warne.

Potter, Beatrix. (1904). *The tale of Benjamin Bunny*. London: Warne.

Potter, Beatrix. (1964). *The tale of Squirrel Nutkin*. London: Frederick Warne.

Powell, Jillian. (1999). *Talking about disability*. Austin, TX: Raintree Steck-Vaughn.

Preller, James. (2002). *The case of the golden key*. New York: Scholastic.

Prelutsky, Jack. (1976). *Nightmares: Poems to trouble your sleep* (Arnold Lobel, Illus.). New York: Greenwillow.

Prelutsky, Jack. (1980). *Rainy rainy Saturday* (Marilyn Hafner, Illus.). New York: Greenwillow.

Prelutsky, Jack. (1983a). *It's Valentine's Day* (Yossi Abolafia, Illus.). New York: Mulberry Books.

Prelutsky, Jack. (1983b). *The Random House book of poetry* (Arnold Lobel, Illus.). New York: Random House.

Prelutsky, Jack. (1983c). *Zoo doings* (Paul O. Zelinsky, Illus.). New York: Greenwillow.

Prelutsky, Jack. (1984). *The new kid on the block* (James Stevenson, Illus.). New York: Greenwillow.

Prelutsky, Jack. (1985). *My parents think I'm sleeping* (Yossi Abolafia, Illus.). New York: Greenwillow.

Prelutsky, Jack. (1986). *Ride a purple pelican*. New York: Greenwillow.

Prelutsky, Jack. (1990a). *Beneath a blue umbrella*. New York: Greenwillow.

Prelutsky, Jack. (1990b). *Something big has been here*. New York: Morrow.

Prelutsky, Jack. (1991). *For laughing out loud: Poems to tickle your funny bone*. New York: Knopf.

Prelutsky, Jack. (1992). *Tyrannosaurus was a beast*. New York: HarperTrophy.

Prelutsky, Jack. (1996a). *It's Halloween* (Marilyn Hafner, Illus.). New York: Mulberry Books.

Prelutsky, Jack. (1996b). *It's Thanksgiving* (Marilyn Hafner, Illus.). New York: Mulberry Books.

Prelutsky, Jack. (1996c). *A pizza the size of the sun*. New York: Greenwillow.

Prelutsky, Jack. (2000). *It's raining pigs and noodles*. New York: Greenwillow.

Price, Leontyne. (1990). *Aida* (Leo Dillon & Diane Dillon, Illus.). San Diego: Harcourt Brace.

Priceman, Marjorie. (2001). *Little red riding hood*. New York: Simon & Schuster.

Pringle, Laurence. (1995). *Dolphin man: Exploring the world of dolphins* (Randall S. Wells & Chicago Zoological Society, Photog.). Honesdale, PA: Boyds Mills Press.

Pringle, Laurence. (1997). *An extraordinary life: The story of a Monarch butterfly* (Bob Marstall, Illus.). New York: Orchard Books.

Pringle, Laurence. (2001). *A dragon in the sky: The story of a green darner dragonfly* (Bob Marstall, Illus.). New York: Orchard Books.

Pringle, Laurence. (2002a). *Crows! Strange and wonderful*. Honesdale, PA: Boyds Mills Press.

Pringle, Laurence. (2002b). *Dog of discovery: A Newfoundland's adventures with Lewis and Clark*. Honesdale, PA: Boyds Mills Press.

Pringle, Laurence. (2003). *Come to the ocean's edge: A nature cycle book* (Michael Chesworth, Illus.). Honesdale, PA: Boyds Mills Press.

Prior, Natalie Jane. (2002). *The encyclopedia of preserved people: Pickled, frozen, and mummified corpses from around the world* (Karen Carter, Illus.). New York: Crown.

Pullman, Philip. (1996). *The golden compass*. New York: Knopf.

Pullman, Philip. (1997). *The subtle knife*. New York: Knopf.

Pullman, Philip. (2000). *The amber spyglass*. New York: Knopf.

Pyle, Howard. (1986). *King Stork* (Trina Schart Hyman, Illus.). Boston: Little, Brown.

Pyle, Howard. (1997). *Bearskin* (Trina Schart Hyman, Illus.). New York: Morrow.

Quarles, Heather. (1998). *A door near here*. New York: Delacorte.

Quie, S. (1998). *Myths and civilization of ancient Egyptians*. New York: Peter Bedrick.

Raboff, Ernest. (1973). *Van Gogh*. New York: Doubleday.

Raffi. (1987). *Down by the bay* (Nadine Bernard Westcott, Illus.). New York: Crown.

Rand, Gloria. (1992). *Prince William* (Ted Rand, Illus.). New York: Henry Holt.

Rappaport, Doreen. (2000). *Freedom River* (Bryan Collier, Illus.). New York: Hyperion Books.

Rappaport, Doreen. (2001). *Martin's big words: The life of Dr. Martin Luther King, Jr.* (Bryan Collier, Illus.). New York: Scholastic.

Rappaport, Doreen. (2002). *No more! Stories and songs of slave resistance* (Shane W. Evans, Illus.). Cambridge, MA: Candlewick Press.

Raskin, Ellen. (1978). *The westing game*. New York: Dutton.

Rathmann, Peggy. (1995). *Officer Buckle and Gloria*. New York: Putnam.

Rawls, Wilson. (1961). *Where the red fern grows*. New York: Doubleday.

Ray, Delia. (1991). *Behind the blue and gray: The soldier's life in the Civil War*. New York: Lodestar Books.

Raynor, Mary. (1976). *Mr. and Mrs. Pig's evening out*. New York: Atheneum.

Reeder, Carolyn. (1989). *Shades of gray*. New York: Macmillan.

Reeder, Carolyn. (1998). *Foster's war*. New York: Scholastic.

Reeves, C. N. (2001). *Into the mummy's tomb*. New York: Scholastic.

Reinhard, Johan. (1998). *Discovering the Inca ice maiden: My adventures on Ampato*. Washington, DC: National Geographic Society.

Reiss, Johanna. (1972). *The upstairs room*. New York: HarperCollins.

Reit, Seymour. (1998). *Behind rebel lines*. New York: Gulliver Books.

Relf, Pat (with the Sue Science Team of the Field Museum). (2000). *A dinosaur named Sue: The story of the colossal fossil, the world's most complete T. Rex*. New York: Scholastic.

Rey, H. A. (1958). *Curious George*. Boston: Houghton Mifflin.

Reynolds, Cynthia Furlong. (2001). *L is for lobster: A Maine alphabet* (Jeannie Brett, Illus.). Chelsea, MI: Sleeping Bear Press.

Richards, Laura E. (1955). *Tirra lirra, rhymes old and new*. Boston: Little, Brown.

Richter, Hans Peter. (1970). *Friedrich*. New York: Holt, Rinehart and Winston.

Richter, Hans Peter. (1987). *I was there*. New York: Penguin.

Riciutti, Edward. (1998). *Rocks and minerals* (National Audubon Society first field guide). New York: Scholastic.

Ridlon, Marci. (1996). *Sun through the window* (Tom Gillner, Illus.). Honesdale, PA: Boyds Mills Press.

Riggio, Anita. (1997). *Secret signs: Along the Underground Railroad*. Honesdale, PA: Boyds Mills Press.

Rinaldi, Ann. (1995). *A stitch in time* (Quilt Trilogy series #1). New York: Scholastic.

Rinaldi, Ann. (1996). *Hang a thousand trees with ribbons: The story of Phillis Wheatley*. San Diego: Harcourt Brace.

Rinaldi, Ann. (1998). *Mine eyes have seen*. New York: Scholastic.

Rinaldi, Ann. (2001). *The coffin quilt: The feud between the Hatfields and the McCoys*. San Diego: Harcourt Brace.

Rinaldi, Ann. (2003). *Or give me death: A novel of Patrick Henry's family*. Orlando, FL: Harcourt Brace.

Ringgold, Faith. (1991). *Tar beach*. New York: Crown.

Ringgold, Faith. (1992). *Aunt Harriet's underground railroad in the sky*. New York: Crown.

Ringgold, Faith. (1999). *The invisible princess*. New York: Crown.

Riordan, James. (1985). *The woman in the moon and other tales of forgotten heroines* (Angela Barrett, Illus.). New York: Dial Books.

Ritter, John H. (2003). *The boy who saved baseball*. New York: Philomel.

Robbins, Ken. (2002). *Apples*. New York: Atheneum.

Roberts, Willo Davis. (1975). *A view from the cherry tree*. New York: Atheneum.

Robinet, Harriette Gillem. (2000). *Walking to the bus-rider blues*. New York: Atheneum.

Robinson, Barbara. (1972). *The best Christmas pageant ever* (Judith Gwyn Brown, Illus.). New York: Harper & Row.

Robson, Eric. (1999). *Two-Can golden books—WOLVES*. London: Golden Book.

Roche, Denis. (1998). *Art around the world: Loo-loo, boo, and more art you can do*. Boston: Houghton Mifflin.

Rockwell, Anne. (2000). *Only passing through: The story of Sojourner Truth* (R. Gregory Christie, Illus.). New York: Knopf.

Rockwell, Thomas. (1973). *How to eat fried worms*. New York: Watts.

Rockwood, Joyce. (1976). *To spoil the sun*. New York: Holt, Rinehart and Winston.

Rogasky, Barbara. (Ed.). (1994). *Winter poems*. New York: Scholastic.

Rogasky, Barbara. (2001). *Leaf by leaf: Autumn poems*. New York: Scholastic.

Rogers, Fred. (2000). *Extraordinary friends*. New York: Putnam.

Rol, Ruud van der, & Verhoeven, Rian. (1993). *Anne Frank beyond the diary: A photographic remembrance*. New York: Penguin.

Rose, LaVera. (1999). *Grandchildren of the Lakota* (Cheryl Walsh Bellville, Photog.). Minneapolis: Carolrhoda.

Rosen, Michael. (Ed.). (1992a). *Itsy-bitsy beasties: Poems from around the world*. Minneapolis: Carolrhoda.

Rosen, Michael. (Reteller.) (1992b). *We're going on a bear hunt* (Helen Oxenbury, Illus.). New York: Aladdin Books.

Rosenberg, Liz. (1993). *Monster mama* (Stephen Gammell, Illus.). New York: Philomel.

Ross, Kathy. (1999a). *Crafts to make in the winter* (Vicky Enright, Illus.). Brookfield, CT: Millbrook Press.

Ross, Kathy. (1999b). *The best birthday parties ever!: A kid's do-it-yourself guide* (Sharon Lane Holm, Illus.). Brookfield, CT: Millbrook Press.

Rostkowski, Margaret I. (1986). *After the dancing days*. New York: Harper & Row.

Roth, Arthur J. (1974). *Iceberg hermit*. New York: Dell.

Rowling, J. K. (1997). *Harry Potter and the sorcerer's stone*. New York: Scholastic.

Rowling, J. K. (1998). *Harry Potter and the chamber of secrets*. New York: Scholastic.

Rowling, J. K. (1999). *Harry Potter and the prisoner of Azkaban*. New York: Scholastic.

Rowling, J. K. (2000). *Harry Potter and the goblet of fire*. New York: Levine.

Rowling, J. K. (2003). *Harry Potter and the order of the Phoenix*. New York: Scholastic.

Rubin, Susan Goldman. (1998). *Toilets, toasters & telephones: The how and why of everyday objects* (Elsa Warnick, Illus.). New York: Harcourt Brace.

Rubin, Susan Goldman. (2001). *The yellow house: Vincent van Gogh and Paul Gauguin side by side*. New York: Abrams.

Rubinetti, Donald. (1996). *Cappy the lonely camel*. New Jersey: Silver Press.

Ruckman, Ivy. (1984). *Night of the twisters*. New York: HarperCollins.

Ryan, Pam Muñoz, & Pallotta, Jerry. (1996). *The crayon counting book* (Frank Mazzola Jr., Illus.). Boston: Charlesbridge.

Ryder, Joanne. (1982). *The snail's spell* (Lynne Cherry, Illus.). New York: Puffin Books.

Ryder, Joanne. (1987). *Chipmunk song* (Lynne Cherry, Illus.). New York: Dutton.

Ryder, Joanne. (1989). *Where butterflies grow* (Lynne Cherry, Illus.). New York: Lodestar Books.

Rylant, Cynthia. (1982). *When I was young in the mountains* (Diane Goode, Illus.). New York: Dutton.

Rylant, Cynthia. (1985). *The relatives came*. New York: Bradbury Press.

Rylant, Cynthia. (1988). *All I see* (Peter Catalanotto, Illus.). New York: Orchard Books.

Rylant, Cynthia. (1991). *Appalachia: The voices of sleeping birds* (Barry Moser, Illus.). San Diego: Harcourt Brace.

Rylant, Cynthia. (1992). *Missing May*. New York: Orchard Books.

Rylant, Cynthia. (2001). *Waiting to waltz*. New York: Atheneum.

Sabuda, Robert. (1997). *Cookie count: A tasty pop-up*. New York: Little Simon.

Sabuda, Robert. (1999). *The moveable Mother Goose*. New York: Simon & Schuster.

Sabuda, Robert, & Reinhart, Matthew. (2001a). *Young naturalist's pop-up handbook: Beetles*. New York: Hyperion Books.

Sabuda, Robert, & Reinhart, Matthew. (2001b). *Young naturalist's pop-up handbook: Butterflies*. New York: Hyperion Books.

Sachar, Louis. (1978). *Sideways stories from Wayside School* (Dennis Hockerman, Illus.). New York: Random House.

Sachar, Louis. (1989). *Sideways arithmetic from Wayside School*. New York: Scholastic.

Sachar, Louis. (1996). *Wayside School gets a little stranger*. New York: HarperTrophy.

Sachar, Louis. (1998a). *Holes*. New York: Farrar, Straus & Giroux.

Sachar, Louis. (1998b). *Wayside School is falling down*. New York: HarperTrophy.

Salisbury, Graham. (1995). *Under the blood-red sun*. New York: Delacorte.

Salisbury, Graham. (2001). *Lord of the deep*. New York: Delacorte.

Salley, Colleen. (2002). *Epossumondas* (Janet Stevens, Illus.). San Diego: Harcourt Brace.

Saltman, Judith. (Ed.). (1985). *The Riverside anthology of children's literature (6th edition)*. Boston: Houghton Mifflin.

Sandburg, Carl. (1950). *Complete poems*. New York: Harcourt Brace.

Sanders, Pete. (1992). *Let's talk about disabled people*. New York: Gloucester Press.

Sanders, Pete, & Myers, Steve. (1998). *What do you know about people with disabilities?* London: Watts.

Sandler, Martin. (2003). *America's great disasters*. New York: HarperCollins.

Sauer, Julia. (1986). *Fog magic*. New York: Puffin Books.

Say, Allan. (1991). *Tree of cranes*. Boston: Houghton Mifflin.

Say, Allan. (1993). *Grandfather's journey*. Boston: Houghton Mifflin.

Say, Allan. (1995). *Stranger in the mirror*. Boston: Houghton Mifflin.

Sayre, April Pulley. (2002). *Secrets of sound: Studying the calls and songs of whales, elephants, and birds*. Boston: Houghton Mifflin.

Schachner, Judith Byron. (1999). *The grannyman*. New York: Dutton.

Schertle, Alice. (1991a). *William and Grandpa* (Lydia Dabcovich, Illus.). New York: HarperCollins.

Schertle, Alice. (1991b). *Witch Hazel* (Margot Tomes, Illus.). New York: HarperCollins.

Schertle, Alice. (1992). *Little frog's song* (Everett Fisher, Illus.). New York: HarperCollins.

Schertle, Alice. (1995). *Advice for a frog* (Norman Green, Illus.). New York: HarperCollins.

Schertle, Alice. (1998). *How now, brown cow?* New York: Harcourt.

Schertle, Alice. (1999a). *I am the cat* (Mark Buehner, Illus.). New York: HarperCollins.

Schertle, Alice. (1999b). *Keepers* (Mark Buehner, Illus.). New York: HarperCollins.

Schertle, Alice. (1999c). *A lucky thing* (Wendell Minor, Illus.). New York: Harcourt.

Schertle, Alice. (2000). *Down the road* (Earl Lewis, Illus.). New York: Harcourt.

Schmidt, Gary D. (2001). *Straw into gold*. New York: Clarion Books.

Schnur, Steven. (1997). *Autumn: An alphabet acrostic*. New York: Clarion Books.

Schnur, Steven. (1999). *Spring: An alphabet acrostic*. New York: Clarion Books.

Schnur, Steven. (2001). *Summer: An alphabet acrostic*. New York: Clarion Books.

Schnur, Steven. (2002). *Winter: An alphabet acrostic*. New York: Clarion Books.

Schroeder, Alan. (2000). *Minty: A story of young Harriet Tubman* (Jerry Pinkney, Illus.). New York: Viking.

Schwartz, Alvin. (1981). *Scary stories to tell in the dark* (Stephen Gammell, Illus.). New York: Harper.

Schwartz, Alvin. (1992). *And the green grass grew all around: Folk poetry from everyone* (Sue Truesdell, Illus.). New York: HarperCollins.

Schwartz, David. (1998). *G is for googol: A math alphabet book* (Marissa Moss, Illus.). New York: Tricycle.

Schwartz, David. (2001). *Q is for quark: A science alphabet book* (Kim Doner, Illus.). New York: Tricycle.

Scieszka, Jon. (1989). *The true story of the 3 little pigs!* (Lane Smith, Illus.). New York: Viking.

Scieszka, Jon. (1991). *The frog prince continued*. New York: Viking.

Scieszka, Jon. (1992). *The stinky cheese man*. New York: Viking.

Scieszka, Jon. (1995). *Math curse* (Lane Smith, Illus.). New York: Viking.

Scieszka, Jon. (1998). *Squids will be squids*. New York: Viking.

Seeger, Pete. (1986). *Abiyoyo: Based on a South African lullaby and folk story* (Michael Hayes, Illus.). New York: Macmillan.

Sendak, Maurice. (1962). *Chicken soup with rice*. New York: Scholastic.

Sendak, Maurice. (1963). *Where the wild things are*. New York: HarperCollins.

Service, Robert W. (1961). *Collected poems*. New York: Dodd, Mead.

Service, Robert W. (1997). *The cremation of Sam McGee* (Ted Harrison, Illus.). New York: Greenwillow.

Seuling, Barbara. (1985). *What kind of family is this? A book about stepfamilies* (Ellen Dolce, Illus.). New York: Golden Book.

Seuss, Dr. (1937). *And to think that I saw it on Mulberry Street*. New York: Vanguard Press.

Seuss, Dr. (1957). *The cat in the hat*. New York: Random House.

Seuss, Dr. (1961). *The Sneetches and other stories*. New York: Random House.

Seuss, Dr. (1976). *The Lorax*. New York: Random House.

Seuss, Dr. (1984). *The butter battle book*. New York: Random House.

Sewell, Anna. (1970). *Black Beauty*. New York: Penguin.

Shange, Ntozake. (1997). *Whitewash* (Michael Sporn, Illus.). New York: Walker.

Sharmat, Marjorie W. (1977). *Nate the great*. New York: Yearling Books.

Sharmat, Marjorie W. (1990). *Gila monsters meet you at the airport*. New York: Simon & Schuster.

Shea, Pegi Deitz. (1995). *The whispering cloth* (Anita Riggio, Illus.). Honesdale, PA: Boyds Mills Press.

Sheldrake, Rupert. (2000). *Dogs that know when their owners are coming home: And other unexplained powers of animals*. New York: Crown.

Shields, Carol Diggory. (1995). *Lunch money and other poems about school*. New York: Dutton.

Shuter, Jane. (2001). *People who made history in ancient Egypt*. Austin, TX: Raintree Steck-Vaughn.

Siebert, Diane. (1988). *Mojave*. New York: HarperCollins.

Siebert, Diane. (1996). *Heartland* (Wendell Minor, Illus.). New York: HarperCollins.

Siebert, Diane. (2000). *Cave* (Wayne McLoughlin, Illus.). New York: HarperCollins.

Sierra, Judy. (1998). *Antarctic antics*. San Diego: Gulliver Books.

Sierra, Judy. (2002). *Can you guess my name? Traditional tales around the world* (Stefano Vitale, Illus.). New York: Clarion Books.

Silverstein, Shel. (1974). *Where the sidewalk ends: The poems and drawings of Shel Silverstein*. New York: Harper.

Silverstein, Shel. (1981). *A light in the attic*. New York: Harper.

Silverstein, Shel. (1996). *Falling up*. New York: Harper.

Sim, Dorrith M. (1996). *In my pocket* (Gerald Fitzgerald, Illus.). New York: Harcourt Brace.

Simon, Seymour. (1990). *Oceans*. New York: Morrow.

Simon, Seymour. (1993). *Wolves*. New York: HarperCollins.

Simon, Seymour. (1997). *The brain: Our nervous system*. New York: Morrow.

Simon, Seymour. (1999). *Crocodiles and alligators*. New York: HarperCollins.

Simon, Seymour. (2003). *The moon*. New York: Simon & Schuster.

Singer, Marilyn. (1989). *Turtle in July* (Jerry Pinkney, Illus.). New York: Macmillan.

Sleator, William. (1981). *The green futures of Tycho*. New York: Dutton.

Sleator, William. (1986). *The boy who reversed himself*. New York: Dutton.

Sleator, William. (1991). *The spirit house*. New York: Dutton.

Sleator, William. (1993). *Oddballs*. New York: Dutton.

Sleator, William. (1995). *Dangerous wishes*. New York: Dutton.

Sleator, William. (1997). *The beasties*. New York: Dutton.

Sleator, William. (1998). *The boxes*. New York: Dutton.

Sleator, William. (1999a). *Boltzman!* New York: Dutton.

Sleator, William. (1999b). *Rewind*. New York: Dutton.

Slepian, Jan. (1990). *Risk n' roses*. New York: Scholastic.

Sloat, Teri. (1990). *The eye of the needle*. New York: Dutton.

Slote, Alfred. (1984). *Finding Buck McHenry*. New York: HarperCollins.

Slote, Alfred. (1990). *The trading game*. New York: Lippincott.

Smith, Charles R., Jr. (1999). *Rimshots: Basketball pix, rolls, and rhythms*. New York: Dutton.

Smith, Charles R., Jr. (2001). *Short takes: Fast-break basketball poetry*. New York: Dutton.

Smith, David J. (2002). *If the world were a village: A book about the world's people* (Shelagh Armstrong, Illus.). New York: Kids Can Press.

Smith, Doris Buchanan. (1973). *A taste of blackberries* (Charles Robinson, Illus.). New York: Crowell.

Smith, Doris Buchanan. (1975). *Kelly's creek*. New York: Crowell.

Smith, Robert Kimmel. (1984). *The war with Grandpa*. New York: Delacorte.

Smith, Will. (2001). *Just the two of us* (Kadir Nelson, Illus.). New York: Scholastic.

Smith, William Jay. (1991). *Laughing time: Collected nonsense*. New York: Farrar, Straus & Giroux.

Snyder, Zilpha Keatley. (1969). *Today is Saturday* (John Arms, Illus.). New York: Atheneum.

Snyder, Zilpha Keatley. (1996). *The Egypt game*. New York: Laurel Leaf.

Sobol, Donald. (1978). *Encyclopedia Brown, boy detective*. New York: Bantam.

Solheim, James. (1998). *It's disgusting and we ate it: True food facts from around the world and throughout history!* (Eric Brace, Illus.). New York: Simon & Schuster.

Solway, Andrew. (2003). *Rome: In spectacular cross-section* (Stephen Biesty, Illus.). Oxford: Oxford University Press.

Soto, Gary. (1990). *Baseball in April and other stories*. New York: Harcourt Brace.

Soto, Gary. (1992). *Neighborhood odes*. San Diego: Harcourt Brace.

Soto, Gary. (1993a). *The pool party*. New York: Delacorte.

Soto, Gary. (1993b). *Too many tamales* (Ed Martinez, Illus.). New York: Putnam.

Soto, Gary. (1994). *Crazy weekend*. New York: Scholastic.

Soto, Gary. (1995). *Canto familiar*. San Diego: Harcourt Brace.

Soto, Gary. (2002). *Fearless Fernie: Hanging out with Fernie and me*. New York: Putnam.

Speare, Elizabeth George. (1958). *The witch of Blackbird Pond*. New York: Dell.

Speare, Elizabeth George. (1983). *The sign of the beaver*. Boston: Houghton Mifflin.

Sperry, Armstrong. (1968). *Call it courage*. New York: Macmillan.

Spies, Karen Bornemann. (1992). *Our money*. Brookfield, CT: Millbrook Press.

Spinelli, Eileen. (1991). *Somebody loves you, Mr. Hatch*. New York: Macmillan.

Spinelli, Jerry. (1990). *Maniac Magee*. New York: HarperCollins.

Spinelli, Jerry. (1991). *Fourth grade rats*. New York: Scholastic.

Spinelli, Jerry. (1997). *Wringer*. New York: Scholastic.

Spinelli, Jerry. (2000). *Stargirl*. New York: Knopf.

Splear, Elsie Lee. (2000). *Growing seasons* (Ken Stark, Illus.). New York: Putnam.

Editors of *Sports Illustrated for Kids*. (2003). *Sports Illustrated for kids year in sports 2004*. New York: Scholastic.

Stadler, John. (1983). *Hector the accordian-nosed dog*. Scarsdale, NY: Bradbury Press.

Stadler, John. (1984). *Hooray for Snail*. New York: Harper & Row.

Stadler, John. (1986). *Animal café*. New York: Simon & Schuster.

Stadler, John. (1993). *The adventures of Snail at school*. New York: HarperTrophy.

Stadler, John. (1996). *Ready, set, GO!* New York: HarperCollins.

Stadler, John. (1997). *The cats of Mrs. Calamari*. New York: Orchard Books.

Stadler, John. (1999). *One seal*. New York: Orchard Books.

Stadler, John. (2001). *What's so scary?* New York: Scholastic.

Stamm, Claus. (1990). *Three strong women: A tall tale from Japan*. New York: Viking.

Stanchak, John E. (2000). *Civil War*. New York: DK Publishing.

Stanley, Diane. (1988). *Shaka: King of the Zulus*. New York: Morrow.

Stanley, Diane. (1992). *Bard of Avon*. New York: Morrow.

Stanley, Diane. (1993). *Charles Dickens*. New York: Morrow.

Stanley, Diane. (1996a). *Leonardo da Vinci*. New York: Morrow.

Stanley, Diane. (1996b). *Saving Sweetness*. New York: Morrow.

Stanley, Diane. (1997). *Rumpelstiltskin's daughter*. New York: Morrow.

Stanley, Diane. (1998). *Joan of Arc*. New York: Morrow.

Stanley, Diane. (1999). *A time apart*. New York: Morrow.

Stanley, Diane. (2000). *Michelangelo*. New York: HarperCollins.

Stanley, Diane, & Vennema, Peter. (1994). *Cleopatra*. New York: Morrow.

Stanley, Jerry. (1992). *Children of the Dust Bowl: The true story of the school at Weedpatch Camp*. New York: Crown.

Staples, Suzanne Fisher. (1989). *Shabanu: Daughter of the wind*. New York: Knopf.

Starbird, Kaye. (1963). *Don't ever cross a crocodile, and other poems* (Kit Dalton, Illus.). Philadelphia: Lippincott.

Steig, William. (1969). *Sylvester and the magic pebble*. New York: Windmill Books/Wanderer.

Steig, William. (1982). *Doctor Desoto*. New York: Farrar, Straus & Giroux.

Steptoe, Javaka. (1997). *In Daddy's arms I am tall: African Americans celebrating fathers*. New York: Lee & Low.

Steptoe, John. (1987). *Mufaro's beautiful daughters: An African tale*. New York: Morrow.

Stevens, Janet. (1987). *The three billy goats gruff*. San Diego: Harcourt Brace.

Stevenson, Augusta. (1983). *Ben Franklin, young printer*. New York: Aladdin Books.

Stevenson, Burton E. (1953). *The home book of modern verse, American and English*. New York, Holt.

Stevenson, Harvey. (2003). *Looking at liberty*. New York: HarperCollins.

Stevenson, James. (1995). *The bones in the cliff*. New York: Greenwillow.

Stevenson, James. (1998a). *Candy corn*. New York: Greenwillow.

Stevenson, James. (1998b). *Cornflakes*. New York: Greenwillow.

Stevenson, James. (1998c). *Popcorn*. New York: Morrow.

Stevenson, James. (1998d). *Sweet corn*. New York: Greenwillow.

Stevenson, Robert Louis. (1966). *A child's garden of verses* (Brian Wildsmith, Illus.). New York: Watts.

Stewart, David. (2001). *You wouldn't want to be an Egyptian mummy! Disgusting things you'd rather not know*. New York: Scholastic.

Stolz, Mary. (1994). *Cezanne Pinto: A memoir*. New York: Knopf.

Stowe, Harriet Beecher. (1852/1983). *Uncle Tom's cabin*. New York: Bantam.

Strickland, Dorothy, & Strickland, Michael. (1994). *Families: Poems celebrating the African American experience*. Honesdale, PA: Wordsong/Boyds Mills Press.

Strickland, Michael. (1997). *My own song: And other poems to groove to*. Honesdale, PA: Boyds Mills Press.

Super, Gretchen. (1991a). *What is a family?* (Kees de Kiefte, Illus.). Frederick, MD: Twenty-first Century Books.

Super, Gretchen. (1991b). *What kind of family do you have?* (Kees de Kiefte, Illus.). Frederick, MD: Twenty-first Century Books.

Sutcliff, Rosemary. (1995). *The outcast*. New York: Farrar, Straus & Giroux.

Swann, Brian. (1998a). *The house with no door: African riddle-poems*. San Diego: Harcourt Brace.

Swann, Brian. (1998b). *Touching the distance: Native American riddle-poems*. San Diego: Browndeer Press.

Swanson, Diane. (1994). *Safari beneath the sea*. San Francisco: Sierra Club.

Swanson, Diane. (1995). *Coyotes in the crosswalk: True tales of the animal life in the wilds of the city!* (Douglas Penhale, Illus.). New York: Voyageur.

Swinburne, Stephen R. (1998). *In good hands: Behind the scenes at a center for orphaned and injured birds*. San Francisco: Sierra Club.

Swinburne, Stephen R. (1999). *Once a wolf* (Jim Brandenburg, Photog.). Boston: Houghton Mifflin.

Swinburne, Stephen R. (2002a). *Go, go, go! Kids on the move*. Honesdale, PA: Boyds Mills Press.

Swinburne, Stephen, R. (2002b). *The woods scientist* (Susan C. Morse, Photog.). Boston: Houghton Mifflin.

Taback, Simms. (1997). *There was an old lady who swallowed a fly*. New York: Viking.

Taback, Simms. (1999). *Joseph had a little overcoat*. New York: Viking.

Tadjo, Véronique. (2003). *Talking drums: A selection of poems from Africa south of the Sahara*. New York: Bloomsbury.

Tallchief, Maria, with Rosemary Wells. (1999). *Tallchief: America's prima ballerina* (Gary Kelley, Illus.). New York: Viking.

Tanaka, Shelley. (1999). *Secrets of the mummies: Uncovering the bodies of ancient Egyptians*. Toronto, ON: Madison Press.

Tapahonso, Luci. (1999). *Songs of Shiprock Fair*. Walnut, CA: Kiva.

Tate, Eleanora. (1990). *Thank you, Dr. Martin Luther King, Jr.* New York: Bantam.

Taylor, Mildred D. (1976). *Roll of thunder, hear my cry*. New York: Dial Books.

Taylor, Mildred D. (1981). *Let the circle be unbroken*. New York: Dial Books.

Taylor, Mildred D. (1987a). *The friendship* (Max Ginsburg, Illus.). New York: Dial Books.

Taylor, Mildred D. (1987b). *The gold Cadillac*. New York: Puffin Books.

Taylor, Mildred D. (1990). *The road to Memphis*. New York: Trumpet.

Taylor, Mildred D. (1995). *The well: David's story*. New York: Dial Books.

Taylor, Mildred D. (1997). *Song of the trees* (Jerry Pinkney, Illus.). New York: Bantam.

Temple, Frances. (1995). *Tonight, by sea: A novel*. New York: Orchard Books.

Temple, Frances. (1998). *Tiger soup*. New York: Orchard Books.

Terasaki, Stanley Todd. (2002). *Ghosts for breakfast*. (Shelley Shinjo, Illus.). New York: Lee & Low.

Terris, Susan. (1996). *Nell's quilt*. New York: Farrar, Straus & Giroux.

Testa, Maria. (2002). *Becoming Joe DiMaggio* (Scott Hunt, Illus.). Cambridge, MA: Candlewick Press.

Thesman, Jean. (1996). *The ornament tree*. Boston: Houghton Mifflin.

Thomas, Jane Resh. (1998). *Behind the mask: The life of Queen Elizabeth I*. New York: Clarion Books.

Thomas, Joyce Carol. (1993). *Brown honey in broomwheat tea* (Floyd Cooper, Illus.). New York: HarperCollins.

Thomas, Joyce Carol. (1995). *Gingerbread days*. New York: HarperCollins.

Thompson, Kay. (2002). *Eloise takes a bawth* (Hilary Knight, Illus.). New York: Simon & Schuster.

Thompson, Myra. (Sel.). (1993). *Jump for joy: Over 375 creative movement activities for young children*. West Nyack, NY: Parker.

Thurman, Judith. (1976). *Flashlight, and other poems* (Reina Rubel, Illus.). New York: Atheneum.

Tillage, Leon. (1997). *Leon's story* (Susan L. Roth, Illus.). New York: Farrar, Straus & Giroux.

Toft, Kim Michelle. (1998). *One less fish*. Boston: Charlesbridge.

Tohe, Laura. (1999). *No parole today*. New Mexico: University of New Mexico Press.

Tolhurst, Marilyn. (1991). *Somebody and the three Blairs* (Simone Abel, Illus.). New York: Orchard Books.

Tolkien, J. R. R. (1991). *Lord of the rings*. Boston: Houghton Mifflin.

Tomecek, Stephen, M. (2003). *What a great idea! Inventions that changed the world* (Dan Stuckenschneider, Illus.). New York: Scholastic.

Towle, Wendy. (1993). *The real McCoy*. New York: Scholastic.

Travers, P. L. (1997). *Mary Poppins* (Mary Shepard, Illus.). San Diego: Harcourt Brace.

Trivizas, Eugene. (1993). *The three little wolves and the big bad pig* (Helen Oxenbury, Illus.). New York: McElderry.

Trussell-Cullen, Alan. (2000). *Aladdin and the magic lamp* (Carol Daniel, Illus.). Carlsbad, CA: Dominie Press.

Tsuchiya, Yukio. (1990). *The faithful elephants: A true story of animals, people, and war* (Ted Lewin, Illus.) New York: Trumpet.

Tunnell, Michael. (1997). *Mailing May*. New York: Greenwillow.

Turner, Ann Warren. (1985). *Dakota dugout* (Ronald Himler, Illus.). New York: Macmillan.

Turner, Ann Warren. (1989). *Grasshopper summer*. New York: Macmillan.

Turner, Ann Warren. (1990). *Through moon and stars and night sky* (James Graham Hale, Illus.). New York: Harper & Row.

Turner, Ann Warren. (1991). *Rosemary's witch*. New York: HarperCollins.

Turner, Ann Warren. (1992). *Katie's trunk* (Ronald Himler, Illus.). New York: Macmillan.

Turner, Ann Warren. (1993). *Apple Valley year* (Sandi Wickersham Resnick, Illus.). New York: Macmillan.

Turner, Ann Warren. (1994a). *A moon for seasons*. New York: Simon & Schuster.

Turner, Ann Warren. (1994b). *Sewing quilts* (Thomas B. Allen, Illus.). New York: Macmillan.

Turner, Ann Warren. (1995). *Dust for dinner* (Robert Barrett, Illus.). New York: HarperCollins.

Turner, Ann Warren. (1997a). *Mississippi mud: Three prairie journals* (Robert J. Blake, Illus.). New York: HarperCollins.

Turner, Ann Warren. (1997b). *Shaker hearts* (Wendell Minor, Illus.). New York: HarperCollins.

Turner, Ann Warren. (1999). *Red flower goes west* (Dennis Nolin, Illus.). New York: Hyperion Books.

Turner, Ann Warren. (2000). *Secrets from the dollhouse* (Raul Colón, Illus.). New York: HarperCollins.

Twain, Mark. (1876). *The adventures of Tom Sawyer*. Hartford, CT: American.

Uchida, Yoshiko. (1971). *Journey to Topaz* (Donald Carrick, Illus.). Berkeley, CA: Creative Arts Press.

Uchida, Yoshiko. (1992). *Journey home* (Charles Robinson, Illus.). New York: Macmillan.

Uchida, Yoshiko. (1993). *The bracelet* (Joanna Yardley, Illus.). New York: Philomel.

Underwood, Paula. (1991). *Who speaks for wolf?* San Anselmo, CA: A Tribe of Two Press.

Underwood, Paula. (1994). *Many circles, many paths: A Native American learning story*. San Anselmo, CA: A Tribe of Two Press.

Unobagha, Uzo. (2000). *Off to the sweet shores of Africa and other talking drum rhymes*. San Francisco: Chronicle Books.

Urquhart, Jennifer. (1991). *The pets you love*. Washington, DC: National Geographic Society.

Valovkova, Hana. (1993). *I never saw another butterfly: Children's drawings and poems from Terezin Concentration Camp 1942–1944*. New York: Schocken Books.

Van Allsburg, Chris. (1981). *Jumanji*. Boston: Houghton Mifflin.

Van Allsburg, Chris. (1983). *The zephyr*. Boston: Houghton Mifflin.

Van Allsburg, Chris. (1985). *The polar express*. Boston: Houghton Mifflin.

Van Allsburg, Chris. (1986). *The stranger*. Boston: Houghton Mifflin.

Van Allsburg, Chris. (1990). *Just a dream*. Boston: Houghton Mifflin.

Van Allsburg, Chris. (1993). *The sweetest fig*. Boston: Houghton Mifflin.

Van Allsburg, Chris. (1996). *The mysteries of Harris Burdick*. Boston: Houghton Mifflin.

Van Allsburg, Chris. (2002). *Zathura*. Boston: Houghton Mifflin.

VanCleave, Janice. (1996). *Oceans for every kid: Easy activities that make learning science fun*. New York: Wiley.

Van Laan, Nancy. (1995). *Sleep, sleep, sleep: A lullaby for little ones around the world* (Holly Meade, Illus.). Boston: Little, Brown.

Van Laan, Nancy. (1998). *With a whoop and a holler*. New York: Atheneum.

Van Laan, Nancy. (2000). *When winter comes*. New York: Atheneum.

Van Rynbach, Iris. (2003). *Safely to shore: America's lighthouses*. Watertown, MA: Charlesbridge.

Vaughan, Marcia K. (1984). *Wombat stew*. (Pamela Lofts, Illus.). Sydney, Australia: Ashton Scholastic.

Vaughan, Marcia K. (2001). *The secret to freedom* (Larry Johnson, Illus.). New York: Lee & Low.

Venezia, Mike. (1988). *Van Gogh: Getting to know the world's greatest artists*. Chicago: Children's Press.

Venezia, Mike. (1990). *Monet: Getting to know the world's greatest artists*. Chicago: Children's Press.

Vigna, Judith. (1987). *Mommy and me by ourselves again*. Niles, IL: Albert Whitman.

Viorst, Judith. (1969). *I'll fix Anthony*. New York: Harper & Row.

Viorst, Judith. (1971). *The tenth good thing about Barney*. New York: Macmillan.

Viorst, Judith. (1972). *Alexander and the terrible, horrible, no good, very bad day* (Ray Cruz, Illus.). New York: Atheneum.

Viorst, Judith. (1973). *My mama says there aren't any zombies, ghosts, vampires, creatures, demons, monsters, fiends, goblins, or things* (Kay Chorao, Illus.). New York: Atheneum.

Viorst, Judith. (1978). *Alexander, who used to be rich last Sunday* (Ray Cruz, Illus.). New York: Atheneum.

Viorst, Judith. (1995). *Alexander, who's not (Do you hear me? I mean it!) going to move* (Robin Preiss Glasser, Illus.). New York: Atheneum.

Voigt, Cynthia. (1981). *Homecoming*. New York: Atheneum.

Voigt, Cynthia. (1982). *Dicey's song*. New York: Random House.

Voigt, Cynthia. (1983). *A solitary blue*. New York: Atheneum.

Voigt, Cynthia. (1985). *The runner*. New York: Ballantine Books.

Voigt, Cynthia. (1986a). *Come a stranger*. New York: Simon & Schuster.

Voigt, Cynthia. (1986b). *Izzy willy nilly*. New York: Atheneum.

Voigt, Cynthia. (1987). *Sons from afar*. New York: Atheneum.

Voigt, Cynthia. (1989). *Seventeen against the dealer*. New York: Atheneum.

Voigt, Cynthia. (1990). *On fortune's wheel*. New York: Atheneum.

Voigt, Cynthia. (1997). *Bad, badder, baddest*. New York: Scholastic.

Voigt, Cynthia. (2000). *Tree by leaf*. New York: Aladdin Books.

Waber, Bernard. (1962). *Lyle, lyle, crocodile*. Boston: Houghton Mifflin.

Waber, Bernard. (1972). *Ira sleeps over*. Boston: Houghton Mifflin.

Waber, Bernard. (1988). *Ira says goodbye*. Boston: Houghton Mifflin.

Waddell, Martin, & Dale, Penny. (1989). *Once there were giants*. New York: Delacorte.

Waldman, Neil. (1999). *The starry night*. Honesdale, PA: Boyds Mills Press.

Wallace, Barbara B. (2000). *Ghosts in the gallery*. New York: Atheneum.

Walsh, Jill Paton. (1988). *The green book*. New York: Farrar, Straus & Giroux.

Walsh, Vivian. (2002). *Gluey. A snall tale* (J. Otto Seibold, Illus.). San Diego: Harcourt Brace.

Walter, Mildred Pitts. (1986). *Justin and the best biscuits in the world*. New York: Lothrop, Lee & Shepard.

Ward, Cindy. (1988). *Cookie's week* (Tomie dePaola, Illus.). New York: Scholastic.

Ward, Nathalie. (1997). *Do whales ever . . . ? What you really want to know about whales, porpoises and dolphins* (Tessa Morgan, Illus.). Boston: Downeast Books.

Warren, Andrea. (1998). *Pioneer girl: Growing up on the prairie*. New York: Morrow.

Warren, Andrea. (2001). *We rode the orphan trains*. Boston: Houghton Mifflin.

Watkins, Yoko Kawashima. (1986). *So far from the bamboo grove*. New York: Lothrop, Lee & Shepard.

Waugh, Sylvia. (1993). *The Mennyms*. New York: Random House.

Wayland, April Halprin. (2002). *Girl coming in for a landing: A novel in poems* (Elaine Clayton, Illus.). New York: Knopf.

Weatherford, Carole Boston. (2002). *Remember the bridge: Poems of a people*. New York: Philomel.

Webb, Sophie. (2000). *My season with penguins: An Antarctic journal*. Houghton Mifflin.

Weber, Valerie. (1992). *The wonder of whales*. New York: Gareth Stevens.

Weidensaul, Scott. (1998). *National Audubon Society first field guide to birds*. New York: Scholastic.

Weitzman, David. (2002). *Model T: How Henry Ford built a legend*. New York: Crown.

Wells, Rosemary. (1979). *Max's first word*. New York: Dial Books.

Wells, Rosemary. (1992). *Voyage to the bunny planet*. New York: Dial Books.

Wells, Rosemary. (1997). *Bunny cakes*. New York: Hyperion Books.

Wells, Rosemary. (1998a). *Mary on horseback* (Peter McCarty, Illus.). New York: Dial Books.

Wells, Rosemary. (1998b). *Yoko*. New York: Dial Books.

Wells, Rosemary. (2000). *Emily's first hundred days of school*. New York: Hyperion Books.

Whelan, Gloria. (2000). *Homeless bird*. New York: HarperCollins.

White, E. B. (1945). *Stuart Little*. New York: Harper & Row.

White, E. B. (1952). *Charlotte's web*. New York: Harper & Row.

White, E. B. (2000). *The trumpet of the swan* (Fred Marcellino, Illus.). New York: HarperCollins.

White, Ellen. (1990). *Jim Abbott: Against all odds*. New York: Scholastic.

White, Robb. (1946). *The lion's paw* (Ralph Ray, Illus.). Garden City, NY: Doubleday.

White, Robb. (1972). *Deathwatch*. New York: Doubleday.

White, Ruth. (1996). *Belle Prater's boy*. New York: Farrar, Straus & Giroux.

White, Ruth. (2000). *Memories of summer*. New York: Farrar, Straus & Giroux.

Whybrow, Ian. (2001). *Wish, change, friend* (Tiphanie Beeke, Illus.). New York: McElderry.

Wick, Walter. (1997). *A drop of water: A book of science and wonder*. New York: Scholastic.

Wiesner, David. (1987). *Free fall*. New York: Lothrop, Lee & Shepard.

Wiesner, David. (1991). *Tuesday*. New York: Clarion Books.

Wiesner, David. (1999). *Sector 7*. New York: Clarion Books.

Wild, Margaret. (1994a). *Our granny* (Julie Vivas, Illus.). New York: Ticknor & Fields.

Wild, Margaret. (1994b). *Toby*. New York: Ticknor & Fields.

Wilder, Laura Ingalls. (1953a). *By the shores of Silver Lake*. New York: HarperCollins.

Wilder, Laura Ingalls. (1953b). *Farmer boy*. New York: HarperCollins.

Wilder, Laura Ingalls. (1953c). *Little town on the prairie*. New York: HarperCollins.

Wilder, Laura Ingalls. (1953d). *On the banks of Plum Creek*. New York: HarperCollins.

Wilder, Laura Ingalls. (1953e). *These happy golden years*. New York: HarperCollins.

Wilder, Laura Ingalls. (1971). *Little house in the big woods* (Garth Williams, Illus.). New York: HarperTrophy.

Wilder, Laura Ingalls. (1972a). *Little house on the prairie*. New York: Harper & Row.

Wilder, Laura Ingalls. (1972b). *The long winter*. New York: Harper & Row.

Wilkes, Angela. (2002). *Question time: Explore and discover birds*. New York: Kingfisher.

Willard, Nancy. (1981). *A visit to William Blake's inn* (Alice Provensen & Martin Provensen, Illus.). New York: Harcourt Brace.

Willard, Nancy. (2001). *The Moon and Riddles Diner and the Sunnyside Café*. San Diego: Harcourt Brace.

Williams, Margery. (1922/1986). *The velveteen rabbit*. New York: Knopf.

Williams, Rozanne Lanczak. (2001). *The coin counting book*. Boston: Charlesbridge.

Williams, Sue. (1996). *I went walking* (Julie Vivas, Illus.). San Diego: Harcourt Brace.

Williams, Vera B. (1982). *A chair for my mother*. New York: Greenwillow.

Windham, Sophie. (1994). *The mermaid and other sea poems*. New York: Scholastic.

Winnick, Karen B. (1996). *Mr. Lincoln's whiskers*. Honesdale, PA: Boyds Mills Press.

Winter, Jeanette. (1988). *Follow the drinking gourd*. New York: Knopf.

Winthrop, Elizabeth. (1986). *The castle in the attic*. New York: Yearling.

Winton, Tim. (1999). *Lockie Leonard, scumbuster*. New York: McElderry.

Wisniewski, David. (1996). *Golem*. New York: Clarion Books.

Wolf, Bernard. (2003). *Coming to America: A Muslim family's story*. New York: Lee & Low.

Wolff, Virginia Euwer. (1993). *Make lemonade*. New York: Holt.

Wolfman, Judy. (2002). *Life on a crop farm* (David Lorenz Winston, Photog.). Minneapolis: Carolrhoda.

Wong, Janet S. (1994). *Good luck gold and other poems*. New York: McElderry.

Wong, Janet S. (1996). *A suitcase of seaweed, and other poems*. New York: McElderry.

Wong, Janet S. (1999). *The rainbow hand: Poems about mothers and children*. New York: McElderry.

Wong, Janet S. (2000). *Night garden: Poems from the world of dreams*. New York: McElderry.

Wood, Audrey. (1984). *The napping house* (Don Wood, Illus.). New York: Harcourt.

Wood, Audrey. (1990). *Weird parents*. New York: Penguin.

Wood, Ted. (1996). *Iditarod dream: Dusty and his sled dogs compete in Alaska's Jr. Iditarod*. New York: Walker.

Woodruff, Elvira. (2000). *Dear Austin: Letters from the Underground Railroad*. Los Angeles: Knopf.

Woods, Brenda. (2002). *The red rose box*. New York: Putnam.

Woodson, Jacqueline. (1994). *I hadn't meant to tell you this*. New York: Delacorte.

Woodson, Jacqueline. (1997). *The house you pass on the way*. New York: Delacorte.

Woodson, Jacqueline. (2001a). *Miracle's boys*. New York: Scholastic.

Woodson, Jacqueline. (2001b). *The other side* (E. B. Lewis, Illus.). New York: Putnam.

Woodson, Jacqueline. (2002). *Visiting day* (James Ransome, Illus.). New York: Scholastic.

Worth, Valerie. (1992). *At Christmastime* (Antonio Frasconi, Illus.). New York: HarperCollins.

Worth, Valerie. (1994). *All the small poems and fourteen more*. New York, Farrar, Straus & Giroux.

Worth, Valerie. (2000). *Peacock*. New York: Farrar, Straus & Giroux.

Wright, Betty Ren. (1983). *The dollhouse murders*. New York: Holiday House.

Wright, Betty Ren. (1994). *The ghost comes calling*. New York: Scholastic.

Wright-Frierson, Virginia. (1996). *A desert scrapbook: Dawn to dusk in the Sonoran desert*. New York: Simon & Schuster.

Wright-Frierson, Virginia. (1998). *An island scrapbook: Dawn to dusk on a barrier island*. New York: Simon & Schuster.

Wright-Frierson, Virginia. (1999). *A North American rain forest scrapbook*. New York: Walker.

Wynne-Jones, Tim. (1999). *Lord of the fries and other stories*. New York: DK Publishing.

Yagawa, Sumiko. (1981). *The crane wife* (Suekichi Akaba, Illus., Katherine Paterson, Trans.). New York: Morrow.

Yashima, Taro. (1955). *Crow boy*. New York: Viking.

Yates, Elizabeth. (1950). *Amos Fortune, free man* (Nora S. Unwin, Illus.). New York: Dutton.

Yep, Laurence. (1975). *Dragonwings*. New York: Harper & Row.

Yep, Laurence. (1977). *Child of the owl*. New York: HarperCollins.

Yep, Laurence. (1984). *Serpent's children*. New York: Harper & Row.

Yep, Lawrence. (1985). *Mountain light*. New York: Harper & Row.

Yep, Laurence. (1993a). *Dragon's gate*. New York: HarperCollins.

Yep, Laurence. (1993b). *The man who tricked a ghost* (Isadore Seltzer, Illus.). Mahwah, NJ: Bridgewater Press.

Yep, Laurence. (1994). *The boy who swallowed snakes* (Jean Tseng & Mou-Sien Tseng, Illus.). New York: Scholastic.

Yep, Laurence. (1995a). *Later gator*. New York: Hyperion Books.

Yep, Laurence. (1995b). *Thief of hearts*. New York: HarperCollins.

Yep, Laurence. (1997). *Dragon prince* (Kam Mak, Illus.). New York: HarperCollins.

Yep, Laurence. (1998). *The case of the lion dance*. New York: HarperCollins.

Yep, Laurence. (1999a). *The case of the firecrackers*. New York: HarperCollins.

Yep, Laurence. (1999b). *The imp ate my homework* (Benrei Huang, Illus.). New York: HarperCollins.

Yep, Laurence. (2000a). *Cockroach cooties*. New York: Hyperion Books.

Yep, Laurence. (2000b). *The magic paintbrush* (Suling Wang, Illus.). New York: HarperCollins.

Yolen, Jane. (1987). *Owl moon*. New York: Philomel.

Yolen, Jane. (1991). *The devil's arithmetic*. New York: Trumpet.

Yolen, Jane. (1992a). *Briar rose*. New York: Tom Doherty.

Yolen, Jane. (1992b). *Encounter*. San Diego: Harcourt Brace.

Yolen, Jane. (1992c). *Street rhymes around the world* (various artists, Illus.). Honesdale, PA: Boyds Mills Press.

Yolen, Jane. (1993a). *Weather report*. Honesdale, PA: Boyds Mills Press.

Yolen, Jane. (1993b). *Welcome to the green house* (Laura Regan, Illus.). New York: Putnam.

Yolen, Jane. (Ed.). (1994). *Sleep rhymes around the world*. Honesdale, PA: Wordsong/Boyds Mills Press.

Yolen, Jane. (1996). *Sea watch: A book of poetry* (Ted Lewin, Illus.). New York: Putnam.

Yolen, Jane. (1997). *Once upon ice: And other frozen poems*. Honesdale, PA: Boyds Mills Press.

Yolen, Jane. (1998). *Snow, snow: Winter poems for children*. Honesdale, PA: Boyds Mills Press.

Yolen, Jane, & Harris, R. (2000). *The queen's own fool*. New York: Philomel.

Yolen, Jane. (2003a). *Color me a rhyme: Poems for young people*. Honesdale, PA: Boyds Mills Press.

Yolen, Jane. (2003b). *Least things: Poems about small natures*. Honesdale, PA: Boyds Mills Press.

Yolen, Jane, & Stemple, Heidi. (2001). *Dear mother, dear daughter*. Honesdale, PA: Boyds Mills Press.

Yorinks, Arthur. (1986). *Hey, Al* (Richard Egielski, Illus.). New York: Farrar, Straus & Giroux.

Yorinks, Arthur. (1990). *Ugh* (Richard Egielski, Illus.). New York: Farrar, Straus & Giroux.

Young, Ed. (1989). *Lon Po Po: A Red-Riding Hood story from China*. New York: Scholastic.

Young, Karen Romano. (2002). *Small worlds: Maps and mapmaking*. New York: Scholastic.

Young, Mark C. (2002). *The Guinness book of world records*. New York: Bantam.

Young, Robert. (1998). *Money*. Minneapolis: Carolrhoda.

Yumoto, Kazumi. (1998). *The friends*. New York: Yearling.

Zelinsky, Paul O. (1986). *Rumpelstiltskin*. New York: Dutton.

Zindel, Paul. (1968). *The pigman*. New York: Bantam Books.

Zion, Gene. (2002). *Harry, the dirty dog* (Margaret Bloy Graham, Illus.). New York: HarperCollins.

Zoller, Arthur David. (2000). *Fish counting*. Watertown, MA: Charlesbridge.

Zolotow, Charlotte. (1962). *Mr. Rabbit and the lovely present* (Maurice Sendak, Illus.). New York: Harper & Row.

Zolotow, Charlotte. (1965). *Someday*. New York: HarperCollins.

Zolotow, Charlotte. (1972). *William's doll* (William Pène du Bois, Illus.). New York: Scholastic.

Zolotow, Charlotte. (1980). *Say it!* (James Stevenson, Illus.). New York: Greenwillow.

Zolotow, Charlotte. (1993). *Snippets: A gathering of poems, pictures and possibilities*. New York: HarperCollins.

Zolotow, Charlotte. (2002). *Seasons: A book of poems* (Erik Blegvad, Illus.). New York: HarperCollins.

References

Adamson, L. (1998). *Literature connections to world history: Resources to enhance and entice*. Englewood, CO: Libraries Unlimited.

Aiken, J. (1982/1998). *The way to write for children*. New York: St. Martin's Griffin.

Alexander, L. (1983). Fantasy and the human condition. *The New Advocate, 1*(2), 81–83.

Aliki. (1996). The language of my books. In A. A. McClure & J. V. Kristo (Eds.), *Books that invite talk, wonder, and play*. Urbana, IL: National Council of Teachers of English.

Allington, R. (2002). What I've learned about effective reading instruction from a decade of studying exemplary elementary classroom teachers. *Phi Delta Kappan, 83*(10), 740–747.

Allington, R., & McGill-Franzen, A. (1989). Different programs, different instruction. In D. K. Lipsky & A. Gartner (Eds.), *Beyond separate education: Quality education for all* (pp. 75–97). Baltimore, MD: Paul H. Brookes.

Almasi, J. F. (1995). The nature of fourth graders' sociocognitive conflicts in peer-led and teacher-led discussion of literature. *Reading Research Quarterly, 30*(3), 314–351.

Almasi, J. F., & Gambrell, L. B. (1997). Examining conflicts and complexities in peer talk. In J. R. Paratore & R. L. McCormack (Eds.), *Peer talk in the classroom: Learning from research* (pp. 130–155). Newark, DE: International Reading Association.

Anderson, C. (2000). *How's it going? A practical guide to conferring with student writers*. Portsmouth, NH: Heinemann.

Anderson, C. A., Hiebert, E. H., Scott, J. A., & Wilkinson, I. A. G. (1985). *Becoming a nation of readers: The report of the commission on reading*. Washington, DC: The National Academy of Education.

Anderson, R. A., & Pavan, B. N. (1993). *Nongradedness: Helping it to happen*. Lancaster, PA: Technomics.

Applebee, A. N. (1978). *The child's concept of story*. Chicago: University of Chicago Press.

Arhar, H., Holly, M. L., & Kasten, W. C. (2001). *Action research by teachers: Traveling the yellow brick road*. Upper Saddle River, NJ: Merrill/Prentice Hall.

Atwell, N. (1987). *In the middle: Writing, reading, and learning with adolescents*. Portsmouth, NH: Boynton/Cook.

Atwell, N. (1998). *In the middle: New understandings about reading, writing, and learning*. Portsmouth, NH: Boynton/Cook.

Au, K. H. (1993). *Literacy instruction in multicultural settings*. Forth Worth, TX: Harcourt Brace.

Au, K. H., Carroll, J. H., & Scheu, J. A. (1997). *Balanced literacy instruction: A teacher's resource book*. Norwood, MA: Christopher-Gordon.

Au, K. H., & Gallimore, R. (1997). The competence incompetence paradox in the education of minority culture children. In M. Cole, Y. Engestrom, & O. Vasquez (Eds.), *Mind, culture, and activity: Seminal papers from the laboratory of comparative human cognition* (pp. 241–253). Cambridge, UK: Cambridge University Press.

Avery, C. (1993). *And with a light touch: Learning about reading, writing, and teaching with first graders*. Portsmouth, NH: Heinemann.

Avery, C. (1998). Nonfiction books: Naturals for the primary level. In R. A. Bamford & J. V. Kristo (Eds.), *Making facts come alive: Choosing quality nonfiction literature K–8* (pp. 193–203). Norwood, MA: Christopher-Gordon.

Baghban, M. J. M. (1984). *Our daughter learns to read and write: A case study from birth to three*. Newark, DE: International Reading Association.

Bamford, R., & Kristo, J. (2000). *Checking out nonfiction K–8: Good choices for best learning*. Norwood, MA: Christopher-Gordon.

Bamford, R. A., & Kristo, J. V. (2003). An interview with Joanna Cole. In R. A. Bamford & J. V. Kristo (Eds.), *Making facts come alive: Choosing & using nonfiction literature K–8* (p. 282–284). Norwood, MA: Christopher-Gordon.

Bang, M. (1991/2000). *Picture this: How pictures work*. New York: Seastar Books.

Barman, C. (2000). Students' ideas about animals: Results of a national study. *Science and Children, 38*(1), 42–48.

Barnes, D. (1976). *From communication to curriculum*. New York: Penguin.

Barnes, D. (1992). *From communication to curriculum*. (2nd ed.). Portsmouth, NH: Boynton/Cook.

Barnett, J., & Irwin, L. (1994). The effects of classroom activities on elementary students' reading attitudes. *Reading Improvement, 31*(2), 121–133.

Barrs, M. (1993). Introduction: Reading the difference. In M. Barrs & S. Pidgeon (Eds.), *Reading the difference* (pp. i–xx). London: Center for Language in Primary Education.

Barton, B., & Booth, D. (1995). *Mother Goose goes to school: More than 100 rhymes and activities*. Markham, ON: Pembroke.

Bascom, W. (1965, January–March). The forms of folklore: Prose narratives in sacred narrative. *Journal of American Folklore, 78*, 3–20.

Beach, R. (1997). Students' resistance to engagement with multicultural literature. In T. Rogers & A. O. Soter (Eds.), *Reading across cultures: Teaching literature in a diverse society* (pp. 69–94). New York: Teachers College Press.

Beck, I., & McKeown, M. (1991). Conditions of vocabulary acquisition. In R. Barr, M. Kamil, P. Mosenthal, & P. D. Pearson (Eds.), *Handbook of reading research* (Vol. 2, pp. 789–814). White Plains, NY: Longman.

Benton, M. (1992). Poetry response and education. In P. Hunt (Ed.), *Literature for children: Contemporary criticism* (pp. 127–134). London: Routledge.

Berg, E. (2002). *True to Form*. New York: Atria.

Bigelow, B. (1998). Once upon a genocide: Columbus in children's literature. In B. Bigelow & B. Peterson (Eds.), *Rethinking Columbus* (pp. 47–55). Milwaukee: Rethinking Schools.

Bigelow, B., & Peterson, B. (Eds.). (1998). *Rethinking Columbus*. Milwaukee, WI: Rethinking Schools.

Blachowicz, C., & Lee, J. J. (1991). Vocabulary development in the whole literacy classroom. *The Reading Teacher, 45,* 209–282.

Borders, S., & Naylor, A. P. (1993). *Children talking about books.* Phoenix, AZ: Oryx Press.

Brearley, M., & Hitchfield, E. (1973). *A guide to reading Piaget.* New York: Schocken Books.

Bredekamp, S. & Copple, C. (1997). *Developmentally appropriate practice in early childhood programs serving from birth through age 8.* Washington, DC: National Association for Education of Young Children.

Bridge, C., Winograd, P., & Haley, D. (1983). Using predictable materials vs. preprimers to teach beginning sight words. *The Reading Teacher, 36*(9), 884–891.

Britton, J. (1970). *Language and learning.* London: Penguin.

Brooks, G., Waterman, R., & Allington, R. (2003). A national survey of teachers' reports of children's favorite series books. *The Dragon Lode, 21*(2), 8–14.

Brooks, J. G., & Brooks, M. G. (1993). *The case for constructivist classrooms.* Alexandria, VA: ASCD.

Brown, D. F. (2002). *Becoming a successful urban teacher.* Portsmouth, NH: Heinemann.

Brown, H., & Cambourne, B.(1987). *Read and retell: A strategy for the whole language/natural learning classroom.* Portsmouth, NH: Heinemann.

Brown, J. E., & Stephens, E. C. (Eds.). (2003). *Your reading: An annotated book list for middle school and junior high* (11th ed.). Urbana, IL: National Council of Teachers of English.

Bruner, J. (1979). Notes on a theory of instruction. In A. Floyd (Ed.), *Cognitive development in the school years* (pp. 273–283). New York: Wiley.

Bruner, J. S. (1990). *Acts of meaning.* Cambridge, MA: Harvard University Press.

Bruner, J., & Garton, A. (Eds.). (1978). *Human growth and development.* Oxford: Clarendon Press.

Burch, M. M., & Beech, L. (2001). *Instant file folder games for reading.* New York: Scholastic.

Burns, P. (1998). *Informal reading inventory: Preprimer to twelfth grade.* Boston: Houghton Mifflin.

Burns, P. C., & Roe, B. D. (1993). *Burns and Roe Informal Reading Inventory* (4th ed.). Boston: Houghton Mifflin.

Burns, P. C., & Roe, B. D. (1999). *Informal Reading Inventory: Preprimer to twelfth grade.* Boston: Houghton Mifflin.

Cai, G. (1994). "Who knows not but speaks is not wise; who knows but speaks not is not loyal!" Rhetoric of Philosophical Wisdom in Ancient China. Annual Meeting of the Conference on College Composition and Communication. Nashville, 16–19 March 1994. (ERIC Document Number 372–395).

Calkins, L. M. (1983). *Lessons from a child.* Exeter, NH: Heinemann.

Calkins, L. M. (1986). *The art of teaching writing.* Portsmouth, NH: Heinemann.

Cambourne, B. (1988). *The whole story: Natural language and the acquisition of literacy in the classroom.* Auckland, New Zealand: Ashton Scholastic.

Campbell, J. (1988). *The power of myth.* New York: Doubleday.

Campbell. R. (2001). *Read-alouds with young children.* Newark, DE: International Reading Association.

Canton, J. (2001, February/March). Talking with Christopher Paul Curtis. *Book Links,* 32–35.

Carter, B. (2000). A universe of information: The future of nonfiction. *The Horn Book Magazine, 76*(6), 697–707.

Chambers, A. (1996a). *Tell me: Children, reading and talk.* York, ME: Stenhouse.

Chambers, A. (1996b). *The reading environment: How adults help children enjoy books.* York, ME: Stenhouse.

Champlin, C., & Renfro, N. (1985). *Storytelling with puppets.* Chicago: American Library Association.

Chard, D. J., & Dickson, S. V. (1999). Phonological awareness: Instructional and assessment guidelines. *Intervention in School and Clinic, 34,* 261–270.

Chomsky, C. (1972). Stages in language development and reading exposure. *Harvard Educational Review, 42,* 1–33.

Christensen, L. M. (1999). Critical literacy: Teaching, reading, writing, and outrage. In Carol Edelsy (Ed.). *Making justice our project* (pp. 209–225). Urbana, IL: National Council of Teachers of English.

Clark, M. M. (1976). *Young fluent readers.* London: Heinemann.

Clay, M. (1991). *Becoming literate: The construction of inner control.* Portsmouth, NH: Heinemann.

Cohen, P. A., Kulik, J. A., & Kulik, C. C. (1982). Educational outcomes of tutoring: A meta-analysis. *American Educational Research Journal, 19*(2), 237–248.

Cole, A. D. (2003). *Knee to knee, eye to eye: Circling in on comprehension.* Portsmouth, NH: Heinemann.

Collier, C. (1999). *Brother Sam and all that: Historical context and literary analysis of the novels of James and Christopher Collier.* Orange, CT: Clearwater Press.

Colman, P. (1999). Nonfiction is literature, too. *The New Advocate, 12*(3), 215–223.

Colman, P. (2002). Adventures in nonfiction: Talking with Penny Colman. *Journal of Children's Literature, 28*(2), 58–61.

Combs, M. (2002). *Readers and writers in primary grades: A balanced and integrated approach* (2nd ed.). Upper Saddle River, NJ: Merrill/Prentice Hall.

Committee on the Right to Read of the National Council of Teachers of English. (n.d.). *The Students' Right to Read.* NCTE Guideline Series, article 107616. Retrieved July 2, 2004 from *http://www.ncte.org/about/over/positions/category/cens/107616.htm.*

Conniff, C. (1993). How young readers perceive reading and themselves as readers. *English in Education, 27*(2), 19–25.

Cooper-Mullin, A., & Coye Marmaduke, J. (1998). *Once upon a heroine: 450 books for girls to love.* Lincolnwood, IL: Contemporary Books.

Cornelius, C. (1994). Language as culture. *Native American Expressive Culture, XL*(3/4), 146–150.

Cousin, P., Weekley, T., & Gerard, J. (1993). The functional uses of language & literacy by students with severe language and learning problems. *Language Arts, 70*(7), 548–556.

Cox, C. (1991). The media arts and language arts teaching and learning. In J. Flood, J. M. Jensen, D. Lapp, & J. R. Squire (Eds.), *Handbook of research on teaching the English language arts* (pp. 542–548). New York: Macmillan.

Cox, C., & Many, J. (1992a). Towards an understanding of the aesthetic stance in literature. *Language Arts, 69*(1), 28–33.

Cox, C., & Many, J. (1992b). "Reader stance towards a literary work": Applying the transactional theory to children's responses. *Reading Psychology, 13*(1), 37–72.

Craven, M. A. (1980). *A survey of teacher attitudes and practices regarding the teaching of poetry in the elementary school.* Unpublished doctoral dissertation, Lamar University, Beaumont, TX.

Csikszentmihalyi, M. (1990). *Flow: The psychology of optimal experience.* New York: Basic Books.

Culham, R. (2003). *6 + 1 traits of writing: The complete guide.* New York: Scholastic.

Cullinan, B. (1993). Commentary on research: Perspectives for literature. In K. E. Holland, R. A. Hungerford, & S. B. Ernst (Eds.), *Journeying: Children responding to literature* (pp. 317–322). Portsmouth, NH: Heinemann.

Cullinan, B. E. (1995). *Three voices: An invitation to poetry across the curriculum.* Portland, ME: Stenhouse.

Cullinan, B. E. (Ed.). (1996). *A jar of tiny stars: Poems by NCTE award-winning poets.* Honesdale, PA: Wordsong, Boyds Mills Press.

Cullinan, B. E., & Galda, L. (1994). *Literature and the child.* (3rd ed.). Fort Worth, TX: Harcourt Brace.

Cullinan, B. E., & Galda, L. (1998). *Literature and the child.* (4th ed.). New York: Harcourt.

Cullinan, B. E., & Person, D. G. (Eds.). (2001). *The continuum encyclopedia of children's literature.* New York: Continuum International.

Cunningham, P., & Hall, D. (2001). *Making words: Lessons for home and school.* Greensboro, NC: Carson-Dellosa.

Dahl, K., & Freppon, P. A. (1994). *A comparison of inner city children's interpretations of reading and writing instruction in the early grades in skills based and whole language classrooms.* Washington, DC: Office of Educational Research and Improvement. (ERIC Document Reproduction Service No. ED 370–075)

Dahl, K. L., & Scharer, P. L. (2000). Phonics teaching and learning in whole language classrooms: New evidence from research. *The Reading Teacher, 53,* 584–594.

Dale, P. S. (1976). *Language development: Structure and function* (2nd ed.). New York: Holt, Rinehart, and Winston.

Daniels, H. (2002). *Literature circles: Voice and choice in book clubs and reading groups* (2nd ed.). York, ME: Stenhouse.

Dargan, A., & Zeitlin, S. (1999). The people's poetry gathering: Oral poetry traditions. *Teachers and Writers, 30*(4), 1–11.

Darling-Hammond, L., Ancess, J., & Falk, B. (1995). *Authentic assessment in action: Studies of schools and students at work.* New York: Teachers College Press.

Datlow, E., & Windling, T. (Eds.). (2003). *Swan sister: Fairy tales retold.* New York: Simon & Schuster.

Dauenhauer, R., & Dauenhauer, N. (Eds.). (1987). *Our ancestors, Tlingit oral narratives.* Seattle: University of Washington Press.

Day, F. A. (1994). *Multicultural voices in contemporary literature.* Portsmouth, NH: Heinemann.

Deford, D. (2003). Interactive read-aloud: Supporting and expanding strategies for comprehension. In G. S. Pinnell & P. Scharer (Eds.), *Teaching for comprehension in reading, grades K–2* (pp. 211–224). New York: Scholastic.

DeLawter, J. (1992). Teaching literature: From clerk to explorer. In J. A. Langer (Ed.), *Literature instruction: A focus on student response* (pp. 131–162). Urbana, IL: National Council of Teachers of English.

Delpit, L. (1991). The silenced dialogue: Power and pedagogy in educating other people's children. In M. Minami & B. Kennedy (Eds.), *Language issues in literacy and bilingual multicultural education* (pp. 483–502). Cambridge, MA: Harvard Education Review.

Delpit, L. (1995). *Other people's children: Cultural conflicts in the classroom.* New York: The New Press.

de Villiers, P. A., & de Villiers, J. G. (1980). *Early language.* Cambridge, MA: Harvard University Press.

Dewey, J. (1929). *My pedagogic creed.* Washington, DC: The Progressive Education Society.

Dias, P. X. (1992). Literary reading and classroom constraints: Aligning practice with theory. In J. A. Langer (Ed.), *Literature instruction: A focus on student response* (pp. 131–162). Urbana, IL: National Council of Teachers of English.

Diffily, D. (1996). *The Scholastic books of early childhood learning centers.* New York: Scholastic.

Doake, D. (1985). Reading-like behavior: Its role in learning to read. In A. Jagger & M. T. Smith-Burke (Eds.), *Observing the language learner* (pp. 82–98). Newark, DE: International Reading Association.

Dole, J. A., Sloan, C., & Trathen, W. (1995). Teaching vocabulary within the context of literature. *Journal of Reading, 38*(6), 452–460.

Donelson, K. (1975, January–February). What to do before the censor arrives. *Today's Education,* 22–26.

Dorn, L. J., & Soffos, C. (2001). *Shaping literature minds: Developing self-regulated learners.* Portland, ME: Stenhouse.

Durkin, D. (1966). *Children who read early.* New York: Teachers College Press.

Duthie, C. (1996). *True stories: Nonfiction literacy in the primary classroom.* York, ME: Stenhouse.

Ediger, M. (2000). Phonics and poetry in the curriculum. *Reading Improvement, 37,* 56–60.

Edmiston, B. (1993). Going up the beanstalk: Discovering giant possibilities through literature. In K. E. Holland, R. A. Hungerford, & S. B. Ernst (Eds.), *Journeying: Children responding to literature* (pp. 250–266). Portsmouth, NH: Heinemann.

Edwards, B. (2002). *Using multicultural literature to teach K–4 social studies: A thematic approach.* Boston: Allyn & Bacon.

Eeds, M., & Wells, D. (1989). Grand conversations: An exploration of meaning construction in literature study groups. *Research in the Teaching of English, 23*(1), 4–29.

Eisele, B. (1991). *Managing the whole language classroom: A complete teaching resource guide for K–6 teachers.* New York: Creative Teaching Press.

Eisemon, T., Hallett, M., & Maundu, J. (1986). Primary school literature and folktales in Kenya: What makes a children's story African? *Comparative Education Review, 30*(2), 232–246.

Elley, W. B. (1989). Vocabulary acquisition from listening to stories. *Reading Research Quarterly, 24,* 176–186.

Emig, J. (1981). Writing as a mode of learning. *The writing teacher's sourcebook.* New York: Oxford University Press.

Esbensen, B. J. (1975). *A celebration of bees: Helping children write poetry.* New York: Winston Press.

Feldman, J. R. (1947). *Wonderful rooms where children can bloom! Over 500 innovative ideas and activities for your child-centered classroom.* Peterborough, NH: Crystal Springs Books.

Ferdman, B. (1991). Literacy and cultural identity. In M. Minami (Ed.), *Language issues in bilingual and multicultural education* (pp. 347–372). Cambridge, MA: Harvard Educational Review.

Fienup-Riordan, A. (1994). Clearing the path: Metaphors to live by in Yup'ik Eskimo oral tradition. *American Indian Quarterly, 18*(1), 61–70.

Finney, S. (2000). *Keep the rest of the class reading while you teach small groups.* New York: Dimensions.

Fisher, B. (1991). *Joyful learning: A whole language kindergarten.* Portsmouth, NH: Heinemann.

Fisher, B., & Medvic, E. (2000). *Perspectives on shared reading: Planning and practice.* Portsmouth, NH: Heinemann.

Fisher, C. (1994). Sharing poetry in the classroom: Building a concept of poem. In J. Hickman, B. E. Cullinan, & S. Hepler (Eds.), *Children's literature in the classroom: Extending Charlotte's Web* (pp. 53–65). Norwood, MA: Christopher-Gordon.

Fisher, C., & Natarella, M. (1982). Young children's preferences in poetry: A national survey of first, second, and third graders. *Research in the Teaching of English, 16*(5), 339–355.

Fletcher, R. (1996). *A writer's notebook: Unlocking the writer within you.* New York: Avon Books.

Fletcher, R., & Portalupi, J. (2001). *Writing workshop: The essential guide.* Portsmouth, NH: Heinemann.

Flower, L., & Hayes, J. R. (1981, December). A cognitive process theory of writing. *College Composition and Communication,* 365–387.

Folta, B. (1979). *Effects of three approaches to teaching poetry to sixth grade students.* Unpublished doctoral dissertation, Purdue University, West Lafayette, IN.

Ford, D. J. (2002). More than facts: Reviewing science books. *The Horn Book Magazine, 78*(3), 265–271.

Ford, M., & Opitz, M. (2002). Using centers to engage children during guided reading time. *The Reading Teacher, 55*(8), 710–735.

Foss, A. (2002). Peeling the onion: Teaching critical literacy with students of privilege. *Language Arts, 79*(5), 393–403.

Fountas, I., & Pinnell, G. S. (1996). *Guided reading: Good first teaching for all children.* Portsmouth, NH: Heinemann.

Fountas, I., & Pinnell, G. S. (1999). *Matching books to readers: Using leveled books in guided reading, K–3.* Portsmouth, NH: Heinemann.

Fountas, I., & Pinnell, G. S. (2001). *Guiding readers and writers grades 3–6: Teaching comprehension, genre, and content literacy.* Portsmouth, NH: Heinemann.

Fredericks, A. D., Blake-Kline, B., & Kristo, J. V. (1997). *Teaching the integrated language arts: Process and practice.* New York: Addison-Wesley.

Freeman, D. E., & Freeman, Y. S. (1994). *Between worlds: Access to second language acquisition.* Portsmouth, NH: Heinemann.

Freeman, J. (1995). *More books children will sit still for: A read-aloud guide.* New Providence, NJ: R. R. Bowker.

Freeman, M. (1994). Trope densities, analogy clusters, and metaphor types: Metaphors, similes, and analogues in elementary science textbooks and trade books. *Dissertation Abstracts International, 55*(11), 3436A. (University Microfilms No. AAT9434204)

Freeman, M. S. (2001). *A K–5 school-wide instruction plan based on a continuum of critical writing skills.* Gainesville, FL: Maupin House.

Freeman, M. S., & Kasten, W. C. (1990, February). A secondary model for a young author's conference. *Journal of Reading,* 356–358.

Freeman, Y. S., & Freeman, D. E. (1992). *Whole language for second language learners.* Portsmouth, NH: Heinemann.

Fritz, J. (1990). The teller and the tale. In W. Zinsser (Ed.), *Worlds of childhood: The art and craft of writing for children* (pp. 21–46). Boston: Houghton Mifflin.

Fritz, J. (2001). Nonfiction, 1999. In M. Zarnowski, R. M. Kerper, & J. M. Jensen (Eds.), *The best in children's nonfiction: Reading, writing, & teaching Orbis Pictus award books* (pp. 87–89). Urbana, IL: National Council of Teachers of English.

Frohardt, D. C. (1999). *Teaching art with books kids love: Teaching art appreciation, elements of art, and principles of design with award-winning children's books.* Golden, CO: Fulcrum Resources.

Fromm, E. (1951). *The forgotten language: An introduction to the understanding of dreams, fairy tales and myths.* New York: Grove Press.

Frost, S. E., Jr. (Ed.). (1947). *History of education.* Great Neck, NY: Barron's.

Fry, E. B. (1978). *Fry Readability Scale.* Providence, RI: Jamestown.

Galda, L. (1993). How preferences and expectations influence evaluative responses to literature. In K. E. Holland, R. A. Hungerford, & S. B. Ernst (Eds.), *Journeying: Children responding to literature* (pp. 302–315). Portsmouth, NH: Heinemann.

Galda, L., Ash, G. W., & Cullinan, B. (2000). Children's literature. In M. L. Kamil, P. B. Mosenthal, P. D. Pearson, & R. Barr (Eds.), *Handbook of reading research* (Vol. III, pp. 361–379). Mahwah, NJ: Erlbaum.

Galda, L., & Cullinan, B. (2001). Literature for literacy: What research says about the benefits of using trade books in the classroom. In J. Flood, J. M. Jensen, D. Lapp, & J. R. Squire (Eds.), *Handbook of research on teaching the English language arts* (pp. 529–535). New York: MacMillan.

Galda, L., & Cullinan, B. (2002). *Literature and the child* (5th ed.). Belmont, CA: Wadsworth/Thomson Learning.

Gambrell, L. (1996). What research reveals about discussion. In L. Gambrell, & J. F. Almasi (Eds.), *Lively discussions: Fostering engaged reading* (pp. 25–38). Newark, DE: International Reading Association.

Gambrell, L., & Almasi, J. F. (1996). *Lively discussions: Fostering engaged reading.* Newark, DE: International Reading Association.

Gambrell, L., Codling, R., & Palmer, B. (1996). *Elementary students motivations to read.* Reading Research Report No. 52. Athens, GA: National Reading Research Center.

Gambrell, L., & Morrow, L. M. (1996). Creating contexts for motivating literacy learning. In L. Baker, P. Afflerbach, & D. Reinking (Eds.), *Developing engaged readers in school and home communities* (pp. 115–138). Mahwah, NJ: Erlbaum.

Gardner, H. (1993). *Multiple intelligences: The theory in practice.* New York: Basic Books.

Garza de Cortés, O. (2001). Keeping the democratic process: Critical issues facing today's public libraries. *The New Advocate, 14*(2), 153–156.

Giblin, J. C. (2000). More than just the facts: A hundred years of children's nonfiction. *The Horn Book Magazine, 76*(4), 413–424.

Gilligan, C. (1982). *In a different voice: Psychological theory and women's development.* Cambridge, MA: Harvard University Press.

Gilliland, H. (1988). *Teaching the native American.* Dubuque, IA: Kendall-Hunt.

Gipps, C., & Murphy, P. (1994). *A fair test? Assessment, achievement, and equity.* Philadelphia: Open U. Press.

Goatley, V. J., Brock, C. H., & Raphael, T. E. (1995). Diverse learners participating in regular education "Book Clubs." *Reading Research Quarterly, 30*(3), 352–380.

Goatley, V. J., & Raphael, T. E. (1992). *Non-traditional learners' written and dialogic response to literature.* Fortieth Yearbook of the National Reading Conference. Chicago, IL: National Reading Conference.

Goforth, F. (1998). *Literature & the learner.* Belmont, CA: Wadsworth.

Goodlad, J. (1984) *A place called school.* New York: McGraw-Hill.

Goodlad, J. I., & Anderson, R. H. (1987). *The nongraded elementary school.* New York: Teachers College Press.

Goodman, K. S. (1986). *What's whole in whole language?* Portsmouth, NH: Heinemann.

Goodman, K. S., Bird, L. B., & Goodman, Y. M. (Eds.). (1991). *The whole language catalog.* Santa Rosa, CA: American School Publishers.

Goodman, Y. M. (1987). Kid watching: An alternative to testing. *The National Elementary Principal, 57,* 41–45.

Goodman, Y. M., & Altwerger, B. (1981). *Print awareness in preschool children: A working paper.* (Occasional paper No. 4). Tucson: Arizona Center for Research and Development, University of Arizona.

Goodman, Y., Cox, V., Milz, V., & Haussler, M. (1977). Encouraging young authors and young readers. *Reading Education, 2,* 5–10.

Goodman, Y. M., Watson, D. H., & Burke, C. (1987). *The Reading Miscue Inventory.* Katonah, NY: Richard C. Owen.

Goodman, Y., & Wilde, S. (1992). *Literacy events in a community of young writers.* New York: Teachers College Press.

Gordon, R. (1993). *Peeling the onion: An anthology of poems.* New York: HarperCollins.

Gough, J. (1988). Experiencing a sequence of poem: Ted Hughes' *Season Songs. Children's Literature Association Quarterly, 13,* 191–194.

Graham, J. (1990). *Pictures on the page.* Sheffield, UK: National Association for the Teaching of English.

Graves, D. (1989). *Investigate nonfiction.* Portsmouth, NH: Heinemann.

Graves, M. F., & Graves, B. B. (2003). *Scaffolding reading experiences.* Norwood, MA: Christopher-Gordon.

Gray, P. (1999, September 20). Wild about Harry. *Time Magazine,* 71.

Greenlee, A., Monson, D., & Taylor, B. (1996). The lure of series books: Does it effect appreciation for recommended literature? *The Reading Teacher, 50*(3), 216–224.

Greenman, J. (1988). *Caring spaces, learning spaces: Children's environments that work.* New York: Exchange Place.

Grierson, S. T. (2002). Exploring the past through multigenre writing. *Language Arts, 80*(1), 51–59.

Hade, D. (2002). Living well in a time of terror and tests: A meditation on teaching and learning with literature. *The New Advocate, 15*(4), 293–302.

Hall, S. (1990). *Using picture storybooks to teach literary devices.* Phoenix, AZ: Oryx Press.

Hall, S. (1994). *Using picture storybooks to teach character education.* Phoenix, AZ: Oryx Press.

Hall, S. (2000). *Using picture storybooks to teach character education.* (2nd ed.). Phoenix, AZ: Oryx Press.

Hall, S. (2002). *Using picture storybooks to teach literary devices: Recommended books for children and young adults* (Vol. 3). Westport, CT: Oryx Press.

Halliday, M. A. K. (1978). *Language as a social semiotic.* Baltimore, MD: University Park Press.

Halliland, H., with Reyhner, J. (1988). *Teaching the Native American.* Dubuque, IA: Kendall/Hunt.

Hamilton, S. J. (1995). *My name's not Susie.* Portsmouth, NH: Heinemann/Boynton Cook.

Hancock, M. (1993). Exploring the meaning-making process through the content of literature response journals. *Research in the Teaching of English, 27,* 335–368.

Hansen, J. (2001). *When writers read.* Portsmouth, NH: Heinemann.

Harris, R. (1986). *The origin of writing.* Worcester, UK: Duckworth.

Harris, T. L., & Hodges, R. E. (Eds.). (1995). *The literacy dictionary: The vocabulary of reading and writing.* Newark, DE: International Reading Association.

Harris, V. (1997). *Using multiethnic literature in K–8 classrooms.* New York: Christopher-Gordon.

Harrowven, J. (1977). *The origins of rhymes, songs, and sayings.* London: Kaye & Ward.

Harste, J. C. (2003). What do we mean by literacy now? *Voice in the Middle, 10*(3), 8–12.

Harvey, S. (1998). *Nonfiction matters: Reading, writing and research in grades 3–8.* York, ME: Stenhouse.

Harvey, S., & Goudvis, A. (2000). *Strategies that work: Teaching comprehension to enhance understanding.* Portland, ME: Stenhouse.

Heard, G. (1989). *For the good of the earth and sun: Teaching poetry.* Portsmouth, NH: Heinemann.

Heath, S. B. (1983). *Ways with words: Language, life, and work in communities and classrooms.* Cambridge: Cambridge University Press.

Hecht, S. (1978). *The teaching of poetry in grades seven and eight: A survey of theory, practices, and materials.* Unpublished doctoral dissertation, Boston University, Boston.

Heller, M. F. (1991). *Reading-writing connections: From theory to practice.* New York: Longman.

Helm, J. H., & Katz, L. (2001). *Young investigators: The project approach in the early years.* New York: Teachers College Press.

Hepler, S. (1982). *Patterns of response to literature: A one-year study of a fifth and sixth grade classroom.* Unpublished doctoral dissertation, Ohio State University, Columbus.

Hepler, S. (2002). Nonfiction books for children: New directions, new challenges. In R. A. Bamford & J. V. Kristo (Eds.), *Making facts come alive: Choosing and using quality nonfiction literature K–8* (2nd ed., pp. 3–20). Norwood, MA: Christopher-Gordon.

Hickman, J. (1979). *Response to literature in a school environment, grades K–5.* Unpublished doctoral dissertation, Ohio State University, Columbus.

Hickman, J., Cullinan, B. E., & Hepler, S. (1994). *Children's literature in the classroom: Extending Charlotte's Web.* Norwood, MA: Christopher-Gordon.

Hill, B. C., Johnson, N. J., & Noe, K. L. S. (Eds.). (1995). *Literature circles and response.* Norwood, MA: Christopher-Gordon.

Hill, B. C., Noe, K. L. S., & King, J. A. (2003). *Literature circles in middle school: One teacher's journey.* Norwood, MA: Christopher-Gordon.

Hindley, J. (1996). *In the company of children.* Portland, ME: Stenhouse.

Hoffman, J. V., Roser, N. L., & Battle, J. (1993). Reading aloud in classrooms: From the modal to a "model." *The Reading Teacher, 46,* 496–503.

Holbrook, S. (2002). *Wham! It's a poetry jam: Discovering performance poetry.* Honesdale, PA: Boyds Mills Press.

Holdaway, D. (1979). *The foundations of literacy.* Sydney, Australia: Ashton Scholastic.

Holdaway, D. (1980). *Independence in reading.* Exeter, NH: Heinemann.

Holly, M. L. (1989). *Writing to grow: Keeping a personal-professional journal.* Portsmouth, NH: Heinemann.

Holly, M. L., Arhar, J. A., & Kasten, W. C. (2005). *Action research for teachers: Traveling the yellow brick road.* (2nd ed.). Upper Saddle River, NJ: Merrill/Prentice Hall.

Hoover, M. R., & Fabian, E. M. (2000). Problem solving and struggling readers. *The Reading Teacher, 53,* 474–476.

Huck, C., Hepler, S., Hickman, J., & Kiefer, B. (2001). *Children's literature in the elementary school* (7th ed.). New York: McGraw-Hill.

Huck, C., Hepler, S., & Kiefer, B. (1993). *Children's literature in the elementary school* (4th ed.). Fort Worth, TX: Harcourt Brace.

Huck, C., & Kiefer, B. Z., with Hepler, S., & Hickman, J. (2004). *Children's literature in the elementary school* (8th ed.). Boston: McGraw-Hill.

Hunt, P. (2001). *Children's literature.* Malden, MA: Blackwell.

Ingham, R. (1980). *The poetry preferences of fourth and fifth grade students in a suburban school setting in 1980.* Unpublished doctoral dissertation, University of Houston, Houston, TX.

International Reading Association. (1996). *Standards for the English Language Arts* (with The National Council of Teachers of English). Newark, DE: Author.

International Reading Association. (2002). *What is evidence-based reading instruction?: A position statement of the International Reading Association.* Newark, DE: Author.

Iser, W. (1974). *The implied reader: Patterns of communication in prose fiction from Bunyan to Beckett.* Baltimore, MD: Johns Hopkins University Press.

Jaffe, N. (1996). Reflections on the work of Harold Courlander. *School Library Journal, 42,* 132–133.

Janeczko, P. (Ed.). (1990). *The place my words are looking for: What poets say about and through their work.* New York: Bradbury Press.

Janeczko, P. (1994). *Poetry from A to Z: A guide for young writers.* Scarsdale, NY: Bradbury Press.

Janeczko, P. (2002). *Seeing the blue between: Advice and inspiration for young poets.* Cambridge, MA: Candlewick Press.

Jensen, J. (2001). The quality of prose in Orbis Pictus award books. In M. Zarnowski, R. M. Kerper & J. M. Jensen (Eds.), *The best in children's nonfiction: Reading, writing, and teaching Orbis Pictus award books.* Urbana, IL: National Council of Teachers of English.

Joseph, L. M. (2000). Developing first graders' phonemic awareness, word identification and spelling: A comparison of two contemporary phonic instruction approaches. *Reading Research and Instruction, 39,* 160–169.

Juel, C. (1991). Cross-age tutoring between students, athletes and at-risk children. *The Reading Teacher, 45*(3), 178–186.

Kalman, B. (1995). *How a book is published.* New York: Crabtree.

Kamil, M., Mosenthal, P., Pearson, P. D., & Barr, R. (2000). *The handbook of reading research, Volume III.* Mahwah, NJ: Erlbaum.

Kasten, W. C. (1987). Celebrating child authorship in southwest Florida. *Florida ASCD Journal, 4,* 30–32.

Kasten, W. C. (1991). Books beget books. In K. S. Goodman, L. B. Bird, & Y. M. Goodman (Eds.), *The whole language catalogue* (p. 161). Santa Rosa, CA: American School Publishers.

Kasten, W. C. (1992). Bridging the horizon: American Indian beliefs and whole language. *Anthropology and Education Quarterly, 23*(2), 108–119.

Kasten, W. C. (1995). Literature circles for the teaching of literature-based reading. In M. C. Radencich & L. J. McKay (Eds.), *Flexible grouping for literacy in the elementary grades* (pp. 66–81). Boston: Allyn & Bacon.

Kasten, W. C. (1997). Learning is noisy. In J. R. Paratore & R. L. McCormack (Eds.), *Peer talk in the classroom: Learning from research* (pp. 88–101). Newark, DE: International Reading Association.

Kasten, W. C., & Clarke, B. K. (1993). *The multiage classroom: A family of learners.* Katonah, NY: Richard C. Owen.

Kasten, W. C., & Lolli, E. M. (1998). *Implementing multiage education: A practical guide.* Norwood, MA: Christopher-Gordon.

Kasten, W. C., Lolli, E. M., & VanderWilt, J. (1998). Common roots and threads: Developmentally appropriate practice, whole language, and continuous progress. *Literacy, Teaching, & Learning, 3*(2), 19–40.

Keene, E. O., & Zimmerman, S. (1997). *Mosaic of thought: Teaching comprehension in a reader's workshop.* Portsmouth, NH: Heinemann.

Kehoe, M. (1993). *A book takes root.* Minneapolis: Carolrhoda.

Kerper, R. (2002). Art influencing art: The making of *An extraordinary life. Language Arts, 80*(1), 60–67.

Kerper, R. (2003). Choosing quality nonfiction literature: Examining aspects of design. In R. A. Bamford & J. V. Kristo (Eds.), *Making facts come alive: Choosing & using nonfiction literature K–8* (pp. 65–78). Norwood, MA: Christopher-Gordon.

Kherdian, D. (1992). *Feathers and tails: Animal fables from around the world.* New York: Philomel.

Kibby, M. W. (1995). The organization and teaching of things and the words that signify them. *Journal of Adolescent and Adult Literacy, 39*(3), 208–223.

Kirby, D., & Liner, T. (1981). *Inside out.* Montclair, NJ: Boynton/Cook.

Klesius, J., & Searls, E. (1991). Vocabulary instruction. *Reading Psychology, 12,* 165–171.

Koppenhaver, D., Colman, P., Kalman, S., & Yoder, D. (1992). The implications of emergent literacy research for children with developmental disabilities. *American Journal of Speech-Language Pathology, 1*(1), 38–44.

Kridel, C. (Ed.). (2000). *Review/Books of the century: Louise Rosenblatt's* Literature as Exploration *makes the list.* Retrieved July 21, 2004, from the Association for Supervision and Curriculum Development website: *http://www.ascd.org/publications/ed_lead/200004/kridel.html.*

Kristo, J. V. (1993). Reading aloud in a primary classroom: Reaching and teaching young readers. In K. E. Holland, R. A. Hungerford, & S. B. Ernst (Eds.), *Journeying: Children responding to literature* (pp. 54–71). Portsmouth, NH: Heinemann.

Kristo, J. V. (1996). How come nobody's listening? When reading aloud can go wrong. In B. M. Power & R. S. Hubbard (Eds.), *Oops: What we learn when our teaching fails* (pp. 125–127). York, ME: Stenhouse.

Kristo, J. V., & Bamford, R. A. (2004). *Nonfiction in focus: A comprehensive framework for helping students become independent readers and writers of nonfiction, K–6.* New York: Scholastic.

Krogness, M. (1995). *Just teach me, Mrs. K: Talking, reading and writing with resistant adolescent learners.* Portsmouth, NH: Heinemann.

Kurstedt, R., & Koutras, M. (2000). *Teaching writing with picture books as models.* New York: Scholastic.

Kutiper, K., & Wilson, P. (1993). Updating poetry preferences: A look at the poetry children really like. *The Reading Teacher, 47*(1), 28–35.

Ladson-Billing, G. (1994). *The dreamkeepers: Successful teachers of African American children.* San Francisco, CA: Jossey-Bass.

Lamb, N. (2001). *The writer's guide to crafting stories for children.* Cincinnati: Writer's Digest Books.

Langer, J. (1995). *Envisioning literature: Literary understanding and literature instruction.* New York: Teachers College Press.

Latrobe, K. H., Brodie, C. S., & White, M. (2002). *The children's literature dictionary: Definitions, resources, and learning activities.* New York: Neal-Schuman.

Lauber, P. (1996). Ships sailed the seas. In A. A. McClure & J. V. Kristo (Eds.), *Books that invite talk, wonder, & play* (pp. 262–263). Urbana, IL: National Council of Teachers of English.

Laughlin, M. K., & Swisher, C. L. (1990). *Literature based reading.* Phoenix, AZ: Oryx.

Laughlin, M. K., & Watt, L. S. (1986). *Developing learning skills through children's literature.* Phoenix, AZ: Oryx.

Leal, D. J. (1995). When it comes to informational learning to read. In A. Jagger & M. T. Smith-Burke (Eds.), *Observing the language learner* (pp. 82–98). Newark, DE: International Reading Association.

Lehr, S. (1991). *The child's developing sense of theme: Response to literature.* New York: Teachers College Press.

Leland, C., & Fitzpatrick, R. (1994). Cross-age interaction builds enthusiasm for reading and writing. *The Reading Teacher, 47*(4), 292–301.

Leland, C. H., & Harste, J. C. (1994). Multiple ways of knowing: Curriculum in a new key. *Language Arts, 71*(5), 337–345.

Lenz, L. (1992). Crossroads of literacy and orality: Reading poetry aloud. *Language Arts, 69,* 597–603.

Lewison, M., Flint, A. S., & Van Sluys, K. (2002). Taking on critical literacy: The journey of newcomers and novices. *Language Arts, 79*(5), 382–392.

Lewison, M., Leland, C., Flint, A. S., & Moller, K. J. (2002). Dangerous discourses: Using controversial books to support engagement, diversity, & democracy. *The New Advocate, 15*(3), 215–224.

Lipsky, D., & Gartner, A. (1989). Building the future. In D. Lipsky & A. Gartner (Eds.), *Beyond separate education: Quality education for all.* Baltimore, MD: Paul H. Brookes.

Livingston, M. (1968). "Introduction." *A time beyond us: A collection of poetry.* New York: Harcourt Brace.

Livingston, M. C. (1996). The poem on page 81. In S. Egoff, G. Stubbs, R. Ashley, & W. Sutton (Eds.), *Only connect: Readings on children's literature* (3rd ed., pp. 214–224). New York: Oxford University Press.

Lockward, D. (1996). Poets on teaching poetry. *English Journal, 83,* 65–70.

Locust, C. (1988). Wounding the spirit: Discrimination and traditional American Indian belief systems. *Harvard Educational Review, 58*(3), 315–330.

Lukens, R. J. (1999). *A critical handbook of children's literature.* New York: Longman.

Maccoby, E. (1980). *Social development: Psychological growth and the parent child relationship.* New York: Harcourt Brace.

MacGinitie, W. H., MacGinitie, R. K., Maria, K., & Dreyer, L. G. (2000). *The Gates-MacGinitie Reading Test.* Itasca, IL: Riverside.

Mader, C. (1998). Reverence for the ordinary. *Canadian Journal of Native Education, 22*(2), 171–187.

Many, J. (1990). The effect of reader stance on students' personal understanding of literature. In S. McCormick & J. Zutell (Eds.), *Literary theory and research: Analyses from multiple paradigms* (pp. 51–63) (Thirty-ninth yearbook of the national reading conference). Chicago: National Reading Conference.

Many, J. (1991). The effects of stance and age level on children's literary responses. *Journal of Reading Behavior, 21,* 61–85.

Marcus, L. (1998). *A Caldecott celebration.* New York: Walker.

Marcus, L. (2000). *Author talk*. New York: Simon & Schuster.

Marcus, L. (2002). *Ways of telling: Conversations on the art of the picture book*. New York: Dutton.

Marriott, D., & Kupperstein, J. (2001). *What are the other kids doing while you teach small groups?* New York: Creative Teaching Press.

Martin, B., & Brogan, P. (1996). *Sounds of the storyteller*. New York: Holt, Rinehart and Winston.

Martinez, M., & Roser, N. (1985). Read it again: The value of repeated reading during storytime. *The Reading Teacher, 38*, 782–786.

McCarty, T. L., & Watahomigie, L. J. (1998). Language and literacy in American Indian and Alaska native communities. In B. Perez & T. L. McCarty (Eds.), *Sociocultural contexts of language and literacy* (pp. 69–98). Mahwah, NJ: Erlbaum.

McClure, A. (1985). *Children's responses to poetry in a supportive literary context*. Unpublished doctoral dissertation, Ohio State University, Columbus.

McClure, A. (1990). *Second, third, and fourth grade children's understandings of poetry in supportive literary contexts*. Final Research Report for the Elva Knight Research Grants Program. Newark, DE: International Reading Association.

McClure, A. (1995a). Censorship of children's books. In S. Lehr (Ed.), *Battling dragons: Issues and controversy in children's literature* (pp. 3–30). Portsmouth, NH: Heinemann.

McClure, A. A. (1995b). Choosing quality nonfiction literature. In R. A. Bamford & J. V. Kristo (Eds.), *Making facts come alive: Choosing & using nonfiction literature K–8* (pp. 41–64). Norwood, MA: Christopher-Gordon.

McClure, A. A. (2003). Choosing quality nonfiction literature: Examining aspects of writing style. In R. A. Bamford & J. V. Kristo (Eds.), *Making facts come alive: Choosing & using nonfiction literature K–8* (pp. 79–96). Norwood, MA: Christopher-Gordon.

McClure, A., Harrison, P., & Reed, S. (1989). Poetry in the school: Bringing poetry and children together. In J. Hickman & B. Cullinan (Eds.), *Children's literature in the classroom: Weaving Charlotte's Web* (pp. 173–188). Needham Heights, MA: Christopher-Gordon.

McClure, A., Harrison, P., & Reed, S. (1990). *Sunrises and songs: Reading and writing poetry in an elementary classroom*. Portsmouth, NH: Heinemann.

McClure, A., & Kristo, J. (1996). *Books that invite talk, wonder and play with language*. Urbana, IL: National Council of Teachers of English.

McClure, A., & Kristo, J. V. (2002). *Adventuring with books: A booklist for pre-K–grade 6* (13th ed.). Urbana, IL: National Council of Teachers of English.

McGee, L. M., & Richgels, D. J. (1990). *Literacy's beginnings*. Boston: Allyn & Bacon.

McKenna, M. C., & Kear, D. J. (1990). Measuring attitude toward reading. A new tool for teachers. *The Reading Teacher, 43*, 626–639.

McKindley, E. (1998, Winter). Writing from the inside out: A "chat" with Karen Cushman. *The New Advocate, 11*(1), 1–10.

McLaren, P. L. (1991). Culture or canon? Critical pedagogy and the politics of literacy. In M. Minami & B. Kennedy (Eds.), *Language Issues in Literacy and Multicultural Education* (pp. 286–309). Cambridge, MA: Harvard Educational Review.

McMahon, S. I., & Raphael, T. E. (Eds.), with Pardo, L., & Goatley, V. (1997). *The book club connection: Literacy learning and classroom talk*. New York: Teachers College Press.

McMillan, B. (1993). Accuracy in books for young readers: From first to last check. *The New Advocate, 6*(2), 97–104.

McNeil, J. D. (1992). *Reading comprehension: New directions in classroom practice*. New York: HarperCollins.

Meltzer, M. (1976). Where do all the prizes go?: The case for nonfiction. *The Horn Book Magazine, 52*, 17–23.

Mendoza, A. (1985). Reading to children: Their preference. *The Reading Teacher, 38*, 522–527.

Meyer, B. J., & Rice, G. E. (1984). The structure of text. In P. D. Pearson (Ed.), *Handbook of reading research* (pp. 319–351). New York: Longman.

Meyer, L., Wardrop, J., Stahl, S., & Linn, R. (1994). Effects of reading storybooks aloud to children. *Journal of Educational Research, 88*, 69–85.

Moline, S. (1995). *I see what you mean: Children at work with visual information*. Portland, ME: Stenhouse.

Moline, S. (2002). *Dominie information toolkit*. Carlsbad, CA: Dominie Press.

Moll, L. C. (1994). Mediating knowledge between homes and classrooms. In D. Keller-Cohen (Ed.), *Interdisciplinary conversations* (pp. 385–410). Cresskill, NJ: Hampton Press.

Moll, L., Velez-Ibanez, C., Greenberg, J., & Rivera, C. (1990). *Community knowledge & classroom practice*. United States Department of Education. (ERIC Document Reproduction Service No. ED 341 969)

Monson, D., & Sebesta, S. (1991). Reading preferences. In J. Flood, J. M. Jensen, D. Lapp, & J. R. Squire (Eds.), *Handbook of research on teaching the English language arts* (pp. 664–673). New York: Macmillan.

Montejo, V. (1994). Ancient worlds: Oral tradition and the indigenous people of the Americas. *Native American Expressive Culture, XL*(3/4), 139–145.

Morretta, T. M., & Ambrosini, M. (2000). *Practical approaches for teaching reading and writing in middle schools*. Newark, DE: International Reading Association.

Morrison, T., & Morrison, S. (1999). *The big box*. New York: Hyperion Books.

Morrow, L. (1985). *Promoting voluntary readers in school and home*. Bloomington, IN: Phi Delta Kappa Educational Foundation.

Moss, J. F. (1996). *Teaching literature in the elementary school: A thematic approach*. Norwood, MA: Christopher-Gordon.

Murphy, J. (2001). Serendipity, detective work, and worry: One nonfiction writer's journey through the 90's. In M. Zarnowski, R. M. Kerper, & J. M. Jensen (Eds.), *The best in children's nonfiction: Reading, writing, & teaching Orbis Pictus award books* (pp. 90–98). Urbana, IL: National Council of Teachers of English.

Murphy, S. (1997). Literacy assessment and the politics of identities. *Reading and Writing Quarterly, 13*, 261–275.

Muse, D. (1997). *The New Press guide to multicultural resources for young readers*. New York: New Press.

Nagy, W. E. (1988). *Teaching vocabulary to improve reading comprehension. Center for the Study of Reading*. Urbana, IL: National Council of Teachers of English.

Nagy, W., & Herman, P. A. (1985). Incidental vs. instructional approaches to increasing reading vocabulary. *Educational Perspectives, 23*, 16–21.

Nagy, W., & Herman, P. A. (1996). Incidental vs. instructional approaches to increasing reading. In R. D. Robinson, M. C. McKenna, & J. M. Wedman (Eds.), *Issues and trends in literacy education* (pp. 257–268). Boston: Allyn & Bacon.

National Assessment of Educational Progress. (2000). *NAEP civics consensus project*. Washington, DC: US Department of Education.

National Assessment of Educational Progress. (2003). *The nation's report card: Reading 2002*. Washington, DC: US Department of Education.

National Research Council. (1998). *Preventing reading difficulties in young children*. Washington, DC: National Academy Press.

Nations, S., & Alonso, M. (2001). *Primary literacy centers: Making reading and writing stick*. New York: Maupin House.

Nelson, R. K. (1983). *Make prayers to the raven: A Koyokan view of the northern forest*. Chicago: University of Chicago Press.

Neuman, S. B., Copple, C., & Bredenkamp, S. (2000). *Learning to read and write: Developmentally appropriate practices for young children*. Washington, DC: NAEYC.

Noden, H. R. (1999). *Image grammar*. Portsmouth, NH: Heinemann.

Noonuccal, O. (1990). *Australian legends and landscapes* (Reg Morrison, Photog.). Milsons Point, New South Wales: Random House.

Norton, D. E. (1987). *Through the eyes of a child: An introduction to children's literature* (2nd ed.). Upper Saddle River, NJ: Merrill/Prentice Hall.

Norton, D. E. (1999). *Through the eyes of a child: An introduction to children's literature* (5th ed.). Upper Saddle River, NJ: Merrill/Prentice Hall.

Norton, D. E., & Norton, S. E. (2003). *Through the eyes of a child* (6th ed.). Upper Saddle River, NJ: Merrill/Prentice Hall.

Nye, N. (1994, October). Wind in a bucket: Poetry and energy in young lives. *The Colorado Communicator*, 35–39.

Nystrand, M., Gamoran, A., & Heck, M. (1992). *Using small groups for response to and thinking about literature* [microform]. Washington, DC: US Department of Education, Office of Educational Research and Improvement, Educational Resources Information Center.

Odean, K. (1997). *Great books for girls*. New York: Ballantine Books.

Odean, K. (1998). *Great books for boys*. New York: Ballantine Books.

Ogbu, J. U. (1994). Minority status, cultural frame of reference. In D. Keller-Cohen (Ed.), *Literacy: Interdisciplinary conversations* (pp. 361–384). Creskill, NJ: Hampton Press.

Oleksa, M. (1994). *Communicating across cultures with Father Michael Oleksa* [Video]. J. Lumiansky & R. Burton (Producers), KTOO-TV, Juneau, AK.

Olson, M. W., & Homan, S. P. (Eds.). (1993). *Teacher to teacher: Strategies for the elementary classroom*. Newark, DE: International Reading Association.

O'Neal, S. (1990, November). Leadership in the language arts: Controversial books in the classroom. *Language Arts, 67*, 771–779.

Optiz, M. F. (Ed). (1998). *Literacy instruction for culturally and linguistically diverse students*. Newark, DE: International Reading Association.

Optiz, M. F. (1999). *Learning centers (grades K–4)*. New York: Scholastic.

Ormrod, Jeanne. (2002). *Educational psychology: Developing learners*. Upper Saddle River, NJ: Merrill/Prentice Hall.

Owens, C. V. (1999). Between a rock and a hard place: A natural scientist writes. *Language Arts, 76*, 234–242.

Painter, H. (1970). *Poetry and children*. Newark, DE: International Reading Association.

Pappas, C. (1991). Fostering full access to literacy by including information books. *Language Arts, 68*, 449–462.

Paratore, J., & McCormack, R. (1997). *Peer talk in the classroom*. Newark, DE: International Reading Association.

Parkes, B. (2000). *Read it again! Revisiting shared reading*. York, ME: Stenhouse.

Paterson, K. (1980). Reading as a revolutionary activity. *The Advocate, 1*(1), 137–142.

Paterson, K. (1981). *The gates of excellence*. New York: Dutton.

Paterson, K. (2001). *The invisible child: On reading and writing books for children*. New York: Dutton.

Patterson, L., Santa, C. M., Short, K. G., & Smith, K. (1993). *Teachers are researchers*. Newark, DE: International Reading Association.

Paul, A. (1981). Cultural aspects that affect the Indian student in public schools. *Bilingual Resources, 4*(2–3), 32–34.

Pearson, D. P., & Gallagher, M. C. (1983). *The instruction of reading comprehension*. Champaign, IL: Bolt, Beranek and Newman.

Perez-Stable, M., & Cordier, M. (1994). *Understanding American history through children's literature: Instructional units and activities for grades K–8*. Phoenix, AZ: Oryx Press.

Perfect, K. (1999). Rhyme and reason: Poetry for the heart and head. *The Reading Teacher, 52*, 728–737.

Perl, S. (1980). Understanding composing. *College Composition and Communication, 31*, 363–369.

Perrone, V. (1991). *Expanding student assessment*. Reston, VA: Association for Supervision and Curriculum Development.

Peterson, B. (1998). Columbus and native issues in the elementary classroom. In B. Bigelow & B. Peterson (Eds.), *Rethinking Columbus* (pp. 35–41). Milwaukee: Rethinking Schools.

Peterson, R., & Eeds, M. (1990). *Grand conversations*. New York: Scholastic.

Polanyi, M. (1953). *Personal knowledge: Towards a post-critical philosophy*. Chicago: University of Chicago Press.

Poplin, M. (1988). The reductionist fallacy in learning disabilities: Replicating the past by reducing the present. *Journal of Learning Disabilities, 21*, 389–400.

Post, A. D., Scott, M., & Theberge, M. (2000). *Celebrating children's choices: 25 years of children's favorite books*. Newark, DE: International Reading Association.

Power, B. M. (1996). *Taking note: Improving your observational notetaking*. York, ME: Stenhouse.

Prelutsky, J. (1990). In search of the addle-pated paddlepuss. In W. Zinsser (Ed.), *Worlds of childhood: The art and craft of writing for children* (pp. 99–120). Boston: Houghton Mifflin.

Pullman, P. (1997, Fall/1998, Winter). Myths, folktales and fiction. *SIGNAL* (a journal of the International Reading Association's Special Interest Group on Adolescent Literature), *22*(1), 15–20.

Purves, A. C., Rogers, T., & Soter, A. O. (1990). *How Porcupines Make Love II: Teaching a response-centered literature curriculum*. New York: Longman.

Rabinowitz, P., & Smith, M. (1998). *Authorizing readers: Resistance and respect in the teaching of literature*. New York: Teachers College Press.

Raines, S. C., & Canady, R. J. (1990). *The whole language kindergarten*. New York: Teachers College Press.

Ramirez, G., Jr., & Ramirez, J. L. (1994). *Multiethnic children's literature*. Albany, NY: Delmar.

Rasinski, T., & Padak, N. (2000). *Effective reading strategies: Teaching children who find reading difficult*. Upper Saddle River, NJ: Merrill/Prentice Hall.

Rasinski, T., Padak, N., Linek, W., & Sturtevant, E. (1994). Effects of fluency on urban second-grade readers. *Journal of Educational Research, 87*, 158–165.

Readence, J., Bean, T., & Baldwin, R. (1981). *Content area reading: An integrated approach*. Dubuque, IA: Kendall/Hunt.

Reasoner, C. F. (1976). *Releasing children to literature*. New York: Dell.

Redmond, A. (1978). *Children's response to metaphor in poetry*. Unpublished doctoral dissertation, University of Minnesota, Minneapolis.

Reiner, K. (1998). Developing a kindergarten phonemic awareness program: An action research project. *The Reading Teacher, 53*, 534–539.

Rhodes, R. (1989). Standardized testing of minority students: Navajo and Hopi examples. *Journal of Navajo Education, VI*(2), 29–35.

Richards, M. (2000). Be a good detective: Solve the case of oral reading fluency. *The Reading Teacher, 53*, 534–539.

Robb, L. (2000). *Teaching reading in middle school*. New York: Scholastic.

Robinson, H. M., & Weintraub, S. (1973). Research related to children's interests and to developmental values of reading. *Library Trends, 22*, 81–108.

Rogers, W. C. (1985). Teaching for poetic thought. *The Reading Teacher, 39*, 296–300.

Rosenblatt, L. (1938/1976). *Literature as exploration*. New York: Noble and Noble.

Rosenblatt, L. (1978). *The reader, the text, the poem*. Carbondale, IL: Southern Illinois University Press.

Rosenblatt, L. (1982). The literacy transaction: Evocation and response. *Theory and Practice, 21*(4), 268–277.

Salesi, R. (1992). Reading and writing connection: Supporting content-area literacy through nonfiction trade books. In E. B. Freeman & D. G. Person (Eds.), *Using nonfiction trade books in the elementary classroom* from ants to zeppelins (pp. 86–94). Urbana, IL: National Council of Teachers of English.

Salisbury, L. (1967). Teaching English to Alaska natives. Journal of American Indian Education, VI(2), 1–13.

Samuels, B. (1997). Your reading: A booklist for junior high and middle school students. Urbana, IL: National Council of Teachers of English.

Saul, E. W. (1993). Mediated vs. unmediated texts: Books in the library and the classroom. The New Advocate, 6, 171–181.

Scales, P. (2000). Christopher Paul Curtis. Book notes. New York: Random House.

Schmidt, G. (1991). The story as teller: An interview with Madeleine L'Engle. ALAN Review, 11–14.

Schooley, F. A. (1994). Within class ability grouping and its effect on third grade attitudes toward reading. ERIC Document Clearinghouse ED 371–345.

Schraw, G., Flowerday, T., & Reisetter, M. F. (1998). The role of choice in reader engagement. Journal of Educational Psychology, 90, 705–714.

Scollon, R., & Scollon, S. (1993). The axe handle academy: A proposal for a biogenic, thematic humanities education. Teachers Reflections on Schooling in Rural Alaska, 85–92.

Scott, J., & Nagy, W. E. (1997). Understanding the definition of unfamiliar verbs. Reading Research Quarterly, 32(2), 184–200.

Sendak, M. (1988). Caldecott & Co.: Notes on books & pictures. Toronto, ON: The Noonday Press.

Shapiro, J., & White, W. (1991). Reading attitudes and perceptions in traditional and nontraditional reading programs. Reading Research and Instruction, 30(4), 52–66.

Shapiro, P., & Shapiro, B. (1972). Poetry instruction: Its effect on attitudes toward literature and the ability to write prose. A summary as a paper presented at the annual meeting of the American Educational Research Association, Chicago, April 1972.

Shor, I. (1987). Freire for the classroom. Portsmouth, NH: Heinemann.

Short, K. G., Harste, J. C., & Burke, C. (1996). Creating classrooms for authors and inquirers. Portsmouth, NH: Heinemann.

Shulevitz, U. (1985). Writing with pictures. New York: Watson-Guptill.

Sibberson, F., & Szymusiak, K. (2003). Still learning to read: Teaching students in grades 3–6. Portland, ME: Stenhouse.

Siegel, M. G. (1984). Reading as signification. Unpublished doctoral dissertation, Indiana University, Bloomington.

Siemens, L. (1996). Walking through the time of kids. Going places with poetry. Language Arts, 73, 234–240.

Siemens, L. (1999). A garden of voices: One classroom's story. Primary Voices K–6, 7(4).

Sierra, J. (1991). Fantastic theatre: Puppets and plays for young performers and young audiences. Bronx, NY: H. W. Wilson.

Simmons, M. (1980). Intermediate grade children's preferences in poetry. Unpublished doctoral dissertation, University of Alabama, Tuscaloosa.

Sipe, L. (1998). Learning the language of picture books. Journal of Children's Literature, 24(2), 66–75.

Sloan, G. (1981). Profile: Eve Merriam. Language Arts, 58(8), 957–964.

Smith, F. (1973). Psycholinguistics and reading. New York: Holt, Rinehart and Winston.

Smith, F. (1978). Understanding reading: A psycholinguistic analysis of reading and learning to read (2nd ed.). New York: Holt, Rinehart and Winston.

Smith, F. (1982). Understanding reading (3rd ed.). New York: Holt, Rinehart and Winston.

Smith, F. (1985). Reading without nonsense. New York: Teachers College Press.

Smith, F. (1988). Joining the literacy club: Further essays into education. Portsmouth, NH: Heinemann.

Smith, F. (1990). To think. New York: Teachers College Press.

Smith, J. (1973). Children's understanding of written metaphor. Unpublished doctoral dissertation, University of Alberta, Edmonton.

Smith, J., & Elley, W. (1997). How children learn to read. Katonah, NY: Richard C. Owen.

Smith, M. W., & Wilhelm, J. D. (2002). Reading don't fix no Chevys: Literacy in the lives of young men. Portsmouth, NH: Heinemann.

Smolin, L. I., & Lawless, K. A. (2003). Becoming literate in the technological age: New responsibilities and tools for teachers. The Reading Teacher, 56(6), 570–577.

Starbird, K. (1963). December leaves. In Don't ever cross a crocodile (p. 16). New York: HarperCollins.

Stead, T. (2002). Is that a fact? Teaching nonfiction writing K–3. Portland, ME: Stenhouse.

Steffensen, M. W., Joag-Dev, C., & Anderson, R. C. (1979). A cross-cultural perspective on reading comprehension. Reading Research Quarterly, 15, 10–29.

Stewig, J. W. (1995). Looking at picture books. Fort Atkinson, WI: Highsmith Press.

Stewig, J. W. (2001). The kinds of imagination in picture books. The Dragon Lode, 20(1), 5–9.

Stewig, J. W. (2002). Get the picture? In Association for Library Service to Children, The Newbery and Caldecott awards: A guide to the medal and honor books, (pp. 10–16). Chicago: American Library Association.

Stover, L. T. (1996). Young adult literature: The heart of the middle school curriculum. Portsmouth, NH: Heinemann/Boynton Cook.

Strickland, D. S., Walmsley, S. A., Bronk, G. T., & Weiss, K. (1994). School book clubs and literacy development: A descriptive study (Report 2.22). Albany, NY: National Research Center on Literature Teaching and Learning.

Sulzby, E. (1985). Children's emergent reading of favorite storybooks: A developmental study. Reading Research Quarterly, 20, 458–481.

Sutherland, Z., & Livingston, M. C. (Eds.). (1984). The Scott, Foresman anthology of children's literature. Glenview, IL: Scott, Foresman.

Sweet, A. P., Guthrie, J. T., & Ng, M. M. (1998). Teacher perceptions and student reading motivation. Journal of Educational Psychology, 90, 210–223.

Szymusiak, K., & Sibberson, F. (2001). Beyond leveled books: Supporting transitional readers in grades 2–5. York, ME: Stenhouse.

Taberski, S. (2000). On solid ground: Strategies for teaching reading K–3. Portsmouth, NH: Heinemann.

Taylor, B. M., Graves, M. F., & Van den Broek, P. (2000). Reading for meaning: Fostering comprehension in the middle grades. Newark, DE: International Reading Association/Teachers College Press.

Teale, W. H. (1981). Parents reading to their children: What we know and need to know. Language Arts, 58, 902–911.

Teale, W., & Labbo, L. (1990). Cross-age reading: A strategy for helping poor readers. The Reading Teacher, 43(6), 363–369.

Temple, C., Martinez, M., Yokota, J., & Naylor, A. (2002). Children's books in children's hands: An introduction to their literature. Boston: Allyn & Bacon.

Terry, A. (1974). Children's poetry preferences: A national survey of upper elementary grades. Urbana, IL: National Council of Teachers of English.

Thames, D. G., & Reeves, C. K. (1994). Poor readers' attitudes: Effects of using interests and trade books in an integrated language arts approach. Reading Research and Instruction, 33(4), 293–308.

Thomas, M. A. (Ed.). (1976). Hey, don't forget about me! A report from the Council for Exceptional Children Invisible College on the Severely, Profoundly, & Multiply Handicapped. Reston, VA: The Council for Exceptional Children.

Thompson, S. (1946). The folktale. New York: Dryden Press.

Tiedt, I. M. (2000). Teaching with picture books in the middle school. Newark, DE: International Reading Association.

Tierney, R. J., & Readence, J. E. (2000). Reading strategies and practices (5th ed.). Boston: Allyn & Bacon.

Tierney, R. J., & Shanahan, T. (1996). Research on the reading-writing relationship: Interactions, transactions, and outcomes. In R. Barr, M. L.

Kamil, P. Mosenthal, & P. D. Pearson (Eds.), *Handbook of reading research* (Vol. II, pp. 246–280). Boston: Allyn & Bacon.

Tobitt, J. (Ed.). (1946). *The ditty bag.* New York: Janet E. Tobitt.

Tolkien, J. R. R. (1947). On fairy stories. *Essays presented to Charles Williams.* Oxford: Oxford University Press.

Tomlinson, C., & Lynch-Brown, C. (2002). *Essentials of children's literature* (4th ed.). Boston: Allyn & Bacon.

Tompkins, G. E. (2003). *Literacy for the 21st century* (3rd ed.). Upper Saddle River, NJ: Merrill/Prentice Hall.

Tompkins, G. E. (2004). *Teaching writing: Balancing process and product* (4th ed.). Upper Saddle River, NJ: Merrill/Prentice Hall.

Tompkins, G. E. (2005). *Language arts: Content and teaching strategies* (6th ed.). Upper Saddle River, NJ: Merrill/ Prentice Hall.

Tovani, C. (2000). *I read it, but I don't get it: Comprehension strategies for adolescent readers.* Portland, ME: Stenhouse.

Tovani, C. (2004). *Do I really have to teach reading? Content comprehension, grades 6–12.* Portland, ME: Stenhouse.

Townsend, J. R. (1983). *Written for children.* New York: Lippincott.

Trelease, J. (Ed.). (1992). *Hey! Listen to this: Stories to read aloud.* New York: Penguin.

Trelease, J. (Ed.). (1993). *Read all about it! Great read-aloud stories, poems, and newspaper pieces for preteens and teens.* New York: Penguin.

Trelease, J. (2000). Jim Trelease speaks on reading aloud to children. In N. D. Padak et al. (Eds.), *Distinguished educators on reading: Contributions that have shaped effective literacy instruction* (pp. 233–240). Newark, DE: International Reading Association.

Trelease, J. (2001). *The read-aloud handbook* (5th ed.). New York: Penguin.

Truax, R. R., & Kretschmer, R. R. (1993). Finding new voices in the process of meeting the needs of all children. *Language Arts, 70,* 592–601.

Trudge, J., & Rogoff, B. (1989). Peer influence on cognitive development: Piagetian & Vygotskian perspectives. In M. H. Bornstein & J. S. Bruner (Eds.), *Interaction in human development* (pp. 17–40). Hillsdale, NJ: Erlbaum.

Tunnell, M. O., Calder, J. E. & Phaup, E. S. (1991). Attitudes of young readers. *Reading Improvement, 28*(4), 237–243.

Vacca, J., Vacca, R., & Gove, M. (2000). *Reading and learning to read* (4th ed.). New York: Longman.

Vacca, R., & Rasinski, T. (1992*). Case studies in whole language.* Orlando, FL: Harcourt Brace.

Vacca, R. T., Vacca, J. L., Gove, M. K., Burkey, L. C. Lenhart, L. A., & McKeon, C. A. (2002). *Reading and learning to read.* Boston: Allyn & Bacon.

Valdes, G., & Figueroa, R. A. (1994). *Bilingualism and testing: A special case of bias.* Norwood, NJ: Ablex.

Vardell, S. M. (1998). Using read-aloud to explore the layers of nonfiction. In R. A. Bamford & J. V. Kristo (Eds.), *Making facts come alive: Choosing & using nonfiction literature K–8* (pp. 151–167). Norwood, MA: Christopher-Gordon.

Veatch, J. (1986). Individualized reading: A personal memoir. *Language Arts, 63,* 586–593.

Veatch, J. (1996). From the vantage of retirement. *The Reading Teacher, 49*(7), 510–517.

Veatch, J., & Acinapuro, P. (1966). *Reading in the elementary school.* Katonah, NY: Richard C. Owen.

Vergeront, J. (1987). *Places and spaces for preschool and primary (Indoors).* Washington, DC: NAEYC.

Vygotsky, L. (1978). *Mind in society.* Cambridge, MA: Harvard University Press.

Wade, B. (1989). *Reading for real.* Philadelphia: Open University Press.

Wang, M. C. (1989). Adaptive instruction: An alternative for accommodating student diversity through the curriculum. In D. K. Lipsky & A. Gartner (Eds.), *Beyond separate education: Quality education for all* (pp. 99–119). Baltimore, MD: Paul H. Brookes.

Watson, D. M., Burke, C. & Harste, J. (1989). *Whole language: Inquiring voices.* New York: Scholastic.

Weaver, C. (1994). *Reading process and practice* (2nd ed.). Portsmouth, NH: Heinemann.

Webb, R. A. (1977). *Social development in childhood: Day care programs and research.* Baltimore, MD: Johns Hopkins University Press.

Wells, G. (1986). *The meaning makers.* Portsmouth, NH: Heinemann.

West, M. J., & Donato, R. (1995). Stories and stances: Cross-cultural encounters with African folktales. *Foreign Language Annals, 28*(3), 392–406.

Wheatley, M. (2002). *Turning to one another: Simple conversation to restore hope to the future.* San Francisco: Berrett-Koehler.

Whitehead, J. (1990). *On literacy and gender in knowledge about language: The LINC reader.* New York: Hodder and Stoughton.

Whitmore, K. F., & Goodman, Y. M. (Eds.). (1996). *Whole language voices in teacher education.* York, ME: Stenhouse.

Wilde, S. (Ed.). (1996). *Making a difference: Selected writings of Dorothy Watson.* Portsmouth, NH: Heinemann.

Wilde, S. (2000). *Miscue analysis made easy: Building on student strengths.* Portsmouth, NH: Heinemann.

Wilhelm, J. (1997). *"You gotta be the book." Teaching engaged and reflective reading with adolescents.* New York: Teachers College Press.

Wilhelm, J. (2001). *Improving comprehension with think-aloud strategies.* New York: Scholastic.

Wilhelm, J. (2002a). *Action strategies for deepening comprehension: Role plays, text-structure tableaux, talking statues, and other enactment techniques that engage students with text.* New York: Scholastic.

Wilhelm. J. (2002b, October). Getting boys to read: It's the context! *Instructor,* 16–18.

Wilhelm. J. (2004). *Reading is seeing: Learning to visualize scenes, characters, ideas, and text worlds to improve comprehension and reflective reading.* New York: Scholastic.

Wilhelm, J. D., Baker, T. N., & Dube, J. (2001). *Strategic reading: Guiding students to lifelong literacy 6–12.* Portsmouth, NH: Heinemann.

Wilson, A. (1998). How our stories are told. *Canadian Journal of Native Education, 22*(2), 274–278.

Wilson, L. (2002). *Reading to live: How to teach reading for today's world.* Portsmouth, NH: Heinemann.

Wilson, S. (2001). *Coherence and historical understanding in children's biography and historical nonfiction literature: A content analysis of selected Orbis Pictus books.* Unpublished doctoral dissertation, University of Maine, Orono.

Wood, D. (1988). *How children think and learn.* Cambridge, MA: Basil Blackwell.

Wood, D. (1989). Social interaction as tutoring. In M. H. Bornstein & J. S. Bruner (Eds.), *Interaction in human development* (pp. 59–80). Hillsdale, NJ: Erlbaum.

Wood, D. J., & Middleton, D. (1975). A study of assisted problem solving. *Journal of Child Psychology and Psychiatry, 17,* 89–100.

Wood, K. (1999). *Wondrous words: Writers are writing in the elementary classroom.* Urbana, IL: National Council of Teachers of English.

Wood, K., & Laminack, L. L. (2001). *The writing workshop: Working through the hard parts (and they're all hard parts).* Urbana, IL: National Council of Teachers of English.

Woolsey, D. (2002). Fantasy literature. In A. A. McClure & J. V. Kristo (Eds.), *Adventuring with books: A booklist for pre-K–grade 6* (pp. 278–299). Urbana, IL: National Council of Teachers of English.

Yokota, J. (2001). *Kaleidoscope: A multicultural booklist for grades K–8* (3rd ed.). Urbana, IL: National Council of Teachers of English.

Yopp, R. H., & Yopp, H. K. (2001). *Literature-based reading activities* (3rd ed.). Boston: Allyn & Bacon.

Zarnowski, M. (1995). Learning history with informational books: A social studies educator's perspective. *The New Advocate, 8*, 183–196.

Zarnowski, M., Kerper, R. M., & Jensen, J. M. (Eds.). (2001). *The best in children's nonfiction: Reading, writing, and teaching Orbis Pictus award books*. Urbana, IL: National Council of Teachers of English.

Zinsser, W. (Ed.). (1990). *Worlds of childhood: The art and craft of writing for children*. Boston: Houghton Mifflin.

Zutell, J., & Rasinski, T. R. (1991). Sensitizing teachers to fluency and disfluency in reading. *Theory Into Practice, 30*, 211–217.

Index

Credits

Chapter 1

p. 1 "I Met a Dragon Face to Face" by Jack Prelutsky, from ONCE UPON A TIME by G. P. Putnam's Sons, copyright © 1986 by G. P. Putnam's Sons. Used by permission of G. P. Putnam's Sons, A division of Penguin Young Readers Group, A Member of Penguin Group (USA) Inc., 345 Hudson St., New York, NY 10014. All rights reserved.

Part II

p. 87 "Books in Winter" from A CHILD'S GARDEN OF VERSES by Robert Louis Stevenson. Copyright © 1905 by The Gale Group.

Chapter 5

p. 91 "Shower," from A POCKETFUL OF POEMS by Nikki Grimes. Text copyright © 2001 by Nikki Grimes. Reprinted by permission of Clarion Books/Houghton Mifflin Company. All rights reserved.

p. 91 Quote by Patricia Hubbell from Paul Janeczko (Ed.), *The Place My Words Are Looking For: What Poets Say About and Through Their Work*, New York: Bradbury Press. Copyright (c) 1990 Patricia Hubbell. Reprinted by permission of Marian Reiner for the author.

p. 91 "Sand House." Reprinted with the permission of Atheneum Books for Young Readers, an imprint of Simon & Schuster Children's Publishing Division, from EARTH VERSES AND WATER RHYMES by J. Patrick Lewis. Text copyright © 1991 by J. Patrick Lewis.

p. 92 "Dear Mom." From LOVE LETTERS by Arnold Adoff. Published by the Blue Sky Press/Scholastic Inc. Copyright © 1997 by Arnold Adoff. Reprinted by permission.

Quote by X. J. Kennedy. By permission of X. J. Kennedy. From Paul B. Janeczko, Ed., *The Place My Words Are Looking For* (Simon & Schuster).

p. 93 "Lemonade Sun." Text copyright © 1998 by Rebecca Kai Dotlich from *Lemonade Sun and Other Summer Poems* by Rebecca Kai Dotlich. Published by Wordsong, Boyds Mills Press, Inc. Reprinted by permission.

p. 93 From "A Jamboree for J" in JAMBOREE Rhymes for All Times by Eve Merriam. Copyright © 1962, 1964, 1973, 1984 by Eve Merriam. All rights renewed and reserved. By permission of Marian Reiner.

p. 93 "Brother" from THE LLAMA WHO HAD NO PAJAMA: 100 FAVORITE POEMS, copyright © 1959 and renewed 1987 by Mary Ann Hoberman, reprinted by permission of Harcourt, Inc.

p. 93 Text of "Spring" from IN THE MIDDLE OF THE TREES. Copyright © 1959, renewed 1986 by Karla Kuskin. Reprinted by permission of Scott Treimel NY.

p. 94 "Polliwogs" from THE GREAT FROG RACE AND OTHER POEMS by Kristine O'Connell George. Text copyright © 1997 by Kristine O'Connell George. Reprinted by permission of Clarion Books/Houghton Mifflin Company. All rights reserved.

p. 94–95 "Ocean Rhythms." From SPLASH! POEMS OF OUR WATERY WORLD by Constance Levy. Published by Orchard Books/Scholastic Inc. Copyright © 2002 by Constance Kling Levy. Reprinted by permission.

p. 95 "Flashlight," from FLICKER FLASH by Joan Bransfield Graham. Text copyright © 1999 by Joan Bransfield Graham. Reprinted by permission of Houghton Mifflin Company. All rights reserved.

p. 95 "Brown Honey in Broomwheat Tea." COPYRIGHT © 1993 BY JOYCE CAROL THOMAS. Used by permission of HarperCollins Publishers.

p. 95 Excerpt from "Tent" from BALLOONS AND OTHER POEMS by Deborah Chandra. Published by Farrar, Straus & Giroux, 1990.

p. 110 "Firefly." Text copyright © 1998 by Rebecca Kai Dotlich, from *Lemonade Sun and Other Summer Poems*, written by Rebecca Kai Dotlich. Published by Wordsong, Boyds Mills Press, Inc. Reprinted by permission.

p. 110 "Deer Mouse" from *Turtle in July* by Marilyn Singer 1989. Published by Macmillan.

p. 115 "Cat" from *Near the Window Tree* by Karla Kuskin, © 1975, 1980 by Karla Kuskin. Reprinted by permission of Scott Treimel NY.

p. 116 Quote from Kristine O'Connell George in *Seeing the Blue Between* by Paul Janeczko, 2002, Candlewick Press. For complete text of essay, see www.kristinegeorge.com

p. 117 Bobbi Katz for her words on writing poetry. Copyright © 1994 by Bobbi Katz. Used with permission.

Chapter 6

p. 123 Quote by Terri Windling and Ellen Datlow. Reprinted with the permission of Simon & Schuster Books for Young Readers, an imprint of Simon & Schuster Children's Publishing Division from the Introduction by Terri Windling and Ellen Datlow in SWAN SISTER edited by Ellen Datlow and Terri Windling. Introduction copyright © 2003 Terri Windling.

p. 123 Excerpt from Amy Cohn (Ed.). (1993). *From Sea to Shining Sea: A Treasury of American Folklore and Folk Songs*. New York: Scholastic. Used by permission.

p. 125 Excerpt from *Grannie and the Jumbie*. Text copyright © 2001 by Margaret Hurst. Used by permission of HarperCollins Publishers.

p. 125 Excerpt reprinted with the permission of Atheneum Books for Young Readers, an imprint of Simon & Schuster Children's Publishing Division from BEAUTIFUL BLACKBIRD written and illustrated by Ashley Bryan. Copyright © 2003 by Ashley Bryan.

Chapter 7

p. 158 Excerpt from WHITE DYNAMITE AND CURLY KID by Bill Martin Jr. Reprinted by permission of Bill Martin Jr.

p. 159 From THE BUTTERFLY by Patricia Polacco, copyright © 2000 by Patricia Polacco. Used by permission of Philomel Books, A Division of Penguin Young Readers Group, A Member of Penguin Group (USA) Inc., 345 Hudson Street, New York, NY 10014. All rights reserved.

p. 159 Excerpt from THE KLONDIKE CAT by Julie Lawson. Copyright © 2002 by Kids Can Press.

p. 159 Text copyright © 2002 by Mary Bahr Fritts, from *My Brother Loved Snowflakes*, written by Mary Bahr, illustrated by Laura Jacobsen. published by Boyds Mills Press, Inc. Reprinted by permission.

p. 159 From IRA SAYS GOODBYE by Bernard Waber. Copyright © 1988 by Bernard Waber. Reprinted by permission of Houghton Mifflin Company. All rights reserved.

p. 160 Excerpt from IN COAL COUNTRY by Judith Hendershot. Copyright © 1987 by Alfred A. Knopf. Used by permission.

p. 160 From IRA SLEEPS OVER by Bernard Waber. Copyright © 1972 by Bernard Waber. Reprinted by permission of Houghton Mifflin Company. All rights reserved.

Chapter 8

p. 185 Excerpt from SARAH PLAIN AND TALL. COPYRIGHT © 1985 BY PATRICIA MACLACHLAN. Used by permission of HarperCollins Publishers.

p. 186 Excerpt from Wringer. TEXT COPYRIGHT © BY JERRY SPINELLI. Used by permission of HarperCollins Publisher.

p. 186 Reprinted with the permission of Atheneum Books for Young Readers, an imprint of Simon & Schuster Children's Publishing Division, from ARE YOU THERE GOD? IT'S ME, MARGARET by Judy Blume. Copyright © 1970 by Judy Blume. Copyright renewed © 1998 by Judy Blume. All rights reserved.

Chapter 9

p. 229 From RIVER OF LIFE by Debbie S. Miller. Text copyright © 2000 by Debbie S. Miller. Reprinted by permission of Houghton Mifflin Company. All rights reserved.

p. 229 Excerpt from APPALACHIA: THE VOICES OF SLEEPING BIRDS, copyright © 1991 by Cynthia Rylant, reprinted by permission of Harcourt, Inc.

Chapter 10

p. 258–259 Excerpt from THE READ-ALOUD HAND-BOOK by Jim Trelease. Copyright © 2001 by Penguin Group (USA) Inc. Reprinted by permission.

p. 259 From "Keeping the Democratic Promise: Critical Issues Facing Today's Public Libraries" by Oralia Garza de Cortés, 2001, *The New Advocate, Vol. 14*, (No. 2), p. 153. Copyright © 2001 by Oralia Garza de Cortés. Reprinted by permission.

p. 260 Excerpts from MORE BOOKS KIDS WILL SIT STILL FOR: A READ-ALOUD GUIDE by Judy Freeman. Copyright © 1995 by Reed Elsevier Inc. Reproduced with permission of Greenwood Publishing Group, Inc., Westport, CT.

Chapter 14

p. 318 TOMPKINS, GAIL E., LITERACY FOR THE 21ST CENTURY, 3rd Edition, © 2002. Reprinted by permission of Pearson Education, Inc., Upper Saddle River, NJ.